Intermediate Microeconomics

Second
Edition

INTERMEDIATE
MICROECONOMICS

THEORY AND APPLICATIONS

Alan Griffiths & Stuart Wall

FINANCIAL TIMES
Prentice Hall

An imprint of **Pearson Education**

Harlow, England · London · New York · Reading, Massachusetts · San Francisco
Toronto · Don Mills, Ontario · Sydney · Tokyo · Singapore · Hong Kong · Seoul
Taipei · Cape Town · Madrid · Mexico City · Amsterdam · Munich · Paris · Milan

Pearson Education Limited
Edinburgh Gate
Harlow
Essex CM20 2JE
England

and Associated Companies around the world

Visit us on the World Wide Web at:
www.pearsoneduc.com

First Published 1996
Second edition 2000

© Pearson Education Limited 2000

ISBN 0 582 38226 2

British Library Cataloguing-in-Publication Data
A catalogue record for this book is available from the British Library

Library of Congress Cataloging-in-Publication Data

  Library of Congress Cataloging-in-Publication Data
Griffiths, Alan, 1944-
  Intermediate microeconomics: theory and applications/Alan Griffiths & Stuart Wall.--
  2nd ed.
    p.cm
  Includes bibliographical references and index.
  ISBN 0-582-38226-2 (paper)
    1. Microeconomics. I. Wall, Stuart, 1946- II. Title.

  HB172. G749 2000
  338.5--dc21   99-056831

10 9 8 7 6 5 4 3 2 1
04 03 02 01 00

Typeset by 30
Printed by Ashford Colour Press Ltd., Gosport.

I Sylvia, Anna a fy mam.

ALAN GRIFFITHS

To Eleanor, Rebecca, Jonathan, Suzannah and Elizabeth.

STUART WALL

Contents

A Companion Web Site

accompanies *Intermediate Microeconomics* 2nd Edition

by Griffiths and Wall

Visit the *Intermediate Microeconomics* Companion Web Site at *www.booksites.net/griffithswall/* to find valuable teaching and learning material.

- Links to valuable resources on the World Wide Web
- 25 self-check questions with feedback for every chapter, to help students test their learning as they progress through their course
- A syllabus manager for tutors that will build and host a course web page

In thirteen major chapters and two technical appendices, this book seeks to combine the theoretical rigour of an intermediate microeconomic text with extensive applications involving evidence and data from the UK, Europe and other international sources. While the diversity of the topic areas renders total uniformity of approach unrealistic, all chapters have been arranged in the same format to ease the process of reading and understanding.

Each chapter begins with a section 'Introduction and review' to remind students of the basic ideas and concepts that are a prerequisite for intermediate study of that topic area. It therefore acts as a brief but essential 'primer' to subsequent theory, especially important at a time of increasingly diverse backgrounds for students embarking on intermediate level studies.

The second section in each chapter involves 'Theoretical developments', which take the student into the substance of microeconomic theory and debate, making extensive use of diagrammatic analysis and, where appropriate, mathematical solutions. This is followed by a third section, 'Applications and evidence', alerting the student to contemporary articles and empirical surveys testing the validity of many of the principles previously encountered. On occasions the applications may also involve a theoretical focus on a particular policy issue of contemporary concern. In other words this section attempts to show students that theories can be used as a basis for *thinking* about real-world problems as well as tested empirically to assess whether they have *predictive* value.

Integral to each chapter is a section of 'Review questions', which provide opportunities for student to apply quantitative techniques to a range of microeconomic issues. The review questions are directly related to materials covered in each chapter, and full worked solutions are presented at the end of the book. It is strongly recommended that students seek to conceptualise the problems, where appropriate using diagrams, *before* attempting quantitative solutions. While students should attempt the questions *prior* to checking their work against the solutions, should difficulties be encountered then the full worked solutions will provide a useful aid to inductive learning. It is assumed that students will have completed a first year undergraduate course in basic mathematics and statistics. If this is not the case, then Appendix 1 'Mathematical foundations' and Appendix 2 'Statistical foundations' review much of the material required for tackling these questions.

Each chapter concludes with a graded and comprehensive section of 'Further reading', involving both text and articles, to support the self-learning concept of student participation. Specified chapters in a range of intermediate and advanced texts will help students meet their perceived needs of consolidation, reinforcement or extension of their understanding in a particular topic area. Articles and reports provide access to a still wider range of sources of information and comment. A selection of 'Key terms' is presented at the end of each chapter, with a full definition of these terms in the Glossary at the end of the book.

It is our hope that students will find this book interesting and informative while retaining the analytical rigour so important for a good grounding in microeconomics at the intermediate level.

Alan Griffiths, Stuart Wall. Cambridge 2000

The authors would like to thank Keith Gray, Steven Ison, Glyn Burton and other colleagues for much helpful advice and comment. We would also wish to express our appreciation to Eleanor Wall for copious work in wordprocessing many drafts, and of course to Sylvia and Eleanor, not to mention our children, for enduring frequent absences from key 'events' over a prolonged period.

Alan Griffiths, Stuart Wall

We are grateful to the copyright holders for permission to reproduce copyright material:
Table 2.12 from "What is a good buy?" in *Economic Review* Vol. 9 No. 4, April published by Philip Allan Updates (Gersoki, P. and Toker, S. 1992); Table 3.9 from *Environmental Economics*, Harvester/Wheatsheaf © Kerry Turner, David Pearce and Ian Bateman 1994 (Turner et.al, 1994) reprinted with permission from Pearson Education; Table 4.8 from "The motor industry: an economic overview", *Developments in Economics*. Vol. 15 edited by GBJ Atkinson, Causeway Press Limited, Ormskirk (Rhys, 1999); Table 4.9 and 4.10 adapted from *Development Economics*, Vol. 15 published by Causeway Press Limited, Ormskirk (Rhys, 1999); Table 4.13 and Figure 4.33 from *Journal of Political Economy*, Vol. 102 No. 6, December, University of Chicago Press (Irwin, D.A and Klenow, P.J. 1994); Table 5.5 from *OECD Economic Surveys* (Japan) 1991/2 published and copyright of OECD; Table 5.6 and Figure 5.13 from "Setting business performance and measuring performance" in *European Management Journal*, Vol. 12 No. 2, June, published by Elsevier Science Ltd. (Doyle, P. 1994); Table 7.6 from *Economics*, 3rd Edition, Prentice Hall Europe © 1999 reprinted with permission from Pearson Education (Sloman, 1999); Figure 7.24 from *European Economy: Social Europe*, No. 3, copyright © European Communities, 1993 (Sapir, A. 1993); Figure 7.25 from *Single Market Review, Sub series II: Impact on Services, Air Transport*, Vol. 2 published by Kogan Page/Earthscan; Table 7.3 from *Economics and Business Education*, Vol. 1 Part 1 No. 3, Autumn, published by Economics and Business Education (Myers, G. 1993); Figure 8.18 from "Managerial perceptions of the demand curve: evidence from the multiproduct form", *European Journal of Marketing*, Vol. 27, 9 published by MCB University Press (Diamantopoulos, A. and Matthews, B. 1993); Figure 8.19 from *Journal of Industrial Economics* Vol. XLI, No. 3, September, published by Blackwell Publishers (Domberger, S. and Fiebeg, D. 1993); Table 9.10 from *Foundations of Corporate Success* published and reprinted by permission of Oxford University Press (Kay, 1997); Table 12.2, 12.4 and 12.5 adapted and modified from *OECD Economic Outlook*, June, published by OECD, 1999; Table 13.3a, 13.3b, 13.4 and 13.5 from *Journal of Economic Literature* Vol. XXI, No. 3, September, published by American Economic Association (Winston, C. 1993).
    While every effort has been made to trace the owners of copyright material, in a few cases this has proved impossible, and we take this opportunity to offer our apologies to any copyright holders whose rights we may have unwittingly infringed.

Chapter 1

Consumer behaviour and individual demand

Introduction and review

In this chapter we consider the basic principles underlying the individual consumer decision of what to buy and when to buy it. It may help our later discussions to briefly review some of the ideas you should already be familiar with.

Total and marginal utility

Utility refers to the satisfaction that consumers derive from the consumption of goods and services (commodities). On the assumption that utility can be measured (i.e. is *cardinal*), you will be familiar with curves such as those in Fig. 1.1, reflecting the data in Table 1.1.

Table 1.1 **An individual's utility schedule.**

Drinks consumed	Total utility (units of satisfaction)	Marginal utility (units of satisfaction)
0	0	—
1	27	27
2	39	12
3	47	8
4	52	5
5	55	3
6	57	2
7	58	1
8	58	0
9	56	−2

Fig. 1.1 **Total and marginal utility curves.**

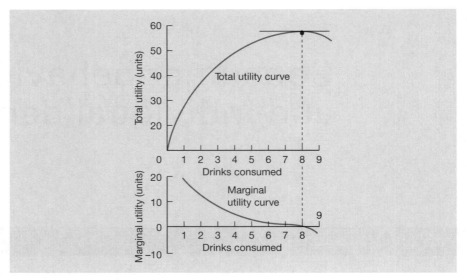

Total utility represents the overall satisfaction to the consumer from consuming a given amount of a good, whereas **marginal utility** represents the change in satisfaction resulting from consuming an extra unit of the good. Here we see that total utility rises up to eight drinks consumed, but falls thereafter. Marginal utility falls after the first drink consumed (the principle of 'diminishing marginal utility'), being zero where total utility is a maximum and negative thereafter.

Indifference curves and maps

Indifference curves are lines representing different combinations of commodities that yield a constant level of utility or satisfaction to the consumer. The consumer is therefore indifferent between the various consumption possibilities denoted by the line. An **indifference map** shows all the indifference curves that rank the preferences of consumers.

On the assumption that more of one good and no less of some other good is a preferred position, indifference curves above and to the right must represent higher levels of utility/satisfaction. For example, in Fig. 1.2, $I_3 > I_2 > I_1$ in terms of utility. Any point in the (shaded) area above and to the right of Z on I_2 is preferred to any point below and to its left. Thus the indifference curve I_3 passing through the upper shaded area must represent a higher level of satisfaction than I_2; similarly the indifference curve I_1 passing through the lower shaded area must represent a lower level of satisfaction than I_2. It also follows that the indifference curve I_2 passing through Z must have a negative slope – generally assumed to be convex to (bowed towards) the origin.

Although, as we shall see, the indifference curves need not be convex to the origin, this is the way they are often presented. In doing so we are assuming a **diminishing marginal rate of substitution** between the goods. It is important that you be familiar with the precise definition of this term. In Fig. 1.3, the **marginal rate of substitution of X for Y** (MRS_{XY}) is the amount of Y that the consumer is willing to give up for an extra unit of X and still achieve the same level of satisfaction (i.e. be on the same indifference curve).

Fig. 1.2 **An indifference map.**

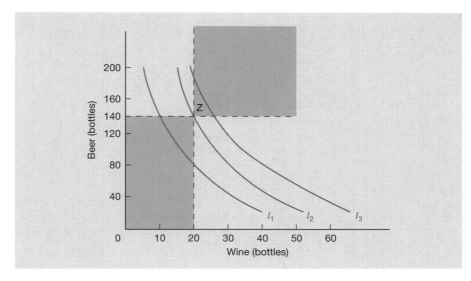

$$MRS_{XY} = \frac{\Delta Y}{\Delta X} \left[\begin{array}{c} \text{along a given indifference} \\ \text{curve where } \Delta X = 1 \end{array} \right]$$

As we can see from Fig. 1.3(a), MRS_{XY} is *diminishing* as the consumer increases consumption of X ($\theta_2 < \theta_1$). The consumer is willing to give up progressively less Y for each extra unit of X, the more of X he or she has already obtained. There is clearly some correspondence between this idea and that of diminishing marginal utility previously encountered.

For those familiar with calculus Fig. 1.3(b) shows that MRS_{XY} can be expressed at a point on the indifference curve as the slope of the tangent to that point:

$$MRS_{XY} = -\frac{dY}{dX} = \text{Slope of indifference curve}$$

Fig. 1.3 **Diminishing marginal rates of substitution between X and Y.**

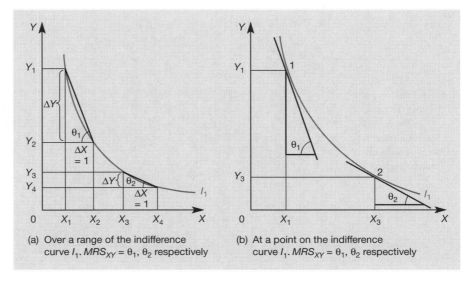

(a) Over a range of the indifference curve I_1. $MRS_{XY} = \theta_1, \theta_2$ respectively

(b) At a point on the indifference curve I_1. $MRS_{XY} = \theta_1, \theta_2$ respectively

Consumer rationality   Throughout our analysis of indifference curves we shall assume that consumers are *rational*, i.e. that they are consistent in their choices. It therefore follows that indifference curves can never intersect, as in Fig. 1.4.

If the indifference curves *were* to intersect, the consumer could not have chosen consistently. For example, in terms of utility or satisfaction:

Combination A = B (both on I_1)
Combination C = D (both on I_2)
Combination A > C (more of both goods)
Combination D > B (more of both goods)

Implies combination A > B (since C = D)

This is clearly inconsistent since we have already seen that A and B are on the same indifference curve. Clearly the intersection of indifference curves is precluded by our assumption that consumers are rational or consistent in their choices.

The budget line   In much of the analysis involving indifference curves we assume that consumers wish to maximise utility subject to a number of constraints, such as the level of household income and the prices of the goods bought. These particular constraints can be represented by the **budget line**.

The *position* of the budget line will depend on the level of household income; the *slope* of the budget line will depend upon the relative prices of the two goods. This can be shown from Fig. 1.5.

Let us suppose the following:

Household income (I) = £200
Price of good X (P_X) =   £20
Price of good Y (P_Y) =   £25

If all the income is spent on X, then we are at point B; if all the income is spent on Y, then we are at point A. The line AB therefore represents the various combinations of X and Y that could be purchased if the *whole* household income was spent on these goods. The slope of this budget line is clearly

$$-\frac{8}{10} = -\frac{20}{25} \text{ i.e. } -\frac{P_X}{P_Y}$$

Fig. 1.4 Indifference curves cannot intersect if consumers are rational (consistent) in their choices.

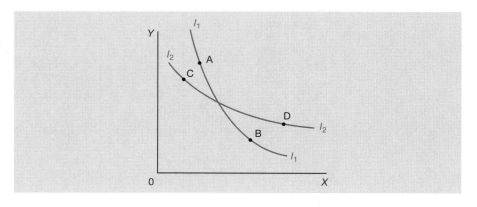

Fig. 1.5 **The budget line. Position depends on household income; slope depends on relative prices.**

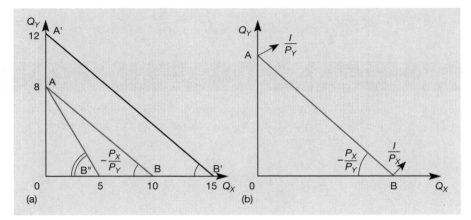

(a)

(b)

A 50% increase in *household income* to £300 would *shift* the position of the budget line to A' B' in Fig. 1.5(a), prices unchanged. A 100% increase in the *price* of X to £40 (income unchanged at the original £200) would cause the budget line to *pivot* to AB" in Fig. 1.5(a).

The budget line can be represented by a linear equation of the following form:

$$P_X Q_X + P_Y Q_Y = I$$

where I = household income; P_X and P_Y = prices of goods X and Y respectively; Q_X and Q_Y = quantities of goods X and Y respectively.

From this expression we can derive the equation for the budget line, by solving for Q_Y:

$$Q_Y = \frac{1}{P_Y} I - \frac{P_X}{P_Y} Q_X$$

If, for example, Q_X is 0, so that the consumer spends all his income (I) on good Y, then he can purchase I/P_Y. On the other hand if Q_Y is 0, so that the consumer spends all his income (I) on good X, then he can purchase I/P_X.

More formally, therefore, the slope of the budget line is

$$\frac{OA}{OB} = \frac{I/P_Y}{I/P_X} = -\frac{P_X}{P_Y}$$

Alternatively, using calculus, the slope of the budget line is the (partial) derivative of the earlier equation for Q_Y:

$$\frac{\partial Q_Y}{\partial Q_X} = -\frac{P_X}{P_Y}$$

We consider the mathematical background to partial differentiation and other useful techniques involving mathematics in Appendix 1.

Theoretical developments

We now develop the framework already outlined into a more comprehensive analysis of consumer behaviour, leading on to the derivation of the individual or household demand curve.

▣ Cardinal utility theory

The **cardinalist** school supposed that utility could be *measured*, either in terms of some abstract quantity (e.g. utils) or in terms of money. In the latter case, utility is expressed in terms of the amount of money that a consumer is willing to sacrifice for an additional unit of a commodity.

Assumptions
- Consumers seek to maximise utility subject to the constraints imposed by their level of income and the prices of the commodities they purchase.
- Utility is measurable in terms of the monetary units that the consumer is willing to sacrifice (pay) for an extra unit of a commodity.
- There is a constant marginal utility of money. For money to function as the standard unit of measurement its marginal utility must remain constant as income increases or decreases.
- There is diminishing marginal utility in the consumption of commodities: i.e. each extra unit of a commodity increases total utility by a progressively smaller amount.
- The total utility (U) of a bundle of commodities depends on the quantities consumed of the individual commodities (X_i) in the bundle consisting of n commodities

$$U = F(X_1, X_2, \ldots, X_n)$$

Equilibrium of the consumer

In a *single* commodity case, the consumer can either buy commodity X or retain his money income. Equilibrium then occurs when the marginal utility of X (MU_X) exactly equals the market price (P_X):

> i.e. $MU_X = P_X$ in equilibrium

If the marginal utility of X is *less than* its price, then the consumer can increase his total satisfaction by reducing his consumption of X (thereby raising MU_X) and keeping more of his income unspent. Similarly, if the marginal utility of X is *greater than* its price, then the consumer can increase his total satisfaction by increasing his consumption of X (thereby reducing MU_X) and retaining less income. Only when $MU_X = P_X$ is total satisfaction maximised. The box on the next page expresses this outcome using calculus.

Individual demand
curve

We can use this simple approach of cardinal utility to derive the consumer demand curve, as in Fig. 1.6.

In Fig. 1.6(a) we have the familiar **total utility** curve, reaching its maximum at quantity X. Only that segment of the total utility curve up to X that has a positive (though declining) marginal utility, as seen in Fig. 1.6(b), is relevant to the consumer demand curve shown in Fig. 1.6(c). Indeed this segment of the **marginal utility** curve *is* the individual consumer demand curve. At price P_1 the consumer will maximise total utility by consuming quantity X_1, at price P_2 will maximise total utility by consuming quantity X_2, and so on. To consume any other quantities will mean that the *difference* between total utility and the cost of purchase will *not* be a maximum. We can illustrate this in terms of Fig. 1.7, which combines Figs 1.6(b) and 1.6(c).

The consumer equilibrium can be expressed using simple calculus.

The utility function is

$$U = F(Q_X)$$

where utility is measured in monetary units. For a purchase of Q_X, the consumer must spend $P_X Q_X$. We assume that the consumer seeks to maximise the *difference* between the utility gained from purchase and the cost of purchase

i.e. maximise $U - P_X Q_X$

The necessary condition for a maximum is that the partial derivative of the function with respect to Q_X be equal to zero.

$$\frac{\partial U}{\partial Q_X} - \frac{\partial (P_X Q_X)}{\partial Q_X} = 0$$

Solving and rearranging we have

$$\frac{\partial U}{\partial Q_X} = P_X$$

i.e. $MU_X = P_X$

Fig. 1.6 **Deriving the consumer demand curve using the cardinalist approach.**

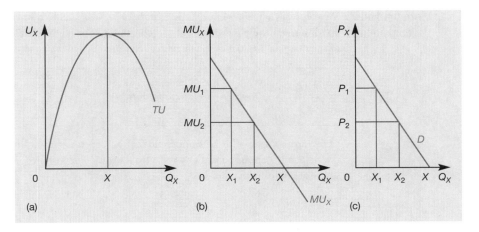

(a) (b) (c)

Fig. 1.7 **Maximising total utility by equating marginal utility to price.**

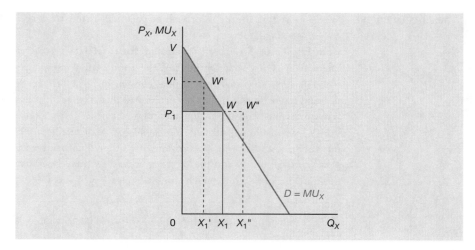

Remembering that total utility is the sum of the individual marginal utilities, we can show the expressions

Total utility at X_1 − cost of purchase of X_1
as
Area $0VWX_1$ − Area $0P_1WX_1$
i.e. Area P_1VW (shaded)

We have already noted that this solution, where $P_X = MU_X$, gives the maximum difference between total utility and cost of purchase. Any other quantity purchased at price P_1 will give a non-maximum solution. For example, if quantity X_1' is purchased at price P_1, the above expression will give area $V'VW'$ ($< P_1VW$) as the solution. Similarly, if quantity X_1'' is purchased at price P_1 we have as our solution $P_1VW − X_1WW''X_1''$, which is clearly $< P_1VW$. Only when $P_X = MU_X$ will our expression of the *difference* between total utility and the cost of purchase be a maximum. Under these conditions the positive segment of the MU curve must be the individual consumer demand curve, telling us how much will be purchased by the (utility maximising) consumer at each and every price.

More than one commodity

We can easily generalise our cardinalist theory of demand to more than one commodity. The condition for the equilibrium of the consumer is now given by the equality of the ratios of the marginal utilities of the individual commodities to their prices. For n commodities:

$$\frac{MU_X}{P_X} = \frac{MU_Y}{P_Y} = \dots \frac{MU_n}{P_n} \text{ in equilibrium}$$

Only in this case will it be impossible for the consumer to reallocate purchases between the respective commodities and raise total utility. For instance, in a two-commodity case suppose the following holds:

$$\frac{MU_X}{P_X} > \frac{MU_Y}{P_Y}$$

In this case the consumer can purchase less of Y, use the money saved to purchase more of X, and thereby increase total utility (with no change in overall household expenditure). Putting numbers into this, suppose $10/4 > 8/8$ then (assuming marginal utilities constant over small changes in output) one less of Y permits two more of X, with a net increase in total utility of 12 ($20 - 8$). Suppose now that the extra purchase of X reduces MU_X (diminishing marginal utility) and raises its price, whereas the reduced purchase of Y raises MU_Y and lowers its price. We may then move to an equilibrium position of, say, $9/6 = 9/6$, where no further reallocation of consumer expenditure can raise total utility. It is only when the ratios of marginal utility to price are equal for all commodities that we have an equilibrium solution in the cardinalist approach.

Ordinal utility theory

Critics of the cardinalist approach to deriving the individual demand curve noted the following:

- It is unrealistic to assume that the marginal utility of money is constant as incomes increase and decrease. The monetary unit cannot, therefore, be used as a standard for measuring utility.
- Other than money, no other standard unit of measurement (e.g. utils) has been credibly proposed.
- Even the principle of diminishing marginal utility has been derived from suppositions rather than from empirical investigation.

As a consequence of such criticisms, economists have sought to use other, more realistic, assumptions as the basis of consumer behaviour. In particular the so-called **ordinalist** approach has replaced the assumption that consumer utility be measurable with the less restrictive assumption that consumer preferences can be *ranked in order of importance*. Here each consumer must be able to rank various bundles of commodities in terms of the satisfaction that they yield. In other words the consumer must be able to determine an *order* of preference between the various bundles of commodities. This is the basis for the indifference curve and revealed preference approaches to consumer behaviour, to which we now turn.

Deriving the individual demand curve

We have already outlined the cardinalist approach to deriving the demand curve of the individual consumer (pp. 6–9). Here we examine the ordinalist approaches to consumer demand. In this chapter we consider indifference curve theory and revealed preference analysis. In the next chapter (p. 73) we consider the characteristics approach.

Indifference curve theory

It will be useful to define at the outset the key assumptions underlying this approach.

1. *Non-satiation.* The consumer is not totally satisfied (satiated) with the amounts of commodities X and Y already obtained. He prefers to have more of both X and Y; in other words 'a good is a good', adding some positive amount to total utility as more of the good is consumed.

2. *Transitivity*. Consumers are consistent in their preference orderings. For example suppose, in terms of utility, we have the following consumer ranking of three bundles of commodities, A, B and C:

A > B
B > C

then via transitivity we can say that

A > C

3. *Diminishing marginal rates of substitution*. As we have seen (p. 3), this refers to the conventional drawing of an indifference curve as convex to the origin. This implies that as more of one good X is consumed, progressively less of the other good Y will be sacrificed for each extra unit of X, if utility or satisfaction is to be unchanged:

$$MRS_{XY} = \text{marginal rate of substitution of } X \text{ for } Y$$
$$= \text{slope of indifference curve} = -\frac{d_Y}{d_X}$$

We have already noted some of the consequences of these assumptions for an indifference map:

- An indifference curve above and to the right of another represents preferred combinations of commodities (by assumption 1).
- An indifference curve has a negative slope (by assumption 1).
- Indifference curves can never intersect (by assumptions 1 and 2).
- The slope of an indifference curve diminishes as we move from left to right along its length (by assumption 3).

Marginal rate of substitution and marginal utilities It is useful at this point to express the MRS_{XY} in terms of the marginal utilities of each commodity. It can be shown that

$$MRS_{XY} = \frac{MU_X}{MU_Y}$$

We can illustrate this property by using Fig. 1.8.

In moving from A to B along the given indifference curve I_1, the consumer gives up AC of Y in return for an extra CB of X, and is *indifferent* to this exchange. The utility loss in giving up AC of Y can be expressed (approximately) as $AC \times MU_Y$. Similarly the utility gain in receiving CB of X can be expressed (approximately) as $CB \times MU_X$. Since the loss and gain exactly offset one another along I_1, we have

$$AC \times MU_Y = CB \times MU_X$$

Note that this equilibrium condition is identical to that of the cardinalist approach, though derived differently (p. 8).

However, although the ordinalist approach of indifference theory implies equality between the slope of each indifference curve at any point and the ratio of the respective marginal utilities, there is no requirement that these marginal utilities be measurable. All that is required to achieve indifference curves convex to the origin is that there be a *diminishing marginal rate of substitution* between the two commodities. Also note that this does not even necessitate the assumption of diminishing marginal utilities for each *separate* commodity.

Price–consumption line We now use our indifference analysis to derive the *individual consumer demand curve*, i.e. the quantities of good X consumed at various prices of X (see Fig. 1.10).

Suppose our household has a weekly income of £48, with the initial price of X (P_X) at £16 and price of Y (P_Y) at £4. This gives us the initial budget line AB and the equilibrium point at E for maximum utility of I_1. At $P_X = £16$, 1 unit of good X is demanded. Suppose now that P_X falls first to £8 and then to £4, other things equal (i.e. household income and P_Y). We can represent this by pivoting the budget line to AB' ($P_X = £8$) and

Fig. 1.10 **The price–consumption line and the individual demand curve.**

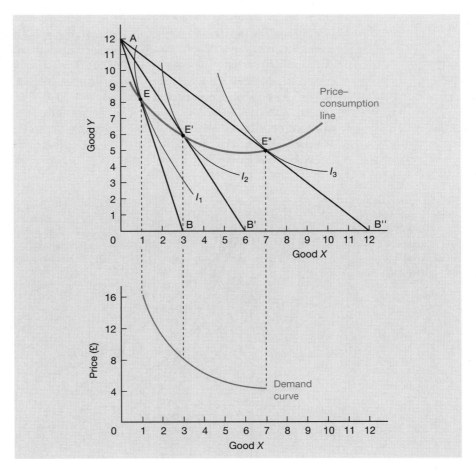

AB" (P_X = £4) respectively. This gives us new equilibrium points of E' and E", where the consumer reaches the highest attainable indifference curves of I_2 and I_3 respectively. So at P_X = £8 we have 3 units of X demanded, and at P_X = £4 we have 7 units of X demanded. Joining all the equilibrium points of tangency between budget lines representing a change in P_X and the highest attainable indifference curves gives us the **price–consumption line** of Fig. 1.10. From this, as is clear from Fig. 1.10, we can derive the **individual demand curve**.

As we shall see, the demand curve for *normal* commodities will always have a negative slope, denoting the **law of demand**, namely that the quantity demanded rises as price falls. It will help at this stage to investigate the conditions that are necessary for this law of demand to hold true.

Income and substitution effects   A reduction in the price of X has, in our analysis, resulted in an overall rise in the quantity demanded of good X, as for instance in the move from E to E' along the price–consumption line in Fig. 1.10 and along the corresponding demand curve. However, this rise in the quantity demanded is the **total price effect**, which may be split into two separate parts: the *substitution effect* and the *income effect*. We now examine each part in turn.

The **substitution effect** refers to the extra purchase of good X now that it is, after the price fall, relatively cheaper than other substitutes in consumption. The **income effect** refers to the rise in real income (purchasing power) now that the price of one commodity is lower within the bundle of commodities purchased by the consumer. This extra real income can potentially be used to buy more of *all* commodities, including X. For analytical purposes it is helpful to deal separately with each effect, and we do this by making use of the *compensated budget line*. In Fig. 1.11 the fall in P_X has caused the budget line to pivot from AB to AB', representing the new price ratio between X and Y. The **total price effect** is shown in the movement from E to E', i.e. the rise in quantity demanded of X from X_1 to X_3. To derive the compensated budget line we reduce the consumer's real income, but retaining the new price ratio after the fall in P_X, so that the

Fig. 1.11 **Income and substitution effects. Law of demand supported – i.e. negatively sloping demand curve.**

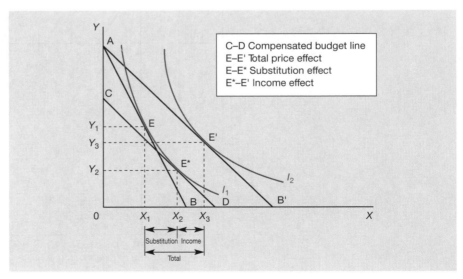

consumer is still only able to achieve the same level of utility as before. We show this by shifting the budget line AB' inwards and parallel to itself (thereby retaining the new price ratio) until it is a tangent to the original indifference curve I_1. This occurs with budget line CD at point E*. We can now say that the movement from E to E* is the *pure substitution effect*, i.e. the extra amount $(X_2 - X_1)$ of X purchased solely as a result of X being cheaper relative to Y, the income effect having been compensated, i.e. eliminated.

If we now allow the income effect to be restored, the budget line returns to AB', moving outwards and parallel to CD. We can now say that the movement from E* to E' is the *income effect*. In this case the income effect is positive $(X_3 - X_2 > 0)$, with still more of X being purchased as a result of a rise in the consumer's real income.

We can therefore state that

> Total price effect ≡ Substitution effect + Income effect

As we shall see below there is a theorem (the Slutsky theorem) that states that the *substitution effect* will always be positive for a fall in P_X.

The income effect can be positive, zero or negative, depending on the type of commodity in question. For *normal* commodities, the income effect will be positive; for *inferior* commodities, the income effect may be negative over certain ranges of income. Inferior commodities are cheap, but poor quality, substitutes for other commodities. As real incomes rise beyond a certain level, consumers will tend to replace the (inferior) commodities with more expensive but better quality alternatives.

We can now explore the situation that will result in the law of demand operating in the conventional manner, i.e. more of X being demanded at a lower price. Clearly when *both* substitution and income effects are positive, then the total price effect will be positive (as in Fig. 1.11) and the law of demand holds. However, if the commodity is inferior, then the total price effect may include a positive substitution effect but a negative income effect, and the overall outcome will be in doubt. Where the commodity is so inferior that the income effect is sufficiently negative to more than outweigh the positive substitution effect, then the total price effect will be negative. In this case a fall in P_X will result in a fall in the demand for X and the law of demand will be violated, with the demand curve sloping upwards from left to right.

Just such an occurrence is shown in Fig. 1.12. The negative income effect $(X_2 - X_3)$ more than outweighs the positive substitution effect $(X_1 - X_2)$, leaving a negative total price effect $(X_1 - X_3)$. The fall in price of X causes demand to *contract* from X_1 to X_3.

Note: Here and subsequently we refer to the substitution effect as positive when more of X is demanded solely because of the fall in P_X relative to P_Y. Technically, this substitution effect for X is negative relative to its price, since a fall in P_X results in a rise in Q_X demanded.

The Slutsky method In this chapter we have followed the method of J. R. Hicks and R. Allen in deriving the compensated budget line and thereby the pure substitution effect. An alternative method for demonstrating the same result was independently devised by Eugene Slutsky.

The compensated budget line (C'D') is rather different in the Slutsky approach. Instead of reducing the consumer's real income at the new set of relative prices (after the fall in P_X) until the consumer's *utility* is unchanged at I_1, Slutsky reduces real income until the consumer can

Fig. 1.12 **Income and substitution effects. Law of demand violated – i.e. positively (upward) sloping demand curve.**

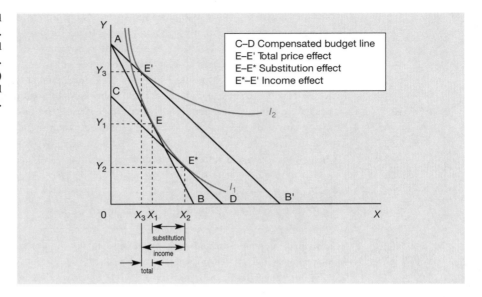

C–D Compensated budget line
E–E' Total price effect
E–E* Substitution effect
E*–E' Income effect

just afford the *original consumption bundle*. In other words, the compensated budget line for Slutsky moves inwards, parallel to AB', until it goes through the original consumption bundle $X_1 Y_1$ at point E. Doing so gives us the budget line C' D', which allows the consumer in equilibrium to reach a higher level of utility I_2, at point E*. The movement along the compensated budget line C' D' from E to E* is the pure substitution effect in this analysis.

In some ways the Slutsky approach to devising the (positive) substitution effect is more easily used in practice than that of Hicks–Allen. For example, the point E* in Figs 1.11 and 1.12 cannot be observed in practice. However, we *can* adjust the money income for a consumer to allow him/her to just afford the original bundle of goods given by point E in Fig. 1.13 at the new set of relative prices. We can then *observe* what the consumer chooses, which is the point E*.

Fig. 1.13 **Substitution and income effects of a price change: the Slutsky method.**

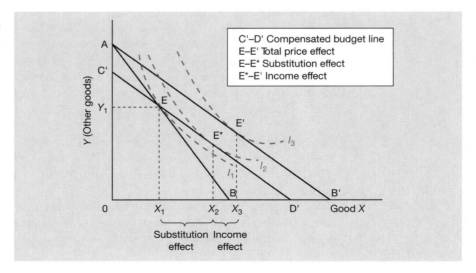

C'–D' Compensated budget line
E–E' Total price effect
E–E* Substitution effect
E*–E' Income effect

Set against this, the Slutsky method involves a movement *between* indifference curves, and does not strictly accord with the conventional idea of the substitution effect as being between goods *along* a given indifference curve, owing to a change in relative prices. In general we can say that the Slutsky approach tends to overestimate the substitution effect and underestimate the income effect.

Giffen goods and inferior goods **Inferior goods** are cheap but poor quality substitutes for other goods. As real incomes rise above a certain 'threshold', consumers tend to substitute the more expensive but better quality alternatives for them. In other words, inferior goods have negative income elasticities of demand (see p. 57) over certain ranges of income.

However, not all inferior goods are **Giffen goods**. These are named after the 19th century economist, Sir Robert Giffen, who claimed to identify an upward sloping demand curve for certain inferior goods. Of course we should now be in a position to explain exactly when an inferior good will become a Giffen good. Remembering our identity

Total price effect $\equiv$ Substitution effect $+$ Income effect

the total price effect will be negative when the positive substitution effect is more than outweighed by the negative income effect. This has already been illustrated in Fig. 1.12. For an inferior good where the degree of inferiority is rather small, so that the negative income effect is outweighed by the positive substitution effect, the law of demand will still hold. In other words a fall in P_X will still result in a rise in Q_X demanded.

Table 1.2 and Fig. 1.14 (p. 18) summarise the various possibilities.

Table 1.2	Type of good	Substitution effect	Income effect	Total effect
Substitution and income effects of a price decline.	Normal	Positive	Positive	Positive
	Inferior (but not Giffen)	Positive	Negative	Positive
	Giffen	Positive	Negative	Negative

Table 1.2 **Substitution and income effects of a price decline.**

Note: in Fig. 1.14 we use the Hicks–Allen variant of the compensated budget line. The starting point in each diagram is a consumer in equilibrium at point E, with budget line AB tangent to the highest attainable indifference curve I_1. The price fall of good X causes the budget line to pivot to AB' in each case, which is then 'compensated' by budget line CD. In Fig. 1.14(a) we have the inferior (but not Giffen) good where the law of demand still applies; in Fig. 1.14(b) we have the Giffen good where the law of demand is violated.

Fig. 1.14 **Inferior and Giffen good.**

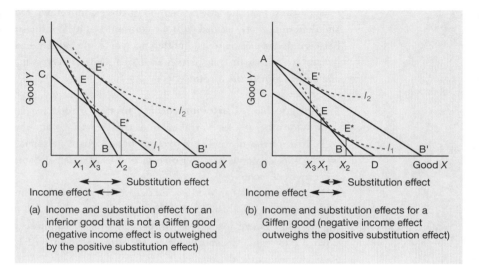

(a) Income and substitution effect for an inferior good that is not a Giffen good (negative income effect is outweighed by the positive substitution effect)

(b) Income and substitution effects for a Giffen good (negative income effect outweighs the positive substitution effect)

The Engel curve The approach involved in deriving the price–consumption line (or curve) in Fig. 1.10 earlier can easily be adapted to deriving the **income–consumption line** and associated **Engel curve** (Fig. 1.15).

Increases in money income (M) lead to parallel shifts of the consumer's budget line away from the origin (Fig. 1.15(a)).

This results in a series of tangency points between budget lines and highest attainable indifference curves. If we join these tangency points together, we derive the **income consumption line**. Plotting consumption of good X on the vertical axis against money income on the horizontal axis gives us the familiar Engel curve of Fig. 1.15(b). We comment further on the nature and shape of the Engel curve in Chapter 2 (p. 63). Here we see that successive rises in money income lead to progressively smaller absolute (and percentage) increases in the quantity of good X demanded.

Fig. 1.15 **Deriving the Engel curve.**

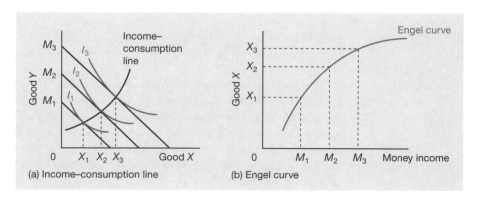

(a) Income–consumption line

(b) Engel curve

Necessary and sufficient conditions for the law of demand From our earlier analysis you should now be in a position to verify the following statements. Check yourself now to see if this is the case.

- The commodity being normal is a sufficient condition for the law of demand to operate.
- The commodity being normal is not a necessary condition for the law of demand to operate.
- The commodity being inferior is a necessary condition for the law of demand to be violated.
- The commodity being inferior is not a sufficient condition for the law of demand to be violated.

Violation of the assumption of diminishing marginal rates of substitution We have already seen that violation of the assumption of transitivity of preferences (p. 10) would lead to indifference curves intersecting. Here we examine the implications of violating the assumption of diminishing marginal rates of substitution (p. 10) between X and Y, which gives us the conventionally shaped indifference curves, which are convex to the origin.

Perfect substitutes and complements. Figure 1.16(a) illustrates straight line indifference curves, with MRS_{XY} constant at 1 for I_1 and 2 for I_2 respectively. A straight line indifference curve means that the consumer treats the two goods as **perfect substitutes** for each other, always being prepared to substitute X for Y at the same rate:

e.g. $1X : 1Y$ on I_1, $1_X : 2_Y$ on I_2

When goods are **perfect complements** the indifference curves are L-shaped, as in Fig. 1.16(b). If X and Y are perfect complements, then the consumer's utility is not increased by extra units of X unless they are accompanied by more Y in some fixed proportion. Thus if $1X$ is a perfect complement for $1Y$, then at $5X:5Y$ we are on I_1 and *remain on* I_1 at $6X:5Y$ and at $5X:6Y$ and so on. This gives us a situation where the level of utility is determined at the corner position of an L-shaped indifference curve. Again MRS_{XY} is constant, this time equal to zero along the horizontal section ($MRS_{YX} = 0$ along the vertical section).

Of course these two cases represent extreme *degrees of substitutability* between commodities: a non-zero constant for perfect substitutes (e.g. $MRS_{XY} = 1$ or 2) and zero for perfect complements ($MRS_{XY} = 0$). More generally, the closer the indifference curve is to a straight line of the type reflecting perfect substitutes, the greater the degree of substitutability between the commodities. In Fig. 1.16(c), consumer A regards X and Y as closer substitutes than does consumer B.

In terms of our earlier analysis on the total price effect of a fall in P_X we can note the following:

- If indifference curves are *straight lines*, there are no income effects, only substitution effects. Tangency between budget line and (straight line) indifference curve can only take place at an *edge position*, i.e. where only one of the two commodities is purchased (except where the budget line lies exactly on top of the straight line indifference curve, where consumer selection is then indeterminate). A compensated budget line can, how-

Fig. 1.16 **Indifference curve under various assumptions.**

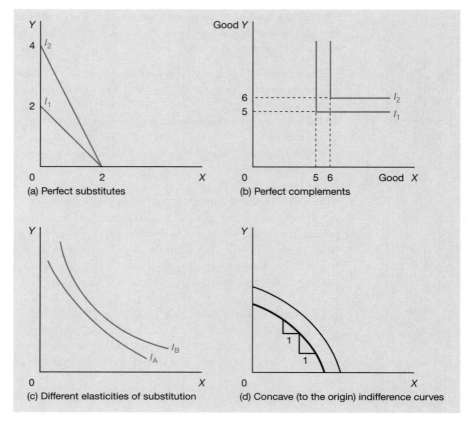

(a) Perfect substitutes

(b) Perfect complements

(c) Different elasticities of substitution

(d) Concave (to the origin) indifference curves

ever, lead to a non-edge solution on the original (straight line) indifference curve (i.e. positive substitution effect). Allowing the income effect to then operate will merely result in a return to the original edge position, with only one commodity consumed.

- If indifference curves are *L-shaped*, there are no substitution effects, only income effects. Tangency between budget line and such indifference curves can only occur at a *corner point*. When we derive the compensated budget line the tangency position will remain at the original corner point.

- The closer indifference curves are to being L-shaped, the less close the goods are as substitutes and the larger is the income effect relative to the substitution effect.

Indifference curves concave to the origin. The final diagram (Fig. 1.16(d)) reflects indifference curves that are concave to the origin rather than convex to the origin. Here we have an increasing MRS_{XY}, i.e. as more of X is purchased the consumer will sacrifice progressively more of Y to achieve each extra unit of X. Again in terms of the total price effect of a fall in P_X, tangency between the budget line and the highest attainable indifference curve will be at an edge position, with only *one* commodity consumed. The usual consumer equilibrium position of equality between relative prices and ratios of marginal utilities (see p. 12) will no longer apply.

Violation of the assumption of non-satiation As we saw earlier (p. 9), one of the conventional assumptions of indifference analysis was **non-satiation**, i.e. a consumer will prefer to have more of a commodity than a lesser quantity. In Fig. 1.17 this implies that the bottom-left quadrant $0X^*SY^*$ (quadrant I) is the relevant quadrant when we take our usual assumption of non-satiation in both commodity X and commodity Y. However, it will be useful to examine the implications of relaxing this assumption for our indifference analysis.

Suppose X^* is the maximum desired quantity of X, and Y^* is the maximum desired quantity of Y. In quadrant I, where the consumer is sated in neither commodity X nor Y, we get the conventionally shaped indifference curve AB. However, in quadrant II at, say, point F the consumer wants more of Y but less of X. To give this consumer still more of X and no less of Y (point G) is actually to confer *disutility* (negative utility), as point G is still further away from X^*, the maximum desired quantity of X. It follows that to compensate the consumer for the disutility of the extra amount (FG) of X, the consumer must receive a positive amount (GH) of Y. In other words a line of constant utility (BD) must slope *upwards* from left to right in this quadrant.

By similar reasoning you should be able to complete the line of constant utility across all four quadrants, as in Fig. 1.17(a). In Fig. 1.17(b) we present a set of indifference curves that are now seen to be *closed contours*, one inside another, which *converge* to the point S. This point S is sometimes called the 'bliss point', at which the consumer possesses exactly the amounts of both X and Y that yield maximum satisfaction (namely X^*Y^*).

A number of implications clearly follow from this analysis:

- If we relax the assumption of satiation, then the conventional indifference curves refer to only one quadrant of the complete indifference map (namely quadrant I). In practical terms, however, this may be quite realistic as most households face income constraints that prevent satiation in commodity consumption.
- The indifference curves in other quadrants may no longer be negatively sloped (e.g. quadrants II and IV). Here we no longer have a diminishing marginal rate of substitution between the commodities.
- Even though the indifference curves are negatively sloped in quadrant III, they are concave (rather than convex) to the origin and we therefore have *increasing* (rather than diminishing) *marginal rates of substitution* between commodities.

Fig. 1.17

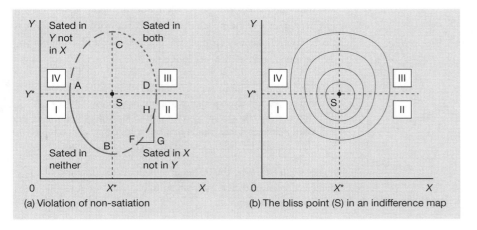

(a) Violation of non-satiation   (b) The bliss point (S) in an indifference map

- At points B and C in Fig. 1.17(a) the marginal rate of substitution of X for Y is zero ($MRS_{XY} = 0$). In other words, because of satiation in commodity X, the consumer is no longer willing to give up any amount of Y whatsoever in order to get an additional unit of X. Effectively the indifference curve is horizontal for infinitely small changes in X at points B and C.

Revealed preference   The idea of revealed preference was introduced into consumer theory by Paul Samuelson in 1938. The **revealed preference hypothesis** has made it possible to establish the law of demand by *direct observation* of consumer behaviour without having to depend on the rather restrictive assumptions that we have noted as being necessary for the use of indifference curve analysis. The weaker assumptions underlying revealed preference can be listed as follows:

Assumptions

- *Non-satiation*. The consumer prefers bundles of commodities that include more of some commodities and no less of any other commodities.
- *Consistency*. The consumer behaves consistently in choosing bundles of commodities. In other words, if bundle A is chosen in preference to bundle B, which was also available, then he will not subsequently choose B in any other situation where A is also available.

  Using notation:

  If $A > B$ then $B \not> A$

- *Transitivity*. The consumer chooses bundles of commodities in such a way that if bundle A is revealed as preferred to bundle B, and in another situation bundle B is revealed as preferred to bundle C, then we can assume that bundle A will be revealed as preferred to bundle C in any situation where A and C are available.

  Using notation:

  If $A > B$ and $B > C$ then $A > C$

However we have not, as yet, introduced the *prices* of commodities into our analysis. If, for example, the prices of commodities in bundle A were lower than those in bundle B, this might be the reason for the consumer choosing A. We could not, then, say that the consumer preferred bundle A to bundle B. In this case the consumer might regret not being able to afford the more expensive bundle B. Price information may help us to remove this uncertainty and allow us to provide a more accurate definition of revealed preference.

> If a consumer chooses some bundle of goods *A*, in preference to other bundles *B, C* and *D*, which are also available, then if none of the latter bundles is more expensive than *A*, we can say that *A* has been *revealed preferred* to the other bundles.

As we have seen, the *budget line* reflects the income of the consumer and the relative prices of commodities. We can now use the budget line to explore further this idea of revealed preference.

Suppose that the consumer facing the budget constraint given by line B_1 in Fig. 1.18(a) chooses bundle A. We can state that A is revealed preferred to bundle C since C has been rejected in favour of A in a situation where C is no more expensive than A, being on the same budget line. By extension, A is revealed preferred to all other bundles *on* the budget line and to all other bundles *inside* the budget line, since each point inside the budget line represents smaller amounts of both commodities than some point on the budget line. Here the consumer is revealing that bundle A maximises the utility of the consumer under present circumstances.

Suppose now that the *relative prices* of commodities X and Y change, a fall in P_X and rise in P_Y causing the budget line to pivot to B_2 in Fig. 1.18(b). Suppose also that the consumer chooses bundle C in a situation where bundle D was available. Although bundles A and D are on *different* budget lines, we can still compare them: namely, we can say that bundle A is revealed preferred to bundle D, using our earlier assumption of transitivity of consumer choices.

Deriving the demand curve Here we use revealed preference to derive the individual consumer demand curve, drawing on the ideas of income and substitution effects mentioned previously.

Assume that the consumer has the budget line AB in Fig. 1.19(a) and reveals his preference for the bundle of commodities denoted by point C. Suppose that the price of X now falls so that the consumer faces the budget line AB_1. We now make a compensating variation of consumer income, i.e. we reduce income so that the consumer has just enough income to continue purchasing the original bundle C if he so wishes, at the *new* set of relative prices (i.e. budget line A_1B_2 through C and parallel to AB_1). Since the bundle C is still available, the consumer will not choose any bundle to the left of C on the segment A_1C because this would be inconsistent, given that in the original situation all these bundles along A_1C were revealed less-preferred (inferior) to C. It follows that the consumer will either continue to buy C (i.e. substitution effect = zero) or choose a

Fig. 1.18 **Revealed preference approach.**

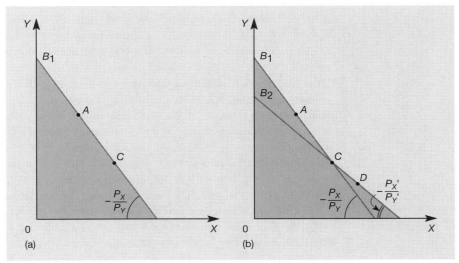

Fig. 1.19 Income and substitution effects using revealed preference analysis.

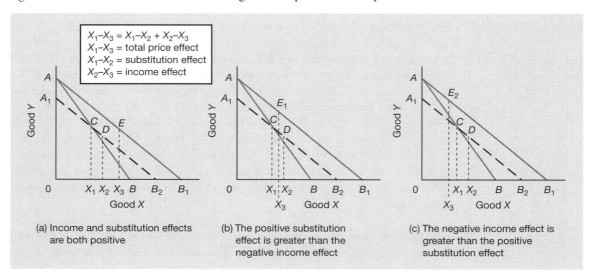

$$X_1-X_3 = X_1-X_2 + X_2-X_3$$
$$X_1-X_3 = \text{total price effect}$$
$$X_1-X_2 = \text{substitution effect}$$
$$X_2-X_3 = \text{income effect}$$

(a) Income and substitution effects are both positive

(b) The positive substitution effect is greater than the negative income effect

(c) The negative income effect is greater than the positive substitution effect

bundle on the segment CB_2, such as D, which includes a larger quantity of X (i.e. substitution effect = positive). Note here that under revealed preference analysis the substitution effect can be zero or positive, whereas under indifference curve analysis it is always positive, given the convexity of the indifference curves to the origin.

If we now restore income to the consumer, allowing the budget line to return to AB_1, he will choose a bundle of commodities (such as E) somewhere to the right of D, provided that commodity X is normal with a positive income effect. The new revealed equilibrium position (E) includes a larger quantity of X (i.e. X_3) resulting from the fall in its price. As with indifference analysis, revealed preference indicates the validity of the law of demand for normal goods: as price of X falls, more of X is purchased.

As before (see Table 1.2 on p. 17) the upward sloping demand curve could be explained for an inferior good in which the negative income effect more than offsets the (zero or positive) substitution effect, which is the case with the Giffen good in Fig. 1.19(c). Even though the good is inferior in Fig. 1.19(b) the law of demand still applies since the negative income effect is outweighed by the positive substitution effect.

Deriving the indifference curves The revealed preference approach has a useful practical application, namely the derivation of the *convex* (to the origin) *indifference curves* used in our earlier analysis. Indifference analysis requires the consumer to rank in a rational and consistent manner *all possible* bundles of commodities. In contrast, revealed preference analysis does not require the consumer to rank his preferences or indeed to provide any information about his tastes. Under this analysis we can construct the consumer indifference map merely by observing consumer behaviour (choices) at various market prices, provided only that we assume (a) that those choices are consistent, (b) that tastes are independent of choices over time, and (c) that more commodities are preferred to fewer.

Suppose the consumer reveals his preference by choosing C along budget line AB in Fig. 1.20(a). All other bundles on, or inside, budget line AB are thereby rejected as less preferred or inferior to bundle C. By drawing the perpendiculars through C, i.e. FC and

CG, we can see that all bundles in segment *FCG* are preferred to *C* because they contain more of at least one commodity and no less of any other. Bundles of goods in the unshaded areas are still not ranked in order of preference, and we call these areas *zones of ignorance*.

We can, however, reduce the extent of these zones of ignorance by *observation*. Suppose, for instance, that the price of *X* falls, with the new set of relative prices giving budget line *A'B'* in Fig. 1.20(b). Here the new budget line intersects the initial budget line at *D* (i.e. below *C*) and allows us to rank bundles of commodities previously in the (lower) zone of ignorance, relative to *C*. To choose any bundle along segment *A'D* of the new budget line would be inconsistent, as all such bundles were previously rejected in favour of *C*. However, the consumer can (consistently) choose either bundle *D* or bundles to the right along segment *DB'* of the new budget line. Assume that the consumer reveals his preference in the new situation by choosing bundle *D* on budget line *A'B'*. We can say:

$$C > D \text{ (in the original situation)}$$
$$D > DBB' \text{ (in the new situation)}$$
Hence $C > DBB'$ (reducing the lower zone of ignorance)

By taking a variety of such observations involving a *fall* in P_X we can gradually rank all the bundles in the lower ignorance zone that are inferior to *C*.

Using a similar line of reasoning, we can take observations following *rises* in the price of *X* relative to *Y*, giving the new budget line *A" B"* through the original point *C* (Fig. 1.20(c)). Consistent consumer choice must then imply remaining at *C* or moving leftwards along the segment *A" C* of the new budget line. Suppose the consumer reveals his preferred bundle as *E*. We can say:

$$E > C \text{ (in the new situation)}$$
$$JELF > E \text{ (in the new situation)}$$
Hence $JELF > C$ (reducing the upper zone of ignorance)

Fig. 1.20 Using revealed preference analysis to identify and remove 'zones of ignorance'.

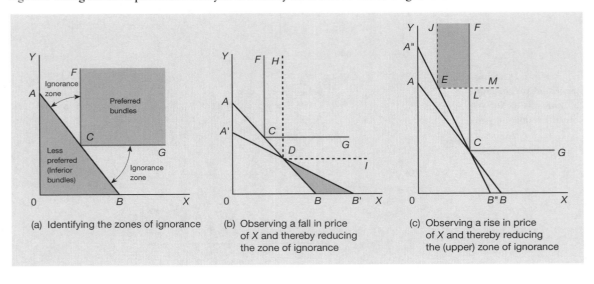

(a) Identifying the zones of ignorance

(b) Observing a fall in price of *X* and thereby reducing the zone of ignorance

(c) Observing a rise in price of *X* and thereby reducing the (upper) zone of ignorance

Again, by taking a variety of such observations involving a rise in P_X, we can gradually rank all the bundles in the upper ignorance zone that are preferred (superior) to C.

By successively reducing these zones of ignorance we can, in effect, use revealed preference analysis to establish the *convexity* of the conventional indifference curve or line of constant utility. From Fig. 1.21 we can observe that the indifference curve through C must pass somewhere through the upper and lower zones of ignorance. However, this indifference curve, I_1, cannot be the straight line AB because the choice of C shows that all the other bundles on AB are inferior to (have lower utility than) bundle C. Neither can the indifference curve through C be a line or curve cutting AB at C, because all bundles below C have already been revealed as inferior to bundle C. Nor can the indifference curve through C be concave to the origin, because all bundles below C have already been revealed as inferior to C. The only remaining possible shape for the indifference (constant utility) curve through C is one that is convex to the origin (i.e. I_1).

The consumer's surplus

An important idea initiated by Arsène Dupuit in 1844 and later developed by Alfred Marshall involved what has become known as **consumer's surplus**. In its most widely used form it measures, in monetary units, the difference between the amount of money that a consumer *actually* pays to buy a certain quantity of commodity X and the amount that he would be *willing to pay* for this quantity of commodity X. In Fig. 1.22 it is given by the area APC, where quantity X_1 is purchased at price P.

It will be useful at this stage, however, to use our earlier analysis to explore the concept of consumer's surplus rather more thoroughly. Take for instance the first rectangle, representing the purchase of the first unit of X. From our earlier analysis (p. 12), we have seen that the equilibrium condition for maximising utility requires that the ratio of the marginal utilities of *commodities* to their prices be equal:

$$\frac{MU_X}{MU_Y} = \frac{P_X}{P_Y}$$

Fig. 1.21 Using revealed preference analysis to derive indifference curves.

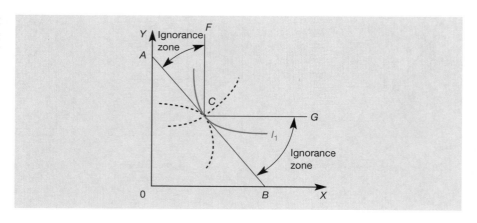

Fig. 1.22 **Consumer surplus.**

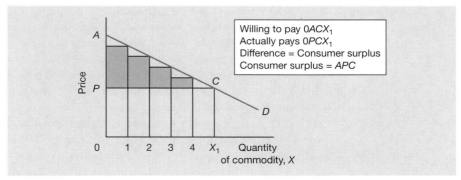

The same principle applies as regards the *money* commodity (M):

$$\frac{MU_X}{MU_M} = \frac{P_X}{P_M}$$

where MU_X / MU_M is the marginal rate of substitution of X for M (MRS_{XM}), i.e. the amount of *money* that the consumer is willing to give up for an extra unit of X. The price of money (P_M) is, of course, unity (how many pounds sterling exchange for one pound sterling?), so we can write $P_M = 1$.

$$\text{Hence } \frac{MU_X}{MU_M} = P_X$$

In other words the marginal utility of an extra unit of X, expressed in terms of the amount of money we are willing to give up to purchase that unit, is equal to its price.

It follows that *each* of the rectangles in Fig. 1.22 represents the marginal utility, in money terms, of purchasing each successive unit of X. Summing all these rectangles then gives us, as an *approximation*, the total utility from purchasing quantity X_1 (i.e. area $0ACX_1$). We now subtract from this area the cost of purchasing X_1, i.e. its price $0P$ times quantity $0X_1$: in other words we subtract the amount the consumer actually pays for X_1 (area $0PCX_1$). The *difference* between the two areas is the **consumer surplus**, i.e. the difference between the money value of the total utility of the purchase by the consumer and the money he actually pays for it. Notice that the smaller the units of purchase, and hence the smaller the rectangles, the more closely will the area under the demand curve approximate to the money value of the total utility of purchase.

As we shall see in Chapter 2, where we can achieve a reliable econometric estimate of the demand curve, we can then measure the area underneath the demand curve as a means of calculating the consumer surplus. Even if our knowledge is restricted to estimating a *segment* of the demand curve only, provided this is the part over which prices are expected to change, then we can still put the idea of consumer surplus into practice.

Non-constant marginal utility of money

So far we have assumed that the marginal utility of money is constant. In this case money can act as a suitable unchanging yardstick (or *numeraire*) by which all other things can be measured. Unfortunately this is unlikely to be the case. At different points on the demand curve the consumer will be left with different amounts of money, and so the value (marginal utility) of money to the consumer will have changed. We can now use indifference curves to examine the implications for measuring consumer surplus of a *non-constant* marginal utility of money income.

In Fig. 1.23(a), commodity X is shown on the horizontal axis and the money commodity on the vertical axis. The budget line of the consumer is MM' and its slope $(-)(P_X/P_M)$ is equal to the price of commodity X since the price (P_M) of one unit of money is 1. Given P_X, the consumer maximises utility at E, buying $0X_1$ of X and paying AM of his income for it, being left with $0A$ amount of money to spend on all other commodities.

We now seek to find the amount of money that the consumer would be willing to pay for $0X_1$ of X rather than do without it. This can be done by drawing an indifference curve I_2 passing through M. If the marginal utility of money income is constant, then the indifference curve I_2 will be vertically parallel to I_1 at each and every quantity of X. For example, at X_1 the slope of I_2 is the same as the slope of I_1.

$$\text{Slope of } I_1 \text{ at quantity } X_1 = MRS_{XM} = \frac{MU_X}{MU_M} = \frac{MU_X}{1} = MU_X$$

$$(\text{given that } MU_M = 1)$$

$$\text{Slope of } I_2 \text{ at quantity } X_1 = MRS_{XM} = \frac{MU_X}{MU_M} = \frac{MU_X}{1} = MU_X$$

In other words, provided that MU_M is constant (here 1), the slopes of the two indifference curves must be equal (at MU_X) for the given quantity X_1 (and for any other given quantity).

The indifference curve I_2 shows that the consumer would be willing to pay $A'M$ for the quantity $0X_1$ since point E' shows that the consumer is indifferent to having $0X_1$ of X

Fig. 1.23

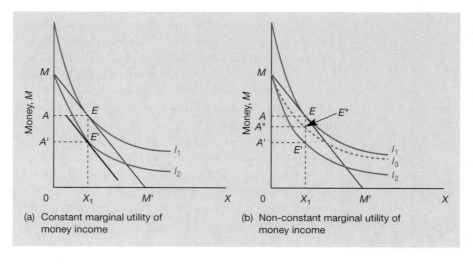

(a) Constant marginal utility of money income

(b) Non-constant marginal utility of money income

and OA' of income to spend on other commodities, or to having none of X and spending all his income 0M on other commodities. That is to say, $A'M$ is the amount of money that the consumer would be willing to pay for $0X_1$ rather than do without it.

We can now represent the **consumer surplus** at X_1 as the difference:

$$A'M - AM = A'A = E'E$$

This is the difference between what the consumer is willing to pay for $0X_1$ ($A'M$) and what he actually pays (AM).

So far we have assumed a constant marginal utility of money income. We can now relax this assumption and use this analysis to investigate the implications of this relaxation for the measurement of consumer surplus.

In Fig. 1.23(b) we now draw a new indifference curve (I_3) through M, representing the fact that there is a **diminishing marginal utility of money income**. Notice that this dashed curve I_3 is flatter than I_1 or I_2 at any given quantity of X. Take, for example, quantity X_1 and compare points E and E''. At each of these points the MU_X is the same, since the quantity of X consumed is the same (namely X_1). However, the marginal utility of the *money commodity* is different at points E and E''. At point E, 0A is the money left to be spent on other commodities. This is greater than at point E'', where only $0A''$ is left to spend on other commodities. Hence at E'' the MU of the money income left is *greater* than at E. It follows that the slope of I_3 is flatter than the slope of I_1 for the given quantity of X (here X_1):

$$\begin{bmatrix} \text{Slope } I_3 \\ \text{at } E'' \end{bmatrix} = \frac{MU_X}{MU_M (A'')} < \frac{MU_X}{MU_M (A)} = \begin{bmatrix} \text{Slope } I_1 \\ \text{at } E \end{bmatrix}$$

It follows from Fig. 1.23(b) that when we allow a diminishing marginal utility of money income (I_3), the consumer would now be willing to pay $A''M$ for quantity X_1 rather than do without. The consumer surplus is the difference:

$$A''M - AM = A''A = E''E$$

This is clearly *smaller* than the consumer surplus ($E'E$) that was obtained on our earlier assumption of constant marginal utility of money income.

It therefore follows that there is a legitimate debate as to exactly how we measure consumer surplus, which will depend in part on the assumptions as to the *rate* of diminishing marginal utility of money income that we build into our analysis. The greater the rate, the smaller our estimated measure of consumer surplus and vice versa.

Clearly we shall have greater confidence in our measure of consumer surplus the more stable is the marginal utility of the money commodity. In other words, we shall have greater confidence the more nearly parallel (vertically) are the indifference curves that we use to map consumer preferences.

Applications and evidence

Although much of the analysis in this chapter might appear rather abstract, there are a wide range of applications for utility theory.

▪ Impact of taxes on incentives

A vital area of policy debate has centred on the allegedly negative impact of higher taxes on incentives to work, save and take risks. Here we focus on the incentives to work aspect, returning to incentives to save and take risks in Chapter 3.

Figure 1.24(a) shows the familiar income–leisure trade-off on the assumptions of flexible daily working time at a constant hourly wage rate. In this useful, if simplistic, presentation, the individual can take OA hours leisure and receive zero income or take zero hours of leisure and receive OB income. The price of leisure in terms of income foregone is given by the *slope* of the budget line, which clearly depends upon the wage rate. At a wage of £7 per hour we have the budget line AB, which pivots inwards to AB', AB'' and AB''' at successively lower hourly wages of £6, £5 and £4 respectively.

The individual's preferences as between income and leisure are indicated by the familiarly shaped indifference curves, such as I_1 and I_2 in Fig. 1.24(b). Each indifference curve represents the combinations of leisure/income that yield a particular level of utility to the individual. The convexity (to the origin) of the indifference curves implies a diminishing marginal rate of substitution between leisure and income: i.e. the more leisure is consumed, the progressively less income the individual is willing to sacrifice for an extra unit of leisure.

A rise in direct tax on earned income can be represented as a reduction in the (net of tax) real wage rate. This can be considered as having two effects, which pull in *opposite directions* (Fig. 1.24(b)). First is a **substitution effect**, with leisure now cheaper via higher taxes, since less real income is sacrificed for each unit of leisure consumed. The positive substitution effect (Hicks–Allen) leads to cheaper leisure being substituted for work, i.e. *less work*. Second is an **income effect**, with real income now reduced via higher taxes. This would mean less consumption of all normal items, in this case leisure, with *more work* now being performed. The overall impact of higher taxes on income clearly depends on the relative strength of the two effects which pull in opposite directions.

Fig. 1.24 Taxes on income and incentives to work.

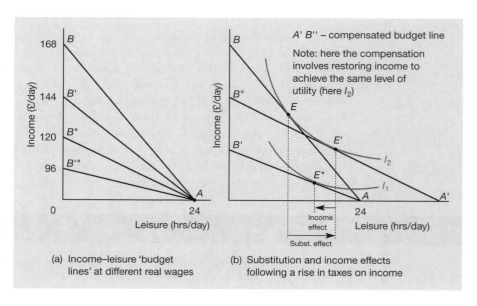

(a) Income–leisure 'budget lines' at different real wages

(b) Substitution and income effects following a rise in taxes on income

In Fig. 1.24(b) the initial equilibrium for the individual is at E with tangency between the income–leisure (budget) line AB and the highest attainable indifference curve, I_2. The higher tax rate on earnings now reduces the real wage, causing the original budget line AB to pivot inwards to AB'. The **total price effect** can be shown as a movement from E to E^*, which can, as usual, be broken down into substitution and income effects. The (Hicks–Allen) *compensated budget line* (see p. 14) $A'B''$ indicates a substitution effect EE', with more of the now cheaper leisure (less work) being consumed. This outweighs the income effect $E'E^*$ of less leisure (more work) being consumed given the reduction in post-tax incomes. The overall result in this case would be less work effort (more leisure) via higher taxes on income.

This analysis yields the familiar upward sloping supply curve of labour with respect to real wages shown in Fig. 1.25(a), reflecting a price–consumption line of the form shown in Fig.1.25(b). Here lower real wages via higher taxes implies less work effort; higher real wages via lower taxes implies more work effort.

Nor would the situation change should the leisure commodity be regarded as inferior. In this case the sign of the income effect could be altered over certain ranges of

Fig. 1.25 **Supply curves of labour and their associated price–consumption lines**

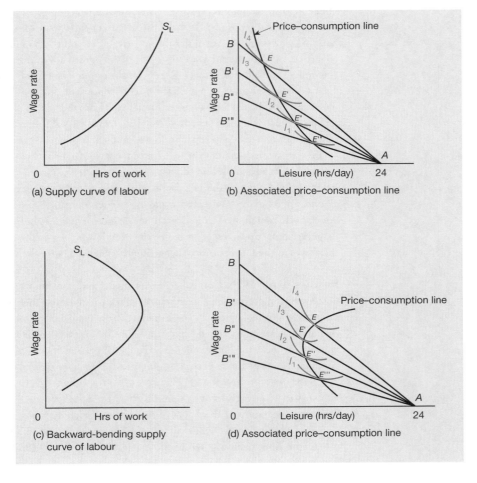

(a) Supply curve of labour

(b) Associated price–consumption line

(c) Backward-bending supply curve of labour

(d) Associated price–consumption line

income. The reduction in real incomes, via higher taxes on earnings, might now *increase* the consumption of leisure, resulting in less work. In this case both substitution and income effects would pull in the *same direction*, with higher taxes invariably reducing work effort.

Clearly it will only be under conditions in which the income effect of higher taxes for a normal leisure commodity outweighs the substitution effect for the leisure commodity that we can expect the *backward bending* labour supply curve of Fig. 1.25(c) and the associated backward bending price consumption line of Fig. 1.25(d). Only under such conditions could we expect higher taxes to lead to more work effort (E to E') and lower taxes to less work effort (E' to E).

Evidence   **Studies up to 1970** Brown and Dawson (1969) conducted an exhaustive review of tax studies in the UK and USA from 1947 to 1968. They concluded that higher taxation had a disincentive effect on work (income effect $<$ substitution effect) for between 5% and 15% of the population. These were mainly people who had the greatest freedom to vary their hours of employment – those without families, the middle-aged, the wealthy and rural workers. In contrast, higher taxation had an incentive effect on work (income effect $>$ substitution effect) for a rather smaller percentage of the population, who were characteristically part of large families, young, less well-off, urban dwellers. From a national viewpoint the small net disincentive effect on the population of higher taxes was regarded by Brown and Dawson as of little significance; over 70% appeared neutral (income $=$ substitution effect) in their work response to higher taxes.

As regards the UK, two of the most important studies reviewed by Brown and Dawson were those based on questionnaires by Break in 1956 and Fields and Stanbury in 1968 (see Brown and Dawson 1969). In 1956, Break found a small net disincentive effect, with an extra 3% of the population claiming higher taxes to be a disincentive to further work than claimed it to be an incentive. In 1968 Fields and Stanbury updated Break's UK study and found the net disincentive effect to have grown to 8% of the population. In both studies the net disincentive effect was greater for higher-income groups, as one might expect with these paying higher marginal taxes (stronger substitution effects). This small growth in overall net disincentive effect between 1956 and 1968, and its being more pronounced at higher-income levels, was really all the empirical support there was in the UK for those suggesting that higher taxes discouraged work effort.

Studies after 1970 Controlled experiments and questionnaire results after 1970 gave no clearer a picture than those before 1970. If, anything, they again pointed to a slight disincentive of higher taxes. For instance, Brown and Levin (see Beenstock 1979) found that an increase in marginal tax rates for 2,000 Scottish workers in 1974 reduced hours worked, at least for higher-income groups. Fiegehen and Reddaway (see Brown 1988) conducted a study on incentives amongst senior managers at board level in 94 companies in 1978, just before the large tax cuts introduced by the (then) newly elected Conservative government a year or so later. Similarly to Break, and to Fields and Stanbury, they showed that 12% of managers reported an incentive effect of high taxation on hours of work, while an equal percentage reported a disincentive effect. The most common response from 41% was 'no reply' or 'don't know'. Fiegehen and

Reddaway concluded: 'It is clear that, in total, any disincentive effects that operated on senior managers had a minimal impact on the activities of British industry.' Such studies were hardly a basis for advocating that tax cuts would lead to an upsurge in work effort!

An important study by the Institute of Fiscal Studies (Dilnot and Kell 1988) tried to assess the effects on tax receipts of the 1979/80 reduction in the top rate of UK income tax from 83% to 60%. The argument used to support these top-rate tax cuts was that the lower income tax rates should provide extra incentives to work harder and thus boost tax revenue. The study found that the subsequent increase in tax revenue during the period to 1985/86 could be explained mostly by factors such as employment growth, growth of earnings and growth of self-employment rather than by any incentive effects. Dilnot and Kell felt that any incentive effect that might have been present could only account, at most, for £1.2 billion or 3% of the total increase in tax revenues over the period studied.

Flemming and Oppenheimer (1996) have also found little evidence to support the suggestion that reduced marginal tax rates at the upper end would unleash entrepreneurial talent and labour effort. They argue that if marginal tax rates for higher skilled workers fell, then one might expect that the *relative price* of their effort, i.e. gross money wage per hour, would fall *vis-à-vis* other lower skilled groups via an increase in relative supply of effort resulting in a decrease in relative price (i.e. gross money wage per hour). However, pre-tax hourly earnings between different skill and occupational levels have widened considerably in the UK over the last 15 years rather than narrowed, indicating that the higher-income earners have *increased* their relative wages. This rather suggests that the higher income, higher skilled segment of the workforce may not have increased the number of hours worked (i.e. the supply of effort) in response to lower marginal tax rates, but may merely have benefited from *demand* changes that have moved in their favour. Interestingly, the disincentive to work resulting from high real marginal rates of tax is arguably more of a problem for those on below-average incomes, as the discussion of the poverty 'trap' indicates (p. 34).

The Laffer curve | Professor Laffer derived a relationship between tax revenue and tax rates of the form shown in Fig. 1.26. The curve was the result of econometric techniques, through which a 'least squares line' was fitted to past UK observations of tax revenue and tax rate. The dotted line indicates the extension of the fitted relationship (continuous line), as there will tend to be zero tax revenue at both 0% and 100% tax rates.

Tax revenue = tax rate × output (income), so that a 0% tax rate yields zero tax revenue, whatever the level of output. A 100% tax rate is assumed to discourage all output, except that for subsistence, again yielding zero tax revenue. Tax revenue must reach a maximum at some intermediate tax rate between these extremes.

The London Business School (Beenstock 1979) has estimated a Laffer curve for the UK using past data. Tax revenue was found to reach a peak at around a 60% 'composite tax rate', i.e. one that includes both direct and indirect taxes, as well as various social security payments, all expressed as a percentage of GDP. If the tax rate rises above 60% then the disincentive effect on output is so strong (i.e. output falls so much) that tax revenue (tax rate × output) actually falls, despite the higher tax rate. The Laffer curve in fact begins to flatten out at around a 45% composite tax rate. In other words, as tax rate rises above

Fig. 1.26 **The Laffer curve.**

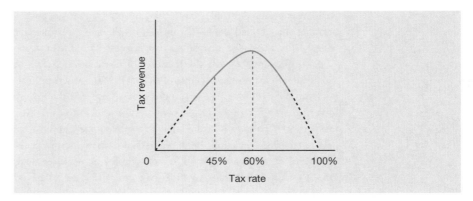

45%, the disincentive effect of higher taxes on output is strong enough to mean that little extra tax revenue results. Econometric studies of this type have given support to those in favour of limiting overall rates of tax. It is interesting to note that shortly after this study, the top rate of tax on earned income in the UK was indeed reduced from 83% to 60%.

Further evidence on the impact of cuts in high rates of British taxation has been provided by Minford and Ashton (see Brown 1988). The latter study concluded that the cut in the higher British tax rates to 40% would increase hours worked by 8% (i.e. income effect < substitution effect).

In summary, those who advocate supply side economics, with tax reduction a key instrument for improving economic incentives, leading to an upsurge of productive activity, receive limited support from empirical studies. Only a small net disincentive effect has been found from studies using questionnaires, such as those by Break and Stanbury. This conclusion was reinforced by the later studies of Dilnot and Kell and Flemming and Oppenheimer. On the other hand, the Laffer curve constructed for the UK by the London Business School, and work by Minford in the UK and Lindsey in the USA, do indicate that reductions in the composite rate of tax below 60% and down as far as around 45% have strong incentive effects on output – the converse of rises in tax rate between 45% and 60% having strong disincentive effects. However, the UK composite tax rate is currently less than 40%, and reductions below this level receive little support from econometric studies.

Poverty and unemployment traps

One area where the facts do strongly suggest that the current level and type of taxation may have eroded incentives concerns the poverty and unemployment traps. The families in these traps are enmeshed in a web of overlapping tax schedules and benefit thresholds.

The *poverty trap* describes a situation where a person on low income may gain very little, or even lose, from an increase in gross earnings. This is because as *gross* earnings rise, the amount of benefits received decreases while income tax deductions increase. In extreme circumstances *net* income may actually fall when a person's *gross* earnings rise, i.e. an implicit marginal tax rate (or marginal net income deduction rate) of over 100%. During the past decade the UK government has tried to resolve the gross disincentive effects of such high rates of deduction by relating benefits to net income after tax. However, as can be seen in Table 1.3 the problems of the poverty trap dilemma still occur, if not to the same extent as before.

	April 1998			
	(£ pw)	(£ pw)	(£ pw)	(£ pw)
Gross earnings	50.00	100.00	150.00	200.00
Plus:				
Child benefit	20.75	20.75	20.75	20.75
Family credit	92.40	81.12	55.49	31.75
Housing benefit	43.73	21.73	14.59	7.98
Council tax benefit	11.07	4.30	2.11	0.07
Less:				
Income tax	0.00	0.00	8.38	19.48
National Insurance	0.00	4.88	9.88	14.88
Net income	217.95	223.02	224.68	226.19

Notes: Calculations are for a married man with two children aged 10 and 14, Local Authority rent of £50 a week and Council Tax of £13 a week
Source: Adapted from DSS, *Tax/ Benefit Model Tables* (April 1998)

Table 1.3 shows the net income situation of a married man with two children in April 1998 when his gross income rises from £50 to £200 per week. We can see that net income rises very little over this range. For example, an increase in income from £100 to £150, i.e. £50 per week, gives only an extra £1.66 in income after deductions, i.e. £48.34 is lost. This results in an implicit marginal tax rate of about 97% (48.34/50). In 1992, using exactly the same family situation and gross income change, the rate was as high as 124%. The improvements in the family credit arrangements since 1992 have eased such extreme situations, but the rates are still very high indeed, and provide little encouragement for those in the area of the poverty trap to work harder. Many are still caught in this poverty trap, with the number of families where the head of the household faces a relatively high implicit marginal tax rate of 70% and over doubling since 1988 to nearly 725,000 by 1998 (HMSO 1998). A high implicit marginal tax rate can therefore act as a major disincentive to low income earners.

As we have noted, the poverty trap relates to people who are *in work* but find little incentive to improve their situation by extra work effort. Some workers never even enter the labour market because of another problem, often called the *unemployment trap*.

The unemployment trap occurs when people find that their income when employed is no better than if they were unemployed. Table 1.4 shows that when the gross wage of the married man in our example is £150 per week, the net income after various allowances and deductions is £224.68. If he was unemployed, his net income would be £195.70: i.e. the *replacement rate* is 87%. The replacement rate measures the proportion of a person's net income that will be 'replaced' by the benefit system if that person loses his or her job. The introduction of family credit in 1988 has helped to decrease the number of people with replacement rates of over 100%. The replacement rate for a person in exactly the same situation as our present example in 1992 was 104%, so things have got marginally better. However, the fact that the income of a person when out of work is still 87% of his income when in work provides little incentive to work. There were still 595,000 people in the UK with replacement rates of 70% and over in 1998 (HMSO 1998).

Table 1.4
Unemployed married couple (one earner previously working more than 30 hours per week) with two children aged 10 and 14.

In work	(£ pw)	Out of work	(£ pw)
Gross earnings	150.00	Jobseeker's allowance	132.70
Child benefit	20.75	Housing benefit	50.00
Family credit	55.49	Council tax benefit	13.00
Housing benefit	14.59		
Council tax benefit	2.11		
Income tax	8.38		
National Insurance	9.88		
Net income	224.68	**Net income**	195.70
Replacement ratio	195.70/224.68 = 87%		

Notes: Calculations are for a married man with two children aged 10 and 14, local authority rent of £50 a week and council tax of £13 a week.
Source: Adapted from DSS, *Tax/Benefit Model Tables* (April 1998)

From these examples, we can see that both poverty and unemployment traps provide a disincentive to work because people caught in these problematic situations find it difficult, if not impossible, to improve their position through their own efforts.

Labour supply curves   We noted (p. 31) the circumstances under which the supply curves of labour would be positively sloped throughout (Fig. 1.25(a)) and negatively sloped (backward bending) over parts of its length (Fig. 1.25(c)). Here we consider a number of empirical studies that take this issue further, many of which make use of econometric techniques.

Econometric studies   Multiple regression analysis (see Appendix 2) has been used to estimate *labour supply elasticities*, i.e. the ratios of percentage change in quantity of labour supplied to percentage change in wage rate. In the UK, cross-sectional data have been collected on a large number of individuals, indicating the number of hours worked per time period and the levels of income received from various sources. Blundell (1994) brings together estimates of labour supply elasticities from a number of econometric studies. Such estimates have tended to distinguish between labour supply elasticities for married women, single parent mothers and husbands in the UK (see Table 1.5).

Table 1.5 **Labour supply elasticities.**

	Uncompensated	Compensated
Married women		
no children	0.37	0.44
young children	0.29	0.50
old children	0.71	0.82
Lone mothers	0.76	1.28
Husbands	−0.23	0.13

Source: Adapted from Blundell (1994)

- *Uncompensated* labour supply elasticities in Table 1.5 represent the 'total wage effect', taking into account both income and substitution effects. As previously noted (p. 30) the uncompensated labour supply elasticities can be positive or negative, depending on the relative magnitude of income and substitution effects.
- *Compensated* labour supply elasticities in Table 1.5 represent only the substitution effect, and must therefore be positive under a Hicks–Allen approach (p. 30).

From Table 1.5 we can see the influence of the negative income effect on the supply of labour in terms of the higher values for the compensated as compared with uncompensated labour supply elasticities. For example, a 1% rise in wages for lone mothers will lead to a 1.28% rise in hours worked when only the substitution effect is taken into account (less leisure and more work since leisure is now relatively more expensive). However, if we now allow the income effect to come into play the 1% rise in wages leads to a 0.52% reduction in hours worked (more leisure and less work via higher income), so that only a 0.76% rise in labour supply results overall from a 1% rise in wages. The (negative) income effect on labour supply of a rise in wages offsets to some extent the positive substitution effect represented by the compensated labour supply elasticities.

Indeed for *husbands* there is evidence of the backward-sloping supply curve of Fig. 1.25(c) (p. 31). Here a 1% rise in wages results in a positive substitution effect on labour supply (+ 0.13%), but this is more than offset by the negative income effect (− 0.36%), giving an overall fall in labour supply of 0.26% from a 1% rise in wages.

◼ Kinked budget line and non-proportionality

The linear and uniform budget lines used so far in the chapter imply a constant wage rate, whether pre- or post-tax. Of course in practice wage rates may vary between standard-time rates and the higher *overtime* rates; similarly taxes may be levied at differential rates from zero upwards, depending on the level of income received. In other words the idea of proportionality embedded in our linear and uniform budget lines is, to some extent, a departure from the reality of corporate and governmental policy action. Here we examine some of the implications of introducing non-proportional taxes and payments into our earlier analysis.

Overtime payments

We have seen that the impact of a higher uniform wage rate may, or may not, increase the supply of work effort. Where the relative strength of the income effect (purchase more leisure) outweighs that of the substitution effect (purchase less of the, now, more expensive leisure), then there will be less work effort. We will be on a backward-bending segment of the supply of labour curve.

One remedy by which firms might ensure an increase in the supply of work effort would be to introduce an element of price discrimination into their wages policy. As we shall see, only the substitution effect would then be in play beyond some threshold level of work effort, ensuring an increased supply of labour and avoiding any surplus or rental (see p. 410) payment to existing units of work effort.

In Fig. 1.27 we are initially in equilibrium at E, with a uniform wage rate giving the income–leisure budget line AB tangent to the individual's highest indifference curve I_1. Here $0L_1$ leisure is consumed, and L_1A hours are worked. A uniform rise in the wage rate, to give budget line AB' may (as here), or may not, yield an increase in the supply of work effort, depending on the relative strengths of substitution and income effects that

Fig. 1.27
Applications of a kinked budget line: overtime payments.

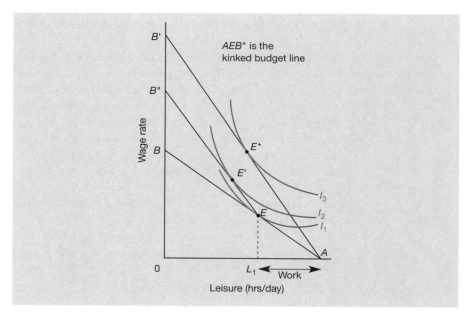

pull in opposite directions. Even where the total price effect of the move from E to $E*$ *does* yield extra work effort, the cost to the employer involves a surplus or rental payment of a higher wage to the L_1A units of work effort already supplied. This might be avoided by consolidating L_1A hours of work effort into the standard time wage rate, and paying higher overtime rates only on any extra hours worked. This gives the new and kinked budget line AEB'' in Fig.1.27 and the new equilibrium position E' with level of utility I_2. The employer gains in at least two respects:

- There is now a degree of certainty that the higher wage will induce more work effort. This follows from the fact that no income effect now results from the original (L_1A) hours of work effort already supplied. The emphasis is on the substitution effect of trading the now dearer leisure for income (i.e. more work). Indeed in a situation where $B''E$ is parallel to $B'A$, $B''E$ can be regarded as the compensated budget line of the Slutsky variety (see p. 15), and the move from E to E' can be regarded as a pure substitution effect giving rise to more work effort.
- There is no need to pay extra to secure the L_1A of work effort already supplied, unlike a situation in which a (higher) uniform wage rate is paid to all. Of course employees secure a lower level of utility via the price discrimination implicit in overtime payment rates. Nevertheless there is a gain in individual utility for those working overtime: hence the focus on the length of the standard working week in many union–employer negotiations.

Fringe benefits versus monetary rewards

Another application of the kinked budget line involves the issue of whether to reward employees with greater (taxed) *monetary rewards* or with enhanced (often untaxed) *fringe benefits* paid for by the employer. Such fringe benefits might include medical services, pension contributions, company cars, and so on.

In Fig. 1.28 we assume that the individual is initially in equilibrium at E, consuming F_1 of the fringe benefit and 0_1 of 'other goods'. The initial budget line is AB, with $0A$ of the fringe benefit potentially purchasable at current prices should the entire income be spent

Fig. 1.28 **Fringe benefits compared with equivalent-value cash payments.**

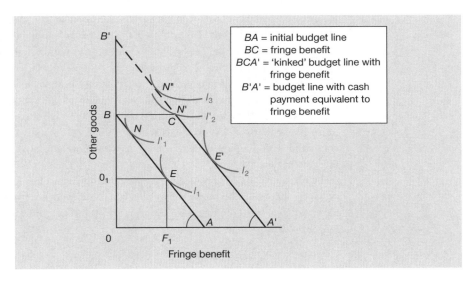

BA = initial budget line
BC = fringe benefit
BCA' = 'kinked' budget line with fringe benefit
B'A' = budget line with cash payment equivalent to fringe benefit

on that item. We can now use Fig. 1.28 to compare the choice between additional income and extra fringe benefit:

- where the fringe benefit is taxed at the prevailing rate;
- where the fringe benefit is untaxed or taxed below the prevailing rate.

If BC units of the fringe benefit are provided whatever the current level of purchase of that item, then the budget line shifts outwards and to the right, giving the new kinked budget line BCA'. The dashed line $B'C$ is irrelevant as (in the absence of resale of the fringe benefit) no more income is available to purchase more 'other goods'.

If, instead, a cash increase of £X in income is on offer to the individual equivalent to the amount needed to purchase the BC units of the fringe benefit, then the budget line shifts outwards and to the right to $A'B'$. Here more of all items are purchasable at the current (unchanged) relative prices, including more 'other goods'.

In this situation we could have a variety of new equilibria. For example, an individual already consuming a significant amount of the fringe benefit may move from E to E', with utility rising from I_1 to I_2. In this case the same gain in utility occurs whether or not the option for remuneration is more fringe benefit or an equivalent amount of cash income.

However, an individual with a weaker preference for the fringe benefit may move from N to N' in a situation of provision of fringe benefit, the latter being a corner point solution with utility rising from I'_1 to I'_2 (see p. 20). However, the option of equivalent payment in cash could yield still higher utility for this individual, who now maximises utility by moving onto the (previously unattainable) dashed segment of the budget line $B'C$ to N'' with utility I_3.

It follows from this analysis that an increase in cash payments as compared with an equivalent increase in fringe benefits will leave the individual either no worse off or better off. There would then seem to be an a priori case in favour of the greater consumer choice implied by the cash payment as a means of remuneration.

However, the analysis so far has assumed that the equivalent income derived from the fringe benefit is taxed at the prevailing rate imposed on the cash payment. If we now relax that assumption, and assume that the fringe benefit is untaxed or taxed at a lower rate, then our conclusion may no longer hold. In this situation £X of free (or less highly taxed) fringe benefit may be worth $>$£X in cash subject to the prevailing rate of tax; put another way, the cash payment (net of tax) will be less than £X of free (or less highly taxed) fringe benefit. As a consequence the new cash equivalent budget line will lie *inside* $A'B'$. This will make I_3 and I_2 unattainable and may even make I'_2 unattainable, depending on consumer tastes and the size of any additional tax incurred by cash payments as opposed to fringe benefit. The greater the tax penalty for cash payment, the more likely that some individuals will be worse off in a situation of cash payment as compared with fringe benefit: i.e. the relatively more attractive the fringe benefit mode of payment becomes.

In situations of high prevailing marginal tax rates and low (or zero) tax rates levied on fringe benefits, the more we would expect payment by fringe benefit to predominate. Our earlier conclusion of an a priori preference in favour of cash payments no longer holds.

Non-price competition Companies such as Hoover, Hotpoint, Philips and Electrolux produce appliances such as washing machines, refrigerators, dishwashers, tumble dryers and vacuum cleaners. In recent years there has been growing interest by firms in the use of free gifts as a means of attracting new or maintaining existing customers. This has been particularly true of promotions involving free Air Miles or air tickets. One such promotion that received a great deal of attention was the Hoover free flight promotion, which (following Ison 1994) we now use as a further application of kinked budget lines.

Households tend to purchase products such as vacuum cleaners only when their existing appliance has irrevocably broken down, or perhaps when they are moving house. The market for such products is therefore by nature rather static, a situation not helped by the economic recession of the early 1990s. Given these factors, Hoover launched a free flight promotion in 1992 as a means of stimulating demand and gaining market share at the expense of its competitors' products. Customers who spent a minimum of £100 on the purchase of one of their products qualified for two free return flights to one of six European cities. This was subsequently extended to include US destinations. In reality consumers had to spend at least £119, since that was the price of the cheapest Hoover product, namely a vacuum cleaner, that qualified for free air tickets.

The notion of free gifts, and in particular the Hoover free flight promotion, can be considered using indifference curve analysis. In brief, available free flights produces a kinked budget line, as shown in Fig. 1.29.

The horizontal axis measures the quantity of Hoover products and free air flights and the vertical axis the quantity of all other goods. In the absence of free air flights the consumer would face a budget line of AF. Given the preference of the consumer there would be an equilibrium at point E where AF is tangential to the highest attainable indifference curve I_1. In this case $0Q_1$ of Hoover products are consumed and $0G$ of all other goods. With the launch of the Hoover offer the consumer who spent a minimum of £100 was eligible for the free flights. The amount of Hoover products purchased for £100 is represented by $Q_1 Q_a$ in Fig. 1.29, i.e. more Hoover appliances are bought and less of other goods. This entitles the consumer to free air flights represented by T, or $Q_a Q_b$ in Fig. 1.29.

Fig. 1.29 **Hoover free flight promotion and kinked budget line.**

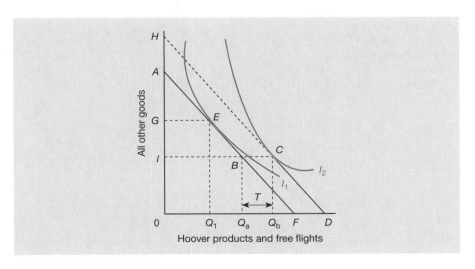

Given the situation illustrated in Fig. 1.29, once the free air flights had been obtained, and provided the price of Hoover products relative to all other goods did not change, then the budget line would continue along a (parallel) line *CD*. Overall therefore, the budget line would be *kinked*, represented by *ABCD*, as opposed to *AF* before the promotion. The free flights offer represents an increase in the consumer's real income but it does not allow the consumer to increase expenditure on other goods. The air tickets cannot be exchanged for cash: thus it is not possible for the consumer to buy more of other goods, i.e. move along the dotted section marked *HC*.

If consumers have indifference curves as illustrated in our diagram then they would be attracted by the offer and would purchase a Hoover product that qualifies them for the free flight. This will have the effect of moving the consumer onto a higher indifference curve, I_2, which results in an increase in the level of satisfaction at a new equilibrium of *C*. At this new equilibrium there will be less spent on other goods: 0*I* as compared with 0*G*. It is likely to be the case that the reduced expenditure on other goods would include appliances produced by Hoover's main competitors.

However, consumers will be affected in different ways by the free flight promotion. For example, the consumer may have indifference curves as illustrated in Fig. 1.30.

In such a situation the consumer would choose *not* to take advantage of the Hoover offer. The indifference curves are relatively flat as compared with Fig. 1.29. It follows that the level of satisfaction is greater in the initial situation, point *E* on indifference curve I_1, than it would be if the consumer took advantage of the offer, point *C* on indifference curve I_2.

It is important to note that Figs 1.29 and 1.30 are based on the fact that the consumer already purchases Hoover products, equal to $0Q_1$, prior to the free offer. However, these figures could easily have been presented on the basis that the consumer did not initially purchase any Hoover product. This would have meant that the consumer indifference curve, I_1, would then have intersected the vertical axis at point A. In practice it soon became apparent to market analysts that Fig. 1.29 more accurately represented consumer preferences.

Fig. 1.30 Impact of consumer preferences on the outcome of the free flight promotion.

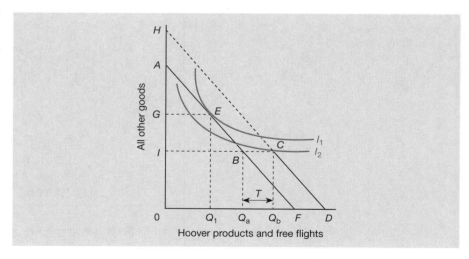

The Hoover promotion was successful in terms of the level of demand it generated, but it created a number of major difficulties. First, additional labour had to be employed and the factory had to be placed on seven-day working in order to meet the increased demand for appliances. Second, it soon became apparent that consumers were buying the product for the free flight offer rather than for the product itself. This became evident from advertisements that began to appear in the second-hand section of local newspapers and *Exchange and Mart* for Hoover appliances, mainly vacuum cleaners, which had been bought but never used. This was hardly a policy aimed at improving brand loyalty! Third, and arguably the most problematic area, was the fact that the offer exceeded all expectations and thus proved to be a costly promotion. With all promotions it is forecast that a good percentage of those buying the product will not actually take up the promotional offer for which they are eligible. For travel-related promotions it is estimated that the level of take up is 10% or below. In terms of the Hoover promotion a higher than expected number of consumers had indifference curve schedules like those illustrated in Fig. 1.29 as opposed to Fig. 1.30. As a result Hoover found it difficult and expensive to cater for the huge demand for free airline tickets for which its customers were now eligible. With hindsight Hoover could have possibly made the offer more restrictive. For example, they could have set the point of eligibility at £200 rather than £100, or offered only one free ticket rather than two. In many promotions the customer has to apply for the offer of a free gift, and this often involves them in having to make additional purchases such as hotel accommodation or restaurant meals. This would have proved to be an additional cost to the customer and could ultimately have acted as a deterrent to taking advantage of the free flight offer.

Fixed quantity subsidy versus voucher systems

Although the comparison between these two approaches can be extended to many commodities, education is frequently the focus for such a debate.

Fixed quantity subsidy The idea of a fixed quantity subsidy is one in which the government will provide a guaranteed quantity of some good or service: for example, free education in the state school system between five years and sixteen years. There is a view that the provision of a guaranteed quantity entitlement can actually result in a *reduced* consumption of educational services. This view can be discussed in the context of Fig. 1.31.

Fig. 1.31 **Fixed quantity subsidy versus voucher systems in the allocation of educational services.**

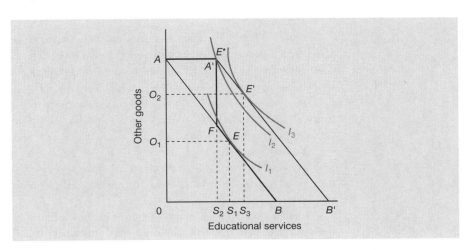

Prior to any such guaranteed entitlement, the assumption is that the individual household can purchase varying quantities of educational services from the private sector at a (here constant) certain price *vis-à-vis* other goods. The budget line *AB* outlines these possibilities and, pre-entitlement, the individual household maximises utility at point E with $0S_1$ educational services consumed.

Suppose now that a fixed quantity entitlement of $0S_2$ educational services is provided (e.g. free schooling at a local state school). This shifts the budget line outwards and parallel to itself, as the individual household can now consume the original $0A$ 'other goods' and $0S_2$ educational services. This gives the kinked budget line *AA' FB*.

To consume more educational services than the free quantity $0S_2$, the household must forgo the state schooling and pay the *full cost* of private schooling along the *FB* segment of the original budget line. The *marginal cost* to the household of consuming more than the $0S_2$ free entitlement is clearly very high. For example, to purchase an extra S_2S_1 educational services it must forgo O_1A 'other goods'.

Faced with the *AA' FB* budget line, the household maximises utility at the (corner) point E^* on the higher indifference curve I_2. This is preferable to the household compared with the original situation E, with indifference curve I_1, yet fewer educational services are being consumed ($0S_2 < 0S_1$). The household has 'traded' $S_1 - S_2$ educational services for O_1A 'other goods'.

Clearly it is possible that some households will consume *fewer* educational services than might have been the case prior to a fixed quantity entitlement. However, other families initially in equilibrium along segment *AF* of the original (pre-entitlement) budget line may now consume *more* educational services than before. The overall outcome cannot be predicted depending, for example, on the relative strength of initial household preferences for educational services *vis-à-vis* 'other goods'.

Voucher system   Much active debate has centred around a *voucher system* proposal, which would seek to reduce the marginal cost to households of consuming more than the minimum entitlement of educational services. There are many versions of the voucher system, but the idea is usually that a given value voucher for educational services is transportable, in the sense that it can be spent on any state or private sector provider, with households able to top up spending beyond the voucher value should they be so inclined.

We can use Fig. 1.31 to discuss such a voucher system, assuming the cash value of the voucher to be the equivalent of purchasing $0S_2$ educational services from the state or private sectors. We now have the kinked budget line *AA' B'*. Since the voucher can only be spent on educational services, no fewer educational services can be purchased than in the previous system. The household may still maximise utility by remaining at E^* but, should it prefer to purchase more educational services, it could move to E' and indifference curve I_3, purchasing $0S_3$ educational services. In Fig. 1.31 it uses the voucher to purchase $0S_2$ educational services and tops up by paying AO_2 of its own income for a further $S_2 - S_3$ educational services. This could be via using the services of schools in the state sector that charge higher fees than the value of voucher available or by using schools in the private sector.

Overall such a voucher system might lead some families to purchase more educational services than they would under a fixed quantity entitlement system. The *marginal cost* of such a purchasing decision has been substantially reduced under this voucher system. Instead of paying AO_1 in terms of other goods for an extra $S_2 - S_1$ of educational services as it would under a fixed quantity subsidy, the household now only pays AO_2 for an extra $S_3 - S_2$ of educational services.

Of course this analysis has avoided the complexities of *supply-side* responses, rather simplistically assuming that the supply of educational services adjusts readily to changes in household demands.

Giffen goods and subsistence

Davies (1994) considers in some detail the circumstances under which a Giffen good (see p. 17) is likely to occur under the *neoclassical* ordinalist approach. It can in fact be demonstrated that the following condition renders a Giffen good more likely to occur, with negative income effects outweighing any positive substitution effect of a price fall, thereby violating the law of demand: namely that indifference curves closer to the origin become progressively steeper and linear (see also Silberberg and Walker 1984). This condition makes corner (or near corner) solutions more likely to result as a final consumer equilibrium, with specialisation (or near specialisation) on a commodity, even one whose price has risen! For the purposes of this analysis we demonstrate the Giffen good case taking a price *rise*, the law of demand being violated by *more* of the commodity whose price has risen being consumed, rather than less.

Davies shows how the *classical* emphasis on subsistence can be incorporated into modern neoclassical analysis, highlighting the reasons for Giffen goods occurring more frequently in earlier times of poverty and less frequently in modern times of rising (average) real incomes. Clearly *calorific intake* becomes a vital element in consumer utility functions when any shortfall of intake can lead to starvation and death. By including calorific intake into consumer utility functions, alongside the more usual price, taste and other commodity attributes, the Giffen good effect in economies close to subsistence can be readily predicted.

Fig. 1.32 **Giffen behaviour with a subsistence constraint and a calorie-modified utility function (see Davies 1994).**

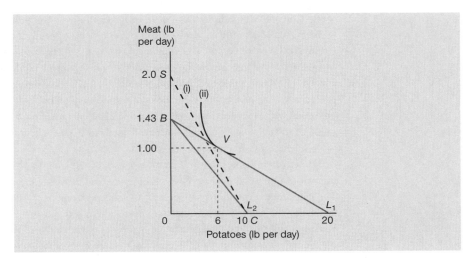

Figure 1.32 illustrates the impact of introducing *both* a minimum calorific subsistence constraint and a calorific attribute to commodities, which influences the rate at which consumers are willing to substitute one for another. The figure represents the commodities widely used in early Giffen good analysis, namely potatoes and meat.

The exposition assumes:

- consumer requires a daily intake of 3,000 calories for survival;
- potatoes yield 300 calories per lb weight;
- meat yields 1,500 calories per lb weight.

The food budget is assumed fixed at $5 per day, with the price of meat $3.50 per lb and the price of potatoes $0.25 per lb. Figure 1.32 presents a **budget line** BL_1, which reflects the $5.00 daily income of the consumer and the respective prices of $3.50 for meat and $0.25 for potatoes. The additional subsistence constraint, SC, is derived from our assumption of the necessity of consuming at least 3,000 calories per day and from the assumed calorific yields of 300 calories per lb for potatoes and 1,500 calories per lb for meat.

Of course the **utility function** is implicit in the shape and position of successive indifference curves. Note here that it would be unrealistic for any indifference curve, in whole or in part, to exist *below* the subsistence constraint SC. Otherwise we should be implying that consumption bundles that are inadequate (in terms of calorific content) to sustain life nevertheless convey pleasure or satisfaction. It follows that the lowest possible indifference curve must either start on the subsistence constraint or else be coincident with the constraint. At this subsistence level, a consumer would only be willing to substitute potatoes for meat if the calorific loss from the latter was counterbalanced by an equivalent calorific gain from the former. Now this trade-off between commodities at rates that just support life exactly mirrors the relationship embodied in the subsistence constraint. Consequently the lowest possible indifference curve must be the subsistence constraint itself. In Fig. 1.32 then, the subsistence constraint, SC, is also designated indifference curve (i). At higher levels of consumption, where neither subsistence nor calorific content is a consideration, the form of the indifference curves will be influenced by the ability of the commodities to yield *other* sources of utility such as taste, texture and so forth. Convexity of indifference curve would doubtless emerge here (see p. 3).

In Fig. 1.32 the initial equilibrium occurs at V, a point *outside* the subsistence constraint. If the price of potatoes now increases to $0.50 per pound, the budget line pivots inward to BL_2. This causes the consumer's real income to fall so substantially that the subsistence constraint, SC, becomes binding. Accordingly the consumer reorders his preferences on the basis of calorific content yielding an equilibrium – which here is synonymous with the identification of an attainable, life-sustaining consumption basket – at point C. In the process, consumption of potatoes has *risen* from 6 to 10 lb following the price *increase*, a Giffen response.

Davies (1994) notes that in common-sense terms, what has happened is that the rise in the price of potatoes both reduces real income and increases the cost of obtaining calories. The consumer responds by substituting the cheapest source of calories – which is still potatoes – for the more expensive source, meat. The result is a corner solution, because a diet consisting solely of potatoes is uniquely the cheapest source of subsistence, and the fall in real income was so large that the consumer effectively had no other choice.

This analysis emphasises a number of key points as regards the emergence of a Giffen good:

- The level of real income necessary for Giffen behaviour to occur is extremely low, namely that level that just sustains biological subsistence.
- The utility function most commonly associated with Giffen goods does not begin at the origin. Rather it begins with a set of consumption bundles (in positive commodity space) reflecting the minimum calorific levels of subsistence.
- Although the lowest indifference curve will be perfectly linear (reflecting this subsistence constraint), the higher indifference curves will possess the usual convexity properties previously associated with Giffen goods.

The approach in Fig. 1.32 can be developed to help explain the observation of Marshall that a large and negative income elasticity for basic foods occurs amongst the poorest (and only the poorest) sections of society. In Fig. 1.33 the initial budget line $B_1 L_1$ represents an extremely low level of income in which complete specialisation in potato consumption occurs at corner point C, with the binding subsistence constraint SC forming the lowest indifference curve (i). We now suppose that incomes progressively rise for these (poor) consumers from $B_1 L_1$ to $B_2 L_2$ and then further to $B_3 L_3$, indicated by parallel outward shifts of the respective budget lines. Successive tangency solutions with highest attainable indifference curves occur at V and W, giving the **income–consumption curve** CVW.

As we can see from Fig. 1.33, the initial increase in income induced a substantial and *negative* income effect (C to V), with subsequent rises of income inducing *positive* income effects (e.g. V to W). The implied Giffen behaviour at low levels of income could equally occur via price rises in potatoes *or* via falls in real incomes of consumers. In the extreme case either of these situations could lead, in this analysis, to complete specialization on potatoes, as at point C.

After reviewing the Irish Potato famine of 1845 as regards Giffen-type behaviour, Davies concludes that *wherever* binding subsistence constraints occur, the consumption patterns of destitute people are likely to display certain Giffen characteristics.

Fig. 1.33 **An income–consumption curve with a subsistence constraint.**

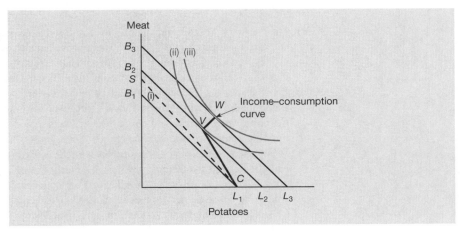

Key terms

Budget line
Cardinalist
Consumer surplus
Diminishing marginal rate of
  substitution
Diminishing marginal utility of
  money income
Engel curve
Giffen goods
Income consumption line
Income effect
Indifference curves

Inferior goods
Marginal rate of substitution of X
  for Y
Marginal utility
Ordinalist
Price–consumption line
Producer surplus
Revealed preference hypothesis
Slutsky equation
Substitution effect
Total price effect

Full definitions can be found in the 'Glossary of terms' (pp. 699–71)

Review questions

1. A student has received a one-off unexpected extra monthly grant allowance of
£38 and has decided to spend it on entertainment. She can spend the money on
tickets to the cinema, concert hall and jazz club, and the prices of the tickets are
£2, £4 and £8 respectively. Her marginal utility functions, measured in utils, are
shown in Table 1.6.

Table 1.6

No. of tickets	Cinema	Concert hall	Jazz club
1	10.0	12.0	25.0
2	8.0	8.0	18.0
3	4.0	6.0	16.0
4	3.5	4.0	12.0
5	3.0	2.0	10.0
6	2.0	1.5	7.0
7	1.0	0.5	5.0
8	0.5	0.25	3.0

(a) How many tickets should she buy for the cinema, concert hall and jazz club if
she is to maximise her total utility, assuming that she wants to spend her extra
money on a spread of entertainment? Explain why this is the only combination
that fulfils all the necessary conditions for utility maximisation.

(b) If the student is told at the box office that there are only two jazz tickets
available, how should she re-allocate the surplus money from the third jazz
ticket between cinema and concert hall tickets in order to achieve a 'second
best' alternative to her original choice?

(c) When the student purchases her ticket at the box office she is also told that,
had she booked two months earlier, she could have bought any number of
jazz tickets at an introductory offer of £6 per ticket. If the student had been
able to book these cheaper tickets would her total utility have been
maximised at a higher level than in part (a) above?

2. A consumer has a budget of £60 per month to spend on clothes or eating out. If the average price of clothes is £12 and the average meal out costs £6 then:

   (a) Write down the general budget expression using Q_c and Q_e for the quantity of clothes and frequency of eating out respectively.
   (b) Derive the budget equation from the budget expression.
   (c) What is the slope of the budget line and the value of the vertical and horizontal intercepts, assuming that quantity of clothes is measured on the vertical axis?

3. A consumer's indifference curve has been constructed using data from questionnaire surveys. A line of 'best fit' that traces the relationship between the two commodities Q_x and Q_y shows a downward–sloping indifference curve, convex to the origin and with an equation of $Q_y = 36/Q_x$. The equation for the consumer's budget line is $Q_y = 12 - Q_x$.

   (a) Calculate how much Q_x and Q_y the consumer should choose in order to maximise satisfaction.
   (b) Prove that the slopes of the indifference curve and the budget line are tangential at these values of Q_x and Q_y.

4. The figures in Table 1.7 relate to two separate indifference curves, and show the combinations of leisure and income between which a worker is indifferent.

Table 1.7

Indifference curve 1		Indifference curve 2	
Income (£/wk)	Leisure (hrs/wk)	Income (£/wk)	Leisure (hrs/wk)
672	20	1,176	35
504	22	840	50
336	38	672	62
252	57	554	75
168	83	454	100
151	102	370	125
133	125	336	150

   (a) Draw the indifference curves as accurately as possible using graph paper.
   (b) Working on the simplified assumption that the individual can spend either all the week enjoying leisure or all the time in work, draw his budget line on the assumption that the rate of pay is £2 per hour. Measure from the graph the approximate income/leisure/work trade-off that ensures maximum satisfaction at this wage rate.
   (c) If the income per hour rose to £6 per hour as a result of a government wage rate subsidy, what would be the new trade-off point that maximised the individual's satisfaction?
   (d) Using the information from (a) and (b) separate the observed total effect of the change in hourly wages into a Hicksian substitution and income effect. Give a general idea of the magnitudes of these figures from the graph. Comment on the results you observe.

5. A consumer is found to have the following utility function:

$$U = Q_x + 8Q_y - Q_x^2 - Q_xQ_y - Q_y^2$$

The budget available to the consumer is £95; the price (P_x) of one unit of Q_x is £10 and the price (P_y) of one unit of Q_y is £5.

Using calculus and the Lagrangian multiplier technique where needed:

(a) Write down the equation for the budget constraint.
(b) Calculate the values of Q_x and Q_y such that the consumer's utility function is maximised given the budget constraint. What is the value of λ?

▓ Further reading

Intermediate texts

Baumol, W. J. (1977), *Economic Theory and Operations Analysis*, 4th edn, Ch. 9, Prentice Hall, Hemel Hempstead.

Browning, E. and Browning, J. (1992), *Microeconomic Theory and Applications*, 4th edn, Chs 2–4, HarperCollins, London.

Dobson, S., Maddala, G. S. and Miller, E. (1995), *Microeconomics*, Chs 2 and 3, McGraw-Hill, Maidenhead.

Hope, S. (1999), *Applied Microeconomics*, Chs 1 and 3, John Wiley, Chichester.

Katz, M. and Rosen, H. (1998), *Microeconomics*, 3rd edn, Chs 2–4, Irwin, Boston, Mass.

Koutsoyiannis, A. (1979), *Modern Microeconomics*, 2nd edn, Ch. 2, Macmillan, Basingstoke.

Laidler, D. and Estrin, S. (1995), *Introduction to Microeconomics*, 4th edn, Chs 2–5, Harvester Wheatsheaf, Hemel Hempstead.

Maddala, G. S. and Miller, E. (1989), *Microeconomics: Theory and Application*, Chs 4 and 5, McGraw-Hill, New York.

Nicholson, W. (1997), *Intermediate Microeconomics and its Application*, 7th edn, Chs 3, 4 and 6, Dryden Press, Fort Worth.

Pindyck, R. and Rubinfeld, D. (1998), *Microeconomics*, 4th edn, Chs 3 and 4, Macmillan, Basingstoke.

Varian, H. (1999), *Intermediate Microeconomics*, 5th edn, Chs 2–9 and 14, Norton, New York.

Advanced texts

Gravelle, H. and Rees, R. (1992), *Microeconomics*, 2nd edn, Chs 3–5, Longman, Harlow.

Mas-Colell, A., Whinston, M. D. and Green, J. R. (1995), *Microeconomic Theory*, Chs 1–3, Oxford University Press, Oxford.

Articles and other sources

Beenstock, M. (1979), 'Taxation and incentives in the UK', *Lloyds Bank Review*, 134, Oct.

Blundell, R. W. (1994), 'Work incentives and labour supply in the UK' in Bryson, A. and McKay, S. (eds) *Is it Worth Working?*, PSI Research Report 766.

Brown, C. V. and Dawson, D. A. (1969), 'Personal taxation incentives and tax reforms', *Political and Economic Planning*.

Brown, C. (1988), 'Will the 1988 income tax cuts either increase work incentives or raise more revenues?', *Fiscal Studies*, 9, 4.

Davies, J. E. (1994), 'Giffen goods, the survival imperative and the Irish potato culture', *Journal of Political Economy*, 102, 3.

Dilnot, A.W. and Kell, M. (1988), 'Top-rate tax cuts and incentives: some empirical evidence', *Fiscal Studies*, 9, 4.

Farrell, L. and Walker, I. (1999), 'The Welfare effects of Lotto: evidence from the UK', *Journal of Public Economics*, 72.

Flemming, J. and Oppenheimer, P. (1996), 'Are Government spending and taxes too high?', *National Institute Economic Review*, 157, July.

Gilley, O. and Karels, G. (1991), 'In search of Giffen behaviour', *Economic Inquiry*, 29, Jan.

HMSO (1998), *The Government's Expenditure Plans 1998/99*, Social Security Department Report.

Ison, S. (1994), 'Competition under oligopoly: Hoover', *British Economy Survey*, Autumn 1994.

ONS (1998), 'The effects of taxes and benefits on household income', *DSS, Tax/Benefit Model Tables*, April, 533.

Silberberg, E. and Walker, D. (1984), 'A modern analysis of Giffens paradox', *International Economic Review*, 25, Oct.

Chapter 2

Market demand

Introduction and review

In Chapter 1 we examined the principles underlying individual consumer behaviour and the law of demand. In this chapter we focus on the demand of *all* consumers in the market, which is, of course, of primary concern to producers. It may help our later discussions to review briefly some of the ideas you should already be familiar with.

Moving from individual to market demand

We derive the **market demand** curve by summing, horizontally, all the individual demand curves, as in Fig. 2.1, where we have a market consisting of three individual consumer demand curves, D_A, D_B and D_C. At each price the quantity of X demanded by the market is the (horizontal) sum of the quantities demanded by each consumer. So, at price £4, the quantity demanded by the *market* (22 units) is the sum of the quantity demanded by each consumer, e.g. by A (no units), by B (8 units), and by C (14 units).

Fig. 2.1 Deriving the market demand curve.

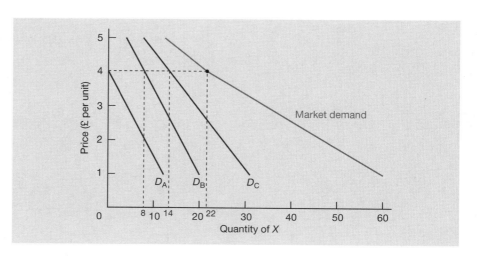

Movements along and shifts in demand curves

Our main concern in economics is with **effective demand**, i.e. the amounts of a commodity that consumers are willing *and able* to purchase at various prices. A desire to purchase will not, by itself, act as a signal to producers unless it is backed up by the means of purchase. Remember also that demand is a *flow* concept, being expressed in units per time period (e.g. tons per month).

As we can see from Fig. 2.2, *movements along* a demand curve, due to a change in the price of the commodity itself, we refer to as either an **expansion** or a **contraction** of demand (Fig. 2.2(a)). *Shifts* in a demand curve, due to a change in the conditions of demand, we refer to as either an **increase** or a **decrease** in demand (Fig. 2.2(b)). For an increase in demand, more of X is purchased at any given price; D_1 shifts to D_2. For a decrease in demand, less of X is purchased at any given price; D_2 shifts to D_1.

The **conditions of demand** are often expressed in a simple functional relationship, as follows:

conditions

$$D_X = F\,(P_X: P_Y;\ I;\ T;\ Y_d;\ Pop;\ \dots\ )$$

where D_X = quantity of X demanded
  P_X = price of X
  P_Y = price of other goods
  I = real income of households in the market
  T = tastes of households in the market
  Y_d = distribution of income between households
  Pop = size and structure of population

You should, of course, be familiar with the way in which changes in any one of the *conditions of demand* will cause the demand curve to shift to the right or left. Take, for instance, a commodity X for which an *increase* in demand is observed, with more of X demanded at each and every price. This could be due to changes in one, or more, of the following conditions of demand:

Fig. 2.2

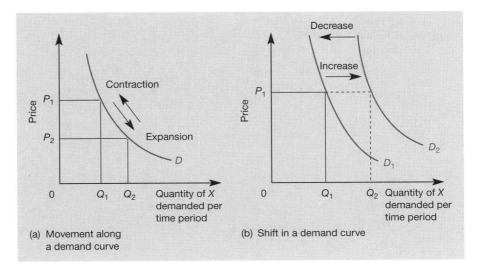

(a) Movement along a demand curve

(b) Shift in a demand curve

- a rise in P_Y, where X and Y are substitutes in consumption;
- a fall in P_Y, where X and Y are complements in consumption;
- a rise in I, where X is a normal good;
- a fall in I, where X is an inferior good (over certain ranges of I);
- a change of tastes (T) in favour of X;
- a change in the distribution of a given level of real income (Y_d) to sections of the population with a higher propensity to purchase X;
- an increase in size of population, or change in structure of population (within a given size), towards those with a higher propensity to purchase X.

Total, average and marginal revenue

As we shall see, there is an important relationship between price elasticity of demand and total revenue. Remember that the demand curve is an **average revenue** curve, telling us the revenue per unit obtained from selling a particular quantity of a commodity. Unless the demand curve is perfectly horizontal, the **marginal revenue** curve will lie inside the demand curve, bisecting the distance between the horizontal axis and the demand curve (Fig. 2.3). The marginal revenue is the addition to total revenue from selling the last unit. **Total revenue** is the total amount spent by consumers on the commodity. It can be obtained by multiplying the price by the quantity sold or by summing all the marginal revenues for each unit sold. When the marginal revenue is zero, the last unit neither adds to, nor subtracts from, total revenue, and so total revenue is a maximum. Check your understanding of these ideas by examining carefully Fig. 2.3.

As price (AR) falls between $0A$ and $0P_1$, we see from Fig. 2.3 that each extra unit adds something positive to total revenue, in that marginal revenue (MR) is positive (but falling). At price $0P_1$ and output $0C$, marginal revenue is zero and total revenue (TR) reaches its maximum value. For further increases in output beyond $0C$, marginal revenue is negative and total revenue falls. At output $0B$, average revenue (price) is zero and so total revenue is zero.

Fig. 2.3 Total, average and marginal revenue.

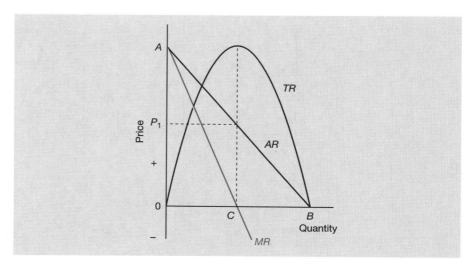

Note that in this example the *AR* and *MR* curves are straight line (linear). The demand (*AR*) curve is linear and of the form

$$P = a - bQ \qquad (1)$$

where P = price, Q = quantity

   a = vertical intercept

   $-b$ = slope of demand (AR) curve

   TR = price × quantity

i.e. $TR = P \times Q = aQ - bQ^2$

Using calculus

$$MR = \frac{\mathrm{d}TR}{\mathrm{d}Q} = a - 2bQ \qquad (2)$$

> In other words a linear demand (*AR*) curve implies a linear *MR* curve.

Setting $P = 0$ and $MR = 0$ respectively gives us the intercept on the *horizontal* (quantity) axis for both *AR* and *MR* curves:

- setting $P = 0$ in equation (1) $\Rightarrow$ horizontal intercept $0B$ is $Q = \dfrac{a}{b}$

- setting $MR = 0$ in equation (2) $\Rightarrow$ horizontal intercept $0C$ is $Q = \dfrac{a}{2b}$

> It follows that $0C = \frac{1}{2} 0B$ in Fig. 2.3; in other words the *MR* curve bisects the horizontal distance between the vertical axis and the demand curve.

Elasticities of demand

Elasticity is a word implying responsiveness. Here we review briefly the responsiveness of market demand for commodity *X* to changes in its own price, changes in real income and changes in the prices of other goods.

- **Price elasticity of demand** (PED) is defined as

$$\mathrm{PED} = \frac{\% \text{ change in quantity demanded of X}}{\% \text{ change in price of X}}$$

Here we consider *movements along* a demand curve in response to a change in price of the commodity. Strictly speaking the sign is negative because of the inverse relationship between quantity demanded and price under the law of demand. However, it is the convention to omit the sign when expressing the numerical value of PED. (See Table 2.1.)

Table 2.1 **Price elasticity of demand, numerical value, terminology and description.**

Numerical value of PED	Terminology	Description
0	Perfectly inelastic demand	Whatever the % change in price (Fig. 2.4(a)) no change in quantity demanded.
>0<1	Relatively inelastic demand	A given % change in price leads to a smaller % change in quantity demanded.
1	Unit elastic demand	A given % change in price leads to exactly the same % change in quantity demanded (Fig. 2.4(b)).
>1< ∞	Relatively elastic demand	A given % change in price leads to a larger % change in quantity demanded.
∞ (infinity)	Perfectly elastic demand	An infinitely small % change in price leads to an infinitely large % change in quantity demanded (Fig. 2.4(c)).

Factors affecting the numerical value of PED for a commodity include the following:

1. *The availability of substitutes in consumption.* The more numerous and closer the substitutes available, the more elastic the demand.
2. *The nature of the need satisfied by the commodity.* The more possible it is to classify the need as being in the luxury category, the more elastic the demand. The more basic or necessary the need, the less elastic the demand.
3. *The time period.* The longer the time period, the more elastic the demand (consumers take time to adjust consumption patterns).
4. *The proportion of income spent on the commodity.* The greater the proportion of income spent on the commodity, the more elastic the demand will tend to be (price changes having a more significant and positive 'income effect' in this case for normal commodities).

Fig. 2.4 **Some important price elasticities of demand.**

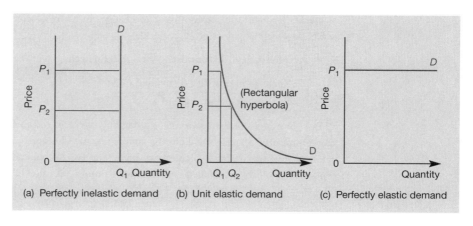

(a) Perfectly inelastic demand   (b) Unit elastic demand   (c) Perfectly elastic demand

5. *The number of uses available to the commodity.* The greater the flexibility of the commodity in terms of the number of uses to which it can be put, the more elastic the demand.

● **Income elasticity of (market) demand** (IED) is defined as

$$\text{IED} = \frac{\% \text{ change in quantity demanded of } X}{\% \text{ change in income}}$$

Here we are considering *shifts* in the demand curve for the commodity. For a *normal* good the sign will be positive: for example, a rise in income increasing demand. For an *inferior* good the sign will be negative over certain ranges of income: for example, a rise in income decreasing demand as consumers use some of the higher income to switch away from the relatively cheap but poor-quality commodity.

As a broad rule of thumb some people regard income elasticity of demand as useful in classifying commodities into 'luxury' and 'necessity' groupings. A commodity is considered a luxury if IED is >1, and a necessity if IED is significantly <1.

Factors affecting the numerical value of IED for a commodity include the following:

1. *The nature of the need satisfied by the commodity.* For some basic needs, e.g. certain types of foodstuff, the proportion of household income spent on commodities satisfying these needs falls as income increases. This has already been considered under the Engel curve (Fig. 1.15(b)). For other, less basic needs, the proportion of household income spent on commodities satisfying these needs rises as income increases.
2. *The time period.* The longer the time period, the more likely it is that consumer expenditure patterns will have adjusted to a change in income, implying a higher IED.
3. *The initial level of national income.* At low levels of *national* income certain commodities will still be largely unattainable for the majority of the population. Changes in national income around such a low level will therefore have little effect on the demand for these commodities (implying a lower IED).

● **Cross-elasticity of demand** (CED) is defined as

$$\text{CED} = \frac{\% \text{ change in quantity demanded of } X}{\% \text{ change in price of } Y}$$

In this case a change in the price of some *other* commodity (Y) will cause a *shift* in the demand for commodity X (i.e. D_X). The cross-elasticity of demand will indicate the direction and magnitude of that shift.

The *direction* of shift will depend upon the relationship in consumption between commodities X and Y. Where X and Y are *substitutes* in consumption, a fall in P_Y will result in a decrease in demand for X, i.e. a leftward shift in D_X. Here the sign of CED will be positive ($-/- = +$). Where X and Y are *complements* in consumption, a fall in P_Y will result in an increase in demand for X, i.e. a rightward shift in D_X. Here the sign will be negative ($+/- = -$).

The *magnitude* of the shift in D_X will depend upon how close X and Y are as substitutes or complements in consumption. The greater the degree of substitutability or complementarity between the two commodities, the greater will be the numerical value of cross-elasticity of demand. In other words, a given fall in price of Y will cause a larger shift to the left in D_X for close substitutes, and a larger shift to the right for close complements.

Theoretical developments

Here we consider some of the aspects of market demand that you must be familiar with at the intermediate level of your studies.

▪ Price elasticity of demand (PED)

An important distinction in our approach to PED is between point elasticity and arc elasticity. We use **point elasticity** in cases where there is an extremely small change in the commodities' own price. We use **arc elasticity** where there is a more substantial change in the commodities' own price.

Point elasticity
of demand

Remember our earlier definition of price elasticity of demand:

$$PED = \frac{\% \text{ change in quantity demanded of } X}{\% \text{ change in price of } X}$$

We can write this as follows:

$$PED = \frac{\Delta Q}{Q} \cdot 100 \div \frac{\Delta P}{P} \cdot 100$$

where ΔQ represents the absolute change in quantity demanded of X
ΔP represents the absolute change in price of X
Q represents the original quantity demanded of X
P represents the original price of X

i.e. $$PED = \frac{\Delta Q}{Q} \div \frac{\Delta P}{P}$$

$$= \frac{\Delta Q}{Q} \cdot \frac{P}{\Delta P}$$

i.e. $$PED = \frac{P}{Q} \cdot \frac{\Delta Q}{\Delta P} \quad \text{(rearranging terms)}$$

Linear (straight line)
demand curve

We can express this result as

$$PED = \frac{P}{Q} \cdot K$$

where K is some constant since the ratio $\Delta Q/\Delta P$ does not change from point to point along a straight-line demand curve. In fact K is the reciprocal of the slope of the demand curve (i.e. $\frac{1}{\theta}$) in Fig. 2.5(a)

Fig. 2.5 **The linear demand curve and price elasticity of demand.**

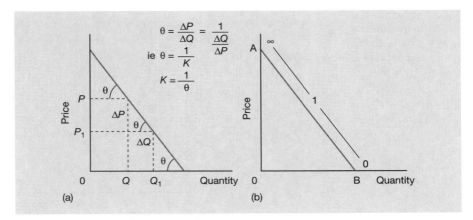

(a)   (b)

- The flatter the demand curve, the smaller is θ and the greater the value of K; the steeper the demand curve, the larger is θ and the smaller the value of K.
- For a straight-line demand curve it follows that price elasticity of demand varies from infinity (∞) at the vertical axis to zero at the horizontal axis (Fig. 2.5(b)). This is because the ratio P/Q becomes infinitely large near point A (and infinity times any constant, K, is infinity), and approaches zero near point B (and zero times any constant, K, is zero).
- For the linear demand curve all we need to know to calculate price elasticity of demand is the original price and quantity and the slope of the demand curve. Our calculation of PED does *not* vary with the direction of price change (rise or fall), nor with the magnitude of price change. Indeed, as we shall see, in the case of the linear demand curve both point and arc elasticity give an identical result.

Non-linear demand curve

It is here that point and arc elasticities differ.

We have seen that price elasticity of demand can be expressed as

$$\text{PED} = \frac{P}{Q} \cdot \frac{\Delta Q}{\Delta P}$$

Clearly the ratio $\Delta Q/\Delta P$ in Fig. 2.6 will now vary depending on the *direction* of price change from P and on the *magnitude* of the price change from P. However, at the point M there is a unique value for price elasticity of demand. In other words, when demand is non-linear, only for infinitely small changes in price around the original price do we have a unique value of PED. We call this **point elasticity of demand**, and it can be expressed as

$$\text{Point elasticity of demand} = \frac{P}{Q} \cdot \frac{\partial Q}{\partial P}$$

$$\left[\text{where } \frac{\partial Q}{\partial P} = \lim_{\Delta P \to 0} \left(\frac{\Delta Q}{\Delta P} \right) \right]$$

Fig. 2.6 **Point and arc elasticities for the non-linear demand curve.**

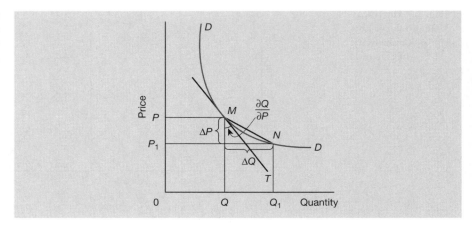

In terms of Fig. 2.6, as N approaches M (ΔP tends to zero), the slope of the chord MN (measured as angle QMN), namely $\Delta Q/\Delta P$, becomes closer and closer to the slope of the tangent MT (measured as angle QMT) at point M. In the *limit*, as N gets extremely close to M, we can regard the two slopes as identical, even though they will never quite be identical so long as N is a separate point from M on the demand curve.

In other words, at the *point* M, price elasticity of demand can be found by multiplying the ratio of initial price to initial quantity by the slope of the tangent (MT) to M. The slope of MT is expressed using *partial* derivatives ($\partial Q/\partial P$) on the assumption that the conditions of demand remain unchanged, with only P_X varying.

For anything other than an infinitely small change in price around the initial price, we must admit that price elasticity of demand will vary with both the direction and magnitude of the price change. It is to this idea of *arc* elasticity of demand that we now turn.

Arc elasticity of demand

Instead of using only the initial price and quantity values in measuring PED, the concept of **arc elasticity** uses the *average* of the initial and final values. If, using Fig. 2.6, P and Q are the initial price and quantity respectively, and P_1 and Q_1 are the final price and quantity, then we can write

$$
\text{Arc elasticity of demand} = \frac{\dfrac{P + P_1}{2}}{\dfrac{Q + Q_1}{2}} \cdot \frac{\Delta Q}{\Delta P}
$$

$$
= \frac{P + P_1}{Q + Q_1} \cdot \frac{\Delta Q}{\Delta P}
$$

The arc elasticity is a measure of *average* elasticity; in Fig. 2.6 it is the elasticity at the mid-point of the chord connecting the two points (M and N) on the demand curve corresponding to the initial and final price levels. Clearly arc elasticity is only an approximation to the true elasticity over a particular segment (MN) of the demand curve. The greater the curvature of the segment of the demand curve being measured, the less accurate will this linear approximation of the true elasticity be.

Price elasticity of demand and revenue

There is an extremely important linkage between price elasticity of demand for a commodity and the **total revenue** from supplying that commodity (see Table 2.2). For a linear demand curve, we can illustrate this relationship as shown in Fig. 2.7.

In Fig. 2.7(a) we can see that with the initial price at $0P$, total revenue (price × quantity) is shown by area $0PVQ$. A fall in price to $0P_1$ will lead to an expansion of demand to $0Q_1$ and a new total revenue indicated by area $0P_1 V_1 Q_1$. Clearly area 1 is common to both total revenue situations, but here area 2 is lost and area 3 gained. The loss of area 2 is due to selling the original $0Q$ units at a now lower price; the gain of area 3 is due to the lower price attracting new consumers for the commodity. The relationships listed in Table 2.2 will hold.

Table 2.2 **Price elasticity of demand and total revenue.**

Numerical value of PED	Relationship between Area 2 and Area 3
1	Area 3 = Area 2
> 1	Area 3 > Area 2
< 1	Area 3 < Area 2

It follows that for *price reductions* along segments of demand curves that are **relatively elastic** (PED > 1 < ∞), total revenue will increase as there is a more than proportionate response of extra consumers to the lower price (Area 3 > Area 2). However, for price reductions along segments of demand curves that are **relatively inelastic** (PED > 0 < 1), total revenue will decrease as there is a less than proportionate response of extra consumers to the now lower price (Area 3 < Area 2). There will be no change in total revenue where price reductions apply to a **unit elastic** demand curve or segment of a demand curve (Area 3 = Area 2).

Of course the opposite situations will apply to *price increases*. Total revenue will fall for price increases where PED > 1 (Area 3 lost > Area 2 gained), will rise for price increases where PED < 1 (Area 3 lost < Area 2 gained), and will be unchanged for price increases where PED = 1 (Area 3 lost = Area 2 gained).

Fig. 2.7 **Price elasticity of demand and total, average and marginal revenue.**

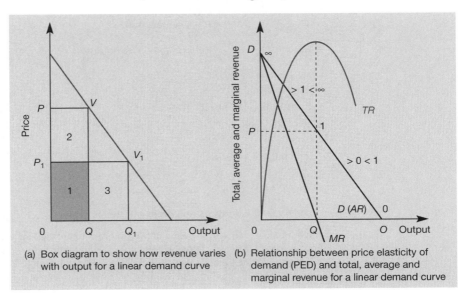

(a) Box diagram to show how revenue varies with output for a linear demand curve

(b) Relationship between price elasticity of demand (PED) and total, average and marginal revenue for a linear demand curve

It is clearly vital that the firm has an accurate estimate of price elasticity of demand over the relevant segment of its demand curve if it is to correctly forecast the revenue consequences of any proposed price change.

Figure 2.7(b) presents the total revenue (*TR*), average revenue (*AR*) and marginal revenue (*MR*) curves corresponding to the values of price elasticity of demand at each point along a linear demand curve. If the initial price is *P*, corresponding to unit elastic demand, then infinitely small changes in price around *P* will leave *TR* unaffected (i.e. *MR* = 0). However, more substantial price reductions below *P* will lead the firm onto a relatively inelastic part of its demand curve, reducing total revenue (*MR* < 0). Price reductions occurring at prices above *P* will take place on a relatively elastic part of the demand curve, raising total revenue (*MR* > 0, but falling). Clearly total revenue is a maximum at the price (*P*) and output (*Q*) corresponding to unit elastic demand.

Relationship between marginal revenue and price elasticity of demand

Various theories of pricing (see Chapter 7) make use of a particular relationship between marginal revenue (MR) and price elasticity of demand:

$$MR = P\left(1 - \frac{1}{e}\right)$$

where P = price = average revenue
        e = (point) price elasticity of demand

Proof: $e = -\dfrac{P}{Q} \cdot \dfrac{dQ}{dP}$ (note the − sign, previously ignored)

Rearranging, we obtain:

$$-e \cdot \frac{Q}{P} = \frac{dQ}{dP}$$

$$-\frac{P}{eQ} = \frac{dP}{dQ} \tag{1}$$

$TR = P \cdot Q$ (where TR = total revenue)

$$MR = P\frac{dQ}{dQ} + Q\frac{dP}{dQ} \quad \text{(differentiation using product rule)}$$

i.e. $MR = P + Q\dfrac{dP}{dQ}$ \tag{2}

Substituting (1) into (2) gives us

$$MR = P - Q \cdot \frac{P}{eQ}$$

$$MR = P - \frac{P}{e}$$

or $MR = P\left(1 - \dfrac{1}{e}\right)$

Note how this formula reinforces our earlier work:

where e = 1, MR = 0   *Note*: although often expressed as above,
where e > 1, MR > 0   technically partial derivatives should be
where e < 1, MR < 0   used (see p. 59 and Appendix 1).

Income elasticity and Engel curves

We noted in Chapter 1 (p. 18) that the **Engel curve** can be derived from the *income–consumption line*, i.e. the locus of tangency points with the highest attainable indifference curves formed by parallel shifts of the budget line. The elasticity of the Engel curve is then the **income elasticity of demand**.

We can use the Engel curve to explore the suggestion that the income elasticity of demand for a commodity will vary over different ranges of income. In this sense, the idea of luxury/necessity can be seen to be a rather imprecise classification, as a *given commodity* could be described by each of these terms over different ranges of income. Indeed that same commodity might even be regarded as inferior at very high levels of income where the purchase of better quality but more expensive alternatives becomes feasible.

Figure 2.8(b) presents an Engel curve in its most general form showing a given commodity being, in turn, luxury, necessity, and inferior good over different ranges of income.

It can easily be shown (Fig. 2.8(a)) that the income elasticity for any *linear* Engel curve passing through the origin is unity. In Fig. 2.8(b) we now construct such a line from the origin, tangent to the *non-linear* Engel curve at point A. Income elasticity is therefore unity at the associated income level M_1. At any point on this Engel curve below M_1 we have income elasticity > 1 (luxury). At any point on this Engel curve between M_1 and M_2 we have income elasticity $> 0 < 1$ (necessity). At M_2 we have zero income elasticity and for income levels above M_2 we have negative income elasticity (inferiority) with the now downward-sloping Engel curve.

Cross-elasticity of demand

Earlier in the chapter (p. 57) we noted that **cross-elasticity of demand** measures the responsiveness of demand for commodity X to changes in the price of another commodity, Y. It is possible to take this concept a little further by adopting the same procedure here as for price elasticity (p. 58), i.e. by expressing cross-elasticity of demand in the form

$$\text{CED} = \frac{\Delta Q_X}{Q_X} \cdot 100 \div \frac{\Delta P_Y}{P_Y} \cdot 100 = \frac{P_Y}{Q_X} \cdot \frac{\Delta Q_X}{\Delta P_Y}$$

or, if measured at a point, by

$$\frac{P_Y}{Q_X} \cdot \frac{\partial Q_X}{\partial P_Y}$$

where Q_X is the quantity demanded of good X, and P_Y is the price of commodity Y.

Fig. 2.8 Engel curves and income elasticity.

Note:
Income E of D =
$\frac{\Delta Q}{Q} \cdot 100 \div \frac{\Delta Y}{Y} \cdot 100$
i.e. Income E of D =
$\frac{Y}{Q} \cdot \frac{\Delta Q}{\Delta Y}$
In move from a to b along E_1, triangles $0aY$, bac are similar with corresponding sides in same ratio
i.e. $0Y : aY = \Delta Y : \Delta Q$
$\Rightarrow Y : Q = \Delta Y : \Delta Q$
$\Rightarrow \frac{Y}{Q} \cdot \frac{\Delta Q}{\Delta Y} = 1$

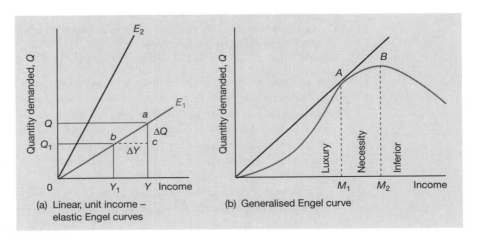

(a) Linear, unit income – elastic Engel curves

(b) Generalised Engel curve

Engel's Law

Ernst Engel was appointed director of the Bureau of Statistics in Prussia and outlined what became known as Engel's Law in a paper published in 1857. The essential idea is that the proportion of income spent on food declines as income rises. In other words food was being regarded as a necessity with an income elasticity of demand less than 1.

Table 2.3 presents data on the spending patterns of 153 Belgian families he studied in 1853. This cross-sectional evidence has subsequently been verified in a range of time-series (longitudinal) data, and cross-country data. For example in nineteenth century America people spent some fifty per cent of their incomes on food compared with less than twenty per cent today. Again, people in the less developed countries spend higher proportions of their income on food than do people in, say, the advanced industrialised countries of the OECD.

Table 2.3 **Percentage of total expenditure on various items by Belgian families in 1853.**

	Annual income		
Expenditure item	$225–$300	$450–$600	$750–1,000
Food	62.0%	55.0%	50.0%
Clothing	16.0	18.0	18.0
Lodging, light, and fuel	17.0	17.0	17.0
Services (education, legal, health)	4.0	7.5	11.5
Comfort and recreation	1.0	2.5	3.5
Total	100.0	100.0	100.0

Source: Adapted from A. Marshall, *Principles of Economics*, 8th edn, London: Macmillan, 1920, p. 97. Some items have been aggregated.

Engel himself was extremely cautious in interpreting his results at the time. Certainly the table data give early support for services of various forms having high income elasticities of demand.

It is worth noting at this stage that a positive or negative *sign* for the cross-elasticity relationship cannot always be relied upon to define, *unambiguously*, situations where commodities are substitutes (+) or complements (−). This is because of the income effects of a price change discussed in Chapter 1. For example, when the price of commodity *Y* falls, the effect on the demand for commodity *X* will depend not only on the tendency to replace *X* by the relatively cheaper *Y*, but also on consumer response to the real income gain from the fall in the price of *Y*, i.e. the income effect.

It follows that although two commodities may be regarded by entrepreneurs and consumers alike as substitutes in consumption, this will not always be reflected in the sign of cross-elasticity. This is because the income effect of the fall in the price of commodity *Y* may lead consumers to demand not only more of commodity Y but also more of the 'substitute' commodity X. Should the income effect of the fall in price of Y be sufficiently large and the income elasticity of demand for (normal) commodity X be sufficiently high, then the sign of the cross-elasticity of demand could be *negative*. In other words the price of Y falls and the quantity demanded of X rises, despite the fact that most observers regard the commodities as obvious substitutes and anticipate a positive cross-elasticity of demand.

Another reason for some ambiguity as to sign and value relates to the fact that cross-elasticity of demand can be defined as *either*

$$\frac{\Delta Q_X}{\Delta P_Y} \cdot \frac{P_Y}{Q_X} \text{ or } \frac{\Delta Q_Y}{\Delta P_X} \cdot \frac{P_X}{Q_Y}$$

depending on whether it is the price of Y or the price of X that is varied. Since the two measures are not identical, then the calculation of cross-elasticity could, technically, result in different signs and values for the *same* pair of commodities depending on the particular expression used.

Clearly we need to examine further the conventional interpretation of any particular sign or value ascribed to a cross-elasticity of demand relationship between any pair of commodities.

Estimating demand functions

We have noted how important it is that the firm be aware of the *price elasticity of demand* when it envisages a change in pricing policy. Any inaccuracy in its estimate of price elasticity of demand can lead to unexpected changes in total revenue following a price adjustment. Similarly, any inaccuracy in its estimate of *income elasticity of demand* can lead to inaccurate projections of future shifts in demand following a rise (or fall) in real national income. Unwise investment decisions in terms of fixed capital equipment or inventories (stocks) might then follow. So too might unwise responses to competitor price strategies if the firm is inaccurate in its estimate of the sign or magnitude of the various *cross-elasticities of demand*.

How then can the firm estimate the demand function for the commodity it produces, given the importance of having such a well-defined estimate of demand?

Interview and survey techniques

A variety of techniques may be used to *interview* consumers directly in order to identify the factors involved in the demand for a commodity. Carefully constructed questionnaires, sensitively handled, are clearly vital if such techniques are to yield useful results. Equally vital will be the selection and location of the sample of respondents to be used in the interviews. Here we first look at the use of buy–response and multi-brand choice tests as examples of this technique.

In **buy–response test**, a large sample of respondents are shown the product and asked 'If you saw this product in your local store, would you pay £x, £y, £z ... etc. for it?' The list will typically contain 10 prices. A large number of responses makes it possible to construct a buy–response curve, giving the percentage of buyers at different price levels. In the example shown in Fig. 2.9, 90% of those willing to buy would pay up to 40 pence for the product, and 35% would pay up to 56 pence. The flatter the buy–response curve, the more control the firm has over price.

In **multi-brand choice test**, respondents are asked to rate the product against similar products. The question may take the form 'If we add this feature to our product, making it different from our competitors, would you pay an *extra* £x, £y, £z … etc. for it?' The aim here is to establish a *relative price* for the product.

The **Gabor–Granger test** is another approach to demand estimation, especially for new products. Here half the respondents are shown a sample of the new product and are asked whether they would purchase the product at each price stated on a random price list. This procedure is then repeated for a product of a similar type already being produced by another firm. The other half of the total number of respondents undertakes the same test, but this time with the established product being surveyed first, before the new product. The idea is to avoid the possible bias of a consumer expressing a willingness to pay a higher price for the first product surveyed on the mistaken assumption that this is exclusive, before becoming aware of a second, competing product.

A widely used survey procedure for estimating the demand for a new product is to use a **test market**. Here the product is sold in a number of geographically separate areas, which nonetheless have similar consumer characteristics. The product is then sold at different prices in each geographical area so that data are built up on consumer demand at a range of possible prices. An advantage over questionnaires is that actual sales behaviour is monitored rather than mere intentions to purchase.

Although widely used, the many interview and survey techniques provide rather subjective and fragmentary evidence as to demand characteristics. Examples of the use of such 'direct' techniques of demand estimation are presented in the next section (pp. 78–82). However, our main attention in this chapter will be on a range of *statistical techniques* that purport to use objective data in demand estimation.

Fig. 2.9 **A typical buy–response curve.**

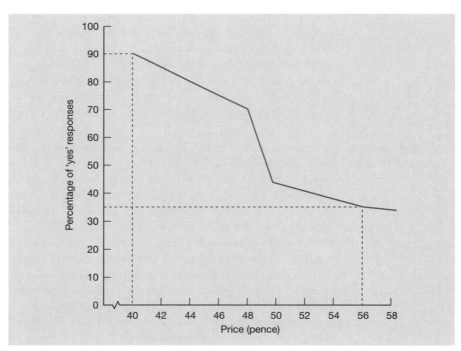

Statistical techniques Many of the **statistical techniques** adopted are based on regression analysis, in which one (dependent) variable is related to (regressed upon) one or more (independent) variables that are believed to affect that variable. The idea here is to estimate the line (or curve) that 'best fits' the data. This is usually taken to be the line (or curve) that minimises the sum of squared deviations from the line or curve. Such a 'least squares' regression line is shown in Fig. 2.10.

In Fig. 2.10, the scatter diagram is only two-dimensional, relating quantity demanded of the commodity (the dependent variable) to its own price (the independent variable). Of course many dimensional relationships can be established using regression analysis: for example quantity demanded may be related to the commodity's own price, the price of other commodities, the real income of consumers, and so on. This could be done by using **multiple regression** analysis. In this case the demand curve will take the form of a plane or surface rather than a line or curve.

Estimating the demand function: multiple regression

The following is an example of the type of result obtained from using multiple (in this case linear) regression techniques. Here the demand for sweet potatoes in the USA over the time period 1949–72 is related to a range of familiar variables expressed in linear (no powers/roots) form (Schrimper and Mathia 1975):

$$Q_X = 7,609 - 1,606P_X + 479P_0 + 947Y + 59N - 271t$$

Q_X = quantity (1000 cwt) of sweet potatoes sold per year in the USA
P_X = real dollar price of sweet potatoes (per cwt)
P_0 = real dollar price of white potatoes (per cwt)
Y = real per capita disposable income ($000)
N = two-year moving average of total US population (in millions)
t = time trend (t = 1 for 1949, 2 for 1950 … 24 for 1972)

* NB 1 cwt = 100 lb

Fig. 2.10 **The 'least squares' regression line.**

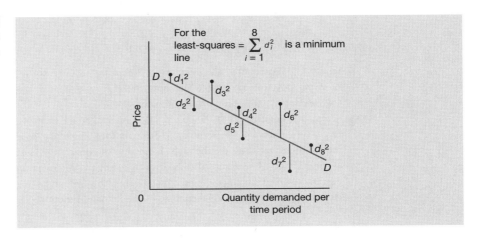

Multiple linear regression has given us a demand function with coefficients and variables that can be related to our earlier analysis. For example, in terms of the product's own price, every $1 rise in price per cwt of sweet potatoes will result in a contraction of demand of 1,606 (000) cwt. Here the own-price coefficient (−1,606) tells us about *movements along* the demand curve for sweet potatoes. However, the coefficients for the other independent variables tell us about *shifts* in the demand curve for sweet potatoes. For example every $1 rise in real price per cwt of white potatoes will result in an increase (shift to right) in demand for sweet potatoes of 479 (000) cwt (clearly the +479 coefficient tells us that sweet and white potatoes are substitutes in consumption). Every $1,000 rise in real per capita disposable income increases demand for sweet potatoes by 947 (000) cwt (clearly the +947 coefficient tells us that sweet potatoes are a normal good over the range of income considered). Again every 1 million extra persons in the US population (as a two-year moving average) increases demand for sweet potatoes by 59 (000) cwt. Finally a time trend in the expression suggests a taste factor progressively reducing (negative coefficient) the demand for sweet potatoes; every extra year over the time period in question decreased demand for new potatoes by 271 (000) cwt.

We can use the coefficients of the independent variables in multiple regression analysis to give us estimates of own-price, income and cross-elasticities of demand. By substituting into our equation particular prices of sweet potatoes we can calculate *percentage changes* in both price and quantity demanded to give an estimate of (arc) own PED. The same procedure can be followed using additional information for prices of white potatoes (cross-elasticity) and real per capita disposal income (income elasticity).

Given the sophisticated techniques of multiple regression analysis available and access to regular data collected over a number of time periods, the statistical approach to demand estimation appears relatively straightforward. By regressing quantity demanded against own-price, prices of substitutes/complements, real incomes, proxy variables for tastes, etc. we can derive a **demand function**. We can then use this demand function for deriving various elasticities and, of course, for forecasting future demand (see also Appendix 2).

It may be useful at this stage to consider the demand function and the demand curve in a little more detail.

Demand function and demand curve

In the use of statistical techniques for demand estimation it is the **demand function** that is the usual outcome of regression techniques. In the case of the demand for sweet potatoes (p. 67), the demand function was expressed in the (general) linear form

$$Q_X = \alpha - \beta_1 P_X + \beta_2 P_0 + \beta_3 Y + \beta_4 N - \beta_5 t \qquad (1)$$

where Q_X represented the demand for sweet potatoes, and the other variables the price of sweet potatoes (P_X), of white potatoes (P_0), real per capita income (Y), population (N), and a time trend (t) reflecting tastes.

It is the coefficients α, β_1, β_2, β_3, β_4 and β_5 that are estimated via regression analysis. However, when we focus on the **demand curve** we are, in effect, subsuming all the independent variables on the right-hand side of equation (1) (except price) into a single term A. This, of course, follows directly from the *ceteris paribus* (other things remain equal) assumption implicit in constructing the demand curve. We now express the **demand curve** as a special subcase of the demand function:

$$Q_X = A + \beta_1 P_X \qquad (2)$$

However, Alfred Marshall, one of the founders of modern microeconomics, placed the independent variable (P_X) on the *vertical* axis for graphical analysis. In effect he used the equation

$$P_X = a + b\, Q_X \tag{3}$$

It is important that we observe the Marshallian convention, although we should keep in mind that Q_X is really the dependent variable and P_X the independent variable. All we have to do to convert the demand function into the Marshallian form is to subtract A from both sides of equation (2) and divide both sides by β_1 to obtain

$$P_X = -\frac{A}{\beta_1} + \frac{1}{\beta_1}\, Q_X \tag{4}$$

Let $A/\beta_1 = a$ and $1/\beta_1 = b$ and we have equation (3). Note that the numerical value of β_1 is negative because of the law of demand. Therefore parameter a will be positive and parameter b negative.

A practical example Suppose that we have used certain estimation techniques to calculate the values of A and β_1 in equation (2) and the result is

$$Q_X = 53.32 - 3.81 P_X$$

Then to convert this expression to the form of equation (3) we have to subtract 53.32 from both sides and divide both sides by -3.81 to find

$$P_X = 13.99 - 0.262 Q_X$$

In this case note that a (13.99) is the *intercept* on the vertical price axis and b (0.262) is the *slope* of the line, i.e. $1/\beta_1$. The intercept on the horizontal axis is, of course, A since this is the value of Q_X when P_X is zero (see Fig. 2.11). A further application of this approach is considered in the next section (pp. 82–84).

Fig. 2.11 **The Marshallian convention for the demand curve.**

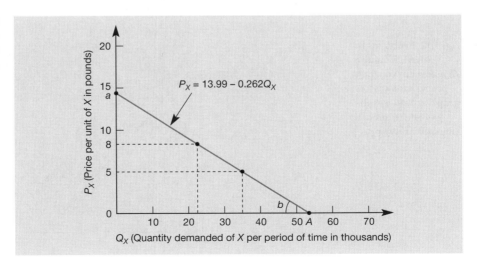

Problems in using statistical techniques for demand estimation

Here we consider a number of problems involved in using statistical techniques to estimate demand functions, and suggest some ways of resolving these problems. A more detailed treatment of such problems and their possible resolution can be found in Appendix 2 (p. 695)

The identification problem We have noted how the points on a scatter diagram can be the basis for estimating the demand curve via regression analysis. Unfortunately, where both demand and supply curves are shifting, fitting the line of best fit to these points on the scatter diagram may not give us an estimate of the true demand curve.

In Fig. 2.12 we have the four observations E_1 to E_4 on a scatter diagram relating price to quantity. If only the supply curve had been shifting from S_1 to S_4, then these points would indeed trace out the true demand curve. If, however, *both* demand and supply curves had been shifting, then the line through (or nearest to) these points would give an inaccurate estimate of demand. In Fig. 2.12 we would be *underestimating* the true own-price elasticity along a given demand curve. The firm might therefore raise price, expecting total revenue to rise (PED < 1), only to find total revenue falling owing to the higher than expected responsiveness of demand to price.

Faced with such an **identification problem** it may still be possible to obtain an estimate of the true and flatter demand curves, say D_2, in Fig. 2.12. One method is to allow the supply changes to take place uncorrected but to correct or adjust for the changes in demand. Starting at point E_2 (S_2 intersecting D_2) extra productivity may have *increased supply* to S_1 whereas, say, a fall in real income together with a fall in price of a substitute in consumption may have *decreased demand* to D_1. However, instead of taking the uncorrected point E_1, we might correct for the change in demand by using various statistical techniques to retain the original real income level and price of substitute that gave the initial demand curve D_2. By allowing supply to change but statistically adjusting in this way for demand, we would obtain a point E'_2 rather than the actual observation E_1. We would thereby obtain a more accurate picture of the true and flatter (dashed) demand curve D_2 than would be obtained by estimating the continuous line connecting the actual observations. Generally speaking, the more volatile the supply relative to the demand, the easier it is to overcome the identification problem for the demand curve.

Fig. 2.12 Problems in identifying the demand curve when points on a scatter graph are the results of shifts in both demand and supply.

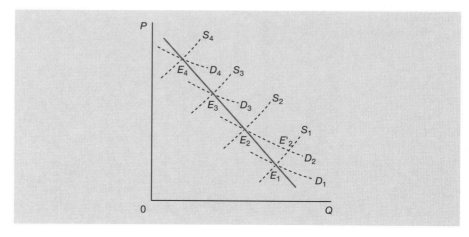

Misspecification   Errors may arise in the **specifications** of the demand function to be estimated. For example it may be the case that one or more important explanatory (independent) variables have been omitted from the right-hand side of the regression equation. For instance the price of white potatoes may not have been specified in the demand for sweet potatoes discussed earlier. By forgetting to include a variable that really does have a significant effect on the demand for sweet potatoes, we introduce inaccuracies into the estimates of the coefficients in front of the other variables. Estimates of price and income elasticities of demand, etc., derived from these regression coefficients will then be misleading. By *omitting important variables* in this way, or indeed by *including irrelevant explanatory variables*, we are likely to derive misleading regression estimates in our demand function.

Another form of misspecification can occur even if we *do* include all the relevant explanatory variables and exclude the irrelevant ones. This would be the case where we assume the *wrong functional form* for the relationship, for example linear instead of non-linear.

Multicollinearity   Multicollinearity occurs where two or more explanatory variables move closely together, i.e. are correlated (or collinear) with each other. The estimated regression coefficient in front of each separate variable is then likely to be inaccurate and misleading. Suppose, for example, that the demand for a commodity depended upon a range of variables, including the level of income of consumers and their educational background. For the population as a whole it is likely that these two explanatory (independent) variables are themselves closely correlated: a rise in incomes increasing demand for education and a rise in education in turn being associated with rising incomes (via greater productivity). In a particular demand equation, the estimated regression coefficients in front of each of these separate variables would therefore be unlikely to capture accurately their separate influences.

If, in a demand function, there are several variables that are highly correlated, it may be sensible to omit all but one in a set of highly correlated variables. However, if the explanatory variables are less than perfectly correlated, a variety of statistical techniques can be used to reduce the impact of this problem: for example principal components or ridge estimators (see, for example, Baumol 1977).

Simultaneity   The problems of identification and multicollinearity are, in essence, part of a more general problem often encountered in a model or system involving **simultaneous equations**. The identification problem for an individual curve can be resolved if we can ascertain particular shock variables that uniquely cause that curve (and that curve only) to shift. In other words, we need to introduce one or more *additional* variables to our simultaneous equation system involving demand and supply. Again, if multicollinearity exists, with a close correlation between two or more variables in the system, then it is likely that these variables are not independent of one another and that at least one additional equation needs to be included in the system that expresses the relationship between these highly correlated variables.

Even if the separate equations in a simultaneous system are identified, a whole range of further problems may be encountered by the statistical analyst. These involve ideas such as deriving *unbiased* estimators where, as we increase the number of samples of a

Simultaneous equations and identification

Here we look at the identification problem from the perspective of solving a system of simultaneous equations.

In the following system we have two equations and three variables. The variables Q_D, Q_S on the left-hand side are conventionally referred to as **endogenous variables** as they are determined by other variable(s) in the system. Since price (P) is itself dependent on $Q_D = Q_S$ in equilibrium, then P is also an endogenous variable in this system.

$$Q_D = a + bP + c$$
$$Q_S = f + gP + h$$

where Q_D = quantity demanded
Q_S = quantity supplied
P = price

In a simple linear model, a and f are the respective intercepts on the vertical axis, c and h are the error terms, and b and g are the coefficients of the price variable, indicating the respective slopes of demand and supply.

In this particular system, neither curve is identified as it is impossible to ascertain shift variables that affect demand or supply uniquely. We are in the situation previously described in Fig. 2.12 as regards equilibrium points E_1 to E_4. In fact we can formalise a *necessary* condition for identification as follows.

For each equation (Q_D, Q_S) the number of variables excluded from that equation but contained in the system must be *at least one less* than the total number of endogenous variables in the system. Put another way, for each equation the number of variables excluded from that equation but contained in the system must be $\geq n - 1$, where n is the number of endogenous variables in the system.

Clearly in our above system neither equation is identified. For Q_D only 1 variable (Q_S) is excluded and $1 \not\geq 3 - 1$. The same applies to Q_S. However, we could introduce *additional (shock) variables* to our system that would fulfil this necessary condition for identification. These would be *exogenous variables* (i.e. determined outside the system), which cause the respective demand and supply curves to shift uniquely:

$$Q_D = a + bP + cY + d$$
$$Q_S = f + gP + hC + i$$

where Y = real income, C = costs of production.

We have three endogenous variables (Q_D, Q_S, P) and two exogenous variables (Y and C).

For Q_D, the number of variables excluded from that equation but contained in the system is 2 (Q_S and C), which fulfils the condition $\geq n - 1$ (i.e. $2 = 3 - 1$ here).

It follows that by introducing appropriate shock or exogenous variables for each equation, we can ascertain unique shifts in the respective curves and thereby identify demand and supply curves respectively. Returning to Fig. 2.12, if we can identify shifts in supply and demand, we can allow the supply shift S_2 to S_1 to occur but *compensate* for the demand shift D_2 to D_1, thereby allowing us to remain on D_2 and move (hypothetically) to the position E'_2 rather than E_1 as actually observed.

given size, the average value of the estimated coefficient becomes nearer and nearer to the true value of that coefficient. Other ideas involve deriving *consistent* estimates, where the value of the *estimated* coefficient becomes nearer and nearer to the *true* value as the sample size *increases*.

We can, of course, be more confident in the results of samples where the estimates are unbiased and consistent. Many methods can be used to more nearly achieve such outcomes in practice, including the use of reduced-form equations, two- or three-stage least squares, or full maximum likelihood techniques. Detailed investigation of such methods is available elsewhere (e.g. Baumol 1977), and they are touched on in Appendix 2.

The characteristics approach

Based on the work of Kelvin Lancaster, the idea here is to focus on the specific **characteristics** or properties of a commodity that yield utility rather than on the whole commodity itself. In Fig. 2.13 we examine a market for a commodity with two key characteristics C_1 and C_2, perhaps sweetness and firmness of texture in the market for apples.

In Fig. 2.13(a) three types or brands of the commodity are currently available, indicated by rays D, E and F from the origin. For example, brand D has a higher ratio of C_1 to C_2 (namely 4:1) than brand E (namely 1:1) or brand F ($1:2\frac{1}{2}$). Each ray joins all the points in characteristics space that can be attained by purchasing more of that brand of commodity.

Table 2.4 presents a fuller picture of the characteristics and prices of the three brands of apple.

Fig. 2.13 **Using the characteristics approach to demand.**

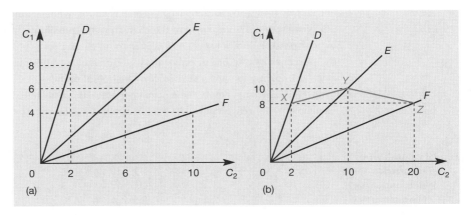

Table 2.4
Characteristics of three brands of apple.

Brand	Sweetness index	Firmness index	Sweetness/Firmness ratio	Price (£ per kg)
D	8	2	4:1	1
E	6	6	1:1	0.6
F	4	10	$1:2\frac{1}{2}$	0.5

If each brand of apple has the characteristics shown, then buying more apples of a single brand will provide the consumer with the combinations of characteristics shown in the straight lines (rays) $0D$, $0E$ and $0F$ in Fig. 2.13(a).

At the prices indicated in Table 2.4, a weekly expenditure of £1 on apples could acquire 1 kg of brand D, $1\frac{2}{3}$ kg of brand E and 2 kg of brand F, giving points X, Y, Z respectively on the characteristic rays in Fig. 2.13(b). By combining different amounts of the different brands the consumer can achieve different *mixes* of the two characteristics for a given expenditure. The line joining points X, Y and Z is therefore a type of budget line, but one that is *segmented*. For example, points on the XY segment of the line show the combinations of characteristics that the consumer can achieve by spending all his income (here £1) on different mixes of brands D and E; points on the YZ segment show the combinations achieved by spending the same amount on brands E and F. Notice that there is also a line (XZ) connecting brands D and F that shows the combinations of characteristics achieved by spending this same sum on differing mixes of brands D and F. However, since this line lies *inside* the frontier set by XYZ it is inoperative, in that it gives the consumer less of both characteristics than can be achieved by spending the same amount on other combinations of brands. We shall call the line XYZ the *characteristics possibility frontier*.

If the price of any brand falls then the relevant point X, Y or Z on the characteristics possibility frontier will shift outwards along its ray, indicating that more characteristics can now be acquired by consumers of that (cheaper) brand for a given expenditure. If consumer expenditure on the commodity rises, then the whole characteristics possibility frontier will shift outwards.

As before, a consumer indifference map can be used to express consumer preferences, this time for characteristics rather than for whole commodities. The maximum utility solution will occur where the characteristics possibility frontier is a tangent to the highest possible indifference curve. This could be at a corner point X, Y or Z, implying the purchase of one brand only or, as in Fig. 2.14, at an intermediate point along the frontier implying the purchase of a combination of brands.

In Fig. 2.14 tangency between the characteristics possibility frontier and the highest attainable indifference curve (I_1) occurs at point K. The precise combination of brands E

Fig. 2.14 Equilibrium in the market for apples under the characteristics approach.

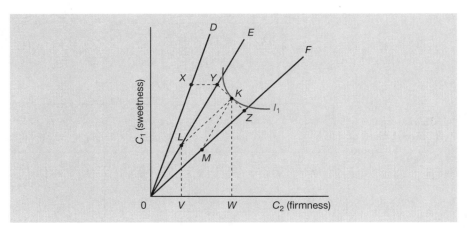

and *F* implied by point *K* can be established using this diagram. First, we draw a line from *K* parallel to the ray 0*F*, intersecting 0*E* at point *L*. We then draw a similar line from *K*, this time parallel to the ray 0*E* and intersecting 0*F* at point *M*. The *optimal brand mix* at point *K* can then be seen to be achieved in either of the following ways:

- purchasing units of brand *E* until we have moved up the characteristics ray for *E* to point *L* and then purchasing units of brand *F* until we move from *L* to *K*,

or

- purchasing units of brand *F* until we have moved up the characteristics ray for *F* to point *M*, and then purchasing units of brand *E* until we move from *M* to *K*.

Both these purchasing patterns are equivalent in that they will yield the characteristics mix given at the optimal position *K*.

Law of demand We can use the characteristics approach to examine the impact of changing prices upon consumer demand. This has many similarities to our earlier use of indifference analysis.

If the price of brand *E falls*, point *Y* will move further out along the ray 0*E*, giving a new characteristics possibility frontier and a new equilibrium position yielding more of both characteristics C_1 and C_2 to the consumer. The new combination of brands can be found using the same technique as before. The impact of a change in price of any brand will depend on the shapes of both the characteristics possibility frontier and the consumer indifference curves. The curvature of the indifference curves suggests that tangency will occur on progressively higher indifference curves at a position *further away* from *Z* (and nearer to the new point *Y*). This suggests, using our earlier technique, purchasing *more* of the now cheaper brand *E* in order to achieve the new optimal brand mix.

In Fig. 2.14 as the price of brand *E rises* then point *Y* will shift inwards along 0*E*. The curvature of the indifference curves suggests that tangency will occur on progressively lower indifference curves at a position *nearer* to *Z* (and further away from the new point *Y*). This suggests, using our earlier technique, purchasing *less* of the now more expensive brand *E* in order to achieve the new optimal brand mix.

The scope for new product development may also be indicated by the characteristics approach. In Fig. 2.14 a new brand of apple offering exactly the characteristics ratio (sweetness: firmness) indicated by point *K* would lead the consumer to spend all his income on that brand alone instead of undertaking the more complex process of mixing brands *E* and *F*.

Figure 2.15 illustrates some of these ideas visually. In Fig. 2.15(a) the fall in price of *E* shifts the characteristics possibility frontier out to *XY'Z*, and the new utility maximizing equilibrium moves to *K'*. This implies attaining the optimal brand-mix at *K'* either via pathway 0*L'K'* or 0*M'K'*, either route implying purchasing more, *Y* to *Y'*, of the (now cheaper) product, *E*, and less, *M* to *M'*, of the (now more expensive) substitute in consumption, *F*.

In Fig. 2.15(b) *new brand G* offering exactly the characteristics ratio indicated by point *K* leads the consumer to spend *all* his income on that brand alone, maximising utility by reaching indifference curve I_2. Even so, a rise in price of this new brand can be shown to

Fig. 2.15 **Further applications of the characteristics approach.**

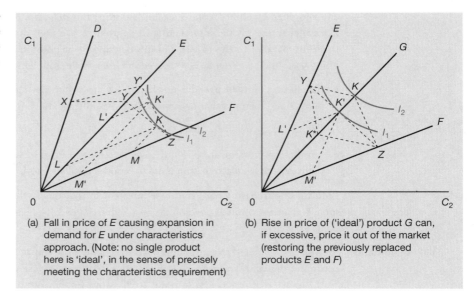

(a) Fall in price of E causing expansion in demand for E under characteristics approach. (Note: no single product here is 'ideal', in the sense of precisely meeting the characteristics requirement)

(b) Rise in price of ('ideal') product G can, if excessive, price it out of the market (restoring the previously replaced products E and F)

price even this 'ideal' brand out of the market. The rise in price of G shifts the characteristics possibility frontier inwards. If G continues to rise in price we eventually have the *straight-line* frontier $YK'Z$. The consumer still maximises utility by purchasing only brand G but can now only reach indifference curve I_1. A still further rise in price of brand G gives the frontier $YK*Z$. In this case purchase of brand G would now be an *inefficient* use of the consumer's budget, since the other brands provide the desired characteristics less expensively. The straight line connecting brands E and F now lies *outside* the frontier set by $YK*Z$ and so this straight-line characteristics possibility frontier becomes operative. The consumer is therefore still able to reach point K' on the straight-line frontier $YK'Z$ by pathway $0L'K'$ or $0M'K'$. In other words the consumer will now prefer to combine brands E and F to maximize utility (reaching indifference curve I_1) from a given income rather than purchase any of (the 'ideal') brand G. In other words, when the price of G is high enough to give the straight-line frontier $YK'Z$, further price rises in G will lead to situations in which only combinations of brands E and F will be selected, with brand G ceasing to be purchased. Thus brand G has been priced out of the market, despite possessing the required characteristics in the preferred ratio.

The income effect under the characteristics approach

A *rise* in income (prices of products unchanged) will shift the characteristics possibility frontier outwards, parallel to itself, as in Fig. 2.16(a). More of all three goods E, G and F can be purchased, since the affordable combinations of characteristics change in the same proportion for each product. A *fall* in income (prices of products unchanged) will of course have the opposite effect, shifting the characteristics possibility frontier inwards parallel to itself.

For simplicity we assume in Fig. 2.16(a) that initially only product G is consumed, as it possesses the required characteristics in *exactly* the preferred ratio. Utility is therefore maximised at point K, with the characteristics possibility frontier YKZ tangent to I_1. A rise in income (prices unchanged) now shifts the frontier to $Y' K' Z'$, with more of product G now purchased at the new equilibrium point K', and the higher indifference curve I_2 now attained. Clearly G is a *normal good* here, a rise in income increasing demand (at least over the range of income considered).

Although more complex to illustrate diagrammatically, G would also be a normal good if that same rise in income increased demand for G in a situation where G was only one of a *combination* of goods consumed in order to achieve the desired characteristics. (You might construct diagrams of your own to illustrate this, following the approach set out on p. 76.)

Figure 2.16(b) shows a situation in which product G exhibits the properties of an *inferior good*. The rise in income (product prices unchanged) this time causes a switch away from G to E. In this rather simplistic case the consumer ceases to purchase any of product G and moves to point Y', reaching I_2 by purchasing *only* product E. The implication here is that the consumer, at the initial equilibrium point K, had approached his/her saturation point as regards characteristic C_2. By reducing intake of characteristic C_2, and increasing intake of characteristic C_1, the consumer can attain the higher indifference curve I_2. In this sense the rise in income allows the consumer to switch away from G, the inferior product, to the now preferred (superior) product E.

To say that the consumer has approached the saturation point for a characteristic is another way of saying that the consumer's *marginal utility* for that characteristic is close to zero. It follows that the income effect for a product can be positive or negative depending on the consumer's relative marginal utilities derived from the characteristics contained in the product. As the marginal utility of a *particular characteristic* approaches zero (the marginal utilities of other characteristics remaining relatively high), that characteristic becomes inferior, as do *products* containing a relatively high proportion of that characteristic.

Our earlier work on indifference curves (p. 3) should have indicated that C_2 is a potentially inferior characteristic in Fig. 2.16. We can see from Fig. 2.16 that the higher indifference curve I_2 is drawn *much flatter* than I_1. This suggests that as we move out along any ray from the origin, the slope of the successive indifference curves is falling:

Fig. 2.16 Income effect under the characteristics approach.

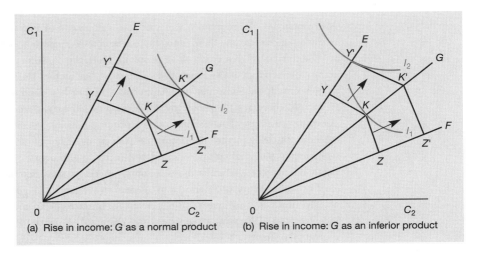

(a) Rise in income: G as a normal product   (b) Rise in income: G as an inferior product

i.e. $MRS_{C_2C_1}$ is falling. In other words the consumer's preferences are such that the more of *both* goods he/she is able to afford, the progressively less of C_1 the consumer is willing to sacrifice for another unit of C_2. Put another way:

$$MRS_{C_2C_1} = \frac{MU_{C_2}}{MU_{C_1}}$$

which implies that a falling $MRS_{C_2C_1}$ means a falling MU_{C_2} in relation to MU_{C_1}.

Applications and evidence

In this section we take further some of the principles and issues mentioned previously. We begin by considering some practical methods used in demand estimation.

Interviews and surveys
These include the most direct methods of demand estimation already discussed (p. 65). Here, buyers or potential buyers are asked how much more or less they would purchase of a particular product if its price or other determinants (e.g. advertising, income, etc.) were varied by a certain amount. Focus groups might be assembled for such discussions, or questionnaires might be administered to a representative sample of buyers. Although this system seems simple, it is fraught with difficulties.

The first problem concerns the *randomness* of the sample. The individuals interviewed or surveyed must represent the market as a whole, so a sufficiently large sample, generated by a random procedure, must be interviewed to form a reasonable and unbiased estimate of the market's reaction to a proposed change. Of course, on occasions the appropriate sample might be non-random, as when a company sees only a discrete segment of the market as its potential customers. In this case *cluster* or other sample types might be selected (see Appendix 2, 'Further reading').

The second problem is the *interview bias*. This is defined as the distortion of the interviewee's response because of the presence of the interviewer. For example, if a question makes the respondent feel foolish or implies greed etc. the respondent may give an incorrect answer. Although telephone and mailed questionnaires avoid eye contact and lessen potential embarrassment, the respondents may be less well chosen or may not give full consideration to the questions because there is no one to whom they are immediately accountable.

The third is the *best of intentions* problem. Here the consumer may have truly intended to buy the product at the time of the interview, but by the time the marketing strategy is implemented, the consumer may have changed his or her mind.

Finally, there are the problems of *confusion* or *misrepresentation* or *unknowable aspects* of consumer response. For example, a new product may be described briefly to a customer who cannot easily picture the product as part of his or her lifestyle. In the early 1980s the estimates of personal computers underestimated the dramatic growth of *business* demand partly because this particular use was not envisaged by many potential buyers of PCs.

To combat these problems, a great deal of research has gone into the problems of questionnaires, interviews and survey formulation. An example appears in Case study 2.1 (p. 79), which considers the results of a particular market strategy for a clothing company.

Simulated market situations

In this situation an artificial market situation is constructed: i.e. a so-called *consumer clinic* is set up. This involves giving (usually) randomly selected participants a sum of 'play' money and asking them to spend this money in an artificial store environment. Often the main group is divided into subgroups, with each subgroup exposed to price changes of different magnitudes, and their reactions are noted. Obviously there are problems with such simulated market situations since some people would spend someone else's money differently from the way they would spend their own money. Also, participants may over-react and feel that they must choose a particular product when the price is reduced to demonstrate that they are thrifty and responsible shoppers. (See Case study 2.2, p. 80.)

Case study 2.1: Use of surveys

A company producing clothing has decided that it must extend its range of shirts. It therefore seeks to estimate the potential demand for a newly designed shirt it has recently developed. The marketing department of the company conducts a question-naire survey using a sample of 1000 people interviewed while shopping in a large store for products similar to the company's new shirt. The interviewees were shown the new shirt and then asked whether they would buy the shirt at each of five price levels. To simplify the procedure for the interviewees, they were asked to choose one out of six possible responses: a = definitely no; b = not likely; c = perhaps; d = quite likely; e = very likely; and f = definitely yes. A breakdown of the responses for each of the six categories is provided in columns (a) to (f) of Table 2.5.

Table 2.5

Price (£)	Responses of interviewees						Expected quantity demanded
	(a)	(b)	(c)	(d)	(e)	(f)	
20	450	350	100	50	50	0	125
19	350	240	205	100	75	30	218
18	200	150	250	200	150	50	345
17	50	100	250	300	200	100	475
16	50	30	150	190	400	180	603

The marketing division has also decided to allocate a probability figure, based on past experience, to each buying response (a) to (f) in Table 2.5. These are 0.0, 0.1, 0.3, 0.5, 0.7 and 1.0 respectively. From this information we can find the *expected value* of the quantity demanded at each price level. (Note: the *expected value* of an event occurring is its probability multiplied by the outcome value.) For example, if the price of the shirt was £20 then the expected value of the quantity demanded would be the sum of the expected values of sales to each group of respondents:

$$E(Q_{20}) = 450.(0.0) + 350.(0.1) + 100.(0.3) + 50.(0.5) + 50.(0.7) + 0.(1.0)$$
$$= 125$$

Proceeding similarly we can calculate the *expected quantity demanded* at each price, which is shown in the last column of Table 2.5. When we have both price and expected demand we can trace out the demand curve. This can be seen in Fig. 2.17, where we plot the demand curve on a simple graph. From this we can see that the price intercept will be approximately £21. We can then calculate the slope of this demand curve by taking, say, a fall in price from £20 to £16 (i.e. of £4) and measuring the expansion of demand as 478 (603 – 125). This gives an approximate slope of – 4/478 or – 0.00837.

Thus the estimated demand curve is $P_x = 21 - 0.00837Q_x$.

To get a more accurate equation we can use regression analysis (see Appendix 2, p. 689). If we use this method we shall get $P_x = 20.912 - 0.00824Q_x$. In other words, the precise intercept is £20.912 and the slope of the demand curve will be –0.00824. The marginal revenue curve (MR) = $20.912 - 0.0165Q_x$ since the price intercept will be the same but the slope will be twice that of the demand curve (see p. 55). The demand and marginal revenue curves are shown in Fig 2.17.

Fig. 2.17

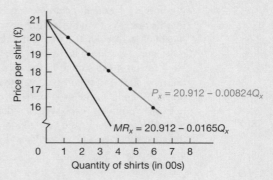

Note that these estimates are based on a *sample* of consumers. If this sample were, say, 1% of the total market for the product, then the expected quantity demanded would be 100 times greater than the sample. This would mean that the demand curve would be 100 times flatter as the quantity demanded at any price level would be 100 times larger. This means we would have a slope of 1/100th of the original one and therefore the estimated *market* demand curve would be $P_x = 20.912 - 0.0000824Q_x$.

Case study 2.2: Simulated market

For example, let us assume that a Swiss company producing a 'gold' brand of cream cheese wants information on the responsiveness of consumer demand to changes in the price of its cheese. One thousand shoppers are organised for the simulated market experiment and divided into five groups, 200 to each group. The membership of each group is chosen such that the socioeconomic characteristics of the groups are roughly the same and similar to the market in total. On the same day, each group is allowed 40 minutes' shopping in a simulated supermarket. Each participant is given £15 in 'play' money to purchase any items on display. The 'gold' brand of cream cheese is displayed prominently alongside the best-selling cream cheeses. For each of the five groups, 'gold' cream cheese is priced at different levels while the prices of all other products are held constant. The price levels and the quantities demanded of 'gold' cream cheese by each of the five groups are as shown in Table 2.6.

Table 2.6
Price levels and quantities of cream cheese demanded by five sample groups.

Group	Price per box (£)	Sample demand (boxes)	Population demand[a] (estimated boxes)
1	1.50	128	12,800
2	1.20	158	15,800
3	1.65	98	9,800
4	1.74	57	5,700
5	1.10	190	19,000

[a]Sample assumed to be 1% of population or market demand.

These data are plotted in Fig. 2.18 with a least-squares regression line estimated and then superimposed onto the scatter diagram.

Fig. 2.18

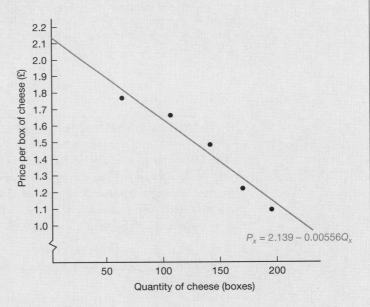

The intercept of this line with the price axis occurs at £2.139, and the slope of the line is –0.00556.

The data generated by the simulated market experiment allow the *sample* demand curve to be estimated as $P_x = 2.139 - 0.00556Q_x$. Assuming a 1% sample of the population, the *market* or *population* demand curve is estimated to be $P_x = 2.139 - 0.0000556Q_x$.

It is possible to calculate the elasticity of market demand for the 'gold' cream cheese from our previous knowledge of the expression for the elasticity of demand for a product:

$$E_d = \frac{\partial Q_x}{\partial P_x} \cdot \frac{P_x}{Q_x}$$

In other words, the elasticity of demand at any point of the demand curve is the reciprocal of the slope of the demand curve (1/–0.0000556 or –17,985.61) times price over quantity demanded at a certain point on the demand curve.

Now, when price (P_x) is £1.65, for example, the demand equation will be

$1.65 = 2.139 - 0.0000556Q_x$

Therefore $Q_x = 8{,}794.96$

Price elasticity of demand at price £1.65 is
$e = -17{,}985.61 \times 1.65/8{,}794.96$
$\quad = -3.374$

It is interesting to note that when price was £1.65 the sample demand indicated 98 packets sold (which is equivalent to 9,800 on the basis of the market or population). However, when we calculated the market or population figures at price £1.65 using our estimated demand curve we obtained a sales figure of 8,794.96. This was because our demand curve is a 'best fit' line. The elasticity is also based on the 'best fit' line and not on the actual data.

Demand for health care in the European Union

An area of vital policy concern for European, as for other, governments has been in identifying the factors underlying the observed surge in demand for health care services. Before considering a *regression-based approach* to identifying the nature and magnitude of the factors involved it will be useful to review briefly a number of widely held perceptions as to the underlying causes of such increases in health care demand.

- *A high income elasticity of demand for health care services*. In most EU economies the rise in health-related spending has grown more than in proportion to any rise in national income.
- *An ageing population*. There has been a rapid increase in the proportion of elderly people in the population of many EU economies. For example, in the UK it has been estimated that, by the year 2011, 17% of the population will be aged over 65 years compared with only 11% in 1951, and 4.5% over 80 years compared with only 1.4% in 1951. Those over 75 years are, together with newborn infants, the main source of increased expenditure on health care services.
- *Increased deprivation/economic recession*. Evidence has begun to accumulate that health care needs are related to aspects of deprivation, such as unemployment and low income.

- *Higher expectations.* With greater awareness by patients of rights and opportunities (e.g. the Patient's Charter in the UK), there is a progressively higher expectation of treatment than in earlier times. Of course advances in medical technology have made new methods and procedures available today to treat conditions that previously would have been left untreated. Indeed some (e.g. Milne and Molana 1991) have argued that the increasing density of physicians per capita in European countries has itself been a factor in stimulating demand for health care services. These physicians have helped overcome the informational assymetries inherent in the health care market by being more accessible to patients than before and directing them towards treatment opportunities, thereby increasing the demand for health care treatment.

- *Bias towards quantity adjustment in health care markets.* In many EU countries, health care services are often either publicly financed or privately financed through insurance. The result is that the price of such services at the point of access is lower than the true cost of provision. Essentially this is a move away from the normal price adjustment of markets to *quantity adjustment.* We can illustrate this in terms of Fig. 2.19.

We assume demand for health care services to be downward sloping with respect to price: i.e. people demand fewer treatments per time period if price rises. If a market were established with demand D_1 and a short-run supply S_1 (here perfectly inelastic supply) then a price P_1 would be established with an equilibrium number of treatments demanded and supplied per year of Q_1. If demand now increases to D_2 then *price adjusts* in the market, rising to P_2 to allocate the unchanged Q_1.

However, in the UK the NHS does not primarily operate by price adjustment but by quantity adjustment (since service is largely free at the point of treatment): with the initial demand D_1, at zero price $0Q_2$ treatments are demanded. This requires the supply curve of treatments to shift rightwards to S_2 if the NHS is to satisfy this demand. If demand now rises to D_2, supply must further increase to S_3 since no price adjustment is permitted. Otherwise $Q_3 - Q_2$ patients would be untreated: i.e. a rise in waiting lists. It is clear that by relying mainly on *quantity adjustments*, health systems such as the NHS must either allocate more resources to health care in the face of increased demand or accept a rise in waiting lists.

Clearly it is of vital policy concern that likely changes in the demand for health care services be accurately forecast and anticipated so that an informed policy response can

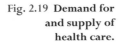

Fig. 2.19 Demand for and supply of health care.

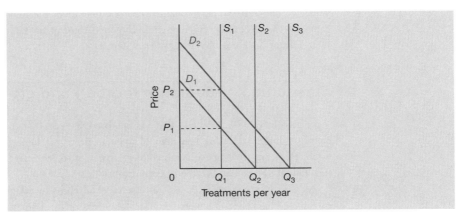

be implemented. Using data from eight EU countries Karatzas (1992) estimated the following relationship for health expenditure:

$$\ln(HE_t) = 19.379 + 0.771 \ln(GDP_t) + 1.283 \ln(DOC_t) + 4.890\ PUO_t$$
$$\qquad\qquad\qquad\quad (2.330) \qquad\qquad\qquad (3.132) \quad\ (1.508)$$
$$R^2 = 0.954$$

where HE_t is expenditure on health care in year t, GDP_t is gross domestic product in year t, DOC_t is the ratio of physicians to the total population in year t, and PUO_t is a ratio of population under 5 and over 65 years of age to the total population in year t.

The *natural logarithmic* form of the equation is such that the coefficients of the respective variables give us the corresponding elasticities directly (unlike the non-logarithmic form of p. 82, where we need to apply numbers to the coefficients to calculate *percentage changes*). The income elasticity coefficient at 0.771 suggests a much lower income elasticity of demand than might have been expected. Rather than being viewed as a luxury, the suggestion here is of health care as a necessity with an income elasticity less than 1. In fact four other regression equations for health care estimated by Karatzas placed the income elasticity coefficient close to 0.9, i.e. less than 1.

An income elasticity coefficient close to 1 is in line with the earlier work of Milne and Molana (1991), who found the demand for health care to be 'homogeneous of degree one in income and the relative price of health care'. In other words, a given percentage increase in income and price leads to the same percentage increase in demand for health care. These findings are in opposition to the suggestion that the demand for health care rises more than in proportion to income. A criticism of this 'luxury' view of health care demand is that it often ignores the relative fall in the price of health care services, thereby overestimating the true income elasticity response.

The impact of demographic factors on health care expenditure is quite strong in the equation. Each percentage increase in the proportion of the population in either the under 5 or over 65 age category leads to an almost 5% increase in expenditure on health care.

The overall fit of the estimated regression line is good, with over 95% of the total variation explained or accounted for by the regression line. The figures in parentheses underneath the estimated coefficients associated with each independent variable give their t statistic scores. These indicate the confidence that we can have in the estimated values of the respective coefficients. The coefficients of the first two variables are significant at a 1% level of confidence while the coefficient of the third (demographic) variable is significant only at a 10% level of confidence.

Elasticities of demand: football and cigarettes

We noted in Table 2.2 (p. 61) that for products with an own-price elasticity of demand having a numerical value less than 1, a rise in price can be expected to raise total revenue. Here we investigate two products that would seem to fall within this category: football attendance and cigarette consumption.

As we can see from Table 2.7, all the football clubs investigated by Simmons (1996) over the period 1962–91 were found to have own-price elasticities of demand less than 1.

Table 2.7 **Estimated own-price elasticities of demand for football clubs in England.**

Club	Price elasticity of demand
Chelsea	−0.40
Everton	−0.97
Manchester United	−0.12
Newcastle	−0.39
Nottingham Forest	−0.57
Tottenham Hotspur	−0.44

Source: Simmons (1996)

The most inelastic demand estimated over the period was that for Manchester United at − 0.12. On the basis of this estimate, a 10% (say) rise in the price of tickets would result in only a 1.2% decrease in the quantity of tickets demanded, and would therefore result in a rise in the value of gate receipts. For Everton, however, the same 10% rise in price would lead to an almost equivalent 9.7% decrease in the quantity of tickets demanded and an approximately unchanged value of gate receipts.

Simmons' study included both season ticket holders and those who 'pay at the gate'. One might expect, other things being equal, that those who 'pay at the gate' would have a higher price elasticity of demand (perhaps less committed supporters!) than those who purchase season tickets. The estimates shown in Table 2.7 are therefore 'averages' across a segmented market place: separate price elasticities of demand might usefully be estimated for each segment if, for example, club directors were considering price changes that might differ for each market segment (here season ticket versus non-season ticket holders). Of course still more price elasticity of demand estimates might be useful if more than two market segments could be identified, such as children, or pensioners, or seats located close to the halfway line.

As regards cigarettes, Cameron (1998) reports a similar array of estimates for own-price elasticities of demand that are less than unity (Table 2.8). The earliest study estimating a demand curve for cigarettes was undertaken in the USA in 1933 by Schoenberg, and a large number of subsequent studies have tended to confirm his findings of a relatively price-inelastic demand. The results of some recent studies are shown in Table 2.8: these are all 'dynamic' studies in the sense that they take account of the addictive properties of cigarettes, with consumption in the current time period assumed to depend in part on consumption in previous time periods. As can be seen, there is considerable evidence of price-inelastic demand, with short-run elasticities usually in the range − 0.2 to − 0.6, and long-run elasticities in the range − 0.5 to − 0.8. The slightly higher long-run elasticities can be ascribed to the positive contribution of time in breaking established habits and the cumulative influence over time of health warnings, advertising restrictions and other regulations (e.g. smoke-free workplaces) in weakening general consumer commitment to cigarettes, and thereby increasing consumer focus on price. Such a viewpoint is supported in the study by Tegene, reported in Table 2.8, which presents short- and long-run price elasticities in *different decades* over the period 1929–86. The results suggest a progressive diminution in both types of price elasticity over time.

Table 2.8 **Cigarette demand estimates: dynamic studies.**

Author/date	Data	Period	Price elasticity (short run/long run)
Chaloupka (1991)	USA	1976–80	− 0.2 / − 0.45
Doroodian and Seldon (1991)	USA	1952–84	− 0.1 / − 0.32
Seldon and Boyd (1991)	USA	1953–84	− 0.22 / − 0.37
Tegene (1991)	USA	1929–86	− 0.66/− 1.23(1956)
			− 0.42/− 0.71(1966)
			− 0.28/− 0.36(1971)
			− 0.15/− 0.17(1985)
Keeler *et al.* (1993)	California	1980–90	− 0.36 / − 0.58
Tansel (1993)	Turkey	1960–88	− 0.21 / − 0.37
Valdes (1993)	Spain	1964–88	− 0.6 / − 0.69
Becker *et al.* (1994)	USA	1955–85	− 0.4 / − 0.75
Sung *et al.* (1994)	USA	1967–90	− 0.4 / − 0.48
Conniffe (1995)	Rep of Ireland	1960–90	− 0.32 / − 0.38
Goel and Morey (1995)	USA	1959–82	− 0.28 / − 0.34

Source: Adapted from Cameron (1998)

With such a unanimity of view as to the price inelasticity of demand for cigarettes, it is hardly surprising that many governments have seen cigarettes as a useful vehicle for generating substantial revenues via increases in indirect taxation.

Elasticities of demand: petrol

Estimates involving elasticities of demand for petrol have been made using statistical techniques of the type outlined above for health care and previously on pp. 67–71. These results are interesting in their own right, and indicate a number of important caveats in the derivation and interpretation of elasticity measures.

Short-run versus long-run elasticities

One of the main features in the following analysis is the importance, for policy analysis, of noting the significant differences that exist between *short-run* and *long-run* elasticity estimates.

Own-price elasticities of demand for petrol

Table 2.9(a) presents the average of a large number of separate estimates of price elasticity of demand for petrol consumption: i.e. the ratio of percentage changes in quantity demanded of petrol with respect to percentage changes in its own price. These estimates are derived from 13 major studies, many European based and covering some 120 separate elasticity estimates. Goodwin noted that although there was some distinction between estimates using *time series* data and those using *cross-sectional* data, the main distinction was between **short-run** estimates and **long-run** estimates. Generally speaking, the short run referred to a period less than one year long. Typically the long run involved time periods around five years (strictly it is the time to the next 'equilibrium' outcome).

Although *all* estimates, independently of data type or time period, demonstrated a *relatively price inelastic* demand for petrol, the long-run estimates were some 50–300% higher than the short-run estimates.

Table 2.9 Summaries of evidence from studies of elasticity of petrol consumption and traffic levels (volume) with respect to price.

(a) Summary of evidence from studies of elasticity of petrol consumption with respect to price

	Short term	Long term
Time series	−0.27 (0.18)	−0.71 (0.41)
Cross-section	−0.28 (0.13)	−0.84 (0.18)

(b) Summary of evidence from studies of elasticity of traffic levels (volume) with respect to petrol price

	Short term	Long term
Time series	−0.16 (0.08)	−0.33 (0.11)
Cross-section	−	−0.29 (0.06)

Figures in parentheses are standard deviations
Source: Adapted from Goodwin (1992)

Cross-elasticities of demand between traffic level and petrol price

Table 2.9(b) presents the *average* of the cross-elasticity of demand estimates from the same studies. This time the relationship is between percentage changes in the volume of traffic and percentage changes in the petrol price. The negative signs for the various cross-elasticity estimates suggest that the products are *complements*, with a rise in the price of petrol leading to a decrease in (demand for) traffic volume, and vice versa.

We might expect the own-price and cross-elasticity estimates to be similar in magnitude in the short run, but less so in the long run. This is because we might expect traffic levels to be broadly proportional to petrol consumption in the short run, but less so in the long run as people take the opportunity to change both the size of the vehicle they own and its petrol efficiency.

Goodwin himself suggested that the elasticities of traffic level and of petrol consumption with respect to petrol price should be broadly equal to each other in the short run. However, they would then diverge over the long run, with the own-price elasticity of demand for petrol growing *faster* than the traffic elasticity (i.e. cross-elasticity). The behavioural basis for suggesting that *both* elasticities would grow over time is that adjustments in terms of trip rates, car ownership, destination to choice and location decisions all take time to implement. The behavioural basis for own-price elasticity of demand for petrol to grow faster than traffic (cross) elasticity over time is the *greater variety of substitution possibilities* in petrol consumption as compared with travel arrangements. For example, mobility (and therefore traffic levels) can be retained and yet substantial switching can occur, over time, between sizes of vehicles (and therefore petrol consumption) and in terms of the petrol efficiency of engines installed within vehicles of any given size.

That the long-run elasticity of petrol consumption *exceeds* that for traffic with respect to petrol price is confirmed by comparing Table 2.9(a) and (b). The long-run elasticity of petrol consumption with regard to its own price is around twice as high as the elasticity of traffic volume with respect to petrol price. However, the evidence also suggests that there is some divergence between the two elasticities even in the short run. In other words, changes in driving styles and speed may occur more rapidly in response to petrol price changes than do changes in distances travelled.

From a policy perspective, the following provides a useful summary of these results. For a sustained, real 10% increase in fuel prices, we can expect:

- in the *short run* a decrease in fuel consumption of around 3% and a decrease in traffic volume of around 1.5%. The *difference* is due to more careful driving and perhaps avoidance of fuel-inefficient journeys;
- in the *longer run* a decrease in fuel consumption of around 7% and a decrease in traffic volume of around 3%. The *difference* here is due in part to the switch to smaller, more fuel-efficient vehicles and to improved engine design as regards fuel economy. Part of the 7% reduction in petrol consumption itself is due to a reduced use of cars, indicated by the reduction in traffic volume of some 3%.

Goodwin notes an important policy implication of these comprehensive elasticity surveys, namely that petrol price adjustment is a more effective policy instrument for conserving fuel than it is for controlling congestion. Further, although averages for all the elasticities under consideration are relatively inelastic, they are nonetheless of a higher magnitude than had hitherto been supposed, again encouraging a renewed emphasis on petrol price adjustment as regards achieving goals involving fuel conservation.

Acutt and Dodgson (1995) present estimates of cross-elasticities of demand for different types of public transport with respect to the price of petrol, and use these to further examine the implications of a 10% increase in fuel prices. The positive signs for the various cross-elasticity estimates in Table 2.10 suggest that they are *substitutes* for petrol, with a rise in price of petrol leading to an increase in (demand for) various types of public transport, and vice versa. As Table 2.10 indicates, a 10% increase in the price of petrol will lead to an extra 1% of passengers on InterCity rail services, an extra 0.9% of passengers on Regional Railways, and an extra 0.4% of passengers on Network South East. There will also be an extra 0.2% of passengers on both London Underground and London buses and 0.1% on other local buses.

Table 2.10 Public transport cross-elasticities of demand with respect to the price of petrol.

InterCity	0.10
Regional Railways	0.09
Network South East	0.04
London Underground	0.02
London buses	0.02
Other local buses	0.01

Source: Adapted from Acutt and Dodgson (1995)

◾ Income elasticity of demand: world trade

The previous application of the elasticity concept focused on own-price and cross-elasticities of demand. Here we review a practical application of the *income elasticity* concept in the context of the growth in world trade.

It is widely recognised that many advanced industrialised economies have a relatively high *income elasticity of demand for imports*. In other words the ratio of percentage change in quantity demanded of imports to percentage change in national income is likely to be considerably greater than 1, with domestic consumers spending a high proportion of any additional income on imported goods and services. Such a situation can present problems for policy makers, with attempts to stimulate economic growth in the domestic economy leading to a rapid growth in imports and a consequent balance of payments problem. Figure 2.20(a) suggests that such concerns are well founded as regards the UK. The 'line of best fit' (see Appendix 2) relating the percentage growth in volume of UK imports (g_m) to the percentage growth of UK GDP (g_y) suggests that each percentage change in income (GDP) leads to a +1.94 percentage change in volume of imports.

Figure 2.20(b) considers the impact of the growth in world trade (here used as a *proxy* variable for growth in world income) on the growth in demand for UK exports. Data on growth of 'world income' are notoriously difficult to derive, but ample evidence exists to suggest a close and positive correlation between growth in world trade and growth in world income, so that growth in world trade can usefully be used as a *proxy variable* for growth in world income.

It can be seen from Fig. 2.20(b) that the UK has a relatively low 'income' elasticity of demand for exports, with each percentage change in 'world income' (g_w) leading to a mere +0.77% change in volume of UK exports (g_x). Arguably this observation further increases the likelihood of a balance of payments constraint on UK economic growth, with a sustained rise in UK and world income providing a greater stimulation to import growth than to export growth.

Fig. 2.20 Income elasticity of demand and UK trade performance.

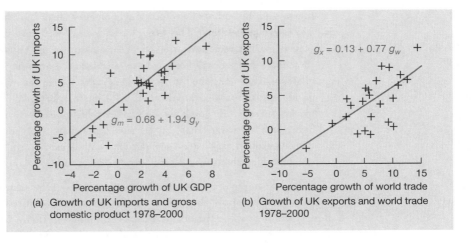

(a) Growth of UK imports and gross domestic product 1978–2000

(b) Growth of UK exports and world trade 1978–2000

■ Characteristics approach: telephone handsets

An interesting application of this approach involved placing a value on individual characteristics embodied in telephone handsets, conducted by Geroski and Toker (1992). They noted that in the early 1990s the UK consumer was faced by over 100 different models of telephone handset on the market, supplied by at least 15 different suppliers and sold mainly through high street shopping outlets. Prices in the early 1990s were seen to range from £10 to over £200.

An extremely large (and increasing) number of characteristics might be embodied in a phone. They may have memory facilities to store frequently used telephone numbers and to redial numbers; they may have a hold option enabling users to interrupt one conversation to have another; they may have a variety of volume control devices, illuminated keyboards, built-in clocks and/or calculators; they may be more or less portable and durable and so on. In fact the Consumers' Association magazine *Which?* listed 43 different characteristics observed in a sample of 34 different phones in 1990. Table 2.11 lists seven of the more important characteristics of these phones, and these seven characteristics will be the focus of the remainder of this analysis.

Geroski and Toker then sought to place a *value* on these seven key characteristics. Two possible approaches were explored:

- *The multi-brand choice test* (see p. 66). Here the consumer is asked how much they would be willing to pay for a little bit more or a little bit less of each different type of characteristic that might be embodied in the good in question. One might, for example, ask how much television viewers would pay to see more movies and less sport, more news and less drama, and so on, and then sum up the values they attach to different types of programme to get an estimate of what a TV licence fee would be worth to one consumer (usually a good deal more than people actually pay for a licence). Averaging across consumers gives a kind of market valuation of the good (or service), which can be compared to its market price.

  This is of course an extremely time-consuming and expensive procedure to follow, and the authors therefore sought an alternative approach.

- *The market process itself.* This provides an *indirect* valuation of characteristics. Goods whose 'market valuation' (i.e. average valuation across all consumers) exactly *equals* their market price will be bought by all of those consumers whose valuation of the characteristics contained in the good is greater than the average valuation. Clearly, goods whose market valuation *exceeds* their market price will command a higher market share, while goods whose market valuation is *less* than their market price will have a smaller market share or, perhaps, will fail and exit from the market. It follows, then, that observing a good's *market price* and its *market share* (success) enables one to say something about what its *market valuation* must be.

If we have a sample of goods with different amounts of the same characteristics, then we can use what we know about their (implicit) market valuations to say something about how consumers value the characteristics embodied in them. Thus, suppose we collect data on a large number of telephone handsets and can identify the different amount each possesses of certain characteristics. If we can then estimate their different market

Table 2.11 **Seven key characteristics of telephone handsets.**

Label	Name of characteristic	Definition
X1	Two-piece phone	A phone with a handset and a cradle with keys on the handset. X1 takes the value 1 if the phone is a two-piece phone and 0 otherwise.
X2	Conventional	A phone with a handset and a cradle with keys on cradle. X2 takes the value 1 if the phone is a conventional phone and 0 otherwise.
X3	Phones with memories	A phone with a facility to store telephone numbers, which can be retrieved and dialled automatically by pressing buttons. X3 takes the value 1 if the phone has memories and 0 otherwise.
X4	Tone-phone	A phone that uses tone dialling as opposed to traditional pulse dialling, and which makes use of electronic exchanges. Tone dialling gives access to BT 'Star Services'. X4 takes the value 1 if the phone is a tone-phone and 0 otherwise.
X5	Weight	Weight of handset including the coiled leads. The Consumers' Association gives a number of letter Hs: the more letters, the heavier is the phone. We give a value 1 for each H.
X6	Display memory	A phone that has the facility to display the numbers as they are dialled or has the facility to display numbers that are stored in the memory. X6 takes the value 1 if the phone has display memory and 0 otherwise.
X7	Hands-off	A loudspeaker phone, which allows hands-free talking, as well as dialling without lifting the handset. X7 takes the value 1 if it has hands-off facility and 0 otherwise.

valuations, then multiple regression analysis (see p. 67) can be used to relate the possession of *individual characteristics* to *market valuations*.

Geroski and Toker collected prices of, and the characteristics embodied in, 76 phones that were on the UK market in 1989 and 1990 and which contained some or all of the seven key characteristics identified. Data limitations forced the authors to assume that the market valuations (which are not observed) of these 76 phones were, on average, just about equal to their market prices (which are observed). The authors then worked backwards to calculate (via multiple regression) what the values of these seven characteristics must have been to account for the price variations observed in the market. Table 2.12 shows the results of this exercise for a small sample of seven telephone handsets.

Table 2.12 Values placed on individual characteristics of telephone handsets.

Phones	X1	X2	X3	X4	X5	X6	X7	Actual price (£)	Estimated value (£)	%
p1	0	0	1	0	1	0	0	10	15.15	−51
p2	1	0	1	0	3	0	0	13	15.42	−19
p3	1	0	0	1	2	0	0	18	20.74	−15
p4	0	1	1	1	4	0	0	35	30.29	+13
p5	0	1	1	1	3	1	0	35	48.81	−39
p6	0	1	1	1	4	0	1	35	43.39	−24
p7	0	1	1	1	1	1	0	100	59.00	+41
Value (£)	10.25	25.02	5.12	5.35	−5.09	13.43	13.09			

Note: The basic characteristics common to all phones are valued at £15.12
Source: Geroski and Toker (1992)

Reading across rows, one discovers that the first phone p1 has only two characteristics, X3 and X5, while p2 has Xl, X3 and 3 units of X5, and so on. Reading down the columns, the (regression) calculations suggest that the value of having a unit of X3 is £5.12 while that of a unit of X5 is −£5.09 (remember that X5 was 'weight', so the negative price here indicates that consumers value lighter phones more than heavy phones, holding other characteristics constant). The basic characteristics that were present in *all* of these seven phones have a total value of £15.12, so that when we add in the values of X3 and X5 we obtain an *estimated market valuation* of phone p1 of £15.15 (£15.12 + £5.12 − £5.09). Since the *actual market price* of p1 is £10, phone p1 seems to be a good buy. Proceeding in this way we see that phones p2, p3, p5 and p6 are all good buys, with estimated market valuations *above* their market price, while phones p4 and p7 are very poor buys, with estimated market valuations *below* actual market price.

The last column of the table expresses the *difference* between each phone's actual market price and its estimated market valuation (via summing the value of its individual characteristics) as a percentage of the actual market price. A *negative* sign indicates an actual market price less than the estimated market value. Clearly the table suggests that phone p1 is particularly good value for money.

It is instructive to ask why phones p4 and p7 are rather poor value for money. Phone p4 is very similar to phone p5 except that it has slightly more of characteristic X5 and lacks characteristic X6. Having one unit more of X5 makes p4 worth £5.09 *less* than phone p5, and not having X6 means that p5 creates £13.43 more value than phone p4. The total difference, therefore, is £18.52 in terms of *estimated market value*, and yet phone p4 has exactly the same *market price* as phone p5! However one looks at it, buying p5 rather than p4 makes sense for almost all consumers (except those who really love characteristic X5 and absolutely hate characteristic X6). Similarly phone p7 looks very much like phone p5, except that it has two units less of X5 (worth −2 × −£5.09 per unit = +£10.18). However, the resulting higher *estimated market value* of p7 over p5 is far overshadowed by the *market price* for p7 being nearly three times that of p5. Again, buying p5 rather than p7 makes sense for most consumers (except for those who absolutely hate characteristic X5, namely heavier handsets). Phone p7 is also similar to phone p6, though lacking three units of X5 (worth $-3 \times -£5.09 = +£15.27$ in total) and X7 (worth £13.09), but containing X6 (worth £13.43). This leaves a net difference in *estimated market valuation* of £15.61, as against a difference in *market price* of £65. Phone p7 looks like worse value than p6 (except for those who hate characteristics X5 and X7 and love characteristic X6).

Valuing enhanced consumer durables /capital items

This type of approach to valuing characteristics has a potentially useful application in establishing values for consumer durable or capital items in situations where *quality is changing* over time. For instance, does a higher price for such an item reflect better quality (more characteristics) or the exploitation of monopoly power by suppliers, etc.? By assigning values to individual characteristics one might then be able to sum these values in order to calculate the *net change* (gain of some characteristics, loss of others) in estimated market valuation for a new vintage of production as against the change in its actual market price.

Suppose, by way of illustration of this idea, that phone p7 in Table 2.12 represents a later vintage of technology than phone p2. The later model (p7) has one unit less of characteristic X1 (i.e. loss of £10.25 in estimated value) and two units less of the (negatively valued) characteristic X5 (i.e. gain of £10.18 in estimated value), as compared with phone p2. So far we have a loss of £0.07 in valuation via the dropping of certain characteristics in the latest model. However, we must also value the benefits of the new characteristics available in the later model p7 as compared with p2, namely one unit extra of characteristics X2 (+£25.02), X4 (+£5.35) and X6 (+£13.43). We then have a net increase in valuation of

$$-£0.07 + £43.80 = £43.73$$

Set against this net increase in *estimated market valuation* of the newly available combination of characteristics in p7, we have an observed increase in *actual market price* of +£90. This might indicate that consumers are paying more for the later model than the revised set of characteristics might warrant, suggesting that some exploitation of monopoly power by suppliers might also be present in addition to enhanced quality of the item purchased.

Pricing new products

This approach, involving the valuing of characteristics, may also help in pricing new products. Suppose that the seven phones in Table 2.12 are all present on the market, and that a new firm decides to enter the telephone handset market. Further suppose that, for whatever reason, the firm decides that it should take phone p4 as its reference point and develop a new handset with all these characteristics *plus* the extra characteristic X6. It therefore produces a phone with characteristics X2, X3, X4, four units of X5, and X6. Its problem now is to choose a price that would make it competitive with the other phones on the market. The most obvious reference price is that for phone p4, and since the new phone is unambiguously better than phone p4 (having X6 plus everything that phone p4 has), it should carry a higher price. The question is: how much higher and, in particular, should it be priced more highly than phone p6, which lacks characteristic X6 but does have X7?

But notice from Table 2.12 that currently phone p4 is a very poor buy, creating a *value* of only £30.29 for consumers as compared with a *price* of £35. The new phone with X6 adds a value of £13.43 to phone p4, giving an estimated market value of £43.72. The new phone also adds £0.33 value to that offered by phone p6 (which is currently a good buy, being worth £43.39 to consumers but costing only £35). Thus, although the new phone offers value to consumers of about £43, choosing a price for it is complicated by the fact that p6 is 'underpriced' and p4 is 'overpriced'. Any price less than £43 will represent good value for money, but if the new entrant wants to compete with phone p6, the price of the new phone will have to be close to £35. At the same time p5, which is also a good buy, is sold at £35 and has one unit less of X5 (an advantage, since X5 is negative) than has the new phone. Setting a price of £35 will almost certainly ensure the new phone a better place on the market in comparison with p6 and perhaps at the expense of phone p4, and will place it very close to p5. In fact, if it were to set a price below £29.91 (£35 − £5.09) then it might prove the best buy of all, the lower price than p5 more than compensating for its being heavier (having one more unit of X5).

Key terms

Arc elasticity	Identification problem
Cross-elasticity	Income elasticity
Conditions of demand	Increase/decrease (demand)
Demand curve	Marginal revenue
Demand function	Point price elasticity
Endogenous variables	Relatively price elastic
Engel curve	Relatively price inelastic
Exogenous variables	Unit elastic
Expansion/contraction (demand)	

Full definitions can be found in the 'Glossary of terms' (pp. 699–710)

Review questions

1. A medium-sized publishing company, Sci-publishers Ltd, produces a specialised journal for the electrical industry. Its monthly market demand schedule is described by the data shown in Table 2.13.

   (a) (i) Draw the demand curve from the data given in the table.
   (ii) Calculate the amount of 'consumer surplus' when the market price is £6.
   (iii) Calculate the *point price elasticity of demand*, first when the price of the journal is £5 and second when the price has been raised to £6.
   (iv) Calculate the *arc price elasticity of demand* when the price rises from £5 to £6.
   Explain the relationships between this result and those obtained from (iii) above.

Table 2.13

Price of journal (£)	Quantity demanded (per month)
11	0
10	100
9	200
8	300
7	400
6	500
5	600
4	700
3	800
2	900
1	1000
0	1100

(b) Another competitor, Electype plc, now enters the market and begins to produce a similar journal to Sci-publishers. In the year 2000, Sci-publishers completes an important market research project, which estimates that its journal has an own-price elasticity of demand of –1, an income elasticity of demand of 2 , and a cross-elasticity of demand with respect to the journal produced by its rival, Electype, of –2. Suppose that Sci-publishers wishes to increase its journal price by 4% in the year 2001 and assumes that (a) consumer income will rise by 3% and (b) the price of the Electype journal will fall by 2%.

(i) If the level of sales in 2000 for Sci-publishers was 550 journals per month, calculate the number of journals that Sci-publishers can expect to sell per month in 2001.

(ii) What price should Sci-publishers charge in 2001 in order to keep its sales unchanged at 550 journals per month?

2. The figures in Table 2.14, obtained from interviews with staff of a large multinational company, show the potential demand for meals at its works canteen over a period of one month. The relevant price and quantity demanded, together with the price elasticities of demand at each price level, have also been calculated.

(a) Calculate total and marginal revenue at each level of demand using the information given in the table.

(b) Draw the demand, total revenue and marginal revenue curves from the data.

(c) Explain the relationships between elasticity, total revenue and marginal revenue as identified in the calculations.

(d) Write down the equation for the demand and marginal revenue curves, and comment on the shape of these functions.

Table 2.14

Price	Quantity demanded	Price elasticity of demand
£6	0	
£5	300	−5
£4	600	−2
£3	900	−1
£2	1200	−0.5
£1	1500	−0.2
£0	1800	0

3. The demand function for woollen sweaters has been derived from a regression analysis based on market research data. The demand function was in the form

$Q_w = 100 - 40P_w + 0.8A + 0.1Y$

where Q_w = demand for woollen sweaters per year

P_w = price of the sweaters in pounds

A = advertising expenditure

Y = per capita income

(a) Using the information contained in the demand function, indicate the change in the number of sweaters purchased per year (i.e. change in Q_w) as the result of a unit increase (e.g. £1) in each of the explanatory variables.

(b) Find the value of Q_w if P_w = £50, A = £6,000, and Y = £20,000.

(c) Derive the equation for the demand *curve* for sweaters from the demand *function* using the relevant information in (b). (Convert the equation into the normal form of a demand curve that has P_w on the left-hand side of the equation and Q_w on the right-hand side.)

(d) Calculate the price and income elasticities of demand for sweaters given the data in (b).

(e) Derive the total and marginal revenue functions for sweaters from the demand curve.

4. A small store specialising in selling jeans found from a market survey that its weekly demand curve for the Levi 501 brand was $P_L = 50 - 0.625Q_L$ where P_L is the price in pounds of the Levi jeans and Q_L is the quantity sold per week.

(a) Calculate the price and quantity values at the points where the demand curve intersects the respective axes.

(b) Using knowledge available from the demand curve, calculate the (point) own-price elasticities of demand for Levi jeans when the price/quantity combinations are 40/16 and 16/80 respectively.

(c) Find the price–quantity combination for which own-price elasticity for Levi jeans is unity. Has this point any special significance on the demand curve?

(d) If the marginal cost of each extra pair of jeans to the store is £20, find the profit-maximising price and quantity for sales of Levi jeans.

5. Research in the London area has found that two brands of chocolate ice cream tend to account for a high percentage of the market for such products. A survey of consumer tastes has also found that the main differences between them are to be found in the attributes of smoothness and flavour. The 'Parma' brand is felt to contain 10 units of smoothness and 5 units of flavour and costs 75p per bar, while the 'Yama' brand contains 5 units of smoothness and 10 units of flavour and costs 60p per bar. However, more recent research has shown that consumers are getting tired of the two dominant brands and would be prepared to try a new type of chocolate ice cream as long as the price was not too high. A new company producing 'Mano' chocolate ice cream seems to be a serious contender since each bar is perceived by consumers to contain 10 units of both smoothness and flavour. For a consumer who has £10 per month to spend on chocolate ice cream and who has the attribute values given:

(a) Draw the attribute rays for 'Parma', 'Yama' and 'Mano' chocolate ice creams and insert the efficiency frontier between the 'Parma' and 'Yama' rays.

(b) Using the approximate values obtained from the graph, calculate the maximum price that can be charged for the 'Mano' brand such that the £10 will buy a combination of attributes that lies on the efficiency frontier.

(c) If we assume that the 'Mano' brand costs 70p a bar, will our consumer switch to the 'Mano' brand or will they stay with 'Parma' or 'Yama'? Give your reasons using the concept of marginal rate of substitution (MRS).

■ Further reading

Intermediate texts

Baumol, W. J. (1977), *Economic Theory and Operations Analysis*, 4th edn, Chs 9 and 10, Prentice Hall, Hemel Hempstead.

Browning, E. and Browning, J. (1992), *Microeconomic Theory and Applications*, 4th edn, Ch. 3, HarperCollins, London.

Dobson, S., Maddala, G. S. and Miller, E. (1995), *Microeconomics*, Chs 1 and 3, McGraw-Hill, Maidenhead.

Hope, S. (1999), *Applied Microeconomics*, Chs 1 and 2, John Wiley, Chichester.

Katz, M. and Rosen, H. (1998), *Microeconomics*, 3rd edn, Ch. 3, Irwin, Boston, Mass.

Koutsoyiannis, A. (1979), *Modern Microeconomics*, 2nd edn, Ch. 2, Macmillan, Basingstoke.

Laidler, D. and Estrin, S. (1995), *Introduction to Microeconomics*, 4th edn, Ch. 9, Harvester Wheatsheaf, Hemel Hempstead.

Maddala, G. S. and Miller, E. (1989), *Microeconomics: Theory and Application*, Chs 4 and 5, McGraw-Hill, New York.

Marshall, A. (1920), *Principles of Economics*, 8th Edition, p.97, London, Macmillan.

Nicholson, W. (1997), *Intermediate Microeconomics and its Application*, 7th edn, Chs 4 and 5, Dryden Press, Fort Worth.

Pindyck, R. and Rubinfeld, D. (1998), *Microeconomics*, 4th edn, Ch. 4, Macmillan, Basingstoke.

Varian, H. (1999), *Intermediate Microeconomics*, 5th edn, Ch. 6, Norton, New York.

Advanced texts   Gravelle, H. and Rees, R. (1992), *Microeconomics*, 2nd edn, Chs 3–5, Longman, Harlow.

Mas-Colell, A., Whinston, M. D. and Green, J. R. (1995), *Microeconomic Theory*, Chs 3 and 4, Oxford University Press, Oxford.

Articles and   Acton. J. P. and Vogelsant, I. (1992), 'Telephone demand over the Atlantic:
other sources   Evidence from country-pair data,' *Journal of Industrial Economics*, XL, 3.

Acutt, M. Z. and Dodgson, J. S. (1995), 'Cross-elasticities of demand for travel', *Transport Policy*, 2, 4, Oct.

Alperovich, G. and Machnes, Y. (1994), 'The role of wealth in the demand for international air travel,' *Journal of Transport Economics and Policy*, XXVIII, 2, May.

Blundell, R., Paschardes, P. and Weber, G. (1993), 'What do we learn about consumer demand patterns from micro data?,' *American Economic Review*, 83, 3.

Cameron, S. (1998), 'Estimation of the demand for cigarettes: a review of the literature', *Economic Issues*, 3, 2, Sept.

Geroski, P. and Toker, S. (1992), 'What is a good buy?', *The Economic Review*, 9, 4, April, Phillip Allan Updates, Oxford.

Goodwin, P. B. (1992), 'A review of new demand elasticities with special reference to short- and long-run effects of price changes,' *Journal of Transport Economics and Policy*, 26, 2.

Harris, A., McAvinchey, I. D. and Yannopoulos, Y. (1993), 'The demand for labour, capital, fuels and electricity: A sectorial model for the UK economy,' *Journal of Economic Studies*, 20, 3.

Karatzas, G. (1992), 'On the effect of income and relative price on the demand for health care – the EC evidence: a comment,' *Applied Economics*, 24.

Milne, R. and Molana, H. (1991), 'On the effect of income and relative price on demand for health care: EC evidence,' *Applied Economics*, 23.

Rosser, M. (1995), 'The demand for durable goods,' *Economic Review*, 12, 3, Feb.

Schrimper, R. and Mathia, G. (1975) 'Reservation and market demand for sweet potatoes at the farm level,' *American Journal of Agricultural Economics*, 57.

Simmons, R. (1996), 'The demand for English League Football: a club level analysis, *Applied Economics*, 28.

Turner, P. (1998), 'Growth and the balance of payments', *Economic Review*, 3, February.

Van Ours, J. C. (1995), 'The price elasticity of hard drugs: the case of opium in the Dutch East Indies,' *Journal of Political Economy*, 103, 2, April.

Chapter 3

Risk, uncertainty and choice

Introduction and review

In the first two chapters of this book we have assumed a 'certain' world, i.e. one in which the consequences of any choice made by the consumer were fully known *before* that choice was made. This is, of course, hardly the case in the real world. In this chapter we introduce the idea of uncertainty and risk, and examine the implications of these for consumer choice.

Although we shall often use the ideas of uncertainty and risk interchangeably, they strictly refer to different situations. **Uncertainty** refers to situations in which many outcomes of a particular choice are possible but the likelihood (or probability) of each outcome is unknown. **Risk** is rather different in that it can only be measured accurately on the assumption that we know all the possible outcomes *and* the likelihood (probability) of each outcome occurring. Of course, as we shall see, risk can be *estimated* in a variety of ways by seeking to assign probabilities to the various possible outcomes.

Expected value

The **expected value** in an uncertain situation is a weighted average of the values (pay-offs) associated with each possible outcome, the probabilities of each outcome being used as weights. For a situation in which there are two possible outcomes having pay-offs X_1 and X_2, with the probabilities of each outcome p_1 and p_2 respectively, then the expected value $E(X)$ is

$$E(X) = p_1 X_1 + p_2 X_2$$

For example, if there is a 60% chance of earning £100 and a 40% chance of earning £500 from an investment, then:

$E(X) = 0.60 \, (£100) + 0.40 \, (£500)$
i.e. $E(X) = £60 + £200 = £260$

More generally, **the expected monetary value** (EMV) of a particular course of action over n possible outcomes can be defined as:

$$EMV = \sum_{i=1}^{n} p_i \cdot X_i$$

where p_i = probability of ith outcome

X_i = value of ith outcome

and $\sum_{i=1}^{n} p_i = 1$

▪ Preference towards risk

We have already considered the ideas of total and marginal utility in Chapter 1. Here we can apply the idea of expected value to *utility curves* in order to identify different preferences towards risk. We can adapt our earlier expression involving n possible outcomes accordingly:

$$\text{Expected utility (EU)} = \sum_{i=1}^{n} p_i \cdot U_i$$

where p_i = probability of ith outcome

U_i = utility of ith outcome

and $\sum_{i=1}^{n} p_i = 1$

Risk averse A person is described as being **risk averse** if he or she prefers a situation in which a given income (pay-off) is certain to a situation yielding the *same expected value* for income but which involves uncertainty. This can be illustrated by the total utility curve in Fig. 3.1(a).

In Fig. 3.1(a), suppose that the consumer can be certain of an income of £20,000, yielding utility level U_3. Suppose also that by choosing an alternative situation the consumer has a 50/50 chance of receiving either £10,000 (U_1) or £30,000 (U_2). We can say that the expected value of this alternative is

$E(X) = 0.5 \,(£10,000) + 0.5 \,(£30,000)$
i.e. $E(X) = £5,000 + £15,000 = £20,000$

The uncertain outcome has the same expected value of income as the certain outcome, namely £20,000. However, the **expected utility** ($\frac{1}{2} U_1 + \frac{1}{2} 2U_2$) of the uncertain situation is indicated at point D, the mid-point of a straight line connecting A to B. This utility (U_4) is clearly less than the utility of the same income in the 'certain' situation

Measures of dispersion and risk

As we consider in rather more detail in Appendix 2 (p. 686), a number of measures of **dispersion** may often be encountered in risk analysis. These uniformly refer to the dispersion (or spread) of data around the **arithmetic mean** or 'simple average' of the data.

- **Mean deviation.** The *average* of the deviations from the mean (ignoring the sign of those deviations).
- **Variance (σ^2).** The average of the *squared* deviations from the mean.
- **Standard deviation (σ).** The *square root* of the average of the squared deviations from the mean.

In other words, standard deviation = $\sqrt{}$ variance.

Absolute and relative dispersion

These are all **absolute** measures of dispersion. Where two sets of data (e.g. two investment projects) have the same arithmetic mean, as in Fig. 3.2(a), then clearly the data set A with the greatest absolute measure of dispersion (here standard deviation σ) contains the greater 'risk'. In other words we can be less sure as to the expected value of an individual item selected at random from data set A, as compared with an individual item selected at random from data set B. In fact under certain circumstances we can quantify that difference in risk. In Fig. 3.2(b) we present certain probabilities associated with being a specified number of standard deviations either side of the arithmetic mean for a 'normal distribution' (see Appendix 2). We can now say that if the standard deviation (σ) for data set A is £6 and that for B is £3, then we can be 68.26% sure that an individual item selected at random will lie within £6 of the arithmetic mean ($\bar{X}$) of £20 for A, but within as little as £3 of the arithmetic mean of £20 for B. Clearly there is greater 'risk' of an individual item being further (in terms of £s) from the arithmetic mean for data set A than is the case for data set B. We can repeat this analysis for ranges between $\pm 2\sigma$, $\pm 3\sigma$ etc. from the respective arithmetic means.

In the above analysis we have compared two data sets with the *same* arithmetic mean. In this circumstance the absolute measure of dispersion is adequate for comparing 'risk' factors. However, when the arithmetic means of the respective data sets *differ*, then we need to use **relative** measures of dispersion.

One such relative measure of dispersion is the **coefficient of variation** (CV). We can define this as

$$CV = \frac{\text{Standard deviation}}{\text{Arithmetic mean}} \times 100 = \frac{\sigma}{\bar{X}} \times 100$$

Here the coefficient of variation is expressed as a percentage, though it is sometimes left in the form of a decimal. Suppose, for example, that the details for data sets A and B are as indicated below:

Data set A
Arithmetic mean ($\bar{X}_A$) = £50
Standard deviation (σ_A) = £6

Data set B
Arithmetic mean ($\bar{X}_B$) = £20
Standard deviation (σ_B) = £3

Fig. 3.2 **Dispersion and risk.**

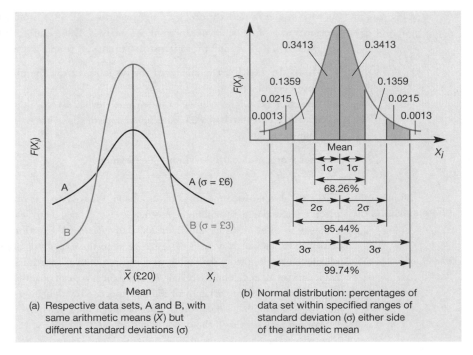

(a) Respective data sets, A and B, with same arithmetic means ($\overline{X}$) but different standard deviations (σ)

(b) Normal distribution: percentages of data set within specified ranges of standard deviation (σ) either side of the arithmetic mean

Then:

$$CV_A = \frac{\sigma_A}{\overline{X}_A} \times 100 = \frac{6}{50} \times 100 = 12\% \ (0.12)$$

$$CV_B = \frac{\sigma_B}{\overline{X}_B} \times 100 = \frac{3}{20} \times 100 = 15\% \ (0.15)$$

We can now see that the **absolute dispersion** for data set A is greater than that for B ($\sigma_A > \sigma_B$), but that the **relative dispersion** is smaller ($CV_A < CV_B$). This is because, in comparative terms, the greater absolute dispersion of data set A takes place around a *still greater* value for the arithmetic mean.

As we shall see (p. 125), when comparing respective investment projects we can usefully apply this concept of relative dispersion to risk analysis.

Theoretical developments

■ Measuring the risk premium

The **risk premium** measures the amount of income that an individual would give up to leave him/her indifferent between a risky choice and a certain one. In Fig. 3.3 we repeat the earlier Fig. 3.1(a) for a risk-averse person. However, in this case we also draw a line

Fig. 3.3 **Measuring
the risk premium
(DE).**

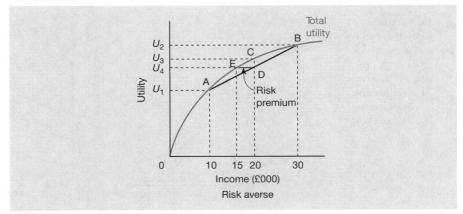

horizontal to the vertical axis from point D, the mid-point of line AB. We have seen that point D reflects the expected value of the uncertain (risky) situation involving the two possible outcomes A and B, each with a 50% probability. The line DE measures the **risk premium,** here £5,000, in that a *certain* income of £15,000 gives the same expected utility (U_4) as the *uncertain* income that has an expected value of £20,000. The consumer is willing to give up £5,000 of expected income from the risky choice in order to be indifferent (have the same utility) between the risky outcome and the certain outcome.

The risk premium is therefore a measure of the *degree* of risk aversion. The more risk averse the person, the greater the risk premium, i.e. the more expected income the person will be willing to give up from the risky choice in order to be indifferent between that and a certain choice.

Indifference curves and attitudes to risk

The **variability** of the likely returns on a particular choice clearly affects the riskiness perceived to be associated with that choice. In Fig. 3.4(a) choices *A* and *B* have the same expected monetary value (E_1), but choice *A* has greater variability around E_1 and therefore is likely to be regarded as the more risky.

As we have seen (p. 103), a common measure of the variability or riskiness of a choice is the variance of the outcomes related to it. Here our formulae take into account the *probabilities* of different outcomes.

$$\text{Variance} = \sum_{i=1}^{n} p_i (X_i - \bar{X})^2$$

where p_i = probability of outcome i
X_i = value of outcome i
n = number of possible outcomes
$\bar{X}$ = arithmetic mean value of all outcomes

The **standard deviation** is also frequently used as a measure of variability or riskiness, and is the square root of the variance.

Fig. 3.4
(a) Variability of
pay-off around a
given expected value
(E_1).
(b) Indifference
curves for risk-
averse decision
markers.

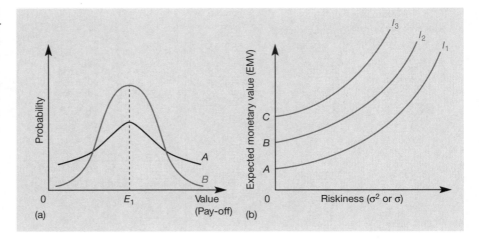

$$\text{Standard deviation} = \sqrt{\sum_{i=1}^{n} p_i (X_i - \bar{X})^2}$$

Both these statistics give a measure of dispersion (or spread) around the expected monetary value of a choice taken under conditions of risk. For example, suppose a firm is about to launch a new product, with the profit outcome expected by the firm depending on the state of the economy at the time of launch. The firm believes the probabilities of a low-growth/stable/high-growth economy at the time of launch to be 0.3, 0.5 and 0.2 respectively. Table 3.1 calculates the arithmetic mean, variance and standard deviation, using our earlier formulae involving probabilities.

Table 3.1 **Expected monetary value (EMV) and measures of risk.**

Economy at launch	Probability p_i	Profit outcome X_i	$p_i X_i$	$(X_i - \bar{X})$	$(X_i - \bar{X})^2$	$p_i(X_i - \bar{X})^2$
Low growth	0.3	4,000	1,200	−900	810,000	243,000
Stable	0.5	5,000	2,500	+100	10,000	5,000
High growth	0.2	6,000	1,200	+1,100	1,210,000	242,000
			$\sum_{i=1}^{3} p_i X_i$ $= 4,900$			$\sum_{i=1}^{3} p_i(X_i - \bar{X})^2$ $= 490,000$

$$\text{(EMV) } \overline{X} = \sum_{i=1}^{n} P_i X_i = 4,900$$

$$\text{Variance } \sigma^2 = \sum_{i=1}^{n} p_i (X_i - \overline{X})^2 = 490,000$$

Standard deviation $\sigma = \sqrt{490,000} = 700$

For this firm the expected monetary value (EMV) or arithmetic mean ($\overline{X}$) of the investment decision is £4,900. We can use either the variance (490,000 square pounds) or the standard deviation (700 pounds) as a measure of dispersion ('riskiness') around this mean value. Such a calculation will give us a particular point or coordinate to place in Fig. 3.4(b).

When deciding between alternative choices, decision makers are weighing different combinations of risk on the one hand (measured by the variance or standard deviation of returns) against different combinations of expected monetary value (EMV) on the other. We can therefore, in principle, use **indifference curves** to reflect the different combinations of risk and return that will leave the decision maker 'indifferent', i.e. will yield the same level of utility.

If we assume decision makers to be **risk averse** then the indifference curves will be similar to those in Fig. 3.4(b). To compensate for greater riskiness (higher variance/standard deviation), the decision maker will require a higher expected return if he is to be indifferent (i.e. achieve the same level of utility). Further, the greater the existing level of exposure to riskiness, the greater must be any *additional* expected return to compensate for each unit increase in riskiness. Hence the indifference curves for those who are risk averse will be convex to the horizontal axis, as shown. Higher indifference curves will correspond to higher levels of utility: for example, a higher expected return from a choice that has the *same riskiness* as another choice will yield higher utility.

The indifference map in Fig. 3.4(b) also illustrates the idea of the **certainty equivalent** of a decision involving risk. This is defined as the sum of money, available with certainty, that would leave the decision maker as satisfied (with the same utility) as if he or she had undertaken the risky action. In terms of our diagram, £A is the certainty equivalent of any combination of risk and return indicated by indifference curve I_1; £B and £C are certainty equivalents corresponding to the combinations of risk and return indicated by indifference curves I_2 and I_3 respectively.

Clearly the *slope* of the respective indifference curves will, in this case, reflect the degree of risk aversion. A decision maker who is **highly risk averse** will require a substantial amount of additional expected return to compensate for a small increase in riskiness: i.e. the slope will be steeper, the more risk averse the decision maker.

A **risk-neutral** decision maker will have *horizontal* indifference curves. Since, by definition, he or she is indifferent between certain and uncertain events with the same expected return, it follows that no additional expected return is required to compensate for an increase in riskiness.

A **risk-loving** decision maker will have indifference curves sloping in the *opposite direction* to those in Fig. 3.4(b), i.e. downwards from left to right. Since the risk lover would prefer a more risky situation associated with any given expected return, he or she is willing to trade off a reduced expected return for an increase in riskiness and yet remain indifferent between the two situations.

Our major interest, in practice, will be with the risk-averse decision maker in Fig. 3.4(b) and with the different curvatures (slopes) of such indifference curves representing different degrees of risk aversion.

■ Insurance and gambling

We can use our analysis to show how the risk-averse decision maker is likely to **insure** and the risk lover to **gamble.** The essence of insurance is that, in return for a premium paid at the start of the period, some agent guarantees to reimburse the decision maker for any loss incurred during the period. In other words, by paying a fee the decision maker can put him or herself in a position of certainty. The trade-off is as follows: by reducing the level of income/wealth with which he or she begins the period by the amount of this fee (**insurance premium**), the decision maker can guarantee that he or she will end the period with the initial level of income/wealth (minus the premium) intact.

In terms of Fig. 3.5, based on our earlier Fig. 3.3, if *not insured* the decision maker faced with possible outcomes A and B, each with a 50% probability, can expect to end up with wealth W_3. In this uncertain situation, the expected wealth W_3 will yield utility $\frac{1}{2}U_1 + \frac{1}{2}U_2 = U_4$. However, should the decision maker expect this level of wealth with certainty, i.e. *be insured,* it would yield utility U_3. The *difference* (CD) between these two utility situations represents the **consumer surplus** that arises from certainty: here from buying insurance that would make the wealth outcome W_3 certain at the end of the period. We have previously noted that W_4 is the **certainty equivalent** level of wealth to W_3, i.e. that wealth which if received with certainty yields the same utility (U_4) as the fifty-fifty gamble. As long as the **insurance premium** is no more than the difference $W_3 - W_4$ (the **risk premium**) then the decision maker will achieve higher utility by insurance than by non-insurance: i.e. will be above E on the total utility curve.

Fig. 3.5 **The insurance decision in a situation of risk aversion (diminishing marginal utility of wealth).**

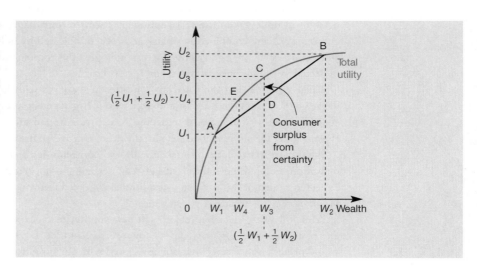

Using our earlier terminology, if the decision maker is **risk averse** then the risk premium is positive and an insurance market can exist (if risk premium > insurance premium).

Put another way, the gap ED in Fig. 3.5 corresponds to the *maximum insurance premium* that would be paid by the decision maker given the degree of risk aversion implied by the shape of the total utility curve in Fig. 3.5. So long as this maximum insurance premium that would be paid by the decision maker is greater than the *minimum insurance premium required* by the insuring agent, then clearly there is scope for an insurance market to exist. Of course the latter calculation will be based by the insuring agent on the 'law of large numbers', which tells us that while single events may be random and unpredictable, the *average* outcome of many similar events can be predicted. It is then an 'actuarial decision', based on statistical probabilities, to calculate the minimum premium that will ensure that, over a large number of events, the total premiums paid in will at least equal the total amount of money paid out in claims (plus administrative costs and required profit margin).

The greater the degree of risk aversion, the greater the concavity to the horizontal axis of the total utility curve and the greater the maximum premium (ED) the decision maker is willing to pay for insurance. In other words the assumption of **diminishing marginal utility of wealth** implicit in the curvature (concave to the origin) of the total utility curve in Fig. 3.5 is crucial to the existence of the insurance market.

If there is a **constant marginal utility of wealth,** as in Fig. 3.6(a), then no such gap (ED) exists: i.e. the *maximum premium* the decision maker is willing to pay for insurance is *zero* since he or she is indifferent between certain and uncertain situations yielding the same expected value.

Using our earlier terminology, if the decision maker is **risk neutral** then the risk premium is zero and no insurance market can exist.

Fig. 3.6 **Constant and increasing marginal utilities of wealth.**

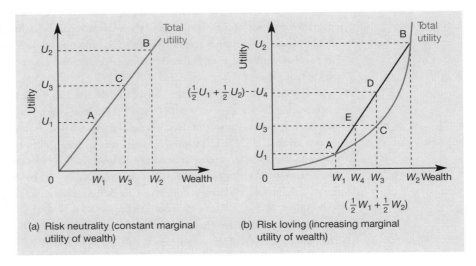

(a) Risk neutrality (constant marginal utility of wealth)

(b) Risk loving (increasing marginal utility of wealth)

Further if we assume that there is **increasing marginal utility of wealth,** i.e. that the decision maker is risk loving, then we can see that he or she is more likely to gamble than insure. In Fig. 3.6(b) a *gain* of wealth ($W_3 - W_2$) will add more to utility than an equal-sized *loss* of wealth ($W_3 - W_1$) takes away from utility. Thus a fifty-fifty chance of such a gain or loss has a higher expected utility (U_4) than the certainty of W_3 (U_3). Only an expected value of W_4 from the gamble is needed to give the same level of utility (U_3) as would derive from the certain level of wealth W_3. Therefore $W_3 - W_4$ measures the money value of the extent to which the uncertain alternative (gamble with expected wealth/utility values W_3/U_4) is preferred.

Clearly in this case of risk loving, with increasing marginal utility of wealth, the decision maker will choose the risky alternative rather than the safe one and will gamble rather than insure against any possible loss.

> Using our earlier terminology, if the decision maker is **risk loving** then the risk premium is negative and no insurance market can exist.

Why some individuals both insure and gamble

So far our analysis implies that decision makers who are risk averse (with a diminishing marginal utility of wealth) will at least consider insuring in any situation of uncertainty, whereas those who are risk loving (increasing marginal utility of wealth) will not insure (i.e. will gamble).

Of course, whether or not risk-averse decision makers *do* insure depends upon the situation being such that risk premium > insurance premium. On the basis of this analysis we should expect that a decision maker who insures against large risks will also insure against small risks, provided the insurance premium is suitably small (< risk premium). We would also expect that a decision maker who does not insure (i.e. gambles) when faced with small risks will not insure when faced with large risks.

In practice, of course, this is *not* what appears to happen. Some people insure against some risks but decline to insure (i.e. gamble) against other risks, even when sophisticated insurance markets exist, offering a variety of premiums for different levels of cover. We now seek to explain in theory why such actual behaviour is observed.

The work of Friedman and Savage provides one possible explanation. The suggestion here is that while the marginal utility of wealth diminishes overall, in 'local situations' it may actually increase (see Fig. 3.7).

In Fig. 3.7 the marginal utility of wealth declines as wealth rises towards W_3, then increases locally for rises in wealth beyond W_3 before continuing to decline. The implication here is that because the decision maker experiences increasing marginal utility of wealth around W_3, for risks involving changes in wealth around that region he or she might be expected to gamble (not insure). However, for risks involving the possibility of more substantial changes in wealth the decision maker can be expected to insure, given the *overall* diminishing marginal utility of wealth associated with risk aversion.

Suppose, in Fig. 3.7, the decision maker is faced with the choice between W_3 with certainty or a fifty-fifty chance of achieving an outcome of W_1 or W_2 from a 'gamble'. The expected value of the gamble is W_3 ($\frac{1}{2}W_1 + \frac{1}{2}W_2$), which for purposes of illustration

Fig. 3.7 **A total utility function showing diminishing then increasing then diminishing marginal utility, as wealth rises.**

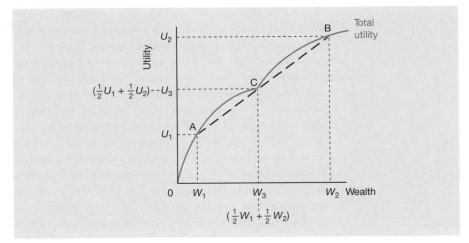

is where there is a 'local' increase in the marginal utility of wealth. Here the expected utility of the gamble $(\frac{1}{2}U_1 + \frac{1}{2}U_2)$ exactly equals the utility (U_3) of receiving wealth W_3 with certainty. For any fifty-fifty gamble *inside* the bounds W_1 and W_2 in Fig. 3.7 with expected value W_3, the expected utility of the gamble $(\frac{1}{2}U_1 + \frac{1}{2}U_2)$ will be *greater* than the certainty equivalent utility U_3. Hence the gamble (non-insurance) will be taken. (You can check this yourself by drawing a straight, dashed line connecting a point on segment AC of the total utility curve with a point on segment CB of that curve.) However, for any fifty-fifty gamble *outside* the bounds W_1 and W_2 in Fig. 3.7 with expected value W_3, the expected utility of the gamble $(\frac{1}{2}U_1 + \frac{1}{2}U_2)$ will be *smaller* than the certainty equivalent utility U_3. Hence insurance will be taken.

This analysis implies that decision makers with a utility function similar to that in Fig. 3.7 will take risks (gamble) by non-insurance when the variations in wealth involved are relatively small in and around points such as C representing *localised* increases in the marginal utility of wealth. However, more substantial changes in wealth are likely to bring the *overall* diminishing marginal utility of wealth more actively into play and result in insurance and the avoidance of risk, rather than non-insurance and the associated gamble.

In practice, however, there seems to be no particular level of wealth (W_3 in Fig. 3.7) around which small prospective changes are more likely to yield non-insuring (gambling) behaviour than larger prospective changes. It seems that at every level of wealth, some decision makers insure against some risks but not against others. Although we have produced a useful analysis, we must look at additional explanatory factors. This brings us to another approach, which stresses the impossibility of the insuring agent offering an entirely 'fair bet' to the decision maker.

Fair bet and administrative costs

We might define a **fair bet** as one for which, should it be repeated an infinite number of times, both insured and insurer would expect to break even. In other words, those insuring against risk would pay as premiums an amount that *exactly equals* the expected pay-out of the insurer over a large number of events.

In practice, of course, the insuring company will be faced with a variety of **administrative costs** in issuing policies, involving infrastructure support (buildings, offices, computer networks), actuarial support (working out risks etc. at head office), local and regional agents, and so on. Many of these costs are likely to be fixed or overhead costs, which do not vary directly with the level or value of business activity. It can be shown that if these administrative costs are apportioned *per unit of activity* (e.g. per insurance contract issued) instead of pro rata to the value of each activity, then this may help explain why larger risks are often insured and smaller risks uninsured.

In Fig. 3.8, *d* represents the administrative cost apportioned as a given sum per insurance contract issued. AB and CD represent gambles with fifty-fifty probabilities; AB corresponds to a gamble with larger risk than CD in terms of dispersion but having the same expected value (W_0) as CD in terms of outcome. The gain to decision makers from insuring as a 'fair bet' is given by G_1 and G_2 respectively (the respective **risk premiums**). With a fixed administrative cost of *d*, clearly only the riskier gamble AB yields a positive *net gain,* i.e. one that is sufficient to cover those costs, so only AB will be undertaken. This analysis would help to explain the observation that some decision makers insure against large risks but gamble by failing to insure against smaller risks.

The demand for risky assets

We have already (p. 106) examined an **indifference map** showing lines of constant utility between different combinations of risk (measured by variance or standard deviation) and expected monetary return. We noted that for a risk-averse decision maker the indifference curves would be convex to the horizontal axis: the greater the degree of risk aversion the greater the degree of convexity. We can now introduce a type of *budget line* to this indifference map that will help us to identify equilibrium solutions for decision makers in terms of the trade-off between risk and expected return.

Fig. 3.8 **How fixed administrative costs (*d*) might favour insuring only against riskier gambles.**

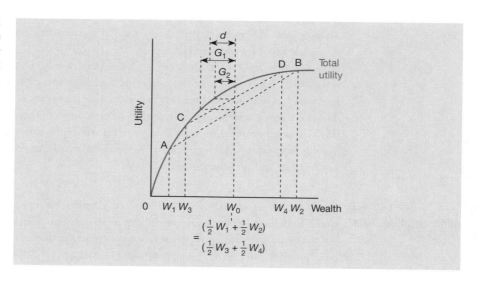

First, however, it will help to define an **asset** as an item that provides a monetary flow to its owner. This monetary flow may in part be **explicit,** such as the rent from a room or building or the interest on a security, and in part **implicit,** such as the increase (or decrease) in market price of the item, i.e. the capital gain (or loss). A **risky asset** is one for which the monetary flow following its purchase cannot be known with certainty. Many assets are of this type, with rental/interest payments and capital values subject to changes in different market conditions. At one extreme, however, we might define a **risk-free asset** as providing a certain monetary flow. Government bonds issued at a specified interest rate are perhaps as close as we can get to a risk-free asset, as the chances of default are minimum and the payments are known. (Even here possible changes in the rate of inflation or in the interest return from alternative sources introduce an element of risk.)

For purposes of this analysis we shall assume that an investor chooses between two types of asset – a risky asset and a risk-free asset. We denote the *expected return* on the **risky asset** as R_m and the *actual return* as r_m with the *expected return* on the **risk-free asset** being R_f and the *actual return* r_f. The risky assets will have a greater variance (σ^2) and standard deviation (σ) in their returns than will the risk-free assets:

$$\sigma^2_m > \sigma^2_f$$

and

$$\sigma_m > \sigma_f$$

If risky assets are to be held then it must be true that $R_m > R_f$ for risk-averse investors. We further suppose that b represents the fraction of the sum available for investment placed in risky assets, with $(1 - b)$ placed in risk-free assets.

The *expected return* on the investor's **total portfolio** (R_p) can now be expressed as a weighted average of the expected return on the two types of asset:

$$R_p = bR_m + (1 - b)\, R_f \qquad (1)$$

It can further be shown (see box, p. 115) that the standard deviation of a **portfolio** (σ_p) consisting of one risky and one risk-free asset is

$$\sigma_p = b\sigma_m \qquad\qquad (2)$$

In other words, the standard deviation of the portfolio (σ_p)is the fraction of the portfolio invested in the risky asset (b) times the standard deviation of that asset (σ_m).

By rearranging equation (1) above we have

$$R_p = R_f + b\, (R_m - R_f) \qquad (3)$$

And by rearranging equation (2) above we have

$$b = \frac{\sigma_p}{\sigma_m} \qquad\qquad (4)$$

Substituting (4) into (3) gives

$$R_p = R_f + \frac{(R_m - R_f)}{\sigma_m} \cdot \sigma_p \qquad (5)$$

This equation (5) is a type of **budget line** because it outlines the trade-off for the portfolio holder between risk (σ_p) and the expected return (R_p). Note that it is the equation of a straight line with (vertical) intercept R_f and slope $(R_m - R_f)/\sigma_m$. This equation (5) is illustrated in Fig. 3.9, and it tells us that the expected return on the portfolio R_p increases as the standard deviation of that return σp increases. We could refer to the *slope* of this budget line, $(R_m - R_f)/\sigma_m$, as the **price of risk,** because it tells us how much extra return the investor requires to accept a further increase in risk.

In Fig. 3.9 the utility-maximising portfolio is at the point where the budget line is tangent to the highest attainable indifference curve U_2, i.e. with expected return for the portfolio R^* and standard deviation σ^*. This solution is somewhere between the two extremes for expected return and standard deviation. One extreme is $(R_f, 0)$ for $b = 0$, i.e. where the investor wants no risk ($\sigma_p = 0$) and expects R_f from investing entirely in the risk-free asset. The other extreme is (R_m, σ_m) for $b = 1$, i.e. where the investor places all his or her funds in the risky asset and expects return R_m and accepts a standard deviation (risk) of σ_m. The equilibrium solution for the portfolio (here R^*, σ^*) is somewhere in between these two extremes, with a higher return ($R^* - R_f$) than the risk-free R_f traded off against some extra risk (σ^*).

We have already indicated that the slope of the budget line indicates the 'price' of risk. Following our earlier work on indifference curves we can say that the optimal portfolio choice between the risk-free and the risky asset involves the **marginal rate of substitution between risk and return** ($MRS_{\sigma,R}$) being equal to the price of risk.

$$MRS_{\sigma,R} = -\frac{\Delta U/\Delta \sigma}{\Delta U/\Delta R} = \frac{R_m - R_f}{\sigma_m} \text{ in equilibrium}$$

Fig. 3.9 **Equilibrium solution in the trade-off between risk and return.**

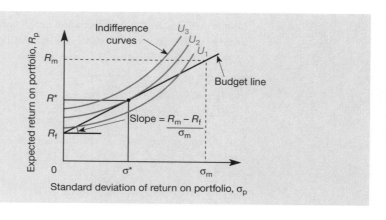

Different degrees of risk aversion between investors

So far we have assumed a single investor with the degree of risk aversion indicated by the curvature of each indifference curve (see p. 109). Suppose now that we have two investors, one more risk averse than the other. Following our earlier analysis we would expect a steeper curvature of the indifference curve (a greater degree of convexity to the origin) for the more risk-averse investor, here investor A. If both investors face the same 'price of risk' given by the slope of the budget line shown in Fig. 3.10, then the more risk-averse investor A will invest a *smaller* proportion of the overall portfolio in the risky asset. We can see that this investor's indifference curve U_A is tangent to the budget line at a point of low risk (σ_A), so he or she will invest almost all the portfolio in the risk-free asset and earn an expected return R_A, just above the risk-free return R_f (for $b = 0$). In contrast the less risk-averse investor B will invest the *greater* proportion of his or her portfolio (remember R_m, σ_m is for $b = 1$) in the risky asset, yielding an expected portfolio return of R_B with risk σ_B. In this case B has a higher expected return than A but incurs greater risk on a portfolio that is weighted towards the more risky assets.

A further note on characteristics of the portfolio

Where the portfolio consists of a risky and a risk-free asset, and where a fraction (b) is invested in the risky asset, the *actual return on the portfolio* (r_p) can be expressed in terms of the actual return on the risky asset (r_m) and the risk-free asset (r_f) as

$$r_p = br_m + (1-b)\, r_f$$

i.e. $r_p = br_m + (1-b)\, R_f$

$$\left[\begin{array}{l} \text{Since } \textit{actual} \text{ return } (r_f) \\ \text{equals } \textit{expected} \text{ return} \\ (R_f) \text{ for a risk-free asset} \end{array} \right]$$

The variance of the portfolio return, σ^2_p, is the average (expected value) of the squared deviations between *actual* (r_p) and *expected* (R_p) portfolio returns.

i.e. $\sigma^2_p = E\,[br_m + (1-b)\, R_f - R_p]^2$

Substituting the earlier equation (1) (p.113) for R_p into the above gives

$$\begin{aligned} \sigma^2_p &= E\,[br_m + (1-b)\, R_f - bR_m - (1-b)\, R_f]^2 \\ \sigma^2_p &= E\,[b\,(r_m - R_m)]^2 \\ \sigma^2_p &= b^2\, \sigma^2_m \\ \text{and } \sigma_p &= b\sigma_m \end{aligned}$$

▨ Discounting and risk

We briefly reviewed the idea of *discounting* in the introduction to this chapter (p. 101). Clearly more risk-averse investors will require a greater **risk premium,** i.e. a higher reward to compensate them for exposure to any given level of risk. Thus investors along U_A in Fig. 3.10 (p. 116) will require a greater risk premium than investors along U_B. We can adjust the discounting process in project appraisal to take account of risk.

Fig. 3.10 **Different portfolio choices between a more risk-averse (U_A) and less risk-averse (U_B) investor. The combination of return/risk (R_f, 0) corresponds to $b = 0$, i.e. none of portfolio invested in risky asset; the combination of return/risk (R_m, σ_m) corresponds to $b = 1$, i.e. all portfolio invested in risky asset.**

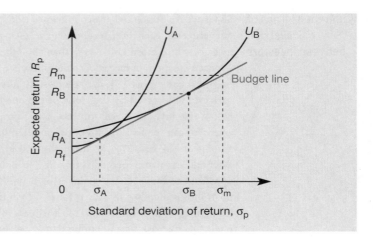

Of course the very process of discounting already makes some allowance for the fact that the further into the future we estimate a return, the more 'risky' that estimate is likely to be. This follows from the *compound* nature of the discounting process. As can be seen from Table 3.2, for any given interest rate (used as a proxy for the discount rate) the **discount factor** by which we multiply the future sum to reduce it to a present-value equivalent falls sharply as the number of years into the future increases. Thus at a 10% interest rate an estimated sum in five years' time will be worth (today) 62.09% of its nominal value; but an estimated sum in 20 years' time will today be worth only 14.86% of its nominal value at that time. Of course the impact of compounding at a still higher interest (discount) rate becomes still more severe in terms of reducing the discount factor over time. Thus at a 20% interest rate an estimated sum in five years' time will be worth (today) only 40.19% of its nominal value, and in twenty years' time will today be worth only 2.61% of its nominal value at that time.

Table 3.2 **Discount factors.**

Years	Interest rate as percentage					
	5	10	15	20	25	30
1	0.9524	0.9091	0.8696	0.8333	0.8000	0.7692
5	0.7835	0.6209	0.4972	0.4019	0.3277	0.2693
10	0.6139	0.3855	0.2472	0.1615	0.1074	0.0725
15	0.4810	0.2394	0.1229	0.0649	0.0352	0.0195
20	0.3769	0.1486	0.0611	0.0261	0.0115	0.0053
25	0.2953	0.0923	0.0304	0.0105	0.0038	0.0014
30	0.2314	0.0573	0.0151	0.0042	0.0012	0.0004

Nevertheless there is further scope for introducing a more finely tuned 'risk element' into the discounting process. We can adjust the discounting equation (p. 102) to make use of a **risk-adjusted discount rate,** as follows:

$$\text{NPV} = \sum_{t=1}^{n} \frac{R_t}{(1 + K)^t} - C_0$$

where K is the risk-adjusted discount rate, and all other variables are as defined on p. 102.

We can make use of Fig. 3.11 to illustrate our argument. Here we have three risk-return trade-off functions, U_1, U_2 and U_3, with a given intercept (10%) on the vertical axis. We could regard this analysis as corresponding to three different firms, with differing degrees of risk aversion: firm 3 is the most risk averse as it requires the highest rate of return of all three firms to compensate it for a given level of risk (σ_1). Indeed we could regard 10% as the risk-free discount rate (i in terms of the original discounting formula, p. 102) for each firm. At perceived risk σ_1 the *discount risk premium* for Firm 1 is shown as 5% (point A), for Firm 2 as 10% (point B), and for Firm 3 as 20% (point C).

The **risk-adjusted discount factor** (K) for the respective firms would, in this case, be the risk-free discount rate (i) + the discount risk premium. It follows that $K_1 = 15\%$; $K_2 = 20\%$; $K_3 = 30\%$

Suppose, now, that all three firms are evaluating an unusual investment project, expected to yield returns at five-yearly intervals, namely £80,000 in each of years 5, 10 and 15. The initial cost is £40,000.

The impact of these risk adjustments in terms of NPV calculations is worked through below (making use of Table 3.2. on p. 116).

Firm 1

$$\text{NPV}_1 = \sum_{t=1}^{3} \frac{R_t}{(1.15)^t} - C_0$$

$$= \sum_{t=1}^{3} \frac{80,000}{(1.15)^t} - 40,000$$

$$= [80,000 \, (0.4972) + 80,000 \, (0.2472) + 80,000 \, (0.1229)] - 40,000$$

i.e. $\text{NPV}_1 = £29,384$ (Firm 1)

Fig. 3.11 Risk-return trade-off functions and discounting for risk.

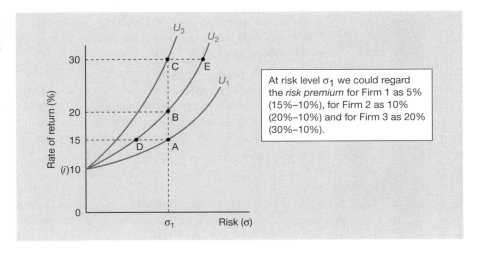

At risk level σ_1 we could regard the *risk premium* for Firm 1 as 5% (15%–10%), for Firm 2 as 10% (20%–10%) and for Firm 3 as 20% (30%–10%).

Firm 2

$$NPV_2 = \sum_{t=1}^{3} \frac{R_t}{(1.20)^t} - C_0$$

$$= \sum_{t=1}^{3} \frac{80,000}{(1.20)^t} - 40,000$$

$$= [80,000\ (0.4019) + 80,000\ (0.1615) + 80,000\ (0.0649)] - 40,000$$

i.e. $NPV_2 = £10,264$ (Firm 2)

Firm 3

$$NPV_3 = \sum_{t=1}^{3} \frac{R_t}{(1.30)t} - C_0$$

$$= \sum_{t=1}^{3} \frac{80,000}{(1.30)^t} - 40,000$$

$$= [80,000\ (0.2693) + 80,000\ (0.0725) + 80,000\ (0.0195)] - 40,000$$

i.e. $NPV_3 = -£11,096$ (Firm 3)

Clearly the more risk-averse firm 3 is much less likely to undertake the given project than the less risk-averse firm 1.

The analysis can easily be adapted to the *same* firm assessing three different investment projects. For example, in terms of Fig. 3.11, Firm 2 may be assessing three projects that it respectively locates at risk/return points D (project 1), B (project 2), and E (project 3) along U_2. Clearly project 3 is regarded as most risky, requiring a discount risk premium of 20%, compared with a discount risk premium of 10% for project 2 and 5% for project 1. The more risky projects may be those involving activities further removed from the 'core' business of Firm 2.

Again, by applying risk-adjusted discount rates to the expected returns from the respective projects, we would have

$$K_3 > K_2 > K_1;\ 30\% > 20\% > 15\%$$

As above, any *given outcome* (say £50,000 in each of three years, with initial cost £40,000) would then be more heavily discounted for the riskier projects and be less likely to be undertaken.

Certainty-equivalent approach   The approach using a risk-adjusted discount rate involves a modification of the discount rate (K) in the denominator of the expression (p. 117). The **certainty-equivalent approach,** in contrast, leaves the denominator unchanged at the risk-free level, i, but modifies the *numerator* of the following expression to account for risk:

$$NPV = \sum_{t=1}^{n} \frac{\alpha R_t}{(1 + i)^t} - C_0$$

where R_t is the expected (risky) return in year t, i is the risk-free discount rate, and α is the *certainty-equivalent coefficient*. The coefficient α will vary from 0 to 1, depending on the perception of the investor. A value of 0 for α implies that the investor perceives the expected future returns as so unlikely to be realized in practice that they can effectively be regarded as zero. A value of 1 for α at the other extreme, implies that the investor views the project as essentially risk-free. The higher the value of α, the smaller the risk perceived by the investor.

Put another way, the certainty equivalent coefficient, α, can be expressed as a quotient, namely that sum (R^*_t) that being received with certainty the investor regards as yielding the same utility as the risky sum (R_t), divided by that risky sum.

$$\alpha = \frac{\text{Equivalent certain sum}}{\text{Expected risky sum}} = \frac{R^*_t}{R_t}$$

For example, if the investor or manager regarded the sum of £40,000 with certainty, as equivalent in terms of utility to the expected (risky) return of £50,000, then

$$\alpha = \frac{£40,000}{£50,000} = 0.8$$

Both risk-adjusted and certainty-equivalent approaches involve a *subjective* assessment of risk by investors. However, the certainty-equivalent approach is favoured by some as more explicitly incorporating investor attitudes towards risk into the decision-making process (see p. 134).

Sequential decision making

In many situations the probability of some future outcome depends in part on the outcome *preceding* it. In corporate activity, for example, the feasibility of a new product line in year 3 may depend on whether or not resources were committed to research and development in year 1! Here we are looking at chance and risk in terms of the *sequence of events* that precede a particular possible outcome and thereby affect the likelihood of that outcome. It is in such situations that the use of **decision trees** can be particularly appropriate.

The decision tree

A decision tree is a diagram that can usefully represent a series of choices and their possible outcomes. Where the outcome is *pure chance,* then the overall probability of 1 will be divided *equally* between all the possible outcomes (e.g. 0.5 for each of two pure chance outcomes). Where the outcome is *uncertain* but where some outcomes are more likely than others, then the decision maker may assign *probabilities* to each possible outcome. The sum of these probabilities over all possible outcomes must, of course, be equal to 1.

The sequence of decisions and outcomes is represented graphically as the branches of the 'tree'. At every point (node) at which a decision must be made or an outcome must occur, the tree branches out further until all the possible outcomes have been displayed. **Boxes** (decision nodes) are usually used to indicate situations where the decision maker consciously selects a particular course of action (strategy), and where the outcome of that action is 'certain'. Branches coming out of these boxes simply indicate the alternative decisions or strategies that might be taken, each of which has a probability of 1 once selected. **Circles** (chance nodes) are usually used to indicate situations reflecting a 'state of nature', i.e. situations whose outcomes are *not* entirely under the conscious control of the decision maker. Branches coming out of such circles show the various possibilities that might occur, together with estimates of their probability of occurrence.

The valuations placed at the end of particular branches emanating from chance nodes are sometimes called **pay-offs.** They are the values that management ascribes to that event or outcome should it actually occur.

In Fig. 3.12, at the *decision node* box, the decision maker must decide between a strategy of increasing price or keeping price unchanged. If this latter strategy is pursued, only one possible profit outcome is possible, which is evaluated at £200,000. If the former strategy (increasing price) is pursued, then the decision maker intends to support the policy change by an active advertising campaign. However, the outcome of such an advertising campaign is not entirely under the control of the decision maker. He estimates that there is a 60% (0.60) chance of the campaign being a success and a 40% (0.40) chance of its being a failure. These two branches are therefore shown as emanating from a *chance node,* indicated by a circle. The firm estimates profits of £800,000 should the advertising campaign (allied to a price increase) be successful, but losses of £600,000 should it fail.

Which branch the firm should choose in order to maximise the expected profit can easily be determined. The process of solving this problem is called **backward induction.** This requires us to begin at the right-hand side of the decision tree, where the profit figures are located. The first step is to calculate the *expected profit* when the firm is situated at the chance node immediately to the left of these pay-off figures.

Because there is a 0.60 probability that the branch culminating in a profit of £800,000 will occur, and a 0.40 probability that the branch culminating in a loss of £600,000 will occur, the expected profit when situated at this chance node is:

0.60 (£800,000) + 0.40 (−£600,000) = £240,000

This number is written above the chance node in question to show that this is the expected profit when located at that node.

Moving further to the left along the decision tree, it is clear that the firm has a choice of two branches, one of which leads to an expected profit of £240,000, the other of which leads to an expected profit of £200,000. If the firm wants to maximise expected profit, it should choose the former branch. In other words, it should increase its price and accompany this with an advertising campaign.

Fig. 3.12 **Decision tree.**

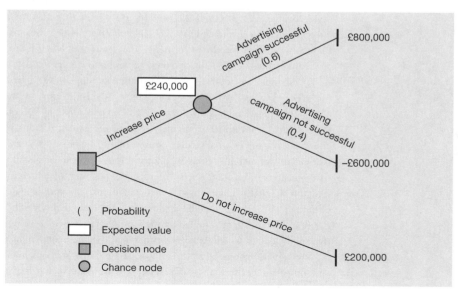

( ) Probability

▢ Expected value

■ Decision node

◯ Chance node

Application of
a decision tree

Suppose that to make a new product a firm must decide whether to buy a larger, more expensive, and more productive machine or a smaller, less expensive, and less productive machine. If the demand for the new product turns out to be at the high end of the range that has been forecast, the purchase of the larger machine may turn out to be profitable; the smaller machine does not possess sufficient capacity to produce large quantities efficiently, and its purchase would require an additional machine to be bought to satisfy such high demand. On the other hand, should the optimistic forecast turn out to be wrong, then the larger machine, if it had been bought, would not be used to capacity. The smaller machine, in this case, would be able to produce the quantities needed efficiently and profitably.

To simplify the analysis we assume that the life of both the project and the machines is two years. In addition all cash flows occurring in the future (i.e. years 1 and 2) have been converted to present values. Table 3.3 shows all the probabilities and forecasts, and Fig. 3.13 illustrates the decision tree with the resulting calculations.

Table 3.3 **Decision tree probabilities and estimated values (pay-offs).**

	Demand forecasts (probabilities)		Cash flow	Costs
Year 1	High 0.50	Low 0.50		
Year 2:				
if Year 1 demand is high	High 0.75	Low 0.25		
if Year 1 demand is low	High 0.25	Low 0.75		
If large machine bought				
Year 1				
if demand is high			150	
if demand is low			−50	
Year 2				
• **if year 1 demand is high**				
and year 2 demand is high			500	
and year 2 demand is low			100	
• **if year 1 demand is low**				
and year 2 demand is high			300	
and year 2 demand is low			−150	
If small machine bought				
Year 1				
if demand is high			100	
if demand is low			30	
Year 2				
• **if year 1 demand is high & 2nd machine bought**				
and year 2 demand is high			400	
and year 2 demand is low			80	
• **if year 1 demand is high & 2nd machine not bought**				
and year 2 demand is high			250	
and year 2 demand is low			120	
• **if year 1 demand is low**				
and year 2 demand is high			150	
and year 2 demand is low			0	
Cost of large machine				**250**
Cost of small machine				**150**

Fig. 3.13 **Decision tree and backward induction.**

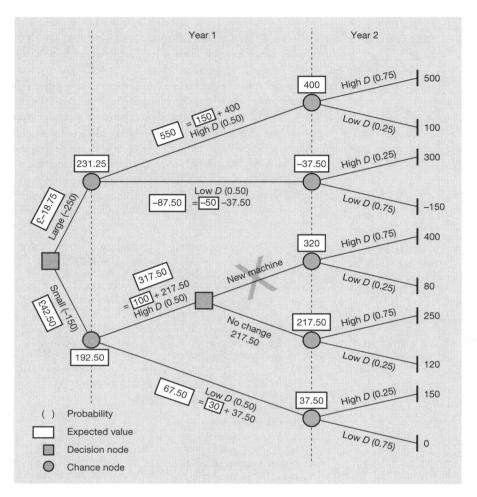

The first step is to set up all the branches of the decision tree. As we move from left to right in Fig. 3.13, we are faced with decision points (e.g. acquire the large machine or small machine) and with outcomes involving chance. For example, the probabilities are fifty-fifty that the demand will be high or low in year 1, and there are certain 'conditional' probabilities as regards demand outcomes in year 2. On the diagram decision nodes are designated with squares and chance nodes with circles. Once the decision tree has been completed, the procedure is to move back from right to left, calculate the value of each branch and, where appropriate, combine or eliminate branches.

Large machine initially purchased We start the analysis in the upper right-hand segment of Fig. 3.13 where it is supposed that the large machine is acquired.

● If year 1 demand is **high**, then there is a 75% probability that the second-year cash flow will be £500 and a 25% probability that it will be £100. Thus the expected value of the year 2 cash flow is

$$(0.75 \times 500) + (0.25 \times l00) = £400$$

> If the first-year demand is high, the cash flow in year 1 will be £150, so the value of the cash flows of years 1 and 2 *combined* will be £550 (£150 + £400).

- If year 1 demand is **low,** then the expected value of the year 2 cash flow is

$$(0.25 \times 300) + (0.75 \times -150) = £-37.50$$

> If the first-year demand is low, the cash flow in year 1 will be –£50, so the value of the cash flows of years 1 and 2 *combined* will be –£87.50 (–£50 + –£37.50)

> Since the probabilities are fifty-fifty that first-year demand will be high/low, the expected value of cash flows if the large machine is purchased is
>
> $(0.5 \times 550) + (0.5 \times -87.50) = £231.25$

From this we must deduct the cost of the large machine (£250), so the net present value of this investment is –£18.75 (–£250+£231.25).

Small machine initially purchased Now we look at the bottom right-hand segment of Fig. 3.13, where it is supposed that the small machine is acquired. A decision must then be made at the end of year 1 whether or not to also buy a second machine.

- If year 1 demand is **high** and the second machine *is* acquired, then the expected value of the year 2 cash flow is

$$(0.75 \times 400) + (0.25 \times 80) = £320$$

- If the year 1 demand is **high** and the second machine is *not* acquired, then the expected value of the year 2 cash flow is

$$(0.75 \times 250) + (0.25 \times 120) = £217.50$$

The cost of a small machine is £150. If the new (second) small machine is bought, the value of the cash flow over two years is £170 (£320 – £150). This is less than the cash flow of £217.50 if the new machine is *not* bought. Therefore the decision at this point would be not to expand productive capacity. A cross is put over the 'new machine' branch in the tree to show that this branch will be ignored as the evaluation is continued.

> If the first-year demand is high, the cash flow in year 1 will be £100, so the value of the cash flows of years 1 and 2 *combined* will be £317.50 (£100 + £217.50).

- If year 1 demand is **low,** then the expected value of the year 2 cash flow is

$$(0.25 \times 150) + (0.75 \times 0) = £37.50.$$

> If the first-year demand is low, the cash flow in year 1 will be £30, so the value of the cash flows of years 1 and 2 combined will be £67.50 (£30 + £37.50).

> Since the probabilities are fifty-fifty that first-year demand will be high/low, the expected value of cash flows if the *small machine* is purchased is
>
> (0.5 × 317.50) + (0.5 × 67.50) = £192.50

From this we must deduct the cost of the first small machine (£150), so the net present value of this investment is £42.50 (£192.50 − £150).

The final step in our analysis is to compare the net present values of the two alternatives. The expected NPV if the large machine is acquired is −£18.75. If the smaller machine is acquired, the expected NPV is £42.50. Thus the smaller machine is the better choice. (In fact, the larger machine would have been unacceptable in any case, as its NPV is negative.)

Expected value, risk and dispersion

The 'expected value' calculations at chance nodes already take into account certain aspects of 'risk', as expressed in the different probabilities assigned to the respective outcomes/pay-offs. However, a further aspect of risk involves the **dispersion** of the pay-offs of the various branches stemming from each chance node, around the arithmetic mean of those pay-offs.

In terms of measuring dispersion in this context, the *standard deviation* is often used. It can be defined here as the square root of the weighted average of the squared deviations of all possible outcomes (pay-offs) from the arithmetic mean of those outcomes:

$$\text{Standard deviation} = \sigma = \sqrt{\sum_{i=1}^{n} p_i \cdot (X_i - \bar{X})^2}$$

where X_i = pay-off for outcome i

p_i = probability of outcome i

$\bar{X}$ = arithmetic mean of the n outcomes

n = number of outcomes

In Table 3.4 we calculate the standard deviation at a chance node involving the listed valuations/pay-offs for five possible outcomes (X_i) with assigned probabilities (p_i) and arithmetic mean $\bar{X}$ = £500.

Having calculated the standard deviation of the possible outcomes/pay-offs at the chance node, this can then be used as a further check on 'risk'. Clearly, if the expected values are the same at two or more chance nodes, then the branch with the lowest (absolute) standard deviation arguably involves less risk. Where, however, the expected values *differ* at two or more chance nodes, then we need a measure of **relative** dispersion. In Table 3.5, pathway A has the higher absolute dispersion at the chance node as measured by the standard deviation, but the lower relative dispersion as measured by the coefficient of variation (see pp. 103–4), using expected value (EV) in the denominator.

Table 3.4 **Finding the standard deviation at a chance node.**

X_i	$(X_i - \bar{X})$	$(X_i - \bar{X})^2$	P_i	$P_i(X_i - \bar{X})^2$
300	−200	40,000	0.1	4,000
400	−100	10,000	0.2	2,000
500	0	0	0.4	0
600	100	10,000	0.2	2,000
700	200	40,000	0.1	4,000
				12,000

$$sd = \sqrt{12,000} = 109.54$$

Table 3.5 **Finding the relative dispersion at a chance node.**

Chance node	Expected value	Standard deviation
Pathway A	200	60
Pathway B	100	40

$$CV_A = \frac{\sigma_A}{EV_A} \times 100 = \frac{60}{200} \times 100 = 30\% \ (0.30)$$

$$CV_B = \frac{\sigma_B}{EV_B} \times 100 = \frac{40}{100} \times 100 = 40\% \ (0.40)$$

The *relative* risk of the pathways at a given chance node is arguably greater for pathway B than for pathway A, further reinforcing the case based on the higher expected value for selecting pathway A at a decision node.

Game-theoretic approaches

As we shall see in Chapter 9, risk or uncertainty can be modelled in terms of a **game** in which each strategy by one player, and counter-strategy by another player, has an expected *pay-off*. Probabilities can be assigned to the likelihood of each player adopting a particular strategy or counter-strategy, and *expected values* of particular courses of action can be derived. This game-theoretic approach is considered in some detail in Chapter 9, where large (oligopolistic) firms recognise interdependence between decisions they themselves take and those taken by competitors.

The strategies (or rules) by which participants play such games can vary. As we shall see (pp. 368–9), the firm may adopt a rather 'conservative' strategy, selecting the best of the 'worst possible outcomes': this is the so-called *maxi-min* strategy. Alternatively the firm may be rather more adventurous, selecting the worst of the 'best possible outcomes': this is the so-called *mini-max* strategy. It may be that other *pure* strategies are adopted, or indeed *mixed* strategies involving elements of various alternative strategies.

This game-theoretic approach is clearly important in resolving many decisions involving risk and uncertainty, but is dealt with in some detail in Chapter 9 rather than here.

Applications and evidence

Much attention has been placed in recent years on attempts to value the *benefits* that individuals place on various risk-reduction measures. These are often set against the *costs* of implementing such measures.

The value of risks to life and health

Labour market surveys

In terms of the labour market, attempts to place a monetary value on risk have often made use of surveys involving questions such as 'What is the *wage premium* workers receive or require for exposing themselves to additional risk?' Of course any such premiums are the result of both labour supply decisions by individuals and labour demand decisions by firms.

In Fig. 3.14 we model labour supply decisions by individuals via an *expected utility curve* (*EU*). This reflects the different combinations of income (wage) and risk yielding a *given level of utility* to the individual. Clearly, there is an assumption of a preference for good health, in that higher income is needed to compensate for greater risk and thereby yield the same utility. As drawn, the expected utility curve is convex to the horizontal axis, suggesting an element of 'risk aversion'. Figure 3.14 also models labour demand decisions via a *wage offer curve* (*WO*). This reflects the different combinations of wage and risk yielding a *given level of profit* to the firm. To maintain the same level of profit, the firm must offer a lower wage rate to offset the additional cost of providing a safer (less risky) work environment. As drawn, the wage offer curve is concave to the horizontal axis, suggesting an increasingly higher cost of successive reductions in risk. Workers will seek to select the available wage–risk combination from the wage-offer curve yielding the maximum expected utility, i.e. point A with job risk q_a and wage w_a.

In empirical attempts to evaluate the risk–money trade-off along *EU*, survey methods are frequently used. The worker's current wage rate (w_a) and assessed job risk (q_a) are, at least in principle, directly observable. Workers are then given information as to a specified *additional* risk to be incorporated into their job description (e.g. handling more toxic chemicals). They are then asked to assess the additional wage rate that they would require to remain on *EU*. In terms of Fig. 3.14, we are seeking to evaluate the additional wage rate ($w_b - w_a$) required to compensate for a specified increase in risk ($q_b - q_a$) associated with a move from A to B along a given expected utility curve (*EU*).

Fig. 3.14 **The employers' wage offer (*WO*) curve and the workers' expected utility (*EU*) curve.**

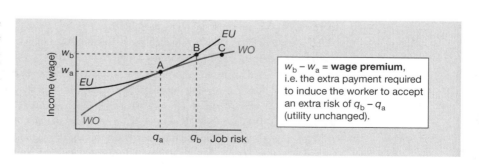

$w_b - w_a$ = **wage premium**, i.e. the extra payment required to induce the worker to accept an extra risk of $q_b - q_a$ (utility unchanged).

Survey evidence of this kind for many workers will clearly yield some kind of scatter diagram relating additional income perceived by workers as being necessary to 'compensate them' (i.e. remain on *EU*) for a specified additional risk. A regression line (or curve) can then be fitted to the scatter diagram to derive an estimate of *EU*.

Of course some of the reasons for particular workers requiring more (or less) compensation than others for a given increase in risk may be due to their possessing differing *individual characteristics*. For example, older workers may be expected to place lower values on a given increase in job risk as they will be exposed to that risk for a shorter working life and, in any case, already face increased morbidity risks from other sources via the ageing process itself. Similarly smokers and those already working in hazardous jobs have been found to place lower values on additional health risks. A *multiple-regression analysis* can (with appropriate data sets) be used to relate the compensating wage increase to differences in these personal characteristics as well as to differences in job risk.

Valuations using labour market surveys

Having identified the monetary value placed by workers on additional exposure to risk, this information can then be used to estimate values of life or values of injury.

The likely impacts of exposure to a particular hazard in terms of death or injury can be calculated in an actuarial sense, based on historical data (see Table 3.6). These probabilities can then be used, together with monetary estimates of the wage premium, to calculate the implicit values of life or injury.

Table 3.6 Hazards and actuarial risks.

Source of risk	Annual fatality risk
Cigarette smoking (per smoker)	1/150
Cancer	1/300
Motor vehicle accident	1/5,000
Work accident (per worker)	1/10,000
Home accident	1/11,000
Poisoning	1/37,000
Fire	1/50,000
Aviation accident (passenger deaths/total population)	1/250,000

Source: Adapted from Viscusi (1993); the smoking risk estimates are averaged over the entire smoking population.

Suppose, for example, that the wage premium for a worker is estimated at £1 for inducing him/her to accept the additional risk of, say, handling a toxic chemical (utility unchanged). Put another way, this *willingness-to-accept* value of £1 to *compensate* for the additional risk of handling the chemical can be equivalently expressed as a *willingness-to-pay* value of £1 for *avoiding* that risk. At least for small risk changes, willingness-to-accept (i.e. the wage premium) and willingness-to-pay values should be equal.

Having estimated that the worker is willing to pay £1 for avoiding the risk of handling the toxic chemical, suppose the **actuarial** risk of death from handling that chemical is 1/1,000,000. It follows that since the worker is willing to pay £1 to reduce (by avoidance) the risk of death by 1/1,000,000, the *implicit value of life* is revealed as £1 million for that worker.

Table 3.7(a) presents some *implicit value-of-life* estimates for various fatal types of injury after exposure to specified hazards. Table 3.7(b) presents some *implicit value-of-injury* estimates for particular types of non-fatal injury after exposure to specified hazards.

Table 3.7(a) **Implicit values of life.**

Author (year)	Sample	Fatal risk variable	Mean risk	Implicit value of life ($ million)
Moore and Viscusi (1989)	Panel study of income dynamics, 1982	National Traumatic Occupational Fatality Survey	0.0001	7.8
Kniesner and Leeth (1991)	Two-digit mfg. data, Japan, 1986	Industrial accident data, Japan	0.00003	7.6
	Two-digit mfg. data, Australia, by state, 1984–85	Industrial accident data, Australia	0.0001	3.3
Douglas, Gegax, Gerking and Schulze (1991)	Authors' mail survey, 1984	Worker's assessed fatality risk at work	0.0009	1.6

Note: All values are in December 1990 dollars   mfg = manufacturing

Clearly the implicit value-of-life estimates in Table 3.7(a) derived from various countries and approaches show some variation. Viscusi (1993) notes that for the USA, over a much wider range of estimates than those shown in the table, the majority fall in the $3 million to $7 million range. Of course the value of life reflects the wage–risk trade-off relevant to the preferences of workers in a particular sample. Where the sample varies in terms of personal characteristics, such as age, smoking propensity, degree of risk already experienced in current job, and indeed mean income, then we should expect some variability in the value-of-life estimates. Indeed when applying value-of-life analyses to samples of air travellers with higher mean incomes than their national counterparts, the value-of-life estimates in all countries tended to rise by upwards of 50%. Clearly such variability warns us against too heavy a reliance on value-of-life estimates.

Table 3.7(b) **Implicit values of injury.**

Author (year)	Sample	Non-fatal risk variable	Mean injury risk	Implicit value of injury
Viscusi and Moore (1987)	Quality of employment survey, 1977	BLS lost workday injury rate, BLS total injury rate	0.038, 0.097	$55,100 lost workday accident; $21,800 for non-pecuniary loss, lost workday accident; $35,400 per accident
Biddle and Zarkin (1988)	Quality of employment survey, 1977	BLS non-fatal lost workday injury incident rate, 1977	0.037	$131,495 (willing to accept), $121,550 (willing to pay)
Garen (1988)	Panel study of income dynamics, 1981–1982	BLS non-fatal injury rate, 1980–81	NA	$21,021
Hersch and Viscusi (1990)	Authors' survey in Eugene, OR, 1987	Workers' assessed injury rate using BLS lost work day incidence rate scale	0.059	$56,537 (full sample); $30,781 (smokers); $92,245 (seatbelt users)
Viscusi and Evans (1990)	Viscusi and O'Connor chemical worker survey, 1982	Utility function estimates using assessed injury and illness rate	0.10	$18,547 (marginal risk change); $28,880 (certain injury)
Kniesner and Leeth (1991)	Current population survey, 1978	BLS lost workday accident rate	0.055	$47,281
French and Kendall (1992)	Current population survey, 1980, railroad industry only	Federal Railroad Administration injury data	0.048	$38,159

Note: All values are in December 1990 dollars BLS = Bureau of Labour Statistics
Source: Adapted from Viscusi (1993)

In Table 3.7(b) the severity of the injuries considered varies within and between studies. Most of the implicit value-of-injury estimates based on aggregate data covering injuries regardless of severity are around the $25,000 to $50,000 range. For more serious injuries leading to the loss of at least one working day, the implicit value-of-injury estimates tend to be higher. Again, some studies highlight the influence of personal characteristics on the wage premium and therefore the implicit value estimates: smokers, as expected, have lower implicit value-of-injury estimates in Viscusi (1993), and seatbelt users (more risk averse) having, as expected, higher estimates.

Non-labour market surveys

So far we have been looking at labour-market survey methods for assessing points such as A and B in Fig. 3.14. The approach has involved contingent valuation, i.e. asking respondents how much they would require as a wage premium contingent on their facing additional risk in the labour market. The questions could be open-ended, or more guided or step by step, with particular values presented to respondents until they indicate indifference.

An alternative survey technique involves presenting subjects with *pairwise comparisons*. In the job risk case, for example, Job 1 might consist of a wage–risk combination of (w_1, q_1), and Job 2 might consist of a wage–risk package of (w_2, q_2). Subjects could indicate their preference between these two jobs, and the packages could be manipulated until indifference is achieved.

■ Costs against benefits

Having established estimates for the *benefits* of avoiding exposure to various hazards causing injury or death, it is clearly important to compare these with the *costs* of reducing such exposure. Policy prescription can then give highest priority to reducing or removing those hazards offering the greatest net benefits in the sense of benefits minus costs.

Information on costs, such as that presented in Table 3.8, can therefore play an important role in policy making.

The right-hand column is found by dividing the cost of reducing exposure to the hazard by a specified extent by the number of lives saved as a result.

Disaster aversion

The degree of aversion we might have to a possible outcome can be built into a model by adjusting the probabilities. For example, suppose we have three possible outcomes for a project: −10 with a 20% chance, +10 with a 50% chance and +40 with a 30% chance.

$$\text{Expected monetary value } (EMV) = (0.2 \times -10) + (0.5 \times 10) + (0.3 \times 40)$$
$$= -2 + 5 + 12$$
$$= +15$$

Table 3.8 **Risks of death in the USA: selected environmental hazards and their cost reduction.**

	Deaths per 1 million people exposed	Cost to avoid 1 death ($ million)
Trihalomethane in drinking water	420	0.2
Radionuclides in uranium mines	6,300	3.4
Benzene fugitive emissions	1,470	3.4
Benzene occupational exposure	39,600	8.9
Asbestos occupational exposure	3,015	8.3
Arsenic/copper exposure	63,000	23.0
Acrylonitrile occupational exposure	42,300	51.5
Coke ovens occupational exposure	7,200	63.5
Hazardous waste land disposal	2	4,190.2
Municipal solid waste landfill standard	1	19,107.0
Hazardous waste: wood preservatives	<1	5,700,000

Source: Adapted from Council on Environmental Quality (1990)

However, if we are three times as averse to a loss as we are to a gain, then we can weight the probabilities accordingly. It might be more appropriate here to speak of *expected utility:*

$$\text{Expected utility} \atop (EU) = (0.2 \times [-10 \times 3]) + (0.5 \times 10) + (0.3 \times 40)$$
$$= -6 + 5 + 12$$
$$= 11$$

We can see in Table 3.9 how such value judgements can be built into calculations to derive how much we are willing to pay to avoid a potential disaster.

Suppose, for argument's sake, we estimate the implicit value of life (v) as £4 million. In other words, society is willing to pay up to £4 million to save a single life, whether in terms of the prevention of illness, road accidents, or whatever. Assume that the disaster in question has a one in a million chance of happening, so the frequency (f) of the event is $1/1,000,000$. Further assume that the disaster might involve any one of three scenarios: 100 deaths, 500 deaths or 1,000 deaths, where N is the number of deaths.

Turner *et al.* (1994) point out that regulatory agencies use a variety of rules in viewing such disasters: for example the *square rule,* whereby in multiple deaths involving, say, 100 persons we should regard them as being equivalent to 100×100 deaths in individual accidents. Another possibility is the *300 rule,* whereby in a multiple death situation we weight each death as being equivalent to 300 deaths in individual accidents, and so on.

The selection of the rule is crucial to assessing the amount that a government, agency or firm will be willing to pay for *disaster aversion* measures. As can be seen from Table 3.9, only £4,000 would be spent to cover a one in a million chance of 1,000 people dying in a single accident if no aversion factor is present, but £4 million if the square rule is used for the aversion factor and £1.2 million if the 300 rule is used.

Table 3.9 **The value of a disaster.**

$f = 1/1,000,000$		
$N = 100$	$N = 500$	$N = 1,000$
$fN = 0.0001$	$fN = 0.0005$	$fN = 0.001$
$fN^2 = 0.01$	$fN^2 = 0.25$	$fN^2 = 1.0$
$300fN = 0.03$	$300fN = 0.15$	$300fN = 0.3$
$vfN = £400$	$vfN = £2,000$	$vfN = £4,000$
$vfN^2 = £40,000$	$vfN^2 = £1,000,000$	$vfN^2 = £4,000,000$
$v300fN = £120,000$	$v300fN = £600,000$	$v300fN = £1,200,000$

Source: Turner *et al.* (1994)

Legal contingency fees and risk aversion

Here we draw on many of the characteristics of our analysis of risk in this chapter to examine the case for lawyers charging their clients **contingency fees.** Following Rickman (1994), we shall seek to demonstrate that contingency fees, whereby lawyers are paid in terms of their 'success' in dealing with a case, are more likely to exist in legal markets where there is a **principal–agent** relationship in which principals find it difficult to properly assess the actions of their agents and in which a conflict of interest might occur. It can also be shown that *full insurance,* whereby the agent pays the principal a fee and takes on the entire risk of litigation (and 100% of any winnings), is more likely to occur where clients are risk averse and lawyers are risk neutral.

It will be useful at the outset to describe the market in which this analysis is set. It involves **personal injury litigation,** i.e. cases involving accidents at work, at home, on the road, etc. Such a market is one in which the payment of contingency fees to lawyers is feasible since most cases are resolved by the payment of financial compensation.

Another characteristic of the personal injury litigation market involves the principal–agent relationship (see also Chapter 5, p. 215), the client being in this market the **principal** and the lawyer, acting on the client's behalf, the **agent.** This relationship is particularly important in situations where the agent has special information about behaviour in the market that is unavailable to the principal. Certainly the majority of individuals or small companies involved in personal injury litigation are likely to have little experience of the legal process and to depend to a large extent on the expertise and advice of lawyers. It may therefore often be true for this market that principals find it difficult to observe and monitor the actions of agents, which could be problematical should the interests of principals and agents diverge. In this case the agents may take decisions that benefit themselves rather than the principal.

We can establish a model for this market by assuming that a **contract** is established in which a fee, *F*, is specified by the principal (client). The agent (lawyer) then agrees to act on the client's behalf, inputting *effort*, *e*, to produce an *outcome* (pay-off), *x*. This outcome depends not only on the agent's effort but also on a *random element*, α, reflecting uncertainty surrounding, perhaps, the abilities of the client's own lawyers, the impact made by the opposition's lawyers, and the court's decision should there be a trial. We can then say that the fee, F, paid by the client will be broadly determined by the following function:

$$F = f(x, e, \alpha)$$
where F = Fee
  x = outcome
  e = agent's (lawyer's) efforts on behalf of the principal
  α = uncertain/random element

Rickman suggests two types of fee arrangement:

- *Output-based fees*, where the fee is based on the output achieved by the agent. Thus the principal pays the agent a fee $F = f(x)$, i.e. a fee that depends upon the outcome (x) achieved, and keeps ($x - F$) himself.
- *Input-based fees*, where the fee is based on the agent's effort. These can be of two types: *fee for service*, where the fee is determined by the amount of effort which is input, and *fixed fees*, where the fee is independent of effort, other than some minimum amount such as initially seeing the client.

Examples of each of these exist in the provision of legal services around the world. The output-based fee is the US-style **contingency fee**. This clearly identifies the lawyer's output, x, as the amount of money he or she recovers for the client. The input-based fee for service is represented by the hourly fee used in the UK and elsewhere, where hours on the case are assumed to be a proxy for the effort expended. Finally, the input-based fixed fee is similar to that used for the remuneration of legal aid services (with government subsidy) to poorer clients in some countries.

We now examine circumstances under which the output-based contingency fee is likely to be the optimal market solution. When the output of the case is the most clearly observable feature to the client (principal) in a principal–agent relationship, then the optimal market solution is likely to involve using that output as the basis for the fee paid to the lawyer (agent). Indeed either of the two types of input-based fee will have potential drawbacks where a principal–agent problem exists:

- There may be an element of *moral hazard* (see also Chapter 12, p. 486), especially where the agent has superior information to that available to the principal. Hidden actions and motives by the agent may then be difficult to observe or monitor by the principal.
- There may be an element of *adverse selection* (see also Chapter 12, p. 483), where the principal has difficulty in identifying the true characteristics of the agent he seeks to act on his behalf. Hidden characteristics of agents may make it difficult for principals to assess quality within the market.

Either of these types of market failure make it difficult for largely inexperienced clients/principals to base the fees they offer on the (difficult to identify) *effort* that is input by the lawyers/agents. The agent may have both the ability and incentive to misrepresent him or herself to the principal to obtain a higher reward.

Establishing the contingency percentage

So far we have considered the characteristics of a market in which an output-based contingency fee is more likely to occur. We now turn to the circumstances that might affect the *percentage* contingency fee offered or accepted.

Full insurance occurs where the lawyer (agent) is willing to pay a fee to the client (principal) to cover all the client's perceived risk. In return the lawyer will take 100% of any winnings from the case. We note that such an outcome is more likely in markets where clients are highly risk averse and lawyers exhibit characteristics of risk neutrality. This is, of course, merely one rather extreme outcome of a litigation market, with the contingency percentage varying depending on the particular characteristics of the market. Nevertheless it will be useful initially to consider the full insurance outcome with a 100% contingency percentage charged by the lawyer.

Arguably the personal injury litigation market and other legal markets can be characterised as containing *risk-averse principals* and *risk-neutral agents*. Certainly there is risk to clients (principals) using the market. The opposition to the litigation may be successful via a counter-claim or an effective defence, and there is a substantial cost associated with the litigation process. This uncertain element (α) is reinforced by the fact that most personal injury plaintiffs (clients) seeking redress are 'one shot' players. In other words they use the judicial process for dealing with a particular problem, being unlikely to return to reuse it in the future.

Figure 3.15(a) indicates a client (plaintiff) who is averse to bearing such risks, with the utility function (U^c) related to wealth level (W) being concave from below. We assume that the client is engaged in litigation which will leave him with nothing ($W = 0$) if he loses and an amount W_w if he wins. Assuming a fifty-fifty chance of 'success', his expected outcome is W_E. The straight line 0A gives the utility that the client expects to receive from the gamble represented by litigation. Clearly, to be *certain* of receiving the same level of utility as might result from the 'gamble' of litigation, the client is willing to give up the claim in return for an amount W_1 (which represents the fee, F, mentioned earlier). In terms of our earlier analysis (p. 105), ED is the **risk premium** the client is willing to pay.

Fig. 3.15 Litigation in which full insurance may occur: i.e. lawyers (agents) paying clients (principals) a fee and taking 100% of any 'winnings' from the 'gamble' of litigation.

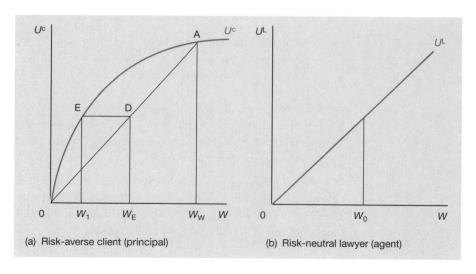

(a) Risk-averse client (principal)

(b) Risk-neutral lawyer (agent)

However, notice here that the client (principal) is receiving the fee to cover the risk premium, and the lawyer (principal) is paying the fee. In other words it is the lawyer (agent) who is buying the claim from the client (principal) and taking any winnings resulting from the gamble.

Figure 3.15(b) indicates a lawyer who is assumed to be risk neutral, as indicated by the utility function (U^L) related to wealth being linear. The suggestion here is that lawyers will be *repeat players* in the market, using the legal system frequently and thereby able to diversify the risks of litigation across a portfolio of cases. They will tend, therefore, to be indifferent between taking the risk of a particular case and not taking that risk. The lawyers' linear utility function U^L suggests that there is no difference between the actual utility received from a certain level of wealth and the expected value of an uncertain gamble, represented by a straight line as in Fig. 3.15(a).

In Fig. 3.15(b) we suppose that the lawyer begins with some initial level of wealth, W_0. He will then be willing to purchase the case from his client at a price W_1 provided that

$$W_0 - W_1 + W_E > W_0$$

In other words, provided that the level of wealth of the lawyer after the purchase is larger than the level before the purchase. Clearly since $W_E > W_1$ in Fig. 3.15(a), this condition is fulfilled. There is therefore scope for a market to exist in which both purchaser and seller of legal cases can benefit. The reason is that the risk-averse seller (client) is equally satisfied with a certain, if smaller, level of wealth, W_1, than an uncertain though larger level of wealth, W_E. The utility loss from the lower pay-off is more than offset by the utility gain from the certainty associated with that lower pay-off. This difference in wealth ($W_E - W_1$) then is available to increase the utility of the risk-neutral lawyer, who, via a diversified portfolio, can expect to receive more wealth via the gamble of taking the case than he must pay to secure the case. In terms of Chapter 11, there is a Pareto efficiency gain via the establishment of a market involving contingency fees: the client is no worse off and the lawyer is better off.

In fact the market we have described so far is an unusual one in which the lawyer sets a contingent percentage on any winnings at 100%. In effect the lawyer is offering the client *full insurance,* by being willing to pay the client a fee yielding at least as much utility as the client would have expected to achieve had he or she gone ahead with the gamble of litigation.

We have, so far, assumed that it is clients (principals) who have difficulties in observing/monitoring lawyers (agents). Rubinfeld and Scotchmer (1993) suggest that this information deficiency is in fact two-way. Clients themselves may be unwilling to reveal all that they know to lawyers for fear they might not take on their case. This information asymmetry can be partially resolved in the market by contingency fees, which enable the client and the lawyers to signal their private information through the size of the contingency fee they are willing to offer or accept. Generally speaking, the more risk either party is willing to bear, the more favourable is likely to be the private information they hold. It therefore follows that good lawyers will generally be willing to offer clients a fee to take on the risk themselves. This is the full insurance offer to clients outlined in Fig. 3.15. Equally, clients with good cases will be willing to accept less than full insurance, i.e. be willing to pay a fee themselves to the lawyer together, perhaps, with some percentage of any winnings. We could then expect a *range* of contingency fee arrangements to be observed in such a market, depending on the distribution of 'good lawyers' and 'good cases' respectively.

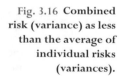
Empirical evidence

The previous analysis has suggested that output-based contingency fees will tend to exist where the principal agent 'problem' is considerable, as when principals are unable to directly observe or monitor the actions of agents. It would therefore follow that contingency-fee arrangements should be used more frequently by clients who are less able to observe or monitor legal processes, such as individuals. In contrast, clients who are better able to observe or monitor legal processes, such as organisations, can be expected to have less need for fee arrangements based on *output*, making use of the 'input-based' payment mechanisms outlined earlier. Kritzer (1990) in his survey data on client–lawyer relationships in the USA found exactly this pattern. In studying tort and contract litigants, he noted that when the plaintiff (client) was an *organization*, hourly fees were used in 81% of the cases. When the plaintiff was an *individual* this figure dropped to 10%, with contingency fees being used by the majority (59%). These results are consistent with the view that organisations are likely to be more experienced users of the legal system than individuals, making them more favourably disposed than individuals to fees based on input as they are better able to observe and monitor their lawyers' work.

Pricing risk: using betas in investment appraisal

Healey (1999) notes that a statistical curiosity of risk theory is that when risky investments are combined, the *average* risk of the combined 'portfolio' of investments is almost invariably reduced. Consider Fig. 3.16, which shows the relationship between expected return and risk for British Gas and Blue Circle Industries (a construction-related company). Because it provides a basic commodity (energy), British Gas generates steady, but unspectacular, revenues. Blue Circle Industries, in contrast, is in a highly cyclical business, in which returns are higher but more variable.

As Fig. 3.16 shows, combining (equal) investments in Blue Circle Industries and British Gas gives a *combined expected return* halfway between the expected returns on the two companies, i.e. at 0A. But the *combined risk* is not halfway between the two variances, i.e. at 0B, but is at the lower value 0C. The fact that the combined variance is

Fig. 3.16 **Combined risk (variance) as less than the average of individual risks (variances).**

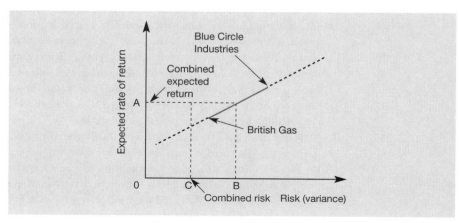

below the average of the two variances reflects the 'benefits' of diversification. Because each company operates in a different market there will be times when an upturn in one industry offsets a downturn in the other industry, and vice versa. This will tend to modify the value of a given measure of dispersion around the combined expected return. Such a 'netting out' of risk lies behind the principle of portfolio diversification.

Figure 3.17(a) illustrates the effect of netting out risk by combining investments. The horizontal dotted line shows the variance of a **market portfolio** in which shares in *all* the FTSE 100 companies are held: i.e. it is a measure of the average riskiness of investing in the top 100 UK companies. The risk associated with holding this market portfolio is σ^2_m, and is an irreducible minimum level of risk from holding shares in the top 100 companies (since no further diversification is possible in this market portfolio). The continuous line sloping downwards from left to right illustrates the way in which the riskiness of any other portfolio falls as shares are randomly added. In practice, even when as few as 20 randomly selected shares are held in a portfolio, the variance (risk) of the portfolio falls close to the market portfolio variance (risk) at σ^2_m.

Of course the FTSE 100 index fluctuates over time, and no amount of diversification can eliminate this risk entirely: σ^2_m in Fig. 3.17(a) is the lowest risk that portfolio diversification alone can ever achieve. The only way in which risk-averse investors can choose a portfolio with a *lower* risk than σ^2_m is to combine the 'market portfolio' with riskless cash (i.e. short-term bank deposits). Figure 3.17(b) shows the trade-offs available, where R_m is the return on the market portfolio and R_f is the return on risk-free assets (here interest rate on short-term bank deposits).

The capital asset pricing model (CAPM)

The CAPM uses the key elements of the analysis we have outlined to 'price' the risk associated with a portfolio investment. The key point in assessing the riskiness of a new share added to the portfolio is not so much the *absolute variance* of its returns but the variance of its returns *relative to the market as a whole*. In the CAPM, this relative performance is measured by the **beta (β) value** of a share (Fig. 3.18). A beta of 1.0 means that the returns on the share move exactly in line with the 'market portfolio' (i.e. the overall index). A beta of 1.5 means that the share moves 1.5% for every 1.0% move in the market

Fig. 3.17

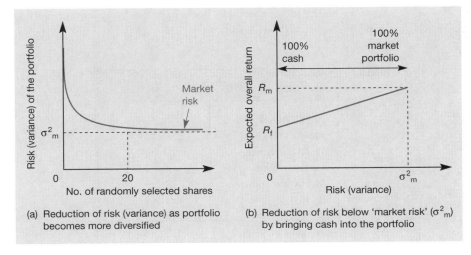

(a) Reduction of risk (variance) as portfolio becomes more diversified

(b) Reduction of risk below 'market risk' (σ^2_m) by bringing cash into the portfolio

Fig. 3.18 **Beta value**
(β) for individual
shares.

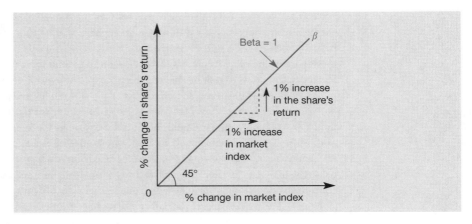

index, outperforming the index in a rising (bull) market and underperforming in a falling (bear) market. Conversely a beta of 0.5 means that the share's return is more stable than that for the market as a whole, with the share moving by only 0.5% for every 1.0% move in the market index: the higher the beta value, the riskier the share and therefore the higher the return required to compensate for this extra risk, and vice versa.

The link between the beta value (β) and the required return (R^*) for a particular company is given by the following expression (see p. 113 and equation (3)):

$$R^* = R_f + \beta (R_m - R_f)$$

For a company that moves in line with the market return we have seen that $\beta = 1$, so that $R^* = R_m$. Beta values can, however, be measured empirically by simply studying past movements of returns and comparing these with movements in the market return. The London Business School's Institute of Finance and Accounting offers a risk measurement service that provides beta values for all the major publicly listed companies. Table 3.10 provides recent estimates for a selection of well-known companies. It shows that British Airways and Lloyds Bank TSB have relatively high beta values, with returns on their shares being highly susceptible to fluctuations in the economy as a whole, while Marks and Spencer and Boots have low beta values, reflecting the relative stability of returns on their shares.

Table 3.10

Company	β
British Airways	1.35
Lloyds TSB Group	1.32
Vodafone Group	1.06
Cadbury-Schweppes	0.93
Marks and Spencer	0.73
Boots Co.	0.65

Source: Healey, N. (1999)

We can use our information on beta values to derive the required rates of return ($R*$) needed to compensate for variations in the perceived 'riskiness' of companies if an investment is to be deemed worthwhile in the share of that company. For example, assuming a risk-free rate of return (R_f) of 5% and a market return (R_m) of 10%, the following required rates of return can be estimated for selected companies:

British Airways $R* = R_f + \beta \; (R_m - R_f) = 5\% + 1.35(10 - 5)\% = 11.8\%$

Vodafone $R* = 5\% + 1.06(10 - 5) = 10.3\%$

Boots Co. $R* = 5\% + 0.65(10 - 5) = 8.3\%$

In this way investors, by knowing beta values, can place a 'price' on risk and calculate the required rates of return if they are to invest in different companies: the higher the β value, the riskier the share, and the higher the return required to compensate for that additional risk.

Key terms

Adverse selection
Budget line
Certainty equivalent
Coefficient of variation
Consumer surplus
Contingency fees
Discount factor
Expected monetary value
Expected utility
Expected value
Fair bet
Full insurance
Gamble
Insurance premium
Marginal rate of substitution
   between risk and return

Moral hazard
Net present value
Pay-offs
Portfolio
Price of risk
Principal–agent problem
Risk
Risk-adjusted discount rate
Risk averse
Risk-free asset
Risk loving
Risk neutral
Risk premium

Full definitions can be found in the 'Glossary of terms' (pp. 699–710)

Review questions

1. An investor has a portfolio composed of two types of asset. The first type consists of risk-free assets such as government stock and the second type consists of more risky assets such as steel company shares. The expected return on government stock is 0.08 and the expected return on steel shares is 0.12. The standard deviation of the returns on the whole portfolio is 0.018 and the standard deviation of the more risky steel shares is 0.09.

   (a) Calculate the proportion of the portfolio that should be invested in government stock and in steel shares and the expected returns on the total portfolio.

   (b) If the expected rate of return on steel shares fell to 0.10 because of a possibility of recession in the future, what would have to be the proportion invested in steel shares in order to maintain the same overall rate of return on the investor's whole portfolio?

(c) From the information presented above, calculate the value of the marginal rate of substitution (*MRS*) between the risky steel shares and the risk-free government stock in order to achieve an optimal portfolio choice.

2. A German exporter of mini–waterpumps used in ornamental fountains has to decide whether or not to lease new capital equipment. The firm realises that the demand for such products in the European market is income elastic so that demand for the pumps will vary strongly with disposable income. The company has enlisted the help of a macroeconomic forecasting team to calculate the various probabilities and profit returns given different demand conditions in Europe. An assessment of the exporter's utility outcomes is also given. The results are tabulated in Table 3.11.

Table 3.11

Demand conditions	Probability	Profits/Utility			
		Leasing		No leasing	
		Pr	Ut	Pr	Ut
Above normal	0.25	80	(92)	60	(76)
Normal	0.50	50	(40)	34	(60)
Below normal	0.25	0	(0)	20	(20)

Pr is profits in 000s DM and Ut is utility in 000s utils.

If the German manager's utility function is $U = 300D - 2D^2$, where U equals total utility and D is profits in Deutschmarks, then complete the following:

(a) Apply simple calculus or any other method to determine whether the German exporter is a risk lover, risk neutral or a risk averter.
(b) Explain the relationship between utility and risk taking that you noticed in (a) above within a business context.
(c) If the German exporter feels disposed to take a gamble and maximise profits regardless of any risks, what project (lease or not lease) should he choose?
(d) However, if the exporter's objectives are to maximise utility would he change his mind about which project to undertake?

3. A pub landlord has decided that to increase his drinks income, he has to buy a gaming machine. There are many machines on the market but two types in particular seem attractive alternatives. Machine 1 will generate a cash income of £4,250 per year over a lifespan of 4 years while machine 2 will generate £6,000 per year over a shorter 3 year lifespan.

(a) If the cost of each machine is £10,000, calculate the net present value (NPV) of each investment assuming that the discount rate chosen is 10%. Which machine should the pub landlord install?
(b) On further study, the landlord finds that machine 2 is of a type that is technologically older, so that the risk of new models coming out is higher. To compensate for this he decides on a risk adjustment discount rate of 20%. Will this affect his investment decision?

4. A major European car manufacturer has to decide which of two strategies it should adopt in order to gain a lead over its competitors at the 'executive' end of the market. It can either modify body design or modify engine specifications. The company's market research division has estimated the potential levels of sales and their probabilities for each strategy; these estimates are shown in Table 3.12. The top management of the company have asked the research department to work on the assumption of a profit-to-sales ratio of 50%.

Table 3.12

Strategy	Potential sales (ecu m)	Probability
Modify body design	10	0.2
	14	0.6
	18	0.2
Modify engine specifications	10	0.3
	12	0.4
	14	0.3

(a) Given the sales and probability figures in the table, calculate the expected level of profits for each strategy.
(b) Determine the variability or riskiness of the strategies by calculating the standard deviation of the profits distribution.
(c) Explain why the company still does not have sufficient information to make a valid decision about that strategy to take.
(d) Suggest a test to measure the risk per ecu of profit for each strategy and use it to solve the dilemma that emerged in (c).
(e) Give your final verdict as to the most appropriate strategy, and indicate whether there were any other clues in the information given that would tend to substantiate your conclusions.

5. A construction company is planning to build a housing complex in the suburbs of a major city. The company is trying to decide whether to build a large complex with extra communal facilities, or build a smaller, more compact scheme. The two major areas for concern involve uncertainty as to future interest rates and future levels of demand. The probability of interest rates being high is 40%, and low, 60%. Similarly the expectations of demand being high, medium or low are 30%, 50% and 20% respectively. Given these figures, the investment needed to build the respective housing schemes and the present value of annual cash flows (revenues – operating costs) for each scheme are given in Table 3.13.

(a) Draw up a decision tree that would help the company to evaluate the potential options, and explain briefly the approach you have used.
(b) Calculate the expected net present value of both schemes and indicate what strategy these figures seem to favour.
(c) Investigate the range of outcomes for the two schemes by comparing the present value figures for each demand scenario with the costs involved. Does this provide any useful information?

Table 3.13

Scheme (investment)	Interest rates	Demand conditions	Present value of cash flows (£m)
Small housing complex (£1m)	High	High	3
		Medium	2
		Low	1
	Low	High	4
		Medium	3
		Low	2
Large housing complex (£5m)	High	High	8
		Medium	6
		Low	3
	Low	High	10
		Medium	8
		Low	5

(d) Use the coefficient of variation statistic to provide the building company with an idea of the risks involved with the two different building schemes. What does this result suggest about the two schemes?

(e) How could the building company take account of these risk differentials when deciding which project to pursue?

▓ Further reading

Intermediate texts

Baumol, W. J. (1977), *Economic Theory and Operations Analysis*, 4th edn, Chs 17–19, Prentice Hall, Hemel Hempstead.

Browning, E. and Browning, J. (1992), *Microeconomic Theory and Applications*, 4th edn, Ch. 13, HarperCollins, London.

Dobson, S., Maddala, G. S. and Miller, E. (1995), *Microeconomics*, Ch. 18, McGraw-Hill, Maidenhead.

Hope, S. (1999), *Applied Microeconomics*, Chs 5 and 6, John Wiley, Chichester.

Katz, M. and Rosen, H. (1998), *Microeconomics*, 3rd edn, Ch. 6, Irwin, Boston, Mass.

Koutsoyiannis, A. (1979), *Modern Microeconomics*, 2nd edn, Ch. 19, Macmillan, Basingstoke.

Laidler, D. and Estrin, S. (1995), *Introduction to Microeconomics*, 4th edn, Ch. 8, Harvester Wheatsheaf, Hemel Hempstead.

Maddala, G. S. and Miller, E. (1989), *Microeconomics: Theory and Applications*, Ch. 21, McGraw-Hill, New York.

Nicholson, W. (1997), *Intermediate Microeconomics and its Application*, 7th edn, Ch. 7, Dryden Press, Fort Worth.

Pindyck, R. and Rubinfeld, D. (1998), *Microeconomics*, 4th edn, Chs 5, 15 and 17, Macmillan, Basingstoke.

Turner, R. K., Pearce, D. and Bateman, I. (1994), *Environmental Economics*, Harvester Wheatsheaf, Hemel Hempstead.

Varian, H. (1999), *Intermediate Microeconomics*, 5th edn, Chs 12, 13 and 34, Norton, New York.

Advanced texts   Dixit, A. K. and Pindyck, R. S. (1994), *Investment Under Uncertainty*, Princeton University Press, Princeton.

Gravelle, H. and Rees, R. (1992), *Microeconomics*, 2nd edn, Chs 19–22, Longman, Harlow.

Mas-Colell, A., Whinston, M. D. and Green, J. R. (1995), *Microeconomic Theory*, Ch. 6, Oxford University Press, Oxford.

Articles and other sources   Chirinko, R. S. (1993), 'Business fixed investment spending: a critical survey of modelling strategies, empirical results and policy implications', *Journal of Economic Literature*, XXXI, Dec.

Cicchetti, C. J. and Dubin, J. A. (1994), 'A microeconometric analysis of risk aversion and the decision to self-insure,' *Journal of Political Economy*, 102, 1, February.

Glenn Hubbard, R. (1994), 'Investment under uncertainty: keeping one's options open', *Journal of Economic Literature*, XXXII, Dec.

Healey, N. (1999), 'Pricing risk: using betas in investment appraisal', *British Economy Survey*, 28, 2.

Klein, M. (1997), 'The risk premium for evaluating public projects', *Oxford Review of Economic Policy*, 13, 4.

Kritzer, H. M. (1990), *The Justice Broker: Lawyers and Ordinary Litigation*, Oxford University Press, Oxford.

Rickman, N. (1994), 'The economics of contingency fees in personal injury litigation', *Oxford Review of Economic Policy*, 10, 1, Spring.

Rubinfeld, D. L. and Scotchmer, S. (1993), 'Contingent fees for attorneys: an economic analysis', *Rand Journal of Economics*, 24.

Simons, R. (1999), 'How risky is your company?', *Harvard Business Review*, May–June.

Viscusi, W. (1993), 'The value of risks to life and health', *Journal of Economic Literature*, XXXI, Dec.

Chapter 4

Production and costs

In this chapter we first concentrate on the techniques of **production** itself; later in the chapter we relate these techniques to the **costs** facing the producer.

Many of the ideas underlying the techniques of production have already been touched upon in the context of the consumer in Chapter 1. For example, instead of lines of constant utility (indifference curves) we have **lines of constant output (isoquants)**; instead of diminishing marginal utility we have **diminishing marginal returns to the variable factor**, and so on. Let us first review some of the ideas you should already have encountered in your introductory courses in economics.

Processes of production

Here we look at the various *processes* that a firm might use in turning *inputs* (factors of production) into *outputs* (products – whether tangible goods or services). For instance, a knitwear manufacturing firm might use various quantities of inputs such as labour (skilled machine operators, unskilled packers, etc.), capital equipment (knitting machines, factory buildings, etc.) and raw materials (wool, thread, dyes, etc.) in producing different types of knitted garments.

Isoquants In producing a given amount of a particular type of knitted garment, the firm may be able to choose between different **processes of production**, i.e. different combinations of capital and labour technically available to the producer. In Table 4.1 the firm might be able to produce one sweater using any one of the processes outlined, where K represents units of capital and L units of labour. Figure 4.1 shows the line or curve connecting these various processes for producing 1 sweater (i.e. one unit of product X).

The curve drawn in Fig. 4.1 is the $1X$ **isoquant**, i.e. the various processes available for producing 1 unit of product X in a *technically efficient* manner. A technically *inefficient* process uses more of one factor of production and no less of any other factor of production than some other process. For instance, process h in Fig. 4.1 is technically inefficient compared

Table 4.1 Alternative processes for producing 1 sweater (1X).

Process	K	L
a	18	2
b	12	3
c	9	4
d	6	6
e	4	9
f	3	12
g	2	18

with process d as it uses more capital than d (9 > 6) but only the same labour (6 = 6). We therefore *exclude* h from the 1X isoquant. Note that process h is also technically inefficient compared with process c, this time using more labour (6 > 4) but the same capital (9 = 9).

Given the present state of technology, to produce more units of product X will require more of at least one factor of production. For example in Fig. 4.2, with K_1/L_1 factor input we can produce $1X$; to produce $2X$ we need either more labour ($L_2 > L_1$) with the given capital K_1, or more capital ($K_2 > K_1$) with the given labour L_1, or more of *both* capital and labour (segment mn of the $2X$ isoquant). Hence we can draw an **isoquant map** with successively higher isoquants, i.e. lines of constant quantity (iso = constant), above and to the right of lower isoquants.

The short-run production function

The **short run** is that period of time for which at least one factor of production is fixed. The factor that takes longest to vary is usually capital. The short run may be a different period of time for different industrial sectors. For example, it may take six months to install and make operational any new equipment in the knitwear industry. We would say that the short run is six months for the knitwear industry, since capital is fixed over this time period. On the other hand it may take ten years to install and make operational a new nuclear power station. We would say that the short run is ten years for the nuclear industry, since capital is fixed over this time period.

Fig. 4.1 The 1X isoquant: i.e. the various processes technically efficient in producing 1 unit of X.

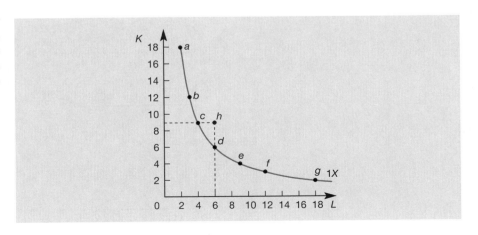

Fig. 4.2 **Higher isoquants lie above and to the right of any given isoquant.**

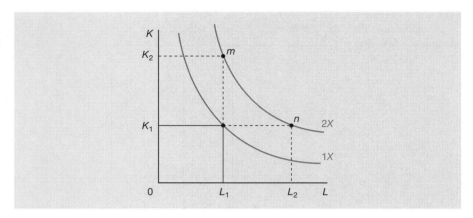

The **production function** describes the relationship between changes in the quantities of the factor inputs and changes in output. For two factors, labour (L) and capital (K), the production function Q can be written as

$$Q = F(L, K)$$

where Q = output
L = labour input
K = capital input

In the short run, with at least one factor of production fixed, we can derive the production function by taking a horizontal or vertical section through the isoquant map (Fig. 4.3).

Fig. 4.3 **Deriving a short-run production function from an isoquant map.**

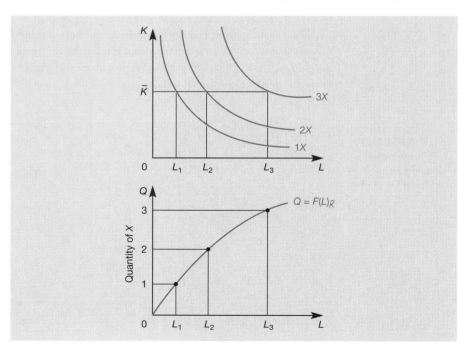

In the example shown, we keep *capital* constant at $\bar{K}$ and allow labour to vary. At $\bar{K}$ this *horizontal* section through the isoquant map gives us the production function below it, showing how output varies with labour, capital constant at $\bar{K}$. Of course if capital was constant at some higher level, $\bar{K}_1$ then we would anticipate higher output for each input of labour, giving us the short-run production function shown in Fig. 4.4.

The procedure could, of course, be altered by keeping *labour* constant at some level $\bar{L}$ and allowing capital to vary: i.e. taking a *vertical* section through the isoquant map.

We consider the factors determining the shape of these respective short-run production functions later in the chapter.

Total, average and marginal products

The production functions shown in Figs 4.3 and 4.4 can be regarded as indicating the **total product** of labour, showing how total output varies with labour input, capital fixed at some designated level. Here we shall also consider the **average product** of any variable factor (i.e. the total product divided by the total input of that factor) and the **marginal product** of any variable factor (i.e. the addition to total product from using one more unit of the variable factor).

Laws of variable proportions

As the variable factor is progressively increased, the *proportions* in which it is combined with the fixed factor will change. The result is that in the short-run time period the so-called '**law of variable proportions**' applies. The idea here is that prior to some optimum proportion of variable to fixed factor (e.g. 1 man:1 machine), we initially have too little of the variable factor. Extra units of the variable factor, here labour, will then be highly productive, making fuller use of 'spare capacity' in the fixed factor. Output rises more than in proportion to the extra input of variable factor, and we say that **increasing returns** have set in. However, beyond the optimum proportion of variable to fixed factor, additional units of the variable factor, here labour, will be progressively less productive, and we now say that **diminishing returns** have set in.

As we can see from Table 4.2, it may be that **diminishing average returns** set in at a different level of input of the variable factor than is the case for **diminishing marginal returns**.

We can see from Table 4.2 that diminishing *average* returns set in after six units of labour, but diminishing *marginal* returns set in earlier, after only five units of labour.

Fig. 4.4 Short-run production functions showing how output varies with labour input, at different levels of the fixed factor capital.

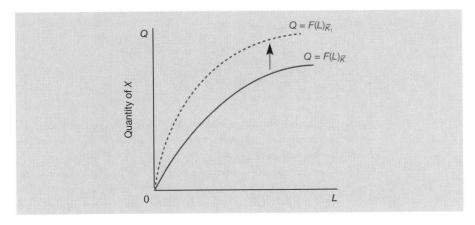

$$\text{Average product of labour} = \frac{\text{Total product}}{\text{Total labour input}} = \frac{Q}{L}$$

$$\text{Marginal product of labour} = \frac{\text{Change in total product}}{\text{Change in labour input}} = \frac{\Delta Q}{\Delta L}$$

Table 4.2 **Total, average and marginal product of labour.**

(1) Number of workers (L)	(2) Total product (TP)	(3) Average product (AP)	(4) Marginal product (MP)
0			
1	4	4	4
2	14	7	10
3	25.5	8.5	11.5
4	40	10	14.5
5	60	12	20
6	72	12	12
7	77	11	5
8	80	10	3
9	81	9	1
10	75	7.5	−6

The general relationships between total, average and marginal products are shown in Fig. 4.5. For example, at point A on the total product curve the **average product of labour** (Q/L) is given by the slope of the line drawn from the origin to point A. The **marginal product of labour** ($\Delta Q/\Delta L$) at point A will, in the limit (i.e. for infinitely small changes in labour input), be shown by the slope of the tangent to A on the total product curve.

$$\text{i.e. } MP_L = \lim_{\Delta L \to 0} \left(\frac{\Delta Q}{\Delta L} \right) = \frac{dQ}{dL}$$

Plotting these respective values for average and marginal product of labour at all points on the total product curve will give us the average and marginal product curves in the lower part of Fig. 4.5.

As it happens the tangent to the total product curve is steepest at point A: i.e. the marginal product reaches its highest value at five units of labour input. After this the total product curve begins to flatten out, and marginal product, while still positive,

Fig. 4.5 **Total, average and marginal product curves for the variable factor (labour).**

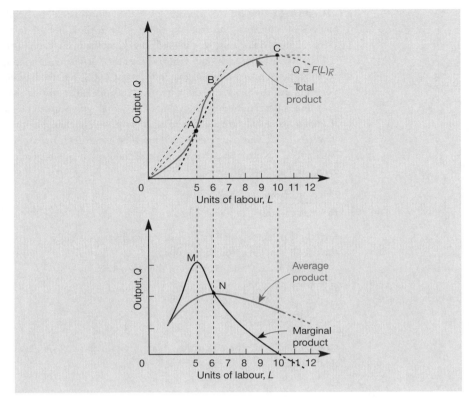

starts to fall. We say that **diminishing marginal returns** set in at five units of labour. Notice that the marginal product is zero at 10 units of labour input, where the total product curve has reached its maximum (point C). This must be so since the slope of the tangent at point C is zero and the slope of the tangent is the marginal product of labour.

Notice that the average product of labour reaches its highest value at point B on the total product curve, i.e. at six units of labour input, falling thereafter. We say that **diminishing average returns** set in at six units of labour.

Notice also that the marginal product of labour curve cuts the average product of labour curve at its highest point (N). If you think of any game, once your last (marginal) score falls below your average, then your average must fall. Similarly once $MP_L < AP_L$, then AP_L must fall.

We return to many of the ideas contained within these laws of variable proportions when we consider costs later in the chapter.

Isocosts Just as isoquants are lines of constant quantity, so **isocosts** are lines of constant costs. They are similar to the budget lines of Chapter 1 except that this time they tell us the different quantities of the *factors of production* that *producers* can purchase for a given expenditure (instead of the different quantities of products that consumers can purchase for a given expenditure).

From all the *technically efficient* processes of production shown as available on the isoquant, a profit-maximising producer is likely to select that process which is most **economically**

efficient, i.e. the least-cost process. In other words it will be helpful to bring together our analysis of isoquants with that of isocosts, thereby linking both technical and economic efficiency. Before doing this, we can usefully review the main features of an isocost line.

The isocost line $\bar{C}_1$ in Fig. 4.6(a) shows the various combinations of capital and labour that can be purchased for an expenditure of £600, where the price of capital (r) is £200 per unit and the price of labour (w) is £100 per unit. Notice that the *position* of the isocost line is determined by the value of the total expenditure of the firm on factor inputs. If expenditure halved to £300 with factor prices unchanged, the isocost line would shift inwards to $\bar{C}_2$, and if expenditure doubled to £1200, the isocost line would shift outwards to $\bar{C}_3$. Notice also that the *slope* of the isocost line is given by the factor price ratio. Here we have the following:

$$\frac{\text{Price of labour}}{\text{Price of capital}} = (-)\frac{w}{r} = \frac{100}{200} = \frac{1}{2}$$

Strictly this factor price ratio is negative, but we usually ignore the sign, as indicated by the use of brackets around the sign.

More formally, the equation of the isocost line is

$$\bar{C} = wL + rK$$

where L and K are the quantities of labour and capital respectively.
Rearranging:

$$\frac{\bar{C}}{r} - \frac{w}{r}L = K$$

$$(-)\frac{w}{r} = \frac{dK}{dL}$$

i.e. the slope of the isocost line is given by the ratio of the factor prices.

Fig. 4.6 Isocost lines.

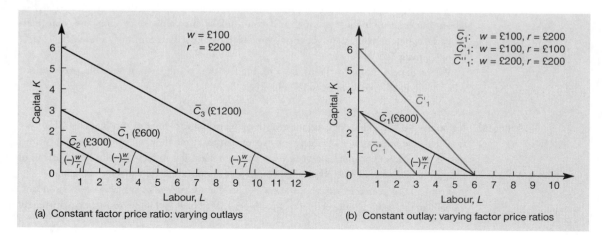

(a) Constant factor price ratio: varying outlays

(b) Constant outlay: varying factor price ratios

Clearly a change in the factor price ratio will cause the isocost line to *pivot*, as in Fig. 4.6(b). If we start with $\bar{C}_1$, a fall in the price of capital (r) will raise the factor price ratio (w/r) and cause the isocost line to pivot from $\bar{C}_1$ to $\bar{C}'_1$. On the other hand, if we start with $\bar{C}_1$, a rise in the price of labour (w) will raise the factor price ratio (w/r) and cause the isocost line to pivot from $\bar{C}_1$ to $\bar{C}''_1$.

■ Types of cost

Later in this chapter we consider the ways in which the following cost curves can be derived from the production function.

Short-run costs Remember, the short run is that period of time for which at least one factor of production is fixed. From your earlier work in economics you should be familiar with the ideas of fixed costs (invariant with output) and variable costs, and with definitions such as the following.

Total cost
Total cost = Total fixed cost + Total variable cost

i.e. $TC = TFC + TVC$

Average cost

Average total cost $(ATC) = \dfrac{\text{Total cost}}{\text{Total output}} = \dfrac{TC}{Q}$

i.e. $ATC = \dfrac{TFC + TVC}{Q} = \dfrac{TFC}{Q} + \dfrac{TVC}{Q}$

$ATC = AFC + AVC$

Marginal cost Marginal cost is the addition to total cost from producing one extra unit of output. Marginal cost is entirely variable cost.

Marginal cost $(MC) = \dfrac{\text{Change in total cost}}{\text{Change in total output}} = \dfrac{\Delta TC}{\Delta Q}$ where $\Delta Q = 1$

In Fig. 4.7 the marginal cost is shown by the slope of the chord PS.
For an *infinitely small* change in output we can write

$MC = \underset{\Delta Q \to 0}{\text{limit}} \left(\dfrac{\Delta TC}{\Delta Q} \right) = \dfrac{dTC}{\delta Q}$

i.e. *MC* is given by the gradient (PV) to the *TC* curve.

Fig. 4.7 **Marginal cost and the total cost curve.**

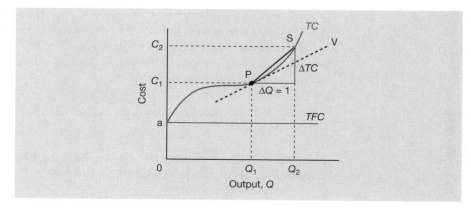

You should also be familiar with conventional diagrams used to illustrate fixed and variable costs, as in Fig. 4.8.

● Note that average fixed costs fall continuously as we divide an unchanged *TFC* with a progressively increasing quantity. This curve is the so-called rectangular hyperbola.
● Note that the *MC* curve slopes downwards initially, with falling marginal costs the mirror image of *increasing marginal returns* to the variable factor in the short run (see the rising part of the marginal product curve in Fig. 4.5 above). At output Q_1 *diminishing marginal returns* set in (see the falling part of the marginal product curve in Fig. 4.5 above) and the *MC* curve begins to rise.

Similarly we initially have *increasing average returns* to the variable factor, with the result that *AVC* falls. At output Q_2 *diminishing average returns* set in (again see Fig. 4.5 earlier) and the *AVC* curve begins to rise.

The *ATC* curve is the vertical sum of the *AFC* and *AVC* curves and this starts to rise after output Q_3, when the rise in *AVC* outweighs the fall in *AFC*.

Note also that, for reasons identical to those previously explained, the *MC* curve cuts the *AVC* and *ATC* curves at their respective minima. As soon as the marginal is above the average, then of course the average must rise: the analogy of a game is that if your last (marginal) score is greater than your average, then your average must rise.

Fig. 4.8 **Short-run cost curves.**

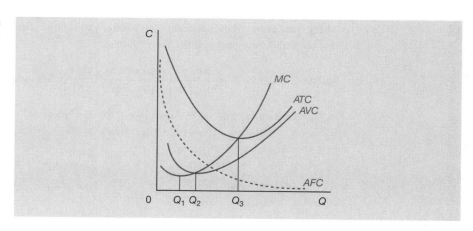

Long-run costs

The **long run** has been described as the period of time in which all factors of production can be varied. We are now in the situation of **returns to scale**.

You should be familiar with the *envelope* curve (Fig. 4.9) from your previous work in economics. Each of the *short-run average cost (SRAC) curves* shows how costs change with output at some given value/level of the fixed factor, here capital. For example, with capital fixed at $\bar{K}_1$, the lowest cost of producing output Q_1 would be C_1. However in the long run we can vary *all* factors, including capital. The lowest cost of producing output Q_1 in the long run would be to change capital to $\bar{K}_2$, when it would be possible to produce Q_1 at cost C_2. So C_2 (and not C_1) is a point on the **long-run average cost curve** (*LRAC*), which shows the lowest cost of producing any output given that all factors can be adjusted to their optimal level. In fact the outer envelope to the family of short-run average cost curves in Fig. 4.9 will constitute *LRAC*. Up to output $Q*$ the *LRAC* is falling, and we call this **economies of scale**; beyond output $Q*$ the *LRAC* is rising, and we call this **diseconomies of scale**. We consider the factors influencing economies and diseconomies of scale later in this chapter (pp. 169–73).

◼ Supply and elasticity

As we note in subsequent chapters, it is the various *cost* curves that underlie many of our notions of the **supply curve** of firm and industry under different market conditions. For example, we identify the *marginal cost curve* as being the basis for the firm and industry supply curve under perfect competition (p. 249).

Movements along and shifts in supply curve

Effective supply refers to the amounts of a commodity that producers are willing *and able* to supply at various prices. As with demand, supply is a *flow* concept, being expressed in units per time period (e.g. tons per month).

As we can see from Fig. 4.10, *movements along* a supply curve, due to a change in the price of the commodity itself, we refer to as either an **expansion** or **contraction** of supply (Fig. 4.10(a)). *Shifts* in a supply curve, due to a change in the conditions of supply,

Fig. 4.9 The long-run average cost (LRAC) curve as the outer 'envelope' to a family of short-run average cost (SRAC) curves.

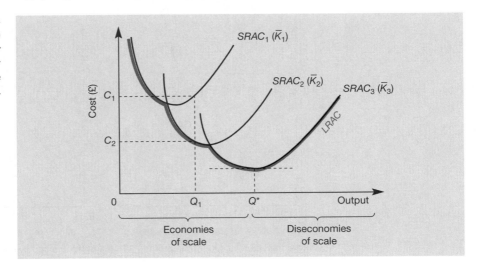

we refer to as either an **increase** or **decrease** in supply (Fig. 4.10(b)). For an increase in supply, more of X is supplied at any given price: S_1 shifts to S_2. For a decrease in supply, less of X is supplied at any given price: S_2 shifts to S_1.

The **conditions of supply** are often expressed in a simple functional relationship, as follows:

$$S_X = F\,(\overbrace{P_X\colon P_Y;\ C;\ T_X;\ Sub_X;\ T\ldots}^{\text{conditions}})$$

where
$$
\begin{aligned}
S_X &= \text{quantity of } X \text{ supplied} \\
P_X &= \text{Price of } X \\
P_Y &= \text{Price of other goods} \\
C &= \text{Costs of production} \\
T_X &= \text{Tax levied on } X \\
Sub_X &= \text{Subsidy provided on } X \\
T &= \text{Tastes of producers}
\end{aligned}
$$

You should, of course, be familiar with the way in which changes in one of the *conditions of supply* will cause the supply curve to shift to the right or left. Take, for instance, a commodity X for which an *increase* in supply is observed, with more of X supplied at each and every price. This could be due to changes in one, or more, of the following conditions of supply:

- a fall in P_Y where X and Y are substitutes in production (i.e. commodities with factors of production in common);
- a rise in P_Y, where X and Y are complements in production (i.e. commodities that are by-products or in joint supply: producing more of Y implies producing more of X, and vice versa);
- a fall in C, costs of production, so that more of X can be supplied at a given price (or a given quantity of X can be supplied at a lower price);

Fig. 4.10

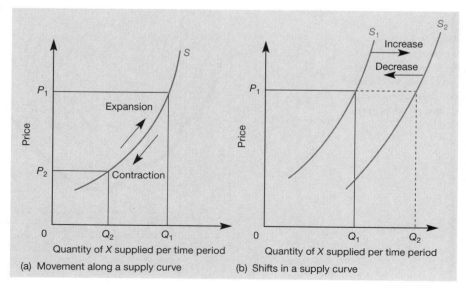

(a) Movement along a supply curve

(b) Shifts in a supply curve

- a fall in T_X, i.e. a fall in any taxes currently levied on X. Remember that the supply curve shifts vertically downwards by the amount of the tax reduction (and, of course, upwards by the amount of any tax imposed). A downward shift is, of course, a right-ward shift in the supply curve. If the tax was a **lump sum**, then the reduction in tax would shift the supply curve downwards in a *parallel* manner, but if **percentage** (ad valorem), then downwards in a *non-parallel* manner;

- an increase in Sub_X, i.e. the granting of a subsidy for the first time on X or the increase in an existing subsidy. Remember that the supply curve shifts vertically downwards by the amount of the additional subsidy (and, of course, upwards by the amount of any subsidy withdrawn). A downward shift again is equivalent to a rightward shift in the supply curve. The same points apply for lump-sum and percentage subsidies as regards parallel and non-parallel shifts in the supply curve;

- a change of producer tastes (T) in favour of X;

    etc.

Elasticity of supply

Unlike the situation of price, income and cross-elasticities of demand, as regards supply we have the single concept of **price elasticity of supply** (*PES*). It is a measure of the responsiveness of supply of X to changes in the price of X, and is defined as

$$PES = \frac{\% \text{ change in quantity supplied of } X}{\% \text{ change in price of } X}$$

The numerical values, terminology, and descriptions outlined in Chapter 2 (p. 56) as regards price elasticity of demand apply equally to supply (Table 4.3). The only difference in the case of elasticity of supply is that the signs are positive rather than negative, given the direct relationship between price and quantity supplied.

Table 4.3 Price elasticity of supply, terminology and description.

Numerical value of *PES*	Terminology	Description
0	Perfectly inelastic supply	Whatever the % change in price (Fig. 4.11(a)) no change in quantity supplied.
$> 0 < 1$	Relatively inelastic supply	A given % change in price leads to a smaller % change in quantity supplied.
1	Unit elastic supply	A given % change in price leads to exactly the same % change in quantity supplied (Fig. 4.11(b)).
$> 1 < \infty$	Relatively elastic supply	A given % change in price leads to a larger % change in quantity supplied.
∞ (infinity)	Perfectly elastic supply	An infinitely small % change in price leads to an infinity large % change in quantity supplied (Fig. 4.11(c)).

Factors affecting the numerical value of *PES* for a commodity include the following:

- *The mobility of factors of production.* The more easily factors of production can be moved between commodity *X* and the supply of other commodities, the more elastic the supply.
- *The time period in question.* The longer the time period under consideration, the more elastic the supply (producers take time to redirect factors of production).
- *Producer's attitude towards risk.* The less risk averse the producer, the more elastic the supply. In other words, if producers are more willing to take risks, they will be more responsive in redirecting factors of production to alternative uses in response to price changes in commodity X.
- *The existence of natural constraints on production.* The less inhibited is production as regards natural constraints (such as fertile land, climate, mineral deposits), the more elastic the supply is likely to be.

The diagram representing *unit elasticity of supply*, as in Fig. 4.11(b), is any straight-line supply curve through the origin. The equivalent diagram for unit elasticity of demand was seen in Chapter 2 to be the rectangular hyperbola (Fig. 2.4(b) p. 56). Before considering the principles behind the shape of the unit elastic supply curve, it will be useful to follow the approach for expressing price elasticity of demand (*PED*) in Chapter 2 (p. 58). We can devise an expression for price elasticity of supply (*PES*) in similar fashion as follows:

$$PES = \frac{P}{Q} \cdot \frac{\Delta Q}{\Delta P}$$

where *P*, *Q* refer to the *original* price and quantity supplied of *X* and ΔP, ΔQ to the *change* in price and quantity supplied of *X*.

Fig. 4.11 **Some important price elasticities of supply.**

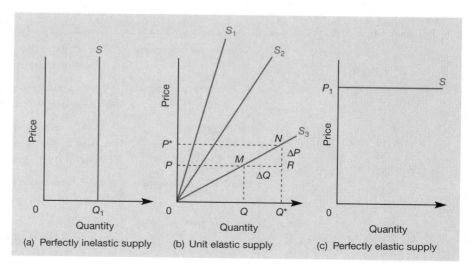

(a) Perfectly inelastic supply   (b) Unit elastic supply   (c) Perfectly elastic supply

We can now see why any straight-line supply curve through the origin has unit elasticity of supply. From Fig. 4.11(b):

Triangles 0MQ, MNR are similar therefore ratios of corresponding sides are equal. So

$$\frac{MQ}{0Q} = \frac{NR}{MR}$$

i.e. $\dfrac{P}{Q} = \dfrac{\Delta P}{\Delta Q}$

rearranging:

$$\frac{P}{Q} \cdot \frac{\Delta Q}{\Delta P} = 1$$

For a *non-linear* supply curve we can use the expression

$$PES = \frac{P}{Q} \cdot \frac{\partial Q}{\partial P}$$

as the price elasticity of supply at any particular *point* on the supply curve. Strictly we use partial derivatives here since, as we move along a given supply curve, we assume that other things (the conditions of supply) remain equal.

The producer surplus   Parallel to the concept of consumer surplus considered in Chapter 1 (p. 26) is that of **producer surplus**. Whereas consumer surplus involves the idea of individuals being willing to pay more than the market price for units of a product, here producers are seen as being willing to offer units of the product at less than market price. In Fig. 4.12, the shared area *PVW* corresponds to the *excess* of revenue received by producers over and above the amount required to induce them to supply 0Q units of the product. It is this excess that we refer to as producer surplus.

Fig. 4.12 **Producer surplus.**

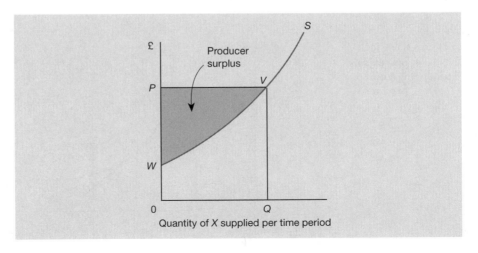

Theoretical developments

■ Technical and economic efficiency

From all the technically efficient processes of production defined by the isoquant the least cost or **economically efficient** process will occur where there is a *tangency* between isoquant and isocost. In other words, for any given output, the profit-maximising firm will select that process which is on an isocost line nearest the origin. This will indicate which, of all the technically efficient processes indicated by the isoquant, is the least cost process given the current factor price ratio.

In Fig. 4.13 if $1X$ is the desired level of output, the lowest cost of producing $1X$ given the current factor price ratio (w/r) is $\bar{C}_1$. This 'least cost' process will involve using capital to labour in the ratio K_1/L_1.

Changes in factor price ratio and factor substitution

The tangency between isocost $\bar{C}_1$ and isoquant $1X$ in Fig. 4.14 is the initial situation, with $\bar{C}_1$ (the isocost line nearest the origin) representing the lowest cost of producing $1X$ at the prevailing factor price ratio w_1/r_1. The process of production used to produce $1X$ in the cheapest way possible has a capital/labour ratio of K_1/L_1. Suppose the price of capital now falls from r_1 to r_2: the isocost line now becomes steeper (since $w_1/r_2 > w_1/r_1$). The new minimum cost of producing $1X$ is $\bar{C}_2$ – i.e. tangency between the $1X$ isoquant and the nearest isocost line to the origin with the new slope w_1/r_2 – giving a capital/labour ratio K_2/L_2. Not surprisingly, standard theory has predicted an increased use of the cheaper capital input, K_2 instead of K_1, and a decreased use of the now relatively more expensive labour input, L_2 instead of L_1.

Of course the analysis only considers factor substitution in producing a *given* level of output ($1X$). If the new cost of production $\bar{C}_2 < \bar{C}_1$, then lower costs may raise the desired (e.g. profit maximising) level of output above $1X$ and lead eventually to more of *both* factors being required.

Fig. 4.13 The least-cost process for producing 1 unit of product X.

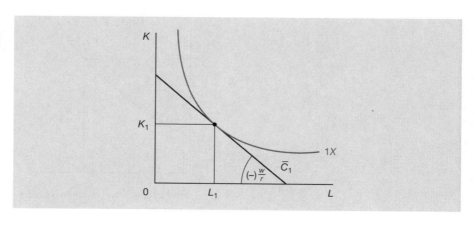

Fig. 4.14 **Factor substitution under changing factor price ratios.**

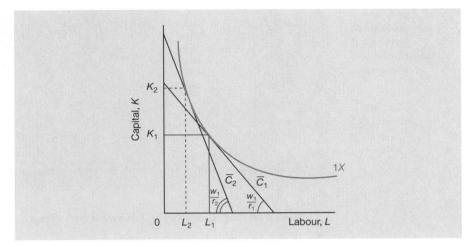

Technology and factor substitution

As well as the factor price ratio, the shape of the isoquant itself will also play an important part in determining factor input. The slope of each isoquant tells us how the firm can trade off the quantity of one input against another input, while keeping output constant. Clearly the present state of technology will influence the trade-off possibilities.

Marginal rate of technical substitution (*MRTS*)

The **marginal rate of technical substitution** of labour for capital ($MRTS_{LK}$) tells us how much capital can be replaced by *one* extra unit of labour, output remaining constant. This idea is similar to the marginal rate of substitution of product X for product Y (MRS_{XY}) already encountered in consumer theory in Chapter 1.

$$MRTS_{LK} = \frac{\text{Change in capital input}}{\text{Change in labour input}}$$

$$\text{i.e. } MRTS_{LK} = \frac{\Delta K}{\Delta L} \text{ (for a fixed level of Q)}$$

Usually we allow $\Delta L = 1$ and ignore the negative sign that follows from the downward sloping isoquant.

As we can see from Fig. 4.15 the conventional drawing of an isoquant as convex to the origin implies a progressively diminishing $MRTS_{LK}$. In other words, as we move from point a to point e along the lX isoquant, the amount of capital replaced by each extra unit of labour falls continuously. The suggestion here is that the productivity possibilities available to any single factor input are limited. Seeking to replace capital by additional units of labour becomes less and less successful: in other words effective production requires a balance of *both* inputs.

Fig. 4.15 **The marginal rate of technical substitution and an isoquant.**

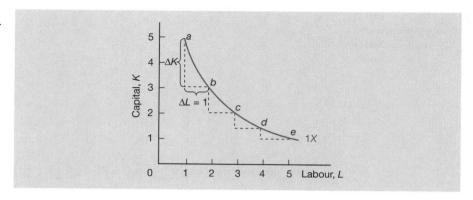

Fig. 4.15 **The marginal rate of technical substitution and an isoquant.**

The discussion here has similarities to that for arc and point elasticity in Chapter 2. At a single point on the isoquant:

$$MRTS_{LK} = \underset{\Delta L \to 0}{\text{limit}} \left(\frac{\Delta K}{\Delta L} \right) = \frac{dK}{dL}$$

In other words, the marginal rate of technical substitution of labour for capital is given by the slope of the tangent to an isoquant at any point. Clearly the convex isoquant of Fig. 4.15 implies a progressively falling $MRTS_{LK}$ (ignoring the negative sign).

Marginal products and MRTS

It will be useful at this point to demonstrate a result that will be of use to us in welfare economics (Chapter 11). In Fig. 4.15 each extra unit of labour (ΔL) replaces a certain amount of capital (ΔK) while keeping output constant.

We can therefore say:

- Additional output from increased use of labour $= (MP_L) \cdot (\Delta L)$
- Reduction in output from decreased use of capital $= (MP_K) \cdot (\Delta K)$

where MP_L and MP_K are the marginal products of labour and capital respectively.

Since output is constant (move along a *given* isoquant):

$$(MP_L) \cdot (\Delta L) + (MP_K) \cdot (\Delta K) = 0$$
$$(MP_L) \cdot (\Delta L) = -(MP_K) \cdot (\Delta K)$$
$$\frac{(MP_L)}{(MP_K)} = -\frac{(\Delta K)}{(\Delta L)} = MRTS_{LK}$$

$$\frac{MP_L}{MP_K} = MRTS_{LK}$$

In other words the slope of the isoquant is given by the ratio of the marginal products, here labour to capital. As we move along the $1X$ isoquant of Fig. 4.15, continually replacing capital with labour in the production process, the marginal product of capital increases and the marginal product of labour decreases. The net result of this is to cause the $MRTS_{LK}$ to progressively fall, as noted earlier.

Figure 4.16 indicates four types of isoquant, each implying a different marginal rate of technical substitution (*MRTS*) between the factors of production.

(a) Figure 4.16(a) presents the **smooth, convex (to the origin) isoquant** we have already considered. The *MRTS* between the factors varies as we move along the isoquant, for example $MRTS_{LK}$ falling as we move downwards from left to right. We usually consider only the sections of the isoquants within the *ridge lines* of Fig. 4.16(a).

The *upper ridge line* is the locus (set) of points where MP_K is zero: processes on a given isoquant beyond points *a*, *b*, *c* in the diagram would imply negative MP_K. The *lower ridge line* is the locus (set) of points where MP_L is zero: processes on *a* given isoquant beyond points *d*, *e*, *f* in the diagram would imply negative MP_L. Outside the ridge lines the marginal products of factors are negative and the processes of production are inefficient since they require more of *both* factors of production for producing a given level of output. We have already noted that such technically inefficient processes are not considered by the theory of production.

Fig. 4.16 Types of isoquant in production theory.

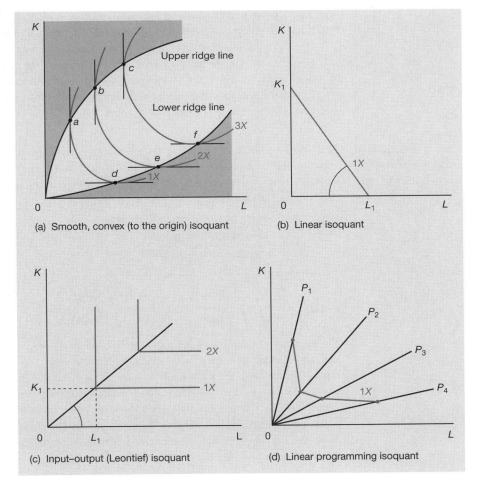

(a) Smooth, convex (to the origin) isoquant

(b) Linear isoquant

(c) Input–output (Leontief) isoquant

(d) Linear programming isoquant

(b) The **linear isoquant** of Fig. 4.16(b) suggests that the marginal rate of technical substitution (*MRTS*) is constant at all points. This means that the rate at which capital and labour can be substituted for each other is the same whatever the respective combinations of factor inputs being used. In terms of Fig. 4.15, each extra unit of labour can be substituted for exactly the same amount of capital and leave output unchanged, no matter how much labour is already being used. We say that **perfect substitutability** exists between the factors of production. In Fig. 4.16(b) a given output (1X) can be produced by using only capital or only labour or any of the infinite number of processes of production along the linear isoquant using the fixed input ratio K_1/L_1.

(c) The **input–output (Leontief) isoquant** of Fig. 4.16(c) assumes **zero substitutability** between the factors of production. Here there is only one technically efficient process of production for any given level of output. The addition of more labour does not increase output; neither does the addition of more capital. Thus MP_L = zero on horizontal segments of the L-shaped isoquants and MPK = zero on vertical segments. Higher output only results when *both* labour and capital are increased in the constant proportion K_1/L_1.

(d) **The linear programming isoquant** of Fig. 4.16(d) assumes **limited substitutability** between the factors of production. There are only a few processes (here P_1 to P_4) for producing the commodity, and capital can only be substituted for labour (or vice versa) at the kink points of a given isoquant. The respective kink points are conventionally connected by straight lines, giving a rather misleading impression of a constant *MRTS* for the factors between the kink points, when in fact no substitution is possible between those kink points.

Elasticity of substitution (*EOS*) between factors

This rather technical concept is sometimes encountered in production theory to describe substitutability between factors. It is defined as the percentage change in the capital/labour ratio divided by the percentage change in the marginal rate of technical substitution between factors.

$$EOS = \frac{\text{percentage change in } K/L}{\text{percentage change in } MRTS_{LK}}$$

i.e. $EOS = \dfrac{\partial(K/L)}{K/L} \Big/ \dfrac{\partial(MRTS_{LK})}{MRTS_{LK}} = \dfrac{\partial(K/L)}{K/L} \Big/ \dfrac{\partial(\partial K/\partial L)}{\partial K/\partial L}$

The elasticity of substitution is a pure number, independent of any unit of measurement. Let us illustrate this idea with an example. For any given percentage fall in the capital/labour ratio, the more easily labour can be substituted for capital, the *smaller* will be the percentage fall in the $MRTS_{LK}$, and the *larger* therefore will be the elasticity of substitution (*EOS*). (Remember that when there is perfect substitutability between factors, as with the linear isoquant, there will be *zero* percentage change in $MRTS_{LK}$ as we move down the isoquant.) A high elasticity of substitution (*EOS*) therefore implies a greater degree of substitutability between the factors of production.

Returns to scale:
production in
the long run

Returns to scale refer to the long-run time period in which we can change *all* the factors of production. The laws of variable proportions need no longer apply – for example we can double *both* capital and labour, keeping the proportion of capital to labour constant. Suppose we start with the production function

$$Q = F(L, K)$$

and in the long-run time period change all the factors by the constant proportion v. We observe the new level of output Q^*, where

$$Q^* = F(vL, vK)$$

- If Q^* increases by the same proportion v as the factor inputs, we have *constant returns to scale*.
- If Q^* increases by less than in proportion to the factor inputs, we have *diminishing returns to scale*.
- If Q^* increases by more than in proportion to the factor inputs, we have *increasing returns to scale*.

Returns to scale are seen graphically in Fig. 4.17. The production process here uses two hours of labour to one hour of capital and the expansion path is along the ray 0C, showing what happens as we increase both capital and labour factor inputs by the same proportion (v).

- Segment 0A exhibits *constant returns to scale*, with successive isoquants the same distance apart (e.g. doubling both inputs from the starting point of one hour capital: two hours labour, exactly doubles output).
- Segment AB exhibits *increasing returns to scale*, with successive isoquants getting closer and closer together (e.g. a 50% increase in both inputs from the starting point of two hours labour: four hours capital, increases output by more than 50%).
- Segment BC exhibits *decreasing returns to scale*, with successive isoquants getting further and further apart (e.g. doubling both inputs from three hours' labour: six hours' capital, less than doubles output).

Fig. 4.17 **Constant, increasing and decreasing returns to scale.**

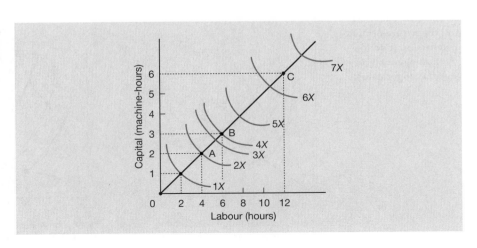

Returns to scale and homogeneity

Here we look at the idea of homogeneity of production functions. Suppose we start from an initial situation

$$Q_0 = F(L, K)$$

and then increase both factors of production by the same proportion v. We now observe the new level of output $Q*$, where

$$Q* = F(vL, vK)$$

- If v can be factored out (that is, taken out of the brackets as a common factor) then the new level of output $Q*$ can be expressed as a function of v (to any power α) and the initial level of output Q_0:

> or
> $$Q* = v^\alpha F(L, K)$$
> $$Q* = v^\alpha Q_0$$

The production function is therefore said to be *homogeneous*.

- If v cannot be factored out, then the production function is said to be *non-homogeneous*.

So a homogeneous production function is one for which, if each of the inputs is multiplied by v, then v can be completely factored out of the production function.

Degree of homogeneity Note also that the power (α) of v is called the degree of homogeneity of the production function, and is a measure of the returns to scale:

If $\alpha = 1$, we have constant returns to scale
If $\alpha > 1$, we have increasing returns to scale
If $\alpha < 1$, we have decreasing returns to scale

Isoclines and homogeneity An *isocline* is a locus of points on different isoquants at which the *MRTS* of factors is constant at a particular value (i.e. the tangents to successive

Fig. 4.18 **Isoclines and the nature of the production function (homogeneous or non-homogeneous).**

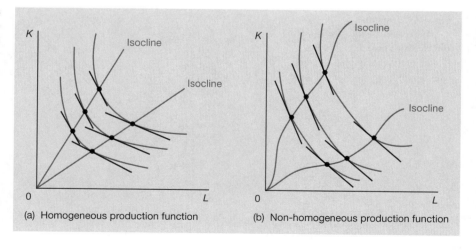

(a) Homogeneous production function

(b) Non-homogeneous production function

isoquants will have the same slope). If the production function is homogeneous, as in Fig. 4.18(a), then the isoclines will be straight lines through the origin. Note that along any one isocline (for a given *MRTS*) the K/L ratio is constant. If the production function is non-homogeneous, then the isoclines will not be straight lines, but irregular lines, as in Fig. 4.18(b). Here the K/L ratio will also vary along each isocline.

Later in this chapter we consider the *reasons* for increasing or decreasing returns to scale and the implications for costs of production (p. 169).

Technical progress and the production function

New or improved processes of production may be developed. This is often referred to as technical progress. In this case technical progress takes the form of *process* innovation as opposed to *product* innovation. The impact of technical progress is illustrated in Fig. 4.19.

Technical progress can be shown as an upward shift of the production function, i.e. more output for any given factor input (a shift from Q to Q^1 in Fig. 4.19(a)). Alternatively technical progress can be shown as a downward shift of an isoquant (X_0 in Fig. 4.19(b)). Here the same output is produced by fewer factor inputs or greater output produced by the same factor inputs.

Of course technical progress may affect the shape of the respective isoquants as well as their position. In fact, following the work of J. Hicks, we can distinguish between three types of technical progress, depending upon the impact of that progress on the *MRTS* (slope of the isoquant).

Capital deepening technical progress This occurs where the marginal product of capital is raised by more than the marginal product of labour. The ratio of marginal products MP_L / MP_K therefore falls (ignoring sign): i.e. the $MRTS_{LK}$ falls (see pp. 159–60), which is of course the slope of the isoquant. We can therefore show capital deepening technical progress as an inward shift of an isoquant such that, at any given K/L ratio (i.e. on a particular isocline), the isoquant becomes *less steep* (see Fig. 4.20(a)).

Labour deepening technical progress The previous analysis holds, except that *labour deepening technical progress* raises MP_L more than MP_K: the ratio MP_L / MP_K therefore rises (ignoring sign) as does the $MRTS_{LK}$, which is the slope of the isoquant. The inward-

Fig. 4.19 Impact of technical progress.

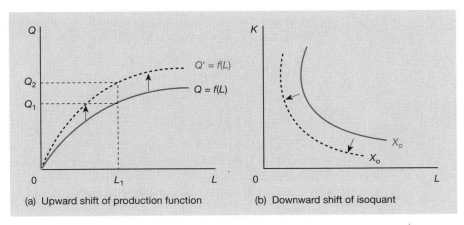

(a) Upward shift of production function   (b) Downward shift of isoquant

Fig. 4.20 **Different types of technical progress.**

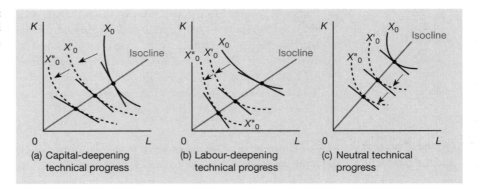

(a) Capital-deepening technical progress

(b) Labour-deepening technical progress

(c) Neutral technical progress

shifting isoquant therefore becomes *steeper* at any given K/L ratio (i.e. on a particular isocline), as shown in Fig. 4.20(b).

Neutral technical progress This occurs where the process innovation raises the marginal products of *both* factors by the same percentage. As a result the ratio of marginal products MP_L/MP_K is unaffected: i.e. $MRTS_{LK}$, the slope of the isoquant, remains constant. Here the inward shifting isoquant remains parallel to its original position at any given K/L, as shown in Fig. 4.20(c).

The Cobb–Douglas production function

This particular production function was first proposed by C. Cobb and P. Douglas in 1928, and is widely used in applied work. In its simplest form, with output Q and two inputs, labour L and capital K, it can be written as

$$Q = b_0 L^{b_1} K^{b_2}$$

or taking logs:

$$\log Q = \log b_0 + b_1 \log L + b_2 \log K$$

b_0 is a constant that depends on the units of measurement of Q, L and K. The coefficients b_1 and b_2 can be interpreted as the elasticities of output with respect to labour and capital inputs respectively.

Further, we can use $b_1 + b_2$ as a measure of the returns to scale. For example, suppose we double L and K, then the new output Q_1 is given by

$$Q_1 = b_0 (2L)^{b_1}(2K)^{b_2} = 2^{(b_1+b_2)} (b_0 LK)$$
$$Q_1 = 2^{(b_1+b_2)} (b_0 L^{b_1} K^{b_2})$$

i.e. $Q_1 = 2^{(b_1+b_2)} Q$ (where Q = original output)

We can now state the following:

- If $b_1 + b_2 = 1$, then doubling inputs will double output $\Rightarrow$ *constant returns to scale.*
- If $b_1 + b_2 > 1$, then doubling inputs will more than double output $\Rightarrow$ *increasing returns to scale.*
- If $b_1 + b_2 < 1$, then doubling inputs will less than double output $\Rightarrow$ *decreasing returns to scale.*

Costs

In the introduction to this chapter we looked at the firm's production technology – namely how factor inputs can be transformed into outputs in a technically efficient manner. These various technical possibilities were summarised by isoquants and production functions for the firm. We also noted that, given the prices of factor inputs, we could use isocost lines to identify the least-cost process of all those that are technically efficient. This least-cost solution would occur in situations of tangency between isoquant and isocost, i.e. where the slope of the isoquant ($MRTS$) exactly equals the factor price ratio: e.g. $MRTS_{LK} = (-) w/r$ in Fig. 4.21.

Minimum cost expansion paths

We can derive *cost curves* from a series of tangency points between isoquants and isocosts, as in Fig. 4.21. The *slope* of the isocost is given by the factor price ratio (here w/r) and the *position* of the isocost by total firm expenditure on factor inputs. In our analysis, we initially assume that the factor price ratio is unchanged as the firm expands output (i.e. parallel isocost lines). In Fig. 4.21 we can now plot the total cost curve from the successive tangency points a, b, c and d between isoquants and isocosts. These represent the least-cost processes (C_1 to C_4) available for producing each level of output ($1X$ to $4X$). The simplified *linear* total cost curve of Fig. 4.21 would only occur where constant (as opposed to increasing or diminishing) returns characterised the production process and where no fixed costs were incurred.

Fig. 4.21 Deriving the total cost curve from the minimum cost expansion path (*MCEP*).

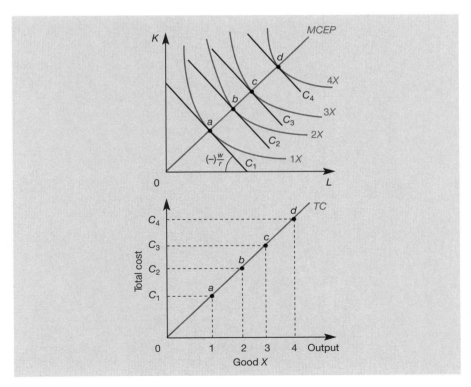

Of course in reality we are often faced with non-constant returns and the presence of fixed costs, giving *non-linear* total, average and marginal cost curves, as in Fig. 4.8 previously (p. 152). Figure 4.22 shows how non-constant returns result in non-linear total cost curves.

The straight-line minimum cost expansion paths (*MCEP*) shown in Figs 4.21 and 4.22 would occur where the production function (summarised by the set of isoquants) was homogeneous – see p. 164. Where the production function was non-homogeneous, the *MCEP* would not be a straight line, as in Fig. 4.23.

As before, *MCEP* shows the least-cost combinations of factors for different output levels, at a given factor price ratio. Where the production function is non-homogeneous, *MCEP* is non-linear as in Fig. 4.23(a). Plotting the resulting total cost curve in Fig. 4.23(b) gives us the typically shaped (assuming no fixed costs) *TC* curve shown. Remember that average total cost (*ATC*) can be derived from the angle (total cost/total output) of any straight line *ray* from the origin to the total cost (*TC*) curve. Remember also that marginal cost (*MC*) can be derived from the *tangent* to the total cost (*TC*) curve at each level of output. It follows that in Fig. 4.23(c) $MC = ATC$ at output Q'; $MC < ATC$ at output levels below Q'; $MC > ATC$ at output levels above Q'.

The reasons for the falling marginal and average variable cost curve in the short-run time period often involve the laws of variable proportions. Increasing the variable factor

Fig. 4.22 Non-constant returns and non-linear total cost curves.

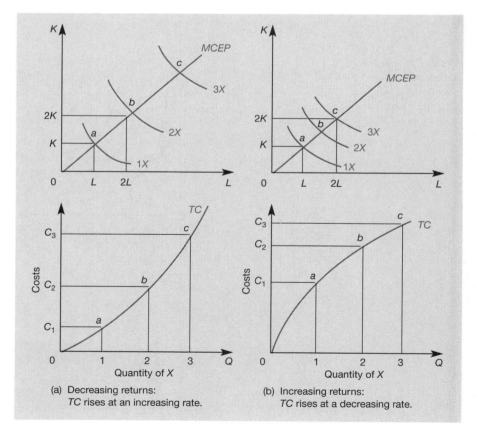

(a) Decreasing returns:
   TC rises at an increasing rate.

(b) Increasing returns:
   TC rises at a decreasing rate.

Fig. 4.23 **Deriving the total, average and marginal cost curves from a non-homogeneous production function.**

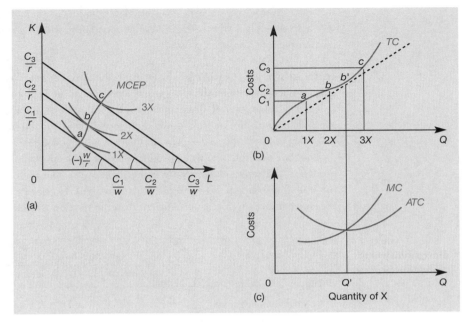

in combination with at least one fixed factor initially moves the production process nearer to some optimal combination of variable and fixed factor(s). As a result both marginal product and average product of the variable factor initially rise, and thereby marginal cost and average variable cost respectively fall. Eventually we attain the optimal combination, when marginal and average variable cost curves are at their minima. We then move further away from the optimal combination of variable to fixed factor(s), when marginal costs and average variable costs begin to rise.

However, in the long run we can, at least in principle, increase *all* factors in the same proportions – doubling, say, labour, land and capital – thereby retaining any initial proportion in which the factors are combined. When we increase all factors in proportion, we talk about changes in the *scale* of production. Why, in this case, do we typically observe ranges of output for the long-run average cost curve (as in Fig. 4.9, p. 153) over which *LRAC* is downward sloping to output Q^*?

▨ Economies of scale

In terms of *production* we have talked about 'increasing returns to scale' in the long-run time period; the counterpart in terms of *costs* is economies of scale. **Economies of scale** describes the downward-sloping segment of the *LRAC* curve. The underlying reasons can be broken down into two broad categories: technical and non-technical economies of scale.

Technical economies of scale — Some of the factors behind these economies of scale involve technical aspects of the production process and so are often given a separate heading. As we have noted, anything that raises average products of (variable) factor inputs as we increase them in proportion will help to explain why average variable costs fall in the long run (we look at marginal costs in the long run later, p. 174).

Indivisibilities Certain processes of production, e.g. mass assembly techniques, can only be operated efficiently at large output volumes and cannot be operated as efficiently at lower outputs, even if all factor inputs are scaled down in proportion to one another. We call this inability to scale down the processes of production without affecting their efficiency of operation, *indivisibility* of the production process.

Take, for example, the three production processes outlined in Table 4.4. For all three processes, the capital/labour ratio is the same at 1:1, and each process is a scaled down (or scaled up) version of one of the other processes. However, the larger-scale processes are clearly more productive or efficient than the smaller-scale processes.

Table 4.4
Indivisibility in the
production process.

Type of process	Factor inputs		Output
	L (men)	K (machines)	X (units)
A. Small-scale process	1	1	1
B. Medium-scale process	100	100	1,000
C. Large-scale process	1,000	1,000	20,000

- For $0 < X < 100$ the *small-scale process* would be used, and constant returns to scale would be experienced as the process is duplicated.
- For $100 < X < 1,000$ the *medium-scale process* would be used, since producing 100 units of X by duplicating the small-scale process would require $100L:100K$, which could produce 1,000 units using the medium-scale process. Provided disposal costs are zero, it will pay to operate the medium-scale process inefficiently (throwing away up to 900 X) rather than duplicate the small-scale process over this range of output.
- For $10,000 < X$ we would switch to the *large-scale process* for reasons similar to the above, even if this means inefficient operation of that process.

We can designate the output levels of 100 and 10,000 as *threshold levels*, in that as output rises beyond them we switch to a more productive, larger-scale process. As a result of this switch, costs can be expected to fall. For example, in Table 4.4, for $X > 100$ a hundredfold increase in both factor inputs (compared with $1X$) leads to a more than hundredfold increase in output as we switch from duplicating process A to process B; similarly, for $X > 10,000$ a tenfold increase in both factor inputs (compared with $1,000X$) leads to a more than tenfold increase in output as we switch from process B (or combinations of processes A and B) to process C. Clearly indivisibility between the various production processes means that we have *increasing* returns for output levels beyond each threshold, rather than constant returns. Provided only that costs of factor inputs do not rise in such a way as to outweigh these increasing (technical) returns, then average (and marginal) costs will initially fall.

Specialisation   As output increases it becomes more possible to use *specialised labour* and capital equipment, with corresponding increases in output per unit of factor input. This is the familiar idea behind Adam Smith's 'division of labour', with the same quantity of labour producing a greater output of pins by specialising in each of four separate processes rather than four persons seeking to perform *all* the processes. Repetition (practice makes perfect), time savings in not having to move between separate processes, and a number of related factors accounted for the greater productivity of labour via specialisation. The same benefits can apply to *specialised equipment* being more productive: for example a more sophisticated machine costing 10 times as much as a simple machine may produce 50 times as much output of the same (or higher) quality. Of course specialisation of labour and capital is limited by the size of the market; only when the market grows beyond a certain size will it be profitable to use the more specialised and productive labour and machinery.

There is some overlap between our first two reasons for economies of scale. However, the first reason (indivisibilities) refers mainly to contrasts between the larger and more productive *flow methods* (or processes) of production, such as assembly lines, and the smaller-scale *batch methods*. The latter reason (specialisation) refers more to increasing returns resulting from individual units of labour or capital becoming more specialised *within any given method* (process) of production.

Technical change involving *process innovation* can, of course, yield economies of scale under both headings. New (indivisible) flow processes may be developed with greater productivity beyond 'threshold' levels of output, or existing larger-scale processes may become still more productive by using more specialised labour or equipment.

Increased dimensions   In many cases production involves *materials* as inputs and *capacity* as intermediate or final output. The economy of *increased dimensions* follows from materials increasing as the square but volume (capacity) increasing as the cube. It follows that material costs per unit of capacity fall with increases in that capacity (output).

Economies of increased dimensions are particularly important in the so-called 'process industries', such as petroleum refining, gas transmission, chemical and cement industries, and glass manufacture. The methods of production in the process industries utilise equipment such as storage tanks, reaction chambers, and connecting pipes, all of which involve the technical-geometric relationship between surface area and volume. Since the material and labour input costs of constructing such equipment increase in proportion to the surface area, but the output of the equipment increases in proportion to the volume (capacity), clearly material and labour costs per unit of output decline with size.

Transport-related industries purchasing and using bulk-carrying vehicles (larger lorries, super-tankers, aeroplanes, etc.) also benefit from economies of increased dimensions.

Linked processes   It may be that the final output results from *linking* or *combining* separate processes. However, it may require a large output before these separate processes can be linked in an optimal way. Suppose, for example, that good X requires three separate processes in its production, each of which needs specialised equipment with the following capacities:

Process A: specialised equipment producing 20 units per hour
Process B: specialised equipment producing 30 units per hour
Process C: specialised equipment producing 40 units per hour

Only when good X is produced at the rate of 120 units per hour will it be possible to avoid the cost of idle capacity (i.e. 6 machines for process A, 4 for B, 3 for C). In other words the *lowest common multiple* from these separate, but linked, processes is a large number. As output rises towards this number we reap the *economy of linked processes*.

Reserve capacity   Firms often build an element of *reserve capacity* into the production process in order to cope with unexpected events, such as breakdown, disruption of supplies of raw materials, or unexpectedly large orders.

Since large firms usually operate a larger number of machines and personnel, proportionately fewer units of equipment or labour need be held in reserve to meet unexpected contingencies. For example, the number of persons required to repair breakdowns in plant and equipment usually increases less than in proportion to the scale of operations.

These reserve capacity economies often extend to stocks of raw materials or output held to smooth out random fluctuations in input requirement or in demand. The law of large numbers usually works to the benefit of large firms in this respect. For example, the larger the existing customer base, the more likely it is that extreme reactions by clients are likely to offset each other, i.e. give a more stable (average) reaction. Larger firms are therefore able to hold a smaller percentage of their output in stock to meet such random changes in demand, thereby reducing stockholding costs per unit of output.

Non-technical economies of scale   The majority of the economies of scale discussed so far involve benefits in *technical* aspects of production related to increases in the size of the *plant or establishment* (production unit). However, a number of other benefits are more closely related to *non-technical* aspects of the firm's operation, such as increases in the size of the firm as an *enterprise* (institutional unit). We have already touched upon these non-technical economies, and we now consider them in rather more detail.

Financial economies   Large firms (enterprises) can often obtain finance at a lower cost per £/$ than smaller firms. For example, lenders often charge a lower interest on loans to larger firms, which are perceived to be more secure or are better able to raise collateral in support of the loan. Further the administrative costs (fees, etc.) of arranging larger loans usually increase less than in proportion to the increased size of loan. Again larger firms often have access to cheaper sources of finance, such as equity capital via share issues (often cheaper than term loans or the issue of debentures). Larger share issues will also help to spread the substantial initial administrative costs, making large share issues cheaper per unit of capital raised than smaller share issues.

Administrative and managerial economies   The administrative and managerial infrastructure of an enterprise (head office, regional offices, functional and area-based managers, etc.) may be able to deal with increased throughput with a less than proportional increase in the administrative/managerial overhead. Clearly progressive developments in office-related information technologies are also having an impact here.

Economies of bulk purchase   Large enterprises may be able to purchase in bulk, with proportionately larger discounts, over a whole range of inputs used in the operation of the enterprise.

Selling and marketing economies Various sales costs increase less than in proportion to the scale of output. For example, the costs of advertising space in newspapers and magazines, or advertising time on television, radio and cinema, increase less than in proportion to scale, thereby reducing advertising costs per unit of output. Similarly a given sales force or distributional network can often handle a larger throughput with a less than proportionate increase in input.

Large firms may also be able to enter into exclusive arrangements with existing dealers to feature their particular product ranges. By saving the cost of establishing such distributional outlets themselves, selling costs per unit may thereby be reduced.

Research and development (R & D) activity may be a vital resource for improving product quality or developing new product lines – key features of a successful marketing strategy. The R & D activity is clearly an expensive overhead affordable only to large firms. However, as such (large) firms grow still further in size, the R & D overhead can be spread over a greater volume and value of output, reducing R & D costs per unit of output.

Internal versus external economies

Sometimes a distinction is made between internal and external economies of scale. **Internal economies** are the result of the *plant or enterprise* itself growing in size, as already outlined. **External economies** are the result of the *industry* growing in size, of which the plant or enterprise is but a part. The suggestion here is that a growth in size of the industry may lead to the development of various infrastructure support services available to *all* the firms within that industry, thereby lowering costs. The benefits of such external economies are particularly substantial where an industry is localized within a particular geographical area. For example, as the industry grows in size:

- specialised *markets* may develop for buying raw materials or selling the finished product (e.g. cotton, corn exchanges);
- specialised *labour skills* may develop, fostered by local college or training agency provision as well as by a local culture as regards the provision of such skills;
- specialised *component suppliers* may develop, providing customised materials;
- specialised *financial services* may develop, catering for the particular needs of firms in that industrial sector.

In these and many other ways, the costs of individual plants and enterprises may fall because the industry grows in size. These external economies occur independently of any change in size of a particular plant or enterprise within the industry.

Diseconomies of scale

The suggestion is often made that beyond some particular level of output (Q^* in Fig. 4.9, p. 153) the *LRAC* begins to rise. The usual explanations for the existence of such *diseconomies of scale* focus on managerial problems in handling growth beyond some optimum size. Larger firms typically have extended and more bureaucratic decision-making processes, leading to time delays and distortions in information flows between the actual marketplace and top management. We explore the evidence for the existence of such diseconomies later in the chapter. What is generally agreed is that there is a levelling of the *LRAC* at particular outputs in different industries. The term *minimum efficient size* is often used to describe the output level at which the *LRAC begins* to level off, and this is considered further later (p. 186).

Long-run marginal cost

So far we have mainly been concerned with economies of scale and the long-run average cost curve (*LRAC*). In this and later chapters of this book we also make use of the *long-run marginal cost curve* (*LRMC*).

Figure 4.24 presents the traditional U-shaped *LRAC* curve shown as an envelope to a family of short-run average cost curves (*SRAC*). As noted earlier (p. 152), each *SRAC* curve is intersected at its lowest point by an associated short-run marginal cost curve (*SMC*). We can now use this diagram to show that the long-run marginal cost curve (*LMC*) is derived from the family of short-run marginal cost curves (*SMC*), but is *not* in this case the 'envelope' to the family of *SMC* curves. In fact we can show that the *LMC* curve is a locus of points formed by the intersection of vertical lines drawn towards the horizontal axis from each tangency point (*a*, *b* and *c* respectively) between an *SRAC* and the *LRAC* envelope and the *SMC* associated with that *SRAC* curve.

We can illustrate the derivation of the *LMC* curve by taking point *a* in Fig. 4.24, which indicates a point of tangency between $SRAC_1$ and *LRAC*. Where the vertical line drawn from point *a* to the horizontal axis (i.e. aQ_1) intersects SMC_1 we have a point on the *LMC* curve. This can be seen to be so by considering points to the left (*a'*) and to the right (*a"*) of point *a* on $SRAC_1$.

- Compare the move from *a'* to *a*

  At point *a'*, $SRAC_1$ > *LRAC*. It follows that at associated output level Q'_1 total cost in the short run is *greater than* total cost in the long run. Now at point *a* and associated output level Q_1 total cost in the short run is *equal to* total cost in the long run at some higher level (since *MC* is positive). It must therefore be the case that the *change in total cost* in the short run (i.e. SMC_1) is *less than* the change in total cost in the long run (i.e. *LMC*).

> i.e. $SMC_1 < LMC$

- Compare the move from *a* to *a"*

  At point *a"*, $SRAC_1$ > *LRAC*. It follows that at the associated output level $Q"_1$ total cost in the short run is *greater than* total cost in the long run at some higher level (since *MC*

Fig. 4.24 Deriving the long-run marginal cost curve (*LMC*).

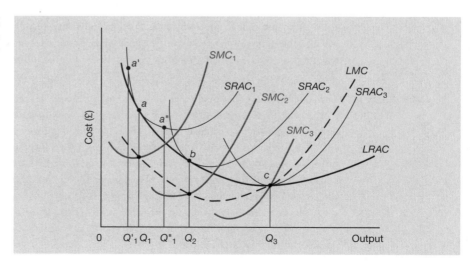

is positive). It must therefore be the case that the *change in total cost* (i.e. SMC_1) in the short run is *greater than* the change in total cost in the long run (i.e. *LMC*):

i.e. $SMC_1 > LMC$

We can therefore say that

- To the left of point *a*, $SMC_1 < LMC$.
- To the right of point *a*, $SMC_1 > LMC$.
- At point *a*, $SMC_1 = LMC$.

If we repeat this procedure for all points of tangency between *SRAC* and *LRAC* curves to the left of the minimum point of the *LRAC* (i.e. Q_3), we obtain the dashed line for *LMC* shown in Fig. 4.24. At the minimum point of *LRAC* (i.e. point *c*), the *LMC* intersects the *LRAC* curve. To the right of point *c*, the *LMC* lies above the *LRAC* curve.

▨ Developments in cost theory

Here we consider a number of developments in cost theory, including some explanations as to why 'real life' cost curves might depart from the smooth, continuous and often U-shaped curves frequently depicted in conventional theory.

Flexibility   The idea here is that a firm may be able to design a plant that allows changes in output over a *specified range* in such a way that average variable cost (*AVC*) is constant. In other words, since entrepreneurs are uncertain as to the precise output they may wish to produce, they bring an element of flexibility into their decision making by building *reserve capacity* into the production process. In Fig. 4.25(b) the firm is shown as being able to

Fig. 4.25 Reserve capacity and cost.

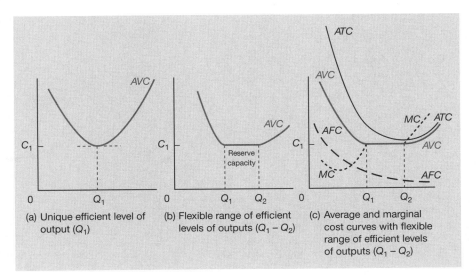

(a) Unique efficient level of output (Q_1)

(b) Flexible range of efficient levels of outputs ($Q_1 - Q_2$)

(c) Average and marginal cost curves with flexible range of efficient levels of outputs ($Q_1 - Q_2$)

vary its output between Q_1 and Q_2 at a constant AVC (namely C_1). This is unlike the more conventional assumption of Fig. 4.25(a), whereby the firm has designed its plant in such a way that Q_1 *alone* is the efficient output at which AVC is a minimum at C_1.

Figure 4.25(c) considers the implications of this idea of reserve capacity for cost. Over the range of reserve capacity $Q_1 - Q_2$, with constant AVC, MC (which is entirely variable cost) must equal AVC. *Below* Q_1, AVC is falling, so $MC < AVC$; *above* Q_2, AVC is rising, so $MC > AVC$.

We clearly have a linear segment for both AVC and MC over the reserve capacity range. ATC becomes progressively closer to AVC as AFC approaches (though never reaches) zero. MC cuts ATC at its minimal point as previously noted (p. 152).

Load factors

Even in situations where ATC curves *are* U-shaped, firms may not always operate at *full capacity*, i.e. at that level of output for which ATC is a minimum. It has been suggested that, in practice, firms often operate at around two thirds or three quarters of full capacity. The term **load factor** reflects the ratio of average actual use to full capacity use.

Assuming the typical load factor of each plant is some two thirds of its full capacity, we then derive an $LRAC$ curve of the type shown in Fig. 4.26(a). On the assumption of a range of alternative plant sizes, the $LRAC$ curve is now a locus of points some two thirds the way along each $SRAC$ curve. The $LRAC$ curve is no longer the envelope curve tangential to a family of $SRAC$ curves.

Further, in the absence of diseconomies of scale, here when plants reach some optimal size $LRAC$ levels out rather than rises. Of course such levelling out could arguably occur whatever the size of the load factor, should constant returns prevail beyond the *minimum efficient size*: i.e. beyond Q_1 with a load factor of two thirds (Fig. 4.26(a)) and beyond Q_2 with a load factor of 1 (Fig. 4.26(b)). We consider the empirical basis for such an L-shaped cost curve later in the chapter (pp. 186–9).

Engineering production functions and cost curves

This approach to deriving cost curves makes use of the fact that only a limited number of production processes are technically efficient. As we have already seen in Fig. 4.16(d), the input–output isoquant may more accurately reflect real-world production

Fig. 4.26 L-shaped LRAC curves.

Note: In Fig. 4.26(b), although each individual firm/plant may operate to full capacity in the short run (load factor = 1), the LRAC is tangent below the full capacity levels of each SRAC, except where constant returns set in (i.e. Q > Q₂).

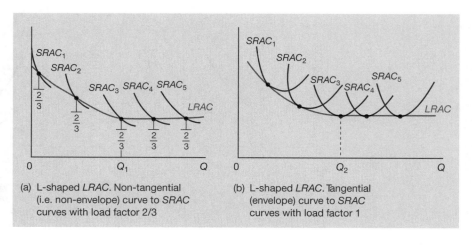

(a) L-shaped *LRAC*. Non-tangential (i.e. non-envelope) curve to *SRAC* curves with load factor 2/3

(b) L-shaped *LRAC*. Tangential (envelope) curve to *SRAC* curves with load factor 1

possibilities than the smooth, convex to the origin, isoquant with its assumption of an unlimited number of technically efficient production processes. The input–output isoquant is kinked, indicating that substitution between factors is limited, occurring only at the kink points on process rays from the origin. The straight-line segments of the input–output isoquant between adjacent production rays indicate the use of a *combination* of the processes represented by these rays.

For example, in Fig. 4.27(a), $1X$ can be produced by using capital/labour in the ratio K_1/L_1. However, this represents a situation in which production is undertaken using a *combination* of processes P_1 and P_2. We can find that combination by drawing parallel lines from P_1 and P_2 respectively to any point on the $1X$ isoquant, suggesting the use of 0A of process P_1 and 0B of process P_2 corresponding to point e (note that this methodology has much in common with the characteristics approach of consumer theory presented in Chapter 2, p. 73).

Of course, as we have already noted, we are interested in economic efficiency as well as technical efficiency: in other words, in selecting the least-cost method of producing any given level of output. We have seen (p. 158) that this involves a tangency between isoquant and an isocost line nearest to the origin. If we assume that the factor price ratio is w/r, then in Fig. 4.27(b) $1X$ will initially be produced at cost C_1. Here the tangency occurs at the kink point a, with $1X$ produced *entirely* via production process P_1 rather than by a combination of the two processes.

However, suppose now that some fixed amount of capital, $\bar{K}$, is available to the firm. Clearly producing $1X$ at a implies *unused capital* of av. If the firm seeks to fully utilise all its resources, then it can produce $2X$ at point e' using $\bar{K}/L_2$ of factor input. It would now use a *combination* of processes P_1 and P_2, namely 0A' and 0B' respectively (found, as before, by drawing parallel lines to P_1 and P_2 from e'). Although strictly speaking there is no single process that can yield $2X$ by the factor input ratio $\bar{K}/L_2$, by *combining* the two processes P_1 and P_2 at the levels specified (0A':0B') we can *indirectly* substitute between capital and labour at intermediate points along the straight-line segments of input–output isoquants. In other words *process substitution* indirectly permits factor substitution along such straight-line segments of isoquants.

Fig. 4.27 Engineering production function approach to costs.

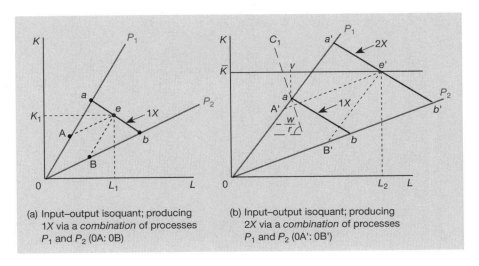

(a) Input–output isoquant; producing
$1X$ via a *combination* of processes
P_1 and P_2 (0A: 0B)

(b) Input–output isoquant; producing
$2X$ via a *combination* of processes
P_1 and P_2 (0A': 0B')

Note that we could *not* produce 2*X* at *a'* by using process P_1 alone (insufficient capital). However, technically we could produce 2*X* at *b'* by using process P_2 alone, although at the prevailing factor price ratio, *w/r*, this would represent an isocost line further from the origin than at *e'* and would therefore be an *economically inefficient* solution.

Engineering costs

Retaining our assumption of some fixed availability of at least one factor of production (e.g. $\bar{K}$ in Fig. 4.27), we can derive the total, average and marginal cost curves related to the engineering production function approach.

In Fig. 4.28(b) we see that the *TC* curve is segmented. The slope of each linear segment is constant, with the ends of each of these segments corresponding to the output level at which one process is replaced entirely by another. For example, in Fig. 4.28(a) it costs C_1 to produce 1*X*, using entirely process P_1 at factor price ratio *w/r*; it costs C_3 to produce 3*X* using entirely process P_2 at that same factor price ratio. These costs and

Fig. 4.28 **Deriving cost curves via the engineering approach.**

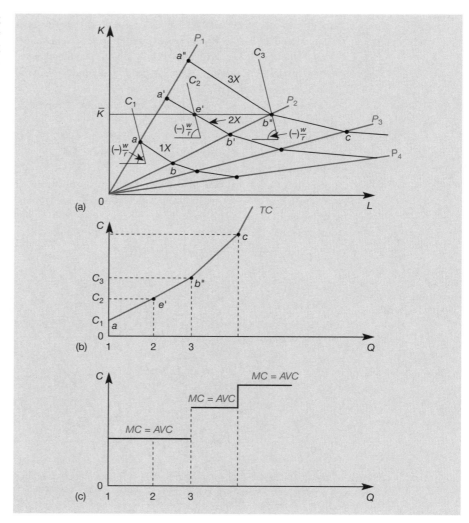

output combinations are reflected as *end points* of the linear segment *ab''* of the *TC* curve in Fig. 4.28(b). *Intermediate points* along the linear segments of the total cost curve reflect the cost of producing higher levels of output using *combinations* of the adjacent production processes. Thus it costs C_2 to produce $2X$ using $0A'$ of process P_1 and $0B'$ of process P_2 (see Fig. 4.27(b), p. 177).

The rise in total cost along any one of these linear (*TC*) segments reflects the *indirect* substitution of labour for capital by varying the combinations of processes at a constant factor price ratio. This gives a constant rate of increase of *TC* along each segment (i.e. *MC* = *AVC*). Note that for a TC curve reflecting *more than two* production processes, each successive linear segment will be steeper than the previous segment. In terms of Fig. 4.28(a) this reflects the fact that it becomes progressively more difficult to substitute labour for capital in producing any given output as we move from processes P_1 to P_4. At a given factor price ratio, total cost therefore rises at a progressively higher (though constant) rate between output levels corresponding to switch-points from one production process to another. It follows that along segment *a–b''* in Fig. 4.28(b), *MC* = *AVC*; along segment *b''–c* in Fig. 4.28(b), *MC* = *AVC* but at *a higher level*. This gives rise to the stepped *MC* and *AVC* curves shown in Fig. 4.28(c).

Survivor technique

G. J. Stigler suggested that the *LRAC* curve can be inferred by observation of the changing *market share* of firms (enterprises) or plants of a given size in a particular industrial sector. The underlying assumption here is that firms or plants with below-average costs within a given industrial sector will survive over time and indeed prosper, thereby increasing their market share. On the other hand firms or plants with above-average costs for that industrial sector will either disappear or experience a falling market share.

To apply this technique, firms or plants in an industrial sector must be *grouped* by size – perhaps in terms of number of employees or share of total sector output. The market share of each size group is then monitored over time. Firm or plant sizes that result in *increased* market share over time are inferred to have *lower average costs*; those firms or plant sizes that result in *decreased* market share over time are inferred to have *higher average costs*. Stigler's study of the US steel industry inferred an *LRAC* curve that was negatively sloped over initial increases in size, then approximately horizontal for a broad range of output before sloping upwards at still higher output levels.

There are, however, a number of problems in inferring average costs via this technique. In particular there may be factors *other than size* that have influenced the firms' success in terms of market share: for example, favourable locational advantages, monopoly or exclusivity access to factor inputs or new technological developments. Further, as we see in Chapter 5, firms may pursue entirely different objectives, which may cause them to grow (or decline) for reasons unrelated to cost and profit. For these and related reasons, the survivor technique can only be regarded as at best a first approximation in inferring cost from the size distribution of firms or plants through time.

Economies of scope

Economies of scale refer to changes in (long run) average cost as a result of proportionate changes in *all* factors of production. For example, doubling inputs of land, labour and capital is a change in the *scale* of production. However, **economies of scope** refer to changes in average costs as a result of changes in the *mix* of production between two or more products.

The suggestion here is that there may be benefits from the *joint production* of two or more products. These may occur for *unrelated* products, as in the joint use of inputs such as management, administration, marketing production or storage facilities yielding cost savings for all the products produced. Of course such joint benefits may also accrue to *related* products, as with those for which there is an element of complementarity in production, such as beef and hide, cars and trucks, teaching and research. Even *by-products* may play a role in generating economies of scope, as with heat from energy production being used in horticulture, etc.

The *production possibility frontier* can be used to illustrate the idea of economies of scope. The frontier O_1 in Fig. 4.29 shows the various combinations of two products, X and Y, obtained from the allocation of some given quantity of factor inputs.

- If the production frontier was the *straight* dashed line this would indicate an *absence* of economies of scope. For example, instead of a single large company producing *both* products, the same resources could be allocated by two smaller companies, each producing a *single* product with no loss of efficiency.
- If the production function was the *concave* (to the origin) continuous line, this would indicate the *presence* of economies of scope. Here a single large company benefits from using the given factor inputs jointly on both products. As a result $0X_1/0Y_2$ is a feasible production outcome, as compared with only $0X_1/0Y_1$ if two smaller companies each specialise in producing a single product, with therefore no opportunities of benefiting from any economies of scope.

Economies of scale can exist independently of the presence or absence of scope economies, and of course vice versa. For example there would be increasing returns to scale if, say, a 50% increase in all resources (O_2) led to more than a 50% increase in output, whether economies of scope were absent (linear production frontier) or present (concave production frontier). It follows that all combinations of scale/scope are possible: economies of scale/but no economies of scope; diseconomies of scale/but economies of scope; and so on.

The extent to which economies of scope exist can be inferred from *cost* as well as from the production frontier. If the single, larger firm can produce more of both products than two smaller specialised firms (using the same overall resources), then costs will

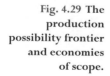

Fig. 4.29 The production possibility frontier and economies of scope.

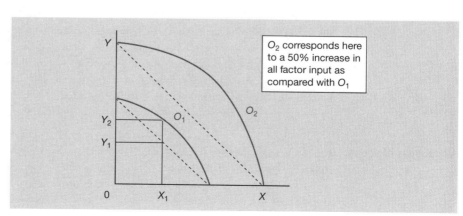

be lower for the larger firm. To measure the *extent* (S) of such economies of scope we can estimate the *percentage cost reduction* via joint production, as follows:

$$S = \frac{C(Q_1) + C(Q_2) - C(Q_1, Q_2)}{C(Q_1, Q_2)}$$

where $C(Q_1)$ represents the cost of producing output Q_1 singly, $C(Q_2)$ the cost of producing output Q_2 singly, and $C(Q_1, Q_2)$ the cost of producing both outputs jointly. Where economies of scope exist, the joint cost is smaller than the sum of the individual costs, so that S is *positive*: the larger the positive value of S, the greater the economies of scope. Of course a *zero* value for S would indicate the absence of economies of scope, while a *negative* value would indicate diseconomies of scope. In this latter case, multi-product output would be less efficient than single-product output.

Sunk costs

A **sunk cost** is a cost of acquiring an asset, whether tangible (e.g. plant) or intangible (e.g. reputation), which *cannot* be recouped by selling that asset or redeploying it to some other market segment. This definition cuts across our earlier breakdown of costs into fixed (indirect) and variable (direct). For example a firm with large fixed costs (such as the airline industry) may incur very few sunk costs in a situation where, say, a thriving second-hand market for aeroplanes exists. Much of any huge initial expenditure on aeroplanes may then be potentially recoverable, thereby incurring only small sunk costs.

The concept of sunk costs is one to which we return in later chapters involving competitive practices. For example the existence of *negligible* sunk costs will encourage entry into an industry, whereas substantial sunk costs may discourage entry into an industry by making the prospect of subsequent exit a more costly outcome.

Experience or learning curves

While economists often explain cost reductions in terms of the familiar economies of scale concept, which we discussed earlier in the chapter, managerial explanations of cost reductions have tended to stress cost savings that result from the **experience curve** (sometimes called the learning curve, improvement curve or progress cost curve). The importance of learning from experience was identified as early as the 1930s, when studies suggested that a doubling of the cumulative production of airframes was accompanied by a 20% reduction in unit labour costs (Griffiths 1994). Initially, such decreases in costs were attributed to two main factors: first, the ability of workers to *improve their performance* of a particular task the more times they repeated it; second, the discovery by workers of *more effective methods* of undertaking such tasks as time passed and labour experience grew.

By the 1960s it began to be better appreciated that a range of technical and non-technical factors underlay the observed linkage between cost and cumulative output:

- learning associated with repetition of labour tasks;
- cost savings due to more appropriate product design;
- gains from solving small problems in production technology as they occurred on the shopfloor (e.g. via team working);

- incremental improvements in the whole operating process – e.g. better use of materials, more efficient use of inventories, more effective distribution systems, better utilisation of research and development systems;
- intergenerational learning or 'spillover' as experience of one generation of technology or product is carried forward to inform the implementation of succeeding generations;
- Improved managerial know-how in organising and operating the business.

In other words the cost reductions obtained from *cumulative* production over time stemmed from both labour and non-labour aspects of production. The term 'experience curve' was then used to cover all the above types of source of cost reductions.

Although both economies of scale and the experience curve attempt to explain the relationship between cost and output, there are important differences between the two concepts. Economies of scale refer to the various factors resulting in a decline in a firm's average cost when it is able to vary *all* factor inputs. For example, when a firm has adjusted all its factor inputs in order to build the optimum plant size, it might find itself in the situation denoted by $SRAC_3$ in Fig. 4.24 (p. 174). Once this optimum plant size has been achieved, the implication is that output $0Q_3$ is produced in each and every time period. Of course as the plant produces the same output ($0Q_3$) repetitively, period after period, its total production experience tends to *accumulate* so that costs may fall still further because of the various learning effects already identified. In other words, the experience or learning effect can be viewed as resulting in a further downward shift of the whole $SRAC_3$ curve in Fig. 4.24.

Definitions of experience curves   An experience curve can be seen in Fig. 4.30(a). Costs per unit are measured on the vertical axis and cumulative output on the horizontal axis. The particular curve shown in Fig. 4.30(a) suggests that for every doubling of cumulative output, costs per unit fall at a constant rate of 80% of their previous level. For example, the first unit cost is £1,000, the second £800, the fourth £640, the eighth £512, the sixteenth £409.60 and so on. Put another way, production costs have declined by 20% for each doubling of cumulative output.

If costs per unit decreased by 30% as cumulative output doubled, then this would be referred to as a 70% experience curve and would be located below the original

Fig. 4.30 **Experience or learning curve: declining average costs as a function of cumulative output.**

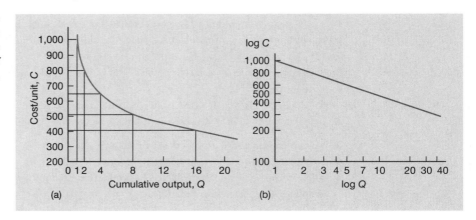

curve discussed above. To calculate the percentage of learning as output doubles we can use the equation

$$L = \frac{C_2}{C_1} \times 100\%$$

where C_1 is the cost of producing the Q_1th unit of output and C_2 is the cost of producing the Q_2th unit of output (where $Q_2 = 2Q_1$). For example, if the cost of producing the thousandth unit (C_1) is £20 and the cost of producing the two thousandth unit (C_2) is £14, then applying the above formula we get $14/20 \times 100\%$, which gives a 70% experience curve.

The experience curve can also be defined in a more precise way by using simple equations. For example, the relationship shown in Fig. 4.30(a) is drawn using the usual *arithmetic scale* on both axes. The experience curve slopes downwards to the right, showing that as cumulative output increases, costs per unit fall. This type of curve can be expressed algebraically as follows:

$$C = aQ^b \tag{1}$$

where C is the average input costs of the Qth unit of output, a is the average cost of the first unit, Q represents the cumulative level of output, and b is the rate of reduction in input costs per unit of output (usually a negative number since costs fall as output increases).

The experience curve equation can also be shown in *logarithmic form* in Fig. 4.30(b) using exactly the same statistics as in Fig. 4.30(a). To do this we merely take logs of the above equation, which gives

$$\log C = \log a + b \log Q \tag{2}$$

Here, both axes are measured in log form. This means that Fig. 4.30(b) shows the *rate of change* of costs as output accumulates. If, as is the case in Fig. 4.30(a), costs fall at a constant rate as output doubles, then the log form of this curve will be a straight line, as shown in Fig. 4.30(b). This shows more clearly than Fig. 4.30(a) that the rate of decrease of costs as cumulative output increases is constant, and that the slope of the line is b.

The shape of actual experience curves may vary for many reasons. For example, M. B. Lieberman (1994), in a study of the chemical industry, found the slopes of experience curves for more capital – intensive and R&D-intensive companies to be *steeper* than those for companies lacking these characteristics. The suggestion here is that as cumulative output rose for such companies, the various learning experiences involving the more productive use of capital and R & D were considerable.

The shape of such experience curves can also be linked to the age of the product. For example, each product goes through its own life cycle, i.e. youth, maturity, old age. In terms of the product life cycle (see p. 219), as a product becomes more mature, the major learning opportunities will already have been identified and exploited.

Applications and evidence

■ The production frontier, technical efficiency: European railways

As we have seen (p. 144), **technical efficiency** underlies the derivation of isoquants and production frontiers. A technically efficient allocation has been taken to mean one on the production function (frontier) itself, such as N or P on the frontier 0F in Fig. 4.31. For any given *input* as much output is being produced as is technically feasible; or for any given *output* the minimum input requirements are being used. Here we consider the empirical application of technical efficiency to a variety of European service industries following the work of Pestieau (1993). It will be useful, at the outset, to consider the *measures* available as regards technical efficiency. From Fig. 4.31(a) we could use one of two measures:

- **Input measure of efficiency**. This refers to the *proportion of the actual input* that would be sufficient to produce a given output if the quantity of input were the minimal (technically efficient) one. In Fig. 4.31(a), for an allocation M, the ratio 0A:0B can be used as an input-efficiency measure. This ratio would be 1 if the allocation M was technically efficient (as for allocations N or P): the greater the divergence from 1, the more technically *inefficient* the allocation. This input measure of technical efficiency uses the respective distances along the input axis.
- **Output measure of efficiency**. This refers to the *proportion of the potential output* that is actually achieved by a given level of input. In Fig. 4.31(a) for the allocation M, the ratio 0C:0D can be used as an output-efficiency measure. This ratio would be 1 if the allocation M was technically efficient (as for allocations N or P): the greater the divergence from 1, the more technically *inefficient* the allocation. This output measure of technical efficiency uses the respective distances along the *output axis*.

Fig. 4.31

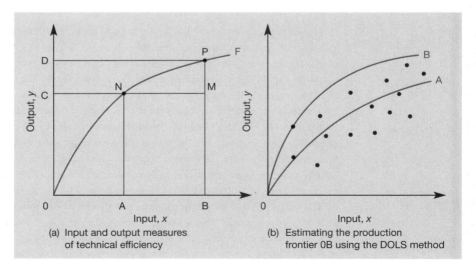

(a) Input and output measures of technical efficiency

(b) Estimating the production frontier 0B using the DOLS method

Of course Fig. 4.31(a) reflects a single input–output relationship. The principles still apply for *multiple* input–output relationships, except that both input and output measures of efficiency would be made radially, along rays (in input or output space respectively) extending from the origin rather than along horizontal or vertical axes.

In the following empirical results the output measure of efficiency is used. Further, the approach to *estimating the production frontier* is indicated in Fig. 4.31(b). This approach is often referred to as displaced ordinary least squares (DOLS). It involves two stages. First, input–output data are used to derive the best-fitting (least squares) line, A in Fig. 4.31(b). Second, some functional form is assumed whereby the least-squares line is moved outwards until it acts as an envelope to the data set: i.e. line B in Fig. 4.31(b). In practice the Cobb–Douglas function (see p. 166) was the functional form assumed in the empirical work. The envelope uses the data set to predict, for any given input, the maximum output technically feasible: i.e. it is our estimated *production frontier*.

Table 4.5 presents efficiency measures using this procedure for European railways over the time period 1962–88. The data set comes from International Railway Statistics published yearly by the UIC (International Union of Railways). It covers the period 1961–88 and includes 18 countries, all European. For each year and each company, the following input–output variables are available: two outputs, y_1 (gross hauled tkm by

Table 4.5 Efficiency measures of European railways (1962–88).

| Railway | Country | Average output (tkm) | | Parametric frontier (DOLS) | |
		Passenger (10^6)	Freight (10^6)	Efficiency 1986–88	Efficiency change 1962–88
BLS	Switzerland	4.9	1.1	0.71	0.35
BR	United Kingdom	343.6	104.2	0.74	0.52
CFF	Switzerland	64.1	28.0	0.73	−0.07
CFL	Luxemburg	2.9	1.5	0.56	−0.34
CH	Greece	12.8	3.2	0.56	−0.16
CIE	Ireland	7.6	4.3	0.73	0.37
CP	Portugal	24.5	6.2	0.69	0.30
DB	Germany	384.7	196.3	0.61	−0.08
DSB	Denmark	35.7	8.3	0.52	−0.34
FS	Italy	210.3	60.3	0.63	−0.03
NS	Netherlands	82.6	15.3	0.79	−0.06
NSB	Norway	22.9	10.2	0.51	0.01
OBB	Austria	56.4	33.6	0.59	−0.13
RENFE	Spain	85.0	44.3	0.64	0.81
SJ	Sweden	64.1	40.7	0.66	0.23
SNCB	Belgium	64.4	21.9	0.62	−0.15
SNCF	France	261.3	204.1	0.73	−0.06
TCDD	Turkey	20.7	18.2	0.76	−0.00
VR	Finland	25.2	18.4	0.65	−0.22

Source: Adapted from International Railway Statistics, UIC.

freight trains) and y_2 (gross hauled tkm by passenger trains); four inputs, x_1 (engines + railcars), x_2 (labour force), x_3 (lines not electrified), and x_4 (lines electrified).

Table 4.5 presents the average value of both outputs, passenger and freight, over the time period in question to given an idea of differences in scale between countries. The *efficiency output measure* is then calculated as an average for the three most recent years (1986–88) in the data set. This efficiency index ranges from 0.79 for the Netherlands, the most efficient, to 0.51 for Norway, the least efficient over the years 1986–88 according to this study.

The column 'Efficiency change' compares the changes in efficiency level for the respective countries over the entire period. A number of patterns can be seen over time. The Netherlands and Norway have been *consistently* first and last respectively, as indicated by little change in their efficiency levels over the period. Spain, the UK and Switzerland have made significant improvements in efficiency levels over the time period, whereas Denmark, Luxemburg and Finland have experienced considerable decline in efficiency levels.

Clearly such results can only be signposts, but they are useful in providing comparative data on technical efficiency across countries, and indicate areas for further analysis: for example, investigations into reasons for apparent increases and decreases in technical efficiency over time.

Economies of scale, scope etc: European and US manufacturing industry

An important summary of recent studies concerning economies of scale in the UK, USA and Germany was carried out in 1987 (Pratten 1987). The study covers various branches of manufacturing industry, and provides information about the **minimum efficient technical scale** (METS), cost gradients, and the nature of the various types of economies of scale (EOS) in general (see p. 169). Table 4.6 lists various branches of industry ranked by the importance of the economies of scale observed in that industry.

METS refers to the level of output at which scale economies are exhausted: i.e. the long-run average cost curve is at a minimum. Strictly speaking METS represents the *production unit* (plant or establishment) that has reached an optimal size in terms of reaping all the *technical* economies available (p. 169). Of course a range of *non-technical* economies (p. 172) may be available at the level of the *industrial unit* (firm or enterprise).

The **cost gradient** represents the *increase* in unit output costs as a result of the production unit (or institutional unit) being only a specified percentage of the optimum size. Here the information relates to the percentage increase in unit output costs where the production unit is only half the METS for that branch of manufacturing industry. Because these industry branches involve a considerable degree of *aggregation* over widely differing types of operation, there is a substantial *range* in the estimates of the cost gradient at half METS. For instance in Branch 36, 'Other means of transport', being 50% smaller than the optimum METS raises costs by 8% for *shipbuilding* but by as much as 20% for *aircraft*. A still finer level of disaggregation of branches of manufacturing industry will be needed to indicate the reasons for the ranges observed (see Pratten 1987).

Branches of manufacturing industry ranked by size of economies of scale.

Table 4.6 **Minimum efficient technical scale (METS), cost gradients, and other economies of scale (EOS).**

NACE code	Branch	Cost gradient at half METS (%)	Remarks
35	Motor vehicles	6–9	Very substantial EOS in production and in development costs.
36	Other means of transport	8–20	Variable EOS: small for cycles and shipbuilding (although economies are possible through series production level), very substantial in aircraft (development costs).
25	Chemical industry	2.5–15	Substantial EOS in production processes. In some segments of the industry (pharmaceutical products), R&D is an important source of EOS.
26	Man-made fibres	5–10	Substantial EOS in general.
22	Metals	>6	Substantial EOS in general for production processes. Also possible in production and series production.
33	Office machinery	3–6	Substantial EOS at product level.
32	Mechanical engineering	3–10	Limited EOS at firm level but substantial for production.
34	Electrical engineering	5–15	Substantial EOS at product level and for development costs.
37	Instrument engineering	5–15	Substantial EOS at product level, via development costs.
47	Paper, printing and publishing	8–36	Substantial EOS in papermills and, in particular, printing (books).
24	Non-metallic mineral products	>6	Substantial EOS in cement and flat glass production processes. In other branches, optimum plant size is small compared with the optimum size for the industry.
31	Metal articles	5–10 (castings)	EOS are lower at plant level but possible at production and series production level.
48	Rubber and plastics	3–6	Moderate EOS in tyre manufacture. Small EOS in factories making rubber and moulded plastic articles but potential for EOS at product and series production level.
41–42	Drink and tobacco	1–6	Moderate EOS in breweries. Small EOS in cigarette factories. In marketing, EOS are considerable.
41–42	Food	3.5–21	Principal source of EOS is the individual plant. EOS at marketing and distribution level.
49	Other manufacturing	n.a.	Plant size is small in these branches. Possible EOS from specialization and the length of production runs.
43	Textile industry	10 (carpets)	EOS are more limited than in the other sectors, but possible economies from specialization and the length of production runs.
46	Timber and wood	n.a.	No EOS for plants in these sectors. Possible EOS from specialization and longer production runs.
45	Footwear and clothing	1 (footwear)	Small EOS at plant level but possible EOS from specialization and longer production runs.
44	Leather and leather goods	n.a.	Small EOS.

Source: European Economy (1988)

Even so we can see some broad trends and patterns from Table 4.6. Economies of scale are clearly larger in transport equipment, chemicals, machinery and instrument manufacture (office machines, electrical equipment, etc.), and in paper and printing. These sectors account for some 55% of industrial production, and 65% of industrial employment in the European Union. They are sectors in which demand has been growing strongly, and which have a high technological content. By contrast, economies of scale are clearly smaller in food, drink and tobacco, textiles, clothing, leather goods and timber. These sectors have been characterised by relatively stagnant demand and low technological content of products.

The final column of Table 4.6 provides a guide to the nature of the general economies of scale available in that branch of manufacturing industry, including both technical and non-technical economies.

It was argued that one of the benefits of the Single European Market would be the creation of a market sufficiently large for companies to benefit from all the potential economies of scale. Clearly any sector where one or both of the following conditions applied would be a particular beneficiary of an extended market:

- the METS was already high in relation to the national market (implying the need for a relatively large market to benefit from cost reductions);
- the cost gradient at half METS was 10% or more (implying significant technical economies at the higher levels of output from an extended market).

The industrial product categories that fulfilled the latter of these two criteria are outlined in Table 4.7, together with data for METS as a percentage of production in the UK and the EU prior to the creation of the Single Market. Here we see that seven product

Products for which the cost slope at (METS) is greater than or equal to 10%

Table 4.7 METS as a percentage of production in UK and EU markets and cost gradients at half METS.

NACE code	Product	METS as % of production UK	METS as % of production EC	Cost gradient at half METS
473	Books	n.a.	n.a.	20–36
241	Bricks	1	0.2	25
251	Dyes	>100	n.a.	17–22
364	Aircraft	>100	n.a.	20
251	Titanium oxide	63	50	8–16
242	Cement	10	1	6–16
251	Synthetic rubber	24	3.5	15
342	Electric motors	60	6	15
471	Kraft paper	11	1.4	13
251	Petrochemicals	23	3	12
26	Nylon	4	1	12
311	Cylinder block castings	3	0.3	10
311	Small cast-iron castings	0.7	0.1	10
438	Carpets	0.3	0.04	10
328	Diesel engines	>100	n.a.	10

Source: European Economy (1988)

categories satisfied *both* criteria: aircraft, chemicals (dyestuffs, titanium oxide, synthetic rubber, petrochemicals), electric motors and possibly paper and printing. If the threshold for the cost gradient was lowered to 5%, then cars and trucks, iron and steel, non-ferrous metals, office machinery, telecommunications equipment and other product categories would also be included.

As well as the important *technical* aspects of economies of scale noted, there has been renewed focus on the potential importance of *non-technical* economies available via an integrated European market. These include sales promotion, financial, marketing, and R & D. For example, cost savings on advertising expenditure might result from the introduction of Community trade marks, which would spread the cost of advertising over a wider audience. Similar benefits were expected as regards development costs (market research for new products, preparation of new catalogues, etc.) since such costs could now be spread over a larger audience, and since technical barriers were to be abolished.

The car industry and scale economies

Having considered the nature and size of scale economies across a range of manufacturing sectors, it may be useful at this point to consider in some detail a particular sector, namely the European car industry. Rhys (1999) has provided many useful insights into and empirical data on the European car industry.

From Table 4.8 it can be seen that the minimum efficient size (MES) in the European car industry is around 2 million units per year. The index of unit average costs suggests that the cost curve is L-shaped, with few additional economies to be gained if production rises above 2 million units per year. The cost gradient was found to be 4% at half MES and 8% at one quarter MES.

Table 4.8 **MES and implied cost gradients in the European car industry.**

Output per year	Index of unit average costs (cars)
100,000	100
250,000	83
500,000	74
1,000,000	70
2,000,000	66

Source: Rhys (1999)

From a theoretical standpoint we have noted that economies of scale can be divided into technical and non-technical economies. As regards **technical economies**, Rhys notes that we must often seek data at as disaggregated a level as is possible. For example, since the manufacture of vehicles involves a number of distinct operations, each of the operations will also have its own optimum scale. This feature is indicated in Table 4.9.

It can be seen from Table 4.9 that the optimum level of output for the pressing of body panels and the casting of engine blocks is much larger than for paint shop and final assembly operations. It follows that in order to achieve output levels securing minimum average costs for pressing body panels and casting engine blocks, firms must use the

Table 4.9 Optimum
scale in various car-
making activities.

	Output per year (volume)
Casting of engine block	1,000,000
Casting of various other parts	100,000–750,000
Power train (engine, transmission, etc.) machining and assembly	600,000
Pressing of various panels	1–2,000,000
Paint shop	250,000
Final assembly	250,000

Source: Adapted from Rhys (1999)

same basic panels or engines over a range of different models. Only after such standardization might they differentiate one model from another by means of different accessories, design features, etc. Another approach is for firms to collaborate and cooperate so that different manufacturers use the same basic components. For example, Peugeot and Fiat use the same body panels in their ranges of people carriers and vans. Other similar agreements between companies to cooperate on the procurement of parts (e.g. Toyota and Nissan) mean that the 'combined' companies would buy basic parts from a common supplier, who would then be able to produce in sufficient volume to benefit from all available economies of scale, thus lowering the cost of these parts to all the companies in the agreement.

As well as the technical economies already noted, there are a variety of **non-technical** economies available in car production, some of which are noted in Table 4.10. Many of these are available at the institutional level (firm or enterprise) rather than the production level (plant or establishment).

It can be seen that the optimum number of cars needed to be produced to benefit fully from economies of scale involving research and development is (at 5 million units per year) very much beyond the optimum level for other technical and non-technical activities. This provides a clue as to why companies such as Renault, Honda, Fiat, Rover and others are actively engaged in cost sharing via joint ventures on design and other aspects of research and development.

Table 4.10 Non-technical economies of car production.

	Optimum output per year (cars)
Advertising	1,000,000
Sales	2,000,000
Risks	1,800,000
Finance	2,500,000
Research and development	5,000,000

Source: Adapted from Rhys (1999)

Economies of
scope in industry

Economies of scope (see p. 179) refer to cost benefits from changing the *mix* of production, and can occur in two main situations:

- Where a number of related commodities or services are produced using *common processing facilities*, thereby decreasing overall costs. For example, large car companies such as Ford and Toyota often produce many different models using common assembly and production equipment. Again Toshiba, the Japanese multinational company, also produces water, gas and electric meters in its instruments division using common facilities and similar raw materials. Cost savings arise because overhead costs are spread over larger output as plant is used more effectively (Griffiths 1994).
- Where the cost of one output falls when the output of another increases, i.e. where *cost complementarity* occurs. The pharmaceutical industry provides good examples of such benefits. As early as the late nineteenth century, German companies such as Bayer, Hoechst and BASF were able to produce hundreds of dyes as well as many pharmaceuticals from the same raw materials and the same set of chemical compounds (Chandler 1990). This was often due to the fact that where chemical X was produced as a by-product of another chemical Y, then an increase in the production of Y decreased the marginal cost of producing X. This phenomenon has also been noted in the petrol-refining industry.

Although the importance of economies of scope is clear, empirical evidence for the phenomenon is sparse since it is difficult to specify the nature of the cost function when it is dependent on multiple output and input configurations. Also it is sometimes difficult to disentangle economies of scale and scope when both processes are simultaneously at work in an industry. We can, however, attempt to provide guidelines as to which industries are most likely to benefit from economies of scope, as in Table 4.11, which refers to the importance of economies of scope in different European industries. The measurement used here for economies of scope is the increase in average costs that results when only half the number of models is produced by companies. In other words, if the number of models decreases, then costs rise because the opportunities to benefit from running many models through common facilities are reduced.

Table 4.11
**Economies of scope
in EU manufacturing.**

Type of activity	Economies of scope[a]
Motor vehicles	8
Pharmaceutical products	5
Electrical machinery	5
Office machinery	5
Domestic-type appliances	5
Man-made fibres	3
Capets	3
Machine tools	1
Cement, lime and plaster	0

[a]Percentage increase in average costs at half the number of models
Source: *European Economy* (1988)

The table indicates a ranking (in descending order) of sectors most likely to benefit from economies of scope. The first five sectors listed include those most likely to use common raw materials or parts and common production facilities, or to enjoy cost complementarity. However, the more specialised the industry, e.g. machine tools, the more difficult it is to produce many models or to use the same process to produce other specialist goods.

Economies of scope and the publications sector

One of the few classical studies that has attempted to measure the importance of economies of scope was carried out for the US publications industry (Baumol and Braunstein 1977). Their study used the cost and output data of a sample of non-profit-making journal publishers (i.e. university presses and professional societies). Each publisher produced a number of different scientific journals, ranging between one and 26 such journals. The result of their regression analysis produced a log-form equation as follows:

$$\log TC = -0.735 + 0.171 D_s + 0.588 \log C + 0.793 \log P - 0.062 \log J$$

where TC is the total cost per journal, C the circulation, P the number of pages per journal, and J the number of different journals per publisher. D_s is a measure used to isolate scientific from non-scientific journals. From an economies of scale perspective, the equation indicated that the total costs increased more slowly with increases in circulation than with increases in the number of pages. From an 'economies of scope' perspective, costs per journal declined as the number of journals published increased. The study found a number of interesting cost gradients. For example, for the same number of pages, circulation and field of expertise, the cost per journal for a publisher producing 36 different scientific journals was 80% of the cost of a publisher who produced only one scientific journal ($36^{-0.062} = 0.8$). The authors concluded from this analysis that the cost benefits of producing a number of different scientific journals (i.e. a multi-product firm) using common facilities were significant.

Economies of scope and the transport sector

The potential for **economies of scope** can also be found in the transport industry. For example, the deregulation of the aircraft industry in the USA after 1978 resulted in significant changes in the structure of carrier operations. Instead of a large number of individual routes between various cities, the carriers redesigned the route system into a *hub and spoke* system reminiscent of a bicycle wheel. Travel was routed from, say, a city positioned at the end of one 'spoke' through a 'hub' or central airport, then out again to another city at the end of another spoke.

For example, in Fig. 4.32(a) we have five point-to-point direct links from cities A to B, C to D, E to F, G to H and I to J respectively. If these are replaced by 10 services from each of the cities to a hub airport, as in Fig. 4.32(b), then the number of city-pairs that can be served rises sharply from 5 to 55. The total number of city-pairs that can be served is given by the formula $n(n+1)/2$, where n is the number of spokes (cities served) emanating from the hub airport. It follows that if the number of spokes from the hub rises to 50, then the number of city-pairs that can be linked rises to 1,275.

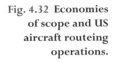

Fig. 4.32 **Economies of scope and US aircraft routeing operations.**

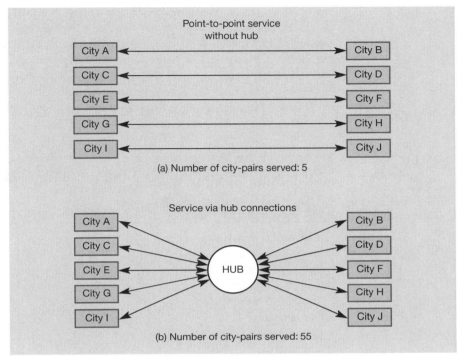

This system has advantages, because all the passengers destined for a city at the end of one spoke will be collected at the hub airport from all the other cities at the end of the other spokes. This means that there will be many more passengers per flight, allowing definite *economies of density*: i.e. larger aircraft can be used, with associated savings in costs. On the marketing side, the hub system also facilitates more departures to a larger number of cities, making the marketing of a more integrated service network a more attractive proposition.

In this way economies of scope are realised. By serving a large number of city-pair markets through the hub, a carrier also provides many different products or combinations of products not previously available. These lead on to further economies as, for instance, airlines are now able to meet travel demands that have *different* characteristics from those previously met. In this case business and vacation travel can use a single network of flights instead of a variety of interconnecting networks of flights. The hub might permit still further 'common carriage' and cost reductions: for example business-oriented routes might become still more cost-effective now that there is a greater chance (with a larger number of spokes) that vacation visitors might also wish to use these business-oriented routes (McGowan and Seabright 1987).

Experience and learning in industry

As noted previously (p. 181), the importance of *learning from experience* originated with studies as early as the 1930s showing that a doubling of the cumulative production of airframes was accompanied by a 20% reduction in unit labour costs. A specific example of the experience curve in such a percentage form involves the Lockheed Corporation, a major US aircraft producer. Lockheed began making the L-1011 Tri Star Airbus in 1970, and their experts estimated that the cumulative average production costs per aircraft would be $15.5 million after producing the 150th plane, but $12.0 million after producing the 300th plane. The experience curve percentage was calculated to be 12.0/15.5 × 100, i.e. 77.4%. They calculated the value of b in the log equation (p. 183) to be 0.369188 and the value of a to be approximately $100 million (Pappas *et al*. 1991).

Table 4.12 outlines a number of experience curve percentage values derived from various studies of industrial sectors since the 1960s.

Table 4.12 Summary of empirical estimates of learning curve percentages in different industrial sectors.

Product	Decrease in costs as output doubles (%)	Learning curve percentage (%)
Electrical components	30	70
Microcomputing	30	70
Ball bearings	27	73
Industrial plastics	25	75
Equipment maintenance	24	76
Life assurance	23	77
Aerospace	20	80
Electricity	20	80
Starters for motor vehicles	15	85
Oil refining	10	90

Source: European Economy (1988)

Three factors seem to influence the learning curve percentage achieved:

- Industrial activities that rely heavily on skilled labour tend to benefit most from learning effects.
- Learning is more pronounced the higher the rate of market growth in the industry.
- Learning percentages are higher in industries where supply and demand are closely interrelated: e.g. where learning brings down costs through increased supply, thereby stimulating demand.

Semiconductors and the learning experience

The semiconductor industry is widely believed to be one in which unit costs fall significantly as production experience (provided by cumulative output) rises. Because semiconductors are produced under exacting standards of precision and cleanliness, it is argued that information gathered from successive production runs can help decrease the number of unusable chips, thereby reducing wastage and cutting average costs. Until recently, the accepted wisdom based upon past surveys was that production costs fall by 28% whenever cumulative output doubles (Baldwin and Krugman 1988). In fact many of the surveys linked cumulative output to price rather than costs, since cost data were difficult to obtain from companies. The implication of this approach is that price–cost margins remain constant over time so that price can be used as a proxy variable for costs.

A more recent analysis of the semiconductor industry between 1974 and 1992 has updated the previous research and given an insight into the 'spill-over' and 'generation' effects of learning (Irwin and Klenow 1994). This research analysed data from a total of 32 firms on the production of seven successive generations of DRAMs (Dynamic Random Access Memory). Figure 4.33(a) plots the average price level over the 18-year period for each generation of DRAM, and Fig. 4.33(b) indicates the production levels of the various generations of DRAM over the same period. Notice that price (a proxy for costs) tends to fall over time as cumulative output increases. Further, each successive DRAM price curve tends to reach a minimum level, which is below the one before. The percentage learning rates for each type of DRAM are indicated in Table 4.13.

Table 4.13 Learning rates for successive generations of DRAM.

	β	$\bar{R}^2$	Observations	Learning rate (%)
4K	−.329(.015)	.91	47	20.4
16K	−.396(.020)	.92	37	24.0
16K−5	−.291(.013)	.95	26	18.3
64K	−.376(.009)	.97	55	22.9
256K	−.332(.015)	.93	40	20.6
1M	−.260(.020)	.86	29	16.5
4M	−.325(.015)	.97	17	20.2
16M	−.251(.014)	.98	6	16.0

Note: standard errors are in parentheses. The learning rate is defined as $1-2^\beta$, i.e. the rate at which costs fall with each doubling of cumulative output.
Source: Irwin and Klenow (1994)

It can be seen that the percentage learning rate associated with each doubling of output varies between 16% and 22.9%, indicating that there are significant benefits from learning through experience in the semiconductor sector, although at a rate smaller than previous studies had suggested.

Using a theoretical model based on Cournot assumptions (p. 333) and stipulating a more complex relationship between price and costs, the study produced two important results:

- Firms learn three times more from an additional unit of their own cumulative production than from an additional unit of another firm's cumulative output. In other words, learning processes *within* firms are more effective than those indirectly encountered outside the firm.
- Intergenerational spillovers are relatively weak. It seems that learning from each previous generation of DRAM was only important as between the 4K and 16K DRAM, and the 256K and 1M DRAM. This observation can perhaps be explained in part by the fact that for other successive generations of DRAM production the industry experienced a relatively rapid emergence of new firms and exit of old ones. Such changes

Fig. 4.33
**Intergenerational
learning effects
and successive
generations of
dynamic random
access memory
(DRAM).**

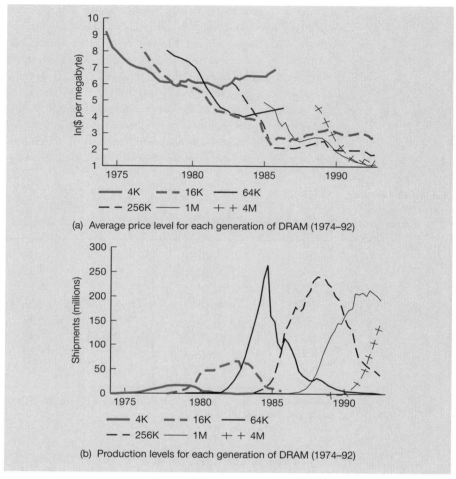

(a) Average price level for each generation of DRAM (1974–92)

(b) Production levels for each generation of DRAM (1974–92)

Source: Irwin and Klenow (1994)

in the industry mean that new firms often start with different ways of approaching semiconductor production, thereby hindering any possibilities of intergenerational spillover in the learning process.

However, a recent study into EPROMs (Erasable Programmable Read Only Memories) by Gruber (1998) found rather stronger evidence of intergenerational spillovers for this type of semiconductor memory chip. This may help to explain the observed ability of Intel to maintain its leadership in product innovation for all generations of EPROMs, with Intel consistently the dominant producer at the beginning of the life cycle of each generation.

Key terms

Average product	Load factor
Average product of labour	Long run
Cost gradient	Marginal product
Diminishing returns	Marginal rate of technical
Diseconomies of scale	substitution
Economies of scale	Minimum efficient scale (*MES*)
Economies of scope	Non-Technical Economies
Expansion/contraction (supply)	Price elasticity of supply
Increase/decrease (supply)	Producer surplus
Increasing returns	Production function
Isocost	Returns to scale
Isoquant	Short run
Law of variable proportions	Sunk cost
Linear isoquant	Technical economies

Full definitions can be found in the 'Glossary of terms' (pp. 699–710)

Review questions

1. A small subcontracting firm, Fabrication Ltd, produces a number of different specialised implements for use in hospitals. Its cost structure for producing a small scalpel used for surgical operations is as shown in Table 4.14.

Table 4.14

Quantity	0	10	20	30	40	50	60	70
Total cost (£)	1,200	1,800	2,000	2,100	2,240	2,600	3,300	4,210

(a) From Table 4.14, derive a full breakdown of the cost structure involved in producing the scalpel. As well as total cost (*TC*), derive all other costs, such as total fixed costs (*TFC*), total variable costs (*TVC*), average fixed costs (*AFC*), average variable costs (*AVC*), average total costs (*ATC*), and marginal costs (*MC*).

(b) Plot, on graph paper, the values of *AVC*, *ATC* and *MC*, and sketch the relevant curves. Since precise valuation of *MC* is difficult, plot the *MC* values you have calculated halfway between the quantity intervals, e.g. at 5, 15, 25, etc.

(c) After completing the tasks in (b), answer the following questions:

  (i) Do the functions shown on the table and graph describe short-run or long-run cost conditions for Fabrication Ltd? Give reasons for your answer.

  (ii) What accounts for the shape of the *ATC* and *AVC* curves, and why is the *ATC* curve positioned at a higher level than the *AVC* curve?

  (iii) How many scalpels should be produced in order for Fabrication Ltd to achieve optimum (least cost) efficiency? If the market price of scalpels was £40 each, what strategy would you recommend to the manufacturer?

2. The production data in Table 4.15 provide estimates of the maximum weekly output of a company producing embroidered shirts, given different combinations of machinery and workers.

Table 4.15

Machinery	Workers					
	10	20	30	40	50	60
60	12	28	32	40	48	50
50	18	30	40	48	52	48
40	18	30	40	48	48	40
30	14	32	36	40	40	30
20	8	24	30	32	30	24
10	2	8	18	24	24	18

If the total cost of producing shirts is £1,200 per week, the wage rate is £20 per week, and the rent of machinery is £60 per week, then complete the following:

(a) From the general equation for the total cost function, derive the expression for the isocost line in the form of a straight line relating K to L.

(b) Write down the actual isocost equation for this company using the total costs and wages/rental information provided above. Draw this information on a graph. If the price of renting machinery halves while the wage rate remains the same, draw the new isocost curve.

(c) Draw the production isoquants at the levels of 18, 30 and 40 shirts per week from the production table given above and connect the points on each isoquant with a smooth curve. Read off from the graph the optimal number of shirts that could be produced when the wage rate is £20 per week and the rental rate of machinery is £60 per week. What would be the optimum weekly output if the rental rate was halved?

(d) What are the values of the marginal rate of technical substitution ($MRTS$) at the optimal points noted in (c)?

(e) Compare the two optimum positions in terms of the machinery and labour used. Does this help us understand the difficulties in using only labour productivity as a measure of efficiency?

3. A subcontractor to a large car manufacturer has been asked to produce 100 units of a specific component every month, and the production function for the process is of the Cobb–Douglas type, where $Q = L^{3/5}K^{1/5}$. The wage of labour is £4 per hour and the rental price of capital goods is £5 per hour.

(a) Express K as a function of L and derive an expression for the marginal rate of technical substitution ($MRTS$) of labour for capital. What type of relationship between capital and labour does this expression describe?

(b) Write down the equation for the total cost function from the wage and rental information given. Using this equation, derive the specific total cost function by substituting for K (which was obtained from (a)) in the total cost function.

Calculate the values of K and L so as to minimise the total costs of producing 100 units of the component.

(c) Suggest another method, using simple calculus and a knowledge of the conditions necessary for optimisation, that could be used to obtain the same result.

4. A medium-sized company producing specialist radar equipment has a production function in the form $Q = 4L^{0.75} K^{0.25}$, where Q is the number of radar units produced per year, L is the number of workers, and K is the value of the capital equipment used, in units of £5,000.

(a) Calculate, to the nearest unit, the value of Q in the first year of production given that $L = 200$ and $K = 100$.

(b) If, in the following year, the company decides to substitute more capital for labour, calculate the value of Q when $L = 190$ and $K = 180$. What is the effect of the substitution on the number of units produced?

(c) If the company had decided to double the amount of labour and capital, use the production function equation to prove that the company would have been operating under constant returns to scale.

(d) Express the marginal product of labour in terms of L and K, and show that it diminishes with output.

(e) If the firm pays a wage equal to the marginal product of labour, by what percentage do wages change between the first and second years?

5. The nitrates division of Agrol, a fertiliser company, finds from statistical studies that its short-run total cost function for producing nitrates is cubic or S-shaped, and is very similar to that postulated by economic theory. The total cost function is in the form $TC = 300 + 50Q - 10Q^2 + Q^3$, where Q is in tonnes per hour of nitrates produced.

(a) Write down the value of fixed costs (FC) and the expressions for the average total cost (ATC), total variable cost (TVC), average variable cost (AVC) and marginal cost (MC) functions.

(b) Show that the AVC curve is U-shaped and that the MC curve will intersect the AVC curve at the lowest point of the latter.

(c) What is the tonnage of nitrates per hour that should be produced to minimise short-run AVC? What will be the average variable cost per tonne of nitrates at this output?

◼ Further reading

Intermediate   Baumol, W. J. (1977), *Economic Theory and Operations Analysis*, 4th edn, Chs 11 and 12, Prentice Hall, Hemel Hempstead.

Browning, E. and Browning, J. (1992), *Microeconomic Theory and Applications*, 4th edn, Chs 6 and 7, HarperCollins, London.

Dobson, S., Maddala, G. S. and Miller, E. (1995), *Microeconomics*, Chs 4 and 5, McGraw-Hill, Maidenhead.

Hope, S. (1999), *Applied Microeconomics*, Ch. 7, John Wiley, Chichester.

Katz, M. and Rosen, H. (1998), *Microeconomics*, 3rd edn, Chs 8 and 9, Irwin, Boston, Mass.

Koutsoyiannis, A. (1979), *Modern Microeconomics*, 2nd edn, Chs 3 and 4, Macmillan, Basingstoke.

Laidler, D. and Estrin, S. (1995), *Introduction to Microeconomics*, 4th edn, Chs 10–12, Harvester Wheatsheaf, Hemel Hempstead.

Maddala, G. S and Miller, E. (1989), *Microeconomics: Theory and Application*, Chs 6 and 7, McGraw-Hill, New York.

Nicholson, W. (1997), *Intermediate Microeconomics and its Application*, 7th edn, Chs 8 and 9, Dryden Press, Fort Worth.

Pindyck, R. and Rubinfeld, D. (1998), *Microeconomics*, 4th edn, Chs 6 and 7, Macmillan, Basingstoke.

Varian, H. (1999), *Intermediate Microeconomics*, 5th edn, Chs 17, 19–22, Norton, New York.

Advanced texts

Gravelle, H. and Rees, R. (1992), *Microeconomics*, 2nd edn, Chs 7 and 8, Longman, Harlow.

Mas-Colell, A., Whinston, M. D. and Green, J. R. (1995), *Microeconomic Theory*, Ch. 5, Oxford University Press, Oxford.

Articles and other sources

Baldwin, R. E. and Krugman, P. R. (1988), 'Market access and international competition: A simulation study of 16K random access memories', *Empirical Methods for International Trade*, R. C. Feenstra (ed.), MIT Press, New York.

Baumol, W. J. and Braunstein, Y. M. (1977), 'Empirical study of scale economies and production complementarities: the case of journal publication', *Journal of Political Economy*, 85, 4, August.

Chandler, A. D. (1990), *Scale and Scope: The Dynamics of Industrial Capitalism*, Harvard University Press, Harvard.

Drake, L. (1992), 'Economics of scale and scope in the UK building societies', *Applied Financial Economics*, 2.

European Economy (1988), 'The economics of 1992', 35, March.

Friedlaender, A. F., Winston, C. and Wang, D. K. (1982), 'Costs, technology and productivity in the US automobile industry', Working paper no. 294 , Department of Economics, Massachusetts Institute of Technology.

Griffiths, A. (1994), 'The roots of corporate competitiveness: the case of Japanese manufacturing companies', *Economics and Business Education* II, 4, 8, Winter.

Gruber, H. (1998), 'Learning by doing and spillovers: Further evidence for the semiconductor industry', *Review of Industrial Organization*, 13.

Hamill, H. (1993), 'Competitive strategies in the world airline industry', *European Management Journal*, 11, 3.

Irwin, D. A. and Klenow, P. J. (1994), 'Learning-by-doing; spillovers in the semiconductor industry', *Journal of Political Economy*, 102, 6, University of Chicago Press, Chicago.

Kurdas, C. (1998), 'Dynamic economies of scope in the pharmaceutical industry', *Industrial and Corporate Change*, 7, 3.

Lieberman, M. B. (1994), 'Learning curves in the chemical processing industry', *Rand Journal*, 15.

McGowan, F. and Seabright, P. (1987), 'Deregulating European airlines', *Economic Policy*, October.

Pappas, J., Brigham, E. and Shipley, B. (1991), *Managerial Economics*, Dryden Press, London.

Pestieau, P. (1993), 'Performance and competition in services', *European Economy*, 3.

Pratten, C. (1987), 'A Survey of the Economies of Scale', Report Prepared for the European Commission.

Rhys, G. (1999), 'The motor industry: an economic overview', *Developments in Economics*, 15, edited by GBJ Atkinson Causeway Press Ltd., Ormskirk, Lancashire.

Chapter 5

Firm objectives and firm behaviour

Economists have put forward various theories as to how firms behave in order to predict their reaction to events. At the heart of such theories are assumptions about firms' objectives, the most usual being that the firm seeks to maximise profits. We initially explore the implications of the profit-maximising assumption for firm price and output. In fact the profit-maximising assumption underpins much of the material in Chapters 6–9 involving different types of market structure. We then move on to identify the various changes in the business environment that have led economists to formulate alternative assumptions as to firms' objectives and behaviour. The chapter concludes by carefully reviewing the empirical evidence for these various alternatives.

■ Marginal analysis and maximisation

The objectives of a firm can be grouped under two main headings: **maximising** goals and **non-maximising** goals. We shall see that *marginal* analysis is particularly important for maximising goals. This is often confusing to the student who, rightly, assumes that few firms can have any detailed knowledge of marginal revenue or marginal cost. However, it should be remembered that marginal analysis does not pretend to describe *how* firms maximise profits or revenue. It simply tells us what the output and price must be if they do succeed in maximising these items, whether by luck or by judgement.

■ Profit maximisation

Much of conventional analysis within microeconomics revolves around the classical firm and its presumed preoccupation with **profit maximisation**. At least five premises can be seen as underlying the profit-maximising assumption:

- that profit can be clearly defined as the excess of revenue over all costs (including opportunity costs) and can be readily measured;

- that a firm behaves as an individual entrepreneur would behave. The entrepreneur is seen as the central figure behind the operation of the business, having complete control and directing the business in his own interests;
- that the firm's utility function has only one variable in it, namely profits;
- that the firm behaves in a rational and consistent way, seeking to maximise its utility, namely by maximising profit;
- that the firm has access to both complete and certain information about the environment within which it operates.

The case for profit maximisation as self-evident is, as we shall see, undermined if any one of these five premises fails to hold true.

Profit is actually maximized where marginal revenue (*MR*) equals marginal cost (*MC*), i.e. where the additional revenue raised from selling an extra unit is exactly equal to the additional cost of producing that extra unit. In Fig. 5.1, total profit (*TP*) is a maximum at output Q_p, where the vertical distance between total revenue (*TR*) and total cost (*TC*) is the greatest ($TP = TR - TC$). To produce one less unit than Q_p would be to forsake making profit on that unit, as it would add more to revenue than to cost. To produce one more unit than Q_p would be to make a loss on the extra unit, as it would add more to cost than to revenue. Only at Q_p, where $MR = MC$, can total profit be a maximum. Notice that the gradients of the total revenue and total cost curves (i.e. *MR* and *MC* respectively) have identical slopes at output Q_p.

Profit maximisation and industry change

Since the Second World War many of the premises that underpin profit maximisation have been increasingly questioned. Major changes in the structure and conduct of industry led many writers to assert that firms operating in the real world did not resemble the 'classical' firm widely regarded as the basis for the profit-maximising model.

- The nature of *ownership* had clearly changed. The emergence in the postwar period of large companies with numerous owners or shareholders, each with limited liability, was quite unlike the single or small group of entrepreneurs with virtually unlimited liability, so readily envisaged by traditional theorists.

Fig. 5.1 **The profit-maximising output, Q_p.**

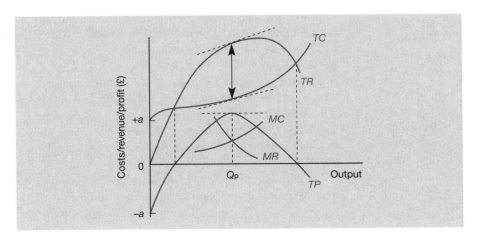

- The nature of *control* had also changed substantially. Shareholders, who were the actual owners of the companies, were clearly unable to run the company individually as their numbers were so large. They therefore had to delegate the day-to-day operation and control of companies to boards of directors, who then acted as their representatives. The fact that ownership (shareholders) and control (managers) had now become separated or 'divorced' from each other was a significant departure from the traditional view of a firm in which ownership and control were securely in the hands of a single individual or small group of individuals.

- As modern businesses grew in size their *organisational structures* often became more hierarchical and complex in nature. For example, the need to coordinate many and varied firm activities became a major problem for many large multi-product companies. Such changes in organisational structure served to highlight the difference between the top strategic managers on the one side, and those engaged in more functional and operational activities on the other. The efficiency of a firm became increasingly dependent on the effectiveness of communication channels within these complex structures. Such organisational problems had been largely absent from the classical firm with its small, cohesive structure.

- As companies grew in size, so too did the potential for *conflict* between departments, divisions and individuals within the organisation. For example, the strategies pursued by directors did not always satisfy other participants in the firm, such as workers or shareholders, creating a need for these conflicting objectives to be reconciled. In the traditional approach no such conflict would arise, the entrepreneur being deemed to be in sole control and having the authority to set profit maximisation as the overriding objective.

- As we have already noted, one of the premises underlying the profit-maximising assumption was that the firm had complete and certain *access to information*. Of course such an outcome is rarely encountered in the world of the modern corporation, given the complexity of the markets and products that firms have to manage.

Managerial capitalism and the theory of the firm

The changing business environment outlined earlier made it inevitable that new theories would be required to account for new behaviour patterns. These often took the form of managerial or behavioural theories of the firm.

Managerial theories revolved around the increasingly apparent fact of the divorce between ownership and control of firm activities, which meant that managers would sometimes pursue their own interests before those of the owners of the company, i.e. the shareholders. Since shareholders were often limited to exercising power during annual general meetings (if at all), it was felt that managers would be tempted to follow strategies that were more closely aligned with their own utility functions. For example, they might be tempted to maximise firm revenue or growth, giving them more power or status, and to pay less attention to maximising profits for the benefit of shareholders. Exponents of these managerial types of theory included W. J. Baumol, O. E. Williamson and R. L. Marris.

On the other hand, many writers developed theories that were based on a recognition that the firm was an *organic structure*. Such **behavioural theories** saw the internal organisation and operation of companies as being of paramount importance in explaining how firms operate in a modern, complex environment. These behavioural theories often stressed the importance of the bargaining process that occurs between various interested parties within companies. Conflict resolution between such internal groups was now seen as having a key role in determining the objectives that firms are likely to pursue. Greater weight was also given to the fact that decisions in the real world were made under conditions of uncertainty. Exponents of these behavioural types of theories included R. M. Cyert, J. G. March and H. A. Simon.

Constraints on non-profit-maximising behaviour

Although criticism of the profit maximisation thesis has been intense, there are still situations where profit clearly remains an important underlying constraint on company behaviour.

First, managers who might want to pursue their own objectives might still feel constrained to achieve 'reasonable' levels of profits in order to secure shareholder utility. Indeed, some have argued that recent changes in the way in which companies are organised may have curbed managerial desires to pursue non-profit-related objectives. For example, O. E. Williamson has argued that cost consciousness has risen as organisations have moved from unitary to multidivisional structures (pp. 207–9), with the renewed focus on efficiency curbing any managerial discretion. Such shifts in company structure are seen as constraining any managerial tendencies to stray too far from profit-related objectives.

Second, contractual and other arrangements may be devised to induce managers to give profit a higher weight in their utility functions. For example, linking managerial remuneration to profit performance may be a way in which shareholders can ensure that their profit-related interests will be reflected in managerial decision making. This is the so-called *principal–agent* problem, in which principals (shareholders) hire others designated as agents (managers) to act on their behalf. Since the principals and agents may want to pursue different objectives, the problem revolves around how the principals can devise suitable packages to induce the agents to act in a manner compatible with the interests of the principals.

The debate about the motivation of firms is far from over, and perhaps revolves around two key issues. First, if firms are maximisers, what objective(s) are they seeking to maximise? Second, if firms are not always maximisers, what are the constraints and inducements affecting firm behaviour? The remaining sections of this chapter will discuss in more depth these and other aspects of firm objective and behaviour.

Theoretical developments

Managerial theories of the firm

We have seen that the divorce of ownership from control in large firms gave managers more potential for controlling the day-to-day operations of such companies. Managerial theories of the firm try to explain the nature of managerial motivation and how this can differ from the motivation of the owner-controlled firm of classical theory. W. Baumol

(1959) has suggested that the management-controlled firm is likely to have **sales revenue maximisation** as a main goal. His argument is that the salaries of top managers and other non-pecuniary benefits, such as managerial status within the firm, are more closely correlated with sales revenue than with profits. Baumol stressed the negative impact for managers of declining sales revenue, such as greater difficulties in raising funds from financial intermediaries.

Sales revenue maximisation: the Baumol model

In terms of Fig. 5.2, a sales-revenue-maximising goal will result in the firm producing output Q_s where total revenue (*TR*) is a maximum and therefore marginal revenue (*MR*) is zero. As already noted, *MR* is the gradient to the total revenue curve at any given output. In this case a different assumption for firm objective will affect firm *output*, the sales-revenue-maximising firm producing more (Q_s) than the profit-maximising firm (Q_p). We might also note that a sales-revenue-maximising firm is likely to have a different pricing policy from that of a profit-maximising firm.

$$\text{Price} = \text{Average revenue} = \frac{\text{Total revenue}}{\text{Total output}}$$

In Fig. 5.2, where Q_p = profit-maximising output and Q_s = sales-revenue-maximising output, the following relationships hold:

- Price in the sales-revenue-maximising firm = $\tan \theta_s = \dfrac{R_1}{Q_s}$

- Price in the profit-maximising firm = $\tan \theta_p = \dfrac{R_2}{Q_p}$

In other words, the price of the sales-revenue-maximising firm is *below* that of the profit-maximising firm.

Constrained sales revenue maximisation

Despite the fact that Baumol believed the primary goal of managers to be sales revenue maximisation, he understood that firms must bear in mind a number of *constraints* when pursuing this goal. For example, to ensure sustained growth of sales revenue in the future it may be necessary for a firm to find sufficient investment funds to finance such

Fig. 5.2 Variation of output and price with firm objective.

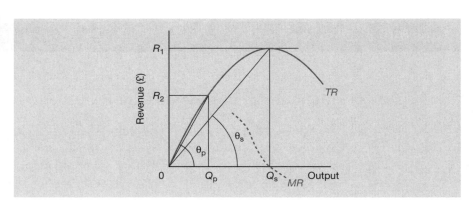

sales growth. Such finance might be derived internally from retained profits or externally from sources such as the capital market. Clearly some internal profit will be attractive to the firm as a secure and low-cost source of investment finance, while a reasonable level of profit is also needed to reassure the capital market that the firm is attractive both to existing and to potentially new investors. However, profit is seen in this model as a means of securing further sales revenue and not as an end in itself. Therefore Baumol's approach is to suggest that firms seek to maximise sales revenue subject to a *minimum profit* constraint. Basically, the large corporation attempts to maximize sales revenue ($p.q$), where p is price and q is quantity, subject to profits being at least π.

The difference that a profit constraint makes to firm output is shown in Fig. 5.3. If π is the minimum profit required by shareholders, then Q'_s is the output that permits the highest total revenue while still meeting the profit constraint. Any output beyond Q'_s up to Q_s would raise total revenue (TR) still further – the major objective – but reduce total profit (TP) below the minimum required (π). In other words Q'_s represents the **constrained sales-revenue-maximising** output.

Utility maximisation: the Williamson model

A second theory, which has its origins in managerial perspectives of firm behaviour, is that of O.E. Williamson. His model is a generalisation of Baumol's model, although there are important differences in the reasoning behind the models. Williamson's general model is based on the idea that managers seek to **maximise a utility function** subject to profits exceeding some minimum acceptable level. He argues that important determinants of managerial utility include salary, status, power, prestige and security. These factors provide the basis for what he calls the 'expense preference' of managers, whereby they gain positive utility by incurring certain types of expense. These include expenditures on staff, and expenditures on emoluments. For example, it is argued that managers derive positive utility from spending directed towards increasing staff numbers, as a greater span of control increases their power, security and salary. Similarly spending on emoluments, such as generous managerial expense accounts, luxurious staff accommodation and other such perquisites, is also seen as increasing managerial utility, especially where such spending is seen as being *above* what is needed to keep existing staff in post. Williamson also saw

Fig. 5.3 Constrained sales-revenue-maximising output (Q^1_s).

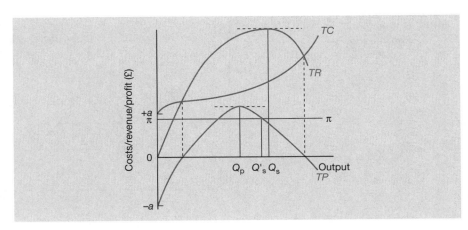

managerial utility as being directly related to *discretionary profits*. This term refers to profits that are above the minimum necessary to keep shareholders happy. Managers are presumed to realise that future expansion and success can be built upon extra profits of this type so that they gain utility from generating such discretionary profits.

The most general model can be expressed as

$$\text{Max } U = U(S, M, \pi_D)$$

where U is managerial utility, S is expenditure on staff, M is expenditure on managerial emoluments, and π_D is discretionary profits. The equation is subject to the constraint that discretionary profits, π_D, should be greater than the level necessary to meet minimum shareholders' needs (π_{min}).

The sign of each variable on the right-hand side is presumed to be positive, indicating that managerial utility varies directly with each of these variables. However, managerial utility is presumed to increase at a diminishing rate with respect to each variable: e.g. more expenditure on staff increases total managerial utility but at a progressively diminishing rate.

In order to maximise U, managers will go on consuming S, M and π_D up to the point where:

$$\frac{MU_S}{£S} = \frac{MU_M}{£M} = \frac{MU\pi_D}{£\pi_D}$$

In other words, if the extra satisfaction achieved *per £ spent* on staff, emoluments and discretionary profits was identical, managerial utility would be at a maximum. Only in this situation would managers no longer be able to reallocate money between the three categories and thereby increase the overall level of managerial utility or satisfaction. Such equality in the above ratios may occur *within* the profit constraint (π_{min}). Alternatively the profit constraint may be 'binding', i.e. come into play *before* the above equalities are fully satisfied. We are then in a situation of **constrained utility maximisation** for managers.

Figure 5.4 gives a partial picture of Williamson's model, with managerial utility shown here as a function of profits and staff size. Profits (π) increase directly with staff size up to S_0, but decrease thereafter. Profits above the profit constraint (π_{min}) are regarded as 'discretionary'.

Fig. 5.4 Managerial utility as a function of profits and staff size.

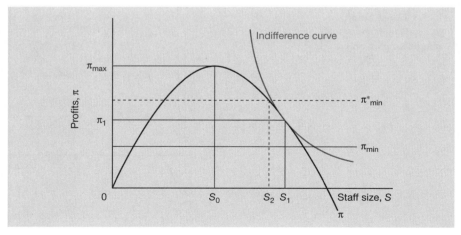

If profit was the only variable in the managerial utility function, then the predicted staff level would be S_0 with profits π_{max}. However, we have seen that in Williamson's model, managerial utility is a function of *more than* the profit variable, and some of the discretionary profit ($\pi_{max} - \pi_{min}$ at S_0) is traded off against a higher staff level in Fig. 5.4 to maximise managerial utility with a staff size of S_1 and profits of π_1. Here the profit constraint (π_{min}) has not influenced the outcome, i.e. it has not proved to be a 'binding' constraint. However, had the profit constraint been the dashed line π^*_{min} in Fig. 5.4, then it would have proved 'binding' and a constrained utility-maximising outcome would have involved staff level S_2 ($< S_1$). In either case (binding or non-binding profits constraint) the outcome is a higher level of staff and a lower level of profits than predicted by a profit-maximising model. A similar conclusion would hold should other variables (e.g. emoluments, discretionary profits weighted *vis-à-vis* non-discretionary profits) appear in the managerial utility function.

This theory has a number of interesting implications:

- It implies that managers are not necessarily cost minimisers, constantly on the lookout to cut costs. Indeed it indicates that there are some costs, such as expenditure on staff, that managers may gain utility by incurring.
- The firm in the Williamson model includes managers who are paid emoluments above the levels necessary to achieve the current level of production, in order to secure additional managerial utility. Consequently costs are higher and profits lower than they could otherwise be. Should a crisis arise and profits fall below the minimum level (π_{min}), there may still be costs currently incurred that can be reduced to help restore profits. Therefore the firm seems to operate with an element of *organisational slack*, reflected in these higher-than-minimum costs.

Growth maximisation: the Marris model

The theories of Baumol and Williamson discussed above tended towards a relatively short-run and static analysis of firm motivation. The growth maximisation model of Marris (1964) shifted the perspective of managerial decision making towards the long run, and incorporated dynamic elements in the analysis. To Marris, managers are motivated not so much by the achievement of absolute size, such as a given value of sales revenue, but rather by *changes* in size. For example, he contends that managers would prefer to expand the firm to a particular size rather than move job to a company that has already achieved such size. The Marris growth model sees the firm as continually diversifying into new products as a key method of maintaining an adequate rate of growth of demand.

Marris identified two main factors as determining managerial utility: growth of the firm and a desire for security. The firm's growth is seen as a way of realising a variety of managerial goals, such as power, prestige, and higher salaries. Security, on the other hand, is seen as instrumental in conserving the manager's role and job description. The most serious threat to a manager's security is seen as emanating from a change of ownership, as in the case of mergers or takeovers. To minimise the risk of such outcomes, managers have an interest in maintaining the market value of the company's shares at a relatively high level, making any takeover more expensive for the predator. However, to achieve this, the managers must pay adequate remuneration to shareholders: in other words pay sufficient dividends to make the shares attractive and keep share value high.

We can express this takeover constraint in terms of the **valuation ratio**, v, which is defined as the ratio of the market value of the shares at any given time (V) to the capital or book value of the shares (K). The capital or book value corresponds to the assessed value of the assets of the firm, namely capital equipment, buildings, etc.

In terms of the above analysis we can express the manager's utility function in the Marris model as

Max $U = U(v, g)$

where v is the valuation ratio and g is the firm growth rate.

This utility function has the usual properties, namely that utility is an increasing function of v and g. It follows that if the valuation ratio, v, rises then managerial security increases, and that if firm growth, g, rises then managerial power, position and income will increase. The relationship between v and g as regards managerial utility is seen as strictly concave from above: i.e. there is a diminishing marginal rate of substitution between the two variables. The suggestion here is that to obtain more growth, g, a higher proportion of profits must be reinvested; but this implies less profits available for distribution to shareholders, resulting in a fall in the value of shares and hence in the valuation ratio, v. Put another way, the *managerial indifference curve* between v and g is seen as sloping downwards from left to right, becoming progressively flatter as it does so.

In order to appreciate the constraints under which policies seeking to maximise managerial utility must operate, we might usefully consider in more detail the relationship between profits, growth and the valuation ratio. Figures 5.5(a) and (b) show the relationship between firm growth and both profit rate and valuation ratio. The shape of the profit rate curve (Fig. 5.5(a)) reflects the fact that in the initial stages of a firm's growth, profits may rise and be reinvested, permitting further growth and a still higher profit rate. However, as growth increases beyond a certain point (g'), costs may begin to rise more

Fig. 5.5 **Relationship between firm growth and both profit rate and valuation ratio.**

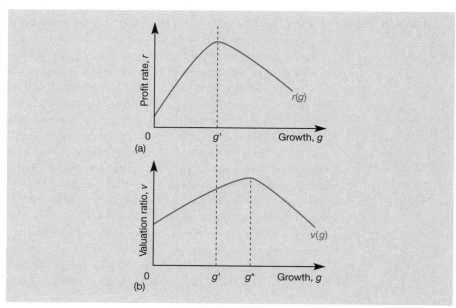

strongly: e.g. the costs of additional advertising, of developing new markets, and of assimilating new staff. All such rises in costs decrease the profit rate, r, as does the exhaustion of the most profitable investment projects open to the firm. The shape of the profit–growth curve in turn affects the shape of the valuation ratio–growth curve seen in Fig. 5.5(b). As the profit rate rises in the early stages, this will increase the demand for shares and push up the price of shares, and therefore the valuation ratio, v. The suggestion here is that when the profit rate, r, starts to fall, the market will not adjust immediately as it does not know whether the fall will be sustained. However, after a lag, the fall in profit rate will eventually decrease the demand for the firm shares, and the valuation ratio will fall in the manner shown in Fig. 5.5(b).

To understand the nature of the constrained maximisation theory of Marris, we must now integrate the managerial utility function with the constraint function, as shown in Fig. 5.6. Here the managerial utility function is displayed in the form of a map of indifference curves having the properties already outlined. The managerial constraint function is also present in the form of the valuation ratio/growth trade-off curve, the shape of which we have just described. The optimum position for managers will be where the highest attainable indifference curve is tangential to the valuation–growth curve. However, we also know that the security of managers depends on the share price (and hence the valuation ratio) being sufficiently high to prevent the possibility of takeover. This minimum required valuation ratio is shown as $\bar{v}$ in Fig. 5.6.

If the managers' indifference curve was I_1, then the equilibrium growth rate would be g_1 with a valuation ratio of v_1. Since v_1 is above the minimum security level ($\bar{v}$) required to prevent the threat of takeover, then A is a possible equilibrium trade-off position. However, if the managerial indifference curve was I_2 then equilibrium would occur at B. This might at first sight appear preferable for managers, as the growth rate would be higher ($g_3 > g_1$) than at A, with associated valuation ratio v_2.

However, this outcome would yield a valuation ratio *below* the security constraint of $\bar{v}$. The highest level of managerial utility consistent with $\bar{v}$ occurs at C, with the lower ($I_3 < I_2$) indifference curve I_3 and the lower ($g_2 < g_3$) firm growth rate g_2.

Fig. 5.6 **Managerial utility and managerial constraints.**

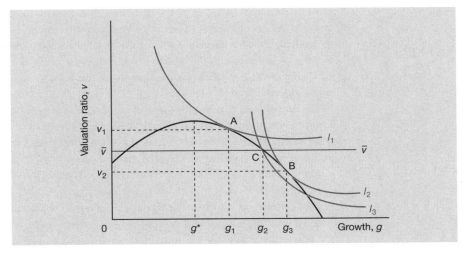

Figure 5.6 therefore usefully indicates the nature of the constraints to managerial util-ity within the Marris model. We should also notice that because of managers' preferences for growth, the 'equilibrium' situations outlined at A, B or C would, in all cases, be above the growth rate (g') in Fig. 5.5 consistent with the highest part of the profit–growth curve $r(g)$. Since this curve reaches a peak at a growth rate (g') *below* that ($g*$) for the valuation–growth curve $v(g)$, then managerial objectives may indeed lead to outcomes different from those of profit maximisation. Nevertheless profit may retain some significance in influencing managerial behaviour, since management may be con-strained from securing still higher growth at the expense of profits by the need to keep the valuation ratio sufficiently high ($\geqslant \bar{v}$) to prevent takeover.

Behavioural theories of the firm

Both the traditional (owner control) and the managerial (non-owner control) theories of the firm assumed that firms attempt to *maximise* the value of a given objective, be it prof-its, sales revenue, managerial utility or growth. More refined versions also recognised that there were constraints that limited the ability of firms to achieve these pure objec-tives. Nevertheless these models were based, in one way or another, on the maximisation of a single objective. The **behaviouralist** view of the firm is rather different, depending not only on the separation of ownership and control, in common with the managerial models, but also on *organisational theory*. In other words, the behaviouralists were much more interested in the internal organisation of firms and how that internal structure could affect firm objectives. For the behaviouralists, the complexity of modern organisa-tions means that the maximisation of any one goal, or even some set of goals, may be impossible to achieve.

Satisficing: the
Simon model

One of the most original contributions to the behaviouralist viewpoint came from H. A. Simon (1959). He argued that the modern firm is not a well-defined 'individual entity' but rather a complex organisation of both individuals and groups of individuals, each with its own goal or set of goals. It follows that decisions must be arrived at through interaction between such groups, often resulting in compromise. Simon argues that only by studying such interactions between the internal components of the firm can we iden-tify the overall motivation of the firm. Indeed *conflicts* between the objectives of various subgroups within the firms mean that an overall firm strategy seeking to maximise a single objective is unlikely.

Simon suggests that the fundamental objective of a firm or organisation is survival. On the operational level, this is translated into a search for a solution that is mutually acceptable to all the different internal groups within the firm. This view of the firm points towards replacing the idea of maximisation by the notion of **satisficing**, i.e. aiming for outcomes that are acceptable or satisfactory for the main internal groups comprising a company, rather than outcomes that are optimal for only one or a few groups within the company. However, this is not to say that satisficing leads to some long-run performance that is less than would otherwise be achieved. Figure 5.7 illus-trates how the attainment of initially limited objectives might subsequently lead to an improved long-run performance.

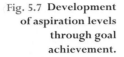

Fig. 5.7 **Development of aspiration levels through goal achievement.**

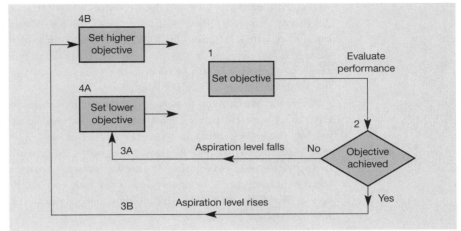

At the starting point, 1, the manager sets some minimum objective and then attempts to achieve it. If, after evaluation, it is found that the objective has been achieved, then this will lead to an increase in aspirational level (3B). A new and higher objective (4B) will then emerge. Thus, by setting achievable objectives, what might be an initial and rather low target turns out to be a prelude to a series of higher targets, perhaps culminating in the achievement of some maximum objective. If, on the other hand, the initial objective is *not* achieved, then aspirational levels are lowered (3A) until achievable objectives are set.

The achievement of objectives has long been recognised as an incentive to improving management performance, and is the basis of the management technique known as management by objectives (MBO). Simon's theory focuses on the *processes* by which firms determine their economic choices, rather than on the outcomes of those choices, as with the earlier maximisation models.

Coalitions and goal formation: the Cyert and March model

The ideas and conceptual apparatus developed by Simon gave rise to the behavioural approach originally associated with R. M. Cyert and J. G. March (1963). If a firm is satisficing, then who are the beneficiaries of the process, and how do these benefits accrue? Cyert and March were rather more specific than Simon in identifying the various groups or coalitions within an organisation. A **coalition** is defined as any group that, at a given moment in time, shares a consensus on the goals to be pursued. Workers may form one coalition, wanting good wages and work conditions and some job security; managers may form another coalition, wanting power and prestige as well as high salaries; shareholders yet another, wanting high profits, with customers wanting prompt delivery, and so on. These various coalitions, with differing goals, may result in intergroup conflicts: e.g. higher wages for workers may mean lower profits for shareholders.

A firm's goals can, from this standpoint, be seen as the outcome of a process of bargaining among potential coalition members. At any point in time a particular coalition may be 'dominant' within a firm: i.e. be in a strong bargaining position to ensure that its goals are implemented. For example, in times of recession, coalitions involving those who seek financial prudence and the avoidance of exposure to insolvency may be able to direct policy towards a focus on core activities and a sustainable cash flow. However, in times of recovery, coalitions involving those who seek growth in revenue and market share may be dominant. In this view no *single* overriding objective can satisfactorily be assigned to a firm, since the firm's objective will clearly change over time, depending on the dominance of any particular coalitions.

Cyert and March go on to suggest that the aim of managers is to set goals that resolve the conflict between opposing groups. For example, two inconsistent goals might be reconciled by adopting satisfactory standards of performance for each of the goals, rather than by seeking to maximise just one of the goals at the expense of another: i.e. by **satisficing** rather than maximising. In this way no single coalition is wholly alienated, a measure of compromise being involved in the final outcome. Profit maximisation is seen here as broadly incompatible with the simultaneous pursuit of alternative goals acceptable to members of other coalitions.

The goals that Cyert and March identify as important for a contemporary firm involve the key areas of production, inventory control, level of sales, market share and profit. However, attempts to attain such goals often create conflict. For example, the inventory goal might imply a desire to avoid running out of stock of the product or of important raw materials required for production. This goal might appeal to the production department but conflict with the interests of the finance department, which might regard the holding of excessive inventories as unprofitable.

To encourage compromise between groups, a number of techniques may be used:

- *Agreed limits*. Some budgets are set at the outset, limiting the area of conflict to how the given 'cake' is to be distributed rather than also involving the size of that cake. This is never more apparent than when strongly enforced cash limits are imposed.
- *Time constraints*. Restricting the bargaining time available creates pressure for compromise between groups.
- *Structure*. Conflict can be reduced by structuring the firm in such a way that group discretion is limited. This may involve clearly demarcated areas of responsibility for each department.
- *Money payments*. Payment in lieu of other demands is often used to reduce conflict. Part of this may well be what Cyert and March call 'organisational slack', i.e. payments in excess of what is necessary to keep the group stable.
- *Sequential problem-solving*. Top management may seize on the process of achieving one goal as a way of limiting the demands of other groups at any given moment. For example, they could use an increase in wages to explain why more equipment could not be purchased.

Once goals have been determined and reconciled, the next process is to set satisfactory levels of performance for the various goals, i.e. to set aspiration levels in terms of Fig. 5.7. These often initially take the form of *targets* based on rules of thumb or on the following specified operational procedures.

For example, a company department might set a target for their sales using a rule of thumb based on past experience. As sales data become available, monitoring and checking may occur to assess whether the department is on target. If the initial sales target *is* achieved, then reordering is likely to occur, again following some standard procedure. If the target is *not* achieved, then other measures might be introduced in an attempt to minimise the damage, e.g. measures that attempt to secure lower prices from suppliers, etc. In the future, of course, the sales target itself may be reduced to accord with a downward revision of aspirational level.

To summarise, these behavioural models developed by Simon and by Cyert and March look at the *process* of decision making. They recognise that the organisation is not synonymous with the owner, nor with any other single individual or group. Rather the firm is an organisational structure containing many different groups. The particular individuals comprising these groups, or coalitions of interest, may change over time, as may the relative strength of any particular group. For example, the financial group is often pre-eminent in times of recession when cash flow is at a premium; however, the marketing group is often pre-eminent in times of recovery and growth, when the future is viewed more optimistically. Hardly surprisingly, the firm objectives are seen here as likely to encompass more than a single goal, and to be fluid through time. Further these varied and changing objectives may often be in conflict, so that management must resort to a number of techniques in order to reduce such conflict. As we have seen, management might resort to organisational slack, i.e. to resolving the conflicts between groups within a company by paying factors of production more than their marginal productivity, as postulated by maximisation theories. The general approach is seen here as being one in which satisficing might be a more realistic description of the way in which firms operate, rather than the more traditional maximising mode of operation. The behaviouralists also tend to stress that much decision making follows routine, fairly simple rules of thumb, rather than the marginalist rules laid down by adherents of a maximising approach.

Principal–agent problem

The so-called 'principal–agent' problem has been advanced as a further reason for non-maximising behaviour by firms. The suggestion has been made that the separation of ownership and control between shareholders and managers in public limited liability companies may lead to decision taking that is contrary to the interests of owners (shareholders). In other words, managers are acting as *agents* of the shareholders (*principals*), and are taking decisions on their behalf. There may be a variety of factors leading to the decisions of agents being 'sub-optimal', at least as regards the viewpoint of principals.

- **Assymetry of information**. Agents may possess information that is not fully available to principals, and which the latter could only acquire, if at all, via extensive and costly monitoring and search activity. As it is unlikely that monitoring and search activity by principals will be sufficient to fully redress any information imbalance, agents will have some freedom to take decisions that best serve their own (rather than the principals') interests.

  We have already noted that managerial objectives may differ from shareholders' objectives. It is often assumed that shareholders seek to maximise *net worth*, defined as the excess of the value of a firm's assets (cash, securities, land, buildings, plant and equipment, etc.) over the value of its liabilities (amounts owed to creditors). By seeking to maximise net worth (assets – liabilities), shareholders are in effect seeking to maximise 'owner's equity'. Of course, we have seen in Chapter 3 that both present and future returns are uncertain. Maximising net worth (or profits as a proxy variable for net worth) may therefore reduce to maximising the *expected present value* of profit. Clearly, such an approach brings probabilities and the use of scenarios directly into play.

Agents, however, may have incentives to pursue goals other than the maximisation of the expected present value of profit. For example, decisions that have a high short-term pay-off may serve to enhance the status of current managers and ensure rapid promotion even if the expected present value of the net worth resulting from these decisions is *below* that of alternative decisions that have their major pay-offs in the future. Again, decisions that either avoid or impose conflict may give an impression of good management, depending on the ethos of the time, thereby securing more rapid promotion even where alternative decisions are the more likely to maximise the expected present value of profit. Payment systems to executives that are *pro rata* to the span of control may yield empire building on the part of managers, which also might be contrary to the principals' primary goals. The same is likely to be true of decisions aiding personal enrichment, as with managers allocating contracts to those within their family or to friendship networks or to those providing bribes. All such actions and decisions by agents may clearly subvert the principals' primary goal. Even aesthetically appealing decisions by managers to protect aspects of the environment, such as creating more pleasant working conditions, may not always be directed towards maximising the expected present value of net worth.

- **Moral hazard** is often applied to insurance situations, where the insured may take inadequate precautions to protect against (recoverable) loss, though the insurer lacks the information to demonstrate that this is the case (see Chapter 12). Here moral hazard occurs where the agent has information superior to that available to the principal. Hidden actions and motives by the agent may then be difficult to observe or monitor by the principal. For example, the principal and agent share the same information only up to the point where the agent *selects* a particular course of action. Since the agent (manager) is selecting innumerable such actions on a day-to-day basis, the principal is only then able to observe the *outcome* of such actions. Yet it is often in the detail and sequence of such actions that the outcome itself is determined. There is clearly an element of moral hazard involved here.

- **Adverse selection** occurs where the principal has difficulty in identifying the true characteristics of the agents who seek to act on his behalf. Hidden characteristics of agents make it difficult for principals to assess quality within the market. For example, adverse selection may occur when the agent (the manager) is privy to information to which the principal (the shareholder or owner) is not. Thus although in this case the principal can observe both the action and the outcome, there is no way in which the principal can judge whether the agent acted optimally. Only the agent has the necessary information to be able accurately to evaluate such situations.

Remedies to the principal–agent problem

At least three approaches are often advanced as a means of overcoming the principal–agent problem:

- Principals must establish procedures for carefully *monitoring* the performance of their agents. For example, independent consultants may be hired to review managerial activities. Minimum acceptable standards might then be set and penalties introduced if those standards are not met. This can help to ensure that the principal's concern for profits and dividends receives more attention than might otherwise be the case.

- In an active capital market, the *threat of takeover* may help to ensure that agents act in concert with principals. By keeping profits high to meet the demands of principals, the agents may have achieved a higher share price, thereby making the company more expensive to buy, and deterring takeover bids. At the same time the principals are less likely to sell their shares to a prospective buyer if their dividends have been high in the past.

- Principals must create *incentives* for agents to act in ways that are consistent with the principal's own interests. Managerial salaries and bonuses (e.g. share options) related to company profitability, share price, etc., have been widely adopted with this end in view. Formal contracts can be devised in ways that seek to bring about a coincidence of interests between principals and agents.

Organisational design

Some writers have argued that the objectives and behaviour of companies may be affected by the ways in which their organisations have been designed. Williamson (1971) traces the changes in organisational design of companies since the 1920s, and puts forward the thesis that a shift from a unitary (U-form) to a multidivisional (M-form) structure has changed the internal system of control and with it the types of objective likely to be pursued. The following sections consider the Williamson approach in more detail.

Unitary (U-form) structure

A **U-form** or unitary structure is generally regarded as being of the type shown in Fig. 5.8(a). The chief executive officer (managing director) is at the top of a hierarchy, and has a responsibility for long-term (strategic) decisions, as well as a key role monitoring the day-to-day operations of the functional departments. The layer below represents heads (general managers) of the functional areas of the firm, such as production, marketing, personnel and finance. Functional managers collect, assess and pass on information to the CEO and in turn receive guidelines or instructions. Linkages between each functional area are usually weak or non-existent.

The suggestion here is that the U-form organisational structure has faced major problems in terms of information and control. These have become more acute as firms have diversified and technology has advanced. The outcome is that firms are increasingly involved with broader and technically more complex product portfolios. Cross-linkages between marketing and production personnel are clearly vital where effective promotion and selling depend on a high degree of technical awareness by those engaged in direct contact with sophisticated consumers. However, as we have seen, the U-form structure is not inherently suited to such cross-functional linkages. As functional managers and the CEO become increasingly involved in facilitating and monitoring functional linkages, there is progressively less time and opportunity for strategic planning. Attempts to resolve problems of information and control within and between functional areas have often involved the addition of extra tiers of management, further divorcing top decision makers from everyday operations. The result may be loss of control by the CEO and top managers, creating opportunities for middle and lower management to create their own subculture and goal sets, which may not fully accord with those at the top of the com-

Fig. 5.8 **Types of organisational structure.**

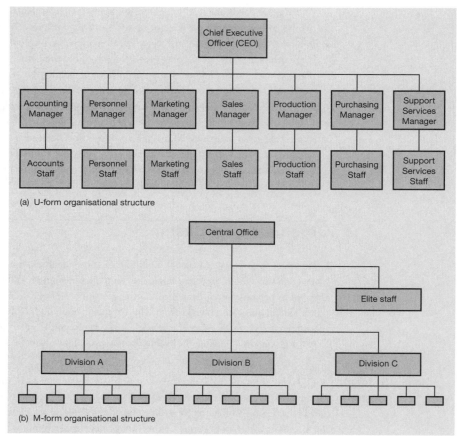

(a) U-form organisational structure

(b) M-form organisational structure

mand structure. This is especially likely where the profitability of functional divisions is difficult to observe and quantify, providing opportunities for managers to expand such divisions beyond their optimal size in terms of corporate profitability.

Multidivisional (M-form) structure

An **M-form** structure is generally regarded as being of the type in Fig. 5.8(b). This multidivisional organisational structure was devised in the 1920s by General Motors and the DuPont company in the USA in an attempt to remedy information and control deficiencies increasingly apparent in the U-form structure.

The M-form structure consists of a central or general office, often with specifically designated (elite) staff to oversee strategic developments and freed from any day-to-day operational involvement. A number of *operating divisions* are overseen by the central office, with each division responsible for a group of related activities. Such groupings could be arranged by product, process, geographical area or type of consumer. Each operating division is self-contained, having access to all the functions deemed necessary for its effective operation.

The alleged advantages of a clearer divorce between those responsible for policy guidance and those involved in operational matters include the former being better able to focus on strategic planning and the latter being more aware of market realities. Growth by diversification can more easily be accommodated by the M-structure, with new divisions created to handle new products. The profitability of each division is arguably more easily observed and monitored, leading to less principal–agent conflict of the type previously considered. Those divisions (profit centres) achieving the most rapid growth in net worth can be allocated additional resources, and vice versa. Such monitoring of divisional profit targets may help to overcome much of the non-profit-oriented behaviour of the U-type organisation. This suggests that profit may be given a higher ranking in terms of firm objective as the design of the organisation shifts away from the U-form and towards the (allegedly) more efficient M-form.

However, where strong *synergies* exist between operating divisions, their separation invariably means some loss of efficiency. To benefit from such synergies may involve extensive information exchange and liaison between divisions. To avoid such time-consuming and costly liaison, interdivisional 'rules' as regards pricing, quality, etc. may be established to give some uniformity of overall approach. However, these rules may themselves inhibit appropriate adaptive responses within individual divisions, leading to suboptimal decisions as regards the maximisation of net worth.

It is clear that neither the U-form, the M-form, nor the many hybrid variants of the two organisational structures, can fully overcome the inherent principal–agent dilemma in all foreseeable circumstances.

Contingency theory

The **contingency theory** of company behaviour suggests that the optimal solutions to organisational problems are derived from matching the *internal* structure and processes of the firm with its *external* environment. However, the external environment is constantly changing as industrial markets become more complex, so that the optimum strategy for a firm will change as the prevailing environmental influences change. The result of this is that firms may not pursue a single goal such as the maximisation of profits or sales, but will have to vary their goals and strategies as the environment changes around them. It has been argued by some economists that there may be as many as 2,000 different strategic behaviour patterns, depending on the nature of the firm and its environment.

▨ Product life cycle and Portfolio planning

Strategies related to the product life cycle and to the approach known as 'portfolio planning' would again seem to cast doubt on the relevance and usefulness of any single, maximising assumption in predicting firm behaviour.

The product life cycle

This extremely important concept, its characteristics and associated strategies are illustrated diagrammatically in Fig. 5.9. The suggestion is that all products brought to the market follow a pattern, which is described as a **life cycle**. This life cycle is normally said to have four stages:

1. *Introduction*. This is a stage in which the product is relatively unknown, sales are low, and profits are not yet being made. The promotion strategy will be designed to inform people that the product is available. The product would normally be stocked in

Fig. 5.9 **Stages in the product life cycle.**

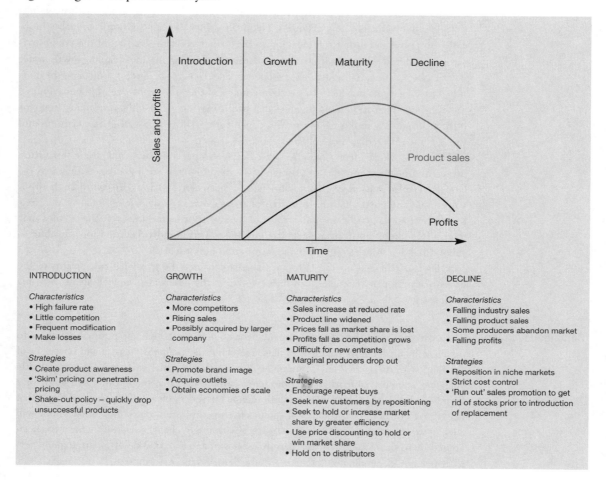

INTRODUCTION

Characteristics
• High failure rate
• Little competition
• Frequent modification
• Make losses

Strategies
• Create product awareness
• 'Skim' pricing or penetration pricing
• Shake-out policy – quickly drop unsuccessful products

GROWTH

Characteristics
• More competitors
• Rising sales
• Possibly acquired by larger company

Strategies
• Promote brand image
• Acquire outlets
• Obtain economies of scale

MATURITY

Characteristics
• Sales increase at reduced rate
• Product line widened
• Prices fall as market share is lost
• Profits fall as competition grows
• Difficult for new entrants
• Marginal producers drop out

Strategies
• Encourage repeat buys
• Seek new customers by repositioning
• Seek to hold or increase market share by greater efficiency
• Use price discounting to hold or win market share
• Hold on to distributors

DECLINE

Characteristics
• Falling industry sales
• Falling product sales
• Some producers abandon market
• Falling profits

Strategies
• Reposition in niche markets
• Strict cost control
• 'Run out' sales promotion to get rid of stocks prior to introduction of replacement

a limited number of outlets, but the firm would try to ensure that there was maximum exposure at these points of sale. Price would be relatively high at this time owing to lack of competition.

2. *Growth*. In this stage there is extremely rapid growth, which attracts the first competitors to the market. Prices are likely to be lowered to attract a wider base of customers and the number of outlets to be increased. The firm will be seeking the new products that will replace this one, or modifications to the existing product that will extend its life cycle. The profits that are starting to be made can be used to support such investments.

3. *Maturity*. The majority of sales are repeat orders in this stage rather than first-time purchases. Fierce competition often forces the firm to reduce prices further. Advertising seeks to persuade customers to buy this, rather than some other, brand of product. The firm will be looking to see whether the product can be sold in other markets – often abroad. Refinements and cosmetic changes are introduced to provide

a competitive edge and maintain sales levels. Replacement products are likely to be introduced. Economies of scale resulting from large-volume production will help to keep unit costs low and profits high.

4. *Decline*. As sales decline, advertising and promotion cease. Prices may be reduced as much as possible to keep at least some sales. Eventually, as the product moves into loss, it is withdrawn from the market.

Although it is widely accepted that most products do have a life cycle, the nature and duration of the life cycle is likely to be different for every product. The life cycle for many commonplace items, such as soap, will be long. For others, such as high-technology products, it may be very short. Life cycles of other products – 'fads' – are extremely unpredictable. Sales will increase dramatically, and there may very well be difficulties in meeting this upsurge in demand. Equally suddenly the surge in demand will ease, leaving manufacturers and retailers with unsaleable stock on their hands.

Portfolio planning   Work in the USA by the Boston Consulting Group on the relationship between market share and industry growth has given rise to an approach to corporate planning known as *portfolio planning*. Firms, especially the larger ones, can be viewed as having a collection or portfolio of different products at different stages in the product life cycle. If a product is at an early stage in its life cycle, it will require a large investment in marketing and product development in order to achieve future levels of high profitability. At the same time another product may have matured and, already possessing a good share of the market, be providing high profits and substantial cash flow.

If a firm is using the portfolio approach in its planning then it may be impossible to predict the firm's behaviour for individual products or market sectors on the basis of a single firm objective. This is because the goals of the firm will change for a given product or market sector *depending on the relative position of that product or market sector within the overall portfolio*. Portfolio planning, along with other behavioural theories, suggest that no single objective is likely to be useful in explaining actual firm behaviour, at least in specific cases.

Firm objectives and the internationalisation of production

We have seen in this chapter that firms often attempt to satisfy a number of objectives, and that conflict can occur between managers and shareholders as to which objectives are most appropriate at any given moment in time. These issues have also been at the heart of more recent discussions on the *internationalisation* of production through the growth of multinational companies.

At this stage it might be useful to investigate briefly why companies have adopted an international approach to the organisation of production. It will be noted that much of the motivation for firms to establish multinational production has been based on the need to increase revenue or reduce costs. This shows that in whatever form we encounter it, the profit motive is still a powerful factor in company behaviour. However, before considering such motivation in detail let us briefly define the term 'multinational'.

The terms 'multinational', 'transnational' and 'international' corporation (or enterprise) are often used interchangeably. A multinational may be defined as a company that owns or controls production or service facilities in more than one country. In other words, a multinational is *not* simply a company that trades internationally by exporting its products (or by licensing overseas producers), it actually *owns* (via a wholly or partly owned subsidiary) *or controls* (via a branch plant, joint venture or minority shareholding) productive facilities in countries outside its home country. Such overseas productive facilities may be acquired by taking over existing locally owned capacity (e.g. Nestlé's famous acquisition of Rowntree in 1988 or BMW's takeover of Rover in 1994), or by investing directly in new (or 'greenfield' site) plant and equipment (e.g. Nissan's plant in Washington or Toyota's car factory in Derby).

Technical definitions of multinationals, however, fail to convey the true scope and diversity of global business, which covers everything from the thousands of medium-sized firms that have overseas operations to the truly gigantic multinationals such as IBM, General Motors and Ford. Some multinationals are vertically integrated, with different stages of the same productive process taking place in different countries (e.g. British Petroleum). Others are horizontally integrated, performing the same basic production operations in each of the countries in which they operate (e.g. Forte, Marks and Spencer). Many multinationals are household names, marketing global brands (e.g. Rothmans International, IBM, British Airways). Others are holding companies for a portfolio of international companies (e.g. Hanson, Diageo) or specialise in capital goods that have little name-recognition in the high street (e.g. BTR, Hawker Siddley, GKN).

This analysis of firm motivation and internationalisation follows closely that of Healey (1999). It will be useful at this stage to distinguish between multinationals that are cost-oriented and those that are market-oriented.

Cost-oriented multinationals

Cost-oriented multinationals are those that internationalise their operations by *vertical integration*: e.g. integrating backwards in search of cheaper or more secure inputs into the productive process. The oil companies such as Exxon, Shell and BP were early examples of this approach. In order to secure control of strategic raw materials in oil fields around the world, they established overseas extraction operations in the early years of the twentieth century with the aim of shipping crude oil back to their home markets for refining and sale. More recently, many US and European companies have integrated forwards by establishing assembly facilities in SE Asia in order to take account of the relative abundance of cheap, high-quality labour. Companies such as America's ITT ship semi-manufactured components to the region, where they are assembled by local labour into finished products, which are then re-exported back to the home market. Such home countries are sometimes termed 'production platforms', which underscores their role as providers of a low-cost input into a global, vertically integrated production process.

Market-oriented multinationals

Market-oriented multinationals are those whose internationalisation is motivated by the promise of new markets and greater sales: i.e. the internationalisation process takes the form of *horizontal* (rather than vertical) *integration* into new geographic markets, with companies gradually switching from exporting (or licensing) to establishing first a sales outlet and finally full production facilities overseas (see Figure 5.10) .

Fig. 5.10 **Evolution of a market–oriented multinational.**

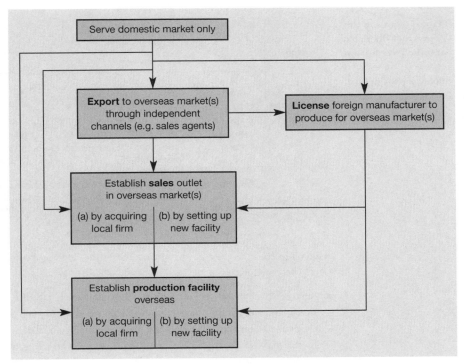

Extending the product life cycle A more subtle variation on this theme is that firms may internationalise in order to extend the product life cycle of their products (p. 220). The link between the product life cycle and internationalisation stems from the fact that a product may be at *different stages of its life cycle* in *different geographic markets*, giving rise to changing configurations of supply and demand that variously favour local production, and/or exporting, and/or importing from cheaper overseas suppliers.

Consider Fig. 5.11, which illustrates one possible scenario for a US manufacturer. In *Phase 1* (introduction), production is concentrated in the USA, with the innovating companies exporting to other countries. As the US market matures and production techniques become standardised, production starts up in the expanding, lower cost European market. These new lower-cost producers are able to initially displace imports from the USA (in *Phase II*) and then increasingly challenge US competitors for a share of developing country markets (in *Phase III*) and finally challenge those competitors in the US market itself (in *Phase IV*). In due course, however, the technology spreads to the developing world, whose producers are gradually able to take on and out-compete higher-cost European companies, first in their own markets (*Phase IV*) and ultimately in the US market as well (*Phase V*). In this way, the product life cycle drives production *out* of the innovating country to lower-cost producers overseas.

Advances in enabling technologies While cost orientation and market orientation clearly provide important motives for investing and producing overseas, the acceleration in the pace of globalisation is also intimately tied up with advances in

Fig. 5.11
Stages/phases in the
product life cycle
and the switch from
domestic to
overseas production.

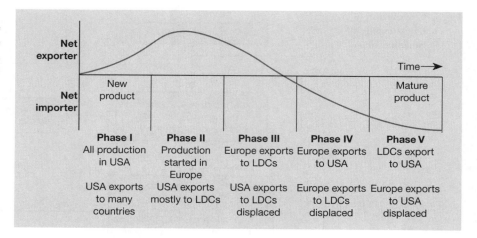

enabling technologies that have reduced the costs of doing business across national frontiers. These include:

- *improved communications*, including cheap air travel, satellite telephone and fax facilities, computers and IT-based communications systems such as the Internet;
- *the globalisation of consumer markets*, through television, video and popular music. These media make it cheaper for established producers to penetrate new markets in developing countries;
- *new organisational technologies*, e.g. the rise of the divisional corporate structure based on product or geographic divisions or matrices. This makes managing complex global companies more feasible.

Benefits of producing overseas compared to exporting   One way of exploring the decision by a domestic company to internationalise its production is to consider the advantages of producing at home *vis-à-vis* overseas.

Consider a **market-oriented** company first. By exporting, the company can concentrate production in a single plant at home, reaping the advantages of the lower production costs that flow from economies of scale and avoiding the costs of managing an overseas facility. By producing overseas, the company can avoid the costs of transporting its products and incurring tariffs. All other things being equal, the greater the scope for economies of scale and the higher the transport, tariff and other costs of managing offshore facilities, the more likely a firm will be to forgo internationalisation in favour of a large domestic plant; conversely, the smaller the scope for economies of scale and the higher the transport costs and tariffs faced when exporting, the greater the incentive to invest directly in overseas capacity.

Figure 5.12(a) illustrates these basic principles graphically. It shows the demand (average revenue) and marginal revenue schedules that the firm faces in its *overseas* market. For simplicity, *the marginal cost of production* (whether at home or abroad) is assumed to be constant at C_1 (n.b., with a given fixed cost, this implies that average total costs decline as production increases). The *marginal cost of supplying the overseas market* from a domestic production platform is C_2, where $C_2 - C_1$ is equal to the unit costs of

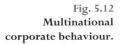

Fig. 5.12
Multinational corporate behaviour.

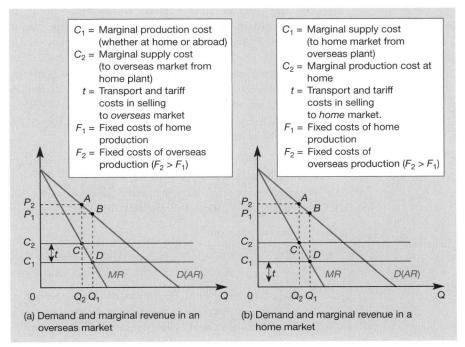

C_1 = Marginal production cost (whether at home or abroad)
C_2 = Marginal supply cost (to overseas market from home plant)
t = Transport and tariff costs in selling to *overseas* market
F_1 = Fixed costs of home production
F_2 = Fixed costs of overseas production ($F_2 > F_1$)

C_1 = Marginal supply cost (to home market from overseas plant)
C_2 = Marginal production cost at home
t = Transport and tariff costs in selling to *home* market.
F_1 = Fixed costs of home production
F_2 = Fixed costs of overseas production ($F_2 > F_1$)

(a) Demand and marginal revenue in an overseas market

(b) Demand and marginal revenue in a home market

transport and *tariffs*. The firm faces *fixed* production costs of F_1 if it produces at home and F_2 if it produces abroad (where F_2 is assumed to be greater than F_1, given the higher costs of managing an overseas production facility).

Consider its options:

- If the firm *exports to the overseas market*, it will set marginal supply cost overseas C_2 equal to marginal revenue, charging a price P_2 and earning profit equal to $P_2 A C C_2 - F_1$.
- If the firm *establishes an overseas production facility*, it will set marginal production cost overseas C_1 equal to marginal revenue, charging a price P_1 and earning profit equal to $P_1 B D C_1 - F_2$.

Clearly, the firm's decision rules are:

1. If $P_2 A C C_2 - F_1 > P_1 B D C_1 - F_2$, then produce at home and export to overseas market.
2. If $P_1 B D C_1 - F_2 > P_2 A C C_2 - F_1$, then produce overseas.

All other things being equal, the *higher the transport costs and/or tariffs levied on exports* to the overseas market (i.e. C_2 compared with C_1), the greater the relative attractiveness of overseas production *vis-à-vis* exporting; similarly, all other things being equal, the *lower the relative fixed costs of producing overseas* (i.e. F_2 compared with F_1), the more attractive overseas production. The gap $F_2 - F_1$ will be reduced by advances in enabling technologies, which, as we have noted, cut the costs of doing business across national frontiers.

Hence the decision for a market-oriented firm to locate overseas rather than export hinges critically on the transport and tariff costs of serving overseas markets and the relative fixed costs of production: the greater the former, and the smaller any gap as regards the latter ($F_2 > F_1$), the more favourable the situation is to multinational activity.

The same diagram can also be reinterpreted to illustrate the decision facing a **cost-oriented multinational**. In this case (Fig. 5.12b) the demand and marginal revenue schedules are drawn for the *home market*. Here C_2 is now the company's marginal cost of producing at home for its domestic market, while C_1 represents the marginal cost of supplying the home market from an overseas production platform, including shipping back to the home market and paying any tariffs imposed. Despite the costs of transport and tariffs, it is assumed here that overseas production is subject to lower supply costs to the home market than would occur via production at home (i.e. $C_1 < C_2$), for example because of lower labour costs.

- If the firm *produces at home*, it sets marginal production cost C_2 equal to marginal revenue, charging a price P_2 and earning profit $P_2ACC_2 - F_1$.
- If the firm *produces abroad*, it sets marginal supply cost C_1 equal to marginal revenue, charging a price P_1 and earning profit $P_1BDC_1 - F_2$.

Its decision rules are now:

1. If $P_2ACC_2 - F_1 > P_1BDC_1 - F_2$, then produce at home.
2. If $P_1BDC_1 - F_2 > P_2ACC_2 - F_1$, then produce overseas and export to home market.

All other things being equal, the *lower the relative marginal costs of supplying from overseas* (i.e. C_1 compared with C_2), the greater the relative attractiveness of overseas production *vis-à-vis* domestic production; similarly, all other things being equal, the *lower the relative fixed costs of producing overseas* (i.e. F_2 compared with F_1) the more attractive is overseas production.

Hence the decision for a cost-oriented firm to serve its home market from an off-shore production facility rather than producing at home hinges on the relative variable costs of overseas production and the relative fixed costs. The greater the (variable) cost discrepancy in favour of overseas supply, and the smaller any adverse gap as regards overseas fixed costs compared with domestic fixed costs (i.e. F_2 compared with F_1), the more favourable the situation is to multinational activity. Clearly any reduction in transport and tariff costs (t) in selling to the home market from overseas will make a variable cost discrepancy in favour of overseas supply more likely.

Applications and evidence

The theoretical models presented in the previous section often tended to concentrate on the role of one or two variables in determining company behaviour. In practice, firms adjust both their behaviour and goals through time in order to survive. As we shall see, there is therefore some element of truth in both the managerial and behavioural theories of the firm. In this section we present some evidence in relation to the various theories of firm motivation and behaviour.

Ownership and control in practice

Profit maximisation is usually based on the assumption that firms are owner controlled, whereas sales and growth maximisation usually assume that there is a separation between ownership and control. The acceptance of these alternative theories was helped by early research into the ownership of firms. Studies in the USA by Berle and Means in the 1930s and by Larner in the 1960s suggested that a substantial proportion of large firms (44% by Berle and Means and 85% by Larner) were manager controlled rather than owner controlled. Later research has, however, challenged the definition of 'owner control' used in these early studies. Whereas Berle and Means assumed that owner control is only present with a shareholding of more than 20% in a public limited company, Nyman and Silberston (1978) used a much lower figure of 5% after research had indicated that effective control could be exercised by owners with this level of shareholding. This would suggest that owner control is far more extensive than previously thought. Leech and Leahy (1991) found that 91% of British public limited companies were owner controlled using the 5% threshold figure, but only 34% were owner controlled using a 20% threshold figure. Clearly the degree of ownership control is somewhat subjective, depending crucially on the threshold figure assigned to shareholding by owners in order to exercise effective control.

A further aspect of owner control involves the role of financial institutions and pension funds. Between them they now own over 76% of the shares of public companies in the UK, compared with only 36% in 1963, while individual share ownership has declined from 54% to around 20% over the same period. Financial institutions are more likely than individuals to bring influence to bear on chief executives, being experienced in the channels of communication and sensitive to indices of firm performance. The effect of this influence is seen by many as moving the firm towards the profit-maximising (owner-controlled) type of objective.

Profit, reward structures and the principal–agent problem

The **principal–agent problem** (p. 215) often emerged as the result of the divorce of ownership from control in large companies. However, if the demands from shareholders for profit could be met, then the tension inherent between the different objectives of shareholders and managers could be partly resolved.

One proposed solution involves formulating a compensation package (including salaries, bonuses and share options) so that managerial pay is closely related to profits, or to profit-related variables such as shareholder wealth and stock performance. Jensen and Murphy (1990) in a survey of 2,213 top US chief executive officers (CEOs) over a period of 50 years found that CEO wealth varied directly with company performance. However, CEO wealth increased by only $3.25 for every $1,000 change in shareholder wealth, as measured by the inflation-adjusted rate of return on ordinary stock. Although bonuses represented as much as 50% of CEO salary, such bonuses were often awarded in ways that were not always sensitive to firm performance. The conclusion of the study was that although there was evidence of a direct relationship between managerial compensation and shareholder wealth, the magnitude of that relationship was too small to be a realistic mechanism for resolving any principal–agent problem.

Some work on compensation and performance sensitivities in the UK is presented in Table 5.1. The term β measures the sensitivity of managerial compensation to company performance across a number of performance measures. The evidence is reasonably consistent across the various empirical studies in that the β values indicate very small pay performance sensitivities. In fact the work of Gregg, Machin and Szymanski (1993) and also Conyon and Gregg (1994) seems to indicate that after the late 1980s there was *no* detectable relationship between executive compensation and company performance. These studies also suggest that there is no effective mechanism in place to induce agents (managers) to act in a manner likely to satisfy principals (shareholders) who have a clear disposition in favour of profit.

Table 5.1 **Studies investigating compensation–performance linkages as indicated by the β parameter.**

Study	Data	Compensation measure	Performance measure	Estimated β (standard error)
Gregg, Machin and Szymanski (1993)	288 UK companies, 1983–91	Change in salary plus bonus of highest-paid director	Change in shareholder returns	1983–88: 0.027 (0.013) 1989–91: –0.024 (0.022)
Main (1992)	512 UK companies, 1969–89	Change in salary plus bonus of highest-paid director	Stock market return	0.038 (0.012)
Main and Johnston (1993)	220 UK companies, 1990	Salary plus bonus of highest-paid director	Risk-adjusted market return	0.100 (0.135)
Conyon and Leech (1994)	294 UK companies, 1983–86	Change in salary plus bonus of highest-paid director	Change in shareholder wealth	0.052 (0.020)
Conyon and Gregg (1994)	169 UK companies, 1985–90	Change in salary plus bonus of highest-paid director	Shareholder return	1985–87: 0.076 (0.032) 1988–90: 0.020 (0.036)
Conyon (1994)	217 UK companies, 1988–93	Change in salary plus bonus of highest-paid director	Shareholder return	–0.016 (0.081)

Source: Adapted from Conyon, Gregg and Machin (1995)

Recent evidence in the UK indicated that in 40% of listed companies the chief executive sits on the company's remuneration committee. Indeed directors of one company often sit as directors on the remuneration committees of other companies, tending to reinforce the view that pay is determined by a 'group coalition' that has its own interests at heart. The Cadbury report (1992) on the governance of British companies recommended that remuneration committees should *not* be composed of executive directors since they should play no part in decisions about their own remuneration. Similarly the Greenbury Report (1995) sought to strengthen shareholder control of corporate remuneration strategy by improving the disclosure of executive remuneration, including pay, pensions and perquisites on an annual basis to shareholders. Chairmen of remuneration committees were to be made answerable to the AGM for pay policy, with shareholder voting to be encouraged on specific aspects of executive pay. Withdrawal of Stock Exchange listing was to be a sanction available should any listed company fail to comply with these recommendations.

Storey *et al.* (1995) also found no evidence of a link between the pay of top managers and the ratio of average pre-tax profits to total assets, confirming this earlier work in the UK, and Barkema and Gomez-Meija (1998) derived similar results in the USA. Table 5.2 confirms this picture, with only one of the firms appearing in the 10 highest profit rankings in the USA being in the list of the ten highest-paid CEOs (namely the CEO of the computer chip manufacturer Intel).

Table 5.2 Ten highest ranked US corporations by profit and CEO remuneration.

Rank	Profit performance	Highest-paid CEOs
1	Microsoft	Travelers Group
2	Intel	Conseco
3	Coca-cola	HealthSouth
4	Schering-Plough	Occidental Petroleum
5	Merck	AlliedSignal
6	Bank of New York	Intel
7	Bristol-Myers Squibb	HBO & Co.
8	CoreState Financial	Monsanto
9	EMC	Morgan Stanley DW
10	Berkshire Hathaway	Cedant

Source: Adapted from *FAME* (1998)

However, the absence of any proven link between the profitability of a firm and the reward structures it offers to its CEO and other top managers does not necessarily mean that profit-related goals are unimportant. Firms increasingly offer top managers a remuneration 'package', with pay but one element of a total remuneration 'package' involving bonus payments and share options as well as salary. In this case higher firm profitability, and therefore dividend earnings per share, may help to raise the share price and with it the value of the total remuneration package. Indeed Ezzamel and Watson (1998) have suggested that the total remuneration package offered to CEOs is directly related to the 'going rate' for corporate profitability. Their findings are in line with an earlier study by Main *et al*. (1996), which found that a 10% increase in shareholder wealth had the effect, via share options, of increasing the pay of the highest-paid director by 8.9%. It may therefore be that top management have more incentives for seeking profit-related goals than might at first be apparent.

Profits and company behaviour

It is obvious to most observers that the creation of **profits** is of vital importance to companies. Profits can be measured in different ways, e.g. in absolute terms or as a ratio such as earnings per share, return on investment (ROI), etc. Unfortunately profit figures depend on the specific type of accounting procedure adopted and on the ways in which companies decide to display their trading outcomes, which are often influenced by tax law. For example, different ways of adjusting for depreciation, valuing stock, utilising exchange rates for expressing holdings of various currencies, accounting for mergers and takeovers, etc. can change reported profits quite substantially. Of course measures such as earnings per share only indicate *past* profit performance, rather than prospects for future profits. Indeed reported profits can often be increased substantially by contemporary actions, such as cutting back on planned investment in plant and machinery. However, such profit-related strategies might jeopardise future growth of the company and with it future profits. The question then arises as to whether firms are seeking to maximise notions of short- or long-run profits.

Given these observations about the complex nature of profit, it may be useful to consider the results of some surveys as regards the role of profit in firm motivation. One of the most comprehensive surveys in the UK was that conducted across 728 UK firms by Shipley (1981).

Profit as a primary objective

As we can see from Table 5.3, Shipley concluded that only 15.9% of his sample of 728 UK firms could be regarded as *true* profit maximisers. This conclusion was reached by cross-tabulating replies to the two questions shown in the table. Because answers to questionnaires can often be given loosely, Shipley considered as 'true' maximisers only those who claimed *both* to maximise profit (answered (a) to Question (1)) and to regard profit as being of overriding importance (answered (d) to Question (2)). Only 15.9% of all the firms replied with both 1(a) and 2(d), and were considered by Shipley as true profit maximisers.

A smaller study of 77 Scottish companies by Hornby (1995), following the Shipley methodology, found that only 24.7% of respondents could be defined as true profit maximisers.

Although these figures seem rather low, it should be remembered that 85% of managers in the Shipley study still felt that a *target* level of profits was either 'of overriding importance' or 'very important' (see Table 5.3).

Given the significance of the profit-maximising assumption in economic analysis, these results may seem surprising. However, some considerations of the decision-making process may serve to explain these low figures for profit maximisation. Traditional theory assumes that firms invest in the most profitable projects first, and then choose

Table 5.3 **Profits and firm objectives.**

	All respondents (%)
(1) Does your firm try to achieve:	
(a) maximum profits,	47.7
(b) 'satisfactory' profits?	52.3
(2) Compared to your firm's other leading objectives, is the achievement of a target profit . . . regarded as being:	
(a) of little importance	2.1
(b) fairly important	12.9
(c) very important	58.9
(d) of overriding importance?	26.1
Those responding with both 1(a) and 2(d)	15.9

Source: Adapted from Shipley (1981)

projects of descending profitability, until the return on the last project just covers the cost of funding that project: i.e. marginal revenue = marginal cost, and profit is maximised. In fact, the process of choosing projects is much more complicated and subject to many influences. First, many companies do not have access to sufficient funds to reach the marginal position. Second, project appraisal is based on perception and educated guesses about how markets will react. Instead of assessing a *single* revenue and cost outcome for the project, to which marginal analysis could be applied, outcome is often evaluated in terms of *scenarios*. In this way, firms are in practice forced away from marginal analysis. In addition, they often rely on preset *hurdle* rates of return for projects, with managers given some minimum rate of return as a criterion for project appraisal. As a result they may not consciously see themselves as profit maximisers, since this phrase suggests marginal analysis. Yet in setting the hurdle rates, top management will be keenly aware of the marginal cost of funding, so that this approach may in some cases relate closely to profit maximisation. In other words, the response of management to questionnaires may understate the true significance of the pursuit of profit.

Profit as part of a 'goal set'

Although few firms appear to set out specifically to maximise it, profit is still seen (even in responses to questionnaires) as an important factor in decision making. In the Shipley study the firms were asked to list their **principal goal** in setting their price and whether any particular pricing objective was part of a broader **goal set**. The results of these questions are reported in Table 5.4.

Table 5.4 shows that *target profit* was easily the goal most frequently cited, with 73% of all firms regarding it as their principal goal. Even more firms (88%) included profit as at least part of their goal set.

Profit: long-term vs short-term

Long-term profit may be even more important than short-term profit in firm objectives. Senior managers are well aware that poor profitability in the long term may lead to their dismissal or the takeover of their firm, quite apart from an increased risk of

Table 5.4 **Pricing objectives: principal objectives and objectives as part of a goal set.**

	Principal goal[a]	Part of goal set
Target profit or ROCE[b]	486	639
Prices fair to firm and customers	94	353
Price similarity with competitors	56	350
Target sales revenue	54	342
Stable volume of sales	37	182
Target market share of sales	16	129
Stable prices	11	120
Other	10	38

[a]Thirty-four respondents cited two or more principal objectives.
[b]Return on capital employed.
Source: Adapted from Shipley (1981)

insolvency. Indeed Shipley found that 59.7% of his sample gave priority to long-term profits, compared with only 20.6% giving priority to short-term profits. Shipley found long-term profit to be a significant influence in all sizes of company, though particularly in those of medium/large size. More recently, a survey by the *Financial Times* (1998) of 77 finance directors of FTSE 100 companies found that 98% considered the priority of investors to be long-term performance of the company rather than its performance in the short term.

Studies of the behaviour of firms in technology-based markets has provided further support for the emphasis on longer-term profit perspectives (Arthur 1996). Arthur suggests that when a technology reaches a certain critical mass of usage the market is 'locked in', and the only rational choice for new users is then to adopt the established technology. He cites Microsoft Windows as being a typical example of this, with the continued increase in use of Windows providing an example of a market system operating positive feedback. Arthur suggests that average (and marginal) revenues might even rise in technology-based markets as volume exceeds the 'critical mass' for that established technology, rather than decline as in standard theory. This phenomenon has often led to a strategy of giving away products reflecting new technologies at their introduction stage in order to create lock-in. The objective of this strategy for technology-based markets might arguably still be profit maximisation, but only in the longer term.

To summarise, therefore, although there may be little open admission in these studies to pursuing the objective of profit maximisation, the strong influence of owners on managed firms, the use of pre-set hurdle rates, and the existence of managerial remuneration 'packages' related to firm profitability may, in the end, lead to an objective or set of objectives in which profit plays an important part, especially in the long term.

International perspectives on profit

A question that naturally arises is whether profit motivation is significant in countries other than the UK. Table 5.5 shows the nature of the management goals recorded in an extensive survey of firm motivation in the USA and Japan (OECD 1993).

Management goal[a]	USA	Japan
Return on investment	2.43	1.24
Higher stock price	1.14	0.02
Market share	0.73	1.43
Improved product portfolio	0.50	0.68
Streamlined production and distribution	0.46	0.71
Higher ratio of net worth	0.38	0.59
Higher ratio of new products	0.21	1.06
Improved image of companies	0.05	0.09
Improved working conditions	0.04	0.09

[a] Figures are averages based on the top three choices: 3 for top place,
2 for second, 1 for third, and 0 for all others.
Source: OECD (1993)

Managers in both countries were asked to ascribe values of between 1 and 3 to each of their three most important goals: 1 to the least important, and 3 to the most important. The averages of these responses are represented for various management goals in Table 5.5. The table suggests that 'return on investment' (i.e. obtaining an adequate rate of profit to satisfy shareholders) was of paramount importance in the USA but was given much less importance in Japan. The reasons for such a difference may depend in part on the nature of shareholder power and on certain strategic behaviour patterns that will be discussed later (p. 235).

A similar survey as to the importance of short-term profits in Japan, the USA and the UK is reported in Table 5.6. From Table 5.6 we see that 'good short-term profits' are seen as much more important in the USA and UK than in Japan. It would appear from Tables 5.5 and 5.6 that the objectives of firms can differ between countries, with motivations other than short-term profit being more important in some countries than in others.

Table 5.6 Emphasis on short-term profit: Japan, USA and UK.

'How well does "good short-term profits are the objective" describe your company?'[a]

Japanese 27%	USA 80%	UK 87%

[a]Statistical significance is at the 5% level.
Source: Doyle (1994)

Managerial theories and non-profit-maximising behaviour

We noted earlier that some of the justification for the **managerial theories** of firm behaviour rested on the progressive divorce of ownership from control, as larger companies became more important within the world economy. It was therefore suggested that managerial motivations based on sales revenue maximisation, utility maximisation or growth maximisation would become increasingly more prominent as compared with pure profit maximisation. It is difficult to provide unambiguous tests of managerial theories because some of the proposed managerial outcomes are interdependent, as is sometimes the case with sales revenue, market share and growth in asset value.

Sales revenue maximisation

Baumol's suggestion that management-controlled firms will wish to maximize sales revenue was based in part on the belief that the earnings of executives are more closely related to firm revenue than to firm profit. A number of studies have tended to support this belief. For example, in a study of 177 firms between 1985 and 1990, Conyon and Gregg (1994) found that the pay of top executives in large companies in the UK was most strongly related to *relative sales revenue growth* (i.e. relative to competitors). They also found such pay to be only weakly related to a long-term profit measure (total shareholder returns) and not at all to current accounting profit. For example, the income of top executives increased by 77% in the same period (1985–90) in which real earnings increased by only 17%. Furthermore, growth in sales resulting from takeovers produced, on average, a lower return for shareholders and an increased liquidity risk. These findings are in line with other recent UK research (Gregg, Machin and Szymanski 1993; Conyon and Leech 1994) and with a study of small UK companies by Conyon and Nicolitsas (1998), which also found sales growth to be closely correlated with the pay of top excutives.

Sales revenue as part of a goal set

The results of Shipley's analysis tell us little about sales revenue maximisation. Nevertheless, Table 5.4 (p. 232) showed that *target sales revenue* was the fourth-ranked principal pricing objective, and that nearly half the firms included sales revenue as at least part of their set of objectives. Larger companies cited sales revenue as an objective most frequently; one-seventh of companies with over 3,000 employees gave sales revenue as a principal goal, compared with only one-fourteenth of all the firms. Since larger companies have greater separation between ownership and management control, this does lend some support to Baumol's assertion. The importance of sales revenue as part of a set of policy objectives was reinforced by a study of 193 UK industrial distributors by Shipley and Bourdon (1990), which found that 88% of these companies included sales revenue as one of a number of objectives. However, we see below that the nature of planning in large organisations must also be considered, and that this may temper our support for sales revenue being itself the major objective, at least in the long term.

Strategic planning and sales revenue

Current thinking on **strategic planning** would support the idea of short-term sales revenue maximisation, but only as a means to other ends (e.g. profitability or growth). Research in the mid-1970s by the US Strategic Planning Institute linked market share – seen here as a proxy for sales revenue – to profitability. These studies found that high market share had a significant and beneficial effect on both return on investment and cash flow, at least in the long term. However, in the short term the high investment and marketing expenditure needed to attain high market share reduces profitability and drains cash flow. Profit has to be sacrificed in the short term if high market share, and hence high future profits, are to be achieved in the long term.

Any observation that firms seek to maximise sales revenue (market share) may then merely reflect tactical short- to medium-term strategy, rather than long-term objective, i.e. a means to an end (higher profits) rather than an end in itself. This does not reduce the value of the theory of sales revenue maximisation for predictive purposes, as long as the timescales involved are recognized. In the short to medium term, sales revenue maximisation may be the most useful assumption for predictive purposes. In the longer term, profit maximisation would still appear to be supreme.

Insofar as there *is* a linkage between sales revenue and market share, then Table 5.5 (p. 233) indicates the importance of this objective in Japan and the USA. For example, market share is seen as the primary managerial goal in Japan, and the third most important managerial goal in the USA.

Constrained sales revenue maximisation

The fact that 88% of all companies in Shipley's study (Table 5.4, p. 232) included profit in their goal set indicates the relevance of the profit constraint to other objectives, including sales revenue. A later study by Shipley and Bourdon (1990) reached a similar conclusion, finding that 93% of the UK industrial distributors surveyed included profit in their goal set.

Growth-maximisation

Perhaps the most fertile ground for testing managerial non-profit-maximising models is to analyse the **growth-maximising** hypothesis put forward by Marris. This is because the growth process can, to some extent, embrace both the sales revenue maximisation and expense preference theories of Baumol and Williamson respectively. On the supply side, Marris's theory involves the growth in such variables as a firm's asset base, including both physical and non-physical assets. On the demand side, Marris recognises that the growth of sales revenue depends on a progressive policy of product diversification. If new products are *not* brought onto the market, then the growth momentum is retarded. The valuation ratio is also regarded as a constraint on the growth process: i.e. there is a threat that if the valuation ratio falls too low, then the firm will become increasingly attractive to those considering a takeover. Thus it becomes important for managers to keep share prices relatively high by providing adequate return to shareholders.

There is some evidence that diversification is indeed an important factor underlying firm growth. Jacquemin and Berry (1979) using information on 460 large US firms found that diversification into new product areas generated faster growth. For the UK, Hassid (1977) in a study of companies with over 100 employees found that diversified firms grew about 50% faster than non-diversified firms. However, such diversification often tends to result in firms' wanting to grow too fast, leading to a variety of subsequent problems. Such problems include higher financial gearing as companies take on more debt. Many companies that pursued arguably excessive rates of diversification and growth in the 1980s, such as Saatchi and Saatchi, WPP, Next, Coloroll and Blue Arrow in the UK, and Texaco, PanAm, Campeau and Interco in the USA, found this to their cost. For example, the excessive focus on growth by the UK advertising firm Saatchi and Saatchi has been linked to the subsequent problems and loss of confidence in the company, resulting in a fall in its market valuation from £7 per share to £0.2 over two years. Many such companies experienced takeovers, buy-outs or liquidations, reinforcing the relevance of the valuation ratio constraint being given such a high profile in the Marris model.

However, it is also worth stressing that it is not only the larger, managerial dominated companies that pursue growth-oriented policies. Hay and Morris (1984), in a study of large unquoted UK companies that were mainly owner controlled, found that owner-controlled firms were as likely to pursue growth-oriented policies as were the managerially controlled companies. The suggestion here is that owner-controlled firms were less open to the threat of takeover than managerially controlled firms if they focused on growth rather than profitability. Additionally, the growth-oriented focus of owner-controlled companies faced less constraint as regards the valuation ratio. Indeed it is suggested that they have incentives to keep dividends and share prices *low* in order to minimise tax bills when shares are transferred or when a shareholder dies. The importance of this study is that it tends to indicate that growth is not necessarily an objective pursued only by the managerially controlled firms.

When we examine the facts there is little to indicate that faster growth really does mean higher profits. If, for the purposes of illustration, we equate profitability with percentage profit margin, we can see from Table 5.7(a) that none of the top 10 UK firms with the highest percentage profit margin are in the top 10 growth firms, with only Cable and Wireless, John Swire and Sons and Diageo close to the top 10 fastest-growing

Table 5.7 Firm profitability and firm growth.

(a) Rank in profitability	Firm	Rank in growth
1	Glaxo Wellcome	80
2	Cable and Wireless	11
3	John Swire & Sons Ltd	40
4	Esso Exploration and Production	40
5	Rio Tinto	66
6	Cadbury Schweppes	72
7	BG plc	92
8	Smithkline Beecham	76
9	Zeneca	73
10	Diageo	19

(b) Rank in growth	Firm	Rank in profitability
1	Granada Group plc	18
2	British Steel	55
3	BAT Industries	46
4	BT	11
5	Rover	96
6	General Motors	84
7	Scottish Power	14
8	British Airways	45
9	Shell International	79
10	BP International	73

Source: Adapted from *Financial Analysis Made Easy (FAME)* (1998)

firms. Moreover, Glaxo Wellcome, the UK firm with the highest profitability ranking, is 80th in the growth ranking. From Table 5.7(b) we can see that none of the top 10 UK firms with the fastest growth (percentage change in total assets over past two years) is in the top 10 most profitable firms, with only BT, Scottish Power and Granada close to such a ranking. The other top ten growth firms are low down in the profitability rankings, such as British Steel, which is second in growth but only 55th in profitability.

Table 5.7 is in line with the results of a study by Whittington (1980), who found that profit levels did not increase as the firm grew in size. This lends some support to those, like Marris, who see growth as a separate objective to profit.

In fast-moving markets, such as high-technology electronics and pharmaceuticals, companies need flexibility to move rapidly to fill market niches. To achieve this, some firms are moving in quite the opposite direction to growth: i.e. they are de-merging. 'De-merging' occurs when the firm splits into smaller units, each separately quoted on the Stock Exchange. For example, since 1996 Hanson plc, the US–UK conglomerate, has de-merged its coal, power, tobacco and chemical interests to concentrate on building materials, rather similar to the situation of ICI which, in 1992, had de-merged its pharmaceutical interests, giving 'birth' to the new company Zeneca. Such de-merging is a clear sign that professional investors do not merely equate larger size with greater profit.

■ Behavioural theories and non-maximising approaches

The theories put forward by Simon (p. 212), and Cyert and March (p. 213) suggested that the motivations of firms may be more diverse than the managerial-led models might indicate. The ideas of coalitions and goal aspirations, together with the importance of satisficing and the use of rules of thumb, began to supersede notions of marginalist doctrine as the hallmark of the decision-making process. Over the past 10 years the debate about the importance of different groups or *stakeholders* in the company has attracted wide interest. Companies are increasingly aware of the need to satisfy shareholders, managers, customers, employees and creditors simultaneously, seeking to resolve conflict between any discernible groups of stakeholders. Indeed companies that pursued excellence, i.e. a very high performance in one single objective, seem to have experienced short lives! Peters and Waterman (1982) found that of the 43 'excellent' companies they studied in the early 1980s, only six were still 'excellent' after eight years, and many had disappeared altogether.

Multi objectives and satisficing

An insight into the nature of multiple objectives and the role of satisficing is provided by Hornby's (1995) study of Scottish companies noted earlier (on p. 230). His work indicated that 29.9% of all firms in his sample had no single objective: i.e. they had multiple objectives. He also found that 51.9% could be defined as satisficers rather than maximisers, in the sense that once an objective or target had been reached, there was no impetus for over half the companies to improve on this (i.e. to maximise). Shipley's results (Table 5.4, p. 232) also indicated the importance of multiple objectives within a goal set.

The importance of the behaviouralist ideas of Simon, and Cyert and March can be illustrated in terms of the concept of **tolerance zones** (Doyle 1994). In Fig. 5.13 the company is shown as having **multiple objectives**, indicated by the outer shaded ring. If a company pushes towards excellence in one objective, it moves outwards from the centre along one objective ray only. This will eventually lead the company into the outer shaded ring, which represents a *disequilibrium* situation or zone. This is because taking one objective too far (thus reaching this disequilibrium zone) has a cost in terms of the inability of the company to meet other important goals along the other rays. Figure 5.13 also displays an inner shaded ring. This also represents a *disequilibrium* zone, this time because the organisation is failing to meet the minimum expectations of the different stakeholders. In between these two disequilibrium zones we find the unshaded area known as the *tolerance zone*. If this tolerance zone is narrow or non-existent, then the firm has little room in which to manoeuvre in order to meet the various conflicting objectives.

The aim of managers is to broaden this tolerance zone by *internal socialisation*: i.e. by focusing on the community of interests among the stakeholders. This may take the form of encouraging mutual respect, introducing bottom-up management, and improving corporate communications. Firms can also minimise the potential conflicts of interests between groups by developing informal networks, as between firms and their suppliers, their distributors, their creditors, etc. involving frequent meetings and discussions. The concept of a 'family of common interests' is evident in the Japanese *Keiretsu* system. This involves close relationships between large firms and their suppliers as a means of broadening the tolerance zone and minimising the possible areas of friction between groups of stakeholders.

Behaviouralists such as Simon, and Cyert and March, stress the complexity of business organisations and the need for companies to be able to deal with many objectives and performance measures simultaneously. Table 5.8 shows the various performance mea-

Fig. 5.13 Tolerance zones and behaviouralist theories.

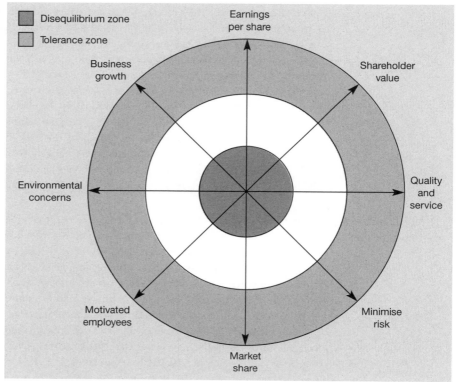

Source: Doyle (1994)

sures used by Proctor & Gamble, the giant US pharmaceutical company. Here we see that the objectives of firms depend on their *particular strategy*. All the main objectives previously considered are included, e.g. profit, sales, market share, size of product line (diversification). In this sense, the large modern firm is a complex, multi-objective entity, which the non-behaviouralist theories find difficult to represent adequately.

Table 5.8 Proctor & Gamble: strategic thrust and performance measures.

Strategic thrust	Performance measurements
1. Concentrate on the profitability of food and and beverages. Divest if necessary.	Sales, profit and margin.
2. Emphasise environmentally friendly products, particularly compact and liquid detergents.	Sales and product mix.
3. Develop OTC product lines.	Size of product line. Overall market share.
4. Increase R&D in process manufacturing.	Production costs and environmental impact.
5. Develop biodegradable diapers.	Time to market.
6. Constantly monitor changes of tastes and health concerns.	Number of consumer surveys and product improvements.
7. Develop geographical strategies for different regions, with emphasis on Latin America, W. Europe, and Asia.	Regional market shares.
8. Develop speciality stores as a channel for prestige care products.	Market share.
9. Improve relationships with suppliers.	Increase percentage of supplier sales to P&G.
10. Encourage communication between market research and product R&D.	Customer-driven product innovations.
11. Develop a full line of men's cometics.	Product line market share.
12. Develop combined products, in both the food and detergent segments.	Number of products, sales, market share.
13. Develop distribution channels through wholesales clubs and discount drugstores.	Market share.
14. Develop entry strategies for China and countries without P&G presence in Eastern Europe, Latin America, and Africa, through distribution alliances.	Market share per product introduced and country.
15. Develop a transnational organization.	Completion of a first proposal.

Source: Adapted from various articles of Proctor & Gamble plc

The M-form organisation and the principal–agent problem

Part of Williamson's thesis was that the arrival of the M-form organisation, with its multidivisional design, was more likely to lead top managers to focus on profits. This was in contrast to the more functional U-form design of companies, which tended to focus more on the individualistic goals of lower management, such as sales, growth or managerial perquisites.

The factors that affect the adoption of the M-form structure have been investigated by Mahoney (1992). The study concludes that firms that decide to diversify (in terms both of products and of geographical location) and which are already large are more likely to take the M-form of organisation. A number of studies have attempted to determine whether the M-form of organisation generates better profits performances than the U-form of organisation. Some argue that profitability has increased under M-form as compared with other organisational designs. A study by Dunsire *et al.* (1991) into organisational status and performance found that a change from a functional U-type to an M-type (profit centre) organisation was indeed associated with improved profit performances in some newly restructured UK companies, such as London Transport, British Aerospace, the Royal Ordnance Factories, Post Office and Telecommunications, and HMSO. This was in line with earlier studies such as Steer and Cable (1978) and Armour and Teece (1978).

However, other studies have pointed to the fact that corporate performance depends more on how effectively firms *adapt* their structures to face uncertainties, rather than on the form of structure (i.e. M or U-form) they decide to introduce. For example, Cable and Yasuki (1985) in a study of 89 Japanese companies found that there was no difference between the profitability of M-form firms and that of firms organised in other ways. However, the study goes on to suggest that the reliance by large firms in Japan on outside subcontractors tends to make internal organisational design less important in Japan as a factor in determining profitability.

It would seem that divisional or similar structures may be a *necessary* condition for increasing the profit performance of large modern companies. However, it may not be a *sufficient* condition, especially as it leaves the principal–agent problem unresolved.

Throughout this chapter we have tried to explain the ways in which the classical view of business organisation and the associated profit maximisation hypothesis have had to be modified to cope with real-world conditions. The behaviour of firms has clearly been influenced by managerial, behavioural and organisational-design factors, as well as by the profit motive. Many of these newer, less profit-oriented theories, while unable to explain all aspects of firm behaviour, have contributed to more realistic insights into the process of decision taking within corporate organisations.

Key terms

Behavioural theories	Moral hazard
Coalition	Portfolio planning
Managerial theories	Principal/agent problem
Mark-up	Satisficing
Maximising theories	U-form structure
M-form structure	Valuation ratio

Full definitions can be found in the 'Glossary of terms' (pp. 699–710)

Review questions

1. A publishing company, Graphco Ltd, produces high-priced specialist medical books for the European market. Its total revenue function $TR = 150Q - 0.5Q^2$ and its total cost function $TC = 1750 - 12Q + 0.5Q^2$. Here both revenue and costs are in pounds and Q is the total output of books in 000's per year.

    (a) What are the levels of output at the lower and upper break-even points?
    (b) Calculate the profit-maximising output, the total profits, and the price per book at this output. Show that when output is at the profit-maximising level, then marginal revenue equals marginal cost.
    (c) If Graphco Ltd decides to maximise its sales revenue, what would be the yearly output of books and the average price per book? Are there any interesting conclusions to be drawn from your calculations as to the profit position of Graphco Ltd at the sales revenue and profit-maximising output levels?

2. Over a relatively short period, Graphco Ltd, the company noted in question 1, finds itself in a changing environment. It needs to invest in a new colour printer, which will result in a new total cost function of $TC = 1850 - 12Q + 0.5Q^2$. At the same time, the new managing director wants to produce the medical books with a minimum profits constraint. Given this new situation, answer the following questions:

    (a) Assuming that the company continues to aim for profit maximisation, calculate the effect on the output level following the investment in new colour printer technology. Give economic explanations for your conclusions.
    (b) If the managing director wants to sell as many books as possible (volume target) but with a profit constraint of £1 million, what will be the output of medical books it needs to produce to meet the profit constraint criterion given that the new investment still goes ahead?

3. A large furniture company, Woodco plc, operating in an inflationary environment, has a medium-term managerial utility function of the form $V = 18/G$ and a general valuation constraint function of $V = 3 + 4G - G^2$, where V is the valuation ratio and G is the growth rate of the economy. With the aid of a diagram and simple calculus where relevant, complete the following:

    (a) Plot the above functions between $G = 0$ and 5 for the valuation constraint function, and between $G = 2$ and 5 for the managerial utility function. Find the rate of growth of the economy that maximises the valuation ratio.
    (b) Show that there is an equilibrium trade-off position between the managerial utility function (the indifference curve) and the valuation constraint function, and indicate
        (i)   the values of V and G at the equilibrium position;
        (ii) the rate of substitution between V and G at the equilibrium position.
        Is this a valid equilibrium point if we assume that the minimum valuation ratio to prevent takeover is 4?
    (c) How does the equilibrium position illustrate the difference between profit-maximising and growth-maximising theories of management behaviour?
    (d) Given that the minimum valuation ratio required to avoid a takeover is 4, what would have been the *desired* growth rate that management would have preferred given the valuation constraint function?

4. A jam manufacturing company, Preserves Ltd, provides a large range of jams for a major supermarket chain. One of its specialist raspberry jams has a demand curve $P = 80 - 0.5Q$, with P, the price per box (£s) and Q being the number of boxes sold per month to the supermarket. The total cost of producing the jam is given by $TC = 160 + 10Q + 0.2Q^2$. The management team has met to determine the price and output strategy for the jam over the next few months. However, there is a disagreement as to the best strategy. The managing director wants to maximise sales revenue but with a profit constraint. On the other hand, the production manager wishes to invest in new technology to gain economies of scope and therefore wants to maximise monthly profits in order to provide funds for reinvestment. The sales manager wants to maximise monthly sales volume of the raspberry jam as his bonus structure for all types of jam produce is geared to total sales revenue.

(a) Calculate the output, price and profits that the production manager would find most suitable for this type of specialist jam.
(b) If the sales manager was to argue that market share was the most relevant current objective, what would be the monthly output, price and profit levels?
(c) The managing director is more conservative and wishes to make sure that a minimum profit of £1,080 per month is made on this type of speciality jam. Calculate the price and output policies that the managing director would advocate.

5. A large UK-based electronics company, Intersound plc, has experienced a significant demand from the USA for one of its low-priced but relatively high-performance amplifiers. Since most of the demand for this product comes from the USA, this market-oriented company is trying to decide whether to produce the amplifier in the UK and export to the USA or shift the whole production base for this type of amplifier to the USA. The demand curve for this type of amplifier in the USA is of the form $P = 100 - 0.001Q$, where P is the price per amplifier (£s) and Q is the quantity of amplifiers sold per month. It has been calculated that the marginal cost of producing each amplifier, including domestic distribution, is constant at £15 per unit in both the UK and the USA. By a consideration of net profits in the UK and USA, answer the following questions.

(a) Where will Intersound produce its amplifiers if transport and tariff levies between the UK and USA are £15 per unit, and fixed costs of production are £0.5 million and £0.7 million in the UK and the USA respectively?
(b) If Intersound follows the economic logic dictated by (a), will it subsequently alter the location of its production given the following changes in the business environment?
  (i) The USA abolishes its tariffs on amplifiers, leaving only transport costs of £2 per amplifier. Give possible reasons why the location decision might be more complicated in this situation, and suggest other factors that Intersound might take into consideration before making a final decision.
  (ii) Following the fall in tariffs, a change in Intersound's corporate structure and communications systems has decreased the fixed costs of managing USA production from £0.7 million down to the level of UK costs.

▨ Further reading

Intermediate texts

Baumol, W. J. (1977), *Economic Theory and Operations Analysis*, 4th edn, Ch. 15, Prentice Hall, Hemel Hempstead.

Browning, E. and Browning, J. (1992), *Microeconomic Theory and Applications*, 4th edn, Ch. 8, HarperCollins, London.

Dobson, S., Maddala, G. S. and Miller, E. (1995), *Microeconomics*, Ch. 6, McGraw-Hill, Maidenhead.

Hope, S. (1999), *Applied Microeconomics*, Ch. 8, Wiley, Chichester.

Katz, M. and Rosen, H. (1998), *Microeconomics*, 3rd edn, Ch. 7, Irwin, Boston, Mass.

Koutsoyiannis, A. (1979), *Modern Microeconomics*, 2nd edn, Chs 11, 12, 15–18, Macmillan, Basingstoke.

Laidler, D. and Estrin, S. (1995), *Introduction to Microeconomics*, 4th edn, Ch. 20, Harvester Wheatsheaf, Hemel Hempstead.

Maddala, G. S. and Miller, E. (1989), *Microeconomics: Theory and Application*, Chs 6 and 8, McGraw-Hill, New York.

Moschandreas, M. (1994), *Business Economics*, Chs 4 and 9, Routledge, London.

Nicholson, W. (1997), *Intermediate Microeconomics and its Application*, 7th edn, Chs 10 and 11, Dryden Press, Fort Worth.

Peters, T. (1988), *Thriving on Chaos*, Macmillan, Basingstoke.

Pindyck, R. and Rubinfeld, D. (1998), *Microeconomics*, 4th edn, Chs 8 and 12, Macmillan, Basingstoke.

Ricketts, M. (1987), *The Economics of Business Enterprise: New Approaches to the Firm*, Harvester Wheatsheaf, Hemel Hempstead.

Sawyer, M. C. (1979), *Theories of the Firm*, Chs 6–10, Weidenfeld & Nicolson, London.

Varian, H. (1999), *Intermediate Microeconomics*, 5th edn, Ch. 18, Norton, New York.

Advanced texts

Baumol, W. J. (1959), *Business Behaviour, Value and Growth*, Macmillan, London.

Cyert, R. M. and March, J. G. (1963), *A Behavioural Theory of the Firm*, Prentice Hall, Hemel Hempstead.

Gravelle, H. and Rees, R. (1992), *Microeconomics*, 2nd edn, Ch. 13, Longman, Harlow.

Hay, D. A. and Morris, D. J. (1991), *Industrial Economics and Organization: Theory and Evidence*, 2nd edn, Chs 9 and 10, Oxford University Press, Oxford.

Hay, D. A. and Morris, D. J. (1984), *Unquoted Companies?*, Macmillan, Basingstoke.

Marris, R. (1964), *The Economic Theory of Managerial Capitalism*, Macmillan, London,

Martin, S. (1993), *Economics of Discretionary Behaviour: Managerial Objectives and a Theory of the Firm*, Kershaw, London.

Articles and other sources

Armour, H. O. and Teece, D. J. (1978), 'Organisational structure and economic performance: a test of the multidivisional hypothesis', *Bell Journal*, 9.

Arthur, W. B. (1996), 'Increasing returns and the new world of business', *Harvard Business Review*, July-Aug.

Barkema, H. G. and Gomez-Meija, L. R (1998), 'Managerial compensation and firm performance', *Academy of Management Journal*, 41, 2.

Cable, J. and Yasuki, H. (1985), 'Internal organization, business groups and corporate performance', *International Journal of Industrial Organization*, 3, (4).

Cadbury, A. (1992), *The Committee on the Financial Aspects of Corporate Governance*, Gee Press.

Caves, R. E. (1998), 'Industrial organization and new findings on the turnover and mobility of firms', *Journal of Economic Literature*, XXXVI, Dec.

Christofides, L. N. and Tapon, R. (1979), 'Discretionary expenditures and profit risk management: the Galbraith-Caves hypothesis', *Quarterly Journal of Economics*, 93.

Conyon, M. and Gregg, P. (1994), 'Pay at the top: a study of the sensitivity of top director remuneration to company specific shocks', *National Institute Economic Review*, 3.

Conyon, M. and Nicolitsas, D. (1998), 'Does the market for top excutives work? CEO pay and turnover in small UK companies', *Small Business Economics*, 11, 2.

Conyon, M. and Leech, D. (1994), 'Executive compensation, corporate performance and ownership structure', *Oxford Bulletin of Economics and Statistics*, 56.

Conyon, M., Gregg, P. and Machin, S. (1995), 'Taking care of business: executive compensation in the UK', *Economic Journal*, 105, 430, May.

Doyle, P. (1994), 'Setting business performance and measuring performance', *European Management Journal*, 12, 2, June, Elsevier science.

Dunsire, A., Hartley, K. and Parker, D. (1991) 'Organisational status and performance; summary of findings', *Public Administration*, 69.

Ezzamel, M. and Watson, R. (1998), 'Market compensation earnings and the bidding-up of executive cash compensation: evidence from the UK', *Academy of Management Journal*, 41, 2.

Financial Analysis Made Easy (FAME) (1998), Oct.

Financial Times (1998), 'Shares in the action', 27 April.

Gregg, P., Machin, S. and Szymanski, S. (1993), 'The disappearing relationship between directors' pay and corporate performance', *British Journal of Industrial Relations*, 31.

Hassid, J. (1977), 'Diversification and the firm's rate of growth', Manchester Business School, 45.

Hax, A. and Majaluf (1994), 'Corporate strategic tasks', *European Management Journal*, 12, 4, December.

Healey, N. (1999), 'The multinational corporation', in Griffiths, A. and Wall, S. (eds) *Applied Economics*, 8th edn, Longman, Harlow.

Hornby, W. (1995), 'The theory of the firm revisited: A Scottish perspective', *Management Decision*, Vol. 33.

Jacquemin, A. P. and Berry, C. H. (1979), 'Entropy, measures of diversification and corporate growth', *Journal of Industrial Economics*, 27.

Jensen, M. and Murphy, K. (1990), 'Performance pay and top management incentives', *Journal of Political Economy*, 98.

Leech, D. and Leahy, J. (1991), 'Ownership structure, control type classification and the performance of large British companies', *Economic Journal*, 101.

Mahoney, J. T. (1992), 'The adoption of the multidivisional form of organisation: a contingency model', *Journal of Management Studies*, 29, January.

Main, B., Bruce, A. and Bucks, T. (1996), 'Total board remuneration and company performance', *Economic Journal*, 106.

MITI (1994), White Paper on International Trade (summary), Tokyo.

Nyman, S. and Silberston, A. (1978), 'The ownership and control of industry', *Oxford Economic Papers*, 30, 1.

OECD (1993), Economic Surveys: Japan, Table 21, Paris.

Peters, T. J. and Waterman, R. H. (1982), *In Search of Excellence*, Harper & Row, New York.

Schoeffler, S., Buzzel, R. D. and Heany, D. F. (1974), 'Impact of strategic planning on profit performance', *Harvard Business Review*, 52, March-April.

Shipley, D. D. (1981), 'Primary objectives of British manufacturing industry', *Journal of Industrial Economics*, 29, 4, June.

Shipley, D. D. and Bourdon, E. (1990), 'Distribution pricing in very competitive markets', *Industrial Marketing Management*, 19.

Simon, H. A. (1959), 'Theories of decision making in economics and behavioural science', *American Economic Review*, 49.

Steer, P. and Cable, J. (1978) 'Internal organization and profit: an empirical analysis of large UK companies', *Journal of Industrial Economics*, 27.

Storey, D., Watson, R. and Wynarczyk, P. (1995), 'The remuneration of non-owner managers in UK unquoted and unlisted securities market enterprises', *Small Business Economics*, 7.

Whittington, G. (1980), 'The profitability and size of UK companies', *Journal of Industrial Economics*, 28, 4.

Williamson, O.E. (1971), 'Managerial discretion, organisation form and the multidivisional hypothesis', in R. Marris and A. Wood (eds), *The Corporate Economy*.

Chapter 6

Competitive and contestable markets

We begin this chapter by reviewing material that you should already have encountered concerning the *extreme* case of a competitive market, namely perfect competition. We then go on to consider the behaviour of the competitive firm and industry under different market conditions, seeking to identify some of the efficiency gains from competitive markets. The *intermediate* case of competitive markets involving imperfect or monopolistic competition is then considered. We then move away from this essentially structure-conduct-performance approach by considering the idea of contestable markets.

Perfect competition

Remember the key assumptions of **perfect competition**:

- Numerous purchasers, none of whom is significant enough to influence market price by an individual purchasing decision.
- Numerous small firms, none of which is significant enough by itself to influence market supply, and all of which produce a homogeneous (identical) product.
- As a consequence, each firm is a *price taker* regarding the demand curve for its product as being perfectly elastic at the going market price. The firm being so small, changes in its output (supply) will be absorbed by demand at the going market price. In other words the demand curve facing the firm is perfectly elastic ($AR = MR$) at that market price.
- Perfect information; effectively the price of the (homogeneous) product conveys all the information required by producers and consumers.
- Freedom of entry into (and exit from) the industry or market.

In terms of the following analysis we initially assume that the firm seeks to maximise profit, which of course could equate to minimising losses in a situation where no profit is feasible.

Short-run equilibrium of firm and industry

In Chapter 4 we defined the **short run** as that period of time in which at least one factor of production is fixed. Over this time period, new firms will be unable to enter the market. The profit-maximising firm will then achieve a short-run equilibrium (balance) by producing that level of output for which the following condition holds:

$$AR = MR = MC$$

If we define (as in Chapter 4) **normal profit** as that which is just sufficient to keep the firm in the industry in the long run, then we can regard normal profit as a *cost* of production. Unless firms earn this level of profit they will ultimately leave the industry. Our condition could therefore result in *supernormal* profits being made, as in Fig. 6.1(a), or *subnormal* profits being made, as in Fig. 6.1(b). Since the firm is maximising

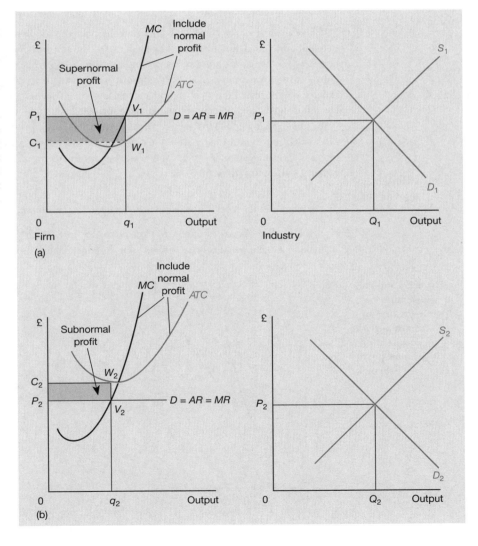

Fig. 6.1 **(a) Short-run equilibrium for a profit-maximising firm in perfect competition: supernormal profit earned. (b) Short-run equilibrium for a profit-maximising firm in perfect competition: subnormal profit earned.**

profits/minimising losses in each case, there is no reason for the firm to alter its output. We are in **short-run equilibrium**.

Long-run equilibrium of firm and industry

In the **long run** all factors of production can be varied, so new firms can enter into (exit from) the industry. If a large number of new (small) firms are attracted into the industry by supernormal profits, then this will have an effect on the (long-run) *industry* supply curve, shifting it to the right in Fig. 6.1(a). New firms will continue to enter the industry until any supernormal profit is competed away: i.e. only normal profit is earned. The mechanism by which the *supernormal* profit is eroded is indicated in Fig. 6.2, and involves the industry price falling (P_1 to P') as industry supply increases (S_1 to S'). Long-run equilibrium will be achieved when the following condition holds true:

$$AR = MR = MC = ATC$$

This can only occur (see Fig. 6.2) when the price-taking firm faces a perfectly elastic demand curve that just touches (is a tangent to) the bottom of its *ATC* curve. Here, and here only, is the condition already outlined satisfied (remember *MC* intersects *ATC* from below at the lowest point of *ATC*). The profit-maximising firm ($MC = MR$) is now earning only normal profit ($ATC = AR$), and no further incentive exists for new firms to enter the industry. We are in **long-run equilibrium**.

In our earlier Fig. 6.1(b), where firms earned *subnormal* profits, then a large number of (small) firms would leave the industry, shifting industry supply to the left in Fig. 6.2 (S_2 to S'), raising price (P_2 to P') and restoring profits to the normal level. Again we are in **long-run equilibrium**.

Benefits of competition

At the introductory level it is usual to note some important *benefits* of competitive markets:

- Price acts as a signal to encourage resources to flow (in the long run) into industries making supernormal profits and out of industries making subnormal profits.

Fig. 6.2 **Long-run equilibrium for a profit-maximising firm in perfect competition: normal profit earned.**

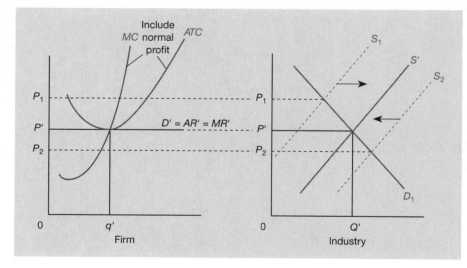

- The absence of barriers to entry permits such resource reallocations to take place.
- The technical optimum (minimum ATC) is achieved in the long run.
- Price in competitive markets will usually be lower (and output higher) than in monopolistic markets (see Chapter 7).

Firm's supply curve

You should also be familiar with the idea of the *firm's* short- and long-run supply curves under perfect competition. A **supply curve** for a firm tells us how much output it will produce at every possible price.

In the short run the firm must be covering its variable or running costs if it is to continue in production. Otherwise it should shut down immediately; to carry on producing is to make an increasing loss, making no contribution to covering the fixed costs already incurred. In Fig. 6.3 the segment AC of the firm's *MC* curve corresponds to its **short-run supply curve**. As a price-taker facing a perfectly elastic demand curve ($D = AR = MR$) at each price, the profit-maximising firm will produce, say, output q_1 at price P_1 ($MR = MC$). Indeed for any given price *above* P^* the profit-maximising firm will equate price to *MC*, and total revenue will be greater than total variable (running) costs. *At* price P^* total revenue just covers total variable costs for the profit-maximising solution. However, at prices *below* P^* the profit-maximising solution ($MR = MC$) will yield total revenue less than total variable (running) costs. P^* is sometimes referred to as the *shut down* price in the short run, in the sense that unless this price is achieved, short-run production will cease altogether.

In the long run the firm must cover *all* its costs, variable and fixed, including normal profit. If the firm does not achieve revenue sufficient to cover all its costs, including that level of profit it deems adequate for continued production in the industry, it will cease production altogether or move to another industry. In other words P' corresponds to the *shut down* price in the long run. Segment AB of the firm's *MC* curve is then the firm's **long-run supply curve**.

Industry supply curve

Clearly segments of the *MC* curve of the firm constitute the supply curve of the firm, depending on the time period in question. If we aggregate the *MC* curves for each and every firm (summing horizontally), we derive the **industry *MC* curve**. Since by aggregating the *MC* curves of each firm we are aggregating their supply curves, we also derive the **industry supply curve**. Figure 6.4 outlines this procedure in a simplified situation in which three firms constitute the industry.

Fig. 6.3 **Short-run (AC) and long-run (AB) supply curves of the firm under perfect competitions.**

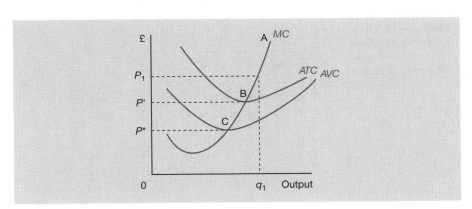

Fig. 6.4 **The industry supply curve is the industry *MC* curve, which in turn is the sum of the firm *MC* curves.**

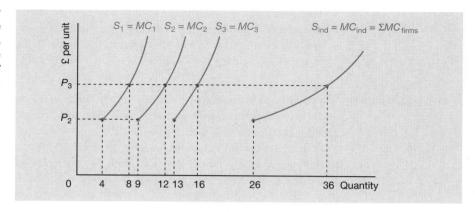

The industry supply curve is therefore the sum of the individual firm *MC* curves in a competitive industry.

Theoretical developments

In the previous section we oversimplified by taking the same *MC* curve to represent both short-run (above *AVC*) and long-run (above *ATC*) supply. Of course, as we saw in Chapter 4, there are entirely different *ATC* and *MC* curves for both short- and long-run time periods.

Long-run equilibrium

The *firm* in Fig. 6.5 has an initial plant size such that the short-run average and marginal cost curves are SAC_1 and SMC_1 respectively. With the market price at P_1 and output q_1 it makes supernormal profit (the shaded rectangle), encouraging it to expand capacity, thereby moving onto a lower average and marginal cost curve. The supernormal profit

Fig. 6.5 **Supernormal profit in short-run equilibrium (q_1) leading to long-run equilibrium (q_2) with increased plant capacity (and new entrants).**

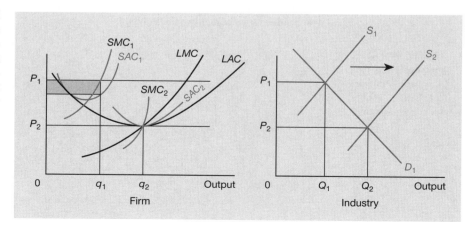

will also, of course, encourage entirely new firms to enter the *industry*. As the *industry supply* increases (shifts to right), the price falls until the long-run equilibrium price P_2 and output Q_2 is reached. Here the capacity of the existing firm has increased such that SAC_2 and SMC_2 are the new short-run average and marginal cost curves respectively.

Note also that the long-run equilibrium of the firm occurs where

> Price = *LMC* = *LAC*

In other words the firm adjusts its plant size so that it now produces that level of output at which the long-run average cost (*LAC*) is the minimum that is technically feasible, given technology and the price of factor inputs. (Remember that *LMC* intersects *LAC* at the lowest point of *LAC* – see p. 174.)

Overall we have the **long-run equilibrium** condition for the *firm* such that

> Price = *SMC* = *SAC* = *LMC* = *LAC*

Unlike the initial situation (q_1) the (short run) *plant* is now being operated at its technical optimum (minimum *SAC*) at output q_2. Of course at q_2 the minimum for both *SAC* and *LAC* coincide.

The *industry* is also in equilibrium at price P_2 but with output Q_2. The **long-run equilibrium** occurs for the industry when all firms are producing at the minimum point of their *LAC* curve and making only normal profit. In this situation there will be neither additional entry into, or exit from, the industry, given present levels of technology and factor prices. In other words the industry is in equilibrium (at rest) with demand D_1 and supply S_2 in Fig. 6.5.

The impact of a change in demand on *industry* equilibrium will depend upon the cost conditions facing the competitive industry. For illustrative purposes we consider an *increase* in industry demand on constant-cost, increasing-cost and decreasing-cost industries, respectively.

Changes in demand and competitive industry equilibrium

Constant-cost industry Here, as output expands, the prices of all factors and other inputs remain *constant* (Fig. 6.6). Suppose the firm is initially in long-run equilibrium when a shift in industry demand from D_1 to D_2 raises price from P_1 to P_2 and firm output from q_1 to q_2. Existing firms find it profitable to raise output by operating plants *beyond* their full capacity (technical optimum) level of output q_1. This increased quantity is shown by a movement along the industry supply curve S_1 from A to C. The *short-run* industry equilibrium Q_1 cannot persist, however, since new entrants are also attracted by the excess profits. As existing firms expand output and new firms enter, the *industry* supply curve shifts rightwards. With **constant-cost** conditions, the extra demand for factors of production does not raise the firm's costs of production. In the long run, therefore, the new entrants face the same *LAC* conditions as do the already established firms. By operating *at* full capacity the new entrants can undercut the price of established firms operating *beyond* full capacity. Entry will continue until the new industry supply

Fig. 6.6 Long-run industry supply (S_L) under constant cost conditions.

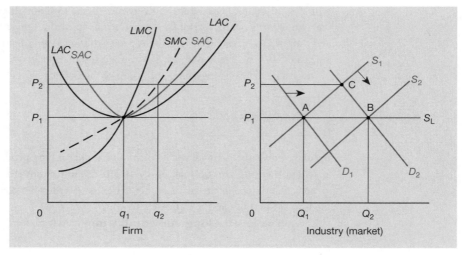

Fig. 6.6 Long-run industry supply (S_L) under constant cost conditions.

curve S_2 intersects D_2 at the original price P_1. The *long-run industry supply curve* is therefore the straight line containing the segment AB at the initial price level P_1. In this long-run equilibrium, existing firms will have cut back their (expensive) operations *beyond* full capacity so that all firms (established and new) now operate *at* full capacity. The industry responds to an increase in demand by producing more output *at the same price* as in the initial situation prior to the demand increase.

Increasing-cost industry   Here, as output expands, the prices of (some) factors and other inputs *rise* (Fig. 6.7). As before, the shift from D_1 to D_2 in industry demand raises price from P_1 to P_2 and (profit maximising) firm output from q_1 to q_2, with existing firms operating plants *beyond* their full-capacity output q_1. Again the *short-run* industry equilibrium Q_1 cannot persist, since new entrants are attracted by the excess profits. As existing firms expand output and new firms enter, the *industry* supply curve shifts rightwards. However, since both existing firms and new entrants face higher input prices, short- and long-run average and marginal cost curves shift upwards. In Fig. 6.7 the industry supply curve will cease shifting to the right when price has fallen from P_2 to P_3, at which both existing and new firms earn only normal profit. The impact of **increasing costs** has been to prevent the industry supply curve from shifting as far to the right as in the constant-cost case, and thereby preventing price falling back to its original level P_1. The *long-run industry supply curve* under increasing costs is therefore a line containing the points A and B in Fig. 6.7 and sloping upwards from left to right. The industry responds to a demand increase by producing more output but only at the higher price needed to compensate for the higher input costs.

Although Fig. 6.7 shows the firm output to be higher (q_3) than initially (q_1), the actual outcome could be a firm output that is smaller, the same or greater than initially, depending on the shift of the cost curves. What can be established is that market price, market output and the number of firms will be greater in the long-run market equilibrium as demand increases.

Fig. 6.7 **Long-run industry supply (S_L) under increasing cost conditions.**

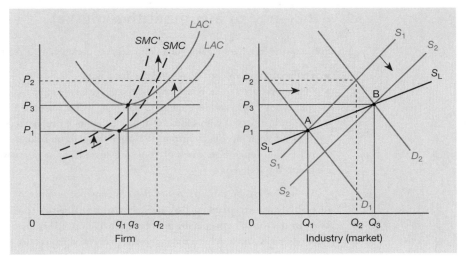

Decreasing-cost industry Here, as output expands, the prices of (some) factors and other inputs *fall* (Fig. 6.8). The previous analysis applies, except this time as existing firms expand output and new firms enter they face lower input prices, so that short- and long-run average and marginal cost curves shift downwards. In Fig. 6.8 the *industry* supply curve will shift further to the right than in the constant- or rising-cost cases, with normal profit only restored for existing and new firms at a price P_3 below the initial price P_1. The *long-run industry supply curve* under **decreasing costs** is therefore a line containing the points A and B in Fig. 6.8 and sloping downwards from left to right. The industry responds to a demand increase by producing more output and at a lower price than in the initial situation prior to the demand increase.

Again, although Fig. 6.8 shows the firm output (q_3) to be higher than initially (q_1), the actual outcome could be a firm output that is smaller than, the same as or greater than initially, depending on the shift of the cost curves. Market price will, however, be lower, market output higher and the number of firms greater in the long-run market equilibrium after the demand increase.

Fig. 6.8 **Long-run industry supply (S_L) under decreasing cost conditions.**

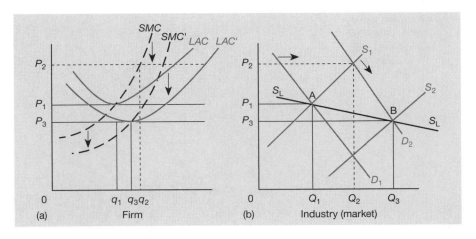

Efficiency of a competitive market

Some of the 'efficiency gains' of a competitive market have already been discussed:

- Firms earn only normal profit in the long run.
- Firms operate at the technical optimum (full capacity) output in the long run, with minimum short- and long-run average cost at that output.
- The industry will respond to changed consumer preferences expressed by increased demand with increased output. Whether this will be sold at the same, higher or lower price will depend on whether constant, increasing or decreasing cost conditions prevail in the long run.

We now develop this analysis of the efficiency of competitive markets, using the ideas of **consumer surplus** (p. 26) and **producer surplus** (p. 157) previously discussed. We can do this by comparing the competitive equilibrium involving market-clearing with other situations where the market is prevented from clearing.

Maximum price set below market-clearing level

In Fig. 6.9 the market-clearing price is P_1, but regulation prevents the actual price from rising above the **maximum** price set at P_2. As a result, industry output falls from Q_1 to Q_2 with consumer surplus falling by area B and producer surplus by area C. Area A is transferred from previously being producers' surplus to now being consumers' surplus, as output $0Q_2$ is now supplied at the lower price P_2. The total welfare loss of market interference is often referred to as *deadweight loss,* and is areas $B + C$. Too little is being produced, and both consumers and producers are, overall, worse off in this analysis.

Minimum price set above market-clearing level

In Fig. 6.10 the market-clearing price is again P_1 but this time regulation prevents the actual price from falling below the **minimum** price set at P_2.

Producers respond to actual demand Producers might desire to produce Q_2 at price P_2 but only Q_3 is actually demanded at this price. If Q_3 is actually produced, then there is a loss of consumers' surplus (area B) and producers' surplus (area C) compared to the market-clearing situation. Because of the higher price some consumers no longer

Fig. 6.9 **Welfare loss with maximum price (P_2) set below market-clearing level (P_1).**

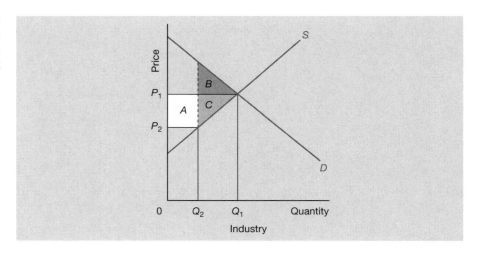

Fig. 6.10 Welfare loss with minimum price (P_2) set above market-clearing level (P_1).

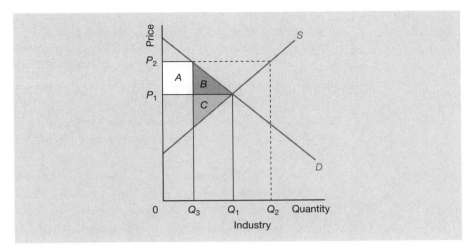

purchase the item and some producers no longer supply it. Area A is transferred from consumers' surplus to producers' surplus, given that producers now receive a higher price (P_2) for output Q_3. The total welfare loss of market interference, i.e. *deadweight loss*, is again areas $B + C$.

Producers ignore actual demand Should producers supply what they desire ($0Q_2$) at price P_2, rather than what is demanded, then the deadweight loss will be even greater (Fig. 6.11). The amount $Q_2 - Q_3$ will go unsold at the minimum price P_2. There is therefore no revenue received to cover the cost of producing $Q_2 - Q_3$. This is the sum of the marginal costs in producing each extra unit over the output range $Q_2 - Q_3$, namely area E in Fig. 6.11 (remember, for a competitive *industry*, the supply curve is the marginal cost curve). This is, effectively, a loss of producers' surplus to be set against the welfare situation when only Q_3 output was produced. The total *deadweight loss* is now

areas $B + C + E$

which is clearly greater than when producers only supplied the amount demanded at the minimum price P_2.

Fig. 6.11 Welfare loss with minimum price (P_2) set above market-clearing level (P_1) *and* producers ignoring actual demand constraint.

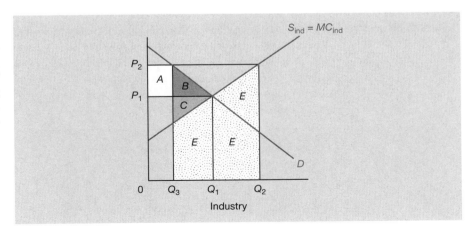

Price support   A possible policy is for a government to announce a certain minimum (intervention) price that it will *support* in the market by purchasing policies. In Fig. 6.12, P_1 is the initial market-clearing price and P_2 the announced support price. The government purchases the excess supply $Q_2 - Q_3$, artificially shifting the demand curve to the right by the quantity purchased (Q_p).

- Change in consumer surplus (ΔCS) = $- A - B$
- Change in producer surplus (ΔPS) = $+ A + B + C$
- Cost to government (ΔG)   = price × quantity purchased
                                             = $P_2.(Q_2 - Q_3)$
  i.e. Cost to government (ΔG)   = area of rectangle mnQ_2Q_3
  Net welfare change   = $\Delta CS + \Delta PS - \Delta G$
                                             = C – area mnQ_2Q_3
  i.e. Net welfare change   = – area $mvnQ_2Q_3$

So in welfare terms, introducing the price support scheme results in society being worse off by the rectangle mnQ_2Q_3 less triangle C. The suggestion here is that a competitive market can suffer a substantial welfare loss via price support policies.

Fig. 6.12 **Welfare loss with a price support scheme at a price (P_2) above the market-clearing level (P_1).**

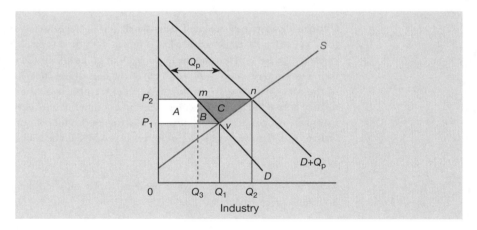

Production quotas   Here we compare the market-clearing equilibrium with a situation involving the setting of **production quotas**. Instead of purchasing any excess production at a specified price (P_2), the government seeks to establish this price by reducing supply, in this case setting *quotas* for the amount each firm can produce. Suppose the *overall* industry quota is set at Q_2, raising price above the market-clearing level P_1 (to P_2) by establishing a new industry supply curve SvS' (Fig. 6.13):

Change in consumer surplus (ΔCS)	= $- A - B$
Change in producer surplus (ΔPS)	= $+ A - C$
Net welfare change	= $\Delta CS + \Delta PS$
	= $- B - C$

Fig. 6.13 Welfare loss with a quota scheme $0Q_2$ raising price (P_2) above the market-clearing level P_1.

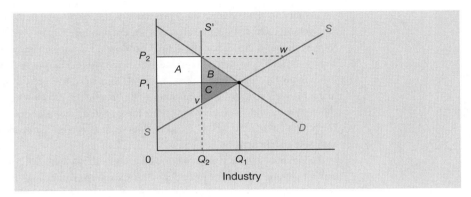

In all the cases considered, intervention in the competitive *industry* imposes negative welfare changes as compared with the market-clearing solution.

Chapters 11, 12 and 13 consider various aspects of welfare gains and losses in rather more detail. Chapter 13 pays particular attention to the issue of regulation versus deregulation. These chapters also adopt a broader *general equilibrium* approach to competitive markets rather than the *partial equilibrium* approach pursued thus far.

Monopolistic competition

So far we have considered the 'extreme' case of a perfectly competitive industry. At this stage it may be useful to contrast the outcomes we have identified with those resulting from the 'intermediate' case of a competitive industry, namely **monopolistic competition** or, as it is sometimes referred to, **imperfect competition**.

The key characteristics of monopolistic competition include the following:

- There are a large number of firms in the market, each acting independently of any other.
- There is freedom of entry into, and exit from, the market.
- Unlike perfect competition, each firm produces non-homogeneous products. In other words the products of each firm differ in some way from those of any other firm: e.g. in quality, appearance, or reputation.

It is this latter characteristic of monopolistic competition that confers an element of monopoly power on the individual firm: the greater the extent of product differentiation, the greater that monopoly power. Again, we shall initially assume that the firm seeks to maximise profits.

Short- and long-run equilibrium

Figure 6.14 usefully summarises the short-run and long-run equilibrium for a profit-maximising firm under monopolistic competition. Notice that, unlike perfect competition, the *firm's* demand curve is downward sloping. If the firm lowers the price of its (differentiated) product it will capture some, but not all, consumers from other firms. Similarly, if the firm raises its price it will lose some, but not all, of its consumers to rival firms.

Loyalty to the differentiated products of the respective firms means that price, while important, is not the sole influence on consumer choice. Hence we have a negatively sloped demand curve for the firm's products. Of course the greater the loyalty to the firm's (unique) product, the greater the price rise needed to induce consumers to switch away from that product to that of a rival. Similarly, the greater the price cut needed to attract (loyal) consumers from other firms' products. It follows that the *greater the product differentiation* and consumer loyalty to the product, the *less price elastic* the demand curve for a particular firm will be, and of course the greater the monopoly power over price available to the firm.

In Fig. 6.14(a) the profit-maximising firm ($MC = MR$) will, in the short run, produce output Q_S and sell this at price P_S, yielding supernormal profit $P_S\,VWC$. This excess profit will, given freedom of entry into the market, attract new entrants. Unlike perfect competition the new entrants do *not* increase the overall market supply of a single, homogeneous product. Rather the new entrants will partly erode the consumer demand for an existing firm's (differentiated) product: i.e. the new entrants will capture some of the customers of the existing firm by offering a still wider variety of differentiated products. It may, of course, be a range of price and non-price factors that cause some consumers to abandon product loyalty. We show this in Fig. 6.14(b) by a leftward shift (decrease) in the existing firm's demand curve.

Only when profit is reduced to normal for firms already in the market will the attraction for new entrants be removed, i.e. when $LAC = AR$. In other words the demand (AR) curve for the existing firm will shift leftwards until it *just touches* the LAC curve. This **long-run equilibrium** occurs with demand curve D' at price P_L and output Q_L in Fig. 6.14(b). At any other output along D', $LAC > AR$ and the firm makes a loss. It must therefore follow that the output Q_L (at which normal profit is earned) is the profit-maximising output, so that MR' must intersect LMC at Q_L. If the demand curve is still to the right of D' in Fig. 6 14(b), then supernormal profits will still be made and new entry will continue. If the demand curve has shifted to the left of D', then subnormal profits

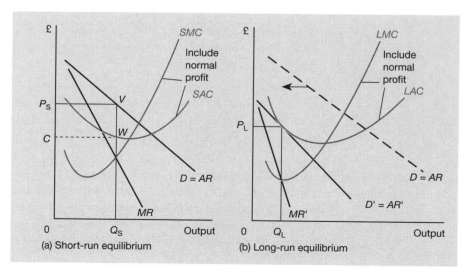

Fig. 6.14 **Equilibrium of the firm under monopolistic competition.**

will be made and some firms will leave the industry (bankruptcy) and the demand curve will shift back to the right. Only at D' will there be no long-run tendency for firms to enter or leave the industry.

Long-run equilibrium under monopolistic competition possesses the following characteristics:

- Only normal profits are earned (as with perfect competition).
- In the long run, output is below, and price above, the levels consistent with the technical optimum, i.e. minimum average cost (unlike perfect competition).
- Price exceeds marginal cost (unlike perfect competition).

Excess capacity   In Fig. 6.14(b) we noted that, in the long run, the firm will produce below the technical optimum (minimum LAC). Put another way, this shortfall in actual output below the technical optimum may be termed *excess capacity*. We can, in fact, decompose this excess capacity into two distinct parts:

- excess capacity via failure to operate the *existing* plant at its technical optimum;
- excess capacity via failure to build the *optimum scale* of plant.

Figure 6.15 will help us to follow through this analysis. $0Q_L$ is long-run equilibrium output sold at price P_L, with the firm earning normal profit and no tendency for new firm entry or existing firm exit. SAC' is the short-run average cost curve corresponding to the optimal plant for output $0Q_L$, and $SAC*$ is the short-run average cost curve corresponding to the optimal plant for output $0Q*$. Note that $0Q*$ is, of course, the long-run technical optimum output, and the plant size corresponding to $SAC*$ is the optimum *scale* of plant.

The overall excess capacity $(Q* - Q_L)$ can be decomposed into two separate parts:

(i) $Q' - Q_L$; that part due to not operating the existing plant at the output level $(0Q')$ consistent with minimum (short-run) average cost;

(ii) $Q* - Q'$; that part due to building a size of plant smaller than the technically optimum scale. In other words, being on SAC' instead of $SAC*$.

Fig. 6.15 **Excess capacity under monopolistic competition.**

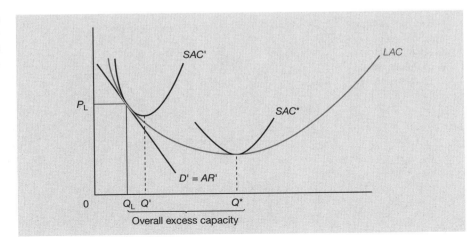

For both these reasons, production costs will be higher than they need be on technical grounds, both in the short run and in the long run.

Notice also that the steeper the demand curve, the greater the overall excess capacity will tend to be in long-run equilibrium. In other words, the greater the success of the firm in product differentiation, the less price elastic will be demand and the greater will be the excess capacity. This is because tangency between AR' and LAC will occur at a lower output than Q_L – and at a higher price!

Of course it can be argued that consumers may be willing to pay for the benefit of greater product differentiation and thereby greater consumer choice. In other words some of the implied welfare losses for consumers of excess capacity, namely higher costs of production, lower firm output, and higher firm prices, may be offset, at least in part, by the greater variety of consumer choice.

In terms of our earlier use of welfare theory (p. 254), the consumer gains from product diversity must be set against the *deadweight loss* of area vwx in Fig. 6.16. This loss results from price *exceeding* marginal cost in the long-run equilibrium solution of monopolistic competition.

Free entry and price competition

So far in our analysis we have assumed that the long-run equilibrium solution of normal profit (Fig. 6.14(b)) was attained via new firm entry eroding the established customer base of existing firms. In fact the adjustment mechanism may be a mixture of this process and of price competition amongst *existing* firms.

In the initial, simplified model of monopolistic competition, firms *perceive* their actions as being independent of those by other firms. In fact all firms in the industry are likely to face similar cost and demand conditions, and are therefore likely to respond in similar ways to an external stimulus. Let us now explore this conflict between perception and reality a little further.

In Fig. 6.17 we have the industry demand curve (D_i). Of course the idea of 'industry' is rather uncertain when each firm produces a differentiated product. Chamberlin preferred to talk about 'product groups' (including all products that are close substitutes) rather than industries. If all firms charge the same price then they will receive identical

Fig. 6.16 Comparison of long-run equilibrium under perfect competition and monopolistic competition.

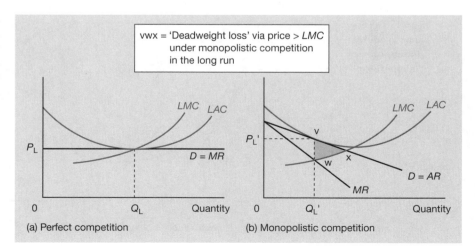

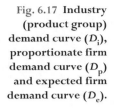

Fig. 6.17 **Industry (product group) demand curve (D_i), proportionate firm demand curve (D_p) and expected firm demand curve (D_e).**

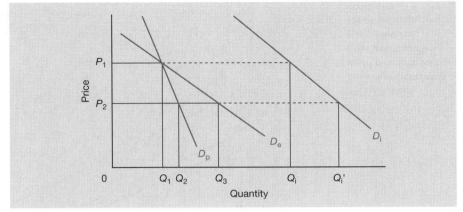

market shares within the product group, as indicated by the **proportionate demand curve** D_p (i.e. D_i at that price divided by the number of firms). Of course if each firm *perceives* that it alone can lower price and gain extra demand, then it may **expect to** face a more elastic demand curve than D_p, namely D_e, where it gains market share at the expense of other firms.

In Fig. 6.17 a reduction in price to P_2 by all existing firms will mean the expanded *industry* demand Q'_i being divided proportionately, to give Q_2 demand for each *firm*. However, if the firm expects it alone to have lowered price to P_2 then it will be the sole beneficiary of the expanded industry or group demand. Its expected demand will therefore be Q_3 at price P_2.

We now use this analysis to consider what the long-run equilibrium solution will be when both free entry (and exit) *and* price competition amongst existing firms are assumed to take place. In our earlier Fig. 6.14(b) we had solution P_L, Q_L with new firms attracted until the *proportionate* demand of any existing firm had been reduced from the short-run equilibrium level Q_S (Fig. 6.14(a)) to the long-run equilibrium level Q_L (Fig. 6.14(b)). However, this will not be an equilibrium solution if the existing firms believe that they can secure a *disproportionate* market share by alone cutting prices. In Fig. 6.18 we see that existing firms have a more elastic **expected demand curve**, D_e , at price P_L than is indicated by the **proportionate demand curve**, D_p.

Of course the firm may well be mistaken in this belief; most firms face similar cost and demand conditions and are likely to react in similar ways to a given set of external circumstances. Nevertheless suppose the individual firm *expects* that a reduction in price to P_1 will raise demand to Q_{1e}, which is clearly profitable (expected $AR > LAC$). In fact suppose that all firms respond by cutting price in similar fashion so that the *actual* outcome for the firm is only to raise demand to Q_1 along the **proportionate demand curve** D_p. It is as though the **expected demand curve** D_e has shifted inwards to D'_e, expectations aligning themselves with reality, at least at price P_1. In effect losses will be made ($AR < LAC$). However, there is still some illusion insofar as D'_e is more elastic than D_p, and the firm still expects that it can make profit by cutting its own price. In effect an equilibrium can only occur when the firm no longer expects that a price-cutting policy can yield enhanced profits: i.e. when the expected demand curve D''_e is tangent to the LAC curve at output Q^* in Fig. 6.18.

Fig. 6.18 **Long-run equilibrium under monopolistic competition with free entry and price competition among existing firms.**

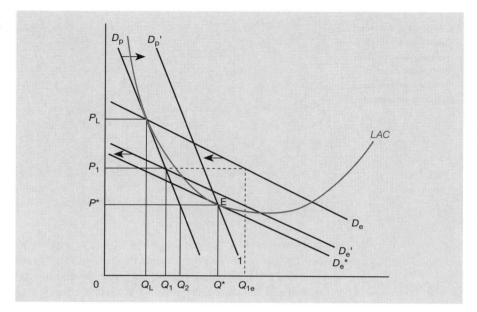

Unfortunately at the corresponding price $P*$ the **proportionate demand curve**, D_p, tells us that only Q_2 will be demanded from each firm! In this situation, as earlier, firms will be making losses and some will be exiting the industry. This reduction in the number of firms will progressively shift the proportionate demand curve to the right, as a given group/industry output at any price is divided between fewer and fewer firms. Exit will continue until D''_e becomes tangent to LAC and D'_p cuts D''_e at the point of tangency, E. We now have a long-run equilibrium, with normal profits earned by all firms and no entry or exit taking place. The equilibrium price is $P*$ with each firm having an expected and actual market share of $0Q*$.

Notice that the inclusion of price competition amongst existing firms alongside new entry has resulted in a lower predicted long-run equilibrium price ($P* < P_L$) and higher predicted output ($Q* > Q_L$), with correspondingly less excess capacity.

Some criticisms of the theory of monopolistic competition outlined previously have, however, been advanced:

- By producing differentiated products, firms will not necessarily face identical cost and demand conditions. They need not, therefore, respond in an identical way to an external stimulus, e.g. all reducing their prices. This casts doubt on the relevance of the *proportionate* demand curve in our earlier analysis.

- If a firm is earning supernormal profits in the short run, it could be argued that these could only be competed away by new entrants producing the *same* (not differentiated) product.

- Differentiated products are often produced by a single (large) firm rather than by a large number of (small) competing firms. Product differentiation is as much a feature of oligopoly (Chapters 8 and 9) as of monopolistic competition.

- It is difficult to empirically identify the boundaries of the 'product group' within which product differentiation occurs. Does the product group *drink* incorporate total soft drinks, soft drinks with a minimum prescribed fruit content, or some other sub-division of the drinks sector? It is difficult to know whether we are faced with a vast array of competing individual drink products, or whether there are clearly bounded categories of drink within which product differentiation and competition effectively take place.

- The predictive content of monopolistic competition theory is less clear cut than that of perfect competition (or indeed monopoly, Chapter 7). For example, imposing a tax on the product of a monopoly, with a highly inelastic demand, will mainly raise firm price rather than reduce firm output. Imposing the same tax on a product group under monopolistic competition will have a much less determinate impact on firm price and output. This is because we shall be unsure whether few or many firms will exit the product group, which, now it is taxed, faces a reduced overall demand. The impact on output and price of firms remaining within the product group is therefore less determinate.

Contestable markets

Baumol (1982) introduced the idea of **contestable markets**, thereby broadening the application of competitive behaviour beyond the structure–conduct–performance approach. In other words, instead of regarding competitive behaviour as existing only, or primarily, in the perfectly or monopolistically competitive *market structures*, it could be exhibited in *any* market structure that was **contestable**. Generally speaking, the fewer the barriers to entry into a market, the more contestable that market. In this sense some monopoly (Chapter 7) and oligopoly (Chapters 8 and 9) markets could be regarded as contestable.

The absence of entry barriers increases the *threat* of new firms entering the market. It is this threat that is assumed to check any tendency by incumbent firms to raise prices substantially above average costs and thereby earn supernormal profit.

It may be useful to illustrate this approach by considering the extreme case of perfect contestability. In a **perfectly contestable market** there are no barriers to entry so that incumbent firms are constrained to keep prices at levels that, in relation to costs, earn only normal profits. Incumbents in perfectly contestable markets therefore earn no supernormal profits, are cost efficient, and cannot cross-subsidise between products or in any way set prices below costs in order to deter new entrants.

An algebraic solution

The solution P^*, Q^* outlined in Fig. 6.18 involves the intersection of both the **proportionate** (D_p) and **expected** (D_e) demand curves. the expected demand curve reflects *perceptions* of firms that they can lower price independently of other firms and gain a disproportionate part of group/industry demand.

The demand conditions of monopolistic competition may be approximated by the linear demand function:

$$p = A - (n - 1)aq^0 - bq \qquad (1)$$

where p and q denote price and quantity for the representative firm, q^0 denotes quantity produced by each of the other members of the group, and n denotes the size of the group (number of producers). This equation represents both the D_p and the D_e curve, depending on wether q^0 is treated as a variable or a constant. Where q^0 is treated as a *variable*, then equation (1) represents the **proportionate** demand curve (D_p), with all firms sharing in the higher group output resulting from a lower price (by the representative and other firms). Where q^0 is treated as a *constant*, then equation (1) represents the **expected** demand curve (D_e), whereby the firm assumes that it alone is the beneficiary of a lower price, other firms being perceived as *not responding* to that lower price.

- The D_p curve has a vertical intercept of A and a slope of $-[(n-1)a + b]$, since q $= q^0 = Q/n$ (Q denoting aggregate group output), and all qs vary uniformly.

- The D_e curve has a vertical intercept of $[A - (n-1) aq^0]$, since q^0 is considered a constant, and a slope of $-b$.

If the parameter values are $A = 200$, $a = 0.01$, $n = 101$, and $b = -1$, the two demand equations become

$$D_p: p = 200 - 2q = 200 - \frac{2Q}{n}$$

and

$$D_e: p = (200 - q^0) - q$$

The location of the D_e curve varies with the output of the group: if $q^0 = 25$, D_e is $p = 175 - q$; if $q^0 = 50$, D_e is $p = 150 - q$, etc. An increase in the group's output effectively shrinks the demand curve for any number, and vice versa.

Fig. 6.19 indicates the equilibrium for this model, with $q^* = 50$ and $p^* = 100$ the intersection point for both D_p and D_e.

Fig. 6.19
Intersection of expected (D_e) and proportionate (D_p) demand curves in long-run equilibrium.

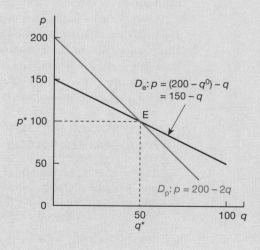

At least three conditions must be fulfilled for a market to be perfectly contestable:

- There must be an absence of sunk costs (see p. 181). Sunk costs are the costs of acquiring an asset (tangible or intangible) that cannot be recouped by selling the asset or redeploying it in another market should the firm exit the industry. The presence of sunk costs, by increasing the costs of exiting the industry, can be assumed to make incumbent firms more determined to *avoid* being forced to exit the industry and therefore more aggressive towards new entrants. They might then seek to resist new entrants by adopting a variety of strategies that essentially constitute a barrier to entry.
- The potential entrant must be at no disadvantage compared with incumbents as regards production technology or perceived product quality. Any lack of access to *equivalent production technology* utilised by incumbents might prevent new entrants from competing on the same cost base or quality-of-product base. This would inhibit the threat of potential new entrants, thereby permitting incumbents to earn and retain supernormal profits. Similarly *perceptions* of consumers (via branding etc.) as to the superiority of incumbent product quality would also inhibit the threat of new entrants and permit incumbents to earn and retain supernormal profits.
- The entrant must be able to engage in 'hit and run' tactics: i.e. to enter a market, make a profit and exit *before* incumbents can adjust their prices downwards. Put another way, existing suppliers can only change their prices with time-lags whereas consumers respond immediately to any lower prices offered by new entrants.

Under these conditions there is a total absence of barriers to entry, and exit from the market is costless. Such a **perfectly contestable market** will ensure that incumbents are unable to earn supernormal profits in the long run, and that price will equate with long-run average total cost (including normal profit). Any rise in price above long-run average cost will attract new entrants, who, by undercutting the price of incumbents, can attract their customers and make a profit before the incumbent can react by reducing price. The new entrant can exit the market at zero cost by such 'hit and run' tactics, having benefited by earning supernormal profits prior to the reaction of incumbents, namely the curbing of their prices back to long-run average cost.

Suppose we take Fig. 6.20 to illustrate a perfectly contestable market fulfilling the three criteria noted above. In this market, the price p^* corresponds to earning normal profits, with long-run average cost (*LAC*) including normal profit being equal to average revenue (*AR*). In fact this market exhibits features of 'natural monopoly' (Chapter 7). The continuously declining *LAC* curve reflects sustained scale economies so that industry costs would be minimised by having just one firm in the industry. Even in this case, we can use Fig. 6.20 to show how the threat of 'hit and run' tactics by potential new entrants might keep the price of the incumbent firm at p^* in the case of perfectly contestability.

We can use Fig. 6.20 to show what might happen if the incumbent were to set a price *above* p^*. Here we suppose the incumbent initially sets the profit-maximising price p^m, with $MC = MR$ at the corresponding output should those curves have been drawn on the diagram. In this case a new entrant operating under the three conditions outlined above could, say, set price at p^c and capture the whole market available at that price, making supernormal profit per period of EFGH. If the incumbent were then to retaliate in the next period by reducing price to below p^c, the new entrant could simply exit the market at zero cost, taking with it the profits already made.

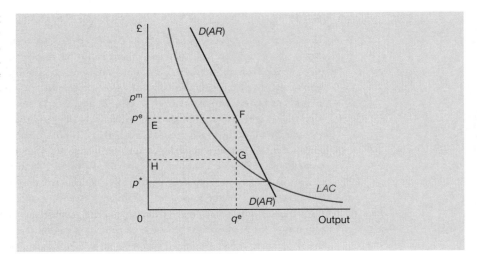

In a perfectly contestable market any price that the incumbent sets above p^* will induce such 'hit and run' entry, thereby giving the incumbent no incentive to charge anything other than the price (p^*) consistent with normal profit (even in this case of 'natural monopoly').

Although such perfect contestability is an ideal rarely, if ever, achieved it sets the context for competitive behaviour in all types of market structure. Even highly monopolistic or oligopolistic markets could, in principle, experience a high degree of contestability, thereby achieving a competitive-type market solution with price close to long-run average costs and profits close to normal. The policy implication of such an approach is to encourage the removal of entry barriers and the lowering of exit costs in all types of market structure in order to increase the degree of contestability.

A rather weaker, but more pragmatic, approach to contestability focuses on *cost* rather than on price contestability. Here the suggestion is that the threat of entry may be more likely to induce incumbents to be *cost efficient* than to set prices equal to long-run average costs. By 'cost efficient' is meant the delivery of a given level of output at the lowest cost technically feasible. This perspective allows cost-efficient incumbents still to make supernormal profits, engage in cross-subsidisation, etc. However, only by keeping costs at the lowest level technically feasible does the incumbent firm retain the *flexibility* to respond to potential new entrants by reducing price to a level consistent with long-run average cost. Being aware of this flexibility acts as a deterrent to potential new entrants even where *price* is currently set above such a cost base by incumbents, thereby earning supernormal profits. As we shall see (Chapter 13), the perspective of 'cost contestability' is a widely used argument in support of *deregulation*, i.e. the opening up of specified markets to potential new entrants as a means of securing efficiency gains via cost cutting by incumbents.

Applications and evidence

■ The stock market and competition

Although strictly speaking there is no particular market that fulfils all the criteria for a perfectly competitive market as previously outlined (p. 246), the **stock market** is arguably the closest approximation. Numerous buyers and sellers are engaged in daily (indeed hourly) transactions of large volumes of stock, whether shares (equities) or bonds (debentures). Prices of stock are known worldwide in *real time*, and electronic facilities permit *contracts* to be established immediately at prevailing prices. The characteristics of the various types of stock are frequently discussed in the financial press, in various specially commissioned *external* reports and surveys, and in a variety of easily accessed *internal* documents.

Taking the London Stock Exchange as an example, over £1,000 billion of purchases and sales of stock occurred in 1994, involving the shares of more than 2,500 companies. For any *new issues* of shares, a full prospectus describing the company and its prospects must be issued, and widely advertised in public. The Stock Exchange Automated Quotation (SEAQ) service allows market makers and others to see competing quotations on their screens, and allows brokers to select the best bid/offer for their clients.

Following Heather (1994) we can consider the changes in share price of a particular (pharmaceutical) company, Wellcome plc, over a period of 18 months from January 1991 to August 1992 as exhibiting many of the characteristics of a perfectly competitive market.

Figure 6.21(a) indicates the observed movements in the share price of Wellcome over this time period. All Wellcome shares had been held in a charitable trust until 1986, when 20% of such shares were sold on the Stock Exchange as a means of raising funds to finance further medical research. As we note below, a further 38% were sold to raise still more funds in July 1992. Clearly the share price proved volatile over the period in

Fig. 6.21(a)
Wellcome's share price movement.

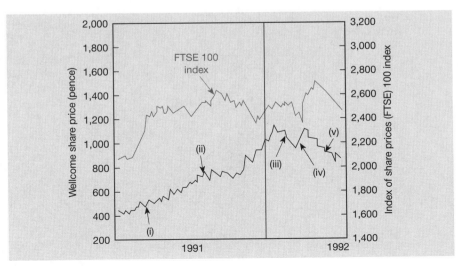

Source: Extel, Heather (1994)

question. Fig. 6.21(b) uses demand–supply analysis to account for five specific examples of volatility in the Wellcome share price identified by numbers (i) to (v) in Fig. 6.21(a). For purposes of comparison with *general* share prices, the FTSE 100 index of share prices is charted directly above that for Wellcome (using the right-hand axis).

(i)   American medical opinion expresses doubts over the effectiveness of Retrovir, a new anti-AIDS drug developed at great expense by Wellcome. There is an increased supply of Wellcome stock. Price falls from P_1 to P_2.

(ii)   A major AIDS conference makes favourable comments on Retrovir. Demand for Wellcome's shares increases. Price rises from P_1 to P_2.

(iii) Enthusiasm for pharmaceutical stocks has been growing; Wellcome had benefited from this, being one of the major drugs companies. Demand had previously risen, but now US investors decide they are over-priced. Supply of Wellcome shares increases. Price falls from P_1 to P_2.

(iv)   Speculation is rife that the recently supplied shares have been *oversold*, confirming the view of a rising market for Wellcome shares. Demand further increases but (sec-ondhand) supply to the market decreases as people speculate on a further rise in price. Price rises from P_1 to P_2 (but quantity of shares traded is little affected).

(v)   The Wellcome trust announces its decision to sell 38% of its shares. The market is taken by surprise. The supply curve shifts sharply to the right at a time when share prices are generally depressed. Wellcome's share price falls from P_1 to P_2.

Of course even the stock market allegedly departs from the ideal of a perfectly competitive market. On occasions perfect information to all market participants is clearly absent, as with instances of *insider trading*. We return to the implications of *market failure* for the perfectly competitive model in Chapter 12.

Fig. 6.21(b) **Using demand–supply analysis in explanation of specific movements in Wellcome's share price.**

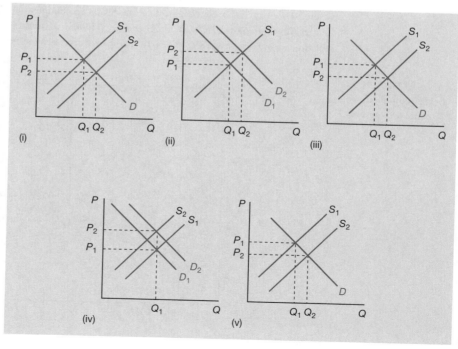

■ Common Agricultural Policy (CAP) and price intervention

Previously (pp. 254–7), we considered the efficiency gains of a competitive market as compared with instances where the market-clearing price was inhibited by interventionist policies. The operation of the Common Agricultural Policy (CAP) of the European Union provides a useful insight into the operation and impact of such interventionist policies. The following discussion is in the context of the *price support* variant for a minimum price set above a market-clearing price, considered on p. 256 and involving Fig. 6.12.

Since one in five of the EU's workers were involved in agricultural production in 1957, it came as no surprise that the depressed agricultural sector became the focus of the first common policy, the CAP, established in 1962. The objectives of this policy were to create a single market for agricultural produce and to protect the agricultural sector from imports, the justification being to ensure dependable supplies of food for the EU and stability of income for those engaged in agriculture.

Both the demand for, and the supply of, agricultural products are, for the most part, inelastic, so that a small shift in either schedule will induce a more than proportionate change in price. Fluctuations in agricultural prices will in turn create fluctuations in agricultural incomes and therefore investment and ultimately output. The CAP seeks to stabilise agricultural prices, and therefore incomes and output in the industry, to the alleged benefit of both producers and consumers.

Method of operation

The formal title for the executive body of the CAP is the European Agricultural Guarantee and Guidance Fund (EAGGF), often known by its French translation Fonds Européen d'Orientation et de Garantie Agricole (FEOGA). As its name implies, it has two essential roles: that of *guaranteeing* farm incomes, and of *guiding* farm production. We shall consider each aspect in turn.

Guarantee system

Different agricultural products are dealt with in slightly different ways, but the basis of the system is the establishment of a *target price* for each product (Fig. 6.22(a)). The target price is *not* set with reference to world prices, but is based upon the price that producers would need to cover costs, including a profit mark-up, in the highest-cost area of production in the EU. The EU then sets an *intervention* or *guaranteed* price for the product in that area, about 7–10% below the target price. Should the price be in danger of falling below this level, the Commission intervenes to buy up production to keep the price at or above the guaranteed level. The Commission then sets separate target and intervention prices for that product in each area of the Community, related broadly to production costs in that area. As long as the market price in a given area (there are 11 such areas in the UK) is above the intervention price, the producer will sell his produce at prevailing market prices. In effect the intervention price sets a *floor* below which market price will not be permitted to fall, and which is therefore the **guaranteed minimum price** to producers.

In Fig. 6.22(b) an increase in supply of agricultural products to S_1 would, if no action were taken, lower the market price from P_1 to P_2 below the intervention or guaranteed price, $P*$. At $P*$ demand is Q' but supply is $Q*$. To keep the price at $P*$ the EAGGF will buy up the excess $Q* - Q'$. In terms of Fig. 6.22(b) the demand curve is artificially increased to D_1 by the EAGGF purchase.

If this system of guaranteed minimum prices is to work, then EU farmers must be protected from low-priced imports from overseas. To this end levies or tariffs are imposed on imports of agricultural products. If in Fig. 6.22(a) the price of imported food were *higher* than the EU target price then, of course, there would be no need for an import tariff. If, however, the import price is below this, say at the *world price* in Fig. 6.22(a), then an appropriate tariff must be calculated. This need not quite cover the difference between *target* and *world* price, since the importer still has to pay transport costs within the EU to get the food to market. The tariff must therefore be large enough to raise the import price at the EU frontier to the target price minus transport costs, i.e. *threshold price*. This calculation takes place in the highest-cost area of production in the EU, so that the import tariff set will more than protect EU producers in areas with lower target prices (i.e. lower-cost areas).

Should an EU producer wish to export an agricultural product and thereby have to sell it at the world price, then an export subsidy will be paid to bring his receipts up to the intervention price (see Fig. 6.22(a)), i.e. the minimum price he would receive in the

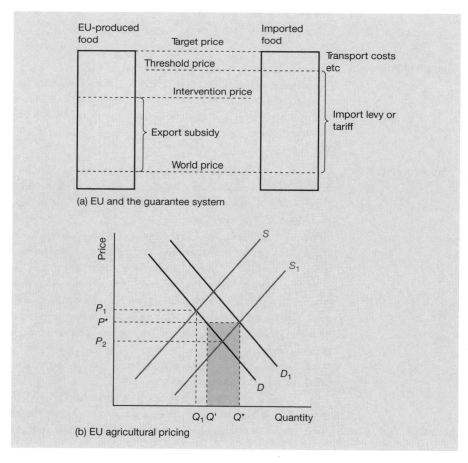

Fig. 6.22 **Intervention and the CAP.**

(a) EU and the guarantee system

(b) EU agricultural pricing

home market. Problems involving this form of subsidy of oilseed exports have been a major threat to dealings between the EU and the USA, with the latter alleging a breach of GATT rules.

The system outlined does not apply to all agricultural products in the EU. About a quarter of these products are covered by different direct subsidy systems, e.g. olive oil and tobacco, and some products, such as potatoes, agricultural alcohol and honey, are not covered by EU regulation at all.

Guidance system

The CAP was, as originally established, a simple price-support system. It soon became obvious that agriculture in the 'Six' required considerable structural change because too much output was being produced by small, high-cost, farming units. In 1968 the Commission published a report called *Agriculture 1980*, more usually known as the *Mansholt Plan* after its originator, the Commissioner for Agriculture, Sicco Mansholt. The plan envisaged taking large amounts of marginal land out of production, reducing the agricultural labour force, and creating larger economic farming units. The plan eventually led to the establishment of a Common Structural Policy in 1972, which for political reasons was to be voluntary and administered by the individual member states. The import levies of the EAGGF were to provide funds to encourage small farmers to leave the land and to promote large-scale farming units.

Empirical evidence

In terms of *theory*, we noted the potential welfare loss of such a price support scheme as area $mvnQ_2Q_3$ in Fig. 6.12 (p. 256). Here we seek to express that loss in alternative ways.

We noted (p. 256) that one part of the overall equation involved a transfer to producers resulting from such price support policies. Figure 6.23(a) indicates the percentage producer subsidy equivalent (PSE) of the price support schemes in the (then) EU 12 and a number of other countries adopting similar policies in the period 1980–90. This is, in effect, a measure of the transfer to producers relative to the farm-gate value of agricultural production. It varies from around 12% of the value of agricultural production in Australia to 70% in Switzerland, with the EU in a middle position with some 40% of the value of agricultural production being absorbed by such producer transfers. As we can see from Fig. 6.23(b), around 90% of that transfer can be ascribed directly to market price support schemes in the (then) EU–12.

Munk *et al.* (1994) use econometric analysis to argue that in recent times the price support system underlying the CAP has incurred still greater welfare losses, in a number of respects:

- The *transfer efficiency* of the price support system has decreased. In other words, a still greater decrease in the real income of the rest of society is now required to increase the income of EU farmers by 1 ecu. In part this is due to the increasing level of protection necessitated under the CAP when guaranteed prices were only *partially* adjusted downwards in response to significant decreases in world market prices. This has, of course, led to the distortion of still greater production of agricultural products in the (relatively inefficient) EU compared with other (relatively efficient) world locations. Further, it has led to greater *budgetary costs* for member governments, which must now fund the additional guarantee payments.

Fig. 6.23 **Transfers to producers via the CAP in the EU, and via similar price (or income) support programmes in other countries.**

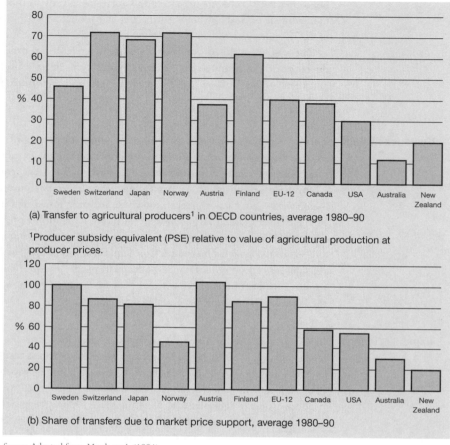

(a) Transfer to agricultural producers[1] in OECD countries, average 1980–90

[1]Producer subsidy equivalent (PSE) relative to value of agricultural production at producer prices.

(b) Share of transfers due to market price support, average 1980–90

Source: Adapted from Munk *et al.* (1994)

These budgetary costs have been further increased by new *administrative costs* required to support the emergence of the EU from being a net importer to a net exporter of most temperate-zone agricultural products. In other words, as well as administering the *tariff* regime on imported agriculture products into the EU, the CAP now also has to administer a wide variety of subsidies to EU agricultural exporters to the rest of the world. In fact any additional revenues from imposing tariffs on agricultural imports into the EU have been more than offset by the additional costs of subsidies to agricultural exports from the EU.

- The redistributional benefits of the CAP have also decreased. There has been a widening of the gap between volumes of production (and associated income support) of small farmers who need such support and large farmers who often do not. It could be said that the latter have received an increase in *economic rent* (p. 410). The increased importance of part-time farming in the EU has also increased the correlation between agricultural earnings and low income.

- The cost of *alternative instruments* other than price support has decreased. Again, this makes the price support system less attractive. For example, the farming population has become a smaller proportion of EU employment, reducing the cost of providing *direct income support* to lower-paid farmers, as an alternative to general price support. Further, a social security net in many member states has now been extended to cover farmers. Arguably the evolution of modern information technology has simplified the gathering and processing of information, making it still more feasible to identify and directly support low-income farmers.

A more recent study confirms many of these criticisms of the CAP. Ritson and Harvey (1997) show that, over the 15-year period from 1979 to 1994, EU prices for a variety of agricultural commodities were consistently above world prices (Fig. 6.24). The EU had therefore to impose a tariff on the imports of such commodities and provide a subsidy to EU exporters, in the manner discussed above (p. 270).

Most of these developments point towards a progressive diminution in reliance by the CAP on a price support scheme, which is in fact the direction in which the EU is seeking to move. The negative externalities imposed on the physical environment by over-production in agriculture further reinforce the need for a switch away from the old system. So too does the reduced impact of the positive externality argument involving social cohesion via CAP price support, now that agriculture plays a significantly smaller part within EU communities.

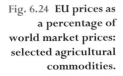

■ European Single Market and competitiveness

So far we have considered the *efficiency losses* associated with perpetuating a regulatory policy for agriculture (the CAP) that, in various respects, *restricts* competition. It may be useful at this stage to consider the *efficiency gains* associated with breaking down previously existing regulations. This was certainly the intention behind the creation of the Single Market for intra-European trade in goods and services in 1987. The Single European Act (1987) created a protected free trade area for trade between some 373 million people. The Act was not aimed simply at removing all frontier controls on trade in goods and services, but at removing all barriers to the movement of goods, people and capital.

Fig. 6.24 EU prices as a percentage of world market prices: selected agricultural commodities.

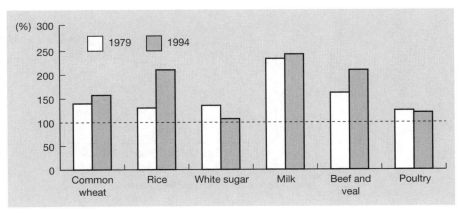

Source: Adapted from Ritson and Harvey (1997)

The Single Market was expected to benefit consumers through increased competition. It was hoped that cost savings resulting from reductions in the cost of trade between EU countries and from greater exploitation of economies of scale would, via competitive pressures, be passed on to consumers in the form of lower prices. The *Single Market Review* (European Commission 1997) sought to check this by measuring price–cost margins across different industrial and service sectors in member states before and after the creation of the Single Market. If the Single Market programme were to have had a broadly pro-competitive effect (bringing firms in different member states into direct competition where previously non-tariff barriers had prevented this) then we would expect price–cost margins to be reduced.

Figure 6.25 presents data for average price–cost margins between 1980 and 1992 across the (then) EU-12 member states, using a data set of some 8,000 cost–price observations. The *price–cost margin* shown in Fig. 6.25 was defined as

$$\frac{\text{Value added} - \text{Labour costs}}{\text{Value added}}$$

The data provide evidence of a sustained fall in price–cost margins in the period following the creation of the Single Market in 1987. The magnitude of this effect is substantial, in the order of a fall of 0.6% per annum in price–cost with an average level of 44%. Over a decade this would correspond to a significant fall of some 6% in the projected price–cost margins.

The airline industry and contestable markets

In the earlier discussion of contestable market theory (p. 263), we saw that this theory broadened the applicability of the perfectly competitive model. The threat of entry could

Fig. 6.25 **Price–cost margins in the EU-12, 1980–92.**

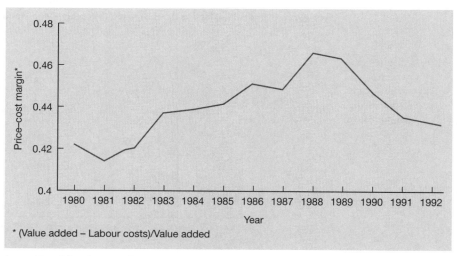

* (Value added – Labour costs)/Value added

Source: Adapted from European Commission (1997)

cause incumbent firms to adopt 'competitive' market behaviour, with price set close to long-run average costs and profits close to normal. Such competitive market behaviour could be expected in highly contestable markets, with few if any barriers to entry, even when the market structure was far from the perfectly competitive ideal.

The theory of contestability followed the earlier ideas of J. S. Bain and P. Sylos-Labini on the effects of *potential* competition on market behaviour and was formulated in a coherent way by Bailey and Panzar (1981), Baumol (1982) and Baumol, Panzar and Willig (1986). At the time, the theory was felt to be particularly relevant to the passenger airline industry, and the pioneering work on contestability was done with reference to the US airline industry in the early and mid 1980s, shortly after the industry had been deregulated. Here we consider the nature of the US airline market and the relevance of contestability theory to the airline industry worldwide.

In the early 1980s the proponents of contestable market theory felt that the US airline industry provided fertile ground for testing the theory:

- First, the industry experienced low sunk costs, with the result that entry and exit could be regarded as virtually costless. The major portion of an airline's costs involves the aircraft itself, and it was widely accepted that few irrecoverable or sunk costs were involved. For example, if one route was closed or found to be unprofitable, then an aircraft could be moved to another route or market at little additional cost.

- Second, an aircraft could fly into an airport, undercut existing prices, make a profit, and then leave, i.e. engage in a 'hit and run' strategy. If airlines already in the industry reacted to new entrants by pushing down prices, the new airline could compete in other geographical locations. In the worst-case scenario the new entrant could sell the aircraft on the (then thriving) secondhand market at very little loss, restarting operations when conditions had improved. This *threat* of entry ensured, according to Bailey and Panzar (1981), that 'local monopolies have been pricing more or less competitively on their long haul routes'. The emergence of new entrants such as Texas Air, People's Express, World Air and President into the US airline business in the mid 1980s seemed to substantiate the contestable markets description of the industry.

Problems of contestability

However, subsequent research has cast some doubt on the applicability of contestability to the airline industry worldwide in a number of respects:

- Sunk costs have been found to be more extensive in the airline industry than had initially been thought. For example, it is now recognised that advertising costs need to be high to persuade travellers to switch to new airlines. Again it has often taken a new entrant some time, and therefore resources, to determine whether a new service is likely to be profitable.

- Even if the sunk costs element *is* smaller in the airline industry than in other industries, other significant barriers to entry in the airline business may negate the relevance of contestable market theory to this activity. These barriers include the fact that landing slots at airports were limited by physical space and time so that existing, large incumbent airlines tended to monopolise the supply of such slots. Further, existing airlines offered 'frequent flyer' programmes under which travellers were offered free flights according to how extensively they used the existing airline's services. These tended to ensure customer loyalty to incumbents using methods that potential or new airlines, with fewer routes, could not readily exploit. Stewart (1998) notes that it has been common practice for incumbent airlines in the USA and Europe to pay a bonus to travel agents if their share of the total flights booked through the agents exceeds some specified level, again creating an entry barrier.

- The 'hit and run' potential within contestable markets is unlikely to be realised when existing firms can lower their prices quickly. For example, Stockton (1988) and Evans and Kessidies (1991) found that incumbent airlines exhibited such flexible responses to competition that the US airline industry experienced up to one million changes in fares per day! In fact the US airlines industry has *not* been characterised by the hit and run tactics of new entrants, with such firms leaving the market after having made positive profits as a result of entry. In the view of Evans and Kessidies, entry could more accurately be described as being of the '*get* hit and run' kind, as with People's Express.

- The assumption that the *threat* of competition is sufficient to control market behaviour has been questioned by the work of Call and Keeler (1985), who noted that *actual* rather than merely potential entry is needed to reduce fares on previously restricted routes. In similar vein, while Morrison and Winston (1987) accept that *potential* competition has an effect on the behaviour of firms already in the industry, they argue that this is not as strong as actual competition on the ground. In their view the number of potential carriers begins to have a significant 'threat' effect on existing companies only if there are at least four newcomers able to enter the market.

- The relevance of the theory of contestability to the airline industry is diminished by the fact that air fares are often a function of market concentration. Research has found that US air fares rose as the degree of concentration rose (Graham *et al*. 1983; Call and Keeler 1985; Hurdle *et al*. 1989; Stewart 1998). In other words, the presence of large incumbent airlines means that profit is rarely at the normal level. Indeed the observed occasional outbreaks of price warfare tend to suggest that it is *actual* competition, rather than potential competition, that keeps profits at reasonable levels.

Here we have considered an attempt to utilise a microeconomic theory in describing an actual market situation. We have seen that, at best, the airline industry was only imperfectly contestable. Perhaps the threat of new competition may have caused incumbent airlines to become more cost conscious, seeking to keep costs low to prevent potential entry (i.e. there may have been some kind of cost contestability). However, incumbent airlines appear less likely to keep profits low (i.e. profit contestability) in the face of the threat of new entry. Indeed excess profits have often been protected by an ability to raise prices where market concentration is high – and by the propensity of incumbents to engage in aggressive price cutting to thwart new entrants, etc. A more extensive review of the barriers to entry still remaining in the air transport industry in Chapter 7 (pp. 318–19) goes some way to explaining these advantages for incumbents over potential new entrants.

■ The rail freight industry and contestable markets

The rail freight industry in the UK was privatised in 1996. Previously the transport of freight by rail had been a separate profit centre within the operations of the state-owned British Rail. Around half of trainload freight is short distance (less than 130 km) and high volume (more than 1 million tonnes per annum), often involving the transport of bulk commodities such as coal, iron ore and various 'aggregates'. The privatisation in 1996 initially established three companies with a broadly geographical base but a vertically separated rail infrastructure (track being the responsibility of a separate company, Railtrack), with its huge sunk costs and economies of density. The idea of 'contestability' lay behind such vertical separation, with new entrants supposedly able to provide (at least potentially) freight services on track that no incumbent freight operator owned. Otherwise the 'sunk costs' and other economies associated with track ownership by incumbents might prove barriers to new firm entry, as previously discussed (p. 263).

Brewer (1996) suggests a number of reasons why the rail freight industry may *not* in fact provide the benefits expected by adherents of contestability theory:

- *Experience economies*. The companies winning the initial contracts immediately after privatisation will already have secured the services of the (scarce) fully trained locomotive drivers previously employed by BR. Subsequent new entrants will face the relatively high costs of recruiting and training new locomotive drivers.
- *Technological indivisibilities*. It may prove difficult to transfer different types of locomotive between different market segments, inhibiting new entrants from moving into rail freight operations from other types of rail operations. In addition much of the existing BR rail locomotive and rolling stock was assigned to the three initial companies on privatisation. Purchasing new stock involves long lead-times and substantial capital expenditure, making it difficult for new entrants to adopt the 'hit and run' practices of contestable market theory. Incomplete driver knowledge as between different types of locomotive and route restrictions arguably constitute further entry barriers favouring incumbents.
- *Safety regulations*. Railtrack, the Health and Safety Executive and the Rail Regulator all lay down strict safety guidelines, which must be met by new applicants for a freight-operating licence. The preparation costs for submissions of such applications, as well as implementation costs and actual licence fees, are likely to act as barriers to entry.
- *Pricing and track access*. Freight contracts typically last for a number of years. Given the various barriers to entry already identified, incumbents will be able to cut contract prices at or before the time of renewal by cross-subsidising within their customer portfolio. New entrants can also be disadvantaged by 'never knowingly undersold' pricing policies of incumbents. Even if new freight operators *do* win contracts by offering lower prices than incumbents, they may fail to secure adequate track access for freight services. Railtrack administers 'path auctions' amongst operators, and given the scarcity of track capacity at certain times and in certain locations, new freight operators may find themselves outbid by incumbents and therefore denied the track access that they need to fulfil the newly secured contracts.

Some of these problems for new entrants are reflected in Table 6.1, which presents the results of a survey by Brewer (1996). This survey sought to identify the *perceived* barriers to entry facing potential operators in the rail freight industry. The 23 barriers identified in Table 6.1 are shown in declining rank order (column 1) according to the number of respondents citing them as significant. For each barrier identified by a respondent as significant, an estimate was requested of its perceived importance, using a scale of 1 (most important) to 5 (least important). Column (2) gives the mean score for each barrier in terms of its perceived severity by those respondents regarding it as significant.

Table 6.1 **Perceived significance of each potential barrier to entry.**

Barrier to entry	(1)	(2)	(3)	(4)
Incumbent operators having first choice of BR traction/rolling stock	1	2.67	9=	1.46
Purchasing new traction involves long lead times and great expense	2	2.61	7	1.36
Cost/time involved in obtaining safety certificates and operator licences	3	2.56	6	1.30
Perceived level of track access charges	4	2.14	1	1.24
No leasing market in motive power	5	3.06	20	1.41
Virtually non-existent secondhand market for 'registered' motive power	6	2.67	9=	1.29
Access to appropriate track paths	7=	2.82	13	1.27
Excessive technical restrictions imposed by Railtrack as part of rolling stock registration	7=	2.35	3	1.12
Incumbent operators having back-up resources enabling better response to changing customer requirements	7=	3.22	23	1.36
Trainload freight operators having experience in running trains, estimating, negotiating and securing contracts	10	2.45	4	1.37
Limited funds available for Track Access Grant	11=	2.74	12	1.46
Presence of economies of density (emphasising the importance of volume in reducing unit costs)	11=	2.62	8	1.37
Method of charging	11=	2.24	2	1.15
Presence of economies of scale (minimising cost of depot/repair facilities)	11=	3.14	22	1.21
Problems of new entrants in obtaining trained drivers and qualified staff	15	2.52	5	1.37
Incumbent cross-subsidies contracts within existing portfolio of traffic	16	2.68	11	1.11
Traction rolling stock having few alternative uses	17	3.03	19	1.40
Limited funds available for Freight Facilities Grant	18	2.90	15	1.52
Physical limitations of traction/rolling stock (trailing weights, route availability, loading gauge, etc.)	19	2.88	14	1.33
Incompatibility of traction from European/US networks due to gauge and power differences	20	3.00	17=	1.48
Incumbent adopts a 'never knowingly undersold' pricing policy	21	3.00	17=	1.41
Incumbent practices 'responsive pricing' (i.e. they react quicker to price differences that may emerge at contract renewal time than do their customers)	22	2.93	16	1.38
Exemption of private siding facilities from access provisions	23	3.08	21	1.38

1. Ranking of the barrier, in terms of number of citations
2. The average severity of the barrier, on a scale of 1 (most important) to 5 (least important)
3. Ranking of the barrier, in terms of average severity
4. Standard deviation of the severity score for each barrier

Source: Adapted from Brewer (1996)

From Table 6.1 it is clear that respondents believe that a number of barriers to entry exist in the rail freight industry to inhibit the 'hit and run' tactics of new entrants under contestable market theory. Seventeen separate barriers were cited by over half the respondents, with 16 barriers receiving an average importance weighting of less than 3.0 (the midpoint of the scale in which a low value implies a more important barrier). The barrier *cited most frequently* by respondents was incumbents having had first choice of the locomotive stock from the previous BR regime. The barrier regarded as *most important* (lowest score) by those mentioning it was the perceived level of track access charges likely to be faced by new entrants. The low measures of dispersion (standard deviation) shown in column (4) indicate a considerable measure of agreement as to barriers of entry in the perceptions of those surveyed.

Key terms	
Allocative efficiency	Normal profit
Barriers to entry	Perfectly contestable market
Consumer surplus	Price regulation
Contestable markets	Producer Surplus
Guaranteed minimum price	Production quota
Imperfect competition	Production efficiency
Industry MC curve	Proportionate demand curve
Industry supply curve	Quality regulations
Long-run	Short-run
Monopolistic competition	

Full definitions can be found in the 'Glossary of terms' (pp. 699–710)

Review questions

1. A competitive industry producing galvanised screws for the building trades has a demand function of the form $Q = 400 - 4P$. Each firm in the industry is operating at its minimum average cost (AC) of $40 - 0.05Q$. If P is the price per screw in pence and Q is the industry's output in thousands then:

   (a) What are the equations for the demand and supply *curves* for this industry? Explain briefly the sort of supply conditions that this industry is experiencing.
   (b) Determine the equilibrium price and output in this market.
   (c) Trace the effect on price and output if the government placed (i) a maximum price of 30p and (ii) a minimum price of 30p on galvanised screws.

2. A small vegetable farm growing carrots in a fertile horticultural area finds that the market for its product has all the symptoms of being perfectly competitive. From simple empirical surveys, the farmer finds that his marginal cost (MC) function is $10 + 0.5Q$ and his average variable cost function (AVC) is $10 + 0.25Q$, where Q represents 20 kg bags of carrots. His total fixed costs have also been calculated to be £1,000.

   (a) If the market price is £30 per bag of carrots, how many bags would the farmer produce?
   (b) At this level of output, is the farmer able to make a profit?

(c) Examine the position of the whole carrot-growing industry in the region. Would the farmer continue to grow carrots in the short run/long run?

3. The handicraft sector of a mature economy is composed of many identical small firms, which are producing high-quality lampshades. The equation for each firm's long-run average cost (LAC) is $Q + 225/Q$ and the long-run marginal cost (LMC) of each firm is $2Q$, where Q is the number of lampshades produced.

   (a) How many lampshades will each firm produce under conditions of long-run equilibrium? What will be the price charged?
   (b) If the market demand function at this optimum level of output for each firm is $Q = 6,000 - 50P$, calculate the market output of lampshades and the number of firms in the industry.
   (c) If there is a short-run increase in the market demand for lampshades so that the new demand function is $Q = 7,000 - 50P$, find the new short-run price level and the total short-run abnormal profits made by each small firm.

4. The market supply and demand functions for the bottom of the range computers are given by

$$Q_S = 2P - 300$$
$$Q_D = 800 - 0.5P$$

   where P is the price per computer and Q is output of computers in thousands. The industry is experiencing a volatile period, with both demand fluctuations and government legislation affecting suppliers' reactions.

   (a) Given the supply and demand functions shown, calculate the price and quantity that will clear the market.
   (b) As a result of a new sales drive, the number of consumers who want to buy the computers doubles. If incomes and tastes remain constant, calculate the new equilibrium level of price and quantity.
   (c) If the government now decides to place a special tax of t per unit on the suppliers of computers, then complete the following:
       (i) Express the supply curve and supply function in terms of t.
       (ii) Express the final equilibrium price and output supplied in terms of t.
       (iii) What does the specific value for t obtained from the equations of (ii) above indicate about the incidence of the tax?
       (iv) If the tax levied is £50 per computer, what are the final post-tax equilibrium price and output levels in the industry?

5. A study of the pensions sector of the financial services industry indicates that competition in this sector is monopolistic in nature. The approximate generalized linear demand equation for firms in this sector is given by

$$P = A - (n - 1)aq^o - bq$$

   where P and q are the price and quantity of contracts per week for a given representative firm in the pensions sector; q^o denotes the quantity of contracts produced by each of the other firms in the pensions sector and n is the number of firms in the sector as a whole.

(a) The equation represents both the DD (proportionate) and dd (expected) curves for the pensions sector under monopolistic competition. Explain clearly the difference between DD and dd.

(b) From your knowledge of the generalised demand equation, explain briefly the meaning of the symbols A, b and a.

(c) Derive the specific DD and dd equations from the generalised equation, and explain what the main parts of the equation mean. Write down the expressions for the two equations assuming that $n = 101$, $A = 120$, $b = -1$, and $a = 0.01$.

(d) Find the short-run equilibrium price and output of pension contracts for the firm on the assumption that each of the 101 firms in the sector has a uniform marginal cost curve of $MC = 50 + 0.5q$.

(e) If the fixed cost element for each firm is £500 prove that the short-run position calculated in (d) is also the long-run equilibrium position.

▓ Further reading

Intermediate texts

Baumol, W. J. (1977), *Economic Theory and Operations Analysis*, 4th edn, Ch. 16, Prentice Hall, Hemel Hempstead.

Browning, E. and Browning, J. (1992), *Microeconomic Theory and Applications*, 4th edn, Chs 9, 10, 12 and 14, HarperCollins, London.

Dobson, S., Maddala, G. S. and Miller, E. (1995), *Microeconomics*, Chs 8 and 11, McGraw-Hill, Maidenhead.

Hope, S. (1999), *Applied Microeconomics*, Ch. 9, Wiley, Chichester.

Katz, M. and Rosen, H. (1998), *Microeconomics*, 3rd edn, Chs 10, 11 and 14, Irwin, Boston, Mass.

Koutsoyiannis, A. (1979), *Modern Microeconomics*, 2nd edn, Chs 5 and 8, Macmillan, London.

Laidler, D. and Estrin, S. (1995), *Introduction to Microeconomics*, 4th edn, Chs 13 and 14, Harvester Wheatsheaf, Hemel Hempstead.

Maddala, G. S. and Miller, E. (1989), *Microeconomics: Theory and Application*, Chs 10 and 13, McGraw-Hill, New York.

Nicholson, W. (1997), *Intermediate Microeconomics and its Application*, 7th edn, Chs 12, 13 and 17, Dryden Press, Fort Worth.

Pindyck, R. and Rubinfeld, D. (1998), *Microeconomics*, 4th edn, Chs 8, 9 and 12, Macmillan, Basingstoke.

Varian, H. (1999), *Intermediate Microeconomics*, 5th edn, Chs 1, 16, 21 and 22, Norton, New York.

Advanced texts

Gravelle, H. and Rees, R. (1992), *Microeconomics*, 2nd edn, Ch. 10, Longman, Harlow.

Mas-Colell, A., Whinston, M. D. and Green, J. R. (1995), *Microeconomic Theory*, Ch. 10, Oxford University Press, Oxford.

Articles and other sources

Bailey, E. and Panzar, J. C. (1981), 'The contestability of airline markets during the transition to deregulation', *Law and Contemporary Problems*, 44, Winter.

Baumol, W. J. (1982), 'Contestable markets: an uprising in the theory of industry structure', *American Economic Review*, 72, 1.

Baumol, W. J., Panzar, J. C. and Willig, R. D. (1986), 'On the theory of contestable markets', in J. E. Stiglitz and F. Mathewson (eds) *New Developments in the Analysis of Market Structure*, MIT Press, Cambridge.

Brewer, P. (1996), 'Contestability in UK rail freight markets', *Transport Policy*, 3, 3.

Call, G. D. and Keeler, T. E. (1985), 'Airline deregulation, fares, and market behaviour: some empirical evidence', in A. F. Daughtey (ed.) *Analytical Studies in Transport Economics*, Cambridge University Press, Cambridge.

European Commission (1997), *Single Market Review Price competition and price convergence*, subseries V, volume 1, Kogan Page.

Evans, W. N. and Kessidies, I. N. (1991), 'Living by the "golden rule": multimarket contact in the US airline industry', Mimeo, 24 January.

Geroski, P. A. (1990), 'Entry, exit and structural adjustment in European industry', *London Business School*, Working Paper Series 85.

Graham, D. R., Kaplan, D. P. and Sibley, D.S. (1983), 'Efficiency and competition in the airline industry', *Bell Journal of Economics*, 14, Spring.

Heather, K. (1994), 'The stock market: a quick way to riches', *Modern Applied Economics*, Harvester Wheatsheaf, Hemel Hempstead.

Hurdle, G. J., Johnson, R. L., Joskow, A. S., Werden, G. J. and Williams, M. A. (1989), 'Concentration, potential entry, and performance in the airline industry', *Journal of Industrial Economics*, 38, (2).

Jovanovic, B. and Macdonald, G. M. (1994), 'Competitive diffusion', *Journal of Political Economy*, 102, 1, February.

Lipsey, R. G. (1995), 'The rediscovery of market economics', *Economics and Business Education*, III, Part 3, 11.

Marsden, C. (1994), 'Towards a responsible free market system', *Economics and Business Education*, II, Part 2, 6.

Matsuyama, K. (1995), 'Complementarities and cumulative processes in models of monopolistic competition', *Journal of Economic Literature*, XXXIII, 2 June.

McGowan, F. and Seabright, P. (1989), 'Deregulating European airlines', *Economic Policy: A European Forum*, October.

Morrison, S. A. and Winston, C. (1987), 'Empirical implications and tests of the contestability hypothesis', *Journal of Law and Economics*, 30, (1).

Munk, K., Blandford, D., Cahil, C. and Koester, U. (1994), 'The economic costs of agricultural policy', *European Economy*, November.

Pye, K. (1995), 'The European Union', in A. Griffiths and S. Wall (eds), *Applied Economics*, 6th edn, Longman, Harlow.

Rayner, T., Hine, R. and Ingersent, K. (1994), 'Will the CAP fit the GATT?', *Economic Review*, 12, 1, September.

Ritson, C. and Harvey, D. (1997) eds., *The Common Agricultural Policy*, Wallingford CAB

Shackelton, J. R. (1995), 'Market structure, competition and contestability', *Economics and Business Education*, III, Part 2, 10.

Stewart, G. (1998), 'Getting off to a flying start', *Economic Review*, 15, 3.

Stockton, W. (1988), 'When eight carriers call the shots', *New York Times*, November 20th.

Chapter 7

Monopoly

Introduction and review

We first consider the opposite extreme to perfect competition, namely **pure monopoly**, with a single seller (or group of sellers) acting as a price setter. We then consider the alleged efficiency losses via monopoly power. The situations under which price discrimination by monopolies might be both practical and profitable are also outlined, as are a variety of pricing practices traditionally associated with the presence of monopoly power.

You should already be familiar with the following aspects of monopoly and the comparisons that can be made between pure monopoly and perfect competition.

Short- and long-run equilibrium

Since the firm *is* the industry under pure monopoly, no distinction need be made between firm and industry equilibrium. It is because of **barriers to entry** under pure monopoly that the short-run equilibrium of the firm may also be the long-run equilibrium.

Such barriers to entry may result from any of the following:

- substantial scale economies – in the extreme case, leading to the *natural monopoly* argument (see p. 286)
- control over raw materials in production
- possession of patents or copyright for products or processes
- high levels of sunk costs (see p. 181)
- market franchises, where exclusive rights are given to sell a particular good or service in a specified area
- pre-emptive price cutting, discouraging potential entry.

Figure 7.1 indicates the short-run equilibrium for a profit-maximising monopolist. As the firm *is* the industry it of necessity faces a downward-sloping demand (average revenue) curve with the marginal revenue curve lying inside it (see pp. 54–5). Price P_1 and output Q_1 is the profit-maximising solution for the monopoly with $MC = MR$. In Fig. 7.1 (a) the firm makes *supernormal* profit ($P_1 VWC$), and may be able to protect this in the long run by resisting new entrants. In Fig. 7.1(b) the firm makes *subnormal* profit ($P_1 VWC$) and will leave the industry in the long run unless this situation can be changed.

Fig. 7.1 Short-run equilibrium: pure monopoly.

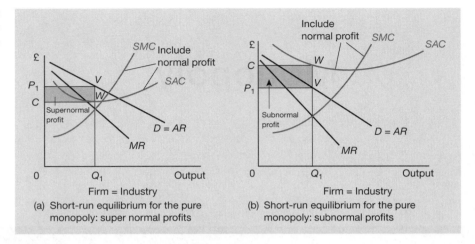

(a) Short-run equilibrium for the pure monopoly: super normal profits

(b) Short-run equilibrium for the pure monopoly: subnormal profits

A more substantial treatment of the possible long-run implications for the monopoly is outlined later (pp. 286–8). Here we simply note that to remain in the industry the monopoly must, in the long run, cover *all* costs including normal profit. In other words price > *LRAC* (including normal profit) is a condition that the monopoly must fulfil in the long run.

Absence of supply curve under monopoly

The marginal cost curve is *not* the supply curve of the monopolist, as it was for the perfectly competitive firm and industry. In fact, as Fig. 7.2 shows, there is no unique relationship for the monopoly between price and the quantity supplied.

In Fig. 7.2(a) different demand conditions lead to the *same output* being supplied at *different prices* by the profit-maximising monopoly. In Fig. 7.2(b) different demand conditions lead to *different outputs* being supplied at the *same price*. In other words the marginal cost curve in monopoly, unlike perfect competition, is no longer the supply curve; it does not define a unique relationship between a single price and a single quantity supplied. In fact under monopoly there is no single curve that can act as a supply curve.

Fig. 7.2 Absence of unique relationship (supply curve) between price and output under monopoly.

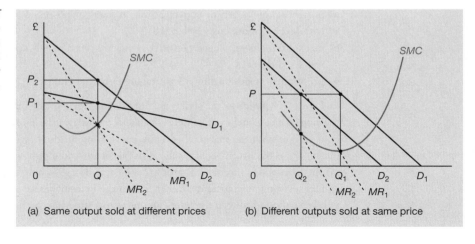

(a) Same output sold at different prices

(b) Different outputs sold at same price

Monopoly and price elasticity of demand (PED)

As a price setter, the monopolist can choose the *price* and leave consumers (via demand) to determine the output that can be sold at that price. Alternatively the monopolist can choose the *output* and leave consumers (via demand) to determine the price at which that output can be sold. The monopolist cannot choose both price and output!

Whether choosing price or output, the profit-maximising equilibrium will occur where $MC = MR$. Since negative MC is unlikely, it follows that the profit-maximising monopolist will produce along the segment ab of the demand curve where $PED > 1$. As we can see from Fig. 7.3, to set a price (or output) where $PED < 1$ would imply negative MR (see pp. 61–2) and therefore negative MC for a profit-maximising equilibrium. Since the negative MC is improbable, the monopolist is likely to set prices at which price elasticity of demand is greater than or equal to unity.

Classical case against monopoly

At the introductory level you are likely to have considered the classical case against monopoly, namely a higher price and lower output under monopoly than under a perfectly competitive market structure. The simplest means of comparison is to take a perfectly competitive industry that is suddenly taken over by a pure monopoly with no (immediate) change in demand or cost conditions. In this case Fig. 7.4 applies.

Remember that the industry supply curve under perfect competition is the industry marginal cost curve (see pp. 249–50). The perfectly competitive *industry* would be in equilibrium at price P_c and output Q_c, where industry supply matches industry demand, each *firm* then being a price-taker at P_c. With the takeover by the pure monopolist, the industry demand and cost conditions now become the *firm* demand and cost conditions, with the profit-maximising ($MC = MR$) solution for the pure monopoly being price P_m and output Q_m. Clearly this indicates a higher price and lower output for the pure monopoly than would occur under the perfectly competitive market structure.

Of course demand and cost conditions may change as a result of the industry being monopolised. In particular, economies of scale may be available to the larger monopoly that were not previously available to the numerous small producers. In this case, the monopoly may, in the long run, be able to move onto a new and lower short-run average cost curve with its associated marginal cost curve. As to whether the classical case against

Fig. 7.3 Why the profit-maximising monopolist produces along the elastic or unit elastic part of the demand curve (segment a–b).

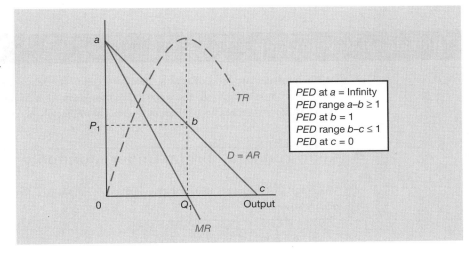

PED at a = Infinity
PED range a–b ≥ 1
PED at b = 1
PED range b–c ≤ 1
PED at c = 0

Fig. 7.4 **Classical case against monopoly: higher price (P_m) and lower output (Q_m) than under perfect competition.**

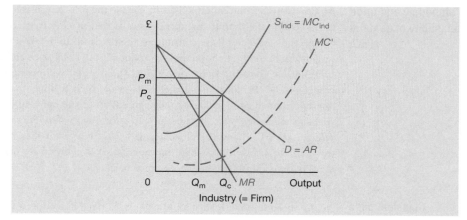

monopoly still holds will depend upon the *extent* of the scale economies available. If the MC curve shifts downwards to MC' in Fig. 7.4, then the profit-maximising pure monopoly will produce exactly the same output and sell it at exactly the same price as the competitive industry. If the MC curve shifts still further downwards, then the pure monopoly will produce a higher output, and sell it at a lower price than the previously competitive industry. In other words, if the economies of scale are large enough, then the classical case against monopoly need not hold.

Note also that whereas price $= MC$ in the perfectly competitive solution, price $> MC$ under monopoly. We return to the welfare implication of this divergence between price and marginal cost (pp. 292–4 and 310–15).

Natural monopoly

Chapter 4 outlined the various sources of economies of scale, both technical and non-technical, and introduced the idea of *minimum efficient size* (MES). The suggestion here is that some industries are **natural monopolies** in that the minimum efficient size of the productive unit or enterprise is so large that the industry can only sustain a single operator. We consider the issue of price regulation in the context of a natural monopoly later in this chapter (p. 296).

Theoretical developments

At the intermediate level of analysis we can explore further some of these propositions about pure monopoly. Indeed we can relax the assumption of pure monopoly and consider market structures with different degrees of monopoly power.

Long-run equilibrium under monopoly

We noted in Chapter 6 that, for the perfectly competitive firm, long-run equilibrium occurs where

$$Price = SMC = SAC = LMC = LAC$$

In other words the firm has adjusted its plant size to the optimal scale (minimum *LAC*) and operates this plant at full capacity (minimum *SAC*) – as in the earlier Fig. 6.5 (p. 250). Under monopoly, of course, new entrants can be excluded, or at least deterred, so that the long-run equilibrium solution is less determinate. Any one of the three long-run solutions shown in Fig. 7.5 may result for the monopoly producer.

In the long run the monopolist can adjust *all* the factor inputs. He has the choice of simply changing the output level at which he runs his **existing plant** or of expanding his plant to a **new scale** of production. Because of barriers to entry facing new competitors, the monopolist may still be able to make supernormal profits by operating his existing plant below (or above) the full capacity level. Nor need he build up his plant to the scale consistent with reaching the minimum point of the *LAC* curve. In fact it will be market demand conditions that will determine both the size of plant and the degree to which that size of plant is utilised.

Restricted demand In Fig. 7.5(a) the **restricted demand** leads the profit-maximising monopolist to produce Q_1 and sell this output at price P_1. The existing plant is *underutilised*, operating at less than full capacity (point a). The size of plant is also *less than the optimal scale*, i.e. less than the plant size consistent with minimum *LAC* (point b). In this case the market size is inadequate to permit the monopolist to move to the 'optimum' solution at b, with minimum *LAC*. Instead the profit-maximising solution (*SMC* = *MR*) is at Q_1 with *SAC* tangent to *LAC* along its falling part, and with *SMC* = *LMC* at this output.

Excessive demand In Fig. 7.5(b) the **excessive demand** leads the profit-maximising monopolist to build a plant *larger in scale than is optimum* (point b) and then to *overutilise* this plant beyond the full capacity output (point a). The profit-maximising solution (*SMC* = *MR*) is output Q_1

Fig. 7.5 Long-run equilibrium for monopoly under different demand conditions.

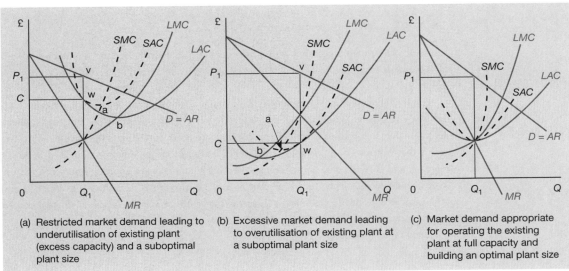

(a) Restricted market demand leading to underutilisation of existing plant (excess capacity) and a suboptimal plant size

(b) Excessive market demand leading to overutilisation of existing plant at a suboptimal plant size

(c) Market demand appropriate for operating the existing plant at full capacity and building an optimal plant size

sold at price P_1. At this output SAC is tangent to LAC along its rising part, and $SMC = LMC$. Here the plant that maximises the monopolist's profits faces higher costs because it is larger than the optimal scale at b and also because it is operated beyond its full capacity level (point a).

Appropriate demand

In Fig. 7.5(c) demand is exactly at the right level (i.e. **appropriate**) for the profit-maximising monopolist to build a plant to the optimum scale (minimises LAC) and to fully utilise that plant by operating it at the full capacity level.

It would be pure coincidence for the situation in Fig. 7.5(c) to be achieved in the long run for the monopolist. There are no market forces bringing such a situation about, as is the case under a perfectly competitive market structure. The more probable outcome is a suboptimal scale of plant, which is then operated either below or above the full capacity output for that plant, depending on the size of the market.

■ The multiplant monopoly

It may be that the monopoly uses *two or more* different plants to produce its total output, with costs varying between these plants.

Whatever the total output produced, the profit-maximising monopolist must organise production so that *marginal costs are identical in each plant*. Otherwise *reallocating* the total output between plants can reduce total costs and therefore raise total profit. If, for example, marginal cost were higher in plant A than in plant B, the firm could produce more units at B and less at A, thereby reducing the total cost of producing the same output.

It must also follow that the profit-maximising monopolist must produce, in total, a level of output at which marginal revenue equals marginal cost. Since marginal costs must be the same at each plant, it therefore follows that the profit-maximising condition for the multiplant firm is where *marginal revenue equals marginal cost in each plant*. In other words, for a two plant monopoly:

$MR_T = MC_A = MC_B$ (for profit maximisation)

These are the profit-maximising conditions where marginal revenue from total output (MR_T) equals marginal cost in each plant, A and B respectively. This solution can be seen in Fig. 7.6.

The total marginal cost curve (MC_T) is obtained by summing horizontally the individual plant marginal cost curves, MC_A and MC_B. The profit-maximising output is where $MC_T = MR_T$, i.e. where marginal cost = marginal revenue for total output, with the result that output Q_{A+B} is sold at price P. This total output must be allocated between plants A and B (with different costs) so that marginal costs are equalised between plants. This occurs with Q_A produced in plant A and Q_B in plant B. The shaded areas abcd and efgh indicate the profit made by each plant, that is the maximum total profit that can be made by the **multiplant monopoly.**

Fig. 7.6 Maximising profit in a two-plant monopoly.

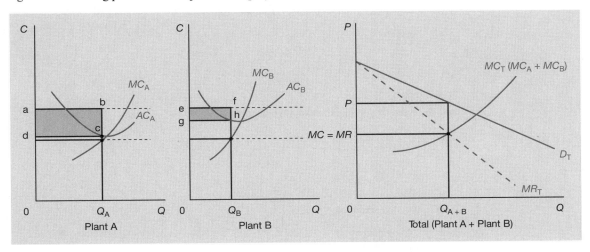

Measuring monopoly power

Much of the discussion so far has implied a pure monopoly, with a single seller. Of course there may be less extreme forms of monopoly power. In the UK **monopoly power** is defined as existing where more than one quarter of output is in the hands of a single firm or group of linked firms.

The Lerner index   A measure of monopoly power was suggested by the economist Abba Lerner, drawing on some of the theoretical principles already considered. For the *perfectly competitive firm* in profit-maximising equilibrium, price = marginal cost; for the *monopoly*, price > marginal cost. It follows that the extent to which the monopoly can raise price (*P*) above marginal cost (*MC*) might be an index of the firm's monopoly power. **Lerner's index** (*L*) can be expressed as

$$L = \frac{P - MC}{P} = 1 - \frac{MC}{P} \qquad (1)$$

L will always have a value in the range 0 to 1. For a perfectly competitive firm, *P* = *MC* so that *L* = 0. The more the firm raises *P* above *MC*, the closer to 1 the index will be. In other words, the larger the value of *L*, the greater the degree of monopoly power.

Of course the implementation of any monopoly power will be constrained by demand considerations, and in particular by the price elasticity of demand facing the firm.

We have already seen in Chapter 2 (p. 62) that

$$MR = P\left(1 - \frac{1}{e}\right)$$

where P = price

e = price elasticity of firm demand (ignoring the strictly negative sign).

It follows that

$$MR = P - \frac{P}{e}$$

and since the firm seeks to maximise profits:

$$MR = MC$$

i.e. $P - \dfrac{P}{e} = MC$

which, when rearranged, gives

$$\frac{P - MC}{P} = \frac{1}{e} \qquad (2)$$

This equation (2) tells us that monopoly power is inversely related to price elasticity of firm demand (e). The left hand side, $(P - MC)/P$, is the mark-up over marginal cost as a proportion of price. The right hand side of the equation, $1/e$, tells us that this mark-up should equal the inverse of price elasticity of firm demand (ignoring the strictly negative sign).

- The *less elastic* is price elasticity of demand, the greater the mark-up as a proportion of price and the greater the monopoly power.
- The *more elastic* is price elasticity of demand, the smaller the mark-up as a proportion of price, and the smaller the monopoly power.

Sources of monopoly power

We are now in a position to examine more carefully the various *sources* of monopoly power, i.e. those factors that give the firm greater freedom to raise its price above its marginal cost of production.

Elasticity of firm and market demand

As we have seen (equation (2)) monopoly power is inversely related to the price elasticity of firm demand: the less elastic that demand, the greater the ability of the firm to raise price above marginal cost (Fig. 7.7). Note that it is price elasticity of *firm demand* that is relevant here. Of course the price elasticity of *market demand* will set a limit below which the firm's price elasticity cannot fall. For example, if several firms compete in a market with price elasticity of $(-)3$, then such competition may raise price elasticity for a single firm above the market figure (e.g. to $(-)5$). However, in the absence of such

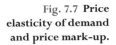

Fig. 7.7 **Price elasticity of demand and price mark-up.**

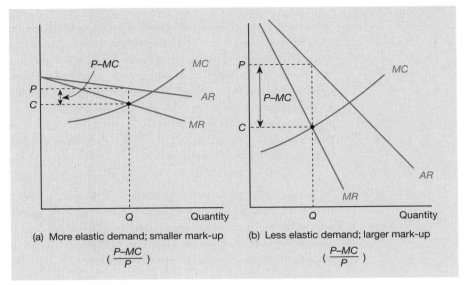

(a) More elastic demand; smaller mark-up $(\frac{P-MC}{P})$

(b) Less elastic demand; larger mark-up $(\frac{P-MC}{P})$

competition, price elasticity of demand for a *single* firm cannot fall below the market figure of (−)3. This must follow since, for a pure monopoly, the price elasticity of demand for a firm will be that for the market. In other words the price elasticity of demand in the market sets a *limit* on the monopoly power available to the firm.

The number of firms   Generally speaking the smaller the number of firms competing in the market, the greater the monopoly power of the firm, and vice versa. Of course it is not simply the number of firms but the number of *key players* that may be most relevant here. A market with fewer firms competing may have less monopoly power than another market with more firms competing. This might be the case where, say, 80% of the market is concentrated in the hands of six key players, compared with another market with more firms in total but where 80% of the market is concentrated in the hands of only two key players. It is the **concentration ratio** involving a specified number of key players that might give a better indication of monopoly power than the total number of firms engaged in the market.

Barriers to entry   Of course the more effective the **barriers** to new entrants, the greater the monopoly power in the hands of existing firms (incumbents). We have already noted that patents and copyright law can protect new products and processes for specified periods of time, deterring new entrants. Entry may also be deterred by pre-emptive price cutting on the part of existing firms or by the existence of substantial scale economies making it prohibitively costly for more than a few firms to supply the entire market. In the extreme case of natural monopoly the minimum efficient size (*MES*) is such that only one large firm can supply the market, if average costs are to fall to the level that is technically feasible.

Interaction among firms

Even if the concentration ratios are identical for two or more industries, there may be different degrees of monopoly power if the key players interact/compete more vigorously in one industry than in another. Where competition is aggressive, the mark-up may be forced down close to the competitive level, and little monopoly power may effectively exist. Of course in industries with the same concentration ratios but less aggressive behaviour by key players, the mark-up may be much higher and substantial monopoly power may effectively exist. Much of the relevant discussion here involves action and reaction between rivals and is covered in the next two chapters involving oligopoly and game theory. In fact where firms cooperate (collude), rather than compete, then monopoly power is usually raised.

Time

As we have seen, it takes varying amounts of **time** for *all* the factors in different industries to be changed. As a result new entrants can only appear over the long-run time period, which may vary from months to years depending on the industrial sector. Monopoly power may therefore be more substantial in the short-run time period than in the long-run time period. This is further reinforced by the fact that price elasticities of demand for products tend to be lower in the short-run time period (enhancing monopoly power) than they are in the long run.

■ Monopoly power and the public interest

We can use our earlier work on consumer surplus (p. 26) and producer surplus (p. 157) to investigate the overall **social costs** of monopoly power. If the classical case against monopoly does hold, namely higher price and lower output than in the perfectly competitive equilibrium, then Fig. 7.8 can be used to indicate the deadweight loss from monopoly power. Here the higher monopoly price (P_m) results in consumers buying less and losing areas $A + B$ in consumer surplus, i.e. giving a change of $-A - B$ in consumer surplus. Those consumers still purchasing at price P_m lose area A and those discouraged from purchasing at this higher price lose area B. At the same time the producers still able to find a market in which to sell at the higher price gain area A of producers' surplus, but those unable to sell at this price lose area C, giving a change of $+A - C$ in producers' surplus.

Fig. 7.8 Deadweight loss as a result of monopoly power raising equilibrium price (P_c to P_m) and lowering equilibrium output (Q_c to Q_m).

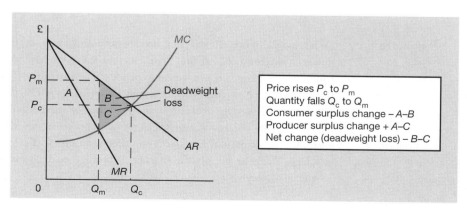

The *net* change (deadweight loss) in aggregate consumer and producer surplus is therefore (Fig. 7.8):

$$-A - B + A - C = -B - C$$

Of course to the extent that the 'classical case' against monopoly of higher price and lower output does *not* hold (see pp. 285–6), then no such deadweight loss need occur.

Of course in the real world industries rarely change from one extreme of perfect competition to the other extreme of pure monopoly, as implied by Fig. 7.8. At this point it may therefore be useful to broaden our approach to consider how a proposed merger, deemed likely to increase industrial concentration and monopoly power, might be regarded in terms of the 'public interest'.

Monopoly and economic efficiency

Two key elements are usually included in definitions of the 'public interest', both relating to the idea of economic efficiency:

- *Productive efficiency.* This involves using the most efficient combination of resources to produce a given level of output. Only when the firm is producing a given level of output with the *least-cost* methods of production available do we regard it as having achieved 'productive efficiency'.
- *Allocative efficiency.* This is often taken to mean setting a price that corresponds to the marginal cost of production. The idea here is that consumers pay firms exactly what it costs them to produce the last (marginal) unit of output: such a pricing strategy can be shown to be a key condition in achieving a so-called 'Pareto optimum' resource allocation (see Chapter 11), where it is no longer possible to make someone better off without making someone else worse off. Any deviation of price *away from* marginal cost is then seen as resulting in 'allocative inefficiency'.

What may pose problems for policy makers is that the impacts of proposed mergers may move these two aspects of economic efficiency in *opposite directions*. For example, economies of scale may result from the merger having increased firm size, with a lower cost of producing any given output thereby improving productive efficiency. However, the greater market power associated with increased size may give the enlarged firm new opportunities to raise price above (or still further above) its costs of production, including marginal costs, thereby reducing allocative efficiency.

We may need to balance the gain in productive efficiency against the loss in allocative efficiency to get a better idea of the overall impact of the merger on the 'public interest'. Figure 7.9 is useful in illustrating the fact that a proposed merger might move productive and allocative efficiencies in opposite directions. For simplicity we assume the curves displayed to be linear, and the firm to be at an initial price/quantity equilibrium of P/Q with marginal cost MC (for a profit-maximising firm MR would have intersected MC at point i). Now suppose that the merger/takeover results in the (enlarged) firm using its market power to raise price from P to P_1, cutting output from Q to Q_1, *but* that at the same time the newly available scale economies cut costs so that MC shifts downwards to MC_1.

Clearly we have to balance a loss of allocative efficiency against a gain in productive efficiency in order to assess the overall impact on the 'public interest'. To do this we can usefully return to the idea of economic welfare, and the associated consumer and producer surpluses.

Fig. 7.9 **Monopoly power and the public interest.**

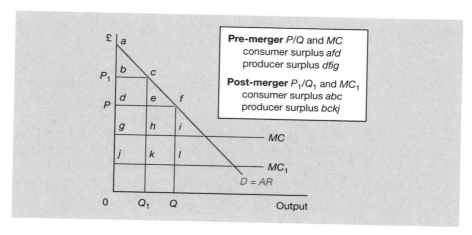

If we regard the total welfare resulting from a resource allocation as being the sum of the consumer surplus and the producer surplus, we have

- pre-merger   *afd* + *dfig*
- post-merger   *abc* + *bckj*

In terms of total welfare (consumer surplus + producer surplus) we can note the following impacts of the merger:

- gain of welfare   *ghkj*
- loss of welfare   *cflk*

The 'gain of welfare' (*ghkj*) represents the improvement in productive efficiency from the merger, as the Q_1 units still produced require less resources than before, now that the scale economies have reduced costs (shifting *MC* down to MC_1).

The 'loss of welfare' (*cflk*) represents the deterioration in allocative efficiency from the merger; price has risen (P to P_1) and marginal costs have fallen (MC to MC_1), further increasing the gap between price and marginal cost. As a result of the price rise from P to P_1, output has fallen from Q to Q_1. This loss of output has reduced economic welfare, since society's willingness to pay for these lost $Q - Q_1$ units (area under the demand curve from Q to Q_1, i.e. *cfQQ$_1$*) exceeds the cost of producing them (sum of all the marginal costs from Q to Q_1, i.e. *klQQ$_1$*) by *cflk*.

Clearly the overall welfare effect (public interest) could be positive or negative, depending on whether the welfare gains exceed the welfare losses or vice versa (in Fig. 7.9 the losses outweigh the gains). No prejudgement can therefore be made that an increase in monopoly power via merger will, or will not, be in the public interest. As Stewart (1996) notes, everything depends on the extent of any price rise and on the demand and cost curve configurations for any proposed merger. It is in this context that a Monopolies and Mergers Commission investigation and other methods of enquiry into particular proposals might be regarded as important in deciding whether any merger should proceed or be abandoned.

■ Price regulation and monopoly power

In the previous chapter (pp. 254–7) we saw that **price regulation** (whether maximum or minimum prices) in a competitive industry inevitably resulted in a deadweight loss. This is by no means the case with price regulation of a monopoly. As we now see, such price regulations can remove any deadweight loss that might otherwise occur. In Fig. 7.10 the classical case is shown, with the monopoly price (P_m) higher than the competitive price (P_c) and the monopoly output (Q_m) lower than the competitive output (Q_c). The regulator now imposes a price ceiling, P_1, for the monopoly.

The firm can now charge no more than P_1, so that the effective *average revenue* curve is the horizontal line P_1V up to output Q_1. For output levels up to Q_1 the *marginal revenue* curve will be identical to the average revenue curve (P_1V). Of course for output levels beyond Q_1 the original average and marginal revenue curves still apply since the firm is permitted to charge *less* than P_1 if it desires to reach those output levels. Effectively the marginal revenue curve is in two segments, P_1V and WZ, with VW a line of discontinuity connecting these two segments.

In Fig. 7.10 the profit-maximising solution ($MC = MR$) will now be output Q_1 at price P_1 for the regulated monopolist. Comparing Fig. 7.10 with Fig. 7.8, it should be readily apparent that the area of deadweight loss under the regulated monopoly is *smaller* than that under the unregulated monopoly:

● *unregulated monopoly:* deadweight loss = 1 + 2 + 3 + 4 + 5
● *regulated monopoly (P_1 as price ceiling):* deadweight loss = 3 + 5

Clearly a reduction of area 1 + 2 + 4 of deadweight loss is achieved by price regulation in this case. Indeed if the price ceiling were set still lower, at the competitive price P_c, then the profit-maximising solution ($MC = MR$) for the regulated monopoly would now be P_c / Q_c with zero deadweight loss.

Fig. 7.10 **Price regulation of monopoly: P_1 as the price ceiling set by the regulator.**

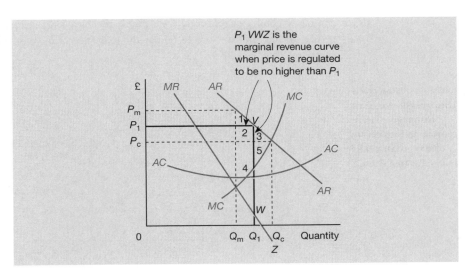

Limits to price regulation

You should be able to see from Fig. 7.10 that if the price ceiling were set *below* the competitive price P_c, then our analysis would predict a profit-maximising output below Q_c. In Fig. 7.11 a reduction in the ceiling from P_c to P_2 results in a profit-maximising output of Q_2, implying a *reduction* in output (from Q_c) and the creation of a *shortage* ($Q'_2 - Q_2$) in the market. Compared with the previous zero deadweight loss at a regulated price of P_c, there is now a *positive* deadweight loss indicated by the shaded area in Fig. 7.11. Any further price reductions below P_2 will increase both the shortage experienced in the market and the area of deadweight loss. The price P_3 is the effective *lower limit* for any price ceiling imposed by a regulator. At a price ceiling of P_3, average (and marginal) revenue is equal to (minimum) average cost, and the firm earns normal profit only. At any lower price the firm ceases to cover normal profits and goes out of business, at least in the long run.

Price regulation and natural monopolies

As we have seen, **natural monopoly** occurs where the minimum efficient size (*MES*) of the firm is at least as large as the total market demand. Put another way, a single firm can meet the entire market demand and still be on the non-increasing part of its average cost curve (Fig. 7.12). To have more than a single firm supplying such a market would clearly increase the total costs incurred in meeting market demand.

In Fig. 7.12 average cost falls continuously so that marginal cost always lies inside it. In the absence of regulation the profit-maximising solution under monopoly is output Q_m (by a single firm) at price P_m. The lowest price the regulator can set in this instance is P_1, with corresponding output Q_1, so that the monopoly still covers its costs, including normal profit. If a price ceiling is set *below* P_1, then the monopoly cannot earn normal profit and will go out of business in the long run.

If, as before, we take the competitive industry price/output solution ($MC_{ind} = S_{ind} = D_{ind}$) as P_c/Q_c, then clearly the regulator is thwarted from being able to eliminate deadweight loss by setting P_c as the price ceiling. At such a price (and output Q_c) $AC > AR$ and the monopoly earns subnormal profits, thereby leaving the industry. At the lowest effective price ceiling available to the regulator, P_1 ($AC = AR$), deadweight loss is still incurred, as indicated by the shaded area in Fig. 7.12. Of course the comparison with a competitive industry solution here is purely technical since the natural monopoly characteristics of the industry would render the existence of many small producers inefficient and unrealistic.

Fig. 7.11 Renewed deadweight loss and shortages where price ceiling set by the regulator falls below P_c (to P_2 here).

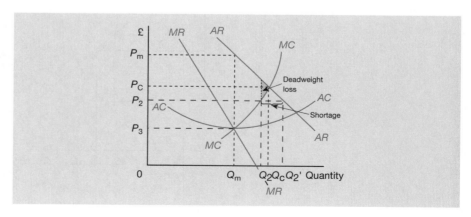

Fig. 7.12
The minimum price ceiling (P_1) available to the regulator under natural monopoly.

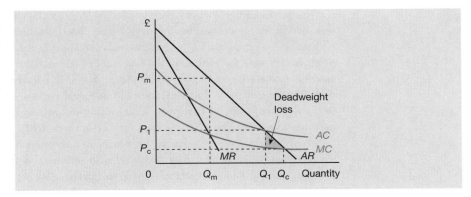

Price discrimination and monopoly power

Price discrimination occurs when the same product is sold at different prices to different buyers for reasons unrelated to cost. An element of monopoly power, implying control over prices, is often associated with price discrimination. Price discrimination is often analysed under three broad headings: first-, second- and third-degree price discrimination respectively.

First-degree price discrimination

Underlying all types of price discrimination is the idea that the firm appropriates to itself more of the consumer surplus than would be possible under a single price policy. In Fig. 7.13 we have the extreme situation where the firm charges a different price to every consumer, the price reflecting that individual consumer's willingness to pay. We call this **first-degree price discrimination.** In this case the extra revenue from each additional unit sold is the price paid for that unit: in other words the demand curve now becomes the marginal revenue curve (Fig. 7.13).

The firm captures, by first-degree price discrimination, area AP_mV. This was previously an area of consumer surplus with the single profit-maximising price of P_m and output Q_m. It is now absorbed as additional total revenue to the firm.

Fig. 7.13 **Consumer surplus (AP_mV) now captured by the firm and additional profit (ANW), both resulting from first-degree price discrimination.**

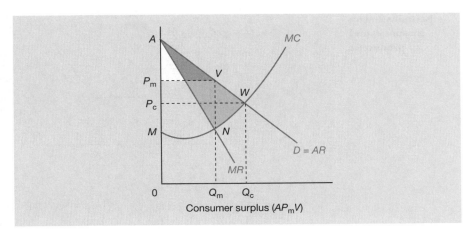

On the assumption that costs are unaffected by price discrimination, we can also see that total profit is increased by first-degree price discrimination. In the single-price case, with price P_m and quantity Q_m, the firm makes total profit equivalent to area AMN. Total profit is of course the sum of all the *marginal profits*, i.e. the sum of all the vertical distances between MR and MC for each of the Q_m units, giving area AMN. We have seen that with first-degree price discrimination the marginal revenue curve now becomes the demand curve itself, so that profit-maximising output rises to Q_c, and total profit becomes area AMW. The *additional profit* is therefore area ANW.

Strictly speaking we are referring here to an increase in total *variable* profit, since only the marginal (i.e. variable) costs associated with additional output have been taken into account, and not the fixed costs underlying that production.

Second-degree price discrimination

In practice, especially where many customers exist, it is impossible to identify the willingness to pay of each individual consumer. However, the firm will be aware that each consumer will be willing to pay *less* for successive units of the product consumed (diminishing marginal utility). A discounting policy may therefore encourage consumption, with different prices charged for different quantities or blocks of the same product. Of course the ability of the producer to offer such discounts may be helped by economies of scale from increased output following a larger volume of consumption.

Second-degree price discrimination is defined as taking place where different prices are charged for different quantities or 'blocks' of the same product. Figure 7.14 illustrates such discrimination using three separate blocks, with prices P_1, P_2 and P_3 charged for the respective blocks.

Here the first Q_1 units of output are each sold at a price of P_1; units between Q_1 and Q_2 are sold at a price of P_2, and units between Q_2 and Q_3 are sold at a price of P_3. As a result the MR curve is the continuous *step function* P_1MLXYW shown in Fig. 7.14. Total output is Q_3, as compared with the profit-maximising output of Q_m resulting from the single price P_m being charged. Second-degree price discrimination has clearly increased output and potentially increased both consumer welfare and firm profit. For example,

Fig. 7.14 **Impact of second-degree price discrimination on consumers and producers.**

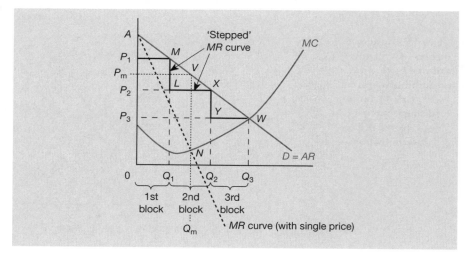

the consumer surplus in the single-price case AP_mV must be set against the *new* consumer surplus with block pricing and enlarged output. In Fig. 7.14 the new consumer surplus would now be given by triangles $AP_1M + MLX + XYW$.

Similarly total (variable) profits may well increase as a result of second-degree price discrimination, though by *less* than ANW. This follows from the fact that consumers this time are also part-beneficiaries of the welfare gain, together with the firm.

The additional welfare gain from second-degree price discrimination results from prices being reduced overall and output expanded, as compared with the single-price monopoly. Of course the greater the economies of scale associated with the expanded output, the greater the net welfare gain from this pricing approach, which is then available for distribution amongst both producers and consumers.

Third-degree price discrimination

This occurs where the monopolist separates out the market into two or more groups of customers, charging a different price to each group. There are two conditions necessary for **third-degree price discrimination:**

- Barriers must exist to restrict the movement of customers from one (the dearer) group to another. Geographical distance, time, customs barriers, personal characteristics, etc. can all be used to prevent customers from transferring themselves to groups purchasing the product at a lower price. This condition makes price discrimination *possible.*
- Price elasticity of demand must be different for each group of customers. This condition makes price discrimination *profitable.*

In Fig. 7.15 we assume that the monopolist produces in one location and sells industry output to two separate groups, A and B, with different price elasticities of demand. Group (market) B has a much higher price elasticity of demand than group (market) A. The corresponding total (industry) marginal and average revenue curves are obtained by summing horizontally the individual group (market) marginal and average revenue curves.

Fig. 7.15 Third-degree price discrimination: charging different prices to different groups of customers.

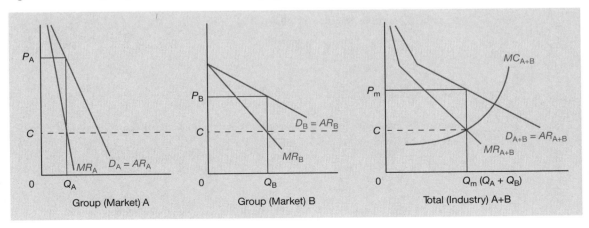

With production in a single location there is one industry MC curve, giving the overall profit-maximising output of Q_m, which might be sold at a single price P_m. However, total profit can, in this situation, be raised by selling this output at a different price to each group (market). The profit-maximising condition is that MC for whole output must equal MR in each separate market:

i.e. $MC_{A+B} = MR_A = MR_B$

In Fig. 7.15, total output Q_m will be allocated so that Q_A goes to group (market) A and Q_B to group (market) B, resulting in respective prices P_A and P_B. Any other allocation of total output Q_m must reduce total revenue and therefore, with unchanged costs, reduce total profit. We can illustrate this by considering a *single unit* reallocated from market A to market B. The *addition* to total revenue (MR_B) of this unit when sold in market B is less than C, whereas the *loss* to total revenue (MR_A) of this unit by not selling it in market A is C. The overall change in total revenue from this unit reallocation is clearly negative, which, with total costs unchanged, must reduce total profit.

As we can see from Fig. 7.15, the implication of third-degree price discrimination is a higher price in the market with lowest price elasticity of demand ($P_A > P_B$)

In Chapter 2 we saw that

$$MR = P\left(1 - \frac{1}{e}\right) \tag{1}$$

where P = price

e = price elasticity of demand

We have stated that for profit maximisation:

$$MR_A = MR_B = MC_{A+B} \tag{2}$$

For the two groups/markets it follows that

$$P_A\left(1 - \frac{1}{e_A}\right) = P_B\left(1 - \frac{1}{e_B}\right) \tag{3}$$

where P_A and P_B are the prices for groups (markets) A and B respectively, and e_A and e_B are price elasticities of demand for each group.

If $e_A < e_B$, then $\dfrac{1}{e_A} > \dfrac{1}{e_B}$ and $\left(1 - \dfrac{1}{e_A}\right) < \left(1 - \dfrac{1}{e_B}\right)$

It follows that P_A must exceed P_B if the equality in (3) is to be fulfilled.

In other words third-degree price discrimination will lead the profit-maximising monopolist to charge higher prices to the groups (markets) with the less elastic demand.

Of course if $e_A = e_B$ in (3), then the profit-maximising solution could be achieved with a uniform price in each market. It is only where price elasticities are *different* among groups of customers that it will be profitable to discriminate in price, thereby raising total revenue and total profit.

Price discrimination and the existence of an industry

There is no unambiguous answer as to the desirability of price discrimination, although consumers in the lower-priced market clearly benefit compared with those in the higher-priced market. However, one of the main ways in which consumers might benefit is when price discrimination enables a monopolist to earn a profit from some activity that might not otherwise be possible, thereby leading to the production of goods and services that might otherwise be denied to the consumer. Figure 7.16 is used as a basis for explanation.

AR and MR depict the monopolist's average and marginal revenue curves while AC and MC depict average and marginal cost. It is clear that if the monopolist charges all consumers the same uniform price, there is no level of output at which a profit could be earned. Indeed the loss-minimising price would be $0P$, giving a loss equal to area b plus area c. Even if the monopolist was prepared to accept a short-run loss, such losses could not be accepted in the long run and production would eventually cease. However, if the monopolist is able to price discriminate and charge some consumers $(0Q_1)$ a price of $0P_1$, while charging other consumers $(Q_1 - Q)$ only $0P$, it becomes profitable for the monopolist to undertake supply of this commodity. This is easily verified since the increase in revenue is equal to area a plus area b, which is *greater than* the loss that is made (area b + area c) when a single price $0P$ is charged (area a > area c).

Fig. 7.16 **Price discrimination and the existence of an industry.**

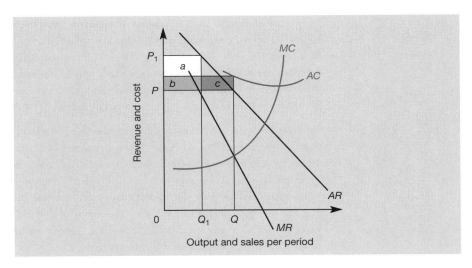

Pricing practices and monopoly power

We now consider a variety of pricing practices or strategies other than price discrimination typically associated with the presence of monopoly power. Of course many of these practices could equally occur in the oligopolistic market structure considered in Chapters 8 and 9.

Mark-up pricing We have already noted when discussing the Lerner index (p. 289) that the greater the degree of monopoly power, the greater the expected **mark-up** of price over marginal cost. We also noted (p. 290) that this mark-up would arguably be greater, the less price elastic the demand for the product of the firm. Mark-up pricing is sometimes referred to as **cost-plus** pricing, and can have a number of variants.

Most cost-plus pricing strategies add a certain percentage profit mark-up to the firm's costs, in order to arrive at a final price. The precise outcome for price will vary from firm to firm for three main reasons:

- There is the problem of selecting which costs to include in the pricing decision. Some firms may include only variable costs in the base for the mark-up. Interestingly this is called *marginal costing* by accountants even when the base is average variable cost. Other firms may include both variable and fixed costs in the base (*full-cost* pricing). Where the firm is producing more than one product, full-cost pricing faces the problem of apportioning total fixed costs between the various products. For instance, if a factory is already producing Product A, and a new Product B is introduced using the same machinery, what part, if any, of the unchanged capital costs should be allocated to B? Product B may be asked to absorb some proportion of the fixed costs already included in the price of A. Different firms will make different decisions on how to absorb fixed costs across their various products.
- Whatever the costs to be included in the base, there is the problem of estimating the normal level of output at which the firm will operate. This estimate is important since *average cost* (both the variable and fixed elements) and therefore the size of the cost base will vary with output, i.e. with capacity utilisation.
- Whatever the costs included, and the estimate of capacity utilisation, there is the problem of calculating the percentage mark-up to be added to costs. Some firms may set a relatively constant percentage mark-up, while others may vary the percentage according to firm objective and market circumstance.

An array of price outcomes is therefore possible for a firm, depending on the practices it adopts in dealing with the three problems outlined. Although mark-up or cost-plus pricing cannot therefore yield precise predictions for firm price, it does put price setting in a particular perspective. The emphasis is upon *costs* influencing price, and then producers selling what they can at that price. Demand has little influence on price setting here, except perhaps in affecting the size of the mark-up to be added to costs. Any extra demand is met from stocks, or by lengthening the order book, rather than by the immediate price rise predicted by market theory.

Two-part tarifff　Under a **two-part tariff**, the firm charges consumers a fixed fee (per time period) that, on payment, gives the consumer the right to purchase the product at a uniform price per unit.

　For example, car rental companies often charge a fixed (lump-sum) fee per day plus an additional mileage charge. Of course the firm must have a degree of monopoly power to enable it to impose a two-part tariff on its product, and must further be able to prevent resale of the product in the cheaper market. In this context it is important to prevent a single consumer from paying the entry fee and then reselling the product to other consumers who have not paid that entry fee.

　Of course charging a *uniform price* is merely a special case of the two-part tariff, namely where the fixed charge is zero. We can expect the two-part tariff to be used in preference to a uniform price in situations where it will generate additional profit.

Single two-part tariff: identical consumers　The ideal scenario for the two-part tariff would be one in which all consumers are identical and their demand curves are known. Figure 7.17(a) presents a single (representative) consumer demand curve, d, with the firm's marginal cost assumed constant at MC. Here the firm can use the two-part tariff to extract all the available consumer surplus, along the lines envisaged under the more complex first-degree price discrimination. A fixed or lump-sum charge can be set equal to T (area APv) in Fig. 7.17(a) and then the (profit-maximising) price P can be set for each unit of usage. Revenue (and profit) will rise by T for each consumer (the previous consumer surplus now expropriated by producers) as compared with the uniform price situation.

Single two-part tariff: non-identical consumers　Suppose, now, that the firm is aware that its customers are *not* identical. For simplicity we assume the firm's customers to be of two types, with the Type 2 customers being willing to purchase more of the product at any given price than the Type 1 customers. This situation is indicated in Fig. 7.17(b).

Fig. 7.17 **The (single) two-part tariff.**

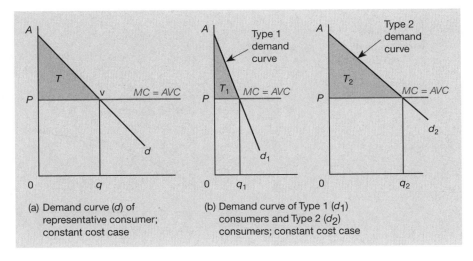

(a) Demand curve (*d*) of representative consumer; constant cost case

(b) Demand curve of Type 1 (*d*₁) consumers and Type 2 (*d*₂) consumers; constant cost case

We initially assume that the firm must select a *single* two-part tariff, as it finds it too complex to charge different combinations of fixed (lump-sum) charge and variable usage charge to each type of customer. In any case the firm may be unable to distinguish in individual cases between the two types of customer, simply being aware that they exist.

If the firm sets the (uniform) usage charge at P, then it cannot impose a fixed charge in excess of T_1. To do so would imply the loss of all Type 1 customers. It could only set a fixed charge in excess of T_1 and retain Type 1 customers by reducing the usage charge below P. In this case the firm fails to cover its variable costs per unit and must set this loss per unit against any additional profit made via the enhanced fixed charge. Clearly the less similar Type 1 customers are to Type 2 customers, the more difficult it is for the firm to extract consumer surplus from the latter via a single two-part tariff. There is no simple method available to yield an optional pricing formula in such situations; only per-haps by an iterative, trial and error approach can the firm reach an appropriate (single) two-part tariff. It may even be the case that the single two-part tariff could yield maxi-mum profit by setting the fixed charge at T_2 and the usage price at P: i.e. by concentrating exclusively on Type 2 customers, letting Type 1 customers choose not to purchase the product.

Multiple two-part tariff: non-identical consumers Suppose that the firm is willing and able to offer different combinations of fixed and usage charges, i.e. more alternatives than the single two-part tariff. Here, for simplicity, we consider *two* alterna-tive schedules for the two-part tariff:

- *schedule 1*: relatively low fixed charge, but relatively high usage charge;
- *schedule 2*: relatively high fixed charge, but relatively low usage charge.

Figure 7.18 indicates these two different two-part tariff schedules. The *intercepts* on the vertical axis indicate fixed charges: T_1, T_2 for schedules 1 and 2 respectively. The *slopes* of the schedules indicate the respective usage charges, U_1 and U_2.

Following this line of reasoning, consumers can be expected to choose the lower envelope of the two schedules, shown by the solid, kinked line in Fig. 7.18.

Fig. 7.18 Alternative two-part tariff schedules.

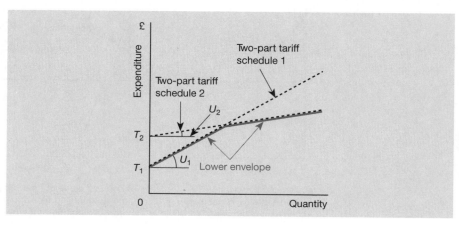

Offering different two-part tariff schedules in this way helps the customers to **self-select** the schedule that yields greatest utility to themselves. This strategy is particularly appropriate where the firm is aware of the varying nature of customer demand curves but cannot itself identify which particular individuals can be categorised by type of customer. By allowing its customers to self-select, however, the firm is still able, say, to lower its usage price to one group without having to pass on the same low price to the other group of customers.

In one sense the above strategy is a way by which the firm can maximise profits in a situation of uncertainty. Had it *known* the type of customer group to which each individual belonged, it could have charged each individual the appropriate fixed/usage charge, namely T_1/U_1 for Type 1 customers or T_2/U_2 for Type 2 customers in Fig. 7.17(b). Instead, where individual customer types are unknown the firm may seek to maximise profits by devising alternative two-part tariff schedules such that customers in any one group do not prefer another group's two-part tariff schedule to that of their own. The firm is then said to be seeking to maximise profits subject to a **self-selection constraint** on behalf of its customers. If, as previously indicated, Type 2 customers have higher demands than Type 1 customers at any given price, then the alternative tariff schedules are likely to possess the following characteristics:

- $T_2 > T_1$: i.e. fixed charge for Type 2 customers greater than that for Type 1 customers;
- $U_2 < U_1$: i.e. usage charge for Type 2 customers less than that for Type 1 customers.

We can illustrate the likely impact of such alternative tariff schedules on *Type 2 customers* using Fig. 7.19. The lower usage charge ($U_2 < U_1$) and higher fixed charge ($T_2 > T_1$) for two-part tariff schedule 2 yield a greater net consumer surplus for large-volume purchases by Type 2 customers, compared with alternative tariff schedule 1. Type 2 customers are therefore likely to *self-select* the two-part tariff schedule 2. In contrast, *Type 1 customers* are likely, via self-selection, to *avoid* two-part tariff schedule 2, since the high fixed charge, T_2, discourages small-volume purchases. Instead they are likely to gain greater (net) consumer surplus by paying a lower fixed charge (T_1) and a higher usage charge (U_1).

Put another way, in our analysis high-volume purchasers (Type 2 customers) value low usage prices more than low-volume purchasers (Type 1 customers). This discrepancy enables the firm to devise alternative two-part tariff schedules whereby customers of each type self-select one schedule in preference to another in order to maximise utility.

Fig. 7.19
(Net) consumer
surplus of Type 2
customers under
alternative two-part
tariff schedules:
schedule 1 (T_1, U_1)
and schedule 2 (T_2,
U_2) such that $T_2 > T_1$
and $U_2 < U_1$.

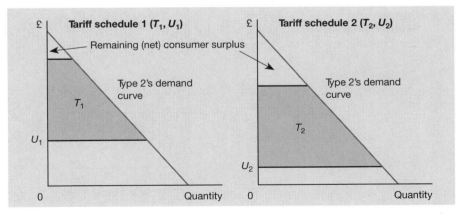

Consumers reveal their (unknown) characteristics by such self-selection, and the firm is able to benefit in terms of higher profit by restricting the lower usage charge to the appropriate type of customer only (here Type 2).

Peak-load pricing The pricing strategies of price discrimination and two-part tariff each assume that different prices are charged for identical products. Profits are thereby raised because of the varying characteristics of separate market segments or customer types. There is no suggestion of the costs of provision differing significantly as regards the supply of these markets/customer types. However, the idea of **peak-load pricing** does take account of potentially significant variations in the costs of supply. In the next section (p. 324) we note the significant differences in the marginal cost of providing electricity at different times of day. Problems of storage of electric power mean that peak period demands (e.g. 4 pm to 6 pm) must largely be met by bringing reserve generating capacity from less efficient plants into operation, thereby raising the marginal costs of supply at such times.

We can use Fig. 7.20 to compare the consequences of some uniform price set by the monopoly with prices set to reflect the different marginal costs of producing the product in the peak and off-peak periods. For simplicity we assume the demand curve for the peak period to be D_1 and that for the off-peak period to be D_2. We further assume a short-run scenario in which the scale of operations has been established (i.e. fixed costs for the desired scale are already incurred), and for which the short-run marginal costs of production are indicated by SMC.

Under certain conditions (see Chapter 11, p. 442) an efficient pricing strategy involves setting prices equal to marginal costs of provision. The implication of such a peak-load pricing solution is the setting of price P_1 in the peak demand period D_1 (with associated output Q_1) and price P_2 in the off-peak demand period D_2 (with associated output Q_2). Suppose we now compare this allocation with that resulting from a *uniform* price, P, set by the monopoly. This might be set to reflect its average costs of production + conventional percentage mark-up, or might even be a uniform price set by an external regulator. Whatever the source of the uniform price, P, we can compare its impact on firm profit and other aspects of resource allocation as compared with the peak/off-peak (marginal cost) pricing solutions P_1, P_2 respectively.

Fig. 7.20 **Peak-period pricing compared with uniform pricing.**

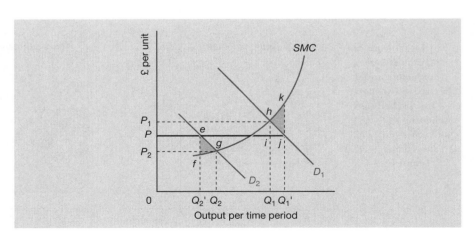

Certainly in the case of utilities, whether public or private, it is likely that there will be a requirement/expectation to meet any demands resulting from the uniform pricing policy. In Fig. 7.20, this will imply output Q'_2 in the off-peak period (D_2) and output Q'_1 in the peak period (D_1).

Impacts of peak-period pricing

- Consumers in each time period are encouraged to purchase less ($Q'_1 - Q_1$) in the peak period and more ($Q_2 - Q_2'$) in the off-peak period. In other words, consumers are encouraged to be more economical in their use of a product in situations where the costs of providing it are highest.
- To the extent that consumers are able and willing to *switch* out of one time period of consumption to another (peak to off-peak), the demand curves D_1, D_2 will shift left and right respectively, further reinforcing this effect.
- There are likely to be other efficiency gains by peak-period pricing, as compared with a uniform pricing regime. In terms of Fig. 7.20, the shaded areas correspond to the *net* efficiency gained via pricing strategies P_1, P_2 as compared with uniform price P. For example, the *reduction* in peak period output from Q'_1 to Q_1 reduces costs by the area under the *SMC* curve, i.e. $Q_1 h k Q'_1$, but benefits by the area under the demand curve, i.e. $Q_1 h j Q'_1$, giving the shaded area *hjk* as the (net) efficiency gain via this reallocation.

    Using similar reasoning, the *increase* in off-peak period output from Q_2' to Q_2 gives the shaded area *efg* as the (net) efficiency gain via this reallocation.

So far we have focused on short-run benefits of peak-period pricing. In the long run there are likely to be still further benefits as firms can cut back on infrastructure and other fixed costs given that they now require a reduced *scale* of output to meet peak period demand.

Of course, the above alleged advantages of peak period pricing must be set against a number of possible disadvantages:

- Some users of the product will be unable to switch their demands from peak to off-peak periods. They will therefore lose via the higher prices now imposed on peak-period users.
- There may be additional administrative, infrastructure and monitoring costs in accurately assessing the period in which consumption actually takes place.

Transfer pricing   In our discussion of price discrimination by monopolies (or indeed the oligopolies of Chapters 8 and 9) we have so far assumed that the price set in the different markets reflects an equality between *MC* of provision and *MR* of sale in markets with differing demand elasticity conditions. In fact there may be situations where the profit-maximising price and output bear little or no relation to the *true* marginal cost of provision or marginal revenue obtained in the market(s). Arguably this may occur where *multinational* corporate activity is involved, especially where different tax regimes apply in different countries.

The suggestion here is that the profit-maximising price may be influenced less by cost or demand elasticity conditions in the intended markets than by the *tax regimes* operating in those markets. We use the term **transfer pricing** where such accountancy-type considerations influence the official price charged in the respective markets (home and overseas).

Following Healey (1999), consider a simplified example in which a multinational's production is vertically integrated, with operations in two countries. Basic manufacture takes place in country A and final assembly and sale in country B (see Table 7.1). In country A, the corporate tax rate is 25%, while in country B it is 50%. Suppose the company's costs (inputs, labour, etc.) in country A are $40 million, and it produces intermediate products with a market value of $50 million; if it were to sell these intermediate products on the *open market*, it would declare a profit of $10 million in country A, incurring a tax liability of $2.5 million in that country.

Table 7.1
Multinational tax avoidance via transfer pricing.

$m	Scenario 1		Scenario 2	
	Country A	Country B	Country A	Country B
Costs	40	90	40	100
Sales	50	100	60	100
Profit	10	10	20	0
Tax liability	2.5	5	5	0
Total tax	7.5		5	

Source: Healey (1999)

However, suppose the products are actually intended for the parent company's subsidiary in country B. In Scenario 1, the transfer price (i.e. the internal price used by the company to calculate profits in different countries) is set at the market price of $50 million in country A for the intermediate products that are now to be shipped to country B for incorporation into the final product. The operation in country B incurs additional costs of $40 million, after which the final product is sold in country B for $100 million: thus the subsidiary will declare a profit of $10 million and incur a tax liability of $5 million. The company as a whole will face a total tax liability of $7.5 million in countries A and B taken together.

Consider an alternative scenario (Scenario 2), in which the company sets a transfer price above the market price for the intermediate products manufactured in the low-tax country, A. With a transfer price of $60 million rather than $50 million and the same costs of $40 million, the subsidiary in country A incurs a higher tax liability (25% of $20 million), but this is more than offset by the lower (in fact, zero) tax liability incurred by the subsidiary in country B. Because the latter is now recording its total costs (including the cost of the intermediate products bought from the subsidiary in country A) as being $100 million rather than $90 million, its profits and tax liability fall to zero. As a result, the total tax liability faced by the company on its international operations is only $5 million under Scenario 2 rather than $7.5 million under Scenario 1.

The basic issue is that the multinational has earned a total profit of $20 million on its vertically integrated operation: i.e. $100 million actual sales revenue in B minus $80 million costs in A + B. However, by setting transfer prices on intra-company sales and purchases of intermediate products appropriately, the company can move this profit to the lowest-tax country, thereby denying the highest-tax country (in this case, country

B) the tax revenue to which it is entitled. Such transfer pricing can, of course, succeed only when there is no active market for the intermediate products being traded. If the tax authorities in country B can refer to an open-market price for the intermediate product, then the inflated transfer price being paid can be identified. However, to the extent that many multinationals internalise cross-border operations because they have ownership-specific advantages (e.g. control of a specific raw material or technology), it may be that comparable intermediate products are not available on the open market. For this reason, high-tax countries may find they lose tax revenues to lower-tax centres as business becomes increasingly globalised. This creates, in turn, an incentive for countries to compete for multinational tax revenues by offering low tax rates; the result of such competition is a transfer of income from national governments to the shareholders of multinational companies.

For the purposes of this chapter, however, the main point is that a profit-maximising solution for the monopolist (or indeed oligopolist) may involve price setting that bears little or no relation to the true marginal costs of provision or marginal revenues from sale in the intended market(s).

Bilateral monopoly

Bilateral monopoly occurs when a monopoly on the *supplier* side is matched by a monopoly on the *buyer* side (**monopsony**). In the extreme case we have one supplier and one buyer, and the market solution will then depend on negotiation between the parties. In Fig. 7.21 we identify the *boundaries* within which the negotiated solution for the pure monopolist (S) and pure monopsonist (B) must lie.

DD is the demand curve; MR_S and MC_S are the marginal revenue curve and the marginal cost curve respectively of the single seller. If the pure monopolist can impose his will on the buyer, then the profit-maximising solution will be output Q_S sold at price P_s. In this case the pure monopolist is making the pure monopsonist behave as if there were many *buyers*. However, if the pure monopsonist can impose his will on the seller, then he can make the pure monopolist behave as if there were many sellers. In the extreme case the single buyer can make the pure monopolist behave in the same way as in a perfectly competitive industry, in which case the marginal cost curve of the single seller (MC_S) becomes the industry supply curve. If this is so, MC_S becomes the average cost curve to the buyer (AC_B), telling him the cost per unit of each quantity purchased. The buyer then becomes aware of the fact that purchasing extra units of the product forces the price of *all* units up. In other words the marginal cost to the buyer (MC_B) of purchasing an extra unit

Fig. 7.21
**Bilateral monopoly:
boundaries within
which the negotiated
solution must lie
(P_S–P_B).**

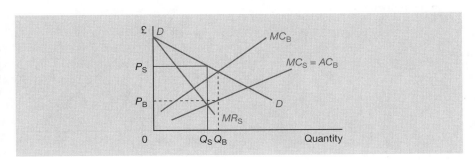

will be greater than the cost of that last unit itself (AC_B). It will be the cost of that last unit plus the additional cost of purchasing all the previous units at the now higher price. Clearly MC_B will lie above AC_B ($= MC_S$). The optimal solution for the buyer is to equate the marginal cost of buying an additional unit (MC_B) with the marginal value of that additional unit to him, the buyer. This is indicated by the demand curve, which reflects the buyer's willingness to pay. The single buyer therefore seeks to purchase Q_B at a cost to him (price) of P_B. Of course in this scenario the single *seller* is behaving like a competitive industry with supply curve MC_S, and is willing to sell Q_B units at a price of P_B.

In this way we have determined not a unique solution but the *boundaries* within which a negotiated solution must lie. Of course it will depend on the relative bargaining strength of the parties to the negotiation as to whether the final price is closer to P_S or P_B.

In conventional economic analysis, bilateral monopolies are regarded as rare in commodity markets but more prevalent in labour markets, with employers' confederations (sellers) and trades unions (buyers) acting as surrogate monopolist/monopsonist respectively. We return to bilateral monopoly when analysing factor markets in Chapter 10.

■ Calculating welfare loss under monopoly

As we noted on p. 286 the traditional or classical case against monopoly is that price is higher and quantity lower than under perfect competition. Here we seek to calculate the deadweight loss (pp. 295–7) or net welfare impacts that might result from the presence of monopoly power, whether regulated or unregulated.

In Fig. 7.22 (which for illustrative purposes assumes constant costs), the perfectly competitive price and output would be $0P_c/0Q_c$, yielding total consumer surplus of areas $1 + 2 + 3$, with total cost of production given by areas $4 + 5$.

With entry barriers and identical demand/cost conditions, the profit-maximising monopoly price and output would be $0P_m/0Q_m$. Consumer surplus is now only area 1 (units Q_m to Q_c are no longer produced), and area 2 switches from consumer to producer surplus.

- The *loss* of area 3 to society is often referred to as an allocative loss or **deadweight loss**.

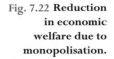

Fig. 7.22 **Reduction in economic welfare due to monopolisation.**

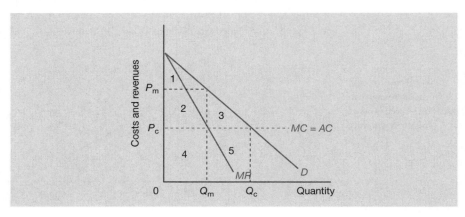

● The *transfer* of area 2 from consumer surplus to producer surplus is more difficult to assess in terms of social impact. It certainly represents a reallocation from consumer surplus to abnormal profit for the monopolist.

The total costs of production are now only area 4, with area 5 representing costs (resources) no longer incurred (utilised) by this firm/sector, i.e. resources that have been released for (potential) use elsewhere.

Following Ferguson and Ferguson (1994), Table 7.2 outlines the changes from perfect competition to monopoly in terms of each designated area from Fig. 7.22. However, we have already noted (p. 293) that the creation of monopoly may permit scale economies and lower costs. This is reflected by the downward shift of the marginal (and average) cost curve in Fig. 7.23 from $MC_c = AC_c$ to $MC_m = AC_m$. The change in price/quantity equilibrium resulting from the competitive industry being monopolised is now from P_c/Q_c to P_m/Q_m. Here price has risen and quantity fallen via monopolisation, though as we indicated earlier (p. 286) this need not be the case where scale economies are more substantial than shown in Fig. 7.23.

Table 7.2 Welfare changes due to monopolisation.

Area in Figure 7.22	Competitive market	Monopoly
1	Consumer surplus	Consumer surplus
2	Consumer surplus	Abnormal profit
3	Consumer surplus	Deadweight loss (i.e. no longer exists)
4	Input costs	Input costs
5	Input costs	Resources used elsewhere in the economy

The monopolist makes abnormal profits, as in Fig. 7.22, but the larger part of these profits can now be termed *production gain* as it stems directly from cost reductions via monopolisation. Some economists would suggest that if this productive gain outweighs the deadweight loss in Fig. 7.23 then society's welfare has improved as a result of monopolisation, even though price is higher and output lower than in the competitive model.

Fig. 7.23 The effects on welfare of a monopoly with costs lower than in perfect competition.

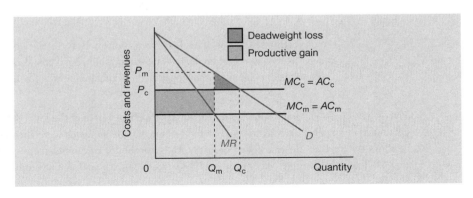

Needham (1978) has shown that only a small reduction in costs need be achieved after monopolisation for 'productive gain' to outweigh 'deadweight loss'. For example, if we take a product with a price elasticity of demand of (−) 2, a cost reduction via monopolisation of only 4% will be required to secure this result, even though price rises by as much as 20%.

Harberger's welfare loss estimates

Returning to Fig. 7.22 and following the analysis of Ferguson and Ferguson (1994), since the area of a triangle is $\frac{1}{2} \times$ base $\times$ height, the deadweight welfare loss (W) of triangular area 3 can be shown to be

$$W = \frac{1}{2} \Delta P \Delta Q \tag{1}$$

where ΔP and ΔQ are respectively the discrete absolute differences in price (P) and in output (Q) between perfect competition and monopoly.

Since arc price elasticity of demand (ε) is defined as

$$\varepsilon = \frac{\Delta Q}{Q} \frac{P}{\Delta P} \tag{2}$$

substituting ΔQ in equation (1) with ΔQ derived from equation (2) gives

$$W = \frac{1}{2} \Delta P \frac{\Delta P}{P} Q \varepsilon \tag{3}$$

This can be rearranged to give the formula used by Harberger (1954) to calculate welfare loss:

$$W = \frac{1}{2} \left(\frac{\Delta P}{P} \right)^2 PQ \varepsilon \tag{4}$$

where W = welfare loss
       P = price
       Q = quantity
       ΔP = change in price via monopolisation
       ε = price elasticity of demand

Having estimated the welfare loss from monopoly for a *market*, the welfare loss for the *economy as a whole* could be derived by summation across markets.

We consider the empirical application of this formula in the next section (p. 322).

Cowling and Mueller's welfare loss estimates

Cowling and Mueller first estimated welfare losses at the level of the *firm*, rather than the market (as was the case with Harberger). These losses were then aggregated across firms within the market or industry. Their method is outlined here; it yields an estimate for the deadweight welfare loss (W) as equivalent to half the amount of monopoly profit. In terms of Fig. 7.22, deadweight welfare loss (W) is given by area 3, which is shown to be half of area 2:

i.e. $W = \dfrac{\pi}{2}$ (1)

where π represents monopoly profits.

According to Cowling and Mueller, the deadweight loss only partly represents the reduction in welfare. For example, the monopoly may have to incur expenditures to establish or maintain a monopoly position. These might take the form of extensive advertising or product differentiation – both of which may imply incurring costs *additional* to production costs. Account must then be taken of these extra costs for the monopoly *vis-à-vis* the competitive firm. The stages involved in deriving this *first* measure (i.e equation (1)) used by Cowling and Mueller to calculate welfare loss via monopolisation are outlined in the box that follows.

Derivation of Cowling and Mueller's first measure of welfare loss

Since total revenue (TR) is equal to selling price (P) multiplied by the quantity sold (Q), or

$$TR = PQ \qquad (1)$$

marginal revenue is

$$MR = \frac{\mathrm{d}TR}{\mathrm{d}Q} = P + Q\,\frac{\mathrm{d}P}{\mathrm{d}Q} \qquad (2)$$

Rearranging gives

$$MR = P\left(1 + \frac{Q}{P}\,\frac{\mathrm{d}P}{\mathrm{d}Q}\right) \qquad (3)$$

Noting that price elasticity of demand (ε), which is invariably negative, is defined as

$$\varepsilon = \frac{\mathrm{d}Q}{Q}\,\frac{P}{\mathrm{d}P} \qquad (4)$$

substituting (4) into (3) gives

$$MR = P\left(1 + \frac{1}{\varepsilon}\right) \qquad (5)$$

For profit maximisation $MC = MR$ therefore equation (5) can be rewritten:

$$MC = P\left(1 + \frac{1}{\varepsilon}\right) \qquad (6)$$

which can be rearranged to give the Lerner condition (see p. 290)

$$\frac{P - MC}{P} = -\frac{1}{\varepsilon} \qquad (7)$$

Hence

$$\varepsilon = - \frac{P}{P - MC} \tag{8}$$

Since $P - MC = \Delta P$ (in absolute terms), equation (8) becomes

$$\varepsilon = (-) \frac{P}{\Delta P} \tag{9}$$

Substituting for ε in equation (2) on p. 312 gives

$$\frac{\Delta Q}{Q} \frac{P}{\Delta P} = \frac{P}{\Delta P} \quad \text{(ignoring the negative sign for } \varepsilon) \tag{10}$$

Dividing both sides by $P/\Delta P$ gives

$$\frac{\Delta Q}{Q} = 1 \tag{11}$$

This can be incorporated into Harberger's equation (1) on p. 312, which now simplifies to

$$W = \frac{1}{2} \Delta PQ \tag{12}$$

Profits in a monopoly (π) are

$$\pi = (P - C)\, Q \tag{13}$$

Where costs are constant, such that average cost $(C) = MC$, then

$$\pi = \Delta PQ \tag{14}$$

Cowling and Mueller's (1978) *first* measure of welfare loss becomes

$$W = \frac{\pi}{2} \tag{15}$$

Cowling and Mueller's second measure of welfare loss includes the *indirect* effects of advertising (A). Compared with perfect competition, it leads to a yet further reduction in output and increase in price. The formula for welfare loss then becomes

$$W = \frac{\pi + A}{2} \tag{2}$$

If advertising expenditure is regarded as undesirable in itself, then a third measure includes the direct *and* indirect effects of advertising and yields a still greater welfare loss equal to:

$$W = A + \frac{\pi + A}{2} \tag{3}$$

Cowling and Mueller suggest a fourth measure for welfare loss if we regard after-tax monopoly profits (π') as being 'used up' in the monopolising process. We then have

$$W = \pi' + A + \frac{\pi + A}{2} \qquad (4)$$

The reasoning here is that any profit return above the (normal) competitive level acts as an incentive for other firms to enter the market to capture the abnormal profit for themselves. But to break down the entry barriers protecting the incumbent monopolist requires extra expenditure, which can also be regarded as reducing society's welfare. Cowling and Mueller assume that these expenditures are equal to after-tax abnormal (monopoly) profits, arguing that it would be rational for rivals to expend up to this amount if they could be certain of capturing the monopoly profits.

The results of empirical calculation of welfare loss using each of the four expressions of Cowling and Mueller are presented in the next section (p. 322).

Applications and evidence

Barriers to entry

We noted (p. 291) that one of the main sources of monopoly power involved **barriers to entry**. Here we consider a variety of empirical evidence for the various types of barrier.

Myers (1993) notes the likelihood of different firms facing different 'heights' of a particular barrier. A distinction is often made between *de novo* entrants, who must make new investments, and those existing firms that are able to enter by diversifying from a related market or modifying existing productive capacity. Take, for example, the barrier of extensive advertising by incumbents in a particular market. A company with a strong brand name in an associated market may find it easier to gain consumer acceptance and so faces a lower entry barrier in this respect: e.g. the use of the Marks and Spencer name, already well known to retail consumers, for its move into consumer finance. Similarly it may be less costly for an existing overseas producer to enter the UK market, because it need not incur the costs of setting up production facilities (i.e. it can enter by imports).

Another important factor in assessing the height of the barrier is the time that it takes for new entrants to enter the industry and become effective competitors. Any particular barrier is likely to be higher in the short run than in the long run. On the supply side, there is likely to be a gestation period between the decision to enter and the act of entry, especially for a *de novo* entrant, e.g. because of the time it takes to build a production plant. On the demand side it is likely to take an entrant some time to build up a customer base and thereby erode consumer loyalty to existing products. In the USA, time is explicitly taken into account by the competition authorities as they only regard firms able to establish themselves in a market within two years as potential competition for incumbents.

Types of barrier

As regards the different types of barrier, Myers suggests that a useful distinction might be drawn between structural and behavioural barriers. **Structural** (or exogenous) barriers are those that are imposed upon the market by external factors, such as government regulation, technology, or consumer preferences. **Behavioural** (or endogenous) barriers arise from the conduct of market participants designed to deter entry, such as acquiring sole use of an input, setting artificially low prices, or over-investing in capacity. In evaluating 37 Monopolies and Mergers Commission Reports in the UK over the period 1980–92, Myers allocates the barriers to entry identified in those reports as shown in Table 7.3.

Table 7.3 **Types of barriers to entry: Monopolies and Mergers Commission Reports 1980–92.**

Category of barrier		Number of reports in which identified	
(I)	**Incumbent dominance**	19	
	(a) pricing		10
	(b) switching costs		7
	(c) excess capacity		3
	(d) acquisitions		2
(II)	**Exclusivity**	18	
	(a) agreements and ties		14
	(b) vertical integration		9
(III)	**Lack of availability of inputs**	12	
	(a) due to strategic behaviour		9
	(b) scarce resource		3
(IV)	**Insufficient market size**	10	
	(a) compared to entry costs		7
	(b) relative to economies of scale		4
(V)	**Brand image**	10	
(VI)	**Government regulations**	9	

Note: The frequencies of the subdivisions in a category may not sum to that category frequency and the category frequencies do not add up to 37 (the number of MMC reports analysed), because a single MMC report will often identify entry barriers in more than one subdivision and category.
Source: Adapted from Myers (1993)

Most of the barriers identified would appear to be *behavioural* in type. Arguably only I (c) (excess capacity), III (b) (scarce resources), IV (insufficient market size) and VI (government regulations) could be regarded as *structural* on the basis of our earlier definition. Under this classification almost 75% of all the entry barriers identified in Table 7.3 could therefore be regarded as behavioural, reflecting conscious actions by incumbent firms to deter new entrants.

European service industry and barriers

Sapir (1993) usefully investigates barriers to entry in the European service industries. He identifies **sunk costs** as an important behavioural/endogenous barrier. Sunk costs are fixed costs associated with irreversible investments and, by increasing exit costs for incumbents, are likely to stimulate incumbent resistance to new entrants. In terms of services, these sunk costs can be of two broad types: investments in *tangible* or physical assets (buildings and equipment) and investments in *intangible* assets. Intangible assets, such as reputation, are likely to be an important sunk cost in service industries. The existence of asymmetric information (e.g. between producers and consumers) in terms of the quality of service provision is likely to place a substantial premium on reputation, especially in the service industries.

As we can see from Fig. 7.24(a), in the nine European service industries investigated it is sunk costs involving intangible assets that provide the more important barrier to entry, as in insurance, banking, airlines and business services. Only telecommunication of the nine service industries has sunk costs as a high entry barrier as regards both tangible and intangible assets. For road transport, distribution, construction and hotels, neither type of sunk cost poses a significant entry barrier.

Government regulation was also identified as an important entry barrier to the European service industries. Regulatory instruments are often classified into our earlier categories as being structural or behavioural in nature. The former affect the structure of the industry and the access opportunities for new entrants directly. The latter affect the conduct or behaviour of existing industry members and thereby access opportunities for new entrants indirectly.

Fig. 7.24(b) indicates the following situations as regards government regulations amongst the nine service industries investigated:

- Four sectors have traditionally been subject to a high degree of both structural and conduct regulations: banking, insurance, airline transport and telecommunications. Stringent rules for new entry have been applied in these sectors, often for prudential reasons.
- Three sectors have been relatively free of government regulation: business services, hotels and construction. The rules for entry into these industries are not very stringent, nor is there much in the way of restriction on the behaviour of their participants.

Fig. 7.24 **(a) Types of sunk costs as entry barriers in nine European service industries. (b) Types of government regulations as entry barriers in nine European service industries.**

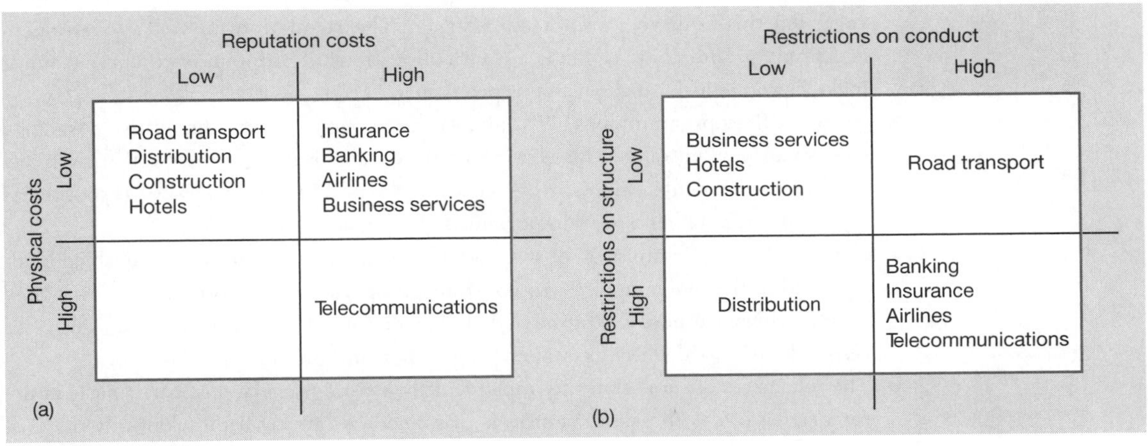

Source: Sapir (1993)

- The distribution sector is subject mostly to structural regulations, though with great differences across subsectors. The subsector most affected has been that of large retail centres, where laws have often been enacted to protect independent retailers. Some degree of conduct regulation also prevails in the guise of restrictions on opening hours.
- Finally, the road transport sector has been subject mostly to conduct regulations. Governments have instituted a number of rules that affect the behaviour of road hauliers, including quantitative restrictions, price controls, and technical standards.

We have already considered economies of scale as a significant barrier to entry in certain industries. Tables 4.5 (p. 185) and 4.6 (p. 187) indicated a variety of industries with significant *cost gradients*, i.e. those for which costs increase substantially when the plant or enterprise is below the minimum efficient size (*MES*) for that industry.

Although **excess capacity** has been identified as a behavioural barrier erected by incumbents to deter new entrants, Lieberman (1987) in his investigation of 38 chemical product industries found little evidence to support this contention. He concluded that in only 3 out of the 38 products was there evidence to suggest that incumbents had indeed over-invested as a means of entry deterrence. When allied to characteristics of slow market growth, high capital intensity and high producer concentration, excess capacity is certainly an effective entry barrier, as with the products magnesium and sorbitol. However, only in rare cases could this be associated with a premeditated corporate strategy by incumbents.

Air transport industry and barriers

We have already cast some doubt as to the air transport industry being 'contestable' (Chapter 6, p. 274). Figure 7.25 reinforces this view by reporting the results of a survey of 18 EU airlines as to the perceived barriers still remaining after the Single European Act of 1987 (European Commission 1997).

The following barriers were identified as deterring new firm entry in this study:

- The lack of peak hour slots at many major airports makes the entry of new carriers on the densest routes, where competition would be most viable, almost impossible. It also inhibits niche carriers from serving regional routes. Over 80% of respondents regarded this as a 'very important' barrier. The regulation on slot allocation, in accepting 'grandfather' rights (i.e. extra allocations in proportion to current holdings), has done little to alleviate this problem.
- Frequent flyer programmes (FFPs) give large carriers a major competitive advantage over small new entrants. This is reinforced by franchising agreements that tie many smaller carriers into one or other larger airlines' FFP. Over 70% of respondents regarded this as either a 'very important' or 'important' barrier.
- Approval by the Commission of state aid with inadequate conditions has enabled high-cost and unprofitable airlines to continue to operate in markets from which they might otherwise have withdrawn. This has distorted competition. Some 60% of respondents regarded this as either a 'very important' or 'important' barrier.
- The reluctance of some states to implement the existing regulations, particularly in the early stages of the liberalisation process, has hindered carriers from taking advantage of

Fig. 7.25 **Importance of various barriers to entry in EU air transport industry.**

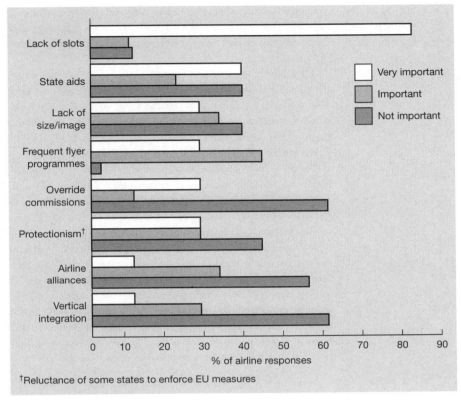

Source: European Commission (1997)

opportunities that are intended to be available. Such 'protectionism' was regarded by around 50% of respondents as either a 'very important' or 'important' barrier.

- Airline alliances make it more difficult for smaller airlines or new entrants to successfully enter established city-pair markets. However, they are regarded by incumbents as an essential means for EU carriers to maintain or enhance their global competitive position. Around 45% of respondents cited this barrier as either 'very important' or 'important'.

- The use of override commissions (i.e. high extra commission usually based on sales volumes) or other incentives by large carriers gives new entrants a competitive disadvantage in selling through travel agents. Some 40% of respondents regarded this barrier as either 'very important' or 'important'.

- Vertical integration between charter airlines and major tour operators within the same country makes new entry into that country's charter market difficult for other Community airlines or indeed start-up airlines from that country. Slightly under 40% of respondents regarded this barrier as either 'very important' or 'important'.

Often the barriers are more powerful in combination: for example, frequent flyer programmes and override commissions, taken together, can be a strong deterrent to entry by new airlines.

European car industry and price discrimination

We considered various types of price discrimination earlier in the chapter (pp.297–301). Figure 7.26(a) and (b) provides evidence of *third-degree price discrimination* in the European car market, with a different price charged for the same product to different groups of consumers.

If we take the example of the VW Golf, Fig. 7.26(a) shows a variation of almost 60% in the price of Golfs between the cheapest (Finland) and most expensive (UK) markets for this model of car. This supports the more general contention that the UK is the most expensive market for cars in Europe. Stewart (1998) reports that the UK was found to be the most expensive market for 61 of the 72 best-selling models, with the lowest European prices found in the Netherlands (for 35 of 72 models) and Portugal (for 14 of 72 models).

Figure 7.26(b) provides further evidence of price differentials throughout Europe. The maximum and minimum prices in euros for a selection of seven different models are presented. Clearly there is a considerable degree of price variation for six of the seven models, the Audi A3 perhaps coming closest to a reasonably uniform price. In fact for 16 of the 72 models investigated by Stewart a price variation of more than 40% was recorded.

We have noted (p. 299) that a *necessary* condition for price discrimination is for barriers to exist inhibiting movement of consumers from dearer to cheaper sources of supply. Stewart reports the results of a series of investigations by the European Commission into Volkswagen and Audi pricing policies across Europe in 1995. Evidence indicated that over 50 authorised dealers had been threatened that their contracts would be terminated if they sold Volkswagen or Audi cars to foreign customers seeking purchases cheaper than those available in their home countries. Dealers found to be in breach of this company policy either had contracts terminated or were penalised by reduced profit margins or

Fig. 7.26 **Price differentials in the EU car market.**

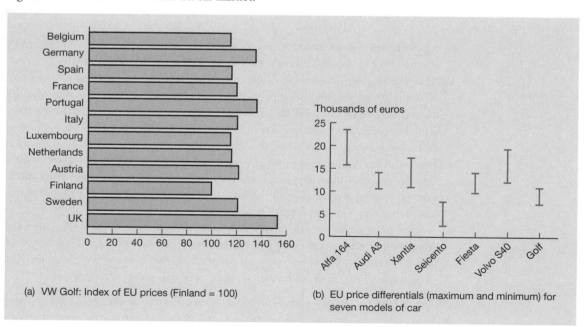

(a) VW Golf: Index of EU prices (Finland = 100)

(b) EU price differentials (maximum and minimum) for seven models of car

Source: European Commission (1999), car price differentials within the EU, D.G.IV, May, adapted.

bonuses. In the case of Volkswagen the European Commission deemed that these practices infringed European Union competition law designed to promote cross-border
trade, and fined Volkswagen 102 million ecus (£68 million) in 1998.

Such 'barriers' between markets are a necessary but *not sufficient* condition for
third–degree price discrimination to be profitable. Insofar as the car companies followed a
profit-related objective, they must have deemed the price elasticity of demand characteristics to have been different as between the various national markets: lower price elasticities of
demand in the markets for which prices were higher, and vice versa (see Fig. 7.15, p. 299).

■ Empirical estimates of welfare loss under monopoly

Harberger's approach   Earlier (p. 312) we noted that deadweight loss (*W*) could be represented in Harberger's
approach by

$$W = \frac{1}{2} \left(\frac{\Delta P}{P} \right)^2 PQ\,\varepsilon$$

where: W = welfare loss

 P = price

 Q = quantity

 ΔP = change in price via monopolisation

 ε = price elasticity of demand

While information on sales revenue (*PQ*) is often readily available from production cen-
suses and published company accounts, the difference between competitive and
monopoly price levels (ΔP) can only be estimated. In his calculations Harberger assumed:

- that the rate of return that firms in competitive markets would earn in long-run equilibrium is equivalent to the *average* rate of return in manufacturing industry. Individual
  industry rates were then compared with this *average* to estimate the price differentials
  due to market power;
- that unit price elasticity of demand (ε) occurs for *all* industries.

His cross-section studies using data aggregated at the industry level indicate that the
activities of the manufacturing sector of the USA in the 1920s resulted in a reduction of
welfare equivalent to 0.1% of GNP. At this time, manufacturing industries accounted for
only about 25% of the USA's output. If market power were present to a similar extent in
other sectors, then the estimate of total welfare loss in the economy would be a mere
0.4%. Such a small estimate of welfare loss inevitably called into question the validity of
policies designed to combat market power.

**Criticisms of the
Harberger approach**   Harberger's study has, however, been the subject of a number of criticisms. Most critics
suggest that Harberger's estimate is a considerable understatement of the true welfare
loss under monopoly:

- It is unlikely that the *average* rate of return in manufacturing industry reflects the *competitive* rate of return (normal profits). Arguably the *average* return in manufacturing
  includes an element of supernormal profit. This would cause the price differential

($\Delta P/P$) in his equation regarded as being due to monopoly to be underestimated. This in turn would mean that his calculation of welfare loss (W) would be underestimated.

- It is unlikely that price elasticity of demand (ϵ) is unity for all industries. Indeed, if it were then $MR = 0$ and the profit-maximising monopoly must produce where $MC = 0$. It is unlikely that MC will be zero for a monopolist. More likely is that price elasticity of demand will tend to be > 1 (i.e. $MR > 0$) in a profit-maximising situation. In terms of Harberger's equation, welfare loss (W) would then again be greater than he estimated.

Cowling and Mueller and the calculation of welfare loss

Methods similar to Harberger's have been used, among others, by Schwartzman (1960), Bell (1968), Worcester (1973), and Siegfried and Tiemann (1974), to give similarly low estimates of welfare losses. By contrast the different approach taken by Cowling and Mueller (1978) suggests that welfare loss may be substantially higher.

Cowling and Mueller's approach We saw (p. 312) that four different expressions for welfare loss could be devised using the approach of Cowling and Mueller. Estimates by Cowling and Mueller for losses in absolute values and as a percentage of gross corporate product are presented in Table 7.4 in both the USA (1963–66) and UK (1968–69). Cowling and Mueller's estimate is much higher (row 2) because of the different techniques used (see p. 323).

Table 7.4 **Estimates of the welfare costs of monopoly.**

	USA ($ million)	UK (£ million)
1. Harberger's estimate	448.2	21.4
2. Harberger corrected	4,527.1	385.8
3. (2) + advertising expenditures	14,005.4	537.4
4. (3) + after tax monopoly profits	14,997.6	719.3
5. (1) as % of gross corporate product	0.4%	0.2%
6. (2) as % of gross corporate product	4.0%	3.3%
7. (4) as % of gross corporate product	13.1%	7.2%

Source: Adapted from Cowling and Mueller (1978)

In addition to correcting Harberger's analysis on the lines previously discussed, Cowling and Mueller included two more corrective elements. One is advertising expenditure (row 3), which they considered to be a social waste, and the other is 'after tax monopoly profits', which they regarded as an indication of resources wasted in the process of gaining monopoly power.

Compared with Harberger's low estimates of 0.4% and 0.2% of welfare loss from monopoly power in the USA and UK respectively, Cowling and Mueller's estimates are much more substantial, whether or not these additional corrective elements are included. From row 2 alone, Cowling and Mueller estimate welfare loss from monopoly power at 4.0% (USA) and 3.3% (UK) of gross corporate product, and from row 4 at as much as 13.1% (USA) and 7.2% (UK) of gross corporate product.

Although there is substance to the argument of Cowling and Mueller that there are costs in monopolisation beyond those that are incurred in production and distribution, it does not necessarily follow that these are a waste to society. For instance, advertising may also provide valuable information.

Summary of various welfare loss estimates

Table 7.5 summarises the various estimates of welfare loss for several economies. Most of these studies use a Harberger-type approach deriving low estimates of welfare reduction. Those that indicate much higher ranges generally use methods similar to those of Cowling and Mueller.

Table 7.5 Summary of empirical studies on the welfare effects of monopoly.

Author	Period	Country	Welfare loss[a]
Harberger (1954)	1924–28	USA	0.1
Schwartzman (1960)	1954	USA	0.1
Kamerschen (1966)	1956–61	USA	5.4–7.6
Bell (1968)	1954	USA	0.02–0.04
Shepherd (1970)	1960–69	USA	2.0–3.0
Worcester (1973)	1956–69	USA	0.2–0.7
Siegfried and Tiemann (1974)	1963	USA	0.07
Cowling and Mueller (1978)	1963–66	USA	4.0–13.1
Masson and Shaanan (1984)	1950–66	USA	2.9
Wahlroos (1984)	1962–75	USA	0.04–0.90
Gisser (1986)	1977	USA	0.1–1.8
Jones and Laudadio (1978)	1965–67	Canada	3.7
Cowling and Mueller (1978)	1968–69	UK	3.3–7.2
Wahlroos (1984)	1970–79	Finland	0.2–0.6
Jenny and Weber (1983)	1967–70	France	0.13–8.85
	1971–74	France	0.21
Pezzoli (1985)	1982–83	Italy	0.4–9.4
Funahashi (1982)	1980	Japan	0.02–3.00
Oh (1986)	1983	Korea	1.16–6.75
Ong'olo (1987)	1977	Kenya	0.26–4.40

[a]Percentage of gross corporate product
Source: Ferguson and Ferguson (1994)

The general inference to be drawn is that the presence of monopoly results in a small deadweight loss. However, where firms' costs are increased as a result of monopolisation, or via extra expenditure incurred to defend the monopoly position, then welfare losses may rise considerably.

The level of aggregation may, however, affect the various results. Aggregation, with its implied averaging, tends to understate the actual variability in price–cost margins following monopolisation. The more highly aggregated the data the more likely it is, therefore, that the welfare losses will be understated. Using the broad two-digit level of the Standard Industrial Classification, Cowling and Mueller demonstrated an estimated welfare loss of only 78% of that reported when the classification of industry is at the narrower firm level. However, even firm-based studies can lead to aggregation errors where firms operate in more than one market and where their market power varies between those markets.

Welfare loss estimates and factor inputs

Browning (1997) adds further weight to the criticism that studies using Harberger's approach essentially underestimate the welfare loss resulting from monopoly power. He argues that by focusing on valuing the 'Harberger triangle' of deadweight loss, only the output–mix distortions of monopoly power are addressed. However, this approach neglects distortions in the quantity of resources supplied when monopoly power affects the prices of factor inputs. Browning argues that monopoly power can be expected to depress factor prices *below* their social marginal revenue products (see Chapter 10). As a result he provides estimates of the true welfare cost of monopoly between 5 and 15 times higher than those of Harberger.

▨ Peak load pricing: electricity

Figure 7.27 indicates the structure of the wholesale market for electricity in England and Wales. *Sales* are made by the producers of electricity (the generators) into what is known as the 'electricity pool'. *Purchases* are made by the suppliers of electricity (regional electricity companies) from that pool. Electricity is *transmitted* via the power lines of the National Grid Company (NGC) to 12 regional distribution companies (usually the regional suppliers themselves), who distribute locally to their customers.

Fig. 7.27 **Wholesale market for UK electricity.**

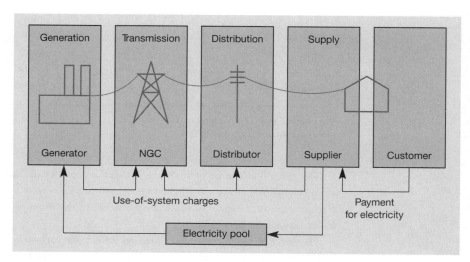

Wholesale market for UK electricity

- The 'pool' is operated by the National Grid Company, seeking to match supply with demand over each of 48 daily half-hour periods.
- The individual generators offer a *provisional selling price* for electricity to the pool for each of these half-hour periods and for each of its power stations. This is provided to the pool by 10.00 am on the day prior to use. This *offer bid* states the price at which each power station will supply electricity to the pool for the half hour in question over the following 24-hour period, together with the quantity it will supply at that price.
- The National Grid (via its subsidiary NGC Settlements Ltd – NGCS) lists the individual power stations in ascending order (from the lowest-price offer of electricity upwards) in terms of the prices of electricity offered to the pool. Quantities available at these prices are also noted.
- The NGCS now seeks to *estimate* likely demand 24 hours hence, based on time factors, weather forecasts, even TV programming etc. It splits the following day into 48 periods of half-hour duration, and seeks to estimate demand in each of these periods.

To ensure that there is sufficient supply to meet the estimated demand in each half-hour period, the NGCS accepts the highest-price power station bid required to match supply with estimated demand. This highest-price bid is known as the **system marginal price** (SMP) for that half-hour period, and is the price paid to *all* the power stations generating electricity in that period.

Table 7.6 outlines the *provisional prices* accepted by NGCS on 16 November 1995 for the generation of 'pool' electricity the next day (17 November) for each of the 48 half-hourly periods. These provisional prices are made available by NGCS to the generators by 16:00 hrs on the day prior to generation.

Final prices for each half-hour period are determined by actual demand on the day in question and may depart (in either direction) from the provisional prices. These, of course, are pool *purchase* prices; the pool *selling* prices to the local/regional distributors or suppliers are in excess of these in order to cover NGCS administrative costs, etc. In addition the suppliers of electricity must pay transmission charges to the NGC and to the local distributors (except that the latter are often themselves!).

Table 7.6 also outlines the final pool purchase and selling prices for trading some four weeks prior to 17 November 1995, namely on 19 October 1995. Looking at the final pool purchase price, we can see that the highest-cost power stations were clearly required on 19 October 1995 in the peak period time slots between 07.30 and 09.00 and between 18.30 and 20.00. The lowest-cost provision at the margin occurred in the off-peak hours between 23.00 and 00.30 and between 03.30 and 06.30. For whatever reason a relatively high price at the margin was required to induce adequate supplies in the off-peak period 01.00 to 02.30.

The data provide evidence of price varying in line with peak and off-peak demands of electricity, broadly reflecting the marginal costs of provision in each time period, as in Fig. 7.20. (Issues involving the regulation of monopoly elements of electricity supply via the Office of Electricity Regulation – OFFER – are addressed in Chapter 13.)

Table 7.6 Price setting in the wholesale market for electricity.

Prices for electricity determined for the purposes of the electricity pooling and settlement arrangements in England and Wales

Half-hour period ending	Provisional prices for trading on 16.11.95 Pool purchase price (£/MWh)	Final prices for trading on 19.10.95 Pool purchase price (£/MWh)	Pool selling price £/MWh
0030	9.07	8.97	8.97
0100	34.53	8.90	8.90
0130	34.53	8.90	8.90
0200	34.53	8.94	8.94
0230	34.53	8.94	8.94
0300	9.04	8.90	8.90
0330	9.02	8.90	8.90
0400	9.02	8.90	8.90
0430	9.02	8.90	8.90
0500	8.98	8.90	8.90
0530	8.97	9.00	9.00
0600	8.98	8.97	8.97
0630	9.07	9.02	9.02
0700	19.74	15.85	17.26
0730	20.71	16.76	18.19
0800	20.96	29.11	30.62
0830	34.84	32.99	34.51
0900	34.86	33.04	34.58
0930	34.87	16.96	18.46
1000	35.86	16.97	18.47
1030	35.86	16.97	18.47
1100	35.87	16.99	18.49
1130	45.15	20.09	21.61
1200	45.18	20.15	21.68
1230	45.18	32.98	34.50
1300	45.18	32.89	34.39
1330	38.78	16.83	18.29
1400	37.23	16.79	18.23
1430	35.86	16.76	18.19
1500	35.86	16.75	18.18
1530	14.87	9.20	9.20
1600	14.91	16.79	18.24
1630	83.07	19.05	20.53
1700	135.28	17.01	18.53
1730	156.24	19.24	20.78
1800	128.58	20.05	21.85
1830	77.98	31.57	34.01
1900	53.10	60.40	62.87
1930	44.29	59.60	61.87
2000	41.44	29.04	30.71
2030	35.93	16.84	18.29
2100	38.14	16.74	18.16
2130	33.69	16.71	18.13
2200	21.06	16.71	18.12
2230	20.71	16.71	18.12
2300	13.07	16.71	18.12
2330	13.07	13.27	14.69
2400	9.00	9.02	9.02

Prices are determined for every half-hour in each 24-hour period.

Prices are in pounds per megawatt-hour, rounded to two decimal places.

Source: Sloman (1999)

Key terms

Allocative efficiency
Barometric-firm leadership
Barriers to entry
Bilateral monopoly
Collusive-price leadership
Cost-oriented multinationals
Deadweight loss
Dominant-firm leadership
First-degree price discrimination
Lerner index
Market-oriented multinationals

Multinational (transnational)
Natural monopoly
Normal profit
Peak period pricing
Price discrimination
Price regulation
Productive efficiency
Second-degree price discrimination
Third-degree price discrimination
Transfer pricing
Two-part tariff

Full definitions can be found in the 'Glossary of terms' (pp. 699–710)

Review questions

1. Glaso Enterprises has a worldwide monopoly in the production of coloured filters for use with theatre lighting equipment. The total cost function is linear, and of the form $TC = 1,000 + 200Q$ where Q is the quantity produced. The company has two distinct markets, Europe and the USA.

   (a) Market research in the USA has found that the price elasticity of demand is –2. Calculate the mark-up above marginal cost that the company should charge in the US market, and indicate the price that should be adopted to maximise profits.

   (b) Similar research in the European market found a price elasticity of –6. Calculate the mark-up above marginal cost and the price that should be charged in this market.

   (c) Discuss the relationship between price elasticity, price, and mark-up under monopoly conditions.

   (d) If research in the Asian market finds that the price elasticity is –0.5, what implications does this have for mark-up and pricing strategies in this market?

2. An econometric study of the salt industry found that the market was dominated by a monopolist firm, Santrac plc, which had total revenue (TR) and total cost (TC) functions of the kind shown:

$$TR = \beta Q - \alpha Q^2$$
$$TC = c + bQ + aQ^2$$

   where Q is the quantity of output in tonnes and α, β, a, b and c are parameters relating to the total revenue and total cost functions.

   (a) In general terms, describe the features of the two functions outlined.

   (b) The government has decided to introduce a specific tax on salt, and wishes to maximise the tax revenue, T, from this source. If the tax revenue function is described as $T = tQ$, where T is the total tax revenue, t the tax in £ per tonne, and Q the monopolist's equilibrium output after the tax, then provide an expression for:

    (i)   the post-tax total cost function;

    (ii) the monopolist's equilibrium output.

(c) Derive the expression for the tax rate (t) that the government should introduce in order to maximise the total tax revenue T.

3. Image plc, a monopolist supplier of specialised ink needed for printing currency notes, has a monthly demand function $Q = 80 - 4P$ and an average cost function of $AC = 40Q^{-1} + 6$, where P is the price per litre of ink and Q is measured in 000s of litres.

(a) Derive the expression for the demand curve from the demand function.

(b) Show that the marginal revenue curve is downward sloping from left to right.

(c) What is the level of output and price when profits are maximised? What is the level of profits?

(d) Calculate the price elasticity of demand at the profit-maximising point on the demand curve.

(e) If the government imposes a lump sum tax of £20,000 on the monthly output of speciality ink, show that this will not alter the profit-maximising level of output but will result in a fall in the total profit.

4. As a result of a series of takeovers, Airocraft plc has become a monopolist supplier of a critical engine part to many of the world's aircraft builders, and has concentrated its production in a single UK plant. The total cost (TC) function for producing the part at its UK factory is $TC = 30Q + 20$. Demand functions for the part in the domestic and overseas market are as follows:

    (i)   domestic market $Q_1 = 20 - 0.4P_1$

    (ii) overseas market $Q_2 = 5.5 - 0.05P_2$

where P is the price per part in ecus and Q is output in 000s. As a result of the different demand conditions, the company has decided to introduce price discrimination between the two markets in an attempt to maximise its returns.

(a) Calculate the profit-maximising price and output levels for each market and the total profit that results from the price discrimination strategy.

(b) Determine the price, output and profit levels if the company had decided to charge a single price based on the output of the single UK factory.

(c) Discuss whether the price discrimination strategy has been successful, and briefly explain the relationship between price elasticity of demand and the pricing policy of Airocraft plc.

5. The production division (P) of Pharma, a multinational drug company producing low side effect sleeping pills, sells its product internally to its marketing division (M), which then packs and distributes the product to its global retail outlets. The marketing division's demand curve for the pills is given by $P_M = 80 - 0.001Q_M$ where P_M is the selling price of the pills per pack in ecus and Q_M is the number

of packs sold (in 000s). The marketing division's total cost function is such that $C_M = 200{,}000 + 10Q_M$ and the production division's total cost function is $C_P = 400{,}000 + 10Q_P + 0.001Q_P^2$.

(a) Assuming that there is no external market for sleeping pills, find the profit-maximising output and price for the product, and calculate:
   (i) the overall market price and output that will maximise Pharma's profits;
   (ii) the optimal transfer price between the production and marketing divisions.

(b) If the sleeping pills could be sold in a perfectly competitive external wholesale market for £45 per packet, calculate:
   (i) the profit-maximising output and price for the production and marketing divisions and the optimal transfer price;
   (ii) how the production division should divide its output between the open market and its own marketing division in order to optimise profits.

■ Further reading

Intermediate texts
Baumol, W. J. (1977), *Economic Theory and Operations Analysis*, 4th edn, Ch. 16, Prentice Hall, Hemel Hempstead.

Browning, E. and Browning, J. (1992), *Microeconomic Theory and Applications*, 4th edn, Chs 11 and 14, HarperCollins, London.

Dobson, S., Maddala, G. S. and Miller, E. (1995), *Microeconomics*, Chs 9, 10 and 12, McGraw-Hill, Maidenhead.

Ferguson, P. R. and Ferguson, G. J. (1994), *Industrial Economics*, 2nd edn, Macmillan, Basingstoke.

Hope, S. (1999), *Applied Microeconomics*, Ch 10, Whiley, Chichester.

Katz, M. and Rosen, H. (1998), *Microeconomics*, 3rd edn, Chs 13 and 14, Irwin, Boston, Mass.

Koutsoyiannis, A. (1979), *Modern Microeconomics*, 2nd edn, Chs 6 and 7, Macmillan, Basingstoke.

Laidler, D. and Estrin, S. (1995), *Introduction to Microeconomics*, 4th edn, Chs 15 and 16, Harvester Wheatsheaf, Hemel Hempstead.

Maddala, G. S. and Miller, E. (1989), *Microeconomics: Theory and Application*, Chs 11 and 12, McGraw-Hill, New York.

Nicholson, W. (1997), *Intermediate Microeconomics and its Application*, 7th edn, Ch. 16, Dryden Press, Fort Worth.

Pindyck, R. and Rubinfeld, D. (1998), *Microeconomics*, 4th edn, Chs 10 and 11, Macmillan, London.

Sloman, J. (2000), *Economics*, 4th edn, Pearson Education, Harlow.

Varian, H. (1999), *Intermediate Microeconomics*, 5th edn, Chs 1, 23 and 24, Norton, New York.

Advanced texts
Gravelle, H. and Rees, (1992), *Microeconomics*, 2nd edn, Ch. 11, Longman, Harlow.

Mas-Colell, A., Whinston, M. D. and Green, J. R. (1995), *Microeconomic Theory*, Ch. 12, Oxford University Press, Oxford.

Articles and
other sources

Bell, W. (1968), 'The effects of monopoly profits and wages on prices and consumers' surplus in US manufacturing', *Western Economic Journal*, 6.

Bishop, M. and Thompson, D. (1992), 'Peak-load pricing in aviation', *Journal of Transport Economics and Policy*, XXVI, 1.

Browning, E. (1997), 'A neglected welfare cost of monopoly – and most other product market distortions', *Journal of Public Economics*, 66.

Cowling, K. and Mueller, D. (1978), 'The social costs of monopoly', *Economic Journal*, 88.

Crew, M. A., Kleindorfer, P. R. and Smith, M. A. (1990), 'Peak-load pricing in postal services', *The Economic Journal*, 100, 402.

European Commission (1997), *Single Market Review: Impact on Services*, Subseries II, Volume 2, Kogan Page and Earthscan.

Fontes, M. (1995), 'Price discrimination and elasticity', *Economic Review*, 12, 4, April.

Harberger, A. (1954), 'Monopoly and resource allocation', *American Economic Review Papers and Proceedings*, 44.

Healey, N. (1999), 'The multinational corporation', in Griffiths, A. and Wall, S. (eds) *Applied Economics*, 8th edn, Pearson Education, Harlow.

Needham, D. (1978), *The Economies of Industrial Structure, Conduct and Performance*, Holt Rinehart and Winston, London.

Lieberman, M. (1987), 'Excess capacity as a barrier to entry: an empirical appraisal', *Journal of Industrial Economics*, XXXV, 4.

Myers, G. (1993), 'Barriers to entry', *Economics and Business Education*, 1, 1, 3.

Pratten, C. (1987), 'A survey of the economics of scale', report prepared for the EC, *European Economy*, 1988, 35, March.

Sapir, A. (1993), 'The structure of services in Europe: a conceptual framework', in *European Economy*, *Market Services and European Integration*, 3, Social Europe, European Communities.

Schwartzman, D. (1960), 'The burden of monopoly', *Journal of Political Economy*, 68.

Siegfried, J. J. and Tiemann, T. K. (1974), 'The welfare costs of monopoly: an interindustry analysis', *Economic Inquiry*, 12.

Stewart, G. (1996), 'Takeovers', *Economic Review*, 14, 1.

Stewart, G. (1998), 'Driving forces', *Economic Review*, 16, 1.

Worcester, D. A. (1973), 'New estimates of the welfare loss to monopoly in the US, 1956–69', *Southern Economic Journal*, 40.

Chapter 8

Oligopoly

Oligopoly is a market structure in which a few firms dominate the industry. Crucially these few firms recognise their rivalry and interdependence, fully aware that any action on their part is likely to induce counter-actions by their rivals. This leads us into a consideration of strategies and counter-strategies between market participants, some of which can be modelled in terms of 'game playing' situations (see Chapter 9). Duopoly, with two sellers, is an extreme form of oligopoly.

The central task of market theory is to predict how firms will set prices and output. In perfect competition and pure monopoly we can make definite predictions. In perfect competition it can be shown that in the long run price will be equal to the lowest possible average costs of the firm – what Adam Smith called 'the natural price'. In pure monopoly the firm seeking to maximise profits will restrict output and raise prices until marginal revenue exactly equals marginal costs. In oligopoly, as we shall see, there can be no such precision.

As with monopolistic competition, oligopoly is a market form intermediate between the two extremes of perfect competition and pure monopoly. However, oligopoly differs from monopolistic competition in a number of ways:

- There are few sellers in oligopoly, and new entry is difficult; there are many sellers in monopolistic competition, and new entry is easy.
- Products in oligopoly may be either homogeneous or non-homogeneous (product differentiation); products in monopolistic competition are invariably non-homogeneous.
- Firms in oligopoly recognise their interdependence; firms in monopolistic competition act independently.
- Prices in oligopoly tend to be 'sticky' or rigid; prices in monopolistic competition tend to be flexible.

It is with regard to this last characteristic of oligopoly markets that the kinked-demand curve model was developed as an explanation of price rigidity.

▪ Kinked demand theory

In 1939 Hall and Hitch in the UK and Sweezy in the USA proposed a theory to explain why prices often remain stable in oligopoly markets, even when costs rise. A central feature of that theory was the existence of a **kinked demand curve**.

To illustrate this we take an oligopolistic market that sells similar, but not identical products, i.e. there is some measure of product differentiation. If one firm raises its price, it will then lose some, though not all, of its custom to rivals. Similarly, if the firm reduces its price it will attract some, though not all, of its rivals' custom. How much custom is lost or gained will depend partly on whether or not the rivals *follow* the initial price change.

Extensive interviews with managers of firms in oligopoly markets led Hall and Hitch to conclude that most firms have learned a common lesson from past experience as to how rivals react: namely, that if the firm were to raise its price above the current level (P in Fig. 8.1), its rivals *would not* follow, content to let the firm lose sales to them. The firm would then expect its demand curve to be relatively elastic (dK) for price rises. However, if the firm were to reduce its price, rivals *would* follow to protect their market share, so that the firm would gain few extra sales. The firm would then expect its demand curve to be relatively inelastic (KD^1) for price reductions. Overall the firm will believe that its demand curve is kinked at the current price P, taking the form of dKD^1 in Fig. 8.1.

One can intuitively see why this belief will lead to price stickiness, since the firm will rapidly lose market share if it raises price, and gain little market share from reducing price. The kinked demand (average revenue) curve of the firm, dKD^1, will have a discontinuity (L–M) in its associated marginal revenue curve directly below the kink point K. This is because two quite separate marginal revenue curves are associated with segments dK and KD^1 of the kinked demand curve, namely dL and MN respectively. The marginal cost curve could then vary between MC_1 and MC_2 *without* causing the firm to alter its profit-maximising price P (or its profit-maximising output Q).

Despite the usefulness of the kinked demand curve model as a descriptive tool in the understanding of oligopoly behaviour, it still faces a number of problems:

● The theory does not explain *how* oligopolists actually set an initial price; merely why a price, once set, might be stable. Kinked demand is not a theory of price determination.

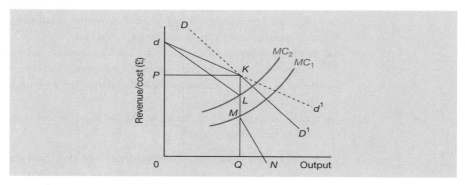

Fig. 8.1 **Kinked demand curve and price stability.**

Notes: d–d^1 = Demand curve when rivals do not follow price changes
  D–D^1 = Demand curve when rivals do dollow price changes
  dkD^1 = Kinked demand curve
  $dLMN$ = Associated marginal revenue curve

- The observed stickiness of prices may have little to do with the rival firm reaction patterns of kinked demand theory. It is, for instance, administratively expensive to change prices too often.
- The assertion, implicit in kinked demand theory, that prices are more sticky under oligopoly than under other market forms has not received strong support from empirical studies. For instance, Stigler, in a sample of 100 firms across 21 industries in the USA, had concluded as early as the 1940s that oligopoly prices hardly merited the description 'sticky'.
- The precise nature of any kink in the demand curve may depend on the economic conditions prevailing at the time. For example, some studies have found that price increases are more likely to be followed during booms, while price reductions are more likely to be followed during times of recession.

We return to attempts to further analyse oligopoly markets in the next section. There we consider a variety of *non-collusive* theories, where firms act independently, while still recognising their interdependence. Kinked demand theory is of this type, as are a variety of game-theoretic solutions. We also consider *collusive theories*, involving elements of agreement between firms, both formal (e.g. cartel) and informal (e.g. tacit agreements), directed towards regulating markets and restricting uncertainty.

Theoretical developments

In the introduction to this chapter we defined oligopoly as competition among the few that may, or may not, also involve product differentiation. A key feature of oligopoly markets is that the number of firms is sufficiently small for each firm to be aware of the pricing policy of its rivals, so that it will have to try to anticipate its rivals' *reactions* to its own pricing decisions. Further, where products *are* differentiated, the firm will have to estimate the degree of brand loyalty that customers have for its products or indeed those of its rivals: the greater that loyalty, the smaller the effect of price changes on consumer demand. This constant need to anticipate the reaction both of rivals and of consumers creates a high degree of uncertainty in oligopoly markets.

Despite this uncertainty, the importance of the oligopoly-type of market structure in modern economies has encouraged the quest for theories to explain and predict firm behaviour. Although little progress seems to have been made in devising a general theory of oligopoly behaviour, some progress has been made in understanding the behaviour of particular firms in particular types of oligopoly situation. We might usefully review a number of such theories, keeping a close eye on firm practice.

Non-collusive oligopoly

First, we consider situations in which each firm decides upon its strategy *without* any formal or even tacit collusion between rivals. There are essentially three approaches that the firm can adopt to handle interdependence when oligopoly is *non-collusive*:

- The firm could assume that whatever it decides to do, its rivals will *not react*, i.e. they will ignore its strategies. This assumption may reasonably be valid for day-to-day, routine decisions, but is hardly realistic for major initiatives. The Cournot duopoly model is, however, of this type. Each firm simply observes what the other does, and then adopts a strategy that maximises its own profits. It makes no attempt to evaluate potential reactions by the rival firm to its own profit-maximising strategy.

- The firm could assume that rivals *will* react to its own strategies, and then use past experience to assess the form that reaction might take. This learning process underlies the reaction-curve model of Stackelberg. It also underlies the kinked demand model considered earlier in the chapter (pp. 332–3), with firms learning that rivals do not match price increases, but certainly do match any price reductions.
- Instead of using past experience to assess future reactions by rivals, the firm itself could try to *identify* the best possible move that the opposition could make to each of its own strategies. The firm could then plan countermeasures if the rival reacts in this (for the rival) optimal way. As we shall see in the next chapter, this is the essence of *game theory*.

We now consider in more detail models consistent with each of these approaches, starting with the Cournot duopoly (two firm) model.

Interdependence unrecognised

Cournot model

The French economist Augustin Cournot developed the earliest duopoly model in 1838. We first consider the original **Cournot model** before looking at the same idea using later conceptual ideas (reaction curves) to express that model.

Cournot assumed there to be two firms, each using a well for mineral water (homogeneous product) and operating with zero costs. Their output is sold on a market with a linear (straight line) demand curve. A key feature of the model is that each firm *observes* the initial action of the other and then seeks to maximise its own profits subject to that initial action.

In Fig. 8.2, assume that Firm A is the first to begin the production and sale of mineral water. Faced with market demand DD_1 it will produce quantity Q_1 at price P_1, where $MR_A = MC_A$ (remember $MC_A = 0$).

At this output, price elasticity of demand = 1, total revenue is a maximum, and marginal revenue = 0. With zero costs, total profit $(TR - TC)$ is also a maximum. (Note that output $0Q_1$ will be half output $0D_1$ – see p. 55.)

Fig. 8.2 **Cournot equilibrium in a duopoly model with zero marginal costs.**

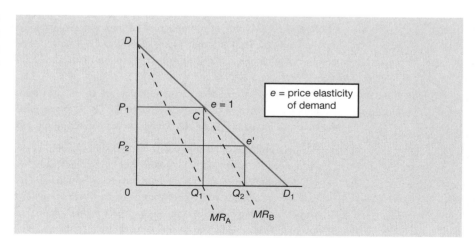

Firm B now assumes that Firm A will keep its output fixed at $0Q_1$. It estimates the (residual) demand available for its product as CD_1 with associated marginal revenue curve MR_B. Firm B will maximise its profits by producing $Q_1 - Q_2$ output at price P_2; (remember $MC_B = 0$). Note that firm B is producing $\frac{1}{2}$ the output not supplied by A (i.e. $\frac{1}{2}$ of Q_1D) to maximise its revenue and therefore profits (with zero costs). In other words, B produces ($\frac{1}{2}$ of $\frac{1}{2}$) = $\frac{1}{4}$ of the total market.

Of course we have not yet found an equilibrium solution since Firm A will now observe that $\frac{1}{4}$ of the market is supplied by Firm B. Firm A will react to this situation. In seeking to maximise profits it will produce $\frac{1}{2}$ of the market *not supplied by B*. Since B supplies $\frac{1}{4}$ of the market, A will now produce $\frac{1}{2}(1 - \frac{1}{4}) = \frac{1}{2} \cdot \frac{3}{4} = \frac{3}{8}$ of the total market.

Firm B in turn observes A's actions of supplying $\frac{3}{8}$ of the market and reacts by now producing $\frac{1}{2}$ of the market *not supplied by A*, i.e. $\frac{1}{2}(1 - \frac{3}{8}) = \frac{5}{16}$.

Long-run equilibrium under Cournot

This action/reaction pattern will continue until, as it turns out, an equilibrium is reached with each firm producing $\frac{1}{3}$ of the total market. The outcome in each of the first four periods of action and reaction of firms A and B is demonstrated here.

- The product of firm A in successive periods is
  period 1: $\frac{1}{2}$
  period 2: $\frac{1}{2}(1 - \frac{1}{4}) = \frac{3}{8} = \frac{1}{2} - \frac{1}{8}$
  period 3: $\frac{1}{2}(1 - \frac{5}{16}) = \frac{13}{22} = \frac{1}{2} - \frac{1}{8} - \frac{1}{32}$
  period 4: $\frac{1}{2}(1 - \frac{42}{128}) = \frac{43}{128} = \frac{1}{2} - \frac{1}{8} - \frac{1}{32} - \frac{1}{128}$

We observe that the output of A declines gradually. We may rewrite this expression as follows:

$$\begin{bmatrix} \text{Product of A} \\ \text{in equilibrium} \end{bmatrix} = \frac{1}{2} - \frac{1}{8} - \frac{1}{32} - \frac{1}{128}\ldots\ldots$$

$$\frac{1}{2} - [\frac{1}{8} + \frac{1}{8} \times \frac{1}{4} + \frac{1}{8} \times (\frac{1}{4})^2 + \frac{1}{8} \times (\frac{1}{4})^3 + \ldots].$$

The section in brackets is a *geometric progression* of the form

$$S_n = a + ar + ar^2 + ar^3 + \ldots ar^{n-1}, \text{ with } n \text{ terms.}$$

Using the formula for the sum of a geometric progression (S_n) with common ratio $r = \frac{1}{4}$, initial term $a = \frac{1}{8}$, and number of periods $= n$:

where $S_n = \dfrac{a(1 - r^n)}{(1 - r)}$

$$S_n = \frac{\frac{1}{8}(1 - \frac{1}{4}^n)}{(1 - \frac{1}{4})}$$

and where n is very large, we have:

$$S_n = \frac{\frac{1}{8}(1 - 0)}{\frac{3}{4}}$$

$$S_n = \frac{1}{8} \times \frac{4}{3} = \frac{4}{34} = \frac{1}{6}$$

So $\begin{bmatrix} \text{Product of A} \\ \text{in equilibrium} \end{bmatrix} = \frac{1}{2} - \frac{1}{6} = \frac{2}{6} = \frac{1}{3}$

- The product of firm B in successive periods is

  period 2: $\frac{1}{2}\left(\frac{1}{2}\right) = \frac{1}{4}$

  period 3: $\frac{1}{2}\left(1 - \frac{3}{8}\right) = \frac{5}{16} = \frac{1}{4} + \frac{1}{16}$

  period 3: $\frac{1}{2}\left(1 - \frac{11}{32}\right) = \frac{21}{64} = \frac{1}{4} + \frac{1}{16} + \frac{1}{64}$

  period 4: $\frac{1}{2}\left(1 - \frac{43}{128}\right) = \frac{85}{256} = \frac{1}{4} + \frac{1}{32} + \frac{1}{32} + \frac{1}{256}$

We observe that B's output increases, but at a declining rate. We may write

$$\begin{bmatrix} \text{Product of B} \\ \text{in equilibrium} \end{bmatrix} = \frac{1}{4} + \frac{1}{4} \times \frac{1}{4} + \frac{1}{4} \times \left(\frac{1}{4}\right)^2 + \frac{1}{4} \times \left(\frac{1}{4}\right)^3 + \dots$$

Applying the above expression for the summation of a declining geometric series over a large n we find:

$$\begin{bmatrix} \text{Product of B} \\ \text{in equilibrium} \end{bmatrix} = \frac{\frac{1}{4}\left(1 - \frac{1}{4}^n\right)}{1 - \frac{1}{4}} = \frac{\frac{1}{4}(1 - 0)}{\frac{3}{4}} = \frac{1}{4} \times \frac{4}{3} = \frac{1}{3}$$

Thus the Cournot solution is stable. Each firm supplies $\frac{1}{3}$ of the market at a common price. Each firm has observed the action of the other firm ($\frac{1}{3}$ output) and maximised its profits subject to that action. There is no reason for either firm now to change what it is doing.

Cournot equilibrium versus monopoly and competitive equilibrium

With $\frac{2}{3}$ of the total market supplied, the equilibrium price will be below P_1 in Fig. 8.2, i.e. below the *monopoly* price. However, the equilibrium price will be above the *competitive* price, which is zero (given zero marginal costs).

Extension of models beyond duopoly

It can be shown that if there are three firms in the industry, each will produce one quarter of the market and all of them together will supply $\frac{3}{4} (= \frac{1}{4} \times 3)$ of the entire market OD_1. In general, if there are n firms in the industry each will provide $[1/(n + 1)]$ of the market, and the industry output will be $[n/(n + 1)] = [1/(n + 1)] n$. It follows that as more firms are assumed to exist in the industry, the greater is the quantity supplied and the lower is the (common) price. Therefore the larger the number of original firms in the market, the closer the equilibrium output and price to the competitive levels.

Criticisms of Cournot

- Firms behave naively. In each time period they simply observe the other firm's action and then seek to maximise profits subject to that action. They do not learn from any past mistakes in predicting competitor actions and reactions.
- The model is *closed* in the sense that we must initially assume a specified number of players (two or more). In other words free entry is not allowed; the number of firms in the first period corresponds exactly to the number of firms in the final period.
- The adjustment period (the total time taken to reach the stable equilibrium) is indeterminate. We do not know how long it will be.

Refinement of Cournot: reaction curve models

We can now impose a later theoretical framework onto the Cournot model, involving isoprofit curves and reaction curves. This approach will be useful in highlighting key features of Cournot and other oligopoly models.

Isoprofit curves   An **isoprofit curve** is the set of points yielding a given (*iso* = constant) level of profit. In a duopoly model an isoprofit curve will indicate the respective levels of output of each firm consistent with a given level of profit for one firm.

In Fig. 8.3 we have a set of isoprofit curves for Firms A and B respectively. Note the following features:

- Each isoprofit curve is *concave* to the axis representing the output of the firm in question. So in Fig. 8.3(a) the isoprofit curves for Firm A are concave to the axis representing output of A (Q_A).
- Each isoprofit curve *further away* from the axis representing the output of the firm in question corresponds to a lower level of profit for that firm.

Let us consider each of these features more carefully before using them to derive the reaction curves of each firm.

Concave isoprofit curves   For firms producing *substitute* commodities, the isoprofit curve will be concave to the axis representing the output of the firm in question (Q_A for Firm A), as shown in Fig. 8.4(a).

Suppose Firm B decides to produce output B_1. Drawing the horizontal line at B_1, parallel to Q_A, we see that this line intersects the isoprofit curve π_1 for Firm A at points f and g. In other words, output combination B_1A_f will give Firm A profit π_1, as will output combination B_1A_g. We now repeat this approach, but this time assume that Firm B decides to produce output level B_2. This time output combinations B_2A_h and B_2A_i will give Firm A profit π_1. We see that initially *both* firms A and B can produce more, consistent with Firm A achieving π_1 level of profits. An elastic market demand curve will allow the fall in price from greater combined output to raise total revenue. Firm A can therefore produce more ($A_f - A_h$) *and* Firm B can produce more ($B_1 - B_2$), yet profits for Firm A are unchanged at π_1, the extra revenue *to A* from increased output exactly offsetting the extra costs of producing increased output. Of course profit is revenue minus cost, so Firm A may also be benefiting from cost reductions via

Fig. 8.3 **Isoprofit maps.**

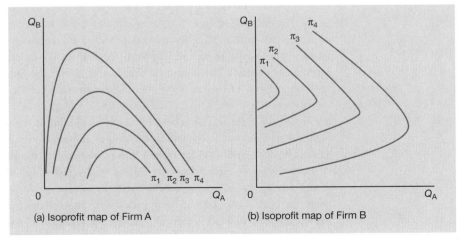

(a) Isoprofit map of Firm A   (b) Isoprofit map of Firm B

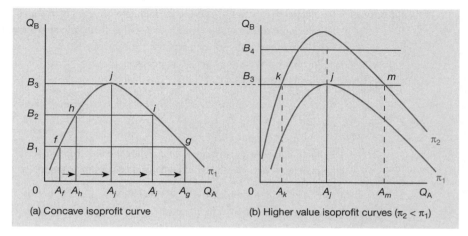

Fig. 8.4 **Key features of the isoprofit map: Firm A.**

(a) Concave isoprofit curve

(b) Higher value isoprofit curves ($\pi_2 < \pi_1$)

scale economies allowing higher output to be consistent with the same profit. This possibility of *both* firms increasing output and Firm A's profits remaining constant at π_1 is exhausted beyond combination B_3A_j. After this, any increased output of A can only yield Firm A the same profit level if the output of Firm B *declines*. We have now exhausted the possibilities (via high price elasticity of demand) of any fall in price via greater combined output raising total revenue for A. Similarly economies of scale have been exhausted with fewer (if any) cost savings available from higher output of A. It follows that more output of Firm A beyond A_j can only be consistent with the given level of profits π_1, if the output of Firm B declines. This pattern yields the concave (to Q_A) isoprofit maps of Figs 8.3 and 8.4.

Higher value isoprofit curves For firms producing *substitute* commodities the successive isoprofit curves will be as shown in Fig. 8.4(b). Each isoprofit curve is further away from the axis representing the output of the firm in question (Q_A for Firm A), corresponding to a lower level of profit ($\pi_2 < \pi_1$).

In Fig. 8.4(b), if Firm B produces output B_3 then the *highest* profit obtained by Firm A is π_1 at point j, producing output A_j. Any other output level by Firm A will yield *lower* profit. For example, if Firm A reduces output from A_j to A_k, then it will receive less revenue (less output at a higher market price on the relatively elastic segment of the demand curve) and therefore less profit (except in the unlikely event of costs falling more than revenue). The output combination B_3A_k will therefore correspond to a lower level of profit (π_2) for Firm A than output combination B_3A_j (π_1). Alternatively if Firm A increases output from A_j to A_m, then it will also receive less revenue (more output at a lower market price on the relatively inelastic segment of the demand curve), and face higher costs from increased output. The output combination B_3A_m will also correspond to a lower level of profit (π_2) for Firm A than output combination B_3A_j (π_1).

Finally, suppose Firm A leaves its output unchanged at A_j, but Firm B raises its output from B_3 to B_4. Again, we can establish that the output combination B_4A_j will yield lower profit for Firm A than output combination B_3A_j. This follows from the fact that increased market output will depress price and reduce the revenue to Firm A from output A_j.

Clearly any output combination horizontally to the left or right of point *j*, or vertically above it, must correspond to a *lower* level of profit for Firm A. Put another way, for any given output that Firm B may produce, there is a unique level of output for Firm A that maximises the profits of Firm A. This unique profit-maximising level of output is obtained at the point of *tangency* between the horizontal line through the given level of output of Firm B and the isoprofit curve for Firm A nearest to its output axis. Isoprofit curves *further from* Q_A will have lower profit ($\pi_2 < \pi_1$), and of course vice versa: isoprofit curves *nearer to* Q_A will have higher profit ($\pi_1 > \pi_2$).

Reaction curves

We can now use our analysis to derive **reaction curves** for each firm. These curves show how each firm determines its output as a reaction to the *given* output decision of the other firm. For a profit-maximising Firm A, its reaction curve will be as shown in Fig. 8.5(a). It is the locus of points of highest profit that Firm A can attain given the level of output of Firm B. As we can see, the highest points of successive isoprofit curves lie to the left of each other as we move further from Q_A in Fig. 8.5(a). Connecting these highest points together gives us Firm A's reaction curve.

Firm B's isoprofit curves in Fig. 8.5(b) are concave to the Q_B axis, and the principles affecting their shape and position are as outlined for Firm A. The highest points on successive isoprofit curves lie to the right of each other as we move further from Q_B. Connecting these highest points together gives us Firm B's reaction curve.

Cournot equilibrium revisited

We now use our analysis to reconsider the equilibrium of Cournot (p. 336). Cournot's equilibrium is shown (in Fig. 8.6) as being determined by the intersection of the two reaction curves at point *e*, giving equilibrium outputs of A_e and B_e for firms A and B respectively.

Stable equilibrium

Provided A's reaction curve is steeper than B's reaction curve, then the Cournot equilibrium will be *stable*, in the sense that any departure from it will lead to events that tend to restore it. For example, if Firm B decided to produce B_1, *less* than the Cournot equilibrium (B_e), then Firm A reacts with (profit-maximising) output A_1. Firm B now assumes that A will keep its output fixed at A_1 and reacts with profit-maximising output B_2, to

Fig. 8.5 **Firm reaction curves.**

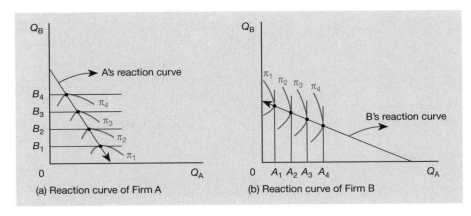

(a) Reaction curve of Firm A

(b) Reaction curve of Firm B

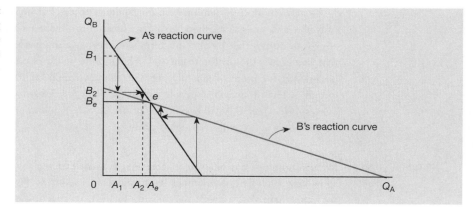

which in turn Firm A reacts with output A_2, eventually restoring the Cournot equilibrium A_eB_e. If the departure had been via one or other firm producing *more* than the Cournot equilibrium, the impact would have been the same, namely return to the equilibrium A_eB_e, which is therefore stable.

Non-profit-maximising equilibrium for the industry

Figure 8.7 helps us to see that the Cournot equilibrium at point *e* does *not* maximise profits for the industry (i.e. joint profits under duopoly).

The '**contract curve**' is the locus (set) of points of tangency between the isoprofit curves of the respective firms. Points **on** the contract curve correspond to situations where profits for the industry are maximised; points **off** the contract curve correspond to non-profit-maximising situations for the industry. Clearly the Cournot equilibrium, *e*, is *off* the contract curve. We can use Fig. 8.7 to show why industry profits would be higher than at *e* for points on the contract curve. For instance, a reallocation of outputs between the firms from *e* to *f* would keep Firm A's profits *constant* at π_{A3} but *raise* Firm B's profits from π_{B3} to π_{B2}. Alternatively a reallocation of outputs from *e* to *g* would keep Firm B's profits constant at π_{B3} but raise Firm A's profits from π_{A3} to π_{A2}.

Fig. 8.7 **Cournot equilibrium and the contract curve.**

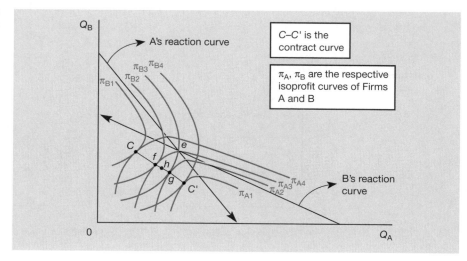

At any intermediate point on the contract curve between f and g, say point h, the real-location of outputs from e would raise the profit of both firms A and B. In other words, only points (output combinations) *on* the contract curve maximise joint or industry profits. Only at these output combinations is it no longer possible to raise the profit of one firm without lowering the profit of the other firm. Why then is the allocation of outputs, e, an equilibrium under Cournot if it does not maximise joint profits? The answer lies in the assumptions for firm behaviour under the Cournot model. Firms simply *observe* the action of their rival and then *react* assuming that the original rival action will remain unchanged whatever they themselves do. Even when past experience tells firms that this is not the case, they continue to behave as though it is. In other words there is *no learning* in the Cournot model from past experience. Each firm acts independently, ignoring any strategic pattern in the actions and reactions of the other firm.

Nash equilibrium

A **Nash equilibrium** occurs when each firm is choosing the strategy that maximises its profit (or achieves some other intended objective), given the strategies of the other firms in the market. In the Cournot duopoly situation, the Nash equilibrium occurs where each firm has selected the output level that maximises its profit in response to an output level that the other firm also regards as maximising its profit: e.g. point e in Fig. 8.7 where the respective firm reaction 'curves' intersect. This is sometimes called a Cournot–Nash duopoly equilibrium or (if more than two firms) a Cournot–Nash oligopoly equilibrium.

Bertrand model

Bertrand argued that it is more realistic to suppose that a rival firm will select the *price* that maximises its profit rather than the output. Each firm then assumes that the rival firm will not change its price. Bertrand further assumes, in duopoly, that each firm has sufficient capacity to meet the *entire* market demand.

In the simplified diagram of Fig. 8.2 (p. 334) with zero marginal costs, we might start with Firm A setting the monopoly price P_1 and selling Q_1. Firm B then enters the market at a lower price than P_1 (say P_2) and this time secures *all* the market demand at that price. Firm A then lowers the price still further and captures the market. The price war concludes when price is zero and the competitive output D_1 is produced.

More realistically we can examine the **Bertrand model** using our reaction curve approach. The difference is this time that *prices* and not outputs are represented on the respective firm axes, as in Fig. 8.8.

This time the isoprofit curves are *convex* to the axis representing the price of the firm in question. In Fig. 8.8(a), each isoprofit curve for Firm A shows the set of *price combinations* of A and B that would yield a given level of profit for A. The shape of A's isoprofit curves are shown as convex to its price axis P_A. In other words, as Firm B reduces its price, Firm A can at first only retain a given level of profit by responding with a price cut. Suppose we start with B setting price P_{B1} and A setting price P_{A1}, giving Firm A profit level π_2. Firm B now cuts its price and firm A responds with price cuts to remain on π_2, at least until point e is reached on π_2. Point e corresponds to B setting price P_{B2} and A setting price P_{A2}. However, any *further* price reduction by B will leave A unable to defend its profit level (hence we reach a minimum turning point of π_2 in Fig. 8.8(a) – i.e. convex shape). If, for example, B cuts its price to P_{B3} and A keeps its price unchanged at P_{A2}, A will now be on an isoprofit curve nearer to its price axis than π_2 (here between π_2 and π_1), corresponding to a *lower* level of profit. This reduction in A's profits is due in

Fig. 8.8 **Isoprofit maps and reaction curves for Bertrand's model.**

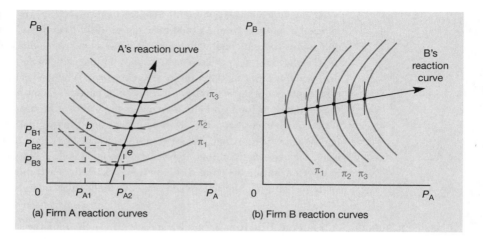

(a) Firm A reaction curves   (b) Firm B reaction curves

part to a fall in B's price taking consumers (and therefore revenue) from A, and possibly in part to higher average costs now facing A (as a result of the loss of output causing existing plant to be run by A at suboptimal levels). It follows that the lower the isoprofit curve, the lower the profit level represented.

Note also that these successive minimum points lie to the right of each other as we move away from that firm's price axis (P_A in Fig. 8.8(a)). This reflects the fact that as Firm A moves to a higher level of profit, it gains some of B's customers because of B's price increases. This is so even though A itself is also increasing its price, though by less than B.

As before, the *reaction curves* can be derived by joining together the turning points of the respective isoprofit curves – this time *minima* rather than maxima as before (see Fig. 8.8(a) and (b)).

Figure 8.9 shows a **stable equilibrium** reached at e in the Bertrand model. Any departure from e sets in motion forces that return the model to e. For example, if Firm A charges a price higher than e, say P_{A1}, Firm B will set its profit-maximising price (given P_{A1}) at P_{B2}. In the next period Firm A responds by setting P_{A2}, and so on, returning us to e. The same forces apply if the initial price is set by A below e.

Fig. 8.9 **The Bertrand (Nash) equilibrium using reaction curve analysis; a stable equilibrium.**

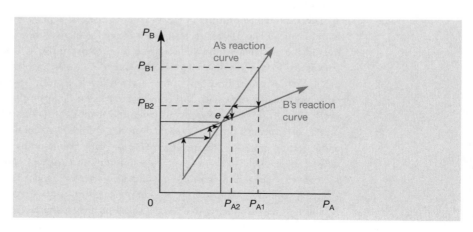

This Bertrand equilibrium at *e* is also a **Nash equilibrium**, with each firm selecting a price level that maximises its profits in response to a price level which the other firm also regards as maximising its profits.

As with Cournot, we can see from Fig. 8.10 that the Bertrand–Nash equilibrium (*e*) is *not* one that maximises industry profits (joint profits in duopoly). At *e*, with the corresponding price combination P_{Ae}, P_{Be}, the profits earned are π_{1A} and π_{1B} for firms A and B respectively. However, each firm can do better *without* the other firm doing any worse. For example, with the price combinations given by point *C*, we have the same profit for B (π_{1B}) but higher profit for A ($\pi_{4A} > \pi_{1A}$). Alternatively, with the price combinations given by point *C'*, we have the same profit for A (π_{1A}) but higher profit for B ($\pi_{4B} > \pi_{1B}$). The contract curve *C–C'* is the set of tangency points between the respective iso-profit curves, and is the set of price combinations that alone will maximise industry (joint) profits. Only at these price combinations will it no longer be possible to raise the profit of one firm without reducing the profit of the other firm.

Criticisms of Bertrand model

- The same 'naivety' of failing to learn from past experience is exhibited here, as under Cournot. Each firm assumes that, under Bertrand, the *price* the rival sets is given and seeks to maximise profits subject to that particular price.
- As with Cournot, industry profits are *not* maximised. It is possible in the Bertrand equilibrium to change the price combination so that at least one firm gains and no other firm loses.
- As with Cournot the model is closed, in the sense that it does not provide for new firm entry.
- The Bertrand–Nash equilibrium is stable, provided A's reaction curve is steeper than B's.
- The Bertrand equilibrium price will be the same as the competitive price. In the original mineral water example of Cournot with zero marginal costs, the equilibrium price will be zero (p. 336). If production is *not* costless, the price will fall to the level which just covers that marginal cost.

Fig. 8.10 **Bertrand (Nash) equilibrium (*e*) and the contract curve.**

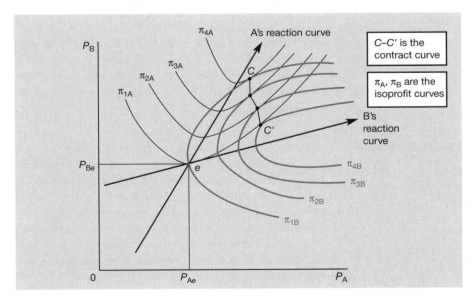

Remember that each firm (in a duopoly) has sufficient capacity to satisfy the entire market demand. Therefore each firm will have the incentive to undercut the price of the other firm and capture the entire demand. Such a situation cannot be a *Nash equilibrium* since the firm that will otherwise lose its entire market will have the incentive to change its price, in turn undercutting its rival. Only when each firm is charging a price covering its marginal costs (including an element for normal profit) will a **Bertrand–Nash equilibrium** result: any further price cut (or price rise) implies a less advantageous outcome for each firm (price cut – losses, i.e. fail to cover normal profits; price rise – losses, i.e. all customers move to the rival).

- The Bertrand equilibrium output occurs at a higher level than the Cournot equilibrium output. For example, in the simplified Cournot duopoly diagram of Fig. 8.2 (on p. 334) with identical (zero) firm marginal costs, each firm supplies $\frac{1}{3}$ of the market. In the Bertrand duopoly representing the same situation, each firm sets a common price = marginal costs (here zero) and supplies an expected $\frac{1}{2}$ of the market.

■ Interdependence recognised

We now begin to explore some of the models that *do* take into account some recognised interdependence between sellers.

Chamberlin's model

Looking back to Fig. 8.2, Firm A initially selects the profit-maximising price–output combination P_1Q_1, and Firm B then produces Q_1Q_2, as in the earlier Cournot model. However, this time A *recognises* that B will change its behaviour in response to any change in the behaviour of A. Since the maximum (joint) profit occurs at output $0Q_1$, Firm A cuts its output to $\frac{1}{2}0Q_1$, leaving B to produce $\frac{1}{2}0Q_1 = Q_1Q_2$. The outcome is a stable solution, which in effect is the profit-maximising monopoly situation. This is achieved without any explicit collusion – simply a recognition of interdependence and mutual benefit.

Sweezy's kinked demand model

Sweezy's kinked demand curve model has already been discussed (p. 332). It has similar features to Chamberlin in that interdependence is recognised in terms of different rival reactions to price rises than to price cuts. As we have seen price stickiness is one of the predictions of this model. We also considered in the earlier text a number of problems with this model.

Stackelberg's model

A more sophisticated model of recognised firm interdependence was proposed by the German economist H.V. Stackelberg, which extends some of the ideas of Cournot.

For simplicity we can illustrate **Stackelberg's oligopoly model** in the two-firm duopoly case. As with Cournot, the firms select *output* levels, giving isoprofit maps and reaction curves as shown in Fig. 8.11 (see also earlier Fig. 8.7).

Unlike Cournot, Stackelberg assumes that one duopolist recognises that the rival firm *acts* on the Cournot assumption. This sophisticated duopolist can then anticipate the reaction curve of the rival and take it into account in seeking its own profit-maximising strategy.

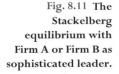

Fig. 8.11 **The Stackelberg equilibrium with Firm A or Firm B as sophisticated leader.**

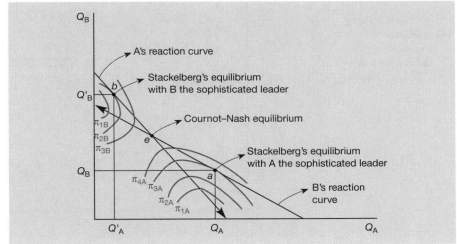

If Firm A is the sophisticated duopolist in Fig. 8.11, the highest level of profit that A can achieve *consistent with B's reactions* is π_{3A} with respective firm outputs Q_A and Q_B. This represents the tangency point *a* between B's reaction curve and A's highest-value (nearest to the origin) isoprofit curve. Firm A produces Q_A, Firm B reacts by producing Q_B, and we have a Nash equilibrium via this Stackelberg model. Essentially Firm A, the sophisticated duopolist, is acting as price leader and Firm B as the (Cournot–type) follower. Firm A, the sophisticated leader, benefits from abandoning naivety since it secures a higher isoprofit level (π_{3A}) than would occur if *both* firms were naive and the Cournot-style Nash equilibrium point *e* resulted. In this case Firm A would be on an isoprofit curve further from its axis and therefore of lower value than π_{3A}. However, Firm B loses as a result of its rival's sophistication, since at point *a* Firm B is on an isoprofit curve further away from its origin (lower value) than at the Cournot–Nash equilibrium point *e*.

Of course the whole situation would be reversed if Firm B was the sophisticated duopolist. Then Firm B would seek to achieve the highest level of profit consistent with its awareness of Firm A's Cournot-type reactions. This occurs at point *b*, with Firm B earning π_{2B}. This solution represents the tangency between A's reaction curve and B's highest value (nearest to its origin) isoprofit curve.

In either case we have a *stable* equilibrium with a leader and a follower, whether the final output combination is at point *a* or point *b*. However, what would be the outcome if *both* firms aspired to be leader and to secure the enhanced profits that result from such a sophisticated reading of the market? We can analyse this situation using Fig. 8.12.

The situation is now one of **disequilibrium** in which no one single solution can be predicted. Several possibilities might result.

- If each firm seeks to act as leader, making the (mistaken) assumption that the rival will act as follower, we get solution *d* with corresponding firm outputs Q''_A, Q''_B. Both firms will lose out in this situation, each being at a lower level of profit than would occur if both acted naively with a Cournot equilibrium *e*.
- A *price war* might result until one of the firms surrendered and allowed the other to act as leader. Eventually point *a* or *b* would then be a solution to the model.

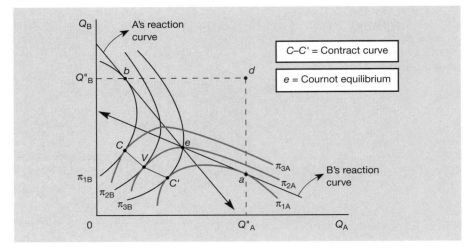

- *Collusion* might occur between the firms, with both firms in a duopoly seeking an agreement that leads each of them to a solution nearer to (or on) the joint profit-maximising contract curve C–C'. In terms of Fig. 8.12, Firm A will seek higher profits than π_{2A} achievable at e, and Firm B higher profits than π_{3B} achievable at e. Any point inside the segment VeC' would be a possible negotiated agreement leaving each better off than at the naive Cournot equilibrium e. The bargaining power of the respective firms will then dictate which is the prime beneficiary of such a collusive agreement.

Game theory   Before looking in detail at the kind of collusive agreements that might be reached in oligopoly situations, we briefly mention **game theory** as also representing situations in which interdependence is explicitly recognised. As with the previous models, this approach initially assumes non-collusive behaviour by rivals. Here interdependence is *recognised*, but instead of using past experience to assess future reactions by rivals, the firm itself tries to identify the possible moves that the rival could make to each of its strategies. The firm can then plan countermeasures if the rival *does* react in one or more of the anticipated ways. Game theory is the subject matter of Chapter 9.

Collusive oligopoly

When oligopoly is non-collusive, the firm uses guesswork and calculation to handle the uncertainty of its rivals' reactions. Another way of handling that uncertainty in markets that are interdependent is by some form of central coordination: in other words, **collusion**. At least two features of collusive oligopoly are worth emphasizing: first, the objectives that are sought through collusion; second, the methods that are used to promote collusion – these may be formal, as in a cartel, or informal, via tacit agreement.

'Perfect' collusion   This term is often used to refer to the **centralised cartel**, usually presumed to have as its key objective the maximisation of joint profits on behalf of its member firms. The firms may therefore seek to use some form of centralised body to coordinate their price, output and other policies to achieve maximum profits for the members of the cartel. In the extreme case the firms may act together as a monopoly, aggregating their marginal costs and equating these with marginal revenue for the whole market. If achieved, the result would be to maximise joint profits, with a unique industry price and output $(P_I Q_I)$, as in the simplified two-firm centralised cartel of Fig. 8.13.

A major problem is, of course, how to achieve the close coordination required. We consider this further later, but we might note from Fig. 8.13 that coordination is required both to *establish* the profit-maximising solution for the industry, $P_I Q_I$, and to *enforce* it once established. For instance, some agreement must be reached on sharing the output between the colluding firms. One solution is to equate marginal revenue for whole output Q_I with marginal cost for each firm, with Firm A producing Q_A and Firm B producing Q_B. A distribution of the joint profit-maximising output such that aggregate $MR = MC$ in each separate market is often called the *ideal* distribution. From Fig. 8.13 we can see that there is no other distribution that will raise total profits for the centralised cartel. For instance, one extra unit produced by Firm B will add more to overall cost than is saved by one less unit produced by Firm A (i.e. $MC_B > MC_A$). With revenue unchanged by such a reallocation of output, overall profit must fall for the centralised cartel. The shaded areas in Fig. 8.13 represent the short-run profits earned by the respective firms, given the quotas Q_A and Q_B. Whether the firms will acquiesce in such a share-out is quite another matter.

Whatever the agreement, it must remain in force – since if any firm produces above its quota, this will raise industry output, depress price and move the centralised cartel away from the joint profit-maximising solution.

Various cartels operate internationally. The most famous is OPEC, in which many, but not all (the UK is not a member), oil-exporting countries meet regularly to agree on prices and set production quotas. The International Air Transport Association (IATA) is the cartel of international airlines, and has sought to set prices for each route. A more recent example of an international cartel was brought to light by investigations during

Fig. 8.13 **Joint profit maximisation via centralised cartel.**

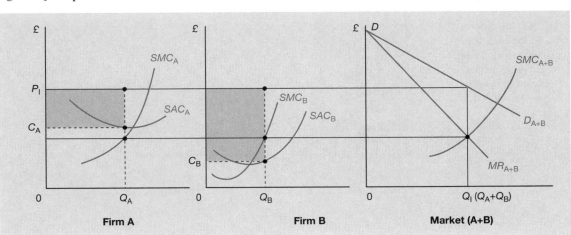

1990 into the activity of the International Telegraph and Telephone Consultative Committee (CCITT), a Geneva-based 'club' consisting of the main international telephone companies of the major industrial countries such as AT & T (USA), British Telecom (UK), Deutsche Bundespost (Germany), France Telecom (France), Telecom Canada (Canada) and KDD (Japan), all of which belong to the group.

The CCITT had a book of 'recommendations' for its member companies, which included two important features. First, it suggested a complicated method of sharing the revenues received from international telephone calls. Second, it suggested that members of the group should not lease too many of their international telephone circuits to other private companies, since this could increase potential competition.

Incentives to breach quotas

The arrangements we have identified for the centralised cartel may create incentives for individual firms to leave the cartel and act independently. Should most other firms remain within the cartel, then a firm acting independently can expect to face a *more price-elastic demand curve* than exists for the market as a whole. In Fig. 8.14 Firm A acts independently and therefore faces a more price-elastic demand curve, $D_A D_A$, than that for market demand, $D_M D_M$. The reason for this is that should Firm A cut price around the originally established cartel price P_I, then it can expect to attract some existing consumers away from firms remaining within the cartel (who continue to charge P_I) as well as attract new consumers to the product. It follows that the marginal revenue for Firm A (MR_A), which operates an independent price-cutting policy around P_I, will be higher than the marginal revenue for the market (MR_M) around market output Q_I.

The original quota assigned to Firm A by the centralised cartel was Q_A, to be sold at the (market-wide) price P_I. However, by cutting price to P^*_A, Firm A benefits from a price-elastic demand response, which results in output Q^*_A. If we assume that the additional output ($Q^*_A - Q_A$) requires no change in fixed costs (e.g. there is spare capacity), then the additional profit can be represented by the shaded area pqr, i.e. the change in total revenue (ΣMR_A) minus the change in total variable cost (ΣMC_A) over this extra output.

Of course, the price-cutting incentives for one firm in the centralised cartel potentially apply to *all* firms. However, any general tendency for firms within the cartel to cut

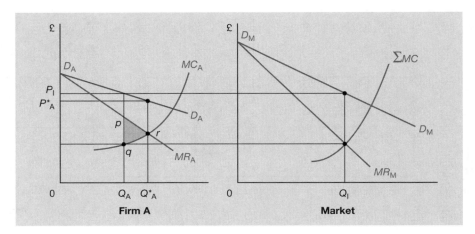

Fig. 8.14 Incentives for individual firms to lower price and increase output, breaking original agreed quota (Q_A).

prices and raise output will increase industry output, lower industry price, and move all firms away from their initial positions within the joint profit-maximising market solution $P_1 Q_1$, with unforeseeable impacts for individual firm profits. The influence of the centralised cartel is thereby weakened, and any previous gains from collusion may be lost.

'Imperfect' collusion Although cartels are illegal in most countries, various forms of **tacit collusion** undoubtedly occur, to which the team 'imperfect' collusion is often applied. In 1776 Adam Smith wrote in his *Wealth of Nations* that entrepreneurs rarely meet together without conspiring to raise prices at the expense of the consumer. Today the most usual method of tacit collusion is **price leadership**, in which one firm sets a price that the others follow. Such price leadership can take a variety of forms.

Price leadership models

Dominant-firm leadership Frequently the price leader is the dominant firm: controlling a major share of the industry output, it is regarded by other by other firms as the *price setter*. It sets the price that meets its primary objective, say maximising profits, and then allows smaller firms in the industry to sell all they wish at that price.

We can use Fig. 8.15 to indicate the price-setting problem faced by the dominant firm. We can effectively regard the smaller firms as *price takers*, so that the short-run supply curve for each of these smaller firms is its marginal cost curve above minimum average variable cost (see pp. 249–50). For the *aggregate* of these smaller firms in the industry (i.e. all but the dominant firm) the supply curve will then be the horizontal sum of these individual marginal cost curves (i.e. MC_S). The industry (or market) demand curve is $D_1 D'_1$. The *dominant* firm is seen here as behaving like a monopolist and equating its marginal revenue (MR_{DF}) to its marginal cost (MC_{DF}) in order to establish its profit-maximising price $0P$.

Fig. 8.15 Price leadership by a dominant firm (DF).

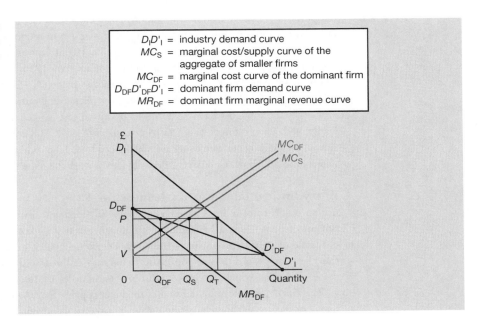

$D_1D'_1$ = industry demand curve
MC_S = marginal cost/supply curve of the aggregate of smaller firms
MC_{DF} = marginal cost curve of the dominant firm
$D_{DF}D'_{DF}D'_1$ = dominant firm demand curve
MR_{DF} = dominant firm marginal revenue curve

To explain this it will help to use Fig. 8.15 to demonstrate how the dominant firm demand curve (and therefore its marginal revenue curve) is established. Note that the demand curve for the dominant firm ($D_{DF}D'_{DF}$) can be regarded here as a *residual* after the smaller firms have supplied (MC_S) all they wish to at a given price. So at price $0V$ and below, when the smaller firms wish to supply zero, *all* the industry demand is available to the dominant firm (i.e. segment $D'_{DF}D'_I$). At the other extreme, for price $0D_{DF}$ and above, when the smaller firms wish to supply all that the industry requires, *none* of the industry demand is available to the dominant firm. For intermediate prices between $0V$ and $0D_{DF}$ the residual demand available to the dominant firm is given by $D_{DF}D'_{DF}$. In other words, between these (extreme) prices the quantity demanded from the dominant firm is the quantity demanded in the whole industry *minus* that quantity supplied by the (aggregate of) smaller firms. For example, at prices $0P$ the quantity demanded from the dominant firm is $0Q_T - 0Q_S = 0Q_{DF}$. The dominant firm's demand curve is then given by segments $D_{DF}D'_{DF}D'_I$ in Fig. 8.15.

Having derived the (residual) dominant firm demand curve, we can construct the associated marginal revenue curve (MR_{DF}) in the usual way. The profit-maximising dominant firm now equates MR_{DF} with MC_{DF} (shown here as $> MC_S$), giving output Q_{DF}. The profit-maximising dominant firm then sets price at $0P$. Note that only by setting price *along* the segment of its demand curve $D_{DF}D'_{DF}$ is the dominant firm acting in a way different from that of a monopolist.

At price $0P$ the dominant firm supplies $0Q_{DF}$ and the aggregate of smaller firms supplies $0Q_S$. It follows that $0P$ is a *market-clearing* price, with industry/total supply matching industry/total demand at that price. This must be so since, by construction $0Q_{DF} + 0Q_S = 0Q_T$, the total quantity demanded at price $0P$.

Low-cost price leadership Here the low-cost firm in the cartel establishes itself as price leader. Figure 8.16 shows how such a leadership might develop, taking a simplified duopoly situation for ease of illustration. Here each firm faces the same demand ($D_A = D_B$) and marginal revenue ($MR_A = MR_B$) curves for a homogeneous product, with the market equivalent curves (D_M, MR_M) being the horizontal summation of these. However, one Firm (A) is a low-cost producer and the other Firm (B) is a high-cost producer. As can be seen from Fig. 8.16, the profit-maximising price (P_A) for the low-cost Firm A is *below* that (P_B) for the high-cost Firm B (and corresponding output is higher, $Q_A > Q_B$).

Clearly the low-cost Firm A, in these circumstances, is likely to establish itself as price leader, with Firm B forced to lower its price from P_B to P_A. Of course this account is highly simplified, with other outcomes possible should we relax our assumption of a homogeneous product, allow for different firm objectives, vary the nature of the market, etc.

Entry limit model of price leadership Firms may seek to coordinate policies, not so much to maximise short-run profit but rather to maximise some longer-run notion of profit (see Chapter 5). A major threat to long-run profit is the potential entrance of new firms into the industry. Economists such as Andrews and Bain have therefore suggested that oligopolistic firms may collude with the objective of setting price below that which maximises joint profits, in order to deter new entrants.

The **limit price** can be defined as the highest price that the established firms believe they can charge without inducing entry. Its precise value will depend upon the nature

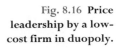

Fig. 8.16 **Price leadership by a low-cost firm in duopoly.**

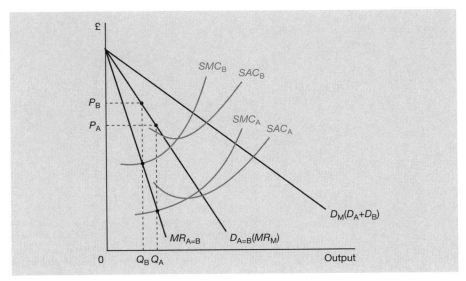

Note: In this simplified diagram $MR_A = MR_B$, $D_A = D_B = MR_M$

and extent of the barriers to entry (see p. 291) for any particular industry: the greater the barriers to entry, the higher the limit price will be.

Substantial economies of scale are a barrier to entry, in that a new firm will usually be smaller than established firms and will therefore be at a cost disadvantage. Product differentiation itself, reinforced by extensive advertising, is also a barrier since product loyalty, once captured, is difficult and expensive for new entrants to dislodge. Other barriers might include legally enforced patents to new technologies in the hands of established firms, and even price-inelastic market demands. The latter is a barrier in that the less price elastic the market demand for the product, the greater will be the price fall from any extra supply contributed by new entrants.

Deterring entry of a high-cost firm. If the potential entrant is expected to have higher costs (SAC_p) than those for existing firms (SAC_e), then the limit price (P_L) may be set (perhaps by the price leader) as shown in Fig. 8.17(a). This price is such that the potential new entrant will be unable, at any output, to earn even normal profit in the short run (normal profit is included in average costs). This will deter entry unless, in the long run, the potential entrant is able to move onto a lower SAC curve. To retain the limit price (P_L) the incumbents must collectively supply no more than ΣQ output to the market.

Deterring entry of a low-cost firm. Suppose, however, that the potential new entrant is at no cost disadvantage *vis-à-vis* existing firms, perhaps having access to the same technology and factor markets as incumbents. We could then regard both existing firms and the potential new entrant as having the same long-run average cost curve (LAC). The strategy of Fig. 8.17(a) no longer applies, since a price set below the average cost of the potential new entrant would now result in *all* firms in the industry earning less than normal profits.

Fig. 8.17 **Limit pricing to deter entry.**

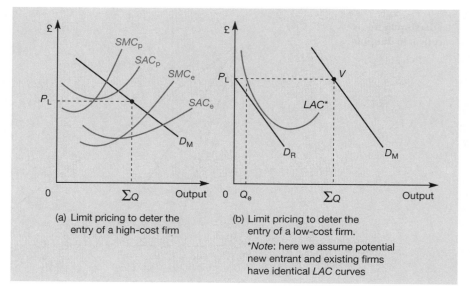

(a) Limit pricing to deter the
entry of a high-cost firm

(b) Limit pricing to deter the
entry of a low-cost firm.

Note: here we assume potential
new entrant and existing firms
have identical *LAC* curves

The suggestion in Fig. 8.17(b) is that the limit price (P_L) might be set by the price leader. At this price the existing oligopoly firms collectively supply ΣQ units of output to meet market demand, with all consumers willing to pay P_L or above already purchasing the product from incumbents. If the potential new entrant believes that existing firms will collectively *maintain* market output at ΣQ, it might regard the only market demand available for its product should it enter as being that implied by segment VD_M of the market demand curve below P_L. This *residual demand* is now transposed to the vertical axis in Fig. 8.17(b) and shown as $P_L D_R$.

> We can now see that the limit price needed to deter the entry of a low-cost firm is the price that results in the residual demand curve (D_R) lying below the *LAC* curve of the potential new entrant throughout its entire length.

The above analysis would apply to a potential new entrant with an *LAC* equivalent to that of existing firms, or even below that of existing firms. Of course the deterrent to entry here is the *threat* that the incumbents will collectively maintain output at ΣQ and maintain price at P_L should the new firm actually enter the market.

If the new firm were to 'call the bluff' of incumbents and actually enter, then the additional market output could be expected to lower price below P_L for all firms. It might then be in the interests of all firms for output levels (individual and collective) to be revised downwards, despite the earlier threats, enabling the price leader to establish a price at which all firms make at least normal profits.

Barometric-firm leadership In some cases the price leader is a small firm, recognised by others to have a close knowledge of prevailing market conditions. The firm acts as a barometer to others of changing market conditions, and its prices are closely followed.

Collusive-price leadership This is a more complicated form of price leadership: essentially it is an informal cartel in which prices change almost simultaneously (see p. 355). In practice it is often difficult to distinguish collusive-price leadership from types in which firms follow price leaders very quickly.

Applications and evidence

Kinked demand curve

We noted (p. 332) the relevance of the kinked demand curve as an explanation of the observed price rigidity in many oligopolistic situations. There is considerable evidence to suggest that firms in oligopoly situations do indeed perceive their demand curves as having differential price elasticity of demand characteristics for price rises (more elastic) as compared with price cuts (less elastic).

Diamantopoulos and Mathews (1993) studied the perception of product managers in 21 distinct product groups (covering over 900 products) of the largely oligopolistic UK medical supplies industry. The oligopolistic nature of these markets is reflected in the fact that the *lowest* three-firm concentration ratio recorded within the 21 product groups was as high as 0.85 (85%).

Product managers were invited to supply information on a range of market descriptors in response to different scenarios of price cuts or rises, ranging in 5% segments from ±50% of the current price set by the firm. These market descriptors included, for each 5% change, demand sensitivity, competitor reactions as regards price/non-price characteristics, etc. Essentially three types of *perceived* demand curve represented the different clusters of responses from the product managers, as indicated in Fig. 8.18. The index of 100 on the vertical axis represents the *current product price*, and the index of 100 on the horizontal axis represents the *current output volume*.

For most product groups there appears to be a price interval around the current price where price changes have little or no effect on volume. Indeed a vertical band extending both above and below the current price was observed for 15 out of the 21 product groups, as in Fig. 8.18(c). This **double-kinked demand curve** resembles that considered by Gutenberg (1984).

It has been suggested that *buyer loyalty* may be a contributory factor to such a vertical band, giving greater pricing discretion to the supplying firm. Again, significant *supplier switching costs* may play a part, with incumbents using these costs of changing from one supplier to another (or, indeed, of transacting with a supplier for the first time) as a barrier to new entry, thereby enhancing their price discretion and the size of the vertical band. Even *product differentiation strategies* have been suggested as contributing to this vertical band, with a different package of characteristics (see Chapter 2, p. 75) only available to consumers by their switching to significantly different product and price categories (i.e. a discrete rather than continuous spectrum of product characteristics available to consumers).

Fig. 8.18 **Types of demand curve: medical supplies product groups.**

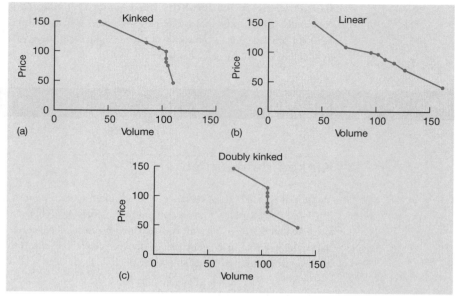

Source: Diamantopoulos and Mathews (1993)

In general, for changes in price of 20% or more for all product groups, demand elasticity was found to be greater for upward rather than downward price changes, in accordance with conventional kinked demand theory. As Morris and Morris (1990) in a separate study concluded, this asymmetric shape of the demand curve suggests that product managers in oligopoly markets appreciate that 'customers may have different elasticities for a price increase compared to a decrease over the same range'.

Further evidence consistent with kinked demand theory is presented by Domberger and Fiebig (1993). They devised measures of skewness of the distribution of price changes around the mean price change, using quarterly data covering 80 industries in the UK across an 11-year time period (1974–85). Their results for the highly oligopolistic industries tended to conform with the distribution shown in Fig. 8.19.

The distribution involving *price decreases* by the oligopoly industry tended to be negatively skewed (tail of distribution to the left). Although the mode (highest frequency) was 'no price change' (i.e. index 1.00) in any given quarter, where price decreases did occur, these tended to be readily followed by other firms who were willing to change price. In contrast the distribution of *price increases* tended to be positively skewed (tail of distribution to right). Again the mode (highest frequency) was 'no price change' in any given quarter, but when price increases did occur these were less readily followed by other firms.

In other words, for the more oligopolistic industries, the distribution of price decreases tended to be more symmetric than those for price increases. This provides indirect evidence in support of the view that oligopolists follow price reductions more readily than they follow price rises, which of course is an essential ingredient of kinked demand theory.

Fig. 8.19
**Distributions of
price changes (1.00 =
no change) for
highly oligopolistic
industries.**

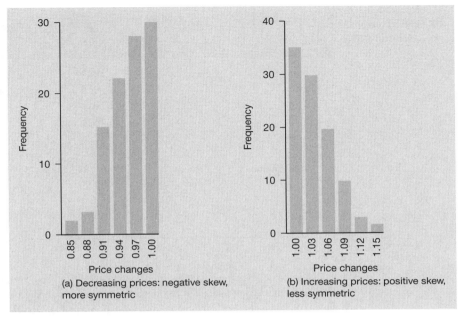

(a) Decreasing prices: negative skew, more symmetric

(b) Increasing prices: positive skew, less symmetric

Source: Domberger and Fiebig (1993)

▦ Collusive price leadership (parallel pricing)

We considered this form of price leadership on p. 353. The objective may be for market participants to rapidly change prices in the same direction and by similar magnitudes in order to defend market share. Such instances are often referred to as **parallel pricing**, and may reflect market share objectives whereby each major participant seeks to prevent others from securing enhanced market shares by responding immediately to any price-cutting strategy they might adopt.

Again we are into action–reaction situations so typical of oligopoly, where firms change price for reasons of strategy rather than to reflect variations in cost. Jobber and Hooley (1987) found that market share pricing objectives were practised more by larger firms in oligopolistic markets. Grant's study of the oligopolistic wholesale petrol market (Grant 1982; see also OFT 1998) is a clear case of market-share strategies exerting a dominant influence on price-setting. As we see from Table 8.1, five firms accounted for over 65% of the volume of petrol sold in the UK in 1988 and four firms for some 59% by 1996.

There is evidence to suggest that these 'major' oil companies have often followed a pattern of *parallel pricing* since the early 1970s, charging roughly the same wholesale price within a geographic region. They have also offered similar discounts for 'solus' agreements, where the retailer takes all his petrol from the one company. As a result the *relative* market share of the individual 'majors' has remained rather static during much of the past 30 years. The *absolute* market share of the 'majors' in petrol refining has, however, fallen substantially over this period from over 78% in 1970 to the 59% recorded in 1996. In recent times the majors have also lost market share in petrol retailing to the superstores (Tesco, Safeway, etc.), which have increased their share of petrol retailing from 5% in 1990 to 23% in 1996 (OFT 1998).

Table 8.1 **Share of UK refined output, 1988 and 1996.**

| | Market share (%) | |
	1988	1996
Esso	18.0	17.9
BP	9.2	⎫
Mobil	10.3	⎬ 17.1
Shell	15.4	13.2
Texaco	12.9	10.7
Total majors	65.8	58.9
Others	34.2	41.1
Total	100.0	100.0

Source: OFT (1998)

Aggressive pricing policies by the majors have sometimes broken out in an attempt to defend their market share against both other majors and the non-majors. For example, Esso launched its 'Price Watch' campaign in January 1996. This saw prices cut to the extent that its margin on the price per litre fell to 1p (OFT 1998). Since petrol is a relatively homogeneous product with little attendant brand loyalty, the other oil majors and the supermarkets also had to cut their prices to support their *relative* market share. When prices are dictated in this way by market-share strategies they may bear little relationship to the costs of production, at least in the short run. This can be seen in Fig. 8.20, where the falling net profit margins for the four majors reflected their commitment to defending their relative market share via aggressive pricing strategies.

From this analysis we can see that parallel pricing has been used by the majors to avoid mutually damaging encroachment on their respective market shares. However, when times get difficult, price wars can still break out. When prices are dictated by market-share strategies they may bear little relationship to costs of production, at least in

Fig. 8.20 **Percentage change in net margins of oil majors in UK refining, wholesaling and retailing operations, 1992–96.**

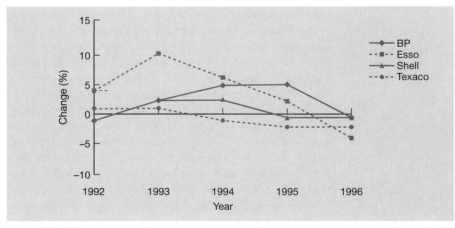

Source: Adapted from OFT (1998)

the short run. This view was confirmed by Hall *et al.* (1996) in a survey of 654 UK companies. Over 65% of companies stated that their most important pricing strategy was 'market-led pricing', with prices set either at the highest level the market could bear or at a level that has taken full account of their competitors' pricing strategies.

Domberger and Fiebig (1993) also noted in their study of 80 industries in the UK over the period 1974–85 that the more oligopolistic the industry, the more symmetric (less skewed) the price changes experienced. In other words, following our earlier analysis (p. 354), price adjustments by market participants would occur more rapidly, in the same direction and by similar magnitudes. This can be illustrated by considering two specific industry examples in the data set used by Domberger and Fiebig. The most highly concentrated oligopoly in the sample was the tobacco industry, with a three-firm concentration ratio of 1.00 (100%). The average skew of the distribution of price changes measured throughout the period was only 0.08, small enough to be consistent with almost simultaneous price adjustments. In similar manner the highly concentrated cement industry exhibited an average skew of only 0.19, sufficiently small to suggest considerable price coordination.

Eurotunnel: finding the Nash equilibrium

We outlined the Bertrand Model (p. 341) as an oligopoly situation involving *pricing* actions and reactions. Here we apply that approach to a Eurotunnel pricing model involving two key participants (i.e. a duopoly), namely the Eurotunnel rail link and the ferry companies, here aggregated and represented as one participant (though in fact some competition exists between the ferry companies themselves). We show how a **Nash equilibrium** (p. 341) might be the outcome of the model, i.e. one in which both participants are achieving the best outcome for themselves given the strategies of the others.

In 1994 the 30-mile tunnel between Britain and France was opened for service. As Britain has become more integrated in the European economy, roll-on/roll-off traffic – in which loaded trucks are carried by ferries between Dover and Felixstowe on one side and Calais or Zeebrugge on the other – has become a significantly larger proportion of total freight movements. Today, Dover is Britain's second largest 'port' (the largest is Heathrow Airport).

While some of this traffic is expected to shift to through-rail services, most of it will continue to be carried in lorries. But since the opening of the Eurotunnel service, lorries have the option of boarding a shuttle train to be carried through the tunnel instead of using a ferry. However, this new and alternative mode of transport does have drawbacks, since time will still be spent loading and unloading lorries at each end. Further, the Dover–Calais route, although short, is not the most direct. In fact one of the reasons why the Felixstowe–Zeebrugge ferry route is so popular is that if a direct road link could be built between the heart of England and the heart of Europe, it would almost certainly cross the sea between those two ports.

Kay (1993) estimated that it cost an average of around 200 ecus to take a lorry between Britain and continental Europe in 1993 via ferry. What, then, should the tunnel charge? If the ferries were to continue to set an average price of 200 ecus, as was the case prior to the opening of the tunnel, then the choice that Eurotunnel faces is described in Fig. 8.21(a) along the continuous '200 ecus' line concave to the horizontal axis. If the price is set too low by Eurotunnel, then its market share will be high but profit margins low. If price is set at higher levels by Eurotunnel, then profit margins will be much greater but the result will be a loss of market share. Kay suggests that if the fer-

Fig. 8.21 A Nash equilibrium: Eurotunnel pricing model.

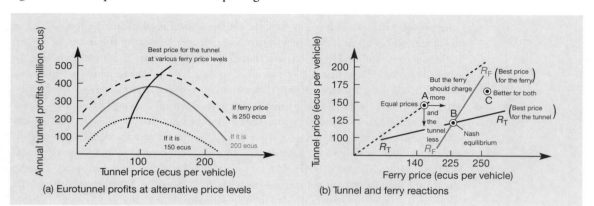

(a) Eurotunnel profits at alternative price levels

(b) Tunnel and ferry reactions

ries were to continue to charge 200 ecus, the tunnel would maximise annual profit by setting a much lower price – perhaps as low as 100 ecus or so. This would be feasible since the tunnel's marginal costs of operation are very low, costing as little as around 15 ecus to transport a lorry, at least until the tunnel is operating at full capacity.

Of course the ferries themselves might choose *not* to continue with their current average pricing strategy of 200 ecus if Eurotunnel were to lower its price significantly below this figure. As we can see from Fig. 8.21(a), the lower the ferry price, the lower the profit (and market share) implied by any given Eurotunnel price. In fact by drawing a line through the *peaks* of the various curves relating Eurotunnel profits to ferry price, we can see that the lower the ferry price, the lower the (profit-maximising) tunnel price should be. As indicated in Fig. 8.21(a), it is clear that this analysis suggests that Eurotunnel will always maximise its profits by setting a price below that set by the ferries.

Of course we have noted that there is a danger of a mutually damaging price war, unless the interdependence between the companies is recognised in some way. Figure 8.21(b) begins to model this interdependence, plotting from Fig. 8.21(a) the locus (set) of tunnel/ferry prices that are best for the tunnel. This gives us the reaction curve R_T in Fig. 8.21(b). A similar procedure can be devised to give us the locus (set) of tunnel/ferry prices that are best for the ferry. This gives us the reaction curve R_F in Fig. 8.21(b).

The use of reaction curves in this way indicates that there may be a pricing solution to the mutual benefit of all participants that avoids a price war. This is the (Nash) equilibrium at B – the pair of strategies in which both the ferry and the tunnel are achieving the best outcome for themselves given the strategies of the other. In this Nash equilibrium, the tunnel price is 120 ecus and the ferry price 225 ecus. The ferries continue to do business, because there are still many users who prefer sea crossings, especially those that take them closer to their destination, but a large proportion of freight traffic now uses the tunnel.

Kay summarises this outcome as follows:

> The nature of this Nash equilibrium illustrates that even in unstable environments competitors do not necessarily pursue each other to mutual destruction. The unstable environment is one in which each party takes no account of the *interests* of the other, but nevertheless considers the *responses* of the other, and that is the key difference. Not to consider other firms' responses would simply be irrational: but to take account of their interests requires a formal or a tacit agreement between the parties.

Of course there is no obvious mechanism, in the absence of collusion, to guarantee that the Bertrand–Nash equilibrium at B is achieved. However, if R_F is steeper than R_T, as here, then by an iterative (step by step) process we might reach B as a stable equilibrium (see also Fig. 8.9, p. 342).

Take for example a starting point of A in Fig. 8.21(b), where Eurotunnel and the ferry companies believe they should charge equal prices. From Fig. 8.21(a) we have already noted that Eurotunnel increases its profits by undercutting the ferry price, and will presumably realise this, thereby reducing its price. Similarly, ferries will presumably realise that they increase profits by raising their prices above those of Eurotunnel. In other words both firms move from A towards their respective reaction curves, and the iterative process may, in this case, then guide them to the Bertrand–Nash equilibrium at B.

Of course it may be that the firms seek to achieve a pricing outcome that maximises industry profits: i.e. seek to achieve a contract curve pricing outcome such as that at C (see also Fig. 8.10, p. 343). Apart from collusion, Kay suggests that this is a less probable outcome of the model than the Bertrand–Nash equilibrium at B. Without collusion, the significant (marginal) cost disparities may persuade, say, the ferries to move away from C. At C they charge a very high price, and one that is still substantially above that charged by Eurotunnel. The implication is that they can do better, in terms of profit, by reducing their price and attracting extra volume, i.e. moving towards their reaction curve R_F. Of course Eurotunnel has incentives to move towards its reaction curve R_T, reducing its prices. Having returned to the reaction curves, the iterative process might then lead the model to the Betrand–Nash equilibrium at B. Only collusion, formal or informal, might persuade the respective companies to remain at the industry profit-maximising solution, C, and not to follow their instincts and move towards the perceived profit enhancing pricing strategy for each company indicated by the respective reaction curves.

'Learning' in terms of the Stackelberg model (p. 344) might induce a solution near to C with one firm accepting the other as dominant (here as price leader). The other firm might then acquiesce in being off its (profit-maximising) reaction curve. Except in this case, or in the event of collusion, the Bertrand–Nash equilibrium B might be a more realistic outcome for the model than the industry profit-maximising solution C.

Symptoms and tests of collusive behaviour

Earlier in this chapter we noted the complexity of oligopoly behaviour patterns and the tendency towards collusive agreements. In practice it is important to find a way of assessing the conditions facilitating the emergence of such collusion. There are four 'schools' of thought in this respect (European Commission 1994):

- There is the *concentration school* already touched on earlier (p. 291). This believes that the growth of concentration ratios in a sector of industry gives a clue as to the ability of firms to coordinate their actions in an oligopolistic way. If the largest four companies have a market share (C_4) in excess of 50%, then the industry is seen as being prone to collusive behaviour.
- There is the *coordination school*, which argues that oligopolistic dominance is not always dependent on market concentration because there are other coordination factors that need consideration. For example, the degree of heterogeneity of the

products of a particular market can have some influence here: the more heterogeneous the products of the group, the less likely it is that large firms will seek to collude. On the other hand, the more 'focal' points there are available, the more likely it is that oligopolistic collusion will emerge. Focal points include aspects such as *price lining*, whereby certain prices are used as norms for different types of goods (and different quality levels of given types of goods) across a variety of companies. *Round-number discounting* is another focal point, e.g. 10% or 15% discounts, as is *rule of thumb pricing*, e.g. cost plus 40%. All these so-called 'focal points' help to provide a common base on which to build collusive coordination between oligopolists. Arguably the pace of technological change will also influence the prospects for such coordination. If technology changes rapidly, then prices and quality levels are likely to change in a complex fashion, making it more difficult for firms to collude.

- The *contestability school* holds that oligopolistic collusion depends on whether or not the market is contestable. As we saw in Chapter 6 (p. 265), contestability depends, among other things, on the nature and existence of any sunk costs or other barriers to entry. If contestability is high, then new firms can enter the industry and prevent or weaken attempts at oligopolistic collusion.

- The *multi-market school* argues that oligopolistic behaviour patterns involving coordination and collusion are more likely to occur when firms compete in multi-markets, rather than compete in a single market. If there are significant cost differences between large firms competing in different markets, then firms may tacitly agree on 'spheres of influence' and withdraw from competition in one market in exchange for receiving (by agreement) a more dominant position in another market.

Elders IXL and Grand Metropolitan plc

In 1989 the UK beer brewing interests of Elders IXL Ltd and Grand Metropolitan plc were involved in a proposed merger, which was referred to the Monopolies and Mergers Commission (MMC 1990). The key issue was whether the reduction of major suppliers from six to five companies would be associated with a risk of collusive oligopolistic behaviour. It was predicted that the merger of both companies would imply shares of Grand Metropolitan and Courage (Elder's UK subsidiary) in the UK beer market as indicated in Table 8.2.

Table 8.2 **National brewers' share of total UK beer sale, 1989.**

Brewer	Total market	Ale	Lager
Grand Metropolitan	11	9	13
Courage	9	9	10
Total	20	18	23
Allied Lyons	12	12	13
Bass	22	20	24
Whitbread	12	12	12
Scottish & Newcastle	10	13	7
All national brewers	77	75	78

Source: MMC's beer report (1989) and Grand Metropolitan Courage estimates

- As far as the *concentration school* was concerned, the C_4 measure gave a reading of 66%, suggesting a serious risk of oligopolistic collusion.

- The *coordination school* held a similar view based on 'focal point' pricing, since the brewers published a wholesale trade price list indicating the price at which beer could be sold to wholesalers and retailers in various parts of the country. With over half the market operation being reflected on the list, this was seen as a focal point on which coordinated pricing could readily be based.

- In contrast there was also concern about collusion from the perspective of the *contestability school*. It emerged from the report that, in addition to the six large brewers, some 60 very small local brewers had entered the market in the 1980s. These local brewers, by using small-scale technologies, had been able to keep sunk costs to a minimum and thereby compete effectively in the market. Unfortunately the small breweries mainly operated in niche markets and were unable to act as an effective price discipline against oligopolistic coordination between the large national players on the main beer market. In this respect the contestability factor was restricted to a fringe segment of a larger market dominated by a group of oligopolists.

- The *multi-market* school of thought also reflected some concern about likely collusion in this market. While the four largest UK brewing companies tended not to compete in multiple *geographic* markets, they were nevertheless active competitors in other related businesses (i.e. multiple *product* markets), e.g. restaurant chains and spirits. This suggests that aggressive price behaviour by one company in, say, the beer market could bring retaliation by other companies in related product markets. In other words a network of threats and counter-threats between competitors in the UK beer and related product markets is possible, with companies using their other related businesses as bargaining weapons. This would tend to make the major companies move towards oligopolistic coordination over all the markets, rather than risk retaliation in a specific market of major concern to the company.

The UK Monopolies and Mergers Commission found that the proposed merger of Elders IXL and Grand Metropolitan as originally conceived could be expected to operate against the public interest. It therefore recommended certain remedies that, if implemented, could prevent the adverse effects of the proposed merger.

Key terms		
Barometric-firm leadership	Kinked demand
Barriers to entry	Limit price
Bertrand-type equilibrium	Maxi-min
Cartel	Mini-max
Collusive oligopoly	Nash equilibrium
Collusive-price leadership	Non-collusive oligopoly
Cournot-type equilibrium	Pay-offs
Dominant-firm leadership	Reaction curves
Dominant strategy	Stable equilibrium
Isocost line/curve	Stackelberg equilibrium
Isoprofit line/curve	Variable sum game
Isoquant	Zero-sum game

Full definitions can be found in the 'Glossary of terms' (pp. 699–710)

Here we have noted that the perspectives of different schools of thought may differ over their assessment of the likely emergence of collusive behaviour. In any particular case, an *overall* assessment may have to weight the differing perspectives and take a judgement that is by no means clear cut.

Review questions

1. Safelock Ltd produces door clips for the security industry, and shares the market with its competitor, Securol plc. In this duopoly situation, Safelock has found that it faces a demand function of $Q_A = 180 - 20P$ for *price increases* and $Q_B = 60 - 5P$ for *price reductions*, where Q is output measured in thousands of units and P is price in pounds sterling. At present the price of the door clips are set by the market leader, Safelock, at £8 each, and Safelock's various cost functions are shown in Table 8.3.

Table 8.3

Q (000s)	SAC_1	SMC_1	SAC_2	SMC_2	SMC_3
10	5.0	4.0	6.0	5.0	7.0
15	4.5	4.5	5.5	5.5	7.5
20	4.9	5.5	5.9	6.5	8.5
25	5.5	7.0	6.5	8.0	10.0
30	6.5	9.0	7.5	10.0	12.0

(a) From the information given in the demand functions, plot on graph paper the respective demand curves and their associated marginal revenue curves. (*Hint*: draw the vertical axis on a scale from zero to £12, and the horizontal output axis from zero to 70(000) only. To save drawing an extended output axis, the value of Q_A at 70(000) can be calculated from the demand function.) Erase the parts of these curves that are not relevant, and show clearly the 'kinked' nature of Safelock's demand curve. Briefly explain why this 'kinked demand curve' exists.

(b) Plot the SAC_1 and SMC_1 curves, and calculate the equilibrium quantity of door clips produced by Safelock and the price per unit. What will total profits be at this level of production?

(c) Safelock's costs rise owing to difficulties in obtaining sufficient tensile steel used to make the clips. This results in a new set of cost structures, SAC_2 and SMC_2. Does this affect the equilibrium output position and the amount of total profits earned?

(d) Owing to increased trade union bargaining pressure, the existing rise in the price of tensile steel is also accompanied by a rise in labour costs, resulting in the marginal cost shifting to SMC_3. Draw this new marginal cost curve on your graph, and explain what will happen to Safelock's price and output strategy.

2. Two companies in the restaurant business, Fastfoods plc and Easymeal plc, dominate the popular eating outlets of a town. The market demand function for their type of meals is given by $Q = 12 - P$, where Q is the output measured in

1,000s of meals per week and P is the price of meals in £s. During the first year, the local authority has decided to subsidise the two companies in order to help encourage visitors to the town. The subsidy is such that each company has in effect zero marginal costs ($MC = 0$), so each will maximise revenue (and profit) where MR is also zero.

(a) Suppose the market was originally satisfied by Fastfoods plc alone. Plot the demand and marginal revenue curves to show that the optimum number of meals per week would be 6(000) at a price of £6 per meal, and that total profit would be £36,000 per week. Also show that for any linear demand curve (such as that of Fastfood), the quantity of meals produced would be $Q/2$ when $MR = 0$.

(b) Now suppose that both companies operate in the market and behave in Cournot fashion. Let the quantity demanded of Fastfoods' products be denoted by Q_F and of Easymeal's by Q_E. Briefly explain the assumptions of the Cournot model, and derive an expression for the total demand market function ($Q = 12 – P$) in terms of Q_F and Q_E. Use this expression to derive the two profit-maximising reaction functions (use the linear demand curve assumptions of part (a). Graph the two functions.

(c) Determine the equilibrium output level of output for each company that satisfies the Cournot condition by reading off the values from the graph. Use simple algebra to check your results. Compare profit levels in the market when Fastfoods had a monopoly in part (a), with profit levels under duopoly conditions in part (b). Explain why they are different.

(d) Suppose now that the situation changes so that Fastfoods becomes a sophisticated leader: i.e. it recognises (in Stackelberg fashion) that Easymeal reacts to its output according to Easymeal's reaction function derived in part (b). Calculate the new equilibrium levels of output for both companies and their respective levels of profit.

3. Two companies, Avionics Ltd and Engineering Enterprises plc, have a joint patent on a minor component part used in the manufacture of flight simulators, which are used to train pilots. The market demand for the component is given by the function $P = 1,000 – Q_M$, where P is the price in ecus and Q_M is the market output. The marginal costs of both companies are identical at $MC = 100$ ecus.

(a) What would be the price and output solutions if the industry operated under (i) competitive or (ii) monopoly conditions?

(b) In reality, the two companies realise that they are in a duopoly situation and begin to behave in a Cournot fashion. Derive the demand curve and marginal revenue curves for each company on the assumption that Avionics and Engineering Enterprises' shares of the market are Q_A and Q_E respectively.

(c) Derive their respective reaction functions and calculate the equilibrium rate of output for both firms on the assumption that they both maximise profits independently. What share of a competitive market output would they each produce?

(d) If Avionics decided to withdraw from the market, how much would Engineering Enterprises supply to the market and at what price?

4. Over time, the relationship between Avionics and Engineering Enterprises changes as the latter company becomes more dominant in the industry. Competition between the two companies begins to resemble the Stackelberg model of competitive behaviour. Given that the same demand and cost functions apply to this situation as in the previous Cournot problem:

   (a) Derive Engineering Enterprises' demand function on the basis that the competition is now of the Stackelberg type.
   (b) Calculate the output and the market price as a result of the dominant behaviour of Engineering Enterprises.
   (c) How much output will be left for Avionics to produce, given Engineering Enterprises strength in the industry?

5. The European market for soda (an essential ingredient for many chemical products) is dominated by a chemical giant, International Chemicals. The rest of the European production is divided between 20 smaller companies. Table 8.4 provides information on market demand, D_M (by relating output, Q, to price, P), the marginal cost of International Chemicals (MC_I), and the combined marginal costs of the other companies (ΣMC_0).

Table 8.4

Q (m tonnes)	0	1	2	3	4	5	6	7
P (£/kg)	12	11	10	9	8	7	6	5
MC_I (£/kg)	1	3	5	7	9	11	13	15
ΣMC_0 (£/kg)	2	3	4	5	6	7	8	9

   (a) Use graph paper to plot D_M, MC_I and ΣMC_0. Use the data to construct the demand and marginal revenue functions for International Chemicals. Assume that, as the dominant company, International Chemicals sets the market price and allows the smaller companies to follow its price leadership, i.e. to sell as much output as they can at this price.
   (b) What is the price charged by International Chemicals? How would the market be shared between the market leader and the smaller companies? Give reasons why the smaller companies would have an incentive to follow the price set by the leader.
   (c) Suppose International Chemicals, as the dominant price leader, decides to exercise its market power and is successful in driving out its smaller competitors. How would you modify your graph in (a) to show the new equilibrium price and output levels in the market?

■ Further reading

Intermediate texts   Baumol, W. J. (1977), *Economic Theory and Operations Analysis*, 4th edn, Ch.16, Prentice Hall, Hemel Hempstead.

Browning, E. and Browning, J. (1992), *Microeconomic Theory and Applications*, 4th edn, Chs 12–14, HarperCollins, London.

Dobson, S., Maddala, G.S. and Miller, E. (1995), *Microeconomics*, Ch. 11, McGraw-Hill, Maidenhead.

Hope, S. (1999), *Applied Microeconomics*, Ch. 11, Wiley, Chichester.

Katz, M. and Rosen, H. (1998), *Microeconomics*, 3rd edn, Ch. 15, Irwin, Boston, Mass.

Kay, J. (1993), *Foundations of Corporate Success*, Oxford University Press, Oxford.

Koutsoyiannis, A. (1979), *Modern Microeconomics*, 2nd edn, Chs 9 and 10, Macmillan, Basingstoke.

Laidler, D. and Estrin, S. (1995), *Introduction to Microeconomics*, 4th edn, Chs 17–19, Harvester Wheatsheaf, Hemel Hempstead.

Maddala, G. S. and Miller, E. (1989), *Microeconomics: Theory and Application*, Chs 13 and 14, McGraw-Hill, Maidenhead.

Nicholson, W. (1997), *Intermediate Microeconomics and its Application*, 7th edn, Chs 17 and 18, Dryden Press, Fort Worth.

Pindyck, R. and Rubinfeld, D. (1998), *Microeconomics*, 4th edn, Chs 12 and 13, Macmillan, Basingstoke.

Varian, H. (1999), *Intermediate Microeconomics*, 5th edn, Chs 26 and 27, Norton, New York.

Advanced texts   Friedman, J. (1986), *Game Theory with Applications to Economics*, Oxford University Press, Oxford.

Fudenberg, D. and Tirole, G. (1991), *Game Theory*, MIT Press, Cambridge, Mass.

Gravelle, H. and Rees, R. (1992), *Microeconomics*, 2nd edn, Ch. 12, Longman, Harlow.

Mas-Colell, A., Whinston, M. D. and Green, J. R. (1995), *Microeconomic Theory*, Chs 7–9, Oxford Universty Press, Oxford.

Articles and other sources   Diamantopoulos, A. and Mathews, B. (1993), 'Managerial perceptions of the demand curve: evidence from a multiproduct firm', *European Journal of Marketing*, 27, 9, MCB University Press.

Domberger, S. and Fiebig, D. (1993), 'The distribution of price changes in oligopoly', *Journal of Industrial Economics*, XLI, 3, Blackwell Publishers Ltd.

European Commission (1994), 'Competition and integration', *European Economy*, 57.

Fuller, E. (1999), 'Pricing in practice', in *Applied Economics*, A. Griffiths and S. Wall (eds), Longman, Harlow.

Gavin, M. and Swann, P. (1994), 'The economics of the Channel Tunnel', *The Economic Review*, 11, 3.

Goodhart, C. A. (1994), 'Game theory for central bankers: a report to the Governor of the Bank of England', *Journal of Economic Literature*, XXXII, 1, March.

Grant, R. M. (1982) 'Pricing behaviour in the UK wholesale market for petrol 1970–80: a 'structure-conduct analysis'', *Journal of Industrial Economics*, 30, 3, March.

Gutenberg, E. (1984), *Grundlagen der Betriebswirtschaftslehre*, Springer Verlag, Berlin.

Hall, R. L. and Hitch, C. J. (1939) 'Price theory and business behaviour', *Oxford University Papers*, 2, May.

Hall, S., Walsh, M. and Yates, T. (1996), 'How do UK companies set prices?', *Bank of England Quarterly Bulletin*, May.

Jobber, D. and Hooley, G. (1987), 'Pricing behaviour in UK manufacturing and service industries', *Managerial and Decision Economics*, 8.

Karni, E. and Levin, D. (1994), 'Social attributes and strategic equilibrium: a restaurant pricing game', *Journal of Political Economy*, 102, 3, August.

MMC (1990), 'Elders IXL and Grand Metropolitan PLC', Cm 1227.

Office of Fair Trading (1998), *Competition in the Supply of Petrol*, OFT 229.

Morris, M. H. and Morris, G. (1990), *Market-Oriented Pricing: Strategies for Management*, Quorum Books, Westport.

Rees, R. (1993), 'Tacit collusion', *Oxford Review of Economic Policy*, 9, 2.

Sweezy, P. M. (1939), 'Demand under conditions of oligopoly', *Journal of Political Economy*, 47, 4.

Williamson, P. J. (1994), 'Oligopolistic dominance and EC merger policy', *European Economy*, 57.

Chapter 9

Game theory

Introduction and review

We noted in Chapter 8 that one of the key features that often characterises oligopoly markets is recognised interdependence between sellers. Whereas the 'reaction curve' models of Chapter 8 use past experience to assess future reactions by rivals, in **game theory** the firm itself tries to identify the possible moves that the rival could make in response to each of its strategies. The firm can then plan counter-strategies if the rival *does* react in one or more of the anticipated ways.

We might introduce the idea of game theory by considering one of the most simple games, namely the 'two-firm zero-sum' game. A game is said to be **zero sum** when any gain to one 'player' is directly offset by an equivalent loss or losses to other players.

It may help to define a few key terms at the outset. A **strategy** is a specific course of action taken by the firm. This will involve the firm in giving clearly defined values to its **policy variables**, i.e. those aspects of its activities that the firm can directly affect. These policy variables will include price, quantity, quality, design, spending on promotion, marketing, research and development, and so on. It follows that one strategy might involve setting a price £v, spending £w on advertising, adopting design x, spending £y on research and development and selling the product range in a set of outlets (say, supermarkets) z. This strategy may, of course, be but one of several possible strategies involving *different* values or options for these policy variables.

For each strategy of this firm its rival (or rivals) may adopt **counter-strategies**. The **pay-off matrix** is the set of net gains that the firm expects to make for each combination of strategy and counter-strategy adopted by it and its rival(s). These net gains will be expressed in terms of the main objective of the firm: thus if profit maximisation is the main objective, the net gains will be profit levels; if market share is the main objective, the net gains will be percentages of market; and so on. The **decision rule** is the guiding principle that the firm uses in selecting between alternative pay-off values in the pay-off matrix.

■ Two-firm zero-sum game

We might usefully illustrate the principles involved by a simple two-firm (duopoly) game, involving market share. By its very nature, a market share game must be 'zero sum', in that any gain by one player must be offset exactly by the loss of the other(s).

Suppose Firm A is considering two possible strategies to raise its market share, either a 20% price cut or a 10% increase in advertising expenditure (note that here each strategy involves only a single policy variable). Whatever initial strategy Firm A adopts, it anticipates that its rival, Firm B, will react by using either a price cut or extra advertising to defend its market share. Firm A now evaluates the market share that it can expect for each initial strategy and each possible counter-strategy by Firm B. The outcomes expected by A are summarised in the pay-off matrix of Table 9.1.

Table 9.1 Firm A's pay-off matrix: market share game.

| | | Firm B's strategies | |
		Price cut	Extra advertising
Firm A's strategies	Price cut	60[a,b]	70[b]
	Extra advertising	50[a]	55

[a] 'Worst' outcome for A of each A strategy.
[b] 'Worst' outcome for B of each B strategy.

If A cuts price, and B responds with a price cut, A receives 60% of the market. However, if B responds with extra advertising, A receives 70% of the market. The 'worst' outcome for A (60% of the market) will occur if B responds with a price cut. If A adopts the strategy of extra advertising, then the 'worst' outcome for A (50% of the market) will again occur if B responds with a price cut rather than extra advertising (55% of the market).

Maxi-min approach to game

If A expects B to play the game astutely, i.e. choose the counter-strategy best for itself (worst for A), then A will choose the price-cut strategy, as this gives it 60% of the market rather than 50%. If A plays the game in this way, selecting the best of the worst possible outcomes for each initial strategy, it is said to be adopting a '**maxi-min**' decision rule or approach to the game.

If B adopts the same maxi-min approach as A, *and* has made the same evaluation of outcomes as A, it also will adopt a price-cut strategy. For instance, if B adopts a price-cut strategy, its 'worst' outcome will occur if A responds with a price cut; B then gets 40% of the market (100% minus 60%) rather than 50% as would be the case if A responds with extra advertising. If B adopts extra advertising, its 'worst' outcome will again occur if A responds with a price cut; B then receives 30% (100% minus 70%). The best of the 'worst possible' outcomes for B occurs if B adopts a price cut, which gives it 40% of the market rather than 30%.

Stable and
unstable equilibrium

In this particular game we have a **stable equilibrium**, without any resort to collusion. Both firms initially cut price, then accept the respective market shares that fulfil their maxi-min targets – namely 60% to A, 40% to B. There could then follow the price stability that we have seen to be a feature of some oligopoly situations. Note that in terms of our earlier analysis (Chapter 8, p. 341) we have here a **Nash equilibrium**, since each firm is doing the best that it can in terms of the objective(s) it has set itself *given the actions of its rivals*. In some games the optimal strategy for each firm may not even have been an initial price cut, but rather non-price competition (such as advertising). Game theory can predict both price stability and extensive non-price competition.

The problem with game theory is that it can equally predict **unstable** solutions, with extensive price as well as non-price competition. An unstable solution might follow if each firm, faced with the pay-off matrix of Table 9.1, adopted *entirely different decision rules* in terms of selecting between alternative strategies. Firm B might not use the maxi-min approach of Firm A, but take more risk. Instead of the price cut it might adopt the extra advertising strategy, hoping to induce an advertising response from Firm A and gain 45% of the market, but risk getting only 30%, which is below its initial expectation of 45%. This might provoke B into alternative strategy formulation, setting off a further chain reaction. The game might then fail to settle down quickly, if at all, to a stable solution, i.e. one in which each firm receives a market share that meets its overall expectation. An unstable solution might also follow if each firm *evaluated the pay-off matrix differently* from the other. Even if they then adopt the same approach to the game, one firm at least will be disappointed, possibly provoking action and counteraction.

Theoretical developments

◼ Multiple strategy games

We can illustrate the greater complexity of possible outcomes to the game in situations where *more than two strategies* must be evaluated by each firm (and, of course, where each strategy might involve more than one policy variable). In Table 9.2 Firm A evaluates four possible strategies for itself and five possible counter-strategies by its rival, Firm B. The numbers within *circles* indicate the 'worst' outcome for A of each A strategy. Here we read along the rows. Thus if Firm A adopts strategy A_1, the 'worst' outcome for A will be if B adopts counter-strategy B_1, giving Firm A 10% of the market (and therefore Firm B 90% of the market). The numbers within *squares* indicate the worst outcome for B of each B strategy. Here we read down the columns. Thus if Firm B adopts strategy B_1, the worst outcome for B will be where A adopts counter-strategy A_2, giving Firm B only 60% (100% − 40%) of the market.

If each firm adopts the **maxi-min** approach, and each firm evaluates its pay-off matrix in the same way, then a *stable* solution may exist for this game: A adopts strategy A_2, and B adopts strategy B_2. Strategy A_2 gives Firm A the highest market share of 30%, given that for each of A's strategies B responds in the worst (for A) possible way. Similarly strategy B_2 gives Firm B the highest market share of 70% (100% − 30%), given

Table 9.2 **Firm A's pay-off matrix: market share game.**

		Firm B's strategies				
		B_1	B_2	B_3	B_4	B_5
Firm A's strategies	A_1	(0.10)	0.20	0.15	0.30	0.25
	A_2	0.40	(0.30)	0.50	0.55	0.45
	A_3	0.35	0.25	(0.20)	0.40	0.50
	A_4	0.25	(0.15)	0.35	0.60	0.20

◯   Worst outcome for A of each A strategy

▢   Worst outcome for B of each B strategy

that for each of B's strategies Firm A responds in the worst (for B) possible way. The solution of strategy A_2/B_2 is clearly one that both firms prefer and therefore can readily accept. It is in this sense that we can accept the solution as stable.

Nash equilibrium and dominant strategies

So far the types of equilibrium solution to the games we have considered have been of the **Nash** variety, in which each firm is doing the best that it can in terms of the objective(s) it has set itself *given the reactions of its rivals*. Thus in the previous game, because Firm A selects strategy A_2 and simultaneously Firm B selects strategy B_2, then neither firm is disappointed by the outcome, namely 30% market share to A and 70% market share to B. It is a Nash equilibrium because, given the decision of its rival, each firm is satisfied that it has made the best decision possible in terms of the objective(s) it has set itself, and has no incentive to alter its decision.

The behavioural rule adopted by each firm in our example is the same: each firm expects the rival to behave in the worst possible way for any strategy it might select. Since a pay-off exists (A_2/B_2) that *simultaneously* provides for each firm the best (maximum) of the worst possible (minimum) outcomes it has evaluated for each strategy, then we have our Nash equilibrium.

It may at this point be useful to distinguish between the Nash equilibrium and a dominant strategy. In terms of duopoly:

- *Nash equilibrium*:   Firm A does the best it can, given what Firm B is doing.
     Firm B does the best it can, given what Firm A is doing.
- *Dominant strategy*:   Firm A does the best it can, no matter what Firm B does.
     Firm B does the best it can, no matter what Firm A does.

Clearly the Nash equilibrium strategy A_2/B_2 is *not*, in this case, a dominant strategy. From our pay-off matrix, Firm A would do best (60% of market) with strategy A_4, if Firm B selected B_4; on the other hand Firm B would do best with strategy B_1 (90% of market), if Firm A selected A_1. It follows that only in specific circumstances will the Nash equilibrium also be the dominant strategy. In other words, a dominant strategy is a special case of the Nash equilibrium. Since oligopoly is all about situations of recognised interdependence between firms, it is with the Nash equilibrium solutions to games that we are most concerned, rather than with dominant strategies.

Alternative decision rules

So far we have assumed that each firm adopts the same decision rule (or approach) to the game, namely a **maxi-min** decision rule that involves selecting the best of the worst possible outcomes from each strategy. Of course other decision rules are possible.

Mini-max
decision rule

Mini-max is a decision rule that involves a more optimistic approach at the outset. Here the firm identifies the *best possible* outcome for each of its strategies. Only in the final selection of its strategy does a note of caution apply, when the firm chooses the *worst* of these best possible outcomes.

Returning to Table 9.2 let us examine a situation in which Firm A adopts a *mini-max* decision rule. In this case the circled numbers would change. For example, if Firm A adopts strategy A_1, the best possible outcome it could expect would be 30% of market share, with Firm B adopting counter-strategy B_4. As a result 0.30 would now be the circled number (best outcome for A of each A strategy). Repeating this procedure for each of the strategies A_1 to A_4, and then selecting the worst of all these best possible outcomes would yield a mini-max solution of strategy A_1 for Firm A, yielding 30% of the market.

Clearly if Firm B retained its original *maxi-min* decision rule then it would still select strategy B_2. This time no pay-off exists that is *simultaneously* preferred by both firms, given the approaches they respectively adopt. In other words there is no Nash equilibrium.

Of course Firm B might itself follow the same (mini-max) decision rule as A now follows. In this case Firm B is more optimistic, assuming Firm A reacts to each strategy in the best way possible for itself (Firm B). Thus for strategy B_1 it assumes Firm A reacts with A_1, giving Firm B 90% of the market, and so on. As a result 0.10 would now be the number in the square for the B_1 column (best outcome for B of each B strategy). Being cautious in the final analysis it selects the worst (mini) of these best possible (maxi) outcomes for itself, namely strategy B_4 giving Firm B 70% of the market. We have already seen that Firm A has selected strategy A_1 under the mini-max approach. We therefore have a pay-off solution (A_1, B_4) that is *simultaneously* preferred by both firms under the mini-max approach, and so is therefore the (unique) Nash equilibrium for this game. Here Firm A achieves 30% of the market and Firm B 70%.

Non-uniform
decision rules

Clearly we must take into account the approach of *each firm* to the game before we can ascertain which, if any, solution or solutions might be found to the game. Any such solution may be a Nash equilibrium or, in specific cases, both a Nash equilibrium *and* a dominant strategy. We have already noted from Table 9.2 that if Firm A adopts a *mini-max* decision rule but Firm B adopts a *maxi-min* decision rule, then the outcome of the game (A_1B_2) is neither a Nash equilibrium nor a dominant strategy for either firm.

Decision rules and mixed strategies

Mixed strategies are those that involve the firm in allotting *probabilities* to the various possible counter-strategies of its rival(s), and to the pay-off values that might then result. The idea of *expected value* considered in Chapter 3 (p. 99) can be used to evaluate the net gains in the pay-off matrix.

In terms of Table 9.1 (p. 368) suppose Firm A estimates the likelihood of Firm B responding with a *price cut* as 40% (0.40) and with *extra advertising* as 60% (0.60).

- The expected value to Firm A of the 'price-cut strategy' in terms of market share would then be

$$EV_{A \text{ price cut}} = 0.40 \, (60\%) + 0.60 \, (70\%)$$

i.e. $EV_{A \text{ price cut}} = 24\% + 42\% = 66\%$

- The expected value to Firm A of the 'extra advertising strategy' in terms of market share would then be

$$EV_{A \text{ extra adv.}} = 0.40 \, (50\%) + 0.60 \, (55\%)$$

i.e. $EV_{A \text{ extra adv.}} = 20\% + 33\% = 53\%$

The evaluation of Firm A's alternative strategies would no longer be in terms of a pay-off value for each of Firm B's 'pure strategy' responses of a price cut or extra advertising, but would now be in terms of a *single* 'weighted average' value, which combines these two possible responses by the rival.

Non-zero sum games

So far we have considered the zero-sum market share game, where any gain (or loss) to one player is matched by an equivalent loss (or gain) to some other player. Here we now consider a **non-zero-sum** game, where different choices by the players may increase or decrease the total pay-out to be distributed. Again, for simplification, we shall use a duopoly game by way of illustration.

Two-firm non-zero-sum game

In this duopoly game we use *profits* in our pay-off matrices. Each firm seeks to choose between two price strategies (£4 and £6) in order to maximise its individual profits (π). Suppose that each firm recognises that it is producing a product that to some degree is a substitute for that of the other firm. Hence each firm's profitability will depend not only on the price it sets, but also on the price set by its rival. The pay-off matrix evaluated by each firm is shown in Table 9.3. It can be seen that any gain (loss) by one rival from a strategy choice is *not* matched by an offsetting loss (gain) by the other. In other words we are in a **variable sum** game.

Table 9.3 **Pay-off matrices for a non-zero-sum game.**

(a) Firm A's pay-off matrix (£s)
(level of profits of A)

Firm A's strategies	Firm B's strategies	
	$P_B = 6$	$P_B = 4$
$P_A = 6$	$\pi_A = 100$	$\pi_A = 50$
$P_A = 4$	$\pi_A = 150$	$\pi_A = 70$

(b) Firm B's pay-off matrix (£s)
(level of profits of B)

Firm A's strategies	Firm B's strategies	
	$P_B = 6$	$P_B = 4$
$P_A = 6$	$\pi_B = 120$	$\pi_B = 140$
$P_A = 4$	$\pi_B = 60$	$\pi_B = 100$

We can now *combine* the respective firm pay-off matrices to give an overall matrix indicating the *joint profit* (π) from the various strategy combinations (Table 9.4).

The nature of any solution that may, or may not, exist for this game will, of course, depend on the decision rule adopted by the respective firms.

Combined pay-off matrix (£s)

Table 9.4 **Combined pay-off matrices and joint profit.**

Firm A's strategies	Firm B's strategies	
	$P_B = 6$	$P_B = 4$
$P_A = 6$	$\pi_A = 100$ $\pi_B = 120$ Joint $\pi = 220$	$\pi_A = 50$ $\pi_B = 140$ Joint $\pi = 190$
$P_A = 4$	$\pi_A = 150$ $\pi_B = 60$ Joint $\pi = 210$	$\pi_A = 70$ $\pi_B = 100$ Joint $\pi = 170$

Both firms adopt maxi-min decision rule Initially we shall assume that both firms adopt a **maxi–min** approach to the game. In other words each firm expects the worst (for it) reaction of the rival to any strategy, before finally selecting the best available from these worst possible outcomes.

If we follow through Firm A's pay-off matrix in Table 9.3(a), then (reading across the rows) we can see that if Firm A sets the price £6, its minimum profit is £50 via Firm B setting price £4; if Firm A sets the price £4, its minimum profit is £70, again via Firm B setting price £4. The maximum available from these minima is £70: i.e. the preferred strategy for Firm A is a price of £4.

If we follow through Firm B's pay-off matrix in Table 9.3(b), then (reading down the columns) we can see that the two minima are £60 and £100 profit. The maximum available from these minima is £100: i.e. the preferred strategy for Firm B is also a price of £4.

We have a **Nash equilibrium** whereby each firm selects a price of £4 and thereby fulfils its own expectations as to how the other firm will react. Thus outcome (P_A = £4, P_B = £4) is a Nash equilibrium, with each firm maximising its profit consistent with its expectation of the rival's reaction. However, this is *not* a dominant strategy, since each firm could have selected an alternative price strategy whereby it achieved still higher levels of profit. For instance, the strategy (P_A = £6, P_B = £6) would have increased their *individual* profits (π_A: 100 > 70; π_B: £120 > £100) and their *joint* profits in Table 9.4 (£220 > £170). Clearly the maxi-min strategy, while yielding a Nash equilibrium, fails to maximise individual or joint (industry) profits.

Both firms adopt a mini-max decision rule   Suppose now that both firms adopt a *mini-max* approach to the game. In other words each firm expects the best (for it) reaction of the rival to any strategy, before finally selecting the worst available (mini) of these best possible (max) outcomes.

From Firm A's pay-off matrix in Table 9.3(a) we see, reading across the rows, that when Firm A sets the price £6 its maximum profit is £100 via Firm B setting price £6; however if Firm A sets the price £4, its maximum profit is £150 via Firm B setting price £6. The minimum available from these maxima is £100: i.e. the preferred strategy for Firm A is a price of £6.

If we follow through Firm B's pay-off matrix in Table 9.3(b) we see, reading down the columns, that the two maxima are £120 profit (P_B = £6) and £140 profit (P_B = £4). The minimum available from these maxima is £120: i.e. the preferred strategy for Firm B is a price of £6.

In terms of our earlier definition (p. 370), the outcome (P_A = £6, P_B = £6) is a 'Nash equilibrium' since a pay-off exists (π_A = £100, π_B = £120) that *simultaneously* provides for each firm achieving the worst (minimum) of the best possible (maximum) profit outcomes it has evaluated for each price strategy. The outcome (P_A = £6, P_B = £6) is also one that maximises joint (industry) profits at £220 (see Table 9.4). However, you should be able to see that this outcome does not reflect one in which each firm has pursued a 'dominant strategy'.

Firms adopt a non-uniform decision rule   Of course each firm might adopt a different decision rule, say one maxi-min and the other mini-max. You should be able to see from the pay-off matrices in Tables 9.3 and 9.4 that a difference of this kind, on either firm's part, will preclude the Nash equilibrium and joint profit-maximising solution of P_A = £6, P_B = £6.

Rather than leave achieving a **joint-profit maximising solution** to the chance occurrence of each firm adopting an appropriate strategy, there is clearly scope for achieving this outcome by other means:

- Firms may *learn* from past experience how to predict the reactions of rivals and thereby avoid mutually damaging outcomes.
- Such learning will be easier in market situations where *tastes and technology change slowly*.
- *Collusion* may occur, whereby firms exchange information or otherwise combine their actions to move directly to a mutually advantageous combination of strategies.

The inherent dangers of a failure to communicate between rivals have been well expressed in the **Prisoner's dilemma**.

Prisoner's dilemma

Games in which strategies selected in isolation are likely to lead to all players being worse off are called **prisoner's dilemma** games. The original presentation of this approach is outlined here.

Two criminals have committed a major robbery and are arrested. However, the prosecuting authorities recognise that the evidence is inadequate to secure a conviction unless one or both criminals confess. The District Attorney is willing to allow plea-bargaining such that if a conviction is secured by *one* person confessing, he will receive no punishment and the convicted criminal will receive a heavy sentence of 20 years. If *both* confess, the sentence of 10 years' imprisonment prescribed by law will apply. Of course if *neither* confesses, they will each go free. Clearly each suspect has two strategies open to himself, with two counter-strategies available to his fellow suspect. The pay-off matrix for prisoners A and B is indicated in Table 9.5.

No confession by prisoner A can lead either to acquittal (if B does not confess) or 20 years' imprisonment (if B confesses). Confession by prisoner A can lead to acquittal (if B does not confess) or 10 years' imprisonment (if B also confesses). The possible pay-off for B is identical to that for A.

Table 9.5 Pay-off matrix (years' imprisonment): Prisoner's dilemma.

Prisoner A's strategies	Prisoner B's strategies			
	No confession		Confession	
	A	B	A	B
No confession	0	0	20	0
Confession	0	20	10	10

Clearly a *maxi-min* (best of the worst possible outcomes) approach by prisoner A will lead to A confessing and receiving 10 years' imprisonment. The same solution will apply to B, so both will confess and receive 10 years' imprisonment each. Clearly the uncertainty that might lead both players to select this suboptimal strategy could have been avoided by the sharing of information between the players or other forms of collusion.

One-shot and repeated games

In the case of the prisoner's dilemma and the other games considered so far, the underlying assumption has been that the decision made was 'once-for-all'. However, such a **one-shot game** may not be typical of many real-life business decisions. Decisions as to price, output, advertising expenditure etc. often have to be made by firms on a *repeated* basis. It will be useful at this stage to consider the different strategies and 'solutions' that might result when we consider **repeated games** rather than one-shot games.

Table 9.6 is a pay-off matrix that expresses the net gains for each of two firms in terms of daily profit. The single policy variable shown here is output level, which can be set high or low, with the pay-off dependent on the rival's reaction. Clearly this is a non-zero sum game since the total daily profit for each combination of policies is a variable rather than a constant.

Table 9.6 **Pay-off matrix (daily profits).**

		Firm B	
		Low output	High output
Firm A	Low output	£3,000; £3,000	£2,000; £4,000
	High output	£4,000; £2,000	£1,500; £1,500

One-shot game   Suppose, initially, that we treat this situation as a **one-shot game**.

- 'High output' would be the *dominant strategy* for each firm, giving both Firm A and Firm B £4,000 in daily profit should the other firm select 'low output'. However, if both firms follow this dominant strategy and select 'high output' then they each receive only £1,500 daily profit.
- If each firm follows a *maxi-min* decision rule, then Firm A selects 'low output' as the best of the worst possible outcomes (£2,000 > £1,500), as does Firm B (£2,000 > £1,500). The combination (low output/low output) will then be a *Nash equilibrium*, with each firm satisfied that it has made the best decision possible in terms of the objective(s) it has set itself (each actually receives £3,000).
- If each firm follows a *mini-max* decision rule, you should be able to show that both Firm A and Firm B will still select 'low output' as the worst of the best possible outcomes (£3,000 < £4,000 for each firm). The combination (low output/low output) remains a *Nash equilibrium*.

Even if one firm follows a maxi-min and the other a mini-max decision rule, the combination (low output/low output) will remain a *Nash* equilibrium in this particular game. We could reasonably describe this output combination (low/low) as a stable, Nash-type equilibrium to our one-shot oligopoly game.

Repeated game   However, should we view the pay-off matrix in Table 9.6 as part of a **repeated game**, then the situation so far described might be subject to considerable change. We might expect the respective firms to alter the strategies they pursue and the game to have a different outcome.

Suppose the firms initially establish the low output/low output 'solution' to the game, whether as the result of a 'Nash equilibrium' or by some form of agreement between the firms. Unlike the one-shot game, a firm in a repeated game can modify its strategy from one period to the next, and can also respond to any changes in strategy by the other firm.

- *Cheating*. If Table 9.6 is now viewed as the pay-off matrix for a repeated game, there would seem to be a possible incentive for either firm to depart from its initial 'low output' policy in the next period. Had the initial 'low output' policy been mutually agreed by the two firms in an attempt to avoid the mutually damaging high output/high output combination should each firm have followed its 'dominant strategy', we might regard such a departure as *cheating* on an agreement. By unexpectedly switching to high output, either firm could benefit by raising daily profit (from £3,000 to £4,000), though the loss of profit (from £3,000 to £2,000) by the other firm might provoke an eventual retaliation in some future time period, resulting in the mutually damaging high output/high output combination.

- *Tit-for-tat strategy*. Whether or not any 'cheating' is likely to benefit a firm will depend on a number of factors, not least the rapidity with which any rival responds to a breach of the agreement: the more rapid the response of the rival, the smaller any net benefits from cheating will be. Suppose, in our example, it takes the other firm 5 days to respond with higher output: then on *each* of these days the cheating firm gains an extra £1,000 in profit from breaching the agreement as compared with upholding the agreement. If the response of the rival were to be more rapid, say 3 days, then only £3,000 rather than £5,000 benefit would accrue. Of course, once the rival has responded *both* firms are damaged in Table 9.6 compared with the pre-cheating situation, losing £1,500 profit per day by the high output/high output combination. This may of course induce both firms to restore the initial agreement. It then follows that the more rapid the restoration of any initial agreement in order to avoid mutual damage, the larger any net benefits from cheating will be.

  If it becomes known that rivals are likely to respond rapidly to any cheating on agreements (or even departures from Nash type equilibria) by adopting *tit-for-tat* strategies, then this may itself deter attempts by either firm to cheat. Provided each firm is sufficiently well informed to be aware of the change of rival strategy, a tit-for-tat response will ensure that any benefits from cheating are of shorter duration. When factored into the decision-making process, the anticipation of a lower profit stream may deter any attempt by either firm to cheat.

- *Discounting and cheating*. It is arguable that the lower the rate of discount applied to future profits, the less likely it is that cheating will occur. The idea here is that the 'penalty' on the cheating firm is the loss of profit in future time periods when the rival actually retaliates, as compared with the profit stream anticipated under the previous agreement. If these *losses* of future profit are heavily discounted, then in present value terms they are worth much less. It follows that a lower rate of discount applied to these future losses of profit will raise their significance in present value terms and act to deter firms from breaking an agreement.

■ Sequential games

In a **sequential game** the moves and countermoves take place in a defined order: one firm makes a move and only then does the rival decide how to react to that move. Table 9.7 is a pay-off matrix showing net gains as profit per period for each of two firms. The individual pay-offs depend on the price (low or high) selected by one firm and the price response of the rival, in this non-zero sum game.

Table 9.7 **Pay-off matrix (profit per period).**

		Firm B	
		Low price	High price
Firm A	Low price	£1,000; £1,000	£3,000; £2,000
	High price	£2,000; £3,000	£500; £500

The *dominant strategy* for both Firm A and Firm B is to set a low price (£3,000 profit), but if they *both* follow this strategy the outcome is mutually damaging (£1,000 profit). You should be able to see that a *maxi-min* decision rule followed by each firm would lead to a Nash equilibrium (low price/low price) in which the expectations of each firm are fulfilled, though a *mini-max* decision rule would yield no such equilibrium.

First-mover advantages

If decisions can only be taken in sequence, an important issue is whether the firm making the *first move* can secure any advantage!

- Suppose Firm A is in a position to move first. It can choose 'low price', forcing Firm B to choose between 'low price' (£1,000) and 'high price' (£2,000). Should (as Firm A expects) Firm B select 'high price', then Firm A receives £3,000 profit per period.
- Suppose Firm B is in a position to move first. It can now choose 'low price' in the expectation that Firm A will respond with 'high price' (£2,000 > £1,000), this time giving Firm B a pay-off of £3,000 profit per period.

Clearly this game does contain 'first-mover' advantages, which lie in anticipating the likely responses of the rival and channelling those responses in a particular direction.

Decision trees

Sequential games can usefully be presented in the form of a 'decision tree' (see Chapter 3), as in Fig. 9.1 for Firm A. Firm A clearly anticipates a higher pay-off by being a 'first mover' and setting a low price in a sequential game. This then channels the choice available to Firm B into one in which its own self-interest would suggest (to Firm A) that it adopts a high-price policy. A makes a *net* benefit of £1,000 (£3,000 > £2,000) by being a 'first mover' and setting a low price as compared with its rival (Firm B) acting as a first

Fig. 9.1 Decision tree for Firm A in a sequential game.

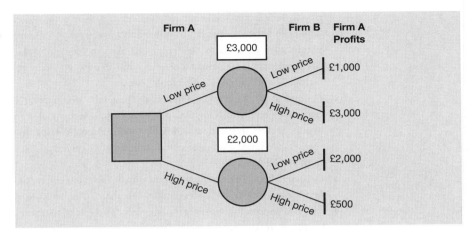

mover and itself setting the low price (check for yourself that the decision tree for Firm B would be as in Fig. 9.1, but with the labels 'Firm A' and 'Firm B' reversed). The 'first-mover' advantage is also apparent as compared with both firms *simultaneously* selecting either a low-price strategy (£3,000 > £1,000) or a high-price strategy (£3,000 > £500).

Of course, 'first-mover' advantages might equally apply in other types of game, such as deterring new firm entry or initiating price warfare to dislodge incumbent firms. The 'success' of first mover strategies may depend on the rival firm(s) being convinced that this first move is 'irreversible', in the sense that the initiating firm's strategy cannot easily be changed by counter-strategies adopted by rivals. Success as a 'first mover' may also depend on the existence of rapid response mechanisms within the operational structure of the firm, and on accurate information on rivals' likely reactions.

Applications and evidence

■ Pay-off matrices and the white salt industry

A number of recent reports and surveys have considered the duopoly situation in the UK market for white salt. In this market two firms produce an essentially homogeneous commodity, with considerable barriers to entry. Rees (1993) outlines the following key characteristics of the industry:

- *Production*. Salt production in the UK consists essentially of the extraction and processing of a non-renewable natural resource. Water is pumped down into salt strata lying underground; this dissolves the salt to form brine, which is then pumped to the surface and transported through a pipeline to, initially, a purification plant. Here chemicals are added to remove unwanted minerals, then the purified brine is pumped to an evaporation plant. After the evaporation process, undried salt is produced, with the consistency of wet sand. Part of this output is shipped immediately to chemical plants, mainly for use in the production of caustic soda and chlorine. The remainder is dried, and then shipped, in bulk or in bags, again to chemical plants for use in the production of sodium chloride, but also to food manufacturing and animal feed preparation plants, and to tanning and dyeing works. Less than 10% of total salt output is sold for cooking or table use.

- *Concentration*. There are effectively just two producers: British Salt (BS), a self-contained but wholly owned subsidiary of an industrial engineering and contracting group, Stavely Industries; and ICI Western Point (WP), a small part of the Mond division of the large chemical conglomerate ICI. BS accounts for some 55% of the UK market; WP around 45%.

- *Capacity*. Each firm experienced considerable excess capacity over the time period considered (1980–84). BS averaged less than 75% capacity; WP around 65% capacity.

- *Entry*. Considerable entry barriers exist. Though salt strata suitable for extraction are common in the UK, a combination of planning controls and high transport costs seems to rule out production outside the Cheshire area in which both BS's and WP's plants are located. The main users are located quite near to the salt plants, while at the prevailing prices imports are not regarded as a threat because of the high cost of transport and transshipment relative to value. The major salt strata in Cheshire are owned by the incumbent firms. Other entry barriers include significant economies of scale and, as we have just seen, significant excess capacity in the market.

- *Costs*. Reducing output raises marginal and average variable costs significantly. For example, restrictions on output mean that firms must reduce the number of evaporation boilers in operation, thereby increasing marginal and average variable costs.

- *Pricing*. There is considerable evidence of parallel pricing (p. 355). The MMC lists the dates and amounts of the 17 changes to list prices made by the two firms between January 1974 and January 1984. The increases are always either exactly or virtually identical. From 1980 each firm made the same percentage increases across all grades of salt; prior to this date, such percentage increases were similar between the companies but varied across grades of salt. In each case one firm announced its price increases and the second firm followed within a month and usually within two weeks. Of the 13 price increases announced from 1974 to 1980, BS led eight times and WP led five times. In each of the years 1981–84, WP was the leader. Typically the leader would inform the follower of its planned price increase a month before it came into effect, and the latter would then inform the leader of its proposed (identical) price change within that period.

Although Rees uses the white salt industry to test a wide variety of models as regards oligopolistic behaviour, here we focus primarily on the use of a **pay-off matrix** to inform the actions/reactions of players in the game. We use Table 9.8 to help explain why the duopolists might regard the observed price coordination in the period as being to their mutual advantage. Clearly the firms were aware of the need to avoid mutually damaging interactions, such as price warfare. In its evidence to the MMC, BS stated that

> if it raised prices by a lesser amount than (WP), and (WP) failed to lower its own price to the same level, there would be an immediate transfer of business to itself. This would lead to a long-term retaliation by (WP) who would seek to take customers from British Salt. (MMC 1986 , para 28:11)

The pay-off matrix in Table 9.8 calculates the outcomes for various courses of action as compared with the price coordination actually observed over the 1980-84 period. All the values (£000) reflect the predicted impact (pay-off) of a marginal price cut (outside the agreement) resulting in a 1% fall in net sales value for the industry as a whole. The values are presented for each firm on the assumption that it is responsible for breaching the agreement. We briefly consider each of the columns in the pay-off matrix.

- *Column 1.* The first period (here quarter) profit differential via breaching the price agreement by marginally (as defined earlier) undercutting that agreement. For example, if in the first quarter of 1984 BS (WP) had undercut the agreed price marginally, it would expect to gain just over £1.63 million (£3.63 million) in additional profit.
- *Column 2.* The following three periods (here the next three quarters) profit differential, via breaching the price agreement by marginally undercutting its rival as compared with adhering to the price agreement. For example, BS (WP) would expect to lose, in present value terms, some £6.04 million (£3.65 million) of profit over the next three quarters as a result of the price war ensuing from breaching the price agreement.

Note that for the five years represented in Table 9.8, and for each company, the pay-off matrix indicates that more will be lost in future profit by breaching the price agreement (column 2) than will be gained immediately by undercutting the rival's price (column 1). In other words, the pay-off matrix is supporting the continuance of a policy of price coordination, however that policy was initially obtained. Although not explaining the origins of the tacit collusion clearly evidenced by pricing behaviour observed for this duopoly in white salt production, the pay-off matrix does support the continuance (stability) of that outcome.

Table 9.8 Pay-off matrix for the white salt duopoly (£000s).

	1 $\pi_i^R - \pi_i^C$		2 $(\pi_i^C/r) - \delta V_i$	
	BS	WP	BS	WP
1980	367	2,015	3,347	3,759
1981	964	2,901	4,172	4,148
1982	800	3,340	5,143	4,006
1983	1,377	3,397	5,041	3,621
1984	1,631	3,633	6,035	3,645

where: π_i^R = maximum profit in 1st period (quarter) via breaching the price agreement.

π_i^C = maximum profit in 1st period (quarter) via adhering to the price agreement.

r (> 0) = per-period interest rate.

τ_i = 'punishment path' of price retaliations by other firms in the three periods (quarters) following any breach by firm i.

V_i = present value (at the date retaliation occurs) of profits to firm i along the 'punishment path'.

$\delta = (1 + r)^{-1}$: i.e. the discount factor.

■ Game theory and world liquidity

Miller and Luangaram (1998) apply game theory in an attempt to justify governmental intervention in world banking and currency markets. The suggestion is that *without* such intervention a 'Prisoner's dilemma' type of situation might occur in world banking currency markets, with the game theory 'solution' likely to be suboptimal for all participants.

The economic principles underlying this particular game involve an assumption that creditors *as a group* are willing to make new loans, but creditors *as individuals* are willing to do so only when convinced that other creditors will do the same. In this situation a game can be established in which the likely 'solution' will be no lending to an illiquid borrower, even when it can be shown to be in the interests of both creditor and borrower for such lending to take place. Only government intervention in the form of *coordinating creditor responses* is then likely to avoid such a mutually damaging outcome.

Table 9.9 reflects a setting in which each of two creditors lends 50 to a borrower who is solvent but illiquid: *solvent* because the project will cover all borrowing and debt service charges (see below) by paying 120 (on the total borrowing of 100) in a year's time, but *illiquid* because there are no payments (e.g. dividends) to creditors in the interim period of time.

Table 9.9 **Pay-off matrix in creditor–debtor game.**

- At the start of the year the borrower must provide a total of 20 to the creditors (10 to each) as *debt service*.
- If *each creditor* is willing to re-lend the 10 of debt service received, then the project will continue and each will receive future payment with a present discounted value of 50.
- If *neither creditor* is willing to re-lend the 10 of debt service (i.e. to 'roll over' the loan), the debtor will default, and the project will collapse with each creditor receiving only 30 from the 'scrap value' of the project.

The pay-offs reflecting these various contingencies are shown in Table 9.9:

- The top-left pay-off (50,50) is where both creditors re-lend the 'debt service' and continue to roll over the loan.
- The bottom-right pay-off (30,30) is where neither creditor is willing to re-lend the 'debt service' and so each receives only the 'scrap value' of 30 as the project collapses.

- The top-right pay-off (20, 30) is where creditor 1 re-lends 10, but not creditor 2. The project will subsequently collapse, with creditor 1 worse off compared with creditor 2, since creditor 1 receives only a net 20 after 'scrapping' the project (30 minus the 10 re-lent and now lost) as compared with 30 for creditor 2.
- The bottom-left pay-off (30, 20) is as above, but where creditor 2 re-lends 10, but not creditor 1.

In terms of our early analysis there are arguably two 'Nash equilibria' to this game: namely (50, 50) with *both creditors lending* and (30, 30) with *neither creditor lending*. Each Nash equilibrium is defined as a situation in which no creditor has an incentive to deviate from his/her strategy given that the other does not deviate from the revealed strategy. The arrows in Table 9.9 show the direction of movement from any initial game solution *other than* one of the two Nash equilibrium solutions. These arrows show that neither creditor would logically choose to behave differently from the other, whether the starting point was 30, 20 or 20, 30.

Of course, the problem with such a *multiple-equilibria game* is in being unable to determine which of the two possible Nash equilibrium solutions will be attained! Clearly the more 'socially efficient' of the two equilibria is lend/lend (50, 50), with the project continuing to the benefit of both creditors and debtors. However, a failure by governments (or international bodies) to coordinate creditor responses may lead to a *self-fulfilling* liquidity crisis in the form of the (30, 30) equilibrium, where neither creditor lends. This is especially likely when general market sentiment moves against debtor firms (or nations). Individual firms (or nations) who might themselves be willing to be creditors provided that others adopt the same outlook, will then select this less socially acceptable Nash equilibrium.

This type of multiple-equilibria game places a premium on governmental and intergovernmental coordination to avoid systemic failure. In the absence of such coordination Radelet and Sachs (1998) have argued that

> 'international loan markets are prone to self-fulfilling crises in which individual creditors may act rationally and yet market outcomes produce sharp, costly and fundamentally unnecessary reversals in capital flows.'

Arguably it is just such coordination of creditor responses by bodies such as the International Monetary Fund and the World Bank that has prevented liquidity crises in East Asia, Brazil and Mexico in the late 1990s from becoming still more severe.

Coke/Pepsi game   Kay (1993) uses actual and simulated data to devise a Coke/Pepsi game. The 'parameters' shown in Table 9.10 broadly reflect the (then) actual market shares and marginal cost situations, together with realistic estimates of price and advertising elasticities (shown here as identical for each company). The 'initial values', though hypothetical, capture the actual circumstance of parallel pricing and similar (here identical) advertising spend, with profit outcomes broadly reflecting the ratio then achieved.

Kay goes on to show that the 'initial values' of this Coke/Pepsi game most definitely do not represent a Nash equilibrium. In other words the observed behaviour of Coke and Pepsi in charging the same price and advertising at similar levels is not an outcome whereby each is taking the best possible decisions given the decisions of its rival. Kay shows how, in a *sequential game*, Pepsi could benefit from *first-mover advantage*. Pepsi could

Table 9.10 **The
Coke/Pepsi game.**

	Coke	Pepsi
Parameters		
Marginal cost (ecus)	0.24	0.24
Market share at parity (%)	70	30
Price response elasticity	5.0	5.0
Adv. spend response elasticity	0.5	0.5
Initial values		
Price (ecus)	0.39	0.39
Ad spend (£000)	630	630
Market share (%)	70	30
Profits (000 ecus)	2,625	765
Nash equilibrium		
Price (ecus)	0.40 (+0.01)	0.35 (−0.04)
Ad spend (£000)	630 (+0)	430 (−200)
Market share (%)	58 (−12)	42 (+12)
Profits (000 ecus)	2,350 (−275)	1,050 (+285)

Source: Kay (1993)

do better by cutting price, thereby securing a higher market share (given the high price-elasticity of demand) and cutting its expenditure on advertising: the latter because, with its low market share (relative to Coke) and the estimated inelasticity of sales with respect to advertising spend, expenditure on advertising adds more to Pepsi's costs in this model than it adds to its revenue.

The Nash equilibrium, where Pepsi secures first-mover advantages in a sequential game, is shown in Table 9.10 with Pepsi reducing prices by 4% (0.04), cutting advertising by 200 (000 pounds), raising market share by 12% and profits by 285 (000 ecus). In this situation Coke, as follower, ends up with its best decisions then being to raise its price by 1% (0.01) and leave advertising unchanged, but even so it loses market share by 12% and suffers reduced profits by 275 (000 ecus). Nevertheless this outcome is seen as Coke's part of a Nash equilibrium in which it acts as follower, making the best decision it can given the first-mover decisions of Pepsi.

The key question then is why the *actual* observations in the marketplace seem to resemble those indicated by the 'initial values' rather than the 'Nash equilibrium' of Table 9.10. Kay suggests that the threat of price warfare, with each rival believing the other will respond with 'tit for tat' strategies, may deter any attempt by either party to secure 'first mover' advantages in a sequential game and thereby discourage their moving away from these initial values. Had the game been 'one off' rather than 'repeated', then Kay suggests the outcome might have been other than the observed similarity of price and advertising spend. However, the concern of mutually damaging action/reaction makes the continuation of the status quo, as given by the 'initial values', an acceptable solution to both parties. Certainly joint profits are not at a maximum at these initial values

(3,390,000 ecus as against 3,400,000 ecus), but the risks associated with either firm's seeking to pursue a 'dominant strategy' would seem to outweigh any additional profit, either individually or jointly. Kay concludes that the competitive environment is such that, despite appearances to the contrary, the 'initial values' constitute a broadly stable solution to the game, since the 'rules' that might allow the two players to charge different prices are simply too hard to implement.

Key terms

Copycat strategy	Prisoner's dilemma
Dominant strategy	Repeated game
First-mover advantages	Sequential game
Maxi-min	Tit-for-tat strategy
Mini-max	Variable-sum game
Mixed strategies	Zero-sum game
One-shot game	

Full definitions can be found in the 'Glossary of terms' (pp. 699–710)

Review questions

1. Summer Delight plc and Golden Dawn plc are major companies competing in the snacks market. They are in the process of updating old popular flavours for their crisps in the hope of creating greater product differentiation and hence increasing their market share of the most popular end of the crisp market. Table 9.11 shows Summer Delight's gain (+) and loss (−) of market shares as a result of the introduction of its most recent tomato, chicken and onion flavoured crisps, given the fact that Golden Dawn will respond to this competition with its own updated cheese, bacon and curry flavoured crisps. Assume that there are only two main companies competing in this part of the snacks industry and that Summer Delight's gain/loss is Golden Dawn's loss/gain.

Summer Delight's Gain (+) or loss (−) of market share (%)

Table 9.11

		Golden Dawn		
		Cheese	Bacon	Curry
Summer Delight	Tomato	+5	−1	−4
	Chicken	+3	+1	+9
	Onion	+4	−2	−6

(a) Explain the meaning of the term *zero–sum* game and maxi-min/mini-max solutions, in the context of the crisp market.

(b) With the use of the table, show the maximum and minimum range of outcomes for both companies, and derive the maxi-min and mini-max solutions.

(c) What is the most likely solution to this type of competition? Why is there no incentive for any of the firms to change their strategy under these oligopoly conditions?

(d) If, for any reason, the market shares in the chicken/cheese and chicken/bacon boxes were reversed, what would be the strategic importance of this change?

2. Saltco plc has dominated the salt-producing industry for years, earning significant monopoly profits. Recently a new company, Westgram plc, has used new technology to become a potential entrant into the salt industry. However, Westgram knows that before it enters the industry it will have to invest £80 million in a new plant to incorporate the new technology. Westgram also knows that Saltco can either respond to Westgram's entry by keeping its price high, or engage in a price war to try to push Westgram out. The profit pay-off matrix that describes the entry/no entry situation is shown in Table 9.12, with Saltco's profits (£m) shown on the left in each square and Westgram's profits (£m) on the right.

Table 9.12 **Profit pay-off matrix (£m).**

		Westgram plc	
		Entry	No entry
Saltco plc	High price	100,20	200,0
	Low price	60, −20	80,0

(a) Describe briefly the situation shown in this pay-off matrix .

(b) What might happen if Saltco threatened a price war (i.e. low price) in an attempt to dissuade Westgram from entering? Do you think Saltco's threat is a credible one?

(c) Saltco now decides to invest £60 million in new capacity *before* Westgram's entry, in order to increase output and bring down price. This new strategy reduces Saltco's profit pay-offs for its 'High price' strategy from 100, 200 respectively to 40, 140 respectively. The new strategy has no impact on Saltco's profit pay-offs for its 'Low price' strategy. Will the new pay-off matrix have any effect on Westgram's prospects for entry?

(d) Is there any other way in which Saltco could deter Westgram from entering the industry without investing in new capacity-creating equipment?

3. Two firms, Proctor plc and Lever plc, dominate the market for washing powder, with Proctor producing their 'Aerol' brand and Lever producing a competing product called 'Nova'. Each firm has decided to investigate the possibility of undertaking a more aggressive advertising campaign in order to maintain its market share in a competitive environment. The possible outcomes of such strategies are shown in the pay-off matrix (Table 9.13) showing yearly profit figures (£m). In each square the profit figures shown on the left relate to Lever and those on the right to Proctor.

Table 9.13 **Profit pay-off matrix (£m).**

		Proctor	
		Advertise	No advertising
Lever	Advertise	11,6	16,0
	No advertising	7,9	11,3

(a) Use the pay-off matrix to explain what is meant by the term 'dominant strategy' for the respective companies.

(b) Suppose the pay-off values in the bottom-right square now change from 11,3 respectively to 22,2. How will this influence the dominant strategy of each firm? Will the Nash equilibrium change?

(c) Consider any strategic implications for either company as a result of the changes in profit pay-offs noted in part (b).

4. Two companies, Deckord Ltd and Tapemech Ltd, make lifting mechanisms for tape decks, which are subsequently incorporated into VCR players. Both companies dominate the industry and, as a result, the market appears duopolistic in nature. Net profits depend on industry output, as shown in Table 9.14.

Table 9.14

Quantity/week (units)	1,000	1,250	1,500	1,750	2,000
Net profits/week (£)	32,000	35,000	30,000	21,000	10,000

Experience has shown that the optimum output for each company involves batches of 500, 750 or 1,000, and that profits are divided in proportion to each firm's share of total output. (In other words if Deckord and Tapemech produce 500 units each, total output will be 1,000 and the total weekly profits of £32,000 will be divided 50:50, i.e. £16,000 each. However, if Deckord produces 750 and Tapemech 1,000, total output will be 1,750 units and the total weekly profits of £21,000 will be divided in the ratio of 3:4: i.e. Deckord gets 3/7 of £21,000 or £9,000 per week and Tapemech gets 4/7 of £21,000 or £12,000 per week.)

(a) Suppose the two companies realise their market power and collude. What total output level would they choose to maximise total joint profits?

(b) Compile a profit pay-off matrix for these two companies with Deckord's three outputs of 500, 750, and 1,000 across the top of the matrix and Tapemech's three outputs of 500, 750 and 1,000 vertically down the left-hand side of the matrix (e.g. the 500/500 square will be on the top-left corner of the matrix). Within each of the nine squares comprising the matrix, enter the net profits of both companies resulting from those output combinations (e.g. the top-left corner square will contain 'Deckord £16,000 and Tapemech £16,000').

(c) Both Deckord and Tapemech take the rival's output as given and choose their own output accordingly (i.e. both companies choose their strategies *simultaneously*). Identify the 'Nash equilibrium', and explain why no other square would fulfil this equilibrium condition.

(d) Suppose now that Deckord announces its production strategy *at the outset* and assumes that Tapemech will then follow by choosing its own optimal response (i.e. the companies choose their strategies *sequentially*). Which production strategy would Deckord choose to follow in this situation? Can you identify any equilibrium outcome in this situation?

(e) Deckord and Tapemech reach an initial agreement giving £20,000 profit to Deckord and £10,000 profit to Tapemech respectively. Is there any incentive for Deckord to break this agreement (i.e. 'cheat')? What might result from such 'cheating' by Deckord?

5. Two companies, Building Supplies Ltd and Metal Trades Ltd are the only suppliers of metal roof supports to the building industry. To improve their combined profits they have formed a cartel, but they are still nervous about their future in a volatile market. Table 9.15 shows that each company has two possible strategies: to maintain the cartel agreement or to break the agreement. The result of breaking the agreement by selling at a lower price in order to gain market share and increase profits is shown in the table. The upper half of each quadrant refers to Metal Trades Ltd and the lower half to Building Supplies Ltd.

(a) The table shows a non–zero–sum game. Briefly explain what this expression means in terms of the table. What are the implications of this fact for our maxi–min and mini–max approaches to game theory?

(b) Explain why there are strong incentives to break the agreement by:
 (i) deriving the information logically from the detail shown in the table;
 (ii) using the relevant maxi–min or mini–max approach.

(c) Explain why breaking the cartel agreement is detrimental to both Metal Trades Ltd and Building Supplies Ltd.

(d) If the two companies have played the cartel game repeatedly in the past, can this have any repercussions on the strategies of both companies?

Table 9.15

Cartel profits game		Metal Trades Ltd (Profits £m)	
		Maintain agreement	Break agreement
Building Supplies Ltd (profits £m)	Maintain agreement	5 / 5	6 / 2
	Break agreement	2 / 6	4 / 4

■ Further reading

Intermediate texts

Baumol, W. J. (1977), *Economic Theory and Operations Analysis*, 4th edn, Ch. 16, Prentice Hall, Hemel Hempstead.

Browning, E. and Browning, J. (1992), *Microeconomic Theory and Applications*, 4th edn, Chs 12–14, HarperCollins, London.

Dobson, S., Maddala, G. S. and Miller, E. (1995), *Microeconomics*, Ch. 11, McGraw-Hill, Maidenhead.

Hope, S. (1999), *Applied Economics*, Ch. 11, Wiley, Chichester.

Katz, M. and Rosen, H. (1998), *Microeconomics*, 3rd edn, Ch. 15, Irwin, Boston, Mass.

Kay, J. (1993), *Foundations of Corporate Success*, Oxford University Press, Oxford.

Koutsoyiannis, A. (1979), *Modern Microeconomics*, 2nd edn, Chs 9 and 10, Macmillan, Basingstoke.

Laidler, D. and Estrin, S. (1995), *Introduction to Microeconomics*, 4th edn, Chs 17–19, Harvester Wheatsheaf, Hemel Hempstead.

Maddala, G. S. and Miller, E. (1989), *Microeconomics: Theory and Application*, Chs 13 and 14, McGraw-Hill, Maidenhead.

Nicholson, W. (1997), *Intermediate Microeconomics and its Application*, 7th edn, Chs 17 and 18, Dryden Press, Fort Worth.

Pindyck, R. and Rubinfeld, D. (1998), *Microeconomics*, 4th edn, Chs 12 and 13, Macmillan, Basingstoke.

Varian, H. (1999), *Intermediate Microeconomics*, 5th edn, Chs 26 and 27, Norton, New York.

Advanced texts

Gardner, R. (1995), *Games for Business and Economics*, Wiley, Chichester.

Heap, S. and Varoufakis, Y. (1995), *Game Theory: A Critical Introduction*, Routledge, London.

Articles and other sources

Ashby, S. G. and Diacon, S. R. (1998), 'The corporate demand for insurance: a strategic perspective', *The Geneva Papers on Risk and Insurance: Issues and Practice*, 86, Jan.

Levenstein, M. (1997), 'Price wars and the stability of collusion: a study of the pre-World War 1 bromine industry', *The Journal of Industrial Economics*, XLV, 2.

Miller, M. and Luangaram, P. (1998), 'Financial crises in East Asia: bank runs, asset bubbles and antidotes', *National Institute Economic Review*, 3, July.

MMC (1986), *White Salt: A Report on the Supply of White Salt in the UK by Producers of such Salt*, HMSO, London.

Radelet, S. and Sachs, J. (1998), 'The onset of the East Asian Financial crisis', *Harvard Institute for International Development*, March.

Rees, R. (1993), 'Collusive equilibrium in the great salt duopoly', *Economic Journal*, 103, 419.

Vulkan, E. (1999), 'Economic implications of agent technology and e-commerce', *The Economic Journal*, 109, 453.

Chapter 10

Factor markets

In this chapter we consider the determination of the price and output of the factors of production, namely labour, land, capital and arguably entrepreneurship. You should, of course, be familiar with the idea that the demand for any factor of production is derived from the demand for the product (good or service) produced by that factor.

In this first section of the chapter we shall illustrate this idea of derived demand in the context of the single factor, labour. We shall initially assume competitive product and labour market conditions, and review a variety of ideas with which you should already be familiar. The next section continues the analysis of labour markets, but takes into account imperfect conditions in the product market and in the market for labour itself. We then go on to broaden the analysis to consider factor markets other than labour.

With the exception of profit, the reward that any factor of production receives is clearly equal to the price that is paid to hire it. As with all prices in competitive markets, the price of any factor of production is determined by supply and demand. However, the factors of production are not demanded in order to obtain ownership, as is the case with consumer goods, but rather because of the stream of services they offer. For example, the demand for labour implies a demand for the mental and physical effort of workers involved in production. Because of this, the demand for labour (and indeed for any factor of production) is referred to as a **derived demand** rather than a direct demand. It is derived from the product, whether a good or a service, that labour (and all other factors) produces.

Marginal productivity theory

The classical theory of income distribution is the **marginal productivity theory**. According to this theory firms will continue to employ factors of production until the employment of the marginal unit of each factor adds as much to revenue as it does to costs. For simplicity it is sometimes assumed that there is perfect competition in the market in which the product is sold so that firms sell their entire output at the *ruling market price*. In these circumstances the contribution of the marginal unit of any factor of production – that is, its marginal revenue product – is equal to the factor's *marginal physical product* multiplied by the *price* at which the product is sold.

We noted in Chapter 4 (p. 147) that the **law of variable proportion** applies in the short run when at least one factor of production is fixed. This law predicts that when labour is the variable factor being applied to some fixed factor (such as land or capital) the marginal physical product at first rises but subsequently falls as the employment of workers increases, as in Table 10.1. **Marginal physical product** (*MPP*) of labour refers to the additional (physical) *output* contributed by the last person employed. We can see from Table 10.1 that *MPP* of labour begins to fall after the sixth worker has been employed. However, employers are less concerned with marginal physical product than with marginal revenue product.

Marginal revenue product (*MRP*) of labour is the additional *value* contributed by the last person employed. In a perfectly competitive product market, *MRP* is found by multiplying the *MPP* by the price of the product; in Table 10.1 the *MRP* is calculated assuming a constant product price of £5 per unit. This is sometimes called the **value marginal product** (*VMP*): see p. 394. Under marginal productivity theory the profit-maximising firm will continue to employ workers until the last person employed adds exactly the same value to revenue as to costs, i.e. until *MRP* from employment = *MC* of employment.

Table 10.1 Returns to labour in the short run.

No. of workers	Total product	Marginal physical product	Marginal revenue product	Marginal cost	Total revenue product	Total variable cost	Total profit
1	12	12	60	100	60	100	−40
2	26	14	70	100	130	200	−70
3	50	24	120	100	250	300	−50
4	90	40	200	100	450	400	50
5	140	50	250	100	700	500	200
6	200	60	300	100	1,000	600	400
7	254	54	270	100	1,270	700	570
8	304	50	250	100	1,520	800	720
9	340	36	180	100	1,700	900	800
10	358	18	90	100	1,790	1,000	790
11	374	16	80	100	1,870	1,100	770
12	378	4	20	100	1,890	1,200	690

For illustrative purposes, as well as assuming a constant product price of £5, Table 10.1 assumes a constant wage rate per person of £100 (i.e. *AC* = *MC* = £100). The only cost in Table 10.1 is labour, i.e. variable cost.

It is clear that after the employment of the second person and up to the employment of the ninth person, each worker adds more to revenue than to cost (*MRP* > *MC*). After the employment of the ninth worker the situation is reversed, and each additional employee adds more to costs than to revenue (*MRP* < *MC*). It follows that profit is maximised when nine people are employed.

■ The individual firm's demand for labour

The general relationship between *MRP*, *ARP* and the number of workers employed at a constant wage rate is set out diagrammatically in Fig 10.1. At a constant wage of $0W$ ($= AC = MC$) the profit-maximising firm will employ $0L$ workers, where $MRP = MC$. If the market wage rate increases to $0W_1$, the number of workers employed by the profit-maximising firm will fall to $0L_1$. It follows that when there is perfect competition in the factor and product markets, the firm's **demand for labour curve** is that part of its *MRP* curve that lies below its *ARP* curve. At wage rates above *ARP* the firm is making a loss and will not undertake production.

Equilibrium in a competitive labour market

A theory of wage determination in competitive markets involves an understanding of the *market demand* and *market supply* conditions that relate to any particular industry or occupation.

Demand for labour

If we know the number of workers that each firm demands at any given wage rate, then we can derive the *industry's* demand for labour by adding together the *individual firms'* demand curves. Because each individual firm's demand for labour will vary inversely with the wage rate, the industry's demand for labour will also vary inversely with the wage rate. In other words, market demand for labour will expand as the wage rate falls.

The **elasticity** of an industry's demand for labour will, as with any factor of production, vary *directly* with:

- the elasticity of demand for the product produced by the industry;
- the proportion of total costs of production accounted for by labour;
- the elasticity of substitution between labour and other factors of production – in other words, the ease with which labour can be substituted by other factors.

The demand for labour will therefore be less elastic:

- the less elastic is the demand for the product it produces;
- the smaller the proportion of total costs accounted for by labour input;
- the less easy it is to substitute labour by capital or by other factors.

Fig. 10.1 **Wage rates and employment in a competitive labour market.**

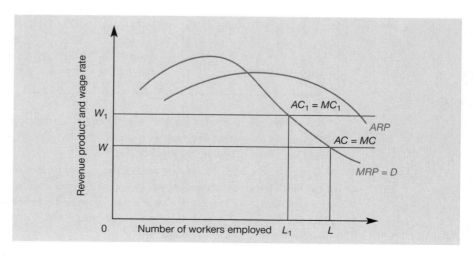

Supply of labour The supply of labour to any particular industry or occupation will vary directly with the wage rate. At higher wage rates more workers will be available for employment in the industry or occupation, and vice versa. However, in certain cases the supply of labour to an occupation might be relatively inelastic in the short run. For example, where the nature of work is highly skilled and requires considerable training, the supply of labour to the occupation will *not* rise substantially, at least initially, as wage rates increase. This is true of doctors and barristers, for example.

The supply of labour to *all* industries or occupations will tend to be more elastic in the long run than in the short run. Where wages increase in particular occupations, more people will be encouraged to undertake the necessary training, so increasing the amount of labour available. In the case of unskilled labour, supply will tend to be relatively elastic in both the short run and the long run, since little, if any, training is required.

Wage determination In competitive labour markets, wage rates are determined by the forces of supply and demand for labour. In these circumstances, different wage rates between occupations will reflect differences in the respective conditions of supply and demand conditions in the two hypothetical labour markets shown in Fig. 10.2.

The higher wage rate in one of these competitive labour markets is due to the fact that *at any given wage rate* demand for labour is *greater* (D_1D_1) and supply of labour is *lower* (S_1S_1) than in the other competitive labour market.

Given a free market and a particular set of supply and demand conditions for labour, only one wage rate is sustainable: that which equates supply of labour with demand for labour. It follows that wages in a particular industry or occupation can change only if there is a prior change in the conditions of supply, or in the conditions of demand, or in both. Furthermore, differences in wage rates between occupations will reflect differences in the conditions of supply and demand for different types of worker.

Fig. 10.2 Equilibrium wage rates and levels of employment in two separate, but competitive, labour markets.

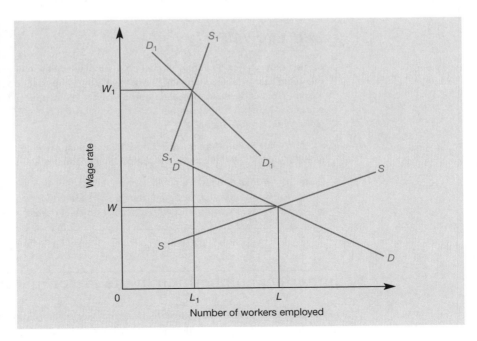

Theoretical developments

So far we have considered the single factor labour, and assumed perfectly competitive conditions in both product and labour markets. In this section we begin to consider the impact on equilibrium wage and levels of employment of various imperfections in the labour market that more closely accord with reality. We also broaden our analysis to take account of other factor markets.

■ Imperfect competition in the product market

Our earlier analysis is fundamentally unchanged if we relax the assumption of perfect competition in the product market. There will still be a tendency for marginal revenue product at first to rise and to pull up average revenue product because of increasing returns. Subsequently, the onset of diminishing returns will mean that *MRP* will fall as successive workers are employed, and this will eventually pull down the *ARP*. However, with **imperfect product markets** there are now two reasons why marginal revenue product declines as employment expands beyond a certain point. Not only is there the onset of diminishing returns, but firms with imperfect product markets facing negatively sloped demand curves must now reduce the price of all units in order to increase sales.

In imperfect markets, then, marginal revenue product is determined both by marginal physical product *and* by the effect on market price of an increase in output. Because price will tend to fall in imperfect markets as output increases, the effect is to make the *MRP* curve fall more steeply than for firms in perfect competition. Nevertheless, where the firm recruits additional workers at a constant wage rate, its demand for labour is still given by its (now steeper) marginal revenue product curve.

MRP and *VMP*

Some texts make a distinction between the **marginal revenue product** (*MRP*) and the **value marginal product** (*VMP*) once we admit imperfections in the product market. This is because increased output lowers the product price so that, strictly speaking, *MRP* no longer equals *MPP* × product price but *MPP* × marginal revenue (*MR*). We therefore have:

- *VMP* = *MPP* × product price (competitive product market)
- *MRP* = *MPP* × *MR* (imperfectly competitive product market)

Certainly *MRP* as defined here will be steeper than, or lie inside, the *VMP* curve. In other words, an *imperfect product market* will mean fewer workers employed for any given wage, as compared with a perfect product market.

■ Imperfect competition in the factor market

In the **factor market** itself, imperfections may occur on the side of both the purchasers of labour and the suppliers of labour. It may be useful to consider each in turn.

Monopsony: imperfection in the purchase of labour

In the analysis underlying Fig. 10.1 (p. 392) we assumed that the firms hiring (purchasing) labour were able to secure all the workers of a given type at the going wage rate. We can therefore state that at a wage rate of, say, W, the average cost (AC) of labour to the firm is equal to W no matter how few or many persons are employed. It follows from this that the wage $W = AC = MC$ to the hiring firm. Hiring the eleventh person in Table 10.1 (p. 391) at a wage of £100 increases total labour cost to the firm from £1,000 to £1,100: i.e. MC of the eleventh unit of labour = £100. The AC of hiring 11 units of labour is £1,100/11 = £100. Clearly for *all* units of labour employed, wage = £100 = $AC = MC$ to the hiring firm.

We now relax this assumption and assume the firm to be a significant purchaser of labour, which, by hiring more labour, pushes up the price of labour. In terms of Figs 10.1 and 10.2 it is as though an increase in the *firm's* demand for labour is significant enough to shift the *industry/occupational* demand curve for labour to the right, thereby raising the equilibrium wage.

When a firm is a significant purchaser of labour, potentially forcing up the price of labour by hiring additional units, we refer to a situation of **monopsony** in the labour market. The result of such monopsony in the purchasing of labour is that the firm will be unable to recruit as many workers as it wishes at the ruling wage rate. Instead it will be compelled to increase wage rates in order to attract more workers, so that the AC curve of labour now slopes upwards from left to right, as in Fig. 10.3. Both the average and the marginal cost of employing additional workers will now rise as employment increases. Indeed, the marginal cost curve will now rise by more than average cost, so that the marginal cost curve will now lie *above* the average cost curve. For example, if hiring the eleventh worker in Table 10.1 now raises the wage rate for all workers from £100 to £110, AC = £110 for hiring 11 workers but the MC of the eleventh worker is £210: the £110 paid to the last worker plus an extra £10, which must (in the absence of discrimination) be paid to the 10 workers already employed. Clearly $MC > AC$, and we have a situation such as that illustrated in Fig. 10.3, with MC lying above AC throughout its length.

Fig. 10.3 **Wage rates and employment.**

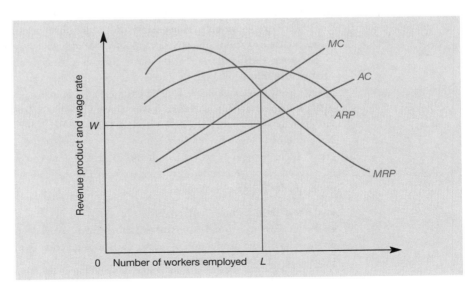

Note that in this case of monopsony, the intersection of *MC* with *MRP* determines the *number of workers employed* (0*L*), and the average cost curve determines the *wage rate* (0*W*) at this level of employment. In other words, because the marginal cost and average cost of employing additional workers are no longer the same, the firm's marginal revenue product curve no longer indicates the demand for labour at any given wage rate.

The conventional criticism of monopsony is that it will reduce both wages and levels of employment in the labour market. In terms of Fig. 10.3, the suggestion here is that, for a *competitive* labour market as regards both purchasing and supplying labour, the industry/occupation solution will be the intersection of supply of labour to the industry (*AC*) with demand for labour by the industry (*MRP*). Clearly *AC* and *MRP* intersect at a higher wage and higher level of employment than would be the case if the industry became a pure monopsony, with a single purchaser of labour. In this case the *MC* curve lies above the *AC* curve (previously the supply of labour curve to the industry) and we have the outcome previously described at wage 0*W* and employment 0*L*.

This criticism of monopsony may, however, be less valid when we admit imperfections on *both* the purchasing and supply of labour sides simultaneously (see p. 402).

Monopoly: imperfections in the supply of labour
If the labour force is now unionised, then the supply of labour to the firm (or industry) may be regulated. We initially assume, however, that the demand for labour remains competitive: i.e. many small firms purchase labour, none of which is significant enough by itself to influence the price of labour. The MRP curve therefore remains the demand curve for labour.

◼ Impacts of trade unions

A **trade union** is usually defined as a group of workers who band together to pursue certain common aims. A trade union can influence the supply of labour to an industry depending on the extent to which the workforce are members of the union. We consider the factors likely to determine the effectiveness of a trade union later in the section (p. 399). Here we initially concentrate on the various *methods* by which a trade union might secure its various objectives, especially that of higher wages for its members.

However, we should note at the outset that even though unions bring an element of **monopoly** into labour supply, theory suggests that they can influence price *or* quantity, but not both. For example, in Fig. 10.1 (p. 392) the union may seek wage rate W_1 instead of *W*, but must accept in return lower employment at L_1 instead of *L*. Alternatively, unions may seek a level of employment *L* instead of L_1, but must then accept a lower wage rate of *W* instead of W_1. Except (see later) where unions are able to force employers off their demand curve for labour (*MRP*), then unions can only raise wages at the cost of reduced employment. However, a *given rise* in wages will reduce employment by less, under the following circumstances:

- the less elastic is final demand for the product;
- the less easy it is to substitute other factors for the workers in question;
- the lower is the proportion of labour costs to total costs of production.

All of these circumstances will make the demand curve for labour (*MRP*) less elastic.

Restricting supply of labour

A union might seek to **restrict supply** by refusing to supply workers below a particular wage rate. The implications of this are examined in Fig. 10.4.

Supply and demand for labour in this industry are initially represented by *SS* and *DD* respectively, and the equilibrium wage rate is $0W$ with $0L$ workers employed. If a trade union now demands a pay rise of WW_1 and refuses to supply labour below $0W_1$, then the effective supply curve of labour to this industry becomes W_1RS. If all other things remain equal, the higher wage rate implies a reduction in the number of workers employed to $0L_1$. However, if demand for the product is rising, perhaps because of a general rise in incomes, it might be possible for the firm to finance the increase in wages by raising the price of the product. The effect of this will be to increase the demand for labour ($MRP = MPP \times$ price) at each and every wage rate. If the increase in demand is sufficiently large (i.e. $\geqslant D_1D_1$), then the higher wage rate $0W_1$ does *not* lead to any reduction in the number of workers employed.

In practice this is often what happens as a result of an increase in wages. Firms are able to pass on the costs of wage increases in the form of higher prices, helped by the fact that incomes in the economy as a whole tend to rise over time. However, when firms are *unable* to pass on the full effect of higher costs to consumers in the form of higher product prices, perhaps because demand is relatively price elastic and income inelastic, then the higher wage increase might lead to some workers losing their jobs.

Higher productivity

Another way in which a trade union might obtain a higher wage rate for its members is by **increasing productivity**. If all other things remain equal, it is possible to increase wage rates by the same percentage as an increase in productivity *without* increasing average costs of production. Of course, because of increased productivity the firm will have a larger output to sell. Provided price remains constant this again implies an increase in the demand for labour as each worker's marginal revenue product increases. Figure 10.5 illustrates that

Fig. 10.4 **The effect of a trade union on wage rates and employment in an industry.**

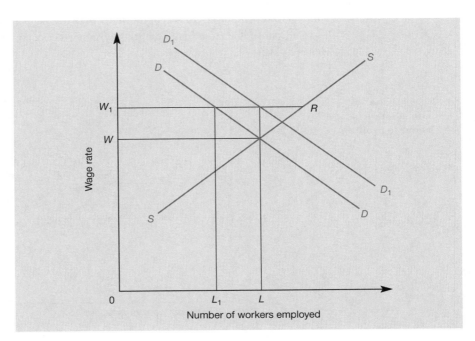

Fig. 10.5 **The effect of
an increase in
productivity where
there is perfect
competition in the
product market.**

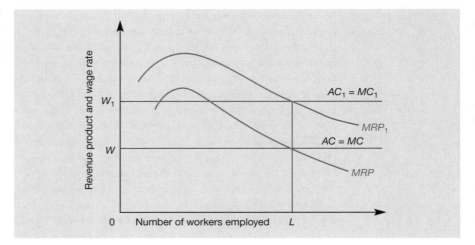

in these circumstances it is possible for a firm to pay higher wages without necessarily
reducing the number of workers employed.

Initially the wage rate is $0W$, and $0L$ workers are employed in the profit-maximising
situation ($MRP = MC$). If an increase in productivity shifts the MRP curve to MRP_1 it is
possible to increase wages to $0W_1$ without there being any reduction in the number of
workers employed. This explains why so much emphasis is attached to productivity deals
when wage increases are negotiated.

**Profit-financed
wage increases**

Even without an increase in marginal revenue productivity it might be possible for a
union to obtain a substantial wage increase for its members. This would be possible if it
could persuade employers to accept a **cut in profits**. Figure 10.6 is used to illustrate
this point, and refers to a firm operating with perfect competition in the factor and
product markets.

Fig. 10.6 **The net
contribution of
labour to profit.**

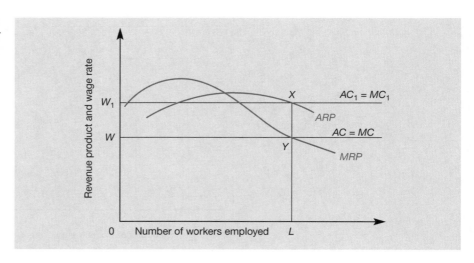

If *ARP* and *MRP* represent the returns to labour, it follows that at the profit-maximising level of employment (*OL*) employers earn a surplus of *XY* per worker. If unions can persuade employers to accept a *smaller* surplus it may be possible to negotiate a higher wage rate above the existing level $0W$, without reducing the number of workers employed. For example, employers might be willing to offer a wage between $0W$ and $0W_1$ rather than risk the union taking industrial action, with a consequent loss of output.

Decreased supply of labour

In the long run unions might be able to **decrease the supply** of labour to the industry without any of its members becoming unemployed. The most obvious way in which this can be achieved is by reducing the number of workers taken on annually. A trade union can do this by curbing the number of trainees or apprentices taken on annually or by insisting on a reduction in the number of part-time workers employed. Over time, as workers leave the industry through retirement and job-changing, this will bring about a decrease in the supply of workers to the industry. The effect of this is illustrated in Fig. 10.7, with the supply curve of labour shifting from SS to $S_1 S_1$. As a result wages rise from $0W$ to $0W_1$, and although employment in the industry falls from $0L$ to $0L_1$ higher wages have not led to union members becoming unemployed. In this sense wage increases might be self-financing, because although the wage rate for those employed has increased, the total wage bill might actually fall given the reduced total of employment.

Unions and bargaining power

We noted on p. 398 that unions may seek to force the employer off his demand curve for labour so that he makes less than maximum profits. It may then be possible for wages to rise from W to W_1 in Fig. 10.7 with no loss of employment: i.e. the union may seek to achieve combination $W_1 L$ rather than $W_1 L_1$, which is clearly above and to the right of the

Fig. 10.7 **The effect on wage rates of a reduction in the supply of labour to a particular occupation.**

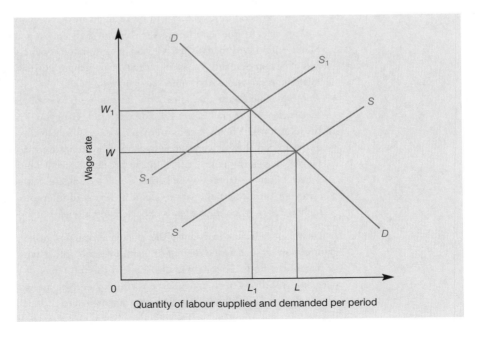

Quantity of labour supplied and demanded per period

firm's demand curve for labour (*MRP*). How effective unions will be in such strategies will depend upon the extent of their bargaining power.

Chamberlain (1951) defines union **bargaining power** as

$$\frac{\text{Management costs of disagreeing (to union terms)}}{\text{Management costs of agreeing (to union terms)}}$$

Although this ratio cannot be measured as it relies on subjective assessments, it is a useful analytical tool. If unions are to exert effective influence on management the ratio must exceed unity. That is to say it must be more costly for management to disagree (e.g. loss of profits, or market share as a result of strike action) than to agree (e.g. higher labour costs and manning levels). The higher the ratio, the more inclined management may then be to agree to the union's terms.

- The *level of the wage demand* will also affect union bargaining power. The more modest the wage claim, the lower the management cost of agreement, and the higher Chamberlain's ratio, i.e. the greater is union bargaining power. This will increase the prospects for securing higher wages with stable employment.
- *Union density* will also affect bargaining power. The greater the proportion of the industry unionised, the less easy it will be to substitute non-union labour. The management costs of disagreeing to union terms will tend to be higher, so that the ratio, i.e. union bargaining power, rises. Equally, the higher union density is in the industry as a whole, the easier it is for any particular company to pass on higher wage demands as price increases to consumers without losing market share. This is because competing firms in the industry will also be facing similar wage-cost conditions. High union density therefore reduces the management costs of agreeing to union terms, and again raises the ratio, i.e. union bargaining power. High union density will therefore also increase the prospects for securing higher wages with stable employment.
- Even macroeconomic factors can be brought into this analysis. The *higher the level of real income* in the economy, the higher will be demand for 'normal' goods. Management will then be able to pass on cost increases as higher prices with relatively less effect on demand. This will reduce management costs of agreeing to union terms, raise the ratio, and with it union bargaining power.
- Another main factor that affects the bargaining power of trade unions is the *degree of competition in the product market*. For example, Gregg and Machin (1991) found that those unionised firms facing increased competition in the market for their product experienced slower wage growth than those unionised firms that did not. In other words, increasing competition in the product market tends *to reduce* the bargaining power of unions to raise wages. This seems to indicate that unions are becoming more aware of the potential costs to them in terms of unemployment if they bargain for higher wages when their firm is experiencing intense competition.

However, one must recognise the existence of many other dimensions to union bargaining power, such as the degree of unanimity or conflict within unions over bargaining goals and methods. Unions will also vary in the militancy of their members and in the bargaining abilities of their leaders. All this makes the assessment of union bargaining power extremely difficult. It is also important to note that the resource theory of the impact of trade unionism on the firm does not accept that the exercise of this bargaining power will necessarily raise production by providing an efficient means for the management and settlement of disputes. Thus collective bargaining reduces the costs of individual expressions of grievances, which may raise the quit rate of key employees and the incidence of absenteeism or of poor-quality work. Further, the 'shock' effect of unions' negotiation of pay rises may force managements to increase efficiency in order to absorb higher costs.

Wages are therefore determined by a variety of factors, of which union bargaining power is but one, admittedly important, element.

Employers' associations

Employers' associations are themselves able to create an element of monopoly on the *demand* side of the labour market (i.e. monopsony). These associations bring together the employers of labour in order to exert greater influence in collective bargaining.

The existence of employers' associations will clearly affect the strength of union bargaining power. The greater the density of their coverage within an industry, the smaller might be the management costs of disagreement: e.g. in the case of a strike there is less likelihood of other domestic firms capturing their markets. By reducing the numerator of the ratio, union bargaining power is reduced.

Standard theory suggests that monopsony in the labour market will, by itself, reduce both wages and employment in the labour market (see p. 395). When monopoly on the demand side (employers' associations) is combined with monopoly on the supply side (trade unions), the wage and employment outcome becomes indeterminate (see p. 404).

■ Determination of wages and other market imperfections

A variety of imperfections may be present in labour markets other than the existence of monopoly and monopsony conditions. Here we briefly review a number of practices and rigidities that may also influence wage rates and levels of employment. Many of these practices and rigidities result in the wage/employment outcome diverging from that which might be expected given the particular labour market (supply/demand) conditions experienced.

- *Spillover and comparability.* The spillover hypothesis argues that wage settlements for one group of workers are transmitted (spilled over) to other groups through the principle of comparability, irrespective of product and labour market conditions. For example, the pay awards achieved by *wage leaders* often give rise to a sequence of similar settlements in the same wage round for other workers. Settlements at Ford and in the coal industry in the UK have often been regarded as important targets for general pay settlements in the private and public sectors respectively. The 'going rate' established by powerful trade unions becomes a 'virility symbol for those who follow' (Taylor 1989), a benchmark against which the performance of union leaders will be measured.
- *Non-pecuniary advantages or disadvantages.* Not all jobs have the same conditions of work. Some are hazardous, dirty, boring, require the working of unsocial hours, or receive various perquisites (perks). These will inevitably form part of the collective bargain, and ultimately affect the wage outcome. In some circumstances wage demands may be modified as the union places greater emphasis on non-wage factors.

- *Cost of living.* The cost of living is an important factor in determining the wage claim, and has even been a formal part of wage settlements. In some arrangements with employers, cost-of-living rises beyond a certain threshold trigger additional payments to employees. When inflation is accelerating, unions become still more preoccupied with securing cost-of-living increases. This can trigger off a wage price spiral when unions overestimate future rates of inflation.

- *Productivity agreements.* Part of the wage bargain may include the abandonment of restrictive practices, and the raising of production in return for higher wages. During the 1960s in the UK a whole series of formalised productivity agreements were concluded. The first and most celebrated of these was negotiated between Esso and the unions at the oil refinery at Fawley. A whole range of restrictive practices, including demarcation rules, excessive overtime and time-wasting, were bought out by management for higher wages. Most of these productivity agreements were negotiated at plant level. In a rather less formal way it soon became accepted practice for unions to trade small concessions on work practices for higher wage increases.

Simultaneous imperfections on purchaser/provider sides of labour market

Much of the discussion has so far considered an imperfection on *one* side of the labour market. Here we consider situations in which a number of imperfections may occur simultaneously on each side of the labour market and, indeed, in the market for the product. In this context it will be useful to draw on the distinction (p. 394) often made between value marginal product (*VMP*), i.e. *MPP* × price when *product* markets are perfect, and marginal revenue product (*MRP*), i.e. *MPP* × *MR* when *product* markets are imperfect.

Figures 10.8(a) and (b) then provide the yardsticks against which subsequent comparisons can be made when we consider simultaneous combinations of market imperfections.

In Fig. 10.8(a) we have our perfectly competitive labour *and* product market, with labour paid (W_c) the value of its marginal product (*VMP*) and with level of employment L_c. In Fig. 10.8(b) we introduce monopoly in the product market only, and derive the equilibrium solution W_m, L_m. In other words, the inward shift of *VMP* to form the *MRP*

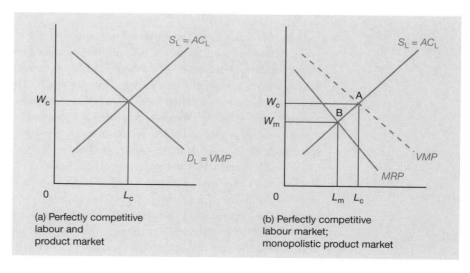

Fig. 10.8 **Different product market conditions.**

(a) Perfectly competitive labour and product market

(b) Perfectly competitive labour market; monopolistic product market

curve ($MPP \times MR$) means that labour is now paid less than its VMP ($W_m < W_c$) and less labour is employed than hitherto ($L_m < L_c$). Arguably these differences can be used as indices of *monopolistic exploitation*, where monopoly here refers to the *product* market.

Monopsony in factor market, monopoly in product market

We now compare the expected outcome for our analysis if monopsony in the labour market occurs simultaneously with monopoly in the product market.

To maximise its profits the firm employs L_e, where the marginal cost of employment (MC_L) equals the marginal revenue to the firm from employment (MRP). This means that the firm must offer a wage W_e to obtain the required volume of labour (L_e). We could arguably suggest that the total exploitation of labour in terms of remuneration, as compared with the perfect labour and product market case (Fig. 10.8(a)), can be split into the following components (Fig. 10.9):

- $W_c - W_e$ total exploitation of labour;
- $W_c - W_m$ exploitation of labour via monopoly in product market;
- $W_m - W_e$ exploitation of labour via monopsony in labour market.

Note that in this situation labour does *not* receive a wage commensurate with its contribution to the value of production ($W_e < MRP$), which was at least the case when the only imperfection was monopoly in the product market.

Monopsony and monopoly in factor market, monopoly in product market

We now add a further imperfection to the analysis, namely monopoly in the *factor* market as well as in the product market. In other words we assume the presence of unionisation. To simplify the analysis we shall assume that all firms are organised in a single employers' association, which acts like a monopsonist (pure monopsony) and all labour is organised in a single union, which acts like a monopolist (pure monopoly). We

Fig. 10.9
Monopsonistic labour market; monopolistic product market.

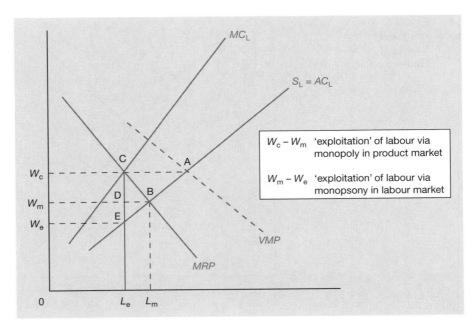

therefore have the typical situation of a **bilateral monopoly** with two monopolies, one involved in purchasing labour, one in supplying labour. As we shall see, as with the case of bilateral monopoly in *product* markets (Chapter 7, p. 309), the outcome of such a situation in *factor* markets is also indeterminate. Figure 10.10 can usefully illustrate our analysis. (Note: the use of the *MRP* rather than *VMP* for labour demand indicates an imperfectly competitive product market.)

In Fig. 10.10 we use the subscript B to refer to the *buyer* of labour (the firm or employers' association); we use the subscript S to refer to the *seller* of labour (the union).

Buyer of labour: monopsonist From the point of view of the *monopsonist* (buyer of labour – B), the supply of labour facing the firm is the upward sloping curve S_L, which indicates the average cost to the buyer (AC_B) of hiring any given quantity of labour. As noted earlier, by pushing up the price of labour, hiring more labour causes the marginal cost to the buyer (MC_B) to *exceed* the average cost (AC_B). Note here that the buyer's demand curve for labour (D_B) is the marginal revenue product curve of labour (MRP_L). It tells the buyer the profit-maximising amount of labour that should be hired at any given wage (However, with monopsony a given quantity of labour may be supplied at a lower wage).

Seller of labour: monopolist From the point of view of the *monopolist* (seller of labour – S), the demand for labour ($D_B = MRP_L$) is the average revenue curve of the seller (AR_S). It tells the seller (here a single union) how much it can expect to receive per person for any given number of persons supplied to the labour market. Of course, by supplying more labour the wage rate is lowered, and therefore the marginal revenue to the seller from supplying the last person (MR_S) will be *inside* the average revenue curve (AR_S).

Note here that the supply of labour curve (S_L) is also designated the marginal cost curve of the seller of labour (MC_S). The suggestion here is that the wage needed to

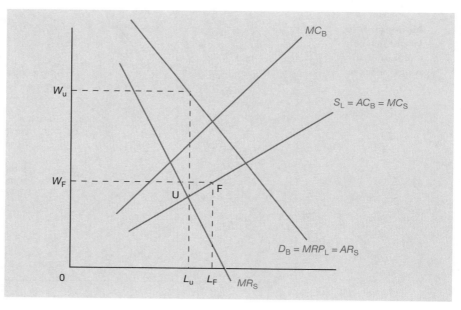

Fig. 10.10 **Pure monopsony and pure monopoly in a labour market.**

encourage the union to supply one extra worker to that labour market is just sufficient to compensate the union for what that worker could earn elsewhere (i.e. his/her opportunity cost). In this sense, S_L can be regarded as the marginal cost to the union (seller) of supplying one extra worker to that labour market (MC_S).

Indeterminate outcome

- The pure monopsonist (firm) buying labour maximises profit with wage W_F and level of employment L_F in Fig. 10.10. Only here is the marginal revenue from offering employment ($MRP_L = D_B$) equal to the marginal cost of employing the last person (MC_B).
- The pure monopolist (union) selling labour maximises returns to itself with wage W_u and level of employment L_u in Fig. 10.10. Only here is the marginal revenue to the union from supplying an additional unit of labour (MR_S) equal to the marginal cost to the union of providing that additional unit (MC_S).

Clearly there is a conflict between the outcomes desired by the pure monopsony (firm) and the pure monopoly (union). In this sense we say that the outcome is *indeterminate*. In other words no unique solution exists to this bilateral-monopoly situation in the labour market. The final outcome will depend upon the *relative bargaining strengths* of the monopsony and monopoly.

■ Statutory minimum wage

We have already considered the impact of setting a *price floor* in Chapter 6, pp. 255–6. Here we return to this issue in the more specific context of the **minimum wage**. A statutory minimum wage already features in a number of European countries, such as France, the Netherlands, Portugal, Spain and Luxembourg, and may eventually become a part of the Social Chapter of the European Union. Here we consider the theoretical case for and against the statutory minimum wage. The next section (p. 426) considers empirical materials relevant to the discussion.

If we consider a single labour market we can analyse the consequences of establishing a legal minimum wage *above* the existing equilibrium wage in this labour market. In Fig. 10.11 demand for labour is represented by DD and supply of labour is represented by SS. The equilibrium wage is $0W$, and $0L$ workers are employed.

If the minimum wage is set above $0W$, for example at $0W_1$, those workers who *receive* the higher wage clearly gain when a minimum wage leads to a reduction in the number of workers employed, which now falls from $0L$ to $0L_1$. In other words, fewer workers are employed at a higher wage. In terms of economic theory, they lose employment because their marginal revenue productivity is less than the statutory minimum wage. If we add together all the labour markets affected in this way, then this implies an increase in unemployment nationally should a legal minimum wage be established. So setting a legal minimum wage may raise the earnings of the low-paid workers still employed, but make those that become unemployed worse off.

Arguably the fall in employment from L to L_1 understates the unemployment impact of the minimum wage. From Fig. 10.11 we can see that at wage $0W_1$, $0L_2$ seek employment but only $0L_1$ obtain it (i.e. $L_1 - L_2$ 'unemployment').

Fig. 10.11 **Impact of a minimum wage set above the market clearing wage.**

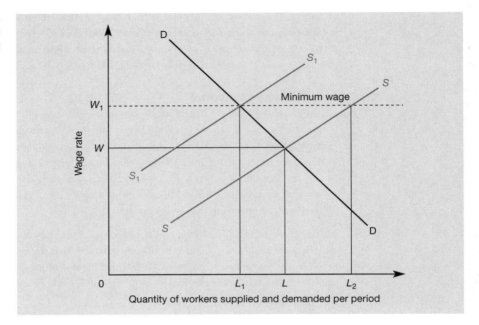

Elasticity of demand for labour The *extent* to which unemployment rises as a result of the minimum wage depends on the *elasticity of demand for labour*. As we have noted (p. 396), the elasticity of demand for labour in each market will in turn depend on:

- the elasticity of demand for the product which that labour produces;
- the ease with which other factors of production can be substituted for labour;
- the proportion of total costs that is made up of labour costs.

The more elastic the demand for the product, the more easily other factors can be substituted for labour, and the greater the proportion of total costs involving the factor labour, the more elastic we would anticipate the demand for labour to be. Of course, any given rise in the minimum wage will then have a more significant impact on the levels of employment and unemployment.

Labour force impacts Often a major reason for introducing a minimum wage is an attempt to help **low-paid workers**. Since low-paid workers are often *unskilled* there is likely to be some substitutability between factors. In addition, low-paid workers are often employed in *labour-intensive occupations*, such as local authority ancillaries, cleaners and canteen staff. In these cases labour costs form a large proportion of total costs. Both of these factors will tend to make the demand for low-paid workers *relatively elastic*. The greater the elasticity of demand for labour, the greater will be the impact of a legal minimum wage on the numbers employed.

Another factor to consider is the effect of **school leavers** on employment. If the minimum wage applies to all workers, this will reduce the incentive of firms to take on and train young workers since their higher wage will represent an effective increase in training costs. This may have serious implications in terms of youth unemployment, and could lead to major skill shortages in the future and a consequently slower growth of productivity.

Another possible consequence of a statutory minimum wage is a reduction in the **mobility of labour**. The price mechanism functions in the labour market (as well as in product markets) and discharges its role of allocating workers to the highest bidders. By *reducing the differentials* available from changing jobs, a statutory minimum wage might arguably reduce the incentive of workers to seek better-paid alternatives. Here again productivity might be adversely affected in the future, because expanding industries might not be able to offer a wide enough differential to persuade workers to leave their existing jobs.

Inflationary impacts The establishment of a statutory minimum wage might also lead to wage demands from trade unions in order to safeguard their established differentials. If pay awards are granted in excess of productivity, this will generate **inflation** and might well leave the *real wage* of the low-paid unchanged, even after the establishment of a legal minimum wage. In fact the relative position of the low-paid might be adversely affected as a result of such pay awards!

If inflation is generated it is also possible that a statutory minimum wage will adversely affect the position of the low-paid workers in another way. Higher prices in the domestic market will make exports less competitive and imports more competitive. This will lead to unemployment in the domestic economy. To the extent that those workers who become unemployed were previously employed in low-wage occupations, they will be adversely affected by the statutory minimum wage. Furthermore, any lack of competitiveness might encourage employers to offer smaller pay increases to their workers in an attempt to restore competitiveness.

Minimum wages and monopsony

We have already considered (Figs. 10.9 and 10.10) the impact of monopsony on the labour market equilibrium. We can now take this analysis further, showing that the introduction of a minimum wage in monopsonistic labour markets might, in theory, increase *both* the wages of workers and the level of employment.

Figure 10.12 replicates part of the earlier Fig. 10.9, using the same letters and symbols to ease comparison. The monopsonistic outcome was a level of employment L_e, at which the marginal cost to the firm of employing the last person (MC_L) exactly matched the marginal revenue to the firm from employing that person (MRP). The wage needed to get L_e workers to supply themselves to the firm is W_e.

We now suppose that a minimum wage, $\overline{W}$, is imposed on the labour market. Since no labour is supplied below the minimum wage $\overline{W}$, the supply curve of labour is now $\overline{W}MQ$. Further, since the wage rate is constant at $\overline{W}$ over the range $\overline{W}M$, then $MC_L = AC_L$ over this range. After point M, however, the S_L and MC_L curves are as they were *before* the minimum wage was imposed. This gives us the new marginal cost of labour (MC_L) curve $\overline{W}MNP$.

We can now analyse the impacts of a statutory minimum wage imposed on a monopsonistic labour market. The key thing to remember is that with a minimum wage the new MC_L curve will be horizontal until it meets the supply curve, at which point it becomes vertical until joining the original MC_L curve. Also remember that in monopsony, the *level of employment* is determined by the intersection of the MC_L and MRP curves, with *wages* then determined from the corresponding point on the labour supply curve, S_L.

Fig. 10.12 Impact of minimum wage ($\overline{W}$) in monopsonistic labour market.

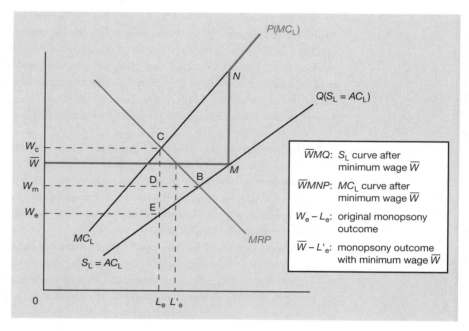

In Fig. 10.12, when the minimum wage is $\overline{W}$, the level of employment will be given by the intersection of the new MC_L curve $\overline{W}MNP$ and the MRP curve: i.e. at level of employment L'_e. The new labour supply curve is $\overline{W}MQ$, which gives the wage outcome at $\overline{W}$. Clearly, by setting a minimum wage of $\overline{W}$ we have a higher wage ($\overline{W} > W_e$) and a higher level of employment ($L'_e > L_e$) compared with the original monopsonistic equilibrium.

Of course a variety of outcomes are possible, depending on the *particular level* of the minimum wage set:

- $\overline{W} = W_e$: if the minimum wage is set at the *original* monopsony wage W_e, then there will be no change from the original outcome W_e / L_e.
- $\overline{W} = W_c$: if the minimum wage is set at W_c, then this gives the highest wage level consistent with no reduction in the original level of employment (L_e).
- $\overline{W} = W_m$: if the minimum wage is set at W_m, then this gives the highest level of employment consistent with prevailing labour market conditions.

Note here that any minimum wage ($\overline{W}$) set between W_e and W_c ($\overline{W} > W_e$ but $\leqslant W_c$) will raise *both* level of employment and wages as compared with the original monopsonistic outcome (W_e / L_e). Any minimum wage set above W_c will, however, while raising wages reduce employment below L_e. Any minimum wage set above W_c will, however, while raising wages reduce employment below L_e. Any minimum wage set below W_e will have no influence on the original outcome.

Wages, marginal productivity and discrimination

Our main concern here is to consider the theoretical case for wages departing from marginal productivity in the context of discrimination. Although, following Tzannatos (1990), the context is that of male/female wage differentials, the principles are applicable to any situation in which wages depart from marginal productivity on the basis of *perceived* labour characteristics unrelated to actual labour performance.

The labour market position of women and men can be represented as follows with respect to the determination of pay. Assume that the personal attributes of a woman can be usefully summarised as X^f and those of a man as X^m. Then their respective pay, W^f and W^m, relates to these attributes or characteristics according to the following formulae:

$$W^m = a.X^m$$
$$W^f = b.X^f$$

This means that the man's attributes are paid by the market according to the coefficient a and those of the woman according to the coefficient b. If there were no discrimination, a would equal b so that a man and a woman with identical attributes would receive identical pay.

If we take the difference between these two equations and rearrange the right-hand side, we can identify the part of any pay differentials as between men and women due to possessing *different characteristics* and the part due to different market rewards for possessing a *given characteristic*:

$$W^m - W^f = a.X^m - b.X^f$$
i.e. $$W^m - W^f = a.X^m - a.X^f + a.X^f - b.X^f$$
so $$W^m - W^f = a.(X^m - X^f) + X^f.(a - b)$$

or $$\frac{\text{Wage}}{\text{differential}} = \frac{\text{Justified}}{\text{discrimination}} + \frac{\text{Unjustified}}{\text{discrimination}}$$

The first component on the right-hand side measures that part of the pay differential that is usually called **justified discrimination**, since it relates to genuine differences in attributes or characteristics. The second component on the right-hand side measures that part of the pay differential that is usually called **unjustified discrimination**, since it relates to men and women being rewarded differently in the market for identical attributes or characteristics. Figure 10.13 helps to illustrate these points.

Fig. 10.13 **Measuring discrimination.**

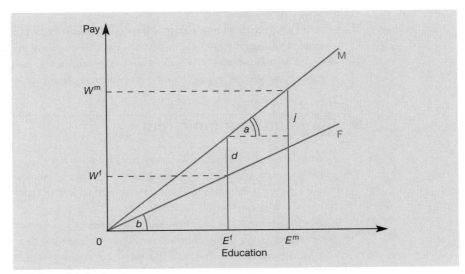

The horizontal axis measures the productivity of an employee resulting from the possession of some appropriate characteristic, e.g. education. The vertical axis measures the reward for possessing such a characteristic, say pay. The two rays from the origin show how pay varies between women (OF) and men (OM) when possessing different levels of the characteristic, here education, and when possessing the same levels of the characteristic.

Let us examine the implications of Fig. 10.13 with reference to pay and education. Assume that women have less education than men, namely E^f (in terms of volume or quality) for women, as compared with (E^m) for men, and that female pay is W^f and male pay W^m. The total pay difference ($W^m - W^f$) is due to the fact that, first, women are rewarded less than men of the same educational standard (distance d) and, second, women receive less reward bcause they have less education than men (distance j). With respect to the equation above, the first component of the right-hand side relates to j and the second component to d. Clearly if a and b were identical, then unjustified discrimination (d) would be zero.

Both components of the differential, namely d and j, can be the concern of public policy. In practice, legislation can deal more effectively with d (this part is often called *direct discrimination*). This is particularly true when pay structures are organised and are known to the public.

One should, however, warn that the abolition of differential wage rates from collective agreements has *not* resulted in the elimination of the distance d in many countries. Research in the UK suggests that between one-third and one-half of the remaining differential in male/female pay since the Equal Pay Act of 1970 cannot be accounted for by differences in the endowment of productive characteristics between women and men. Put another way, the abolition of different wage rates from collective agreements has eliminated only between two-thirds and one-half of the unjustified pay differential previously experienced in the UK.

Tackling the 'justified' discrimination, j, may be still more difficult since there may, of course, be all manner of cultural and economic barriers preventing a particular group of workers (here women) from acquiring as much of the characteristic associated with productivity (here education) as other groups of workers.

Other issues involving labour markets have also been considered elsewhere. For example in Chapter 1 we examined the impact of overtime payments, tax regimes, etc. on work-leisure incentives. We now turn to the issue of *rent* payments, which, as we shall see, can be applied in principle to the returns to any factor of production.

Rent and economic rent

Economic rent is defined as a *surplus* earned by any factor of production over and above the minimum price at which that factor would be supplied. The minimum price at which a factor will be supplied is referred to as its **supply price**, and hence economic rent is a surplus over supply price.

The supply price of a factor of production might also be referred to as a factor's **transfer earnings**. Any factor of production that is offered less than the amount it is aware it could receive in its next best paid alternative employment will transfer to that alternative. Figure 10.14 is used to illustrate the concepts of economic rent and transfer earnings.

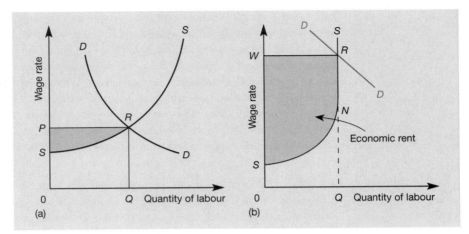

Fig. 10.14
(a) Economic rent
(PRS) and transfer
earnings (OSRQ).
(b) Economic rent
and elasticity of
supply.

In Fig. 10.14(a), *SS* and *DD* represent the relevant supply and demand curves for any factor of production. In this market the equilibrium price is *P*. However, all units except the last unit employed would have been prepared to accept a lower price than *P*. In fact, the very first unit would have been supplied at a price of approximately *S*. All units except the last unit supplied therefore receive an amount in excess of their supply price or transfer earnings. Because of this the area *PRS* is referred to as *economic rent* and the area *OSRQ* is referred to as *transfer earnings*.

Sources of economic rent

For any factor of production, economic rent is determined by demand for that factor of production and its supply characteristics, which in turn are related to its transfer earnings. However, in the case of labour a small number of individuals receive incomes that are sometimes many times greater than the average income. In these cases the transfer earnings of the individuals concerned are often relatively low so that the bulk of their earnings consist of economic rent. The most often quoted examples are probably film stars and pop singers. These individuals possess unique qualities, the supply of which is inelastic in the sense that their abilities cannot be duplicated.

However, it is not sufficient to possess unique abilities to earn relatively high rewards. Instead it is necessary to possess those unique abilities that are demanded by others and for which people are prepared to pay. It is, therefore, demand that accounts for the relatively large earnings of pop singers, film stars and some individuals from the sporting and entertainment world. In this sense economic rent is largely demand determined. Figure 10.14(b) is used to illustrate this point. Above some relatively low rate of pay, the supply of this individual's services become totally inelastic. The actual rate of pay is determined by the intersection of supply and demand at *W*, but, because of the inelastic supply, the bulk of this person's earnings consist of economic rent, equal to *WRNS*.

For some types of land, economic rent forms a large part of the income that owners receive. In recent years large tracts of agricultural land have been turned over to building land; once planning permission is granted on a particular piece of land its value rises substantially over and above what it can earn as agricultural land. In such cases the rise in land values is clearly economic rent, since landowners do nothing to improve the quality of the land; they simply obtain permission for its use to be changed!

It is clear that any factor of production can earn economic rent, and the main determinant of such rent is *demand* for the factor of production. However, *elasticity of supply* is also an important determinant of economic rent. When rising demand drives up factor earnings, the higher level of earnings will attract other units of the factor into the industry, unless there are barriers to entry that prevent this. If no barriers exist, then supply of the factor will be relatively elastic, and this will mitigate the effect of increasing demand on factor incomes and, therefore, on the level of economic rent earned.

Quasi rent   Sometimes factors of production earn economic rent in the short run that is eliminated in the long run. In this case economic rent is referred to as **quasi rent**. For example, during a housing boom the earnings of building site workers may rise substantially, the increase consisting largely of economic rent. However, for many of the jobs performed on building sites there are no long-run barriers to the entry of new workers. It follows that as new workers enter the industry the higher earnings in part disappear and are therefore seen to be quasi rent.

Part of the earnings of capital might also consist of economic rent. Some types of capital equipment are highly specific and cannot be transferred to an alternative use. For example, it is doubtful that a dockyard or a coal mine have many alternative uses! Conventional theory of the firm teaches us that, in the short run, firms will continue in production as long as earnings at least cover the variable costs of production. Because of this, the transfer earnings of fixed capital in the short run are the *variable costs of operating it*, and the entire earnings of fixed capital such as dockyards and coal mines *in excess of this* might be considered economic rent. However, earnings must ultimately cover depreciation, so it is only the excess over and above this *plus* the variable costs of operation that can be considered economic rent in the long run.

The entrepreneur might also earn economic rent in the form of supernormal profit. The minimum reward acceptable to the entrepreneur in the long run is *normal profit*. Any entrepreneur not earning at least normal profit will transfer to an alternative occupation. Normal profit is therefore the *transfer earnings* of the entrepreneur, and anything in excess of this is *supernormal profit* or *economic rent*. For many entrepreneurs, however, supernormal profit turns out to be nothing more than quasi rent. Unless an entrepreneur patents a particular process, ideas can often be copied by others, and supernormal profits are consequently competed away in the long run. Where patents or other barriers to entry exist, however, an entrepreneur might have a monopoly position, and economic rent can be earned for as long as barriers to entry prevent the emergence of competition. In the pharmaceutical industry, for example, patents prevent rival firms from producing identical drugs. The government has issued guidelines on target rates of return for drug companies to aim at, so as to avoid the NHS paying an excessive amount for drugs and conferring economic rent on drug producers.

Urban rents and city centre prices   It is sometimes alleged that retail prices in outlets occupying city centre locations are higher than they are for the same items sold in outlets located away from the city centre, because city centre rents are higher than elsewhere. It is certainly true that city centre rents are generally higher than elsewhere but it is not always true that retail prices are higher in the city centre. Even in cases where retail prices *are* higher this is not necessarily because retailers pay higher rents in the city centre.

Any higher prices that are observed for goods sold in city centres are as likely to be the result of the greater demand for the products of retail outlets in such locations as of the higher *cost* factors due to higher rents. Indeed, the main reason why costs (rents) are higher is the increased (derived) demand amongst retailers for the favourable city centre sites, which are in relatively inelastic supply.

Should economic rent be taxed? It is often suggested that economic rent should be taxed. The reasoning behind this is that since economic rent is a *surplus* rather than a *cost of supply*, a tax on economic rent will be borne entirely by the factor of production receiving economic rent. This will leave the supply of that factor, and therefore the output it produces, unchanged.

The case for taxing economic rent is therefore a powerful one. However, there are major difficulties with implementing such a tax. In the first place it is extremely difficult to identify economic rent. If a tax exceeds the value of the surplus, then the supply of the factor of production will be reduced and its price, along with the price of whatever it produces, will be increased. Another problem is that not all economic rent that is earned is true economic rent; it might simply be quasi rent. Quasi rent refers to income that is entirely a surplus in the short run, but part of which is a transfer earning in the long run. Taxing this will reduce the long-run supply of the factor of production. Here again the result might be rising prices.

▪ Interest

In Chapter 12, we consider in some detail the suggestion that the interest rate is largely determined by intertemporal utilities of consumers and producers. In other words, *consumers* realise that they can trade consumer products today (via interest on savings) into larger quantities of consumer goods in the future. Similarly producers realise that they can increase future output by devoting some of today's resources (via investment) into more productive capital equipment for use in future periods. Interest paid on borrowings is the price offered by producers (and others) to encourage the postponement of current consumption by consumers. The interest rate is then seen, in such models, as equating the respective rates of time preference between consumers and producers. Figures 12.12 (p. 489) and 12.13 (p. 490) take this argument further.

Of course many other models seek to express interest rates as the outcome of demands and supplies of various forms of assets, including the most liquid of assets, money. This brings into focus ideas of transactions, precautionary and speculative demands for money. Institutional attempts to set or manipulate interest rates may also play a role in interest rate determination.

The influence of various market imperfections on interest rate determination is also considered further in Chapter 12.

■ Profit

Profit is seen in some models as the return to the factor entrepreneurship, in recognition of the role involved in organising production and risk-taking. Again, we have considered in detail elsewhere the role of profit in managerial motivation (Chapter 5) and as an outcome of different types of market structure (Chapters 6–9), in both short- and long-run time periods.

Arguably *normal profit*, which is just sufficient to keep the firm in the industry in the long run, can be regarded as a cost of continued production. Excess or *supernormal* profit is regarded by some as a deadweight loss, diminishing welfare (see Chapter 6, p. 254).

The situations in which such excess or supernormal profits are likely to occur include the following:

1. perfectly and monopolistically competitive industries in the short run;
2. monopolistic and oligopolistic industries in both the short and the long run;
3. industries characterised by risk and uncertainty.

Schumpeter (1934) related profits to the successful application of product and process innovations, often by new entrants to an industry. This would correspond to both (1) and (2), with the long-run retention of profits the result of entry barriers of one form or another (e.g. patents on new innovations).

Knight (1921) argued that profits could primarily be regarded as the reward for risk-taking by entrepreneurs. Only by the prospect of profit could entrepreneurs be induced to undertake activities and innovations that carried real possibilities of loss as well as gain. In this sense, Knight's view of profit accords with point (3).

Applications and evidence

■ Distribution of factor incomes

In analysing the share of income between the factors labour, capital and land there are initial problems of definition. First, under labour do we include workers and managers, thereby combining wages and salaries, since both are paid in return for work? Some argue that salaries for managers include a profit element, since they exert direct control over capital and they carry entrepreneurial risks. In practice it is impossible to separate any profit element in salaries, and payments to workers and managers are counted together. More difficult still is the income of the self-employed, since this undoubtedly includes payment for both labour and capital services; a separate category is, in fact, usually made for the self-employed.

Table 10.2 shows pre-tax income to various factors as a percentage of total income in the UK since 1973. The share for labour has tended to increase, at least until recently. It has been estimated that, at the beginning of the century, labour's share was only 50%. This increase has not, however, been at the expense of profits but of rent, which has declined from about 25% to a negligible proportion (part of 'other income' in Table 10.2). This follows mainly from the decline in the relative importance of agriculture, and the rise in owner-occupation of dwellings. It is, however, of note that relatively high levels of unemployment since 1981, and a sustained upturn in the economy, contributed to a significant shift of income away from employment and towards corporate profit. However, there was then a shift away from profits under the impact of economic recession between 1989 and 1992 (when the share of company profits fell from 15.2% to 11.9%) before recovering to 14.9% by 1998. The privatisation programme (see Chapter 13) has also reduced the share of public corporations and general government enterprises, within gross trading profits.

Table 10.2 **Factor shares as a percentage of total income.**

	1973	1977	1981	1989	1998
Income from employment	66.9	67.2	69.1	64.5	63.2
Income from self-employment	10.2	8.4	8.4	10.9	10.7
Gross trading profits					
Companies	12.5	13.0	10.9	15.2	14.9
Public corporations and general government enterprises	3.1	3.8	3.3	1.5	0.6
Other income[a]	7.3	7.6	8.3	7.8	10.6
	100.0	100.0	100.0	100.0	100.0

[a]Rent income, and an imputed charge for consumption of non-trading capital.

Source: Adapted from ONS (1999) *Economic Trends* (April) and previous issues

One may question the importance of factor shares to aspects of equality or inequality in the overall income distribution. If it was the case that all income from self-employment, profits, interest and rent went to a small group, the very rich, then even though only 36.8% of income could possibly come from these sources in 1998 (Table 10.2), it would still be a major cause of inequality.

In fact these sources of income are enjoyed by *all* groups, although there is a bias in favour of the very rich. The richest 1% in the UK received 28.2% of their income from self-employment, and 20.5% from investment and occupational pensions. The top 25% received 8% of their income from self-employment, and 6.3% from investment and occupational pensions. However, the bottom 25%, though receiving only 2.3% of their income from self-employment, gained as much as 10.2% from investment and occupational pensions. Thus profits, however defined, are arguably *not* the major cause of income inequality.

There are two main types of theoretical explanation of factor shares. The first emphasizes the role of market forces and starts with a microeconomic analysis of factor markets. If there is perfect competition in goods and factor markets, each factor will receive precisely its marginal revenue (value) product; in other words, it will receive income in proportion to its contribution to production. The rising share to the factor labour would be viewed, from this standpoint, as reward for a greater contribution to overall production.

An alternative approach has been to explain factor shares in terms of power. Marx saw capitalists as exploiting labour, receiving surplus value from the fact that the efforts of workers yield returns over and above their wages. Marx believed that this exploitation would increase as production became more capital-intensive and labour was displaced, creating a pool of unemployment that would depress wages, and therefore the share of labour in national income. Eventually, the decline in people's ability to purchase the output of the capitalist factories, combined with the workers' resentment at their poverty, would cause crisis and revolution.

Neither theory is wholly adequate. Assumptions, such as perfect competition in labour markets, required by orthodox theory are clearly unrealistic. Similarly, Marx's prediction of a declining wage and factor share for labour has not been fulfilled.

The earnings distribution

Since over 63% of total income accrues to the factor labour, it follows that differing returns to the various factors (labour, capital or land) are unlikely to be the main explanation of income inequality. Rather, we must turn our attention to variations in income between different groups *within* the factor labour, i.e. to the **earnings distribution**.

Earnings by occupation   Table 10.3 shows the relative earnings of the main occupational groups in the UK according to the Standard Occupational Classification (SOC), introduced for the first time in 1991. Each figure represents the average earnings of the members of that group as a percentage of overall average male earnings. We can see that the first three categories of non-manual workers earn significantly more than the average. These categories include: managers in industry and in local/central government; professionals, such as engineers, teachers, scientists and solicitors; and associate professional and technical employees such as technicians, surveyors and computer programmers. However, it is also true that non-manual workers in occupations such as clerical and secretarial earn, on average, less than manual occupations such as craft workers and machine operators. Indeed a more detailed analysis also reveals that certain

Table 10.3 Earnings of occupational groups. Average (gross weekly) earnings of full-time male employees in selected occupations, as a percentage of average (gross weekly) earnings of all full-time male employees (April 1999).

Non-manual	
Managers and administrators	146
Professional occupations	133
Associate professional and technical	121
Sales	80
Personal and protection services	80
Clerical and secretarial	68
Manual	
Craft and related occupations	84
Plant and machine operators	78
Other occupations	66

Source: Adapted from ONS (1999) *New Earnings Survey*, *Part A*

manual occupations, such as plant drivers and scaffolders, earn as much as teachers and certain classes of management. Although the overall picture is complicated, it can be seen that inequalities of earnings are clearly present in UK society.

A hidden source of inequality between occupations is the difference in value of fringe benefits and pension entitlement. As early as 1979 the Diamond Commission found that this typically adds 36% to the pre-tax salary of a senior manager, and 18% to that of a foreman, while unskilled workers enjoy little or no such benefits.

Earnings by sex Table 10.4 shows female earnings in relation to male earnings in the UK. The position of women improved significantly during the 1970s – a period that saw the introduction of equal pay legislation – though women continued to earn substantially less than men. The momentum towards equal pay seems to have slowed down during the 1980s and early 1990s, with the earnings of both manual and non-manual females making little further progress as compared with males.

Table 10.4 **Average gross weekly female earnings as a percentage of average male earnings.**

	1970	1976	1998
Manual	50	62	64
Non-manual	51	61	65

Source: Adapted from ONS (1999) *New Earnings Survey, Part A*, and previous issues

Earnings trends

Figure 10.15 shows that there have been significant changes over time in the real earnings gap between high and low wage earners. The figure traces the growth in real hourly (male) earnings between 1966 and 1998 of people positioned at three different points on the income distribution scale. The fiftieth percentile line traces the increases in the real hourly earnings of workers receiving the median (average) wage over the period. Similarly, the ninetieth percentile represents the growth of real hourly earn-

Fig. 10.15 **Real hourly male earnings by percentile (Index 1996 = 100).**

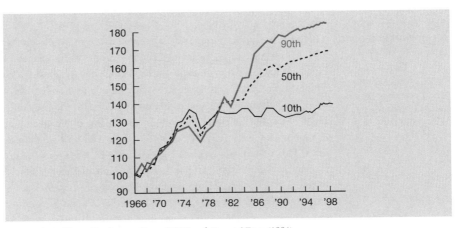

Source: Adapted from *New Earnings Survey* (1999) and *Financial Times* (1994)

ings of workers who are 90% of the way up the income distribution, while the tenth percentile shows the growth of real hourly earnings for those whose income is only 10% of the way up the income distribution. Of course the ninetieth percentile is likely to include some of the people in the non-manual managers and administrators category in Table 10.3, while the tenth percentile will include some of those in the manual 'other occupations' category.

Between 1966 and 1978 the three categories moved roughly in line with each other. However, major differences have emerged since then between those on low and high pay. For example, the real pay for average earners (fiftieth percentile) increased by 38% between 1978 and 1998, while the real pay for those near the top of the income scale (ninetieth percentile) increased by over 50% during the same time period. On the other hand, those with earnings near the bottom of the income scale (tenth percentile) did not benefit at all over this period. The relative position of workers near the bottom of the income scale was in fact the lowest since records began in 1886.

The study by Gottshalk and Smeeding (1997) on the '90/10 ratio' (see p. 423) confirms this pattern for the UK, and considers the same ratio in other countries. The '90/10 ratio' compares incomes at the ninetieth percentile of the income distribution with incomes at the tenth percentile. Using this ratio they found that the USA had the highest *increase* in earnings inequality (rise in the ratio) between 1979 and the early 1990s for males, compared with other industrial countries. Their results show that the UK's increase in earnings inequality over the period was just over 80% of that of the US, followed by Canada and Australia (in the range 50% and 80% of the US figure) and France, Japan, the Netherlands, Sweden and Finland (in the range 10–50% of the US figure). Finally, Italy and Germany experienced no measurable increase in earnings inequality. From these figures we note that the growth of male earnings inequality in the UK has been second only to the USA over the recent past.

■ Explanation of earnings differentials

In seeking to explain the earnings distribution there are two main theoretical approaches, similar to those we considered for factor shares.

Market theory   The first, the *market theory*, starts from an assumption of equality in **net advantages** for all jobs: i.e. that money earnings and the money value placed on working conditions are equal for all jobs. It also assumes that labour has a high degree of occupational and geographical mobility, so that if there is any inequality in net advantages, labour will move to the more advantageous jobs until equality is restored. Thus differences in actual earnings must be caused by compensating differences in other advantages. Job satisfaction is one compensating advantage: enjoyable or safe jobs will be paid less than irksome or risky ones. This may partly explain the relatively high wages of manual workers such as coalface miners and chemical, gas and petroleum plant operators. Still more important are differences in training. Training and education are regarded as investments in human capital, in which the individual forfeits immediate earnings, and bears the cost of training, in the prospect of higher future earnings: this may in part explain the high earnings of professional groups. Market theory therefore proposes that relative occupational earnings reflect non-monetary advantages between occupations, and the varying length and cost of any required training.

Proponents of this theory agree that it is not wholly adequate, and would recognise differences in natural ability as also affecting earnings. However, others, while still broadly advocating market theory, have suggested a more fundamental objection, namely that labour is in fact highly immobile. The most recent study of income immobility among the rich and poor found that groups of people at the extreme ends of the income distribution tend to be subject to intergenerational immobility (Johnson and Reed 1996). This research attempted to assess whether the income level and unemployment experiences of fathers were related to the subsequent experiences of their sons. The results were interesting in that the sons of those fathers who were unemployed were also more likely to end up being unemployed. Indeed, the sons of fathers whose income was in the bottom 20% of income earners were three times more likely to remain in the same income group than those sons whose fathers' incomes were above average. Similarly, the sons of fathers whose income was in the top 20% of earners were three times more likely to remain in the same income group as their fathers than those sons whose fathers' incomes were in the bottom 20% of income earners. However, the survey also showed that the more able children of poor parents do have a better chance of moving into higher income bands than less able children, making it very important to make sure that good-quality education is available to all.

From what we have noted above, a combination of social, occupational and geographic immobility can have a significant effect on the earnings distribution, especially at the upper and lower ends of the distribution, contrary to the simple predictions of market theory.

Segmented markets   The second theoretical approach places 'immobility' at the very centre of its analysis. This approach sees the labour market as 'segmented': i.e. one that is divided into a series of largely separate (non-competing) occupational groups, with earnings determined by **bargaining power** within each group. Some groups, especially professional bodies, have control over the supply of labour to their occupations, so that they can limit supply and maintain high earnings. Other occupational groups have differing degrees of unionisation and industrial power. The relatively high earnings of the relatively small number of printworkers and coalminers in the UK may be explained in part by their history of effective and forceful collective bargaining, while the fragmented nature of agricultural and catering work may have contributed to their low pay. In this approach bargaining power is held to outweigh the effects of free market forces.

These two theoretical approaches to the distribution of earnings need not be regarded as mutually exclusive. Market theory can itself be used to analyse bargaining power, with professional bodies and trade unions affecting the supply of labour, and the elasticity of labour demand determining the employment effects of their activities. More fundamentally, it may be suggested that labour, while fairly immobile in the short run, is highly mobile in the long run. Thus, while the exertion of bargaining power may affect differentials in the short run, in the long run labour will move in response to market forces, and thereby erode such differentials.

However, it is obvious from Fig. 10.15 that the wage differential between those on low and those on high wages has not been eroded; in fact it actually widened in the UK between 1978 and 1998. Although the reasons for such a trend are complex, they seem to lie in both inter-industry and intra-industry shifts that have occurred in the UK labour market (Gregg and Machin 1994). For example, the *inter-industry* employment shift from manufacturing to services has tended to increase the number of lower-paid jobs. However, there also seem to have been *intra-industry* employment shifts, namely a shift in demand within industries in favour of non-manual, better educated workers. Even when the proportion of workers in the UK with degrees rose from 8% to 11% during the 1980s, their wages continued to rise as demand for such workers rose even faster than their supply. At the other end of the scale, although the percentage of workers with no qualifications fell from 46% to 32%, the unemployment rate among this group actually rose from 6.5% to 16.4% over the 1980s. In other words the demand for such workers fell even faster than the fall in their supply. The drive towards international cost competitiveness and the introduction of new technology has increased the demands for a more skilled and flexible workforce (Casey *et al*. 1999; OECD 1996), leaving workers with low skills, poor family backgrounds and inflexible work attitudes to occupy the low-paid jobs. Berman *et al*. (1994) in the USA and Haskel and Heden (1999) in the UK found that technological developments involving computerisation have substantially reduced demand for unskilled labour in all branches of manufacturing.

Another interesting theory linked to the segmented market hypothesis has been suggested by Daniel Cohen (Cohen 1998). He suggests that there is no longer a single market even for a particular kind of skill or occupation, i.e. there is an *intra-skill* dimension to earnings differentials. For example, top law firms may require secretaries whose pay will reflect their value to the company while secretaries of similar capabilities working for less profitable law firms will earn considerably less. In other words, an individual's earnings prospects may depend on the nature and profitability of the company which employs them, so that even modest differences in skill may be magnified into significant earnings differentials. In this sense earnings differentials may substantially exceed any skill differentials, even within a given occupation.

These attempts to explain the presence of wage differentials did not explicitly seek to clarify the reasons for earnings differentials by sex, so clearly shown in Table 10.4. Such differentials could be due, for example, to some element of **unjustified discrimination** (see p. 409) that might exist in the labour market between men and women, even though they are identical workers. For instance, until December 1975, when it was made illegal, collective agreements between employers and employees often included clauses that prescribed that female wage rates should not exceed a certain proportion of the male wage. The examples of wage differentials noted in Table 10.4 were made possible because of the preponderance of males in most unions concluding such collective agreements. The state has also been active in allowing this wage differential to exist. For example, up to 1970 when the Equal Pay Act was passed in the UK, the police pay structure provided for a differential wage structure for men and women up to the rank of ordinary sergeant, while the pay structure for more senior sergeant ranks included only male rates. Obviously, female police officers were felt to be only able to achieve the lower grades, and even here were not seen as being of equal value to males (Tzannatos 1990).

On the other hand, the observed differentials could be regarded as being due to *genuine differences* that exist (or are perceived to exist) between male and female labour. This is the element of **justified discrimination** considered on p. 409. For instance it is often observed that employers make certain assumptions about the average female worker, i.e. as being one who will not be working for long before leaving to have a child. As a result employers may be more reluctant to train female workers, who are then placed at a disadvantage compared with their male counterparts. By acquiring fewer skills, the female worker inevitably receives less pay. Again, female workers are often constrained in competing with male workers by the need to seek employment in the catchment area of their partners' employment. Such restrictions can again result in a lower wage compared with that received by the more mobile male counterpart.

Whatever the causes of wage differentials between males and females, there is no doubt that they still exist, even after the initial improvements in the early 1970s following the Equal Pay Act of 1970 and the Sex Discrimination Act of 1975.

Lorenz curves, Gini coefficients and inequality

The conventional means of illustrating income distribution is the **Lorenz curve**, shown in Fig. 10.16. The horizontal axis shows the cumulative percentage of population, and the vertical axis the cumulative percentage of total income they receive. The diagonal is the line of perfect equality where, say, 20% of all people receive 20% of all income.

The data for the UK in 1991 are plotted in Fig. 10.16 as a continuous line, which is known as the Lorenz curve. The degree of inequality can be judged by the extent to which the Lorenz curve deviates from the diagonal. For instance, the bottom 20% received only 7.6% of total income in 1991, so that the vertical difference between the

Fig. 10.16 **Lorenz curve and Gini coefficient.**

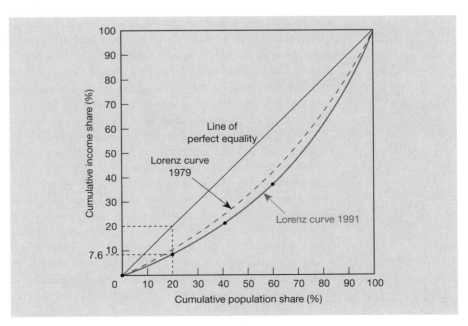

Lorenz curve and the diagonal represents inequality. To assess inequality over the whole range of the income distribution, the **Gini coefficient** is calculated. It is the ratio of the enclosed area between the Lorenz curve and the diagonal to the total area underneath the diagonal. If there was no inequality (i.e. perfect equality), the Lorenz curve would coincide with the diagonal, and the ratio would be zero. If there was perfect inequality (all the income going to the last person) then the Lorenz curve would coincide with the horizontal axis until that last person, and the ratio would be 1. The Gini coefficient therefore ranges from zero to 1, with a rise in the Gini coefficient suggesting less equality.

The value of the Gini coefficient for the UK in 1979 was 0.25; by 1991 it had risen to 0.33, suggesting less equality (greater inequality). Indeed we can see that the UK Lorenz curve is further away from the diagonal (line of perfect equality) at all points of the income distribution in 1991 than in 1979, suggesting an unambiguous rise in inequality. However, when Lorenz curves for different time periods intersect, we may have to weigh greater equality at some parts of the income distribution (Lorenz curve nearer diagonal) against less equality at other parts of the income distribution (Lorenz curve further from diagonal).

International comparisons

International comparisons of income distributions and their associated Gini coefficients have been difficult to undertake because the various countries have different definitions of income and different methods of collecting data. However, recent work by A. B. Atkinson has provided an important insight into income distribution in both Europe and the USA (Atkinson 1996). Table 10.5 presents the income distribution for various countries in the late 1980s, using cumulative decile shares and Gini coefficients. For example, the income distribution for Finland shows that the bottom 10% of income earners (S_{10}) earn 4.5% of all income, whereas the bottom 20% of income earners (S_{20}) earn 10.8% of all income, and so on. The Gini coefficient for the entire distribution is given in the last column on the right (G_0). If these figures were drawn for each country then we would have a series of Lorenz curves of the kind shown in Fig. 10.16 with each Lorenz curve representing a country's income distribution. The countries in Table 10.5 are ranked from low to high inequality, using the share of the bottom decile income group as the initial indicator: i.e. the greater the share of income accounted for by the bottom 10% of income earners, the less inequality we initially assume to occur in that country's distribution of income. Of course we know that the Lorenz curves can intersect each other, making generalisations about the bottom decile less useful.

The Gini coefficients based on the whole distribution are given on the right of Table 10.5 and yield a similar ranking (from low to high) of inequality to that implied by the bottom decile of income earners, although the ordering is not exactly the same. Despite these problems, useful conclusions can be drawn from such tables. For example if all the Lorenz curves were mapped, there would be a clear group of mainland Northern European countries at the top (Finland, Belgium, Luxembourg, Norway and Sweden), i.e. with the lowest income inequalities. In the middle would be countries such as France, Italy and Portugal, and at the bottom, i.e. with the highest income inequalities, would be a grouping containing Switzerland, Spain, the UK and Ireland, together with the USA. The Gini coefficient for the USA suggests the least equal distribution of income of all the countries considered. The weighted average Gini coefficient for Europe was 0.288 compared with that for the USA of 0.341, indicating that inequality of income in

Table 10.5 **Income distribution in European countries and the USA in the 1980s: cumulative decile shares of total income (%).**

	S_{10}	S_{20}	S_{30}	S_{40}	S_{50}	S_{60}	S_{70}	S_{80}	S_{90}	G_0
Finland	4.5	10.8	18.1	26.4	35.6	45.6	56.6	68.6	82.2	0.207
Luxembourg	4.3	10.2	17.1	24.8	33.5	43.1	53.9	66.0	80.4	0.238
Belgium	4.2	10.2	17.1	25.0	33.8	43.5	54.3	66.4	80.3	0.235
Netherlands	4.1	10.1	16.9	24.5	33.0	42.5	53.2	65.3	79.4	0.268
Germany	4.0	9.8	16.6	24.2	32.9	42.5	53.2	65.3	79.4	0.250
Norway	3.9	9.8	16.9	24.9	33.9	43.7	54.6	66.7	80.6	0.234
Portugal	3.4	8.0	13.9	20.9	28.9	38.1	48.5	60.8	75.8	0.310
Sweden	3.3	9.5	16.9	25.3	34.6	44.8	55.9	68.2	81.9	0.220
Italy	3.1	8.0	13.9	20.7	28.7	38.0	48.7	61.2	76.2	0.310
France	3.0	8.3	14.6	21.8	29.9	39.1	49.5	61.6	76.3	0.296
Switzerland	2.8	8.0	14.1	21.0	29.0	37.8	47.7	58.9	72.5	0.323
Spain	2.8	7.4	13.2	20.1	28.2	37.5	47.9	60.2	75.5	0.320
UK	2.5	7.5	13.5	20.5	28.7	38.2	49.1	61.8	77.1	0.304
Ireland	2.5	7.1	12.6	19.3	27.1	36.3	47.0	59.6	75.1	0.330
USA	1.9	5.7	11.2	18.0	26.2	35.7	46.9	60.2	76.3	0.341

Source: Adapted from Atkinson (1996)

Europe as a whole is still less than such income inequality in the USA. Interestingly, this 5% (0.053) difference in Gini coefficient between Europe and the USA is less than the difference between some European countries. For example, when comparing Finland with Switzerland or Sweden with Ireland, we find the differences in Gini coefficients are closer to 10%. The UK has more inequality in terms of the overall Gini coefficient (0.304) than has Europe as a whole (0.288), though some six countries (see Table 10.5) have still greater inequality than the UK. However, in terms of the bottom 10% of income earners, the UK's ranking is lower still, with only Ireland equivalent to it and the USA below it, suggesting that this group of income earners is particularly vulnerable in the UK.

These trends have been substantiated by another major cross-country comparison of income inequality (Gottshalk and Smeeding 1997). They calculate an inequality measure that they call the '90/10 ratio'. The 90 refers to the ratio of the income of a person at the ninetieth percentile to the median income for the whole country, whereas the 10 refers to the ratio of the income of a person at the tenth percentile to the median income. By dividing these two ratios we derive the 90/10 ratio for the UK in the mid-1990s as 206/44 or 4.67, suggesting that a person at the ninetieth percentile enjoys nearly five times the income of a person at the tenth percentile. Only the ratio for the USA at 5.78 was found to be higher than the UK's, while the ratio for most European countries varied within the range from Finland (2.74) to Ireland (4.30).

Trade unions and collective bargaining

The process of collective bargaining has had a number of important effects on the UK labour market.

A number of studies have suggested a significant pay differential between unionised and non-unionised workers. During the 1980s, studies by economists such as Nickell and Andrews placed this differential as high as 20% in favour of unionised workers, though studies in the 1990s by Metcalf (1994) suggested a lower figure of around 10%. The more recent research of Blanchflower (1996) also suggests a pay differential of around 10% between unionised and non-unionised workers. The evidence also suggests that such differentials have decreased over time and that they depend, in part, on the degree of union density across sectors: the greater the union density, the greater the pay differential (Addison and Siebert 1998).

However, the nature of the pay differential observed between union and non-union labour may be due to more than simply collective bargaining. First, union labour may be of higher quality than non-union labour, with some of the pay differential due to the higher marginal revenue product of union labour. Second, employers may raise the wages of non-union labour in an attempt to forestall unionisation, thereby eroding the pay differential. Third, incomes policies imposed by governments may affect the union/non-union pay differential. Flat-rate norms, which are often a part of incomes policy, will compress the pay differential that union bargaining power might otherwise have secured.

In practice, the particular effect of trade unions on pay is very difficult to disentangle from those of other labour market conditions. It is interesting to note, however, that both union and non-union workers have on average been able to secure very large increases in real wages, even during periods of high unemployment. This may suggest a fall in the price elasticity of demand for labour as the capital/labour ratio has increased, thereby reducing labour costs as a proportion of total costs (see above), and may also indicate a low and negative unemployment elasticity of real wages. In fact, unemployed workers have perhaps ceased to exert a permanent influence on wage determination.

It has been suggested that the process of collective bargaining reinforces the unions' perception that they have 'property rights'. These rights may include a variety of established practices that have been used to protect jobs or earnings. These practices have important consequences for labour utilisation, and may form part of the collective bargain. They include the closed shop, minimum manning levels, demarcation rules, seniority principles, and strikes. We briefly review a number of the most important 'restrictive practices' in the UK.

The closed shop

Closed shops confer a number of advantages on trade unions. First, they permit monopoly control over labour supply. This increases the union's ability to disrupt production through industrial action, and therefore raises its 'bargaining power'. In terms of Chamberlain's ratio above, it raises the 'management cost of disagreeing', and therefore union bargaining power. Second, closed shops prevent the 'free rider' problem, whereby non-union labour benefits from union bargaining power. Third, closed shops make it easier to enforce agreements reached between unions and management. Indeed, despite restricting the freedom of employers to choose whom they will employ, the closed shop has the benefit of bringing more order and certainty to industrial relations.

As we have seen, legislation in the UK since 1979 has made the closed shop legally unenforceable, reflecting the government's desire to reduce union bargaining power and to protect the right of an individual not to join a trade union. The incidence of closed shops has decreased rapidly since 1979, with contemporary estimates suggesting that only some 9% of firms continue to have some form of closed-shop agreement with unions.

Established practices In industries such as printing, the railways, and car production, unions often have, by tradition, some control over manning levels, job speeds, the introduction of new technologies, and demarcation issues: in other words, which type or grade of workers should undertake particular types of work. As a result, management decisions over the allocation of labour within an enterprise are subject to union influence.

Interestingly, Daniel (1987) found that trade union opposition to investment in advanced, new technology was unusual, though highly publicised when it did occur. In fact, where there was an association between change and working practices, it was *positive*: i.e. unionised firms in the survey were *more likely* to introduce technical and other forms of change than companies where unions were not recognised.

The seniority principle This is the principle whereby union members with the longest service in a firm are the first to be promoted and the last to be made redundant. This principle may conflict with the firm's desire to employ younger, more flexible and cheaper workers. However, companies may sometimes wish to retain senior workers, having already made a substantial investment in them through specific training.

These *restrictive practices* may enter into the collective bargain. Unions may seek to trade them for higher wages – as in the productivity agreements we have already noted. Through buying out restrictive practices in this way, management seeks a more efficient utilisation of labour, and thereby higher productivity.

The strike weapon One of the most powerful 'property rights' perceived by the unions is their ability to affect the collective bargain by withdrawing their labour, i.e. going on strike. This is viewed by some as the ultimate form of restrictive practice. The use of the strike weapon by unions in the UK has been the subject of much research and debate.

Table 10.6 demonstrates that compared to its major economic competitors the UK was less strike-prone than the OECD and EU averages over the whole period shown. It is often in the context of strikes that governments and employers see union 'property rights' as detrimental to Britain's economic performance, while the unions themselves perceive the withdrawel of labour as a response to the failure of management. Disputes over pay are the most common cause of working days lost, accounting for 71% of the total in 1995–97, followed by staffing and redundancy issues (9%) and work allocation issues (7%), although attributing strikes to a single cause often masks the existence of other contributory factors. The threat of industrial action by a trade union may alone be sufficient to achieve its aims, but one must be careful not to overestimate its role or that of actual strike incidence in the process of bargaining. The CBI has reported that both are only rarely given as a reason for employers conceding wage increases.

Although the improvement in Britain's strike record is clear and indisputable, there has been a dramatic rise in notified individual grievances. For example, the Advisory, Conciliation and Arbitration Services (ACAS) has reported a substantial rise in cases received for conciliation, i.e. prior to a hearing by an industrial tribunal. Perhaps the lack of actual strike activity may not be a good indicator of the actual stresses and strains experienced within the labour market!

Table 10.6 **Strikes: international comparisons, 1987–96 (working days lost per thousand employees).**

Country	1987–91	1992–96	1987–96
Spain	630	400	514
Canada	344	172	257
Italy	276	172	225
United Kingdom	126	29	78
France	98	97	97
United States	68	42	55
Denmark	39	46	42
Germany*	5	17	12
Japan	4	2	3
EU average	246	93	167
OECD average	148	65	105

Notes: * From 1993 data covers entire Federal Republic of Germany
Source: Adapted from *Labour Market Trends* (1998) April

Empirical evidence and the minimum wage

We have already noted (pp. 405–8) some of the opportunities and threats arguably resulting from the imposition of the **minimum wage**. Here we consider some of the empirical evidence cited by advocates and critics of the minimum wage.

Although institutional differences make intercountry comparisons hazardous, much attention has been paid to the impact in the USA of the April 1990 increase in the Federal minimum wage. Earlier work by Neumark and Wascher (1992) had examined cross-state data involving changes in the minimum wage over the years 1973–89. They had reached three broad conclusions:

- A higher minimum wage resulted in lower shares of teenage employment within the working population.
- The main impact on employment of a higher minimum wage occurred after a time lag of two years, though a significant impact was also present after one year.
- Where employers are legally able to offer teenagers wages *below* the minimum wage (i.e. a subminimum wage), the payment of such a wage moderates the employment losses linked to the minimum wage.

Card and Krueger (1994) sought to challenge this conventional view by focusing on the increase in the Federal minimum hourly wage from $3.35 to $3.80 in April 1990. Contrary to the prediction of Neumark and Wascher, they found no relationship between the growth rate of teenage employment in a state and the proportion of teenagers within the working population ('affected teenagers') earning between $3.35 and $3.80 per hour *prior* to the increase in the minimum wage. Indeed, those states with a higher proportion of affected teenagers experienced slightly *larger* employment growth, using time lags in excess of one year. Nor did Card and Krueger find evidence to support the wide use of subminimum wages nor to suggest that where used they had a significant spillover effect on other teenage wage levels. In other words there was little, if any, support for subminimum wages as mitigating the employment losses conventionally attributed to the minimum wage.

In similar vein, Katz and Krueger (1992) found few negative impacts in their specific study of the impact of the minimum wage on the US fast food industry. Their study involved a longitudinal survey of fast food restaurants in Texas. As with Card and Krueger, Katz and Krueger found a *positive* linkage between percentage wage increase as a result of introducing the minimum wage and levels of employment. In their main model, a 10% mandated wage increase is predicted to raise relevant employment in full-time equivalents (FTEs) by approximately 25%.

Katz and Krueger found little evidence of relative product price increases in those establishments with larger mandated wage increases. Only some 2% of employers took advantage of a subminimum wage clause whereby teenagers could be paid a 'training' wage equal to 85% of the minimum wage for the first six months of employment. Even where employers did take advantage of this option, there was no discernible spillover effect depressing wages elsewhere or mitigating any adverse employment effects of a minimum wage.

Katz and Krueger noted two important caveats, which should be remembered when interpreting their results. First, their sample was limited to restaurants that were in operation before *and* after the minimum wage increased. It is possible that the higher minimum wage caused some restaurants to close, thereby reducing total employment in the industry. Further, the rate of formation of new restaurants might have slowed down subsequent to introducing the minimum wages. Neither of these eventualities would have been captured in their data set. Second, although the estimated coefficients for the wage variables in their employment equations are statistically significant, they do have relatively large standard errors (see p. 695).

In terms of our earlier theory, we saw (pp. 407–8) that in a monopsony model a statutory minimum wage can increase *both* employment and wages. Certainly the fast food industry in the USA is one in which large employers of low-wage workers can be expected to possess a considerable degree of market power, i.e. exert a monopsonistic influence. Boal and Ransom (1997) conclude that the widespread presence of monopsony conditions in US labour markets makes it impossible to conclude from theory that higher minimum wages must invariably reduce employment. Rather the issue becomes an empirical one to be addressed on an industry-by-industry basis.

Key terms	
Average product of labour	Marginal physical product of labour
Bilateral monopoly	Marginal rate of technical
Diminishing Marginal Rate of	substitution of labour for capital
Substitution	$(MRTS_{LK})$
Diminishing returns	Marginal revenue product (MRP)
Economic rent	Monopsony
Gini coefficient	Quasi rent
Information asymmetry	Unemployment trap
Justified discrimination	Union bargaining power
Law of variable proportions	Unjustified discrimination
Marginal physical product (MPP)	Value Marginal Product (VMP)
Marginal productivity theory	

Full definitions can be found in the 'Glossary of terms' (pp. 699–710)

1. A large trust hospital has a monopsonistic position in the local labour market for maintenance workers. The weekly supply (or average labour cost) function is $S = 100 + Q_L$ and the demand (or marginal revenue product) function is $D = 1,000 - Q_L$. Here Q_L is the quantity of maintenance workers hired.

   (a) Derive the marginal labour cost equation for maintenance workers.
   (b) Calculate the equilibrium profit-maximising weekly wage and employment level for the monopsonistic hospital. What would be the wage rate at this equilibrium level if the workers were paid their true contribution to the hospital?
   (c) Compare the hospital wage and employment levels with those that would prevail if the labour market was a perfect one.

2. The labour market for engineers is composed of both demand and supply elements. The demand curve $D_e = 760 - 0.1Q_e$, and the supply curve $S = 60 + 0.04Q_e$, where Q_e is the quantity of engineers.

   (a) Calculate the competitive market-clearing wage and employment levels.
   (b) If the market becomes influenced by a powerful labour union, calculate the wage and employment levels:
   (i) that the union will demand in order to maximise the total income of its members;
   (ii) that the union will demand to maximise the 'economic rent' of its members, i.e. the maximum possible excess of the workers' actual income over their best alternatives. (Assume that the supply curve for labour is its marginal cost curve.)

3. Arco, a large multinational chemical company, has a demand for specialist labour in the UK that can be expressed as $P_L = 80 - 0.1Q_L$, where P_L is the price of labour and Q_L the quantity of labour demanded. The supply Q_S of such specialist labour is completely inelastic in the short run at a level of 40. Using a diagrammatic approach:

   (a) Determine the equilibrium wage, and the 'rent' element in that wage. Explain the economic rationale behind your conclusion.
   (b) If Arco's demand function for labour falls to $P_L = 60 - 0.1Q_L$, calculate the new wage level and the associated economic rent.
   (c) If the supply function for labour becomes a more normal upward sloping line of the form $P_L = 20 + 0.05Q_L$, calculate the economic rent element in wages assuming that the demand curve has reverted to its original position. Explain fully the economic reasoning behind your conclusions.

4. A person values two things, goods (G) and leisure time (L). If we assume that goods can be bought only out of wage income, all of which is spent, and that the person works H hours a day at a real wage per hour of w, then:

   (a) Give the equations for the person's income/expenditure per day and hours of work per day.
   (b) Write down the expression for the utility function (U) that needs to be maximised.
   (c) Prove that in the optimum position, the person equates the marginal benefit of work against the marginal cost of the leisure forgone.
   (d) If the person's utility function is $U = G + 2L^{1/2}$, derive the labour supply function.

■ Further reading

Intermediate texts

Baumol, W. J. (1977), *Economic Theory and Operations Analysis*, 4th edn, Ch. 24, Prentice Hall, Hemel Hempstead.

Browning, E. and Browning, J. (1992), *Microeconomic Theory and Applications*, 4th edn, Chs 15–17, HarperCollins, London.

Chamberlain, N. W. (1951), *Collective Bargaining*, McGraw-Hill, New York.

Dobson, S., Maddala, G. S. and Miller, E. (1995), *Microeconomics*, Chs 13–15, McGraw-Hill, Maidenhead.

Flanders, A. (1975), *Management and Unions: The Theory of Reform of Industrial Relations*, Faber & Faber, London.

Hope, S. (1999), *Applied Microeconomics*, Chs 13 and 14, Wiley, Chichester.

Katz, M. and Rosen, H. (1998), *Microeconomics*, 3rd edn, Ch. 8, Irwin, Boston, Mass.

Knight, F. A. (1921), *Risk, Uncertainty and Profit*, Houghton Mifflin, Boston.

Koutsoyiannis, A. (1979), *Modern Microeconomics*, 2nd edn, Ch. 21, Macmillan, Basingstoke.

Laidler, D. and Estrin, S. (1995), *Introduction to Microeconomics*, 4th edn, Chs 21–23, Harvester Wheatsheaf, Hemel Hempstead.

Maddala, G. S. and Miller, E. (1989), *Microeconomics: Theory and Application*, Chs 15–17, McGraw-Hill, New York.

Nicholson, W. (1997), *Intermediate Microeconomics and its Application*, 7th edn, Chs 19–21, Dryden Press, Fort Worth.

Pindyck, R. and Rubinfeld, D. (1998), *Microeconomics*, 4th edn, Ch. 14, Macmillan, Basingstoke.

Schumpeter, J. A. (1934), *The Theory of Economic Development: An Enquiry into Profits, Capital, Credit, Interest and Business Cycles*, Harvard University Press, Harvard.

Taylor, R. (1989), *The Fifth Estate: Britain's Unions in the Modern World*, Pan Books, London.

Varian, H. (1999), *Intermediate Microeconomics*, 5th edn, Ch. 25, Norton, New York.

Advanced texts

Gravelle, H. and Rees, R. (1992), *Microeconomics*, 2nd edn, Chs 14 and 15, Longman, Harlow.

Articles and other sources

Addison, J. and Siebert, W. (1998), 'Union security in Britain', *Journal of Labour Research*, xix, 3.

Atkinson, A. B. (1996), 'Income distribution in Europe and the United States', *Oxford Review of Economic Policy*, 12, 1.

Berman, E., Bound, J. and Griliches, Z. (1994), 'Changes in the demand for skilled labour within US manufacturing industries', *Quarterly Journal of Economies*, 2, 109.

Blanchflower, D. (1996), 'The role and influence of trade unions within the OECD', *L.S.E. Discussion Paper*, 10.

Boal, W. and Ransom, M. (1997), 'Monopsony in the labour market', *Journal of Economic Literature*, xxxv, March.

Bosworth, D. and Simpson, P. (1995), 'Skills, training and economic performance', *Economics and Business Education*, III, Part 3, 11.

Card, D. and Krueger, A. B. (1994), 'Minimum wages and employment: a case study of the fast food industry in New Jersey and Pennsylvania', *The American Economic Review*, September.

Casey, B., Keep, E. and Mayhew, K. (1999), 'Flexibility, quality and competitiveness', *National Institute Economic Review*, 168, April.

Chalkley, M. (1994), 'How much do minimum wages reduce employment?', *The Economic Review*, 12, 1, September.

Cohen, D. (1998), *The Wealth of the World and the Poverty of Nations*, MIT Press, Cambridge, Massachusetts.

Daniel, W. W. (1987), *Workplace Industrial Relations and Technical Change*, Frances Pinter and PSI, London.

Disney, R. (1994), 'The decline of unions in Britain', *The Economic Review*, 12, 2, November.

Fenwick, P. (1999), 'Trade unions, wages and collective bargaining', in A. Griffiths and S. Wall (eds) *Applied Economics*, Pearson Education, Harlow.

Goodman, A. and Webb, S. (1994), 'For richer, for poorer: the changing distribution of income in the UK, 1961–91', *Institute for Fiscal Studies*, Commentary No. 42.

Gottshalk, P. and Smeeding, M. (1997), 'Cross national comparisons of earnings and income inequality', *Journal of Economic Literature*, 35, 2.

Gregg, P. and Machin, S. (1991) 'Changes in union status, increased competition and wage growth in the 1980s', *British Journal of Industrial Relations*, 29, 4, December.

Gregg, G. and Machin, S. (1994) 'Is the UK rise in inequality different?' in R. Barrell (ed.) *The UK Labour Market*, Cambridge University Press, Cambridge.

Haskel, J. and Heden, Y. (1999), 'Computers and the demand for skilled labour', *The Economic Journal*, 109, March.

Jain, S. (1975), *Size distribution of income*, World Bank, Washington.

Jenkins, S. P. (1994), 'Winners and losers: a portrait of the UK income distribution during the 1980's', *University of Swansea Economic Discussion Paper*, No 94–07.

Johnson, P. and Reed, H. (1996), 'Intergenerational mobility among the rich and poor: results from the National Child Development Survey', *Oxford Review of Economic Policy*, 12, 1.

Katz, L. and Krueger, A. (1992), 'The effect of the minimum wage on the fast food industry', *Industrial and Labour Relations Review*, 46, 1, October.

Metcalf, D. (1994), 'Transformation of British Industrial Relations?, Institutions, conduct and outcomes 1980–1990', in R. Barrell (ed.) (1994) *The UK Labour Market*, Cambridge University Press, Cambridge.

Neumark, D. and Wascher, W. (1992), 'Employment effects of minimum and subminimum wages: panel data on state minimum wage laws', *Industrial and Labour Relations Review*, 46, 1 October.

Nolan, P. (1995), 'Trade unions and British economic performance', *Developments in Economics*, 11.

OECD (1996), *Technology, Productitivity and Job Creation*, April, Paris.

Oswald, A. J. (1986), 'Wage determination and recession: A report on recent work', *British Journal of Industrial Relations*, 21, 1, March.

Stewart, M. (1981) *Relative Earnings and Individual Union Membership in the UK*, London School of Economics Centre for Labour Economics, University of London discussion paper 110.

Stewart, M. (1993), 'Do changes in collective bargaining imply declining union wages?', Quoted in Metcalf (1994).

Thomas, B. (1994), 'The labour market and European social measures', *Developments in Economics*, 10.

Tzannatos, Z. (1990), 'Sex differentials in the labour market', *The Economic Review*, May.

Chapter 11

General equilibrium, economic efficiency and social welfare

Introduction and review

In this chapter we shall bring together a number of ideas and terms encountered in earlier chapters. For example, we shall make extensive use of the indifference (iso-utility) curves and budget lines of Chapter 1 and the isocost and isoquant curves of Chapter 4. Our main concern will be to explore the theoretical basis for the belief that markets can coordinate the decisions of innumerable producers and consumers in such a way as to bring about an efficient allocation of resources. The key signal available to markets for influencing producer and consumer decisions is, of course, *market price*.

■ Partial versus general equilibrium

We shall initially assume the existence of *perfect* markets, in which no market failure occurs. Under these circumstances a set of prices can be established such that all markets achieve an equilibrium simultaneously. It is this idea of clearing (reaching equilibrium in) all markets simultaneously that is the essence of **general equilibrium**. In much of this book we have concentrated on a single market (e.g. product market), and have often assumed that certain other things remain equal (ceteris paribus), e.g. tastes of consumers in demand theory. This more restricted approach has often been termed **partial equilibrium** analysis. Here, however, we acknowledge the interdependence between all markets (e.g. product, consumer and factor markets) and make no restrictive ceteris paribus assumptions. We are thereby adopting a general equilibrium approach.

Having established that a set of prices exists that brings simultaneous equilibrium to all markets, we shall seek to enquire as to whether this solution is efficient. In doing so we make use of a well-known concept of welfare economics, namely **Pareto optimality**. A situation is said to be Pareto optimal when it is *no longer possible* to reallocate resources in such a way that we can make one person better off, without at the same time making someone else worse off. If it *were* possible to make someone better off without anyone else being made worse off, then we should do it; in such a situation the existing allocation of resources would then be non-Pareto optimal. Only when we have exhausted such possibilities so that further resource reallocation brings 'losers' as well as 'winners', can we be said to have a Pareto optimal resource allocation.

Fig. 11.1 **The
production frontier
and Pareto-optimal
resource
allocations.**

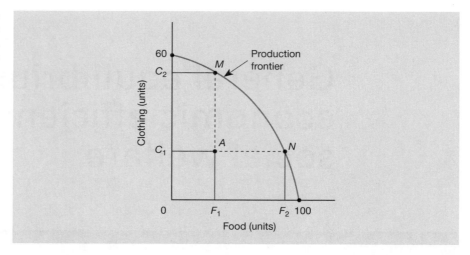

Using the simplified two-good production frontier curve of Fig. 11.1 it is clear that resource allocation A inside the production frontier is non-Pareto optimal. For example, we can move to the frontier at M, produce more clothing (and no less food) and use the extra clothing to make some consumers better off, without making anyone worse off. Similarly, we can move from resource allocation A to that at N, this time using the extra food to make some consumers better off, without making anyone worse off. All resource allocations *inside* the production frontier can be shown to be non-Pareto optimal in this way. However, all allocations *along* the production frontier are Pareto optimal, in the sense that it is no longer possible to reallocate resources so as to make some better off without making some worse off. For example we can move from M to N, but the extra $F_1 F_2$ food is gained only at the sacrifice (opportunity cost) of $C_2 C_1$ clothing. Some consumers will gain extra food *but* some will lose items of clothing. We shall explore Pareto optimality and other ideas of allocative efficiency further in later sections of this chapter.

The chapter goes on to examine the implications of *market failure* for a general equilibrium solution. In other words, if real-world markets depart, in one way or another, from the idealised perfect market solutions of our model, will this affect any of the conclusions we have previously made? As we shall see in this and subsequent chapters of the book, market failure does have significant implications for real-world policy makers.

The chapter concludes by reviewing a number of ideas in the area of welfare economics, including attempts to make the Pareto-optimal criterion more relevant to practical policy making. There is also a brief analysis of the problems involved in trying to develop rules for *aggregating* individual preferences in the attempt to derive social welfare functions.

Theoretical developments

For simplicity, we shall begin our analysis by taking a two-person, two-firm, two-product model and establishing a general equilibrium solution in this simplified case. The principles can be applied to a many-person, many-firm, many-product model, but by assuming only two participants in each model we can make use of (two-dimensional) graphical analysis. This $2 \times 2 \times 2$ general equilibrium model is considered here largely in the context of a *static* analysis, whereby we compare one equilibrium solution with another. At this juncture we are less concerned with *dynamic* analysis, i.e. the precise pathways by which we actually move from one equilibrium to another.

Assumptions of the model

A number of key assumptions will underpin our analysis of the $2 \times 2 \times 2$ model:

- *Two products* are produced, X and Y, under production conditions characterised by isoquants that are smooth and convex to the origin (see Chapter 4, p. 144). This implies diminishing marginal rates of technical substitution between the factors along a given isoquant. Further, the production function for each product is characterised by constant returns to scale, with no external economies (or diseconomies) affecting the production of one product as a result of the production of the other product.
- *Two consumers*, A and B, are active in the market, and their preferences are expressed by (ordinal) indifference curves that are smooth and convex to the origin (see Chapter 1, p. 3). This implies diminishing marginal rates of substitution in consumption between the two products. Consumers are assumed to be independent, in that the consumption pattern of one does not affect the consumption pattern of the other.
- *Two factors of production*, labour (L) and capital (K), are available. These factors are assumed to be both homogeneous and perfectly divisible.
- Producers seek the goal of *profit maximisation*.
- Consumers seek the goal of *utility (satisfaction) maximisation*.
- *Perfect competition* exists in both factor and product markets. Producers and consumers can therefore pursue their goals (objectives) subject to facing the same set of prices in the marketplace.
- There is *perfect information* to both consumers and producers as to the prices and qualities of the products and factors traded.

Terminology used in the model

P_X = price of good X; P_Y = price of good Y
w = price of labour; r = price of capital
X_A, X_B = quantity of product X purchased by consumers A and B respectively
Y_A, Y_B = quantities of product Y purchased by consumers A and B respectively
$\bar{K}, \bar{L}$ = fixed amount of capital and labour respectively available for allocation between products X and Y
K_X, L_X = amounts of capital and labour respectively allocated to product X
K_Y, L_Y = amounts of capital and labour respectively allocated to product Y

Pareto-efficient solutions

A **Pareto-efficient (Pareto-optimal)** allocation of resources is said to occur when the following three conditions exist:

- **Efficient allocation of resources between firms**. It should no longer be possible to reallocate *factor inputs* between *producers* so as to produce more of one product without at the same time producing less of the other product.

- **Efficient allocation of resources between consumers**. It should no longer be possible to reallocate *product outputs* between *consumers* so as to make one consumer better off without at the same time making the other consumer worse off.
- **Efficient combination of products in the economy as a whole**. The combination of outputs of X and Y selected for the economy as a whole should be such that aggregate consumer utility is maximised. In other words, it should no longer be possible to select a *different combination* of outputs of X and Y so as to increase *aggregate consumer utility* $(U_A + U_B)$.

We now seek to explain how, given our earlier assumptions, each of these three conditions can simultaneously be achieved by the price mechanism alone.

Equilibrium in production (efficiency in factor substitution)

The first efficiency condition requires that inputs be allocated amongst producers in such a way that the *combination of factors* is Pareto efficient. To illustrate this first efficiency condition we shall make extensive use of the **Edgeworth–Bowley production box**. This is shown in Fig. 11.2.

The lengths of each side of the production box are determined by the amounts of capital and labour $(\bar{K}, \bar{L})$ available for distribution between the two products X and Y. The more of any factor input allocated to product X, the less is available for product Y, and vice versa.

The isoquants of product X are plotted with the south-west corner of the box as origin. Each X isoquant is smooth and convex to this origin, and the furthest isoquant from the origin (X_5) corresponds to the highest value of output of X available (see Chapter 4, p. 146). In this case *all* the capital and labour available in the economy is devoted to product X (and none to Y).

Fig. 11.2 The Edgeworth–Bowley production box.

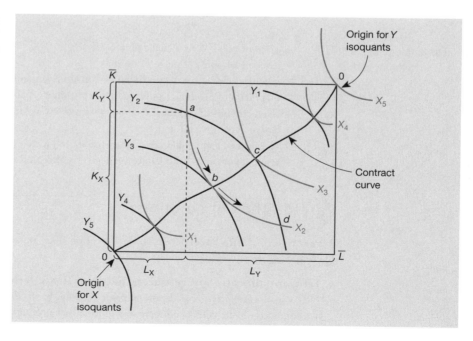

The opposite occurs for product Y; it is as though for Y we turn the same diagram upside down and superimpose it onto our diagram for X. The origin for Y is now the north-east corner of the box. Each Y isoquant is smooth and convex to *this* origin, and the furthest isoquant from the origin (Y_5) corresponds to the highest value of output of Y available. In this case *all* the capital and labour available in the economy is devoted to product Y (and none to X).

We can use the Edgeworth–Bowley production box to identify those resource allocations that are Pareto efficient. Only certain allocations of the total capital ($\bar{K}$) and labour ($\bar{L}$) resources between products X and Y are Pareto efficient. Let us begin by considering the allocation at point a, in which K_X, L_X is the respective capital and labour allocation to product X, and K_Y, L_Y the allocation to product Y. Clearly this allocation is non-Pareto efficient, in the sense that we can reallocate resources so as to make some better off and none worse off. For example, if we slide down the X_2 isoquant to point b, we use *less capital* and *more labour* to produce exactly the same amount of product X, namely X_2. However, by using the residual resources for product Y (now more capital and less labour available to produce Y than the combination K_Y, L_Y at a), we produce more Y ($Y_3 > Y_2$) at point b.

This extra Y (same X) can be used to make some better off, with none worse off. So allocation a is non-Pareto efficient. Note that Y_3 is the highest attainable isoquant for product Y (furthest from the Y origin) in the production box given that we still produce X_2. The allocation at point b is clearly a *tangency position* between the respective X_2 and Y_3 isoquants, and corresponds to a Pareto-efficient allocation. Any *further* reallocation along X_2 in this direction will take us below and to the right of b on X_2, which will mean less of product Y. For example, at point d we again have X_2, Y_2 of each product available, and as we have seen $Y_2 < Y_3$.

It should be clear that *only* tangency positions between the respective isoquants correspond to Pareto-efficient solutions. The line connecting these tangency positions is called the **contract curve**. It is therefore allocations along the contract curve that alone are Pareto efficient in the production box. You might usefully consider why a reallocation of resources from a to c would also achieve a Pareto-efficient solution.

Pareto efficiency in production implies:

$$\frac{\text{Slope of } X}{\text{isoquant}} = \frac{\text{Slope of } Y}{\text{isoquant}}$$

i.e. $MRTS_{LK}$ for $X = MRTS_{LK}$ for Y (see Chapter 4, pp. 159–62)

Prices and Pareto efficiency in production   This first (of three) Pareto-efficiency condition involves production, with the economy attaining an appropriate allocation of resources between firms. We now consider how, under our earlier assumptions, **prices** can provide the *signals* to firms to bring about contract curve allocations of capital and labour between firms.

We have already seen (Chapter 4, p. 150) that the slope of an isocost curve is given by the ratio of factor prices, w/r, where w is the price of labour (wage rate) and r is the price of capital (interest rate). Provided that firms face the *same* factor price ratios (e.g. purchase inputs on perfect factor markets) then they will be faced by isocost curves of *identical slope.* Our earlier assumption of profit maximisation (or loss minimisation) means that the firm must seek to produce the profit-maximising output at minimum feasible cost. In Fig. 11.3(a), if $2X$ is the profit-maximising output, this can be produced at minimum cost ($\bar{C}_1$) where the $2X$ isoquant just touches (is a tangent to) the isocost curve nearest to the product X origin. This implies the use of K_1 capital and L_1 labour. Similarly in Fig. 11.3(b), if $3Y$ is the profit-maximising output, this can be produced at minimum cost ($\bar{C}_2$) where the $3Y$ isoquant is tangent to the isocost curve nearest to the product Y origin. This implies the use of K_2 capital and L_2 labour.

Without any conscious coordination between producers, but simply by individually seeking their own profit-maximising solutions, the two firms have achieved a contract curve allocation of resources (here factor inputs). Provided only that they face the *same* factor price ratio (w/r), they will have equated the slopes of their respective isoquants: i.e. they will be at a solution such as b or c in the earlier Fig. 11.2:

$$\text{i.e. } MRTS^{X}_{LK} = \frac{w}{r} = MRTS^{Y}_{LK}$$

$$\text{or } \frac{\text{Slope of } X}{\text{isoquant}} = \frac{w}{r} = \frac{\text{Slope of } Y}{\text{isoquant}}$$

It is *factor prices* that act as the signal to induce firms to select capital/labour ratios (resource allocations) that are Pareto efficient.

Equilibrium in consumption (efficiency in distribution of products) The second efficiency condition requires that the outputs selected by firms be allocated amongst consumers in such a way that the *distribution of products* is Pareto efficient. We first consider what is involved in a Pareto-efficient distribution of products using an **Edgeworth–Bowley consumption box** then we see how prices can bring about such resource allocations.

Fig. 11.3 Role of factor prices in attaining contract curve (Pareto efficient) solutions.

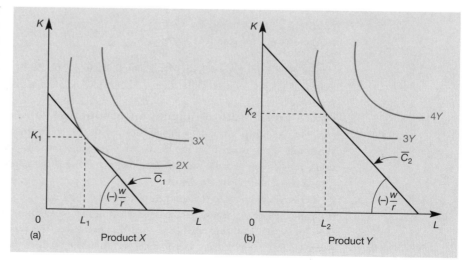

The Edgeworth–Bowley consumption box used in our analysis is shown in Fig. 11.4. The lengths of each side of the consumption box are determined by the amounts of products X and Y $(\bar{X}, \bar{Y})$ available for distribution between the two consumers A and B: the more of one product allocated to consumer A, the less available for consumer B and vice versa.

The indifference curves of consumer A are plotted with the south-west corner of the box as origin. Each A indifference curve is smooth and convex to this origin, and the furthest indifference curve from the origin (A_5) corresponds to the highest level of utility available to A (see Chapter 1, pp. 2–4). In this case *all* the output of products X and Y available in the economy is consumed by A (and none by B).

The opposite occurs for consumer B; it is as though we turn the same diagram for B upside down and superimpose it onto our diagram for A. The origin for B is now the north-east corner of the box. Each B indifference curve is smooth and convex to *this* origin, and the furthest indifference curve from the origin (B_5) corresponds to the highest level of utility available to B. In this case *all* the output of products X and Y available in the economy is consumed by B (and none by A).

This time we use the Edgeworth–Bowley consumption box to identify those distributions of resources that are Pareto efficient. Only certain distributions of the total product $(\bar{X}, \bar{Y})$ between consumers A and B are Pareto efficient. Let us begin by considering the distribution at point a, in which X_A, Y_A are the respective consumptions of products X and Y by consumer A. Clearly *this* distribution is non-Pareto efficient in the sense that we can redistribute output so as to make some better off and none worse off. For example, if we slide down the A_2 indifference curve to point b, we distribute *less product Y* to consumer A but *more product X*, keeping A's utility constant (at A_2). However, by distributing the residual output to consumer B (now more of product Y and less of

Fig. 11.4
**Edgeworth–Bowley
consumption box.**

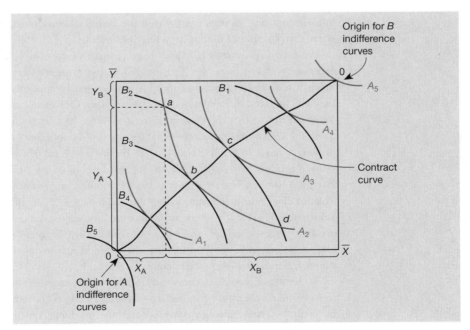

product X available to consumer B than the combination Y_B, X_B at a), we increase B's utility ($B_3 > B_2$) at point b. If consumer B is better off and consumer A is no worse off at b as compared with a, then clearly distribution a is non-Pareto efficient.

Note that B_3 is the highest attainable indifference curve (furthest from the B origin) in the consumption box given that A remains on indifference curve A_2. The distribution at point b is clearly a *tangency position* between the respective A_2 and B_3 indifference curves, and corresponds to a Pareto-efficient distribution of output. Any *further* redistribution of output along A_2 in this direction will take us below and to the right of b on A_2 which will mean lower utility for consumer B. For example, at point d we again have A_2, B_2 levels of utility for each consumer, and as we have seen $B_2 < B_3$.

It should be clear that *only* tangency positions between the respective indifference curves correspond to Pareto-efficient solutions. The line connecting these tangency positions is again called the **contract curve**. It is therefore distributions of output along the contract curve that alone are Pareto efficient in the consumption box. You might usefully consider why a redistribution of resources from a to c would also achieve a Pareto-efficient solution.

Pareto efficiency in consumption implies:

> Slope of A indifference curve $=$ Slope of B indifference curve
>
> i.e. $MRS_{XY}^{A} = MRS_{XY}^{B}$ (see Chapter 1, p. 3)

Prices and Pareto efficiency in consumption This second (of three) Pareto efficiency condition involves the economy attaining an appropriate distribution of output (products X and Y) between consumers (A and B). We now consider how, under our earlier assumptions, **prices** can provide the *signals* to consumers to bring about contract curve distributions of output between themselves.

We have already seen (Chapter 1, p. 4) that the slope of a *budget line* is given by the ratio of product prices, P_X/P_Y. Provided that consumers face the *same* price ratios on product markets (e.g. purchase outputs on perfectly competitive product markets) then they will be faced by budget lines of *identical slope*. Our earlier assumption of utility maximisation means that the consumer must seek the highest attainable indifference curve, given the constraints of income level (position of budget line) and product prices (slope of budget line). In Fig. 11.5(a), if $\bar{M}_1$ is the income level of consumer A, and P_X/P_Y the ratio of product prices, then I_2 is the highest level of utility attainable, where the budget line ($\bar{M}_1$) just touches (is a tangent to) the indifference curve furthest from the origin. This implies consumer A purchasing the combination X_1, Y_1 of the respective products. Similarly in Fig. 11.5(b), if $\bar{M}_2$ is the income level of consumer B, and P_X/P_Y the ratio of product prices, then I_3 is the highest level of utility attainable, where the budget line ($\bar{M}_2$) is a tangent to the indifference curve furthest from the origin. This implies consumer B purchasing the product combination X_2, Y_2.

Without any conscious coordination between consumers, but simply by individually seeking their own utility-maximising solutions, the two consumers have achieved a contract-curve distribution of resources (here the products consumed). Provided only that

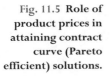

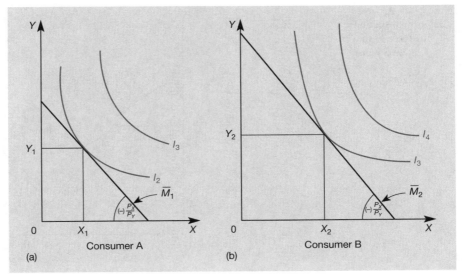

they face the *same* product price ratio (P_X/P_Y), they will have equated the slopes of their respective indifference curves: i.e. they will be at a solution such as *b* or *c* in the earlier Fig. 11.4:

$$\text{i.e.} \quad MRS_{XY}^{A} = \frac{P_X}{P_Y} = MRS_{XY}^{B}$$

$$\text{or} \quad \begin{matrix} \text{Slope of A} \\ \text{indifference} \\ \text{curve} \end{matrix} = \frac{P_X}{P_Y} = \begin{matrix} \text{Slope of B} \\ \text{indifference} \\ \text{curve} \end{matrix}$$

It is *product prices* that act as the signal to induce consumers to select distributions of products X and Y between themselves (resource allocations) that are Pareto efficient.

Efficient combination of product (i.e. product mix in the economy as a whole)

As regards this third efficiency condition we consider *aggregate production* and *aggregate consumer utility*. This condition requires that the product mix selected (i.e. the combination of outputs of *X* and *Y*) be such that no other feasible product mix can increase aggregate consumer utility. We shall see that this implies a tangency solution between the *production frontier* for the whole economy and the *community indifference curve*. The latter is the sum of individual consumer indifference curves (see Chapter 1, p. 2) and in Fig. 11.6 the product mix X_1, Y_1 represents the highest level of utility that the community (society) can attain given the technical production possibilities available for the whole economy.

We have already seen that efficiency in production (the first efficiency condition) requires a contract curve solution in the Edgeworth–Bowley production box, which implies being *on* the production frontier. However, *all* points on the production frontier fulfil this first efficiency condition. Here we are interested in identifying the *particular*

Fig. 11.6 **A Pareto-efficient product mix for the economy as a whole.**

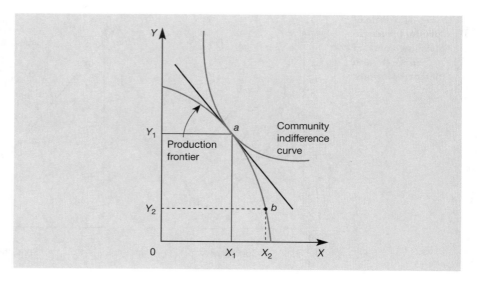

point on the production frontier that maximises the utility of the community (society). This is shown as point a in Fig. 11.6; with the product mix X_1, Y_1 it is no longer possible to change the product mix in order to raise community utility. The product mix X_1, Y_1 is therefore the Pareto-optimal solution, with any other product mix being non-Pareto optimal. For example at b, with product mix X_2, Y_2, we would be on a *lower* community indifference curve; we could then move to point a, producing less X and more Y, thereby raising utility for consumers as a whole.

> Pareto efficiency in product mix implies:
>
> $$\frac{\text{Slope of production frontier}}{} = \frac{\text{Slope of community indifference curve}}{}$$

Of course at point a, with product mix X_1, Y_1, it must not be possible for consumers to *redistribute* this output between themselves to make one consumer better off, without making the other consumer worse off. If it were possible to do this, then aggregate consumer utility would rise and we could not be at the tangency position shown in Fig. 11.6.

As we can see from Fig. 11.7, it is only when the slope of the *production frontier* (at a) is also equal to the slope of the *individual consumer indifference curves* (at a') that we can be sure that we have achieved an efficient product mix. Only in this case will no reallocation of product mix X_1, Y_1 be possible so as to increase the aggregate consumer utility.

Pareto efficiency in product mix therefore also implies:

> $$\frac{\text{Slope of production frontier}}{} = \frac{\text{Slope of individual consumer indifference curves}}{}$$
>
> $$MRPT_{XY} = MRS_{XY}^{A} = MRS_{XY}^{B}$$

Fig. 11.7 Slope of individual consumer indifference curves at *a'* equal slope of production frontier at *a* for Pareto-efficient product mix.

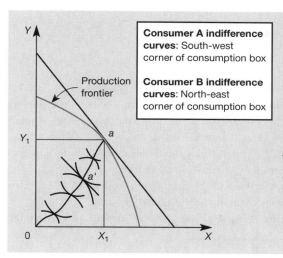

Consumer A indifference curves: South-west corner of consumption box

Consumer B indifference curves: North-east corner of consumption box

Note: For each point on the production function (e.g. *a*) there is a particular Edgeworth–Bowley consumption box (here $0X_1a\,Y_1$) and a particular (here *a'*) Pareto-optimal solution. Of course, a different point on the production frontier would yield a different consumption box and therefore a different Pareto-optimal solution. This *grand utility possibility* curve summarises all these possible outcomes. It is a locus of *all* the feasible Pareto-optimal points of production and consumption.

Prices and Pareto efficiency in product mix   We have so far assumed (p. 433) perfectly competitive markets and a profit-maximising objective. In such markets, prices are set equal to marginal costs. We can use this attribute of competitive markets to demonstrate how *prices* can bring about an efficient product mix.

We have previously seen how the *marginal rate of physical transformation into X of Y* ($MRPT_{XY}$) tells us how much of Y must be given up for each *extra* unit of X. The $MRPT_{XY}$ is given by the *slope of the production frontier* at any point. In Fig. 11.8:

- at *a*, $MRPT_{XY} = 1$
- at *b*, $MRPT_{XY} = 2$

Now it can be shown that:

Slope of production frontier = Ratio of marginal costs

Fig. 11.8 The production frontier and variations in the marginal rate of physical transformation into X of Y ($MRPT_{XY}$).

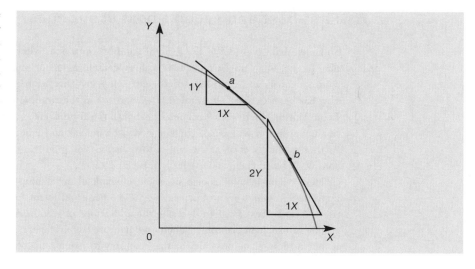

At a: $MRPT_{XY} = 1$ and $\dfrac{MC_X}{MC_Y} = 1$

At b: $MRPT_{XY} = 2$ and $\dfrac{MC_X}{MC_Y} = 2$

In words, we can see from Fig. 11.8 that at point a the slope of the production frontier ($MRPT_{XY}$) is 1. It can also be seen that the *same amount of resources* can produce either 1 extra X *or* 1 extra Y. In other words $MC_X = MC_Y$. At point b, the slope of the production frontier ($MRPT_{XY}$) is 2. It can also be seen that the same amount of resources can produce either 1 extra X *or* 2 extra Y. In other words $MC_X = 2MC_Y$.

Clearly the slope of the production frontier ($MRPT_{XY}$) also tells us the ratio of the marginal costs of production (MC_X / MC_Y).

But if price = marginal cost in competitive markets, then it follows that in equilibrium:

$$\frac{P_X}{P_Y} = \frac{MC_X}{MC_Y} = MRPT_{XY}$$

We have already seen that, under our assumptions, prices fulfil our second Pareto-efficiency condition (consumption):

$$\frac{P_X}{P_Y} = MRS_{XY}^A = MRS_{XY}^B$$

In other words, prices can fulfil the third efficiency condition for product mix:

$$MRPT_{XY} = \frac{MC_X}{MC_Y} = \frac{P_X}{P_Y} = MRS_{XY}^A = MRS_{XY}^B$$

First-best and second-best economies

So far we have considered the general equilibrium model whereby a set of *prices* (product, factor, etc.) might exist that, under certain assumptions, will clear all markets simultaneously and yield Pareto-efficient solutions. This interdependence between markets has been extensively studied elsewhere, as in the simultaneous equation system of Leon Walras. Much work has been devoted to the conditions under which a general equilibrium solution will *exist*, whether it will be *unique*, and whether it will be *stable*. The further reading section at the end of this chapter will guide you into the work of Walras, Arrow, Debreu, Hahn and others in this respect.

Here we initially focus on a situation in which all the assumptions set out on p. 433 *do* apply, and in which a set of prices *does* yield a Pareto-efficient solution in all markets. We use the term **first best** to describe the allocations of resources and the levels of utility attained in such an economy. When one or more of our earlier assumptions *cease to apply* it may no longer be possible for the economy to reach a first-best allocation. The presence of such market failures may mean that only **second-best** allocations are feasible in our economy. It is to a more detailed consideration of first- and second-best resource allocations that we now turn.

Single market failure

In Fig. 11.9 we have a **utility frontier** that is the sum of the individual utilities of our two consumers, A and B. The first-best frontier corresponds to the contract curve solution to the Edgeworth–Bowley consumption box, and all points along it are Pareto efficient. Suppose, however, there was now a *single* market failure on the production side of the economy: e.g. the existence of a public enterprise monopoly violating the competitive markets assumption. We have seen that setting prices equal to marginal costs of production is a key feature for the achievement of Pareto-efficient resource allocations (p. 441); yet the public enterprise will have the market power to set price *above* marginal cost, should it so wish. Suppose that it does this, we are now at point M in Fig. 11.9, inside the first-best (Pareto optimal) utility frontier. Clearly we have a non-Pareto optimal resource allocation, since by moving vertically, horizontally or in a north-east direction, one or both consumers can be made better off, and no one worse off.

For policy-making purposes this *single* market failure can be corrected and a movement from M to the first-best utility frontier can be achieved. This could, of course, be done by breaking up the public enterprise and creating competitive market conditions in which prices equal marginal costs or by regulating the monopoly so that it actually sets prices equal to marginal cost. Whatever the means selected, correcting this single market failure will permit the restoration of a first-best solution.

Two or more market failures

Restrictions on government policy options Suppose now that we have *three* elements of market failure, say two private sector monopolies and one public enterprise monopoly. Suppose also that the government cannot correct all three instances of market

Fig. 11.9 **First-best and second-best utility frontiers.**

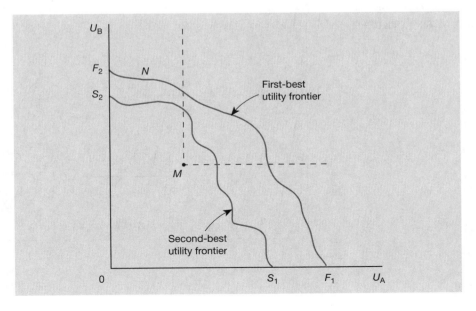

failure. In terms of Fig. 11.9 the economy will *not* be able to move from resources alloca-tion M back to the first-best frontier. However, the government may be able to do something to influence resource allocation. It may, for example, be able to directly influ-ence (by regulation) the pricing policy of the public enterprise monopoly, which might indirectly influence the pricing policy of the private sector monopolies. We shall see that in the presence of such policy restrictions a move from M back to the first-best utility frontier may be impossible. However, a move to the second-best utility frontier in Fig. 11.9 may be feasible. Here we consider the types of policy that might bring about such a second-best solution. We shall see that achieving such a solution sometimes requires rather surprising policy initiatives: for example moving further away from the first-best marginal cost pricing principle rather than towards it.

To illustrate this idea of the second best we shall consider three industries in our economy, which initially is in a first-best equilibrium solution with a set of prices (p^0_1, p^0_2, p^0_3) and quantities (q^0_1, q^0_2, q^0_3) for the respective industries. Initially we assume industries 1 and 2 to be private sector and competitive, but industry 3 to be a public enterprise monopoly regulated so as to set prices = marginal costs. In Fig. 11.10, the continuous lines show the demand, marginal revenue and marginal cost curves of each industry, together with the first-best set of prices (p^0_1, p^0_2, p^0_3) and quantities (q^0_1, q^0_2, q^0_3). In this analysis we closely follow the work of Rees (1983).

Now suppose that the private sector industries 1 and 2 become *monopolised*, with no change in marginal costs. To maximise profits the private sector monopolists raise their prices to p^*_1 and p^*_2 respectively ($MC_1 = MR_1$; $MC_2 = MR_2$), and their outputs corre-spondingly fall to q^*_1 and q^*_2. For simplicity, we assume that the cross-elasticities of demand between the products of the first two industries are zero, so that the respective price increases have no effects on the positions of the demand curves of those industries.

Fig. 11.10 **Finding a second-best solution involving prices (p^*_1, p^*_2, p'_3) and quantities (q^*_1, q^*_2, q'_3).**

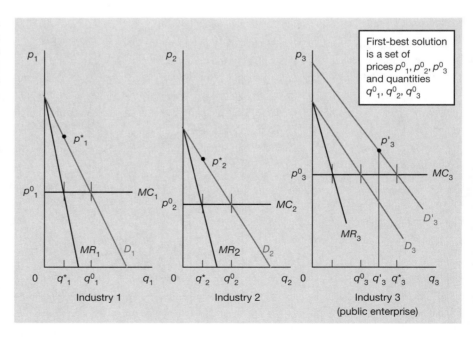

Suppose, however, that both products 1 and 2 are *substitutes* in consumption for product 3, the output of the public enterprise industry. In this case the increase in p_1 and p_2 will cause increased demand for product 3, so that the demand curve D_3 shifts upwards and outwards, say to D'_3. If the public enterprise industry continues to set price equal to marginal cost (i.e. p^0_3), its output will be $q*_3$. Assuming continued full employment in the economy, the effect of the monopolisation has been to release from the first two industries the resources that were required to produce outputs $(q^0_1 - q*_1)$ and $(q^0_2 - q*_2)$ respectively, and these are then absorbed into industry 3 to produce the output increase $(q*_3 - q^0_3)$. The resulting set of prices $(p*_1, p*_2$ and $p^0_3)$ and of outputs $(q*_1, q*_2, q*_3)$ and the associated resource allocation is *not* Pareto optimal; it corresponds to points such as M in Fig. 11.9. The reason is, of course, that the respective price ratios are *unequal* to the corresponding marginal cost ratios. In particular,

$$\frac{p^*_1}{p^0_3} > \frac{MC_1}{MC_3} \quad \text{and} \quad \frac{p^*_2}{p^0_3} > \frac{MC_2}{MC_3}$$

We know, therefore, that it is possible to make everyone better off in this economy by reallocating resources out of industry 3 and into industries 1 and 2. Put another way, consumers of products 1 and 2 would be in a position to benefit from bribing consumers of product 3 to release resources: the former consumers could fully compensate the latter for their loss of consumption, and still experience a net gain in utility. The market mechanism fails to organise such exchanges, however, because of the intervention of the monopolists who control industries 1 and 2. This is the situation that confronts the policy maker at resource allocation M in Fig. 11.9.

We first suppose that the policy maker cannot influence the price–output decisions of the private monopolies directly, but can only do so indirectly through the policies of the public enterprises under his control. In this case the pricing policies of the public enterprises would be the only available instruments of second-best policy. The policy maker will want to choose the price regime for the public enterprise(s) in such a way as to achieve a Pareto-optimum allocation, but subject to the constraint that the monopolists are free to determine their own price (and output) behaviour.

Given the resource allocation with prices $(p*_1, p*_2, p^0_3)$ and outputs $(q*_1, q*_2, q*_3)$, the planner is aware that welfare gains can be made by reallocating resources away from industry 3 and towards industries 1 and 2. Since he is constrained to act only on product 3, he can instruct the public enterprise to raise its price, say to p'_3. This will cause demand to fall along D'_3 to q'_3. Since products 1 and 2 are substitutes for product 3, their demands will now increase (shift upwards and outwards), and resources will be diverted into their production as the planner intends. The problem of determining the final optimum position in the three industries is quite complex; however, Fig. 11.10 gives a flavour of the result. It shows that by varying the price of product 3, the planner is able to cause demand variations and price changes in the other markets in the required direction, as the monopolists adjust their profit-maximising positions in response to the change in the public enterprise price and output. This process may continue until finally a resource allocation is achieved such that no consumer can be made better off without making another worse off, given the policy instruments (public enterprise price) available to the policy makers. This resource allocation, when achieved, would be a second-best Pareto optimum with price deliberately raised above marginal cost in industry 3.

No restrictions on government policy options Of course if *no restrictions* existed as regards government policy towards the three industries, then it might be possible to move from M directly to the first-best frontier. Since we assume that the government can now act *directly* on the monopolies, we have the result that by a suitable choice of policy it can attain a first-best resource allocation. Thus, suppose the policy maker can enforce a marginal cost pricing policy on the public enterprise *and* the private sector monopolists. Their prices now fall to p^0_1 and p^0_2 respectively, and demand for product 3 falls from D'_3 back to D_3, so that the initial first-best situation is restored. In effect, we have an economy consisting of two *regulated* monopolies and a public enterprise, with marginal cost pricing as the optimal policy for each participant in the economy.

In the case of moving to either the second-best or first-best frontiers, we may not necessarily end up at a point *along either frontier* that is contained on, or within, the dashed lines extending from *M* in Fig. 11.9. In the case of the first-best frontier, suppose we move from *M* to *N*. We would be moving to a resource allocation that intrinsically is Pareto efficient as it represents a contract curve position (being on the first-best utility frontier). However, in moving from *M* to *N* consumer B gains utility but consumer A loses utility. *N* is *Pareto efficient* but cannot be said to be *Pareto preferred* compared with the initial allocation *M*. It could only be Pareto preferred if someone was better off and no one was worse off.

We now consider ways in which the Pareto-efficient idea might be extended to enable us to compare resource allocations that involve both winners and losers.

■ Criteria for welfare judgements

The Pareto criterion

In the simple two-person community, the **Pareto criterion** will only help us compare resource allocations of the type shown in Fig. 11.11. Only movements directly east, north or north-east from the initial allocation can be said to be *Pareto preferred* to the initial allocation at *M*. For example *C*, *D* and *E* are Pareto preferred to *M*, with allocations *C* and *D* having one consumer better off and the other no worse off than at *M*, and allocation *E* having both consumers better off than at *M*. However, we *cannot* use the Pareto criterion to compare allocation *F* with the initial allocation *M*, even though allocation *F* is Pareto efficient (*on* the utility frontier and therefore the contract curve) and allocation *M* is non-Pareto efficient. The reason is that at *F*, consumer B is better off but consumer A is worse off, and the very rationale of the Pareto criterion is to *avoid* interpersonal comparisons of utility: in other words to avoid weighing the gains to some against the losses to others. Of course, in many practical policy areas projects under consideration *will* involve changes in resource allocations in which there are winners and losers. The economist N. Kaldor saw that the problem of interpersonal comparisons of utility must be addressed if welfare criteria are to play a role in real-world policy formation.

The Kaldor criterion

In order to allow comparisons between allocations such as *M* and *F* in Fig. 11.11, **Kaldor** proposed that individual B (the winner) be asked how much he/she would be willing to pay (the maximum amount) *rather than forgo* the move from *M* to *F*. Let us suppose this to be a certain amount K_B. Similarly, individual A (the loser) could be asked

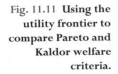

Fig. 11.11 **Using the utility frontier to compare Pareto and Kaldor welfare criteria.**

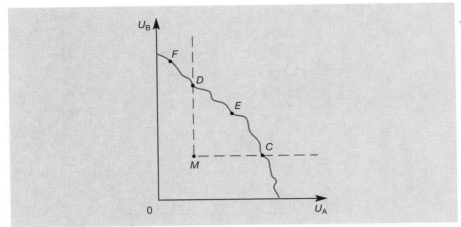

how much he/she would be willing to pay (the maximum amount) *to prevent* this reallocation of resources. Let us suppose this to be a certain amount K_A. Then if $K_B > K_A$, Kaldor would propose that the reallocation go ahead on the grounds that B could *compensate* A for any loss in welfare and still have a surplus to keep for him or herself or for others. In other words, the proposed reallocation of resources yields a *net gain* available to make some better off after the losers have been compensated. Here Kaldor does not actually require that the compensation be paid to the losers; simply that there is *potential* for such payment. (If the payment were actually paid and there were no losers, even the unreconstructed Pareto criterion would regard that outcome as preferred to the original resource allocation.)

> **Kaldor criterion:** a resource reallocation is preferred if those who gain evaluate their gains more highly than those who lose evaluate their losses.

In terms of Fig. 11.11, a reallocation of resources from *M* to *F* is preferred under the Kaldor criterion. There is the *potential* to redistribute resources between the two consumers along the utility frontier so that someone gains and no one loses as a result of the change (e.g. move from *F* to *D* or *E* or *C*). Using the Kaldor criterion, any reallocation from a point such as *M inside* the utility frontier to one such as *F on* the utility frontier is preferred if and only if *M* lies underneath the utility frontier through point *F*.

The Scitovsky double criterion

T. Scitovsky indicated a possible flaw in the use of the Kaldor criterion where the proposed policy change not only affects the individual's utility but also *shifts* the whole utility frontier. In Fig. 11.12(a) the reallocation of resources from *G* to *H* would be considered preferred using the Kaldor criterion; unfortunately the reverse movement from *H* to *G* would also be considered preferred. This situation can occur where the respective economy-wide utility frontiers intersect each other as a consequence of shifting (and pivoting) via the resource reallocation. In Fig. 11.12(a) *G* lies underneath the utility frontier through point *H*, *but H* also lies underneath the utility frontier through point *G*.

Fig. 11.12

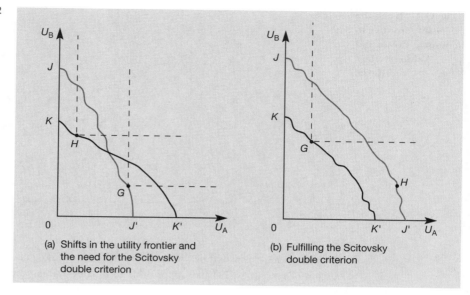

(a) Shifts in the utility frontier and
the need for the Scitovsky
double criterion

(b) Fulfilling the Scitovsky
double criterion

To avoid this situation Scitovsky proposed his **double criterion**. This stricter test for preferred allocations involves two parts:

- fulfilling the Kaldor criterion to show that the move from the initial allocation to the new allocation is preferred;
- showing that the reverse move from the new allocation back to the original allocation *does not* fulfil the Kaldor criterion.

If and only if the move from one allocation to another passes *both* parts of the test, will Scitovsky's double criterion regard the new allocation as preferred.

In Fig. 11.12(b) the move from G to H would pass the Scitovsky double criterion. Here the utility frontiers have shifted as a result of the policy change yielding the resource reallocation, but the frontiers have *not* intersected. The move from G to H fulfils the Kaldor criterion but the reverse move from H to G does not.

Figure 11.12(b) helps, however, to indicate a serious criticism made by many economists of both the Kaldor and Scitovsky criteria: namely that they still require an *interpersonal comparison of utilities*, although one that is somewhat concealed. The move from G to H in Fig. 11.12(b) may be such that A (the winner) is willing to pay up to £500 to secure it, whereas B (the loser) may only be willing to pay £100 to avoid it. Nevertheless if B is relatively poorer (in income or wealth) than A, £100 to B may be a significant sum and correspond to considerable utility to B, whereas £500 to A may be an insignificant sum and correspond to little utility to A. If the compensation is not actually paid, then using these money values of *willingness to pay* for the respective individuals may fail to reflect actual changes in overall (community) utility. If the compensation *is* actually paid, then we are back to the original Pareto criterion and have no need of the Kaldor/Scitovsky refinements! In other words there is a presumption of a *constant marginal utility of money income* (see Chapter 1, p. 28) underlying the use of both the Kaldor and Scitovsky criteria. They essentially accept the existing distribution of income and wealth and ignore its impact on individual utilities. This is the type of implicit interpersonal comparison that many welfare economists seek to avoid.

The Bergson criterion

A. Bergson stresses that interpersonal comparison is inevitable in comparing utility levels resulting from changes in resource allocation. His point is that these comparisons should be made *explicit* (e.g. £1A = £0.60B over certain ranges of income) and be the basis for developing a **social welfare function**. In other words, explicit rules can be laid down for interpersonal comparisons as the basis for developing a map involving community indifference curves ranked in order of utility.

The use of **cost–benefit analysis** can be regarded as following the pattern of Bergson, being an attempt to lay down specific ground rules for interpersonal comparisons when evaluating under what circumstances a reallocation of resources can be regarded as of *net benefit* to society. We consider the principles and practice of cost–benefit analysis in more detail on pp. 455–60.

■ Democratic group decisions and social welfare functions

Much attention has been paid in recent years to the process of deriving *aggregate (group) decision rules from individual decision rules*: in other words, finding social welfare functions from expressions of individual preferences. The work of Kenneth Arrow has been important in this respect, and we briefly review it here.

Arrow's impossibility theorem

Arrow sought to derive a rule for aggregating individual preferences that would meet four, in his view, minimal conditions. The social choices resulting from this rule must be:

- **consistent (transitive)**, such that if allocation A is preferred to B, and allocation B to C, then C will not be selected by the rule in preference to A when A is also available;
- **non-dictatorial**: in other words the (group) rule must not be dictated by any single individual within the group or outside the group;
- **non-perverse**: an allocation that would otherwise be selected by the (group) rule must never be rejected when the only change is that some members of the group come to regard it more favourably;
- **independence of irrelevant alternatives**: a (group) rule that involves selecting between two alternative allocations A and B must depend only on the ranking of these alternatives by members of the group. In other words, any change in the ranking of other alternative allocations by members of the group must *not* affect the ranking of these two allocations, A and B.

These four criteria have been seen by many as essential ingredients for any democratic decision-making rule. However, Arrow has shown that it is *impossible* to derive a rule that meets all four requirements simultaneously! In other words, social choice rules must violate aspects of consistency or democracy. We can illustrate Arrow's point by looking more carefully at conditions 1 and 4 respectively.

Violation of consistency (transitivity)

It can be shown that using even that most democratic of procedures, the *ballot*, as a means of achieving group decisions can violate this first condition. Here we assume that a majority rule applies (or 'first past the post'), with three individuals Brown, Smith and Jones choosing between three alternative allocations A, B and C. Table 11.1 indicates their individual preferences, with 3 being the number assigned to their first choice, 2 to their second choice and 1 to their least preferred choice. As we shall see, even if each individual voter exhibits transitive preferences, the group decision rule based on majority voting may not.

Table 11.1

	A	B	C
Brown	3	2	1
Smith	2	1	3
Jones	1	3	2

From the table we can see that both Brown and Smith prefer A to B, that Brown and Jones prefer B to C, and that Smith and Jones prefer C to A. Clearly the majority prefers A to B and B to C, but unfortunately that majority also prefers C to A! Majority voting can therefore lead to intransitive (inconsistent) group decision rules.

Violation of independence of irrelevant alternatives

As we have seen, this condition states that only individual preferences between the alternatives under consideration should affect the group decision rule. Again, we can use the voting analogy to illustrate this idea.

In Table 11.2, four allocations are ranked by our three individuals in terms of preference (4 is the point score for the most preferred). In that table, A is most preferred over all with a total point score of 10 points, and C next with 8 points. If we concentrate on the comparison between allocations A and C, we can regard B, for example, as irrelevant. Table 11.3 therefore drops B from consideration. Ranking the remaining allocations with the point scores 3, 2, 1 respectively now gives a total point score in which A and C are tied, with 7 points each. Whether or not this (irrelevant) option B is offered to voters does affect the choice between A and C, which is clearly a violation of condition 4.

In fact this fourth condition is rather strong, as it implies a disregard for all public preferences other than those between the alternatives under consideration. Indeed many would question whether the presence of this fourth condition is democratic at all! In political terms, the condition is stating that the presence (or absence) of a particular political party (choice B in Table 11.2) in an election should have no influence on the decision between the major parties A and C. On the contrary, many voters and political commentators expressly desire that the minor parties should have an influence on the outcome of the democratic process.

Further, to satisfy this fourth condition implies that the *intensity* of individual preferences be disregarded, and primacy given instead to the *ranking* of preferences. Thus in our table no distinction is made between situations where, say, Brown might have a strong preference for allocation A over any other but Smith only barely prefers A to the

Table 11.2

	A	B	C	D
Brown	4	3	2	1
Smith	4	3	2	1
Jones	2	1	4	3
Total point vote	10	7	8	5

Table 11.3

	A	C	D
Brown	3	2	1
Smith	3	2	1
Jones	1	3	2
Total point vote	7	7	4

alternatives available. Again, in practical policy ranking the intensity of preferences would be regarded by many as an element to be *incorporated* into a decision rule, rather than avoided.

Despite these criticisms Arrow has usefully highlighted the problems that might be encountered when seeking to define a social welfare function based on a mathematical rule combining individual preferences.

Applications and evidence

■ Efficiency versus equity trade-off

In Fig. 11.6 we noted that the third efficiency condition required an equality between the slopes of the production frontier and highest attainable community indifference curve, sometimes called the social welfare function. It is this outcome that is often referred to as the **first-best social optimum**. As we have previously noted, any resource allocation along the production frontier is Pareto efficient, but only one allocation (*a* in Fig. 11.6) is the social optimum.

The classical assumption in welfare economics is that if market price acts as an appropriate signal to achieve *any* Pareto-efficient allocation along the production frontier, then an appropriate fiscal policy can be imposed by government to achieve the social optimum allocation *a*. In other words appropriate lump-sum transfers and taxes can be imposed by government that have no effect on the underlying economic realities (i.e. do not affect incentives to agents and therefore outcomes). In this view the fiscal policy merely changes the *distribution of income* rather than the position of the production frontier; we might then be able to move from *b* to *a* in Fig. 11.13. Essentially what is being suggested is that there is *no* inevitable trade-off between efficiency and equity. Competitive markets can be left to yield price regimes that lead to Pareto-efficient allocations somewhere along the production frontier (e.g. *b*). If governments believe the resulting income distribution to be incompatible with the social optimum (e.g. *a*), then redistributive fiscal polices can be implemented as appropriate. In the context of Fig. 11.13, non-farmers will be required to lose some real income in favour of farmers, as we move from income distribution NF_2/F_2 at *b* to NF_1/F_1 at the social optimum *a*.

As we have seen, to achieve both a Pareto efficient allocation along the production frontier and a Pareto-efficient distribution of that allocation amongst consumers, we must satisfy the first and second efficiency conditions (p. 434 and p. 436 respectively). In other words, a necessary condition for a market economy to be Pareto efficient under first-best conditions is that the marginal rate of transformation/substitution between any pair of factors and products must be the same for all agents in the economy. Intervention by governments to fix prices at levels other than market-clearing involves a breach of these conditions. Adherents of this approach would therefore advocate non-intervention by government in the agricultural sector, and favour free trade in agricultural products (as the foreign sector is considered as just another production sector). The policy prescription here is that competitive agricultural markets will satisfy the conditions required to achieve Pareto efficiency, and that any adverse income distribution between the agricultural and non-agricultural sectors can be corrected by appropriate fiscal policy at no resource cost. However, modern public finance theory casts doubt on the feasibility of lump-sum taxes and transfers that have *no* resource cost. Rather it suggests (e.g. Atkinson and Stiglitz 1980) that attempts to transfer income by taxes and subsidies inevitably impinge on economic incentives and therefore on productive outcomes. So in terms of Fig. 11.14, attempts to move from the Pareto-efficient allocation *b* to the social optimum allocation *a*, by redistributing income away from the non-farm sector and towards farm-

Fig. 11.13

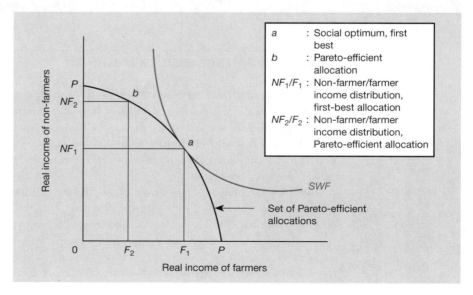

ers, will have an adverse influence on output. Here the production frontier pivots inwards from *PbP* to *PbP'* (around the initial Pareto-efficient allocation *b*) as a result of attempts to use redistributive fiscal policy in favour of the agricultural sector. The *constrained social optimum* solution is then *b'*, where there is a tangency between production frontier *PbP'* and the highest attainable social welfare function *SWF'*.

We are now in the realm of a feasible second-best social optimum at *b'* as opposed to a hypothetical (since unattainable) first-best social optimum at *a*. The rules for achieving such a second-best outcome at *b'* may deviate from those we have seen apply in first-best situations. For example, this second-best social optimum allocation at *b'* need not be characterised by competitive agricultural product markets in which market-clearing prices are sacrosanct. Indeed, the Common Agricultural Policy (CAP) arrangements of the European Union (see Chapter 6. p. 269), which seek to transfer income to farmers, essentially by intervening in product markets, may be justifiable from such a second-best perspective. As Newbery (1990) concludes, in second-best situations there is no a priori reason why governments in countries where the transaction costs of fiscal transfer instruments like income tax and means-tested social benefit schemes are very high should not intervene in agricultural markets to influence prices. For example, we have already seen (p. 444) that prices *can* diverge from marginal costs in product markets under second-best conditions.

Figure 11.14 shows that a trade-off now clearly exists between efficiency and equity. Where attempts at income redistribution via fiscal policies impose significant costs, as where taxes and subsidies influence incentives, and where monitoring and enforcement are required, etc., then they *do* have a resource impact, causing the production frontier to shift/pivot inwards. With a second-best policy framework now implied in order to reach the constrained social optimum allocation *b'*, there could be some justification for various types of interventionist policies in *product* markets in order to sustain the farming sector, such as taxing imports, or subsidising exports.

Fig. 11.14

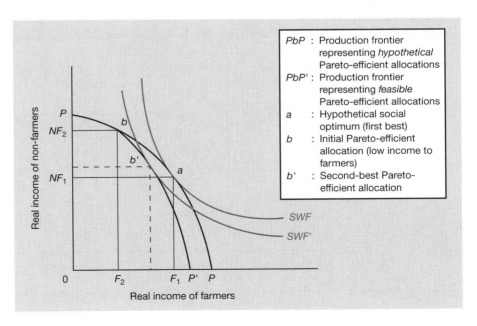

As Munk *et al.* (1994) have noted, all OECD countries have provided significant support to their agricultural sectors during the 1980s. The most commonly used method to support farm income has been a system of market price support. Throughout the OECD countries in 1990, support of this type accounted for 80% of all assistance granted to the sector as measured by the PSE (producer subsidy equivalent). Domestic prices are often *in excess of* market-clearing levels through border measures such as tariffs on imported commodities, and overseas prices *below* the market-clearing levels through border measures such as subsidies for exported commodities. Excess supplies that are not exported are disposed of in various ways – by destruction, as food aid to developing countries, as subsidised input to industry, or as subsidised food for certain consumer groups. Public storage also plays an important role. Direct subsidies to agricultural producers and subsidies for the use of intermediate inputs in the agricultural sector are much less used.

It is only second-best analyses of the type considered that could justify such practices. Indeed, as Table 11.4 indicates, countries with the greatest disparities between agricultural and non-agricultural incomes tend to provide the highest levels of agricultural assistance, much of this taking the form of price support via intervention in agricultural product markets. In Norway and Japan, where gross value added (GVA) per person employed in agriculture was only about 26% of that in the rest of the economy, the level of agricultural assistance was extremely high. Some 71% and 67% of farm income could be attributed in the respective countries to some form of producer subsidy equivalent (PSE). On the other hand, countries with the smallest disparities between agricultural and non-agricultural incomes (i.e with much higher farm to non-farm incomes) engaged in much less income transfer to the agricultural sector by intervention in agricultural product markets. In the USA, Australia and New Zealand, all having gross value added (GVA) per person employed in agriculture at over 60% of the rest of the economy, the

Table 11.4 Relative income of farmers, producer subsidy equivalent (PSE) to farmers, and contribution of market-price support schemes: OECD averages 1980–90.

	Relative income[a] (%)	Farmers' PSE[b] (%)	Share of market price support[c] (%)
Canada	39.8	36.3	58.5
USA	64.0	30.3	55.0
Japan	25.5	67.3	81.9
Australia	62.9	12.0	30.2
New Zealand	61.8	18.8	20.1
Austria	39.1	37.8	104.9
Finland	30.4	62.5	88.1
Norway	26.7	71.8	43.9
Sweden	26.7	48.1	100.4
Switzerland	41.7	71.5	88.0
EUR-12	36.4	39.9	90.9
OECD	41.4	45.1	69.3

[a] Percentage of gross value added (per person employed) from agriculture
[b] Percentage of farm income via producer subsidy equivalent (PSE)
[c] Percentage share of market-price support in PSE and other income transfers to farmers
Source: Adapted from Munk *et al.* (1994)

level of agricultural assistance was extremely low. Only some 30%, 12% and 18% of farm income could be attributed in the respective countries to some form of producer subsidy equivalent (PSE). As the final column of Table 11.4 indicates, much of this assistance takes the form of price support via intervention in product markets.

Cost–benefit: practical applications

We noted (p. 448) that explicit attempts to account for *interpersonal comparisons* underlie the practical use of **cost–benefit** analysis. Monetary values are placed on the gains and losses to different individuals and groups, often weighted according to some perception of the contribution of these individuals or groups to social utility/welfare. If the proposed reallocation of resources via new investment in some project is evaluated as creating a monetary value that is greater to winners than the costs imposed on losers, then the project is potentially viable. In other words, if the net present value of a project is positive, then the project is at least worthy of consideration. Whether or not it will be undertaken may depend upon what restrictions, if any, apply to the level of finance available. If finance is limited and must be rationed, then of course only those projects with the highest (positive) net present values may be selected.

Here we consider some practical applications of specific interpersonal comparisons involved in cost–benefit analysis, in the manner considered by Bergson (p. 449).

Transport and cost–benefit analysis

Cost–benefit analysis (CBA) enables comparisons to be made between the costs of a road scheme and the benefits to road users so that decisions can be made regarding the viability of the project. CBA was first used in a transport context in the UK during the 1960s to evaluate the M1 motorway. It led to the development of a computer-based technique called COBA used by the Department of Transport. This has been modified over the years, and is applied to inter-urban road schemes. COBA acts as a benchmark, since it places monetary values on certain road user benefits, but the values *exclude* non-user or environmental costs and benefits (see Chapter 12), namely pollution, noise, and community severance, because of the difficulty in calculating them accurately. For example, it is difficult to determine what aspects of noise cause disutility. Is it loud noise, intermittent noise or persistent noise? Even if this could be determined, what monetary value should be put on the disutility? As well as excluding the environmental factors, no attempt is made to evaluate the direct costs and benefits of particular road projects to the regional or national economy, because these are also considered to be too difficult to estimate. The following analysis focuses on the ways in which monetary values are placed on those costs and benefits that *are* evaluated in COBA and similar models in the transport context. Much of the discussion is based on Ison (1999).

Costs

When considering the COBA appraisal, the costs of any new road scheme can be divided into two distinct headings:

- *The construction and preparation of roads.* A major component of cost is the construction work undertaken, involving earthworks, bridge building, noise abatement measures, and the acquisition of land, possibly through compulsory purchase. There is also the cost of public consultation and enquiry.

- *Maintenance costs.* The construction of any new road will lead to changes in the costs of road maintenance. Such costs will be incurred on items such as lighting (which is not directly related to the traffic flow) and resurfacing (which *is* directly related to the traffic flow). Maintenance work itself subjects the road user to delays and thereby results in time, accident and vehicle operating costs while the maintenance is underway.

Benefits   Road user benefits included in COBA cover journey time savings, accident cost savings, and savings in vehicle operating costs.

Journey time savings Forecasts have to be made as to the *type* of journey (e.g. for work or for leisure) and how many trips of each type are undertaken, so that an estimate of the time savings can be made. Such time savings are divided into working time savings and leisure time savings, and together they comprise the major benefit of new road schemes.

Working time savings are valued as a benefit to the employer, because it is assumed that they can be used in the production of a good or service. These savings are estimated by using the national average wage rate as a measure of the value of any unit of time saved. However, it is debatable whether small increments of time saved have real economic value when aggregated over a large number of vehicles. For example, it is quite obvious that one hour saved on a work journey can be of benefit in terms of the output that could have been produced in that time, but it is less clear how important a time saving of one minute would be. Also it is unclear, for example, whether a saving of one minute to 60 road users is equivalent to a time saving of one hour for one road user.

Non-working time savings are still more difficult to calculate because there is no economic market for leisure time. The way such leisure time savings are calculated is by observing actual travel behaviour and establishing individual preferences, as expressed through interviews and surveys (see p. 492). This technique involves asking individual travellers hypothetical questions in order to obtain information about what they would be prepared to pay in order to save time when undertaking journeys. On this basis the valuation of non-working (leisure) time is estimated to be 40% of the value used for working time.

Accident cost savings In the UK until quite recently, the *human capital approach* was used to place a monetary value on accidents (see also Chapter 3, p. 126). This approach placed a value on the gross contribution (in terms of lost output) that the victim of an accident would have made to the economy. It also included the direct cost in terms of damage to vehicles, plus the associated police and medical costs. An allowance, which was quite arbitrary, was also made for the pain, grief and suffering incurred by the victim.

Although the human capital approach is still used in a number of European countries, Britain now uses the *willingness to pay* approach. This approach assigns monetary values to fatal and non-fatal accidents. The values are based on research surveys that established what individuals would be prepared to pay to reduce the risk of fatal accidents. Basically, individuals are asked to place a value on safety. To this is added an allowance for things such as medical costs and vehicle damage. This new method of valuation places a higher value on accidents than does the human capital approach. Therefore, the benefits from accident savings will, in future, increase on average from 15% to 25% of the total benefit of any COBA scheme.

Table 11.5 compares the cost of a road accident fatality for various countries that use the two approaches. By the late 1990s the average cost per casualty in the UK was £812,010 for a fatality, £92,570 for a serious casualty and £7,170 for a slight casualty. This gave an average for all casualties of £29,080.

Table 11.5 The cost of road accident fatalities.

Country	$000
USA[a]	2,600
Sweden[a]	1,236
New Zealand[a]	1,150
Britain[a]	1,100
Germany[b]	928
Belgium[b]	400
France[b]	350
Holland[b]	130
Portugal[b]	20

Notes: [a]Willingness to pay basis.
[b]Human capital approach.
Source: Adapted from *The Economist*, 4 December 1993

Vehicle operating costs

Vehicle operating costs are a function of distance and speed, and comprise fuel, tyres, oil maintenance and depreciation. Unlike the benefits of time savings and savings brought about by reduced accidents, overall vehicle operating costs as a result of a new road scheme can be either positive or negative.

Discounting

We have already considered aspects of **discounting** in Chapter 3 (p. 115). When undertaking a road scheme the majority of the costs will be incurred first, followed by a number of years of benefit, and this time profile must be taken into account when assessing a road investment scheme. However, because costs and benefits occur in different years it is necessary to express their values in terms of a particular year, i.e. the *present value year*. The technique of discounting is used to obtain the net present value (*NPV*) of a stream of future costs and benefits from a particular scheme, covering a 30-year period from the time the road is opened. The equation for the *NPV* can be shown as:

$$NPV = (B - C)_0 + \frac{(B - C)_1}{(1 + r)^1} + \frac{(B - C)_2}{(1 + r)^2} + \ldots + \frac{(B - C)_n}{(1 + r)^n}$$

In the equation, *B* refers to the benefits and *C* the costs (including the capital costs) of the particular road scheme. The *subscripts* 0, 1, ..., *n*, refer to the number of years over which the costs and benefits are said to occur (namely 30 years), and *r* is the discount rate (which is currently set by the Department of Transport at 8 per cent). The benefits (*B*) are assessed on a 'do-minimum and do-something' basis. The *do-minimum* scheme is the existing road network with only minor improvements, and the *do-something* scheme is the existing road network plus the new road being proposed. There will be user costs associated with each network, namely the time it takes to travel on the route, the number of accidents, and the operating costs of the vehicles. The *difference* between the user costs on the do-minimum and the do-something network is discounted to form the user benefit (*B*) of the new road scheme being proposed.

The costs (*C*) as stated above comprise the purchase of land, construction and maintenance costs. In terms of the equation, if the *NPV* is *positive* then it indicates that the scheme is economically justified. In order to compare projects that are of different sizes, it is necessary to divide the *NPV* by the capital costs, thus producing the *NPV/C* ratio, which can be used as a means of ranking projects. As stated in the UK government's Expenditure Plans for Transport, 'The average benefit:cost ratio of schemes in the national road programme, which have reached the stage of having a validated cost benefit assessment based on current traffic forecasts is 2.3:1.'

As noted previously, the major benefits of a new road scheme are the savings in terms of time and reduced accidents, and these are based on *estimates* of future traffic flows. It is important therefore to obtain figures on *actual* flows once a road scheme is in operation, in order to establish how successful the original Department of Transport forecasts have been.

With the growth in the UK of vehicle-kilometres being 43% between 1983 and 1993, the increase in the length of all public roads of only 5.4% (15% for motorways) would appear to suggest that road construction has *not* kept pace with the growth in vehicle-kilometres, especially since the motorway traffic flows were 99% higher in 1993 than they were in 1983. Road space is therefore a valuable and scarce resource, and if road congestion is to be controlled it follows that policies need to be pursued either to ration the existing road space (e.g. by introducing a road pricing policy) or to expand the road space available.

Placing a value on congestion

Congestion costs arise because the addition of more vehicles onto a road network reduces the speed of other vehicles and so increases the average time it takes to complete any particular journey.

It is possible to gain some understanding of congestion by studying the relationship between speed and flow along a particular route. Figure 11.15 shows a **speed–flow curve** for the movement of vehicles along a particular road. It shows how motorists interact and impose delays and costs on each other. In a free-flow situation (around point A) there is little or no interaction between vehicles, and therefore speeds (subject to the legal speed limit) are relatively high. However, as extra vehicles join the road, average speed is reduced; nevertheless an increased flow will still occur until point B is reached. The flow of vehicles depends upon the number of vehicles joining the road and the speed of the traffic. For the *individual user*, maximum efficiency is where the speed is at its highest, i.e. point A. In terms of the *system as a whole*, however, the maximum efficiency is at point B, before the speed–flow curve turns back on itself (i.e. where the maximum flow

Fig. 11.15
Speed–flow curve.

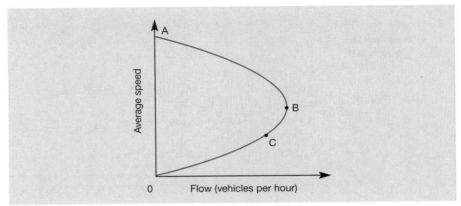

of vehicles is achieved). Once at point B, the road is said to have reached its *capacity* at the maximum flow level. Motorists may continue to enter the road after B because they may lack perfect information, thus slowing down the whole flow. Point C may therefore be used to represent the speed–flow situation during a peak period. At this point the traffic is in a stop–start situation, perhaps where the traffic flow is subject to a bottle-neck. This gives rise to high *external costs*, which the motorist is not taking into account. These costs will tend to increase the closer the road is to full capacity (the zero origin).

Costs of congestion It is clear that a major strategy is needed to tackle the conges-tion problem, not only in urban areas, but also on inter-urban routes. Congestion undermines competitiveness and hinders certain conurbations, particularly London, from attracting people and business. It also imposes a financial cost on the business com-munity in terms of increased commuter times and delays in the delivery of goods. One estimate calculated congestion costs at over £3 billion per year in London and the six major English conurbations alone, and suggested that the total national congestion bill could be in the region of £10 billion per year (British Road Federation 1988).

The Confederation of British Industry estimates that delays on the M25 cost £1 billion per year, and that London's inadequate transport system costs the nation around £15 bil-lion per annum, almost two thirds of which relates to London and the South East. In the CBI report *The Capital at Risk*, published in 1989, the figures in Table 11.6 were given for the average additional costs incurred in London and the South East. This information was compiled from data provided by those national companies that could compare their dis-tribution costs in London and the South East with those in other areas. The results are shown in Table 11.6, and reveal that the £15 billion per annum consists of, amongst other things, increased staff and vehicle requirements and additional fuel costs.

Specific businesses such as British Telecom and the Royal Mail put the cost of conges-tion to themselves at £7.25 million and £10.4 million per annum respectively. These costs were measured in terms of fleet inefficiency, lost drivers' time, and extra vehicle costs. According to the CBI, every British household has to spend at least £5 per week *more than it needs to* on goods and services in order to meet the costs to business of road and rail congestion. This is equal to 2 pence on the basic rate of income tax. The CBI

Table 11.6
Congestion costs in London and the South East.

Average additional costs due to congestion in London/South East	(%)
Productivity lost due to lateness of staff	1
Delivery time and cost penalties within M25	30
Additional staff/drivers needed to beat congestion	20
Additional vehicles needed	20
Additional vehicle service/repair costs	20
Additional fuel costs	10
Estimated total additional transportation costs in the London area	20

Statistics were compiled from information provided by national organisations that could compare distribution costs in London and the South East with other areas.
Source: Adapted from Confederation of British Industry, *The Capital at Risk* (1989)

estimates that if traffic delays could be reduced, thereby raising average speeds by 1.5 mph, then London's economy would be better off by £1 million per day.

In terms of traffic speeds, the situation has worsened over the past 20 years. In Central London, the morning and evening peak period travel speeds were 12.7 and 11.8 mph respectively in 1968–70, whereas by 1998 they had fallen (according to the Department of Transport) to 10.2 and 10.3 mph respectively. Figure 11.16 gives some indication of the causes of congestion. There has been a dramatic rise in the number of licensed vehicles over the period 1951–97, made up almost entirely of 'private and light goods vehicles', in which category the private car predominates.

Fig. 11.16 **Number of vehicles licensed: by type.**

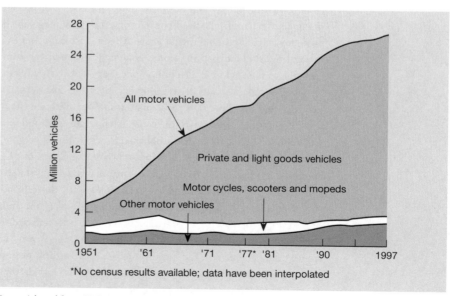

*No census results available; data have been interpolated

Source: Adapted from ONS Transport Statistics (1998)

Full definitions can be found in the 'Glossary of terms' (pp. 699–710)

Key terms

Cost–benefit analysis
Discounting
Edgeworth–Bowley consumption
  box
Edgeworth–Bowley production box
First best
General equilibrium
Kaldor criterion

Pareto optimum
Pareto's Law
Partial equilibrium
Scitovsky double criterion
Second best
Social welfare function
Utility frontier

Review questions

1. An economy produces two goods, A and B, with inputs of capital (K) and labour (L). The total amount of capital and labour available is $60L$ and $70K$. The production isoquants that describe the production process are given by A_1, A_2, A_3 and B_1, B_2, B_3 and are shown in Table 11.7.

Table 11.7

A's isoquants						B's isoquants					
A_1		A_2		A_3		B_1		B_2		B_3	
L	K	L	K	L	K	L	K	L	K	L	K
5	55	25	45	15	65	5	20	10	50	35	60
15	25	35	35	40	55	20	15	25	35	45	45
30	15	50	30	55	55	55	15	40	35	55	40

(a) Use the information contained in the table to construct an Edgeworth–Bowley production box diagram for products A and B.

(b) From the box diagram identify the point at which isoquants A_1 and B_1 intersect as I.

   (i) Explain why I is not an optimum position even though the production isoquants meet. What makes the points of tangency between the A and B isoquants optimal positions?

  (ii) If the respective coordinates of the tangency line between A_2 and B_2 are in terms of K and L ($25K$, $55L$) as measured from the A origin and ($22.5K$, $50L$) as measured from the B origin, calculate the $MRTS_{LK}$ at the point of tangency between the two isoquants.

(c) Draw the contract curve for the production box from the information provided, and comment on its features.

2. The values of the isoquants A and B in question 1 are as follows: $A_1 = 40A$, $A_2 = 100A$, $A_3 = 120A$ and $B_1 = 30B$, $B_2 = 60B$, $B_3 = 90B$.

   (a) Draw the transformation curve (production frontier) that reflects the contract curve of question 1 and explain the relevance of the curve to general equilibrium theory.

   (b) Locate the points X, Y, Z and I of question 1 onto the transformation curve diagram and explain what point I illustrates about the economy in question.

   (c) Efficiency in general equilibrium in both production and exchange requires that each consumer's MRS is identical to the economy's MRT. Use the diagram to illustrate the meaning of this equilibrium condition.

3. If commodities A and B are being produced with the aid of capital (K) and labour (L), and the general form of the production functions for A and B is $A = f(K^A L^A)$ and $B = f(K^B L^B)$ then:

   (a) Prove, with the use of differential calculus, that the slopes of the isoquants A and B are equivalent to the ratio of the marginal products of labour and capital respectively.

   (b) Give the efficiency criterion for the *production* of A and B.

   (c) Explain what happens when efficient production is *not* met.

4. In an economy, the production frontier or transformation curve shows the various combinations of goods X and Y which that economy can produce by fully utilising all its fixed amount of labour (L) and capital (K). This is given by the equation $X^2 + 9Y^2 = 100$, where X and Y are measured in thousands.

   (a) Provide an expression for the marginal rate of physical transformation into X of Y (i.e. $MRPT_{XY}$).

   (b) Prove that the transformation curve is concave to the origin.

   (c) If, for two consumers A and B, one of the points on the consumption contract curve located in the Edgeworth box diagram (i.e. where $MRS^A_{XY} = MRS^B_{XY}$) has a value of $-4/7$, calculate the amount of X and Y that would be required to achieve *simultaneously* a general equilibrium for both production and exchange (consumption).

5. An economy has three social welfare functions (or community indifference curves) as shown in Table 11.8, where U_A and U_B measure the utility of consumer A and consumer B respectively (in utils).

Table 11.8

SW_1		SW_2		SW_3	
U_A	U_B	U_A	U_B	U_A	U_B
50	900	150	900	300	900
100	700	240	600	400	600
200	400	400	400	600	400
700	100	1000	200	1000	300

(a) Draw the three social welfare functions and thereby form a community indifference map (with U_B on the vertical axis and U_A on the horizontal axis). Explain what the community indifference map means.

(b) Explain the relationship between the utility possibility curve and a consumption contract curve. Outline the conditions necessary to obtain, simultaneously, an optimum outcome in terms of both production and consumption.

(c) Explain how the 'grand utility possibility curve' can be derived from a knowledge of part (b) above (see Fig. 11.7, p. 441).

(d) If the grand utility possibility curve was of the form $U_B = 700 - \frac{7}{9}U_A$ then calculate the utility values for U_A and U_B that provide the point of maximum social welfare.

Further reading

Intermediate texts

Baumol, W. J. (1977), *Economic Theory and Operations Analysis*, 4th edn, Chs 21 and 23, Prentice Hall, Hemel Hempstead.

Browning, E. and Browning, J. (1992), *Microeconomic Theory and Applications*, 4th edn, Chs 18 and 19, HarperCollins, London.

Dobson, S., Maddala, G. S. and Miller, E. (1995), *Microeconomics*, Ch. 7, McGraw-Hill, Maidenhead.

Hope, S. (1999), *Applied Microeconomics*, Ch. 16, Wiley, Chichester.

Katz, M. and Rosen, H. (1998), *Microeconomics*, 3rd edn, Ch. 12, Irwin, Boston, Mass.

Koutsoyiannis, A. (1979), *Modern Microeconomics*, 2nd edn, Chs 22 and 23, Macmillan, Basingstoke.

Laidler, D. and Estrin, S. (1995), *Introduction to Microeconomics*, 4th edn, Chs 27–30, Harvester Wheatsheaf, Hemel Hempstead.

Maddala, G. S. and Miller, E. (1989), *Microeconomics: Theory and Application*, Ch. 18, McGraw-Hill, New York.

Nicholson, W. (1997), *Intermediate Microeconomics and its Application*, 7th edn, Chs 22 and 23, Dryden Press, Fort Worth.

Pindyck, R. and Rubinfeld, D. (1998), *Microeconomics*, 4th edn, Ch. 16, Macmillan, Basingstoke.

Varian, H. (1999), *Intermediate Microeconomics*, 5th edn, Chs 28–30, Norton, New York.

Advanced texts

Gravelle, H. and Rees, R. (1992), *Microeconomics*, 2nd edn, Ch. 17, Longman, Harlow.

Mas-Colell, A., Whinston, M. D. and Green, J. R. (1995), *Microeconomic Theory*, Chs 15–18, Oxford University Press, Oxford.

Articles and other sources

Atkinson, A. B. and Stiglitz, J. E. (1980), *Lectures in Public Economics*, McGraw-Hill, Maidenhead.

Confederation of British Industry (1989), *The Capital at Risk: Transport in London Task Force Report*.

Ison, S. (1999), 'Transport', in A. Griffiths and S. Wall (eds) (1995) *Applied Economics*, 8th edn, Longman, Harlow.

Levinson, D., Gillen, D. and Kanafani, A. (1998), 'The social costs of intercity transportation: a review and comparison of air and highway', *Transport Review*, 18, 3.

Munk, K., Blandford, D., Cahil, C. and Koester, U. (1994), 'The economic costs of agricultural policy', *European Economy*, November.

Newbery, D. M. (1990), 'Pricing and congestion: economic principles relevant to pricing roads', *Oxford Review of Economic Policy*, 6, 2, Summer.

Powell, M. (1996), 'Road policy and welfare economics', *Economics and Business Education*, IV, 4, 16.

Rees, R. (1983), *Public Enterprise Economics*, Longman, Harlow.

Rees, R. (1993), *The Economics of Regulation and Public Enterprises*, Harvester Wheatsheaf, Hemel Hempstead.

Chapter 12

Externalities, public goods and market failures

Introduction and review

In the previous chapter we saw how market failure, in the sense of a breakdown in one or more of the assumptions necessary for a Pareto-efficient allocation of resources (see p. 433), can have important implications for policy makers. It may no longer be possible to correct for such market failures and reach a first-best Pareto-efficient solution. Indeed, even achieving a second-best solution may require imagination on the part of policy makers: e.g. encouraging prices in certain sectors to *deviate* from marginal cost by specified amounts rather than simply restoring marginal cost pricing. The remaining chapters in this part of the book deal with specific types of market failure and consider various policy options for correcting such market failures. The following types of market failure will be considered:

- externalities, such as pollution and congestion;
- public goods, such as defence;
- common property rights;
- imperfect information;
- monopoly;
- intertemporal (between time periods) market failure, including differences between private and social time preference rates.

Some issues, such as monopoly (Chapter 7) and time preference rates (Chapter 3) have already been addressed, and cross-reference to earlier materials will be made wherever appropriate, to avoid repetition. Throughout this part of the book, constantly bear in mind the *three efficiency conditions* necessary for achieving a first-best (Pareto efficient) resource allocation (p. 433).

In this chapter we look in close detail at the common types of market failure we have listed, and especially at the presence of externalities and public good characteristics in an economy. Having considered some of the general principles underlying such market failures, the 'Applications and evidence' section of the chapter focuses on the environment as a context for considering corrective policy application. The environment has served as a useful testbed for many governments seeking policies to correct for the adverse effects of perceived market failures.

◼ Externalities

From your earlier studies you should have some familiarity with the idea of externalities. **Externalities** occur when economic decisions create costs or benefits for people *other than* the decision-taker; these are called *external costs* or *external benefits*. For example, a firm producing textiles may emit industrial effluent polluting nearby rivers and causing a loss of amenity. The true cost to society is then more than the (scarce) resources of labour and capital used up by the firm in producing textiles. To these **private costs** of firm production, reflected by wage bill, interest payments, etc., we must add any **external costs** that do not appear in the firm's balance sheet but which have resource implications for society, if we are to assess the true **social costs** of production. In terms of the widely used concept of marginal cost, we can say that:

Marginal social cost = Marginal private cost + Marginal external cost

i.e. $MSC = MPC + MEC$

Sometimes those who impose external costs in this way can be controlled by legislation (pollution controls, Clean Air Acts, etc.) or can be penalised through taxation. The parties affected might be compensated, using the revenue raised from taxing those firms creating social costs. On the other hand, firms creating social benefits may be rewarded by the receipt of subsidies. If the industry is run in the public interest, it might be expected that full account will be taken of any externalities. For instance, it can be argued that railways reduce road usage, creating social benefits by relieving urban congestion, pollution and traffic accidents. This is one aspect of the case for subsidising railways so that they can continue to offer some loss-making services. We return to possible policy prescriptions to account for externalities later in the chapter.

You should also be familiar with the general idea that the presence of externalities may distort the signals conveyed by prices in a market economy. Although at first sight it may seem a contradiction, when marginal social cost is higher than marginal private cost ($MSC > MPC$) because of the existence of a positive marginal external cost ($MEC > 0$), we use the team **negative externality**. This is the situation shown in Fig. 12.1, where we can see that the *marginal social cost* of production lies above the *marginal private cost*. In this case the firm that seeks to maximise its *private surplus* (profit) will fail to maximise *social surplus*. This can be illustrated in the case of a monopoly in Fig. 12.1.

Of course the presence of a monopoly market structure means that we are concerned more with second-best rather than first-best solutions (see p. 442). Even these will be elusive in the presence of uncorrected externalities. The profit-maximising firm in Fig. 12.1 will produce output $0Q_1$ at price $0P_1$, since marginal private cost = marginal revenue (marginal private benefit) at this output. Total profit can be regarded as *total private surplus*, and this is a maximum, given by area *JKL* in the diagram. To produce one extra unit beyond $0Q_1$ would reduce total private surplus, as the extra unit would incur a loss ($MPC > MR$); to produce one fewer unit than $0Q_1$ would also reduce this total private surplus, since that unit would have yielded a profit ($MR > MPC$) had it been produced. Unfortunately, this output Q_1 is *not* the output that maximises total social surplus. This

Fig. 12.1 Total private surplus (*JKL*) for a profit-maximising monopoly creating negative (production) externalities contrasted with maximum social surplus (*JMN*).

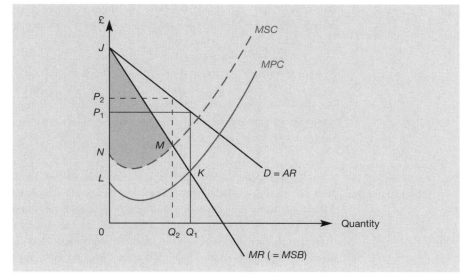

occurs where the marginal social benefit of production, *MSB* (here shown as being the same as *MR*), equals the marginal social cost of production, *MSC*. This occurs at output $0Q_2$ with total social surplus a maximum at area *JMN*, using the same reasoning as before. Clearly this situation, if uncorrected, is one in which prices are conveying inappropriate signals to (monopoly) producers. They are leading to profit maximisers producing too much of the product and selling it at too low a price, as compared with the needs of society as a whole. Externalities of both a negative and even positive (beneficial) type can have major impacts on resource allocation if left uncorrected.

You should be able to use Fig. 12.1 to consider the implications of a **positive externality** (*MSC* < *MPC*) on monopoly output. This time price signals, if uncorrected, are leading to profit maximisers producing too little of the product and selling it at too high a price, as compared with the needs of society as a whole.

Provision of public goods

A **public good** has a number of characteristics. One is *non-excludability*, which means that they cannot be provided for one citizen without simultaneously becoming available to others. In other words, once a public good is provided it is often difficult to actually stop a person consuming an extra unit if they wish to do so. This is true in the case of a lighthouse or street lighting for example. If a lighthouse is constructed, it is impossible to stop shipping in its vicinity from using it. Similarly if street lighting is provided, it is impossible to prevent any passer-by from taking advantage of it. Charges cannot, therefore, be levied on public goods because the benefits cannot be denied to those who refuse to pay.

Another characteristic of public goods is *non-exhaustibility*, which means that consumption of an extra unit by one person does not diminish the amount available for consumption by others. In other words, once the public good is provided, the additional cost of making it available to an extra consumer is zero. Defence and law and order are often called public goods. An extra person can usually be defended by the armed forces, or be protected by the police and judiciary, at no extra cost! Since the true marginal cost (opportunity cost) is zero, the Pareto-efficiency conditions for a first-best economy (see p. 442) require a *zero price* to be charged for such goods. Of course private markets directed by the profit motive are hardly likely to exist in situations where goods are provided free of charge! It is therefore often argued that the only way of providing such goods at the (zero) efficiency price is via the public sector, the goods being cross-subsidised by general tax revenue.

The provision of merit goods

As well as providing public goods, the government also undertakes to provide many other goods and services that add to the quality of life but which are not pure public goods. **Merit goods** such as education and health care do not possess the same characteristics as public goods: for instance people *can* be excluded from consuming them. They could therefore be provided through the market mechanism. However, many are deliberately provided free of charge through public bodies because their consumption arguably confers relatively large social benefits on society that far outweigh their costs of provision.

Arguments for state provision of merit goods

- State provision encourages a greater consumption of goods that confer benefits on society as a whole. For example, using tax revenues to provide education freely to children and health care freely to all produces a more skilled and healthier workforce. The absence of these would seriously reduce labour productivity and adversely affect living standards. Similarly, economic efficiency, and hence living standards, would be reduced if the state did not provide an adequate road network, and so on.
- In the absence of such state provision, inequality of income would limit the availability of merit goods to lower income groups. In this sense the provision of merit goods redistributes income in favour of the poorer members of society. This is one of the main reasons for the provision of municipal housing.

Arguments against state provision Despite these arguments it is important to remember that there is also a case against the provision of merit goods (and indeed public goods) by the state.

- Such goods might be freely available to consumers, but they nevertheless must be paid for by the state. This involves higher levels of taxation or government borrowing than might otherwise be the case. The former might have disincentive effects, while the latter might be a cause of inflation.
- To provide merit goods freely to all makes no distinction between those who can afford to pay and those who cannot. It might also encourage over-consumption (in relation to the most efficient use of resources) and consequently divert resources away from other, more productive, activities. After all, if something is provided free of charge there is no opportunity cost to the consumer of additional consumption. Because of this, resources might be diverted into activities that, were the consumers asked to pay the true cost of provision, they might opt *not* to have, preferring instead some alternative that they feel offers better value for money. In other words, a deci-

sion by the state to provide merit goods limits consumer choice since it reduces the resources available to produce other goods and services. Providing merit goods through the state might, therefore, lead to a misallocation of resources away from those uses that confer greatest benefit on society.

You should already be broadly familiar with the above ideas and concepts. We now explore these and related ideas involving market failure in rather more depth before considering corrective policy measures in the context of environmental considerations.

Theoretical developments

Externalities

As we noted earlier, **externalities** arise where private costs and benefits fail to coincide with social costs and benefits. As a result, individual agents in an economy maximise profit or utility subject to inappropriate prices or signals within the economy. This yields sub-optimum allocations of resources.

In Fig. 12.2, the producer imposes costs on others (social costs) that are not experienced by himself (private costs): e.g. a chemical discharge from a plant polluting a river without penalty. This is represented by the marginal social cost (MSC) being above the marginal private cost (MPC).

We could use Fig. 12.2 to represent an industry rather than a single firm. Suppose this industry is perfectly competitive: then the *sum* of the individual firm marginal private cost curves is the industry MPC curve (MPC_{ind}), which is the industry *supply* curve (S_{ind}). The industry *demand* curve is an average revenue curve that represents the consumer's willingness to pay (WTP) for various amounts of the product. The competitive industry

Fig. 12.2 **Welfare loss for a perfectly competitive industry via negative externalities.**

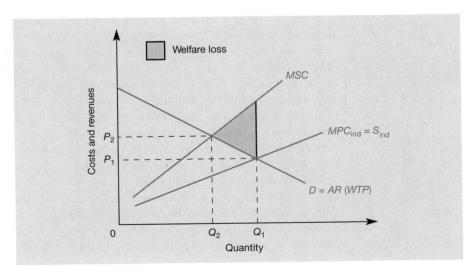

will produce output $0Q_1$ at price $0P_1$, whereas the socially optimum solution is output $0Q_2$ and price P_2. For each unit produced beyond $0Q_2$, the cost imposed on society *exceeds* society's willingness to pay for that unit. We then have the (shaded) area of welfare loss indicated in Fig. 12.2. Much of the debate on externalities has centred on what policies might help in achieving an $0Q_2$-type solution.

Strictly speaking, for a *multi-product* economy, the (Pareto) efficiency condition can be expressed as follows:

$$\frac{MSB_X}{MSC_X} = \frac{MSB_Y}{MSC_Y} = \ldots \frac{MSB_n}{MSC_n} = 1$$

where X, Y, ..., n are the various product categories.

In other words, a necessary condition for a first-best allocation of resources is that marginal social benefits and costs are equalised across the various product categories.

Taxes and standards

Pigouvian tax An allegedly 'ideal' way of dealing with a negative externality is to set a tax on the producer exactly equal to the *marginal external costs* imposed. In terms of Fig. 12.2 this would mean a tax that shifts *MPC* vertically upwards so that it becomes equivalent to *MSC* in the diagram. The producer now faces private costs (including tax) that incorporate the damages imposed on others at each and every level of output, and the profit-maximising solution now becomes $0Q_2$, which is the socially optimum output.

Of course in practice it is extremely difficult to measure the marginal external cost imposed at various levels of output. It is even more difficult to assign a tax rate that *automatically* varies in direct proportion to the marginal external costs imposed. In terms of Fig. 12.2, an 'ideal' Pigouvian tax would automatically rise as output increases. More typically any Pigouvian tax will be 'non-ideal', with its magnitude only assessed once the target output has been identified. In Fig. 12.2, the value of the **Pigouvian tax** at the social optimum output ($0Q_2$) would be given by the *vertical distance* between *MSC* and *MPC* at $0Q_2$ – call this tax t^*.

It may be useful, at this point, to consider the idea of **marginal abatement costs** and **marginal damage costs**, which we will use in various parts of this chapter to help identify the target output. Clearly *avoiding* emitting a pollutant will impose costs on the firm or industry – we call these *abatement costs*. They might include, for example, the cost of installing expensive flue-desulphurisation plants in coal-burning power stations to reduce toxic emissions, etc. The marginal abatement cost (*MAC*) curve in Fig. 12.3 represents the extra cost to the firm of avoiding emitting the last unit of pollutant. The *MAC* curve is shown as sloping upwards from right to left, suggesting that initial cuts in emissions of the pollutant can be achieved at little cost, but that it becomes increasingly costly at the margin to achieve progressively larger cuts in emissions of the pollutant.

The socially optimum level of emission of pollutants is where marginal damage (external) costs exactly equal marginal abatement costs for society, i.e. output Q_s in Fig. 12.3. To emit more pollutants would imply marginal damage costs *greater than* the marginal cost to society of abating that damage. Society is clearly disadvantaged by any emissions in excess of Q_s. Equally, to emit less than Q_s, would imply marginal damage

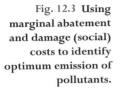

Fig. 12.3 **Using marginal abatement and damage (social) costs to identify optimum emission of pollutants.**

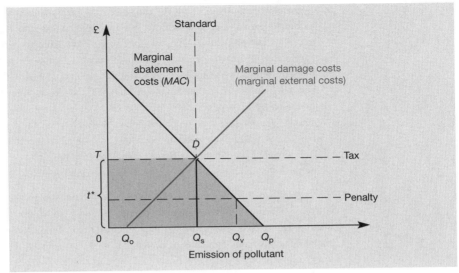

costs to society *less than* the marginal cost to society of abating that damage. In this case society is disadvantaged by seeking to cut emissions below Q_s.

A tax t^* per unit of emission of the pollutant will internalise the marginal damage costs such that the profit-maximising private producer will seek emission level Q_s. To produce less pollutants (than Q_s) will imply greater private costs of abatement (avoidance of pollution) than of emission. To produce more pollutants (than Q_s) will imply greater private costs of emission (the tax t^*) than of abatement. Clearly the profit-maximising solution is pollution level Q_s. Since, for the target output Q_s, tax t^* equals the marginal external cost imposed on society *at that output*, it can be regarded as a Pigouvian tax. Of course in its 'non-ideal' form it could be imposed as a lump-sum tax, yielding $OTDQ_S$ in tax revenue rather than the $Q_O DQ_S$ tax revenue had the 'ideal' Pigouvian tax been implemented.

Standards versus taxes

We can now turn to the issue of tax versus standards in achieving this solution. An equivalent means of achieving the social optimum would be to set standards that limit the maximum emission of the pollutant to Q_s in Fig. 12.3.

- *Firm perspective.* From the point of view of the *firm* the use of standards might seem to be the more attractive option. We can see from Fig. 12.3 that standards would be less costly for the firm to implement in achieving the social optimum, Q_s. This is because under the *tax regime*, the firm would pay $0TDQ_s$ to the government as tax revenue, and itself pay Q_sDQ_p in costs to abate pollution damage from Q_p to Q_s. Any unit of output beyond Q_s would of course, if produced, cause the firm to spend more in tax payment than in abatement cost. The shaded area $0TDQ_p$ represents the costs faced by the firm in achieving the social optimum level of emission, Q_s, under a tax regime. However, under a *standards regime*, with emissions fixed at level Q_s, the firm would only face abatement costs Q_sDQ_p.

- *Government perspective*. From the point of view of *government* the use of tax might seem to be the more attractive option. For example, under the standards regime the government forfeits the $0TDQ_S$ of tax revenue available to it under the tax regime. A further complication that might make standards less attractive is the fact that the firms might fail to comply. Unless the penalty associated with breaking the standards was both sufficiently certain and sufficiently extensive, then the standards might not prove to be binding. For example, even if all offenders were caught, if the penalty actually imposed by the courts was less than $0T$, then the firm would have no incentive to cut pollutant emissions back to Q_s. In Fig. 12.3 the dashed penalty line would only provide incentives for firms to reduce emissions to Q_v. It would cost less to pay penalties on emissions Q_s to Q_v than to pay abatement costs to avoid those penalties.

Standards are therefore only likely to be effective where there is a substantial probability of being caught for any breach, and an adequate deterrent payment. There is, of course, the further disadvantage to government of dependence on standards in having then to establish and fund a *bureaucracy* that will be required to set and monitor the standards regime.

Another argument governments may use in favour of a tax regime is that once a pollution standard has been set, a firm has no incentives to reduce pollution below this level. This is not the case with pollution taxes, which always provide an incentive for further reductions in emissions, as reducing the level of emissions reduces the amount of tax the firm is liable to pay. In this way, taxes may provide firms with greater incentives to invest in the research and development of new pollution abatement technologies or less pollution-intensive processes of production.

Governments may also favour a tax regime because of the higher resources costs they might expect to face in order to achieve the same result should they adopt a standards regime. We now explore this issue in rather more detail.

Standard setting with multiple firms

In practice policy makers may be faced with an alternative of setting a *single tax* or a *single standard* to be imposed on all firms. It is unlikely that a standards regime would be sufficiently well informed, or flexible enough, to impose a *variable standard* on each and every firm. Figure 12.4 indicates how an inflexible standards regime of this kind might achieve the same result as a tax regime, but at greater cost to the participating firms.

In Fig. 12.4, left to its own devices each firm will itself produce 14 units of pollutant, 28 in total. Suppose the government seeks 14 units of pollutant in total. This could be achieved *either* by the tax OT imposed on each firm or by restricting each firm to emitting 7 units of pollutant (we assume there to be inadequate information to apportion different levels of pollution emission to each firm). We can see that the **tax regime** would achieve the overall 14 units emission total by Firm A producing 6 units and Firm B producing 8 units, with each firm equating its respective marginal abatement costs to the tax rate, $0T$. However, if, under a **standards regime**, each firm were instructed to produce no more than 7 units of emission, then the shaded portions of Fig. 12.4 indicate that Firm B would incur increased abatement costs by having to reduce emissions from 8 to 7, whereas Firm A would incur reduced abatement costs by no longer having to reduce emissions to 6 but only to 7. In our diagram, the increased abatement costs to B are greater than the reduced abatement costs to A. In other words, compared with the

Fig. 12.4 **Extra cost of achieving a given level of emissions (14 units) via common standards on each firm as compared with a tax.**

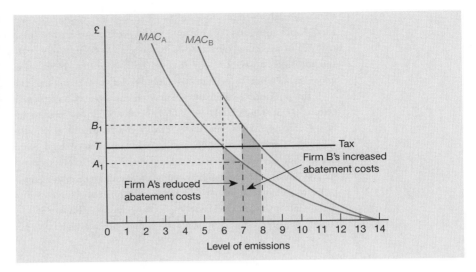

tax regime, our standards regime, in which a fixed standard is apportioned to each firm, is more costly in achieving a given result. The flatter the respective MAC curves, the smaller this cost differential will be.

Tradeable permits

One means of allocating a given overall standard in a more flexible manner between firms is the idea of **tradeable permits**. Permits equivalent to a total level of emission deemed acceptable are distributed between member firms in an industry. These permits can then be traded – bought and sold – on the market. In this way some additional flexibility can be given to the use of a standards regime. In Fig. 12.4 above, suppose each firm receives a 1 unit tradeable permit. Firm B, which faces a relatively high cost of abatement, will be willing to pay up to price B_1 to purchase the unit permit, thereby allowing it to avoid abating the eighth unit. Firm A, which faces a relatively low cost of abatement, will only need to receive as little as price A_1 to compensate it for having to abate the seventh unit after selling its 1 unit permit. Clearly there is scope for the market being able to establish a *price* at which the 1 unit permit is traded to both firms' advantage, that price being somewhere between A_1 and B_1. In this case both firms are better off with a fixed standards regime augmented by tradeable permits than with a fixed standard without this element of flexibility. Note that the use of tradeable permits brings about these efficiency gains by *equalising marginal abatement costs* across firms (see also pp. 497–9). We return to consider further the use of such permits later in the chapter (p. 500).

Negotiation and property rights

Another suggested method for dealing with externalities involves adopting a **negotiated solution**. The precise outcome of any negotiation is influenced by the way in which the law ascribes property rights. By **property rights** we mean the legal rules that determine what individuals or firms may do with their property. We now consider this approach in more detail, using Fig. 12.5.

Fig. 12.5 captures many of the ideas already discussed. Here we consider product output, rather than pollutant emission, though it is assumed that the level of pollutant varies directly with product output. The *marginal external (damage) cost (MEC)* curve therefore slopes upwards from left to right. At the same time the *marginal net private benefit (MNPB)* of each unit of output is assumed to vary inversely with product output. *MNPB* is the addition to private benefit received by the firm from selling the last unit of output *minus* the addition to private costs incurred by producing that last unit of output.

If the pollution externality was *not* taken into account, then firms would produce up to output Q_p at which $MNPB = 0$. Only here would total net private benefit (i.e. total profit) be a maximum. However, the **socially optimum** level of output is Q_s, where $MNPB = MEC$. Each unit of output beyond Q_s adds more in damage costs to society than it does to net private benefit, and is therefore socially inefficient to produce. Equally it would be socially inefficient to forsake producing any units up to Q_s, since each of these units adds more to net private benefit than to pollution costs for society. Note that in this analysis the social optimum does not imply zero damage. Rather it suggests that the benefits to society are greatest at output Q_s, with marginal damage costs being positive at $Q_s X$.

The Coase theorem   If we now introduce property rights into the situation outlined in Fig. 12.5, then there may be prospects for a *negotiated solution* at the social optimum output, Q_s. We initially assume that both polluter and sufferer (of pollution) are aware of the situation described in Fig. 12.5.

Property rights assigned to sufferer   In this case there will be incentives for the polluter to offer side-payments (bribes) to the sufferer. For example, if the polluter is liable to pay compensation for any damage caused, then it will no longer seek the Q_p solution, with $MNPB = 0$. To do so would incur *total private benefit* of $a + b + c$, but *total compensation liability* of $b + c + d$. Since $d > a$, this will result in *loss* for the producer (polluter), who may therefore seek a negotiated settlement. The polluter can afford to offer inducements to the sufferer for all units of output up to Q_s for which $MNPB > MEC$. Up to Q_s the polluter's marginal gains exceed the sufferer's marginal losses.

Fig. 12.5 Finding a negotiated solution to the externality problem.

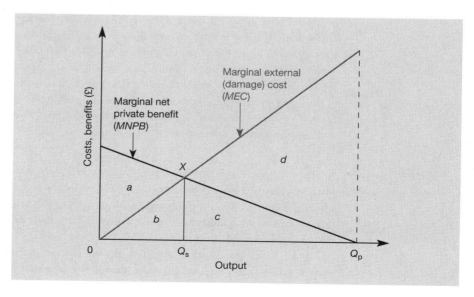

Beyond Q_s there is no scope for such negotiation, since $MNPB < MEC$: i.e. the polluter's marginal gains are less than the sufferer's marginal losses.

This negotiated outcome would yield a total private benefit of a to the polluter and total compensation of b to the sufferer.

Property rights assigned to polluter In Fig. 12.5 there is scope for the same (socially optimum) outcome Q_s as previously, except with a different distribution of income between polluter and sufferer.

In this case it is the sufferer who may have the incentive to offer inducements to the polluter to limit the degree of pollution. With no negotiation and output Q_p, the polluter's *total private benefit* is $a + b + c$ and the sufferer's *total damage incurred* is $b + c + d$. Since each marginal unit beyond Q_s imposes more damage costs on the sufferer than it yields benefit to the polluter ($MEC > MNPB$), there is clearly scope for the sufferer to offer side-payments (bribes) to encourage the polluter to desist. In fact it is only when the polluter has cut output to Q_s that the scope for such negotiation disappears; for any further cuts in output below Q_s, $MEC < MNPB$ and the sufferer will no longer have the means/incentive to fully compensate the polluter. This outcome would yield a minimum total private benefit of $a + b + c$ to the polluter (c via the inducement *not* to produce); of course this would be greater should the sufferer offer side-payments 'over the odds' (i.e. $> c$) for the polluter curbing output beyond Q_s. The sufferer no longer receives any compensation but this time pays out a minimum of c, but gains as compared with the *no negotiation situation* since the losses are now no longer $b + c + d$ but $b + c +$ any 'over the odds' (i.e. $> c$) inducements to the polluter.

In these ways *negotiations* can lead to the socially optimum allocation of resources. The manner in which any negotiations will take place, and the income distribution that follows from any negotiation, will depend crucially upon the *types* of property rights ascribed in the economy. The previous analysis also assumed *zero transactions costs*. Any deviation from this assumption may also influence the prospects for a negotiated solution.

Of course the previous analysis assumed that both polluter and sufferer were aware of the situation depicted in Fig. 12.5: in other words, that information is *symmetrical*. In practice information is often asymmetrical, with one party being aware of things that are obscure to the other party. We look more carefully at the implications of *asymmetrical information* later in this section (p. 479).

■ Public goods

We can summarise our earlier definition of **public goods** (p. 467) by stating that their two key characteristics involve being non-rival and non-exclusive.

By **non-rivalry** in consumption we mean that consumption by one individual does not reduce the quantity available to others. As a result we can sum individual demand curves *vertically* (rather than horizontally) in deriving market or aggregate demand. The provision of, say, a defence infrastructure can protect both you and others simultaneously. The overall willingness to pay for any given level of defence provision can therefore be identified by summing the valuation of each individual for that level of provision. Thus in Fig. 12.6 we can identify the marginal social benefit (MSB) of an extra unit of the public good by summing the individual demand (WTP) curves corresponding to that unit vertically ($MSB = D_A + D_B$).

By **non-exclusivity** in consumption we mean that it is impossible to exclude from consumption individuals who have not paid for the product. Defence is again a classic example of a non-exclusive good. Once a nation has provided for its natural defence, all citizens enjoy its benefits!

Pure public goods

Goods that satisfy *both* these characteristics, such as defence, street lighting, lighthouses, are often called **pure public goods**. In this case we should have a situation similar to that shown in Fig. 12.6, with two consumers for simplicity.

Strictly speaking, the marginal social cost (*MSC*) of providing an extra unit of the pure public good to another consumer is zero. This follows from the non-rivalry characteristic: once provided for one person, someone else can also consume that unit without reducing the first person's ability to consume that same unit. In this case we can regard the *MSC* curve as zero, coinciding with the horizontal axis.

Fig. 12.6(a) **Pure public goods and the socially optimum output.**

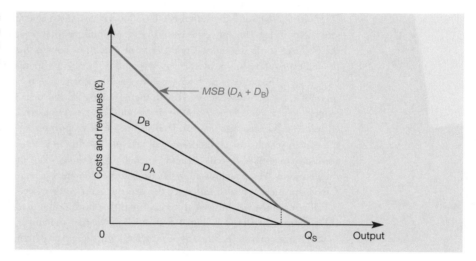

Fig. 12.6(b) **Mixed public goods and the socially optimum output.**

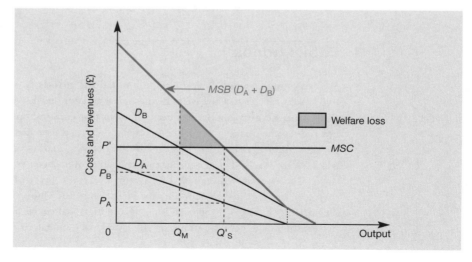

The *socially optimum* (Pareto efficient) solution is where $MSB = MSC$, i.e. output Q_s in Fig. 12.6(a). In this extreme case we can see that a Pareto-efficient solution requires a zero price! Clearly private markets, driven by the profit motive, will have no incentive to be established under these conditions: hence the suggestion that these are *public* goods. Only if general tax receipts are used to fund such goods will they be provided.

Mixed public goods

The suggestion here is that a broader category of goods will have elements of these characteristics, while not fully meeting the criteria for a pure public good. For example, many goods may be non-rival in the sense that, at least up to the congestion point, extra people can consume that good without detracting from existing consumers' ability to benefit from it: e.g. use of a motorway, a bridge, or a scenic view.

However, the non-exclusivity condition may not apply, since it may be possible to exclude consumers from that good: e.g. tolls on motorways and bridges, or fencing (with admission charges) around scenic views. So a market could be established for such a **mixed public good**, with a non-zero price charged. Moreover, at least beyond the congestion point, the marginal social cost of provision is also non-zero: extra cars cause existing users to slow down on roads and bridges, and extra people hinder the enjoyment of the scenic view.

In Fig. 12.6(b), the socially optimum output ($MSB = MSC$) occurs at Q'_s with market price P'. This price might be composed of two parts (were price discrimination possible in the market) equivalent to the individual valuation of each consumer of output Q'_s, namely P_A and P_B. Of course there is the practical problem of identifying what sum of money each person is really willing to pay for this output. If consumers want the good but understate their true preferences in the hope that they can 'free ride', then this social optimum output Q'_s may not occur. For example, if only consumer B reveals his true preference/willingness to pay in Fig. 12.6(b) (perhaps via response to a questionnaire) then the *market* solution might be output Q_M, with the shaded area corresponding to the welfare loss resulting from the free rider problem.

This analysis highlights one of the problems with public goods: namely that everyone has an incentive to rely on their neighbours to provide them, rather than provide them themselves. A shipping company may desire a lighthouse to guide its ships, as may other shipping companies. Unfortunately all may delay any investment decision, hoping that a rival builds the lighthouse, on which they can then 'free ride'. Eventually, perhaps, one company for whom the lighthouse has most value may relent and begin construction, but the level of provision may be less than optimal. This is because it is only the (vertical) sum of the marginal valuations of all consumers to the good that can help to determine the social optimum solution. If any consumer fails to express their true marginal valuation (i.e. attempts to free ride), then we have the sub-optimal type of solution shown in Fig. 12.6(b).

Of course there are many combinations of characteristics that goods might possess: non-rival and non-exclusive (pure public good); rival and exclusive (pure private good); non-rival (up to congestion point) and exclusive (quasi public good) and so on. A more detailed classification of public goods is outlined in Fig. 12.7. We briefly consider alternative means of **monetary valuation** of benefits where market prices are not readily available on p. 492; such devices are often required for products that are other than pure private goods.

Fig. 12.7 Spectrum of private and public goods.

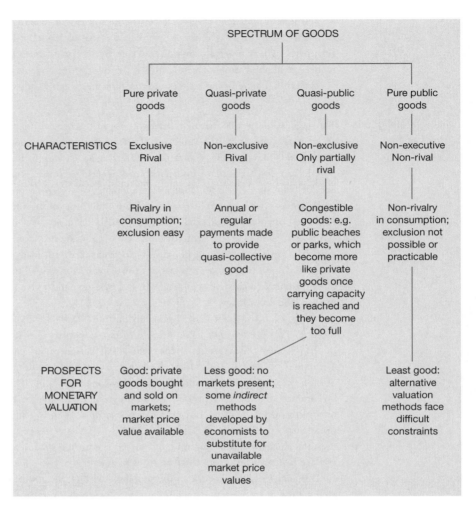

Common property resources

In the case of **common property resources**, property rights are not assigned to individuals but are held in common. In these circumstances access to the resources is often free, with the result that they become overutilised. Fishing on the high seas or in lakes, or livestock grazing on common land, are typical examples. In terms of Fig. 12.7 above we could regard such situations as being in the category quasi-private or quasi-public goods. This is because although the absence of property rights prevents exclusion, there is some element of rivalry in that overfishing or overgrazing is technically possible.

The root problem is again associated with that of the free rider. One co-owner may have little or no reason to consider the impacts of his action on other co-owners of the property rights. Even if conservation of the resource is regarded as desirable, he may hope to free-ride by using the resource to the full himself while others voluntarily restrict their access. Alternatively, he may regard (given imperfect information) collective agreements to conserve as being unrealistic and/or unenforceable, thereby supporting any inclination he might already have to pursue his own self-interest, regardless of its impact on others. Any investment the individual might make in the common property resource (e.g. desisting from overuse; re-stocking fish supplies; re-seeding grazing land) is discouraged by the fact that any returns on that investment cannot be wholly appropriated by that individual because of the absence of property rights.

Take the example of fishing in international waters. Each fisherman (trawler owner) fishes up to the point at which the marginal private benefit = marginal private cost. But since the high seas are a common property resource, the fisherman has no incentive to take into account the impact of his fishing on others. As a result the fisherman's marginal private cost (*MPC*) understates the true marginal social cost (*MSC*) of his activity. In the competitive market for fish (horizontal demand curve) shown in Fig. 12.8, the outcome is likely to be overfishing. The *profit-maximising* solution (*MPB = MPC*) yields F_p fish per time period; the *socially optimum* solution (*MSB = MSC*) is only F_s fish per time period.

The main source of this particular market failure involves the institutional environment in which transactions take place. A simple remedy is therefore to change that institutional environment: e.g. let a single owner manage the resource. Again we would then be internalising the externality. The owner can now charge those using the resource for any costs they impose on the resource; here the *excess* of *MSC* over *MPC*. A Pigouvian-type charge for using the resource (e.g. depleting fish stocks) would shift *MPC* vertically upwards to *MSC*, leading to the socially optimum fishing volume of F_s with a charge $a - b$ per fish (Fig. 12.8).

Of course in practice many common property resources are huge, with single private ownership impractical. In this case *public ownership* or public regulation of private ownership may be more realistic (see Chapter 13).

Imperfect information

The conditions necessary for a first-best allocation of resources (p. 433) included the requirement for perfect information in markets: for example, as to the prices and quality of the products and factors traded.

Fig. 12.8
**Overutilising a
common property
resource.**

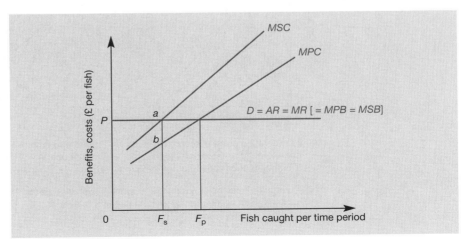

Imperfect information as to product price

Figure 12.9(a) shows how **imperfect information** in *product markets* means that prices would no longer be able to act as appropriate signals for bringing about a contract curve (Pareto efficient) solution in terms of the Edgeworth–Bowley consumption box. Remember how we noted (p. 437) that simply by maximising their own utility subject to the product prices they faced and the incomes they possessed, consumers would equate the slopes of their respective indifference curves and bring about a contract curve solution. In Fig. 12.9(a), however, the absence of such perfect information means that consumer A maximises utility subject to a *different set of product prices* than those faced by consumer B.

Suppose consumer A is *less aware* (perhaps via less search activity) of the availability of a cheaper source of product Y than is consumer B, so that he faces a higher price for Y and therefore a *lower* product price ratio (P_X/P_Y) than does consumer B. This implies a flatter budget line (*AM*) for consumer A than for B. Clearly from Fig. 12.9(a) we can see that in maximising utility by equating their respective budget lines with the highest attainable indifference curves, consumers A and B are in a *non-contract curve* situation. In other words, imperfect information as to product prices means that price signals fail to bring about a (first best) Pareto-efficient allocation of resources in *product markets* as regards consumers (exchange).

Figure 12.9(a) is drawn on the assumption that both consumers have identical incomes, but differential access to information as regards the price of product Y. This simplifying assumption results in the respective consumer budget lines having the same intercept on the horizontal axis (i.e. *M*). It also helps to illustrate the *welfare loss* to the consumer possessing imperfect information. For example, if consumer A were to receive the *same* product price information as consumer B, then his budget line would pivot from *AM* to *BM* and he would be able to attain a higher indifference curve (such as *B'*).

Fig. 12.9 **Imperfect information as to prices and market failure.**

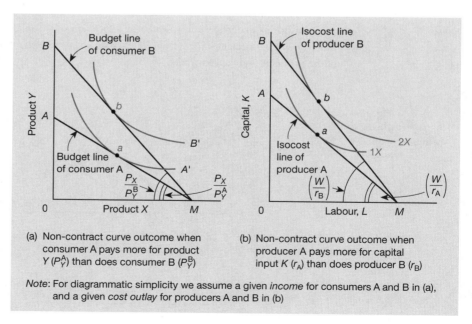

(a) Non-contract curve outcome when consumer A pays more for product Y (P_Y^A) than does consumer B (P_Y^B)

(b) Non-contract curve outcome when producer A pays more for capital input K (r_A) than does producer B (r_B)

Note: For diagrammatic simplicity we assume a given *income* for consumers A and B in (a), and a given *cost outlay* for producers A and B in (b)

Imperfect information as to factor price

Figure 12.9(b) shows how imperfect information in *factor markets* results in a *non-contract curve* situation in terms of the Edgeworth–Bowley production box. If producer A is less aware than producer B of a cheaper source of supply of a factor input (capital), then he will be faced with a higher price of capital, r, and therefore a *lower* factor price ratio (w/r). This implies a flatter isocost line (AM) for producer A than for B. Clearly from Fig. 12.9(b) we can see that in maximising profit by equating their respective isocost lines with the highest attainable isoquant, producers of X and Y are in a *non-contract curve* situation. In other words, imperfect information as to *factor prices* means that price signals fail to bring about a (first best) Pareto-efficient allocation of resources in *factor markets*.

Figure 12.9(b) is drawn on the assumption that both producers have identical *cost outlays*, but differential access to information as regards the price of the factor, capital (K). This simplifying assumption results in the respective isocost lines having the same intercept on the horizontal axis (i.e. M). It also helps to illustrate the *profit loss* to the producer possessing imperfect information. For example, if producer A were to receive the *same* factor price information as producer B, then his isocost line would pivot from AM to BM and he would be able to attain a higher isoquant curve (such as $2X$).

Imperfect information as to the existence of a product

The lack of information may involve a consumer being unaware of the existence of a product. Suppose the consumer is unaware of the existence of product Y, then his indifference curves and budget line will be as in Fig. 12.10(a). Point M will indicate the amount of product X purchased with budget line AM, indifference curve I_1 being attained. However, should the consumer become aware of the existence of Y, then Fig. 12.10(a) would indicate utility as being maximised at point a, indifference curve I_2 being attained. The consumer loss due to imperfect information is described by the *difference* between utility I_2 and I_1.

Fig. 12.10 **Imperfect information as to the existence and quality of products and market failure.**

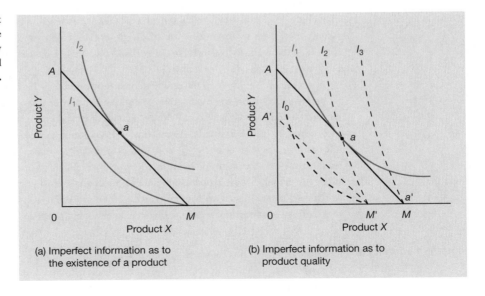

(a) Imperfect information as to the existence of a product

(b) Imperfect information as to product quality

Imperfect information as to the existence of a factor   Although less likely, should a producer be unaware of the existence of a factor of production, then an analysis similar to that conducted for a product can be undertaken, simply substituting isocost for budget line and isoquant for indifference (iso-utility) curve. You should be able to demonstrate a loss of profit via the lack of information to the producer, output produced for a given cost being *lower* than would otherwise be the case were the producer to be fully informed.

Imperfect information as to quality of product   Figure 12.10(b) shows how imperfect information as to the *quality* of a product may also result in a non-contract curve outcome for the Edgeworth–Bowley consumption box.

Here we suppose that consumer A has exaggerated expectations as to the quality of product Y, believing his indifference curves to be as indicated by the continuous curves in Fig. 12.10(b) as opposed to (what is actually the case) the dashed curves. As a consequence he initially selects allocation a, with tangency between budget line AM and continuous indifference curve I_1. However, on *actually consuming* product Y the consumer realises the unwarranted nature of his expectations as to the quality of that product. This downward revision of expectations as regards product Y means that, in effect, at point a the consumer only attained the dashed indifference curve I_2. In fact given the curvature of the set of the dashed indifference curves in Fig. 12.10(b), consumer A would have maximised utility by consuming exclusively product X at point a', yielding indifference curve I_3. The *difference* in utility level, I_3–I_2, is arguably the *loss of utility* as a consequence of the consumer's unwise initial commodity selection resulting from imperfect information as to the quality of product Y.

The loss of utility (welfare) outlined is the loss expressed in terms of *realised* qualities of the products. In terms of (false) *expectations* at the time of purchase, this loss could be expressed as I_1–I_0; in other words the initial (realised) level of utility I_2 could have been achieved (at M') with less income at the current set of relative prices (i.e. budget line $A'M'$). At M' the (false) perceptions as to product quality would yield utility level I_0, the difference between these (false) expected levels of utility being an alternative expression of welfare loss. However, expected or perceived welfare loss based on false premises is largely irrelevant to the evaluation of the potential gains from correct information. It is therefore the welfare loss in terms of realised qualities of the products that is of most relevance here.

In terms of the Edgeworth–Bowley consumption box of Fig. 11.4 (p. 437), any initial tangency solution between consumer A and B indifference curves (i.e. contract curve situation) would now be revised by A's awareness of mistaken expectations as to the quality of product Y. In other words, it would now be possible via a redistribution of the initial allocation of products between consumers A and B to make one consumer better off without the other consumer being made worse off. In this sense the initial allocation no longer represents a Pareto-optimal allocation as a result of imperfect information as to product quality. Prices no longer convey *all* the information required by *consumers* to make utility-maximising decisions that are, at the same time, socially efficient.

Imperfect information as to quality of factor input   In a similar way to the above, if a *producer* was mistaken in his perception of the quality of a particular factor input, an initial allocation of factor inputs within the Edgeworth–Bowley production box could prove to be a non-contract curve situation. A reallocation of the available factor input between producers could then raise the output of some without reducing the output of others. Again, prices no longer convey *all* the information required by *producers* to make profit-maximising decisions that are, at the same time, socially efficient.

Adverse selection, moral hazard and information asymmetry

We have already touched on the issue of **adverse selection** in Chapter 3 (p. 133). It results directly from some agents in a market being better informed than others: i.e. from **information asymmetry**. The insurance market has been widely cited as providing examples of adverse selection since potential *buyers* of insurance are likely to be better informed about their individual characteristics than are potential *sellers* of insurance. If the buyers of insurance exploit this information asymmetry by not disclosing their true characteristics, then the probability of any insured risk actually occurring will be greater than that taken into account by the sellers of insurance in setting their premiums. Premiums will therefore have to be increased, and potential buyers of insurance with good risk characteristics may find themselves driven from the market. The market may become progressively characterised by those with poor risk characteristics as premiums rise, and eventually such a market may cease to exist.

Adverse selection   In markets where only those with *adverse* characteristics select themselves to remain in the market, clearly the earlier Pareto efficiency conditions will be violated. Quite apart from the possibility of no price signal existing at all should the market cease to exist, even if a market is retained price is likely to deviate from marginal cost, violating the third Pareto efficiency condition (p. 442). Akerlof (1970) demonstrated how price is more likely to reflect *average cost* in his analysis of the market for lemons. Here the word 'lemon' was used as a euphemism for a defective product, and the second-hand car market was used by way of illustration. Information asymmetry is seen as rife in that market, since potential sellers of second-hand cars are likely to be far better informed about the true quality of their cars than are potential buyers. As a result the market price of used cars will depend on the *average quality* of the used cars available for sale. Those who sell a 'lemon' (defective product) receive more than their used car is worth; those who sell a good quality car, receive less. The suggestion here is that buyers will be reluctant to pay prices that reflect the true quality of the individual product because of uncertainty and a lack of information on their part. Owners of high-quality used cars are then likely to withdraw their cars from the market, so that the pool of used cars available deteriorates, and as the average quality declines so does the average price that buyers are willing to pay. Again, adverse selection within such a market will violate the Pareto efficiency conditions and prevent prices from acting as an appropriate signal to bring about an optimal allocation of resources.

Adverse selection and insurance

Suppose that the insurance market can be subdivided into two groups:

- those with high-risk characteristics, H in number;
- those with low-risk characteristics, L in number.

The respective probabilities of an illness or accident are:

- P_H for the high-risk individuals;
- P_L for the low-risk individuals.

The *weighted average probability* of illness or accident for the whole group is $\bar{P}$, where:

$$\bar{P} = P_H \cdot \frac{H}{H + L} + P_L \cdot \frac{L}{H + L}$$

and $P_H > \bar{P} > P_L$.

Suppose the cost of an illness or accident to the insurance company is denoted by C. Then the *insurance premium*, I, that must be charged to cover all costs must be such that

$$I \geqslant C \cdot \bar{P}$$

If the difference between $\bar{P}$ and P_L is significant, and the low-risk individuals are aware of this fact, then they may drop out of the insurance market. Of course, high-risk individuals with $P_H > \bar{P}$ are likely to remain in the market.

As the pool of those remaining within the market becomes progressively dominated by high-risk individuals, then $\bar{P}$, the weighted average, will rise and I, the insurance premium, is also likely to rise to reflect the increase in $C\bar{P}$. This process of adverse selection might, in the extreme, lead to such high premiums that the market ceases to exist altogether.

Remedies to information asymmetry

A number of *remedies* have been suggested to counteract this particular type of market failure involving information asymmetry and adverse selection.

Self-selection Here the insurance company provides incentives for low-risk individuals to reveal themselves. Those able to demonstrate specified criteria (e.g. age, health certification, time without accident) can be offered more favourable terms. In this sense price can move away from average to marginal characteristics. Of course any improvement in the pool of risks will also reduce $\bar{P}$, and thereby average (as well as marginal) premiums.

Market-makers Dealers and other market-makers may interpose themselves between buyers and sellers, using their own expertise and name to guarantee minimum standards of product or service. Reputable second-hand car dealers, independent automobile service centres for checking second-hand cars, etc., could perform this function in the market investigated by Akerlof.

Branding The use of brand names is another means of offsetting uncertainty as to product quality, for both direct and indirect (e.g. franchising) production. The consumer may pay a premium for this quality guarantee in terms of a higher price for the branded product.

Signalling The suggestion here is that sellers of a high-quality product may be able to acquire specific attributes, which then serve as *signals* to buyers to help them differentiate products in terms of quality. Spence (1973) suggested that a specified attribute is more likely to serve as a signal if it costs less when acquired by the high-quality seller than by the low-quality seller.

Spence illustrated his idea in terms of education, which, for simplicity, he assumed made no difference to the productivity of workers but acted merely as a **signal** to purchasers of labour, i.e. employers. We can make use of our earlier equation (p. 484), except this time we assume:

- P_H to represent the *productivity* of high-quality workers, which are H in number;
- P_L to represent the *productivity* of low-quality workers, which are L in number.

The weighted average productivity of any employee selected at random by a particular employer is $\bar{P}$, where:

$$\bar{P} = P_H \cdot \frac{H}{H + L} + P_L \cdot \frac{L}{H + L}$$

and $P_H > \bar{P} > P_L$.

As previously noted, where employers are unable to distinguish (information asymmetry) between high- and low-productivity workers they may pay each worker $\bar{P}$, representing *average* rather than marginal productivity and violating the Pareto efficiency conditions.

However, suppose that education, though adding nothing to productivity, costs less to acquire for H-type workers than for L-type workers. It might then act as a signal whereby H-type workers could increase their prospects of being paid a wage that reflects their true marginal productivity. Employers learn from experience to associate educated workers with being H-type workers and pay them accordingly; they act in the opposite direction as regards uneducated workers whom, lacking this signal, employers assume to be L-type workers and pay them accordingly.

Spence showed that a number of conditions must be fulfilled if education is to act successfully as a signalling device in the job market: i.e. to bring about a sustainable equilibrium where employers are not disappointed in their hiring and remuneration policies and find that they *do* in fact pay workers the value of their marginal products.

Taking C_H to be the cost of education for high-productivity workers and C_L the cost of education for low-productivity workers, these conditions include the following:

- $C_H < C_L$ (1)
  (*costs more* for low-productivity workers to acquire education)
- $C_L > P_H - P_L$ (2)
  (so that low-productivity workers do not have the incentive to invest in the education 'signal'; *costs more* for them to acquire the signal than the differential in productivity deemed to follow from possessing that signal)
- $C_H < P_H - P_L$ (3)
  (so that high-productivity workers actually benefit from investing in the education 'signal'; *costs less* for them to acquire the signal than the differential in productivity deemed to follow from possessing that signal).

Those having invested in the educational signal are paid a wage $W_H = P_H$; those *not* having invested in the educational signal are paid a wage $W_L = P_L$.

It follows from equations (1) to (3) that

$$C_H < (P_H - P_L) < C_L \tag{4}$$

The equilibrium outlined in equation (4) is sometimes referred to as the **separating equilibrium**. It indicates how the two groups of workers separate themselves by investing or not investing in the signal, here education.

This condition is a *necessary* but not sufficient condition for the success of education as a signalling device. Still stricter conditions may need to be devised for *sufficiency*. For example, suppose equation (4) is fulfilled but all workers prior to any education are paid a wage corresponding to their average productivity, $\bar{P}$. Since $C_L > P_H - P_L$, then low-productivity workers will not find it worthwhile to invest in education. However, even where $C_H < P_H - P_L$, if at the same time $C_H > P_H - \bar{P}$ then high-productivity workers will also be in a situation where they will not find it worthwhile to invest in education. Here the wage differential $(P_H - \bar{P})$ from being deemed a high-quality worker by investing in the educational signal is smaller (given that they are currently paid $\bar{P}$) than the cost of acquiring that signal. In this case the equilibrium solution will involve neither type of worker acquiring the signal. Hence equation (4) is a necessary but not a sufficient condition for the success of education as a signalling device.

Of course even if education were successful in this role, it would represent a social waste in the example given. By assuming education to have no impact on true productivity but merely on perceived productivity, high-productivity workers are induced to spend periods out of direct employment simply to acquire appropriate signals. The *efficiency gain* is that of a more appropriate allocation of high-productivity employees after the education signal is acquired; the *efficiency loss* is the resources used up by society in providing some individuals with educational opportunities merely to serve as a non-productive signalling device and, of course, the *opportunity cost* of work forgone by high-productivity workers during the educational process.

Moral hazard **Moral hazard** (p. 133) is also related to information asymmetry. It occurs when the probability distribution of an individual's set of possible actions is directly affected by the existence and nature of some contractual relationship. For example, if the existence of an insurance policy means that an individual drives less carefully, or takes fewer precautions to protect a vehicle from theft, then moral hazard is said to occur. Moral hazard involves information asymmetry in an insurance market in that the *buyer* of insurance may be aware of the behaviour change but the *seller* may not. Again the possibility exists that such market failure may cause prices to reflect *average* rather than *marginal* costs, violating the Pareto efficiency conditions. Further, in extreme cases the existence of moral hazard may so force up premiums that good risks are priced out of the market, with the market ultimately ceasing to exist.

■ Monopoly

We have already noted in Chapter 7 various aspects of welfare loss resulting from the presence of **monopoly power**. Chapter 11 has indicated how the presence of monopoly may preclude a first-best Pareto-efficient resource allocation, leaving only second-best allocations available to policy makers. Here we consider this latter situation in rather more detail. We note how conventional policies to correct market failure may turn out to be inappropriate in the presence of monopoly power. In particular we show how the market-based policy instrument of Pigouvian taxes (p. 470) to correct for the presence of a negative externality may fail to secure even a second-best resource allocation when monopoly power is also present.

To illustrate this point we consider a situation in which a *negative externality* (e.g. pollution) is generated by a monopoly producer. In Fig. 12.11 we initially assume a first-best economy with no market failure. This would entail, among other things, perfectly competitive industries with no divergence between private and social costs. For the industry shown in Fig. 12.11, social welfare is then maximised where $MSB = MSC$, i.e. price P_1 and quantity Q_1 (note here that it is the demand curve or willingness-to-pay curve that is regarded as the MSB curve). If the industry was perfectly competitive with no externalities then $MSC_{ind} = MPC_{ind} = S_{ind}$ and the market would yield the social optimum solution P_1, Q_1. However, suppose there is now the single market failure of a negative externality ($MSC > MPC$): then in this case demand and supply are in equality at price P_2 and quantity Q_2. This is clearly no longer the first-best Pareto-efficient solution.

If we then use a Pigouvian tax of t^* (equal to $P_1 - P_7$) to internalise the externality, it would indeed do so by shifting the MPC curve vertically upwards so that it becomes coincident once more with the MSC curve. If no other market failure were present, then the

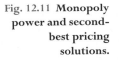

Fig. 12.11 **Monopoly power and second-best pricing solutions.**

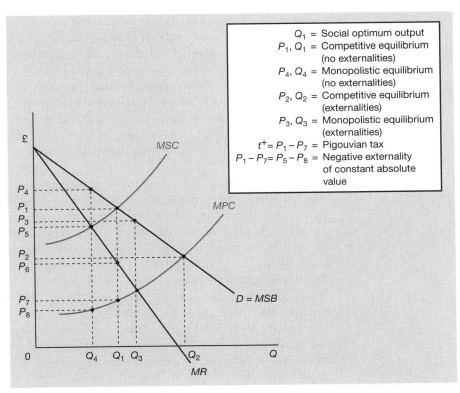

Q_1 = Social optimum output
P_1, Q_1 = Competitive equilibrium (no externalities)
P_4, Q_4 = Monopolistic equilibrium (no externalities)
P_2, Q_2 = Competitive equilibrium (externalities)
P_3, Q_3 = Monopolistic equilibrium (externalities)
$t^+ = P_1 - P_7$ = Pigouvian tax
$P_1 - P_7 = P_5 - P_8$ = Negative externality of constant absolute value

first-best Pareto-efficient resource allocation would be restored at P_1, Q_1 by the Pigouvian tax.

Suppose, however, that in addition to the negative externality of pollution there is a *second* market failure, namely the presence of monopoly power. In this case the profit-maximising monopoly solution in the presence of the negative externality is P_3, Q_3 where $MR = MPC$. This is clearly a socially inefficient allocation of resources ($MSB < MSC$). However, to use the Pigouvian tax $t*$ to correct for this market failure will *not* restore the socially efficient allocation $MSC = MSB$. In fact such a Pigouvian tax ($t* = P_1 - P_7 = P_5 - P_8$), while equating MPC with MSC, will cause the profit-maximising monopolist to produce output Q_4 at price P_4, which is clearly socially inefficient ($MSB > MSC$). In fact the appropriate tax to bring about the socially optimum allocation ($MSB = MSC$) is $P_6 - P_7$. This would shift MPC vertically upwards just enough for the profit-maximising monopolist to produce output Q_1 at price P_1. Note that the appropriate tax here ($P_6 - P_7$) is *less than* the Pigouvian tax ($P_1 - P_7$) that, by definition, fully compensates the negative externality. In other words the presence of monopoly power dictates that we set a tax rate that does *not*, in full, compensate for the negative externality imposed on society by the producer. In fact it falls short of the Pigouvian tax $t*$ by $P_1 - P_6$.

■ Private versus social time preference

We have already considered the ideas of **time preference** and **discounting** in Chapter 3. In the context of this chapter, market failure can be said to occur where the private and social rates of time preference differ.

For the third efficiency condition to be fulfilled (Chapter 11, p. 442) there must be equality between the marginal rate of physical transformation of X into Y ($MRPT_{XY}$) and the individual consumer marginal rates of substitution of X into Y (MRS_{XY}). We now extend this condition into the **intertemporal context**, bringing saving and investment into the picture. It then follows that the credit and capital markets must, like product and factor markets, provide uniform and unambiguous signals to savers and investors in both current and future time periods. We now explore this intertemporal requirement for Pareto efficiency in rather more detail, before considering the consequences of breakdown.

In an intertemporal context, consumers realise that they can trade consumer products today, via *saving*, for larger quantities of consumer goods in the future. The rate of that trade-off will be determined by the prevailing rate of interest (r). Similarly producers realise that they can increase their output in the future by devoting some of today's resources, via *investment*, to the production of more productive capital goods for use in future periods.

It may be helpful, for the moment, to depart from our previous two-product, two-consumer, two-producer model, to assume a single-product, single-consumer, single-producer model, as in Fig. 12.12. The indifference curves of our consumer (A) correspond to levels of utility from different combinations of consumption of product X in time periods 1 and 2. The transformation curve (TT) shows how the producer can transform any savings of the consumer in time period 1, via investment, into greater output in time period 2.

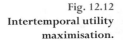

Fig. 12.12
Intertemporal utility maximisation.

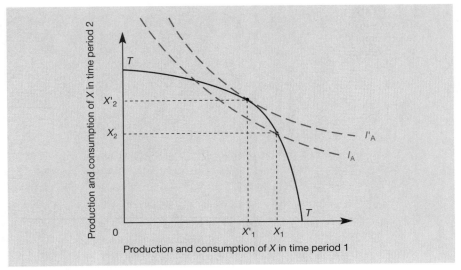

In the initial allocation the consumer chooses combination X_1, X_2 of product X in time periods 1 and 2 respectively, yielding indifference curve I_A. In fact the consumer can maximise utility by consuming less in time period 1 (i.e. saving) and more in time period 2 (moving to combination X'_1, X'_2 and indifference curve I'_A). The producer can (at least in principle) transform the extra saving in time period 1, via investment, into greater output in time period 2 ($X'_2 > X_2$).

In terms of Fig. 12.12, the optimum tangency position can be expressed in terms of equality in marginal rates of substitution and transformation for product X between two time periods as follows:

$$MRS_{X_1,X_2} = MRPT_{X_1,X_2}$$

We now extend our intertemporal analysis to a *market economy* with many producers and consumers. We assume that each consumer can save at a market rate of interest (r). This gives the **intertemporal budget line**, TT, with slope $(1 + r)$ departing from the initial consumer allocation X_1, X_2 in Fig. 12.13. In other words, each unit of X in time period 1 *not consumed* (i.e. saved) can be transformed into $X(1 + r)$ units in time period 2. To achieve maximum utility implies a tangency between the intertemporal budget line and the highest attainable indifference curve, A'.

This occurs by sacrificing (saving) $X_1 - X'_1$ of period 1 consumption in return for $X'_2 - X_2$ additional consumption in period 2. Remember: only contract curve solutions in terms of the Edgeworth–Bowley consumption box (p. 437) achieve a Pareto-efficient resource allocation. It follows that:

- the marginal rate of substitution for product X as between the two time periods must be the *same* for *all consumers* (who save) to achieve a first-best Pareto-efficient solution. *Price*, here the rate of interest r, must be such as to provide the same signal to all consumers and savers seeking to maximise utility as between different time periods.

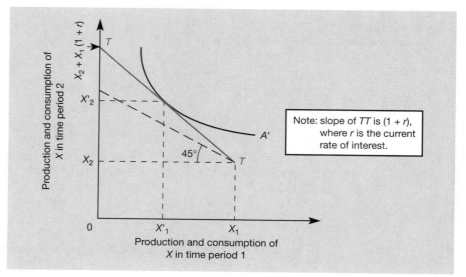

Fig. 12.13 Pareto efficiency in an intertemporal context.

Note: slope of *TT* is $(1 + r)$, where r is the current rate of interest.

To achieve the tangency solution in Fig. 12.13 implies that producers actually use the consumer savings to invest in capital goods to achieve the transformation implied (X'_1, X'_2). In other words, profit-maximising producers who can borrow at the market rate of interest r must invest in capital goods up to the point where the marginal rate of product transformation is made equal to $(1 + r)$. Put another way, they must invest in capital goods up to the point where the rate of return on marginal investments (Keynes' marginal efficiency of investment) exactly coincides with r. It follows that:

- the marginal rate of product transformation as between two time periods must be the *same* for *all producers* (who invest) to achieve a first-best Pareto-efficient solution.

For a first-best Pareto-efficient resource allocation, the credit and capital goods markets must be in equilibrium, providing appropriate signals for *all* savers and investors to achieve the tangency between intertemporal budget lines and indifferences curves shown in Fig. 12.13. Clearly, this implies that all savers *and* investors respectively face the same (equilibrium) price signals of interest rate as to intertemporal consumption and investment decisions. Strictly it also implies that there is perfect information about future markets and prices.

Intertemporal market failure

A number of imperfections may inhibit the achievement of a first-best Pareto-efficient allocation of resources through time:

- A uniform interest rate may not be established for all savers/investors. Some savers may be able to take advantage of higher interest rate opportunities and some investors of lower interest rate opportunities. Imperfections in the credit markets may preclude the achievement of a uniform rate of interest available to all, resulting in an equality in the marginal rates of time preference for both savers and investors.
- Even if such an interest rate were achieved via perfect credit and capital markets there could still exist a discrepancy between the *private* and *social* rates of time preference, and it is to this issue that we now turn.

Private versus social rates of time preference

Figure 12.14 is a useful vehicle for illustrating a number of points. The total output of the economy in terms of a bundle of products in time period 1 is B_1, in which case savings and investments make possible a bundle of products B_2 in time period 2. The trade-off between abstaining from consumption (saving) in time period 1 and additional output (via investment) in time period 2 is given by the transformation curve TT. Suppose, now, that the government has a desired combination of bundles of products between the two time periods, namely the respective bundles B'_1 and B'_2 at point A. This combination yields the highest social welfare function (SWF). The marginal rate of transformation at point A is given by the slope of the tangent to TT at A, which equals 1 plus the return on marginal investments (i) at that point (see p. 490). This is, in effect, the **social marginal rate of time preference** (SMT) between feasible consumption bundles in time periods 1 and 2 respectively. The socially desired level of investment is then $B_1 - B_1'$ in time period 1, yielding additional output $B_2' - B_2$ in time period 2.

If, for whatever reason, the *market rate of interest* (r_m) deviates from the *return on marginal investments* (i) at point A, then the socially desired level of investment will not occur. Only where $r_m = i = SMT - 1$ will the highest attainable social welfare function be achieved at point A.

It follows that wherever $r_m > i$ or $r_m < i$, the market rate of interest will not be suitable as a rate of discount for investment appraisal. For example, suppose $r_m > i$ so that the rate of investment is only $B_1 - B^*$ ($< B_1 - B'_1$) in Fig. 12.14. At the corresponding point on the transformation curve (TT), the slope of that curve (i^*) is steeper than at the social optimum allocation A. The **private marginal rate of time preference** would then be ($1 + i^*$), which is greater than ($1 + i$), the social marginal rate of time preference (SMT). Only when private and social marginal rates of time preference are in accord can we achieve the highest attainable social welfare function.

Fig. 12.14 Equality (at A) between the social and private marginal rates of time preference; and inequality (at B^*) resulting in intertemporal market failure.

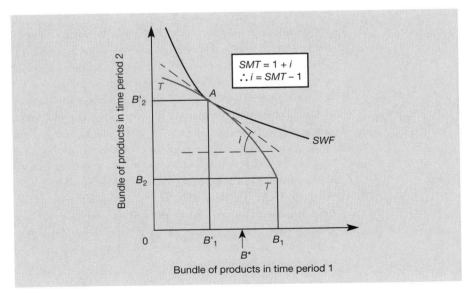

Applications and evidence

The **environment** provides a useful context for exploring the application of the various policy measures available to governments in tackling *externalities* and *public good* problems. Here we look at the important contemporary issue of global warming, and consider ways in which the negative externalities imposed by global warming might be offset.

Before turning to the specific issue of global warming, it will be useful to address the issue of valuation.

The valuation issue

A key element in finding any socially efficient solution to the negative environmental effects of increased production clearly involves placing a *monetary value* on the marginal private and social costs (or benefits) of production. In terms of Fig. 12.1 (p. 467) we need some monetary valuation that will permit us to estimate the *MPC*, *MSC*, *MR*, *AR* and *MSB* curves.

The idea of willingness to pay underlies many of the methods used by economists in an attempt to place a monetary value on benefits and costs, especially where no market prices exist. Individuals are asked, using surveys or questionnaires, how much they would be willing to pay for some specified environmental good, such as improved water quality or the preservation of a threatened local amenity.

For example, in Ukunda, Kenya, residents had three sources of water – door-to-door vendors, kiosks and wells – each requiring residents to pay different costs in money and time. Water from door-to-door vendors cost the most but required the least collection time. A study found that the villagers were willing to pay a substantial share of their incomes – about 8% – in exchange for this greater convenience and for time saved. Such valuations can be helpful in seeking to make the case for extending reliable public water supply even to poorer communities.

Questionnaires and surveys of willingness to pay have been widely used in the UK to evaluate the recreational benefits of environmental amenities (Willis 1991). Other valuation methods may also be used. For example, where no price is charged for entry to recreational sites, economists have searched for private market goods whose consumption is *complementary* to the consumption of the recreational good in question.

One such private complementary good is the **travel costs** incurred by individuals to gain access to recreational sites. The price paid to visit any site is uniquely determined for each visitor by calculating the travel costs from his/her location of origin. By observing people's willingness to pay for the private complementary good it is then possible to infer a price for the non-priced environmental amenity.

In Fig. 12.15 the demand curve D_{VISITS} shows the overall trend relationship between travel costs and visit rates for all the visitors interviewed. Using this information we can estimate the average visitor's (V_1) total recreational value ($V_1 \times P_1$) for the site. Multiplying this by the total number of visitors per annum allows us to estimate the total annual recreational value of the site.

Fig. 12.15 The relationship between the number of visits to a site and the price of the visit.

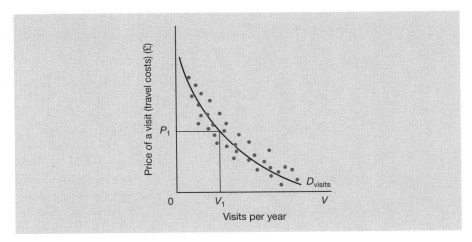

A further technique often used in deriving valuations where no prices exist is the **hedonic-price** method. This estimates the extent to which people are, for example, willing to pay a house price premium for the benefit of living within easy access of an environmental amenity.

Using all such methods, the value of non-priced recreation on the Forestry Commission sites in the UK was estimated to be £53 million per annum in 1988, almost as large as the total income from the sale of timber from those sites.

Total economic value

In recent years there has been considerable discussion as to how to find the *total economic value* (TEV) of an environmental asset. The following identity has been suggested:

Total economic value ≡ Use value + Option value + Existence value

The idea here is that *use value* reflects the practical uses to which an environmental asset is currently being put. For example, the tropical rainforests are used to provide arable land for crop cultivation or to rear cattle in various ranching activities. The forests are also a source of various products, such as timber, rubber, medicines, and nuts. In addition, the forests act as the 'lungs' of the world, absorbing stores of carbon dioxide and releasing oxygen, help to prevent soil erosion, and play an important part in flood control.

There are clear difficulties in placing reliable monetary estimates on all these aspects of the use value of the rainforest. However, it is even more difficult to estimate *option value*, which refers to the value we place on the asset *now* as regards functions which might be exploited some time in the *future*. For example, how much are we willing to pay to preserve the rainforest in case it becomes a still more important source of herbal and other medicines? This is a type of insurance value, seeking to measure the willingness to pay for an environmental asset now, given some probability function of the individual (or group) wishing to use that asset in various ways in the future.

Finally, *existence value* refers to the value we place on an environmental asset as it is today, independently of any current or future use we might make of that asset. This is an attempt to measure our willingness to pay for an environmental asset simply because we wish it to continue to exist in its present form. Many people subscribe to charities to preserve the rainforests, other natural habitats or wildlife even though they may never themselves see those habitats or species. Existence value may involve intergenerational motives, such as wishing to give one's children or grandchildren the opportunity to observe certain species or ecosystems.

Although much remains to be done in estimating TEV, a number of empirical studies have been undertaken. For instance, the Flood Hazard Research Centre in the UK estimated that in 1987/88 people were willing to pay £14 to £18 per annum in taxes in order that recreational beaches (use value) be protected from erosion (Turner 1991). The researchers also surveyed a sample of people who did not use beaches for recreational use. They estimated that these people were willing to pay £21 to £25 per annum in taxes in order to preserve these same beaches (existence value).

Overall, many estimates are finding that the option and existence value of environmental assets often far exceed their use value. For example, existence values for the Grand Canyon were found to outweigh use values by the startling ratio of 60 to l (Pearce 1991). In similar vein, *non-users* of Prince William Sound, Alaska, devastated by the *Exxon Valdez* oil spill in 1989, placed an extremely high value on its existence value (O'Doherty 1994). The amounts that non-users were estimated (via interviews) as willing to pay to *avoid* the damage actually incurred came to $2.8 billion, i.e. $31 per US household. This approach, whereby interviewees are asked about the value of a resource 'contingent' on its not being damaged, is often termed *contingent valuation*.

We now look at applying our early work to the particular issue of global warming.

Global warming: market and non-market policy instruments

Global warming is closely related to the greenhouse effect, which refers to the trapping of heat between the earth's surface and gases in the atmosphere, especially carbon dioxide. Currently some 6 billion tonnes of carbon dioxide (CO_2) are released into the atmosphere each year, largely as a result of burning fossil fuels. Table 12.1 outlines the main sources of the greenhouse gases. A number of studies highlight the rapid projected rate of world growth of CO_2 emissions in the 'no action' case: for example, the OECD (1999) has suggested that CO_2 emissions may rise threefold by 2050, from the current 6 billion tonnes per annum to over 20 billion tonnes. By trapping the sun's heat these gases are in turn raising global temperature (global warming). On present estimates, temperatures are expected to increase by a further 1.3°C by 2020 and 3°C by the year 2070. An increase of merely half a degree in world temperature this century has already contributed to a rise of 10cm in sea levels. Higher sea levels (via melting ice caps), flooding, various climatic changes causing increased desertification and drought, have all been widely linked to global warming.

The various damage costs of global warming are clearly considerable; but so too are the abatement costs of seeking to reduce emissions of CO_2 by use of expensive 'clean' technologies and sometimes less efficient alternative fuels. We take as our starting point Fig. 12.3 on p. 471, and consider a situation in which we seek to reduce emissions of pollutant (here CO_2) from Q_P to the socially optimum level Q_S.

Table 12.1 **Sources of the greenhouse gases.**

Gases	Sources	Percentage of the greenhouse effect
Carbon dioxide	• from burning forests • from burning fossil fuels (e.g. coal, oil) • from cement production, in the crushing of limestone	56
Chlorofluorocarbons (CFCs)	• a type of gas used in refrigerators and air conditioning systems. Used less and less in aerosols and packaging. CFCs are now being replaced by other gases, though these are more expensive alternatives to CFCs	23
Methane	• given off from any vegetation rotting under water (such as rice fields) • given off when animals such as cows and sheep produce waste gases	14
Nitrous oxides	• released during the breakdown of fertilisers, both organic and inorganic	7

Setting the targets   If we are to apply our analysis in practical ways we must seek to *value* both the marginal damage and the marginal abatement cost curves. Again we are faced with the conceptual problem of placing a valuation on variables to which monetary values are at present only rarely attached, if at all. In addition, in a full cost–benefit analysis we must select a rate of discount (see pp. 101 and 115) to enable a comparison to be made between effects in the distant future and the costs of policies introduced today.

Uncertainty will therefore clearly be involved in any attempt to evaluate the costs and benefit of policy action or inaction. The target for reducing CO_2 emissions to the socially optimum level is $(Q_P - Q_S)$ in Fig. 12.3, and this target will clearly be affected by such uncertainty. Analysts often use scenarios of high, medium and low estimates for marginal damage and marginal abatement cost curves. For instance, Nordhaus (1991) estimated each of these marginal cost curves for both CO_2 emissions and for the broader category of greenhouse gases, based on US data. His *high* estimate of marginal damage costs was calculated at $66.00 per tonne of CO_2; his *low* estimate at only $1.83 per tonne of CO_2. We can use Fig. 12.3 (p. 471) to illustrate this analysis. In the high estimate case, the marginal damage cost curve shifts vertically upwards, Q_S falls, and the target reduction in CO_2 emissions (i.e. $Q_P - Q_S$) increases. On this basis Nordhaus advocates reducing CO_2 emissions by 20%. It is hardly surprising (in view of the valuation discrepancy noted) that in his low estimate case, the marginal damage cost curve shifts vertically downwards in Fig. 12.3, Q_S rises, and the target reduction in CO_2 emissions (i.e. $Q_S - Q_P$) falls. On this basis Nordhaus advocates reducing CO_2 emissions by only about 3%.

Kyoto agreement   The Kyoto Protocol calls for greenhouse gas (GHG) emissions expressed in CO_2 equivalents to be reduced in the period 2008–12 by some 5% relative to their 1990 level. The reduction for the more industrialised OECD countries overall is to be around 7%, but with variations among countries – particularly within the European Union (EU) following its (separate) burden-sharing agreement (see Table 12.2). These targets are tighter than they seem because of the growth of emissions that would normally occur in the meantime; relative to this 'business as usual' scenario, the targets imply reductions that may amount to some 30% by 2012. Indeed, by 1995 emissions were higher than in 1990 in the majority of OECD countries.

Table 12.2 **Overview of national emission trends, Kyoto objectives and EU burden-sharing**

	1990 GHG emissions (million tonnes CO_2 equivalent)	Percentage change 1990–95	Kyoto target for 2008–12 (as % of 1990)
Non-EU OECD			
Australia	406	6	8
Canada	558	10	−6
Czech Republic	188	−24	−8
Hungary	102	−24	−6
Iceland	3	5	10
Japan	1,190	8	−6
New Zealand	76	0	0
Norway	49	6	1
Poland	564	−22	−6
Switzerland	54	−2	−8
USA	5,713	5	−7
European Union			
Burden-sharing targets			
Austria	78	1	−13.0
Belgium	139	6	−7.5
Denmark	72	10	−21.0
Finland	65	3	0.0
France	498	0	0.0
Germany	1,204	−12	−21.0
Greece	99	6	25.0
Ireland	57	4	13.0
Italy	532	2	−6.5
Luxembourg	13	−24	−28.0
Netherlands	207	8	−6.0
Portugal	68	6	27.0
Spain	301	2	15.0
Sweden	65	3	4.0
United Kingdom	715	−9	−12.5

Source: OECD (1999)

Achieving the targets   Whatever the targets set for reduced emissions, which policy instruments will be most effective in achieving those targets? The discussion by Ingham and Ulph (1991) is helpful in comparing market and non-market policy instruments. Many different methods are available for bringing about any given total reduction in CO_2 emissions. Users of fossil fuels might switch towards fuels that emit less CO_2 within a given total energy requirement. For instance oil and gas emit, respectively, about 80% and 60% as much CO_2 per unit of energy as coal. Alternatively, the total amount of energy used might be reduced in an attempt to cut CO_2 emissions.

Another issue is whether we seek to impose our target rate of reduction for CO_2 emissions on *all* sectors of the UK economy. Table 12.3 gives the sectoral breakdown of CO_2 emissions.

Table 12.3 UK sectoral breakdown of CO_2 emissions.

Sector	CO_2 emissions (%)
Electricity generation	37
Industry	22
Transport	19
Domestic	15

Source: European Economy (1992)

Equalising marginal abatement costs   Should we then ask for a *uniform* reduction of, say, 25% across all sectors? This is unlikely to be appropriate since *marginal abatement cost* curves are likely to differ across sectors and, indeed, across countries. For instance, it has been estimated that to abate 14% of the air pollution emitted by the textiles sector in the USA will cost $136 million per annum. However, to abate 14% of the air pollution emitted by each of the machinery, electrical equipment and fabricated metals sectors respectively, will cost $572 million, $729 million and $896 million per annum (World Bank 1992). As well as differing between industrial sectors *within* a country, abatement costs will also differ between countries. For example, it has been estimated that a 10% reduction in CO_2 emissions by 2010 (compared with 1988 emission levels) will cost 400 ecus per tonne of CO_2 abated in Italy, but only 200 ecus per tonne abated in Denmark, and less than 20 ecus per tonne abated in the UK, France, Germany and Belgium (*European Economy* 1992).

This point can be illustrated by taking just two sectors in the UK – say electricity generation and transport – and by assuming that they initially emit the same amount of CO_2. Following Ingham and Ulph (1991) suppose that the overall target for reducing CO_2 emissions is the distance O'O in Fig. 12.16.

We must now decide how to allocate this total reduction in emissions between the two sectors. In Fig. 12.16 we measure reductions in CO_2 emissions in electricity generation from left to right, and reductions in CO_2 emissions in transport from right to left. Point A, for example, would divide the total reduction in emissions into OA in electricity generation and O'A in transport. A *marginal abatement cost (MAC)* curve is now calculated for each sector. In Fig. 12.16 we draw the *MAC* curve for electricity generation

Fig. 12.16 Finding the 'efficient' or 'least-cost' solution for reducing CO$_2$ emissions in a two-sector model.

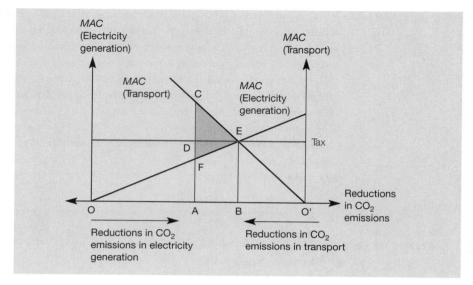

as being lower and flatter than that for transport. This reflects the greater fuel-switching possibilities in electricity generation compared with transport, both within fossil fuels and between fossil and non-fossil (solar, wave, wind) fuels. In other words, any marginal reduction in CO$_2$ emissions in electricity generation is likely to raise overall costs by *less* in electricity generation than in transport. In transport there are far fewer fuel-substitution possibilities; the major means of curbing CO$_2$ emissions in transport are improved techniques for energy efficiency or a switch from private to public transport.

Given these different marginal abatement cost curves for each sector in Fig. 12.16, how then should we allocate our 25% reduction between the two sectors? Clearly we should seek a solution by which the given total reduction in emissions is achieved at the least total cost to society: we shall call this the **efficient** or **least-cost** solution. In Fig. 12.16 this will be where marginal abatement costs are the same in both sectors, i.e. at point B in the diagram. We can explain this by supposing we were initially *not* at B, but at A in Fig. 12.16, with equal reductions in the two sectors. At point A, marginal abatement costs in transport are AC but marginal abatement costs in electricity generation are only AF. So by abating CO$_2$ by one more tonne in electricity generation and one less tonne in transport, we would have the same total reduction in CO$_2$ emissions, but would have saved approximately CF in costs. By moving from point A to the 'efficient' point B, we would save the area CFE in abatement costs.

It follows, therefore, that for any given target for total reduction in CO$_2$ emissions, efficiency will occur only if the marginal cost of abatement is the same across all sectors of the economy (and indeed across all methods of abatement).

The benefits of this principle of equalising marginal abatement costs are further supported by an OECD study on curbing the growth in global emissions of CO$_2$. In seeking to curb growth in CO$_2$ emissions by a given target, namely 2% per annum relative to the 'business as usual' growth path, the cost of achieving that target via *equiproportionate* (equal percentage) cuts across all countries was compared with the cost via *equalising marginal abatement costs*.

Table 12.4 presents this comparison using three separate models over different time periods. The costs shown are expressed as a per cent of GDP. In column (2) these costs represent the equalisation of marginal abatement costs, and are clearly projected as being lower under all three models than those in column (1), which represent equiproportionate cuts. Under the OECD Green model the loss in GDP in OECD countries would be reduced by more than a third, compared with the 'equiproportionate' policy instrument. OECD countries – which have high marginal abatement costs – would contribute only 22% of the total CO_2 abatement sought under the 'equalisation of marginal abatement costs' policy, but 32% under the 'equiproportionate' policy.

Table 12.4 **Cost (% of GDP) of alternative abatement strategies.**

	Edmonds–Reilly model (ERM)		OECD Green model		Manne-Richels Global model (MR)	
	(1)	(2)	(1)	(2)	(1)	(2)
2020	1.9	1.6	1.9	1.0	n.a.	n.a.
2050	3.7	3.3	2.6	1.9	n.a.	n.a.
2100	5.7	5.1	n.a.	n.a.	8.0	7.5

Source: Adapted from OECD (1999,1993)

Policy implications

Environmental policy instruments can be broadly classified into two types: market-based and non-market-based. **Market-based** policy instruments would include setting a tax on emissions of CO_2 or issuing a limited number of permits to emit CO_2 and then allowing a market to be set up in which those permits were traded. **Non-market-based** policy instruments would include regulations and directives. For example, in the UK, the Non-Fossil Fuel Obligation currently imposed on privatised electricity companies requires them to purchase a specified amount of electricity from non-fossil fuel sources.

Market-based instruments

We can use Fig. 12.16 to examine the case for using a tax instrument (market-based) as compared with regulation (non-market-based). A *tax* of BE on CO_2 emissions would lead to the 'efficient' solution B. This is because polluters have a choice of paying the tax on their emissions of CO_2 or of taking steps to abate their emissions. They will have an incentive to abate as long as the marginal cost of abatement is lower than the tax. So electricity generating companies will have incentives to abate to OB, and transport companies to O'B in Fig. 12.16. Since every polluter faces the same tax, they will end up with the same marginal abatement cost. Here prices, amended by tax, are conveying signals to producers in a way that helps to coordinate their (profit maximising) decisions in order to bring about an efficient (least cost) solution.

The alternative policy of *government regulations and directions* (non-market-based instrument), in achieving the efficient solution at B in Fig. 12.16, would be much more complicated. The government would have to estimate the marginal abatement cost curve for *each sector*, given that such curves differ between sectors. It would then have to estimate the different percentage reductions required in each sector in order to equalise marginal abatement costs (the efficient solution). It is hardly reasonable to suppose that the government could achieve such fine tuning in order to reach efficient solutions.

The market-based solution of tax has no administrative overhead. Producers are simply assumed to react to the signals of market prices (amended by taxes) in a way that maximises their own profits. Regulations, on the other hand, imply monitoring, supervision and other bureaucratic procedures. Ingham and Ulph (1991) found that using a tax policy, as compared with seeking an equal proportionate reduction in CO_2 emissions, resulted in total abatement costs being 20% lower than they would have been under the alternative regulatory policy.

More on tradeable permits   As we previously mentioned (p. 473), **tradeable permits** can help to introduce a market-based element into attempts to limit the total amount of environmental damage. Here the polluter receives a permit to emit a specified amount of waste, whether carbon dioxide, sulphur dioxide or whatever. The total amount of permits issued for any pollutant must, of course, be within currently accepted guidelines of 'safe' levels of emission for that pollutant. Within the overall limit of the permits issued, individual polluters can then buy and sell the permits between each other. The distribution of pollution is then market-directed even though the overall total is regulated. The expectation is that those firms that are already able to meet 'clean' standards will benefit by selling permits to those firms that currently find it too difficult or expensive to meet those standards.

Under the United States Clean Air Act legislation it is possible to trade permits. The Tennessee Valley Authority, for example, has agreed to buy allowances to emit 10,000 tons of sulphur dioxide, a key cause of acid rain, from privately owned Wisconsin Power and Light. Similarly, Duquesne Light of Pittsburgh has bought allowances from the same Wisconsin company to emit between 15,000 and 25,000 tons of sulphur dioxide. Under the Clean Air Act, utilities must cut emissions of sulphur dioxide in half by the year 2000, i.e. from a national total of 19 million tons.

There are, arguably, at least two main benefits from this market in tradeable permits. First, costs of production will be lower than they otherwise would be in producing power consistent with the new overall environmental targets. This is because there will be a cost saving for those companies that would otherwise have either to purchase expensive technology (e.g. 'scrubbers') to meet lower sulphur emissions or to change capital equipment to deal with harder, lower-sulphur coal. This cost saving is, arguably, achieved at no overall rise in projected levels of sulphur pollution since the 'cleaner' companies now have an incentive to more than meet the lower targets of sulphur emission, exchanging unneeded permits for cash on the market. In terms of our earlier analysis, these efficiency gains are the result of tradeable permits enabling firms to *equalise marginal abatement costs* (see also Fig. 12.4 and p. 473).

Second, the market in tradeable permits will help to avoid other sources of environmental damage that would otherwise occur. For instance, the market will help to avoid the hazards involved in transporting large amounts of hard, low-sulphur coal from the western states of the USA to the eastern states in which most of the soft, high-sulphur coal is produced, and in which most of the offending power utilities reside. It will now be possible for the power utilities in the east to purchase permits from power utilities elsewhere, thereby avoiding the disruption of adapting capital equipment and working practices, as well as avoiding any environmental costs associated with bulk transport of cargo over long distances.

The Kyoto agreements (see p. 495) raise the profile of tradeable permits as a policy instrument for dealing with global restrictions in emissions of CO_2. The suggestion is that the Kyoto targets for 2008–12 (Table 12.2, p. 496) could be better achieved if *countries* were able to trade CO_2 emission permits between themselves.

Of course, some *initial total* of permits must be agreed on, consistent with the Kyoto targets, and then this total must be allocated amongst the nations according to some agreed formula. **Grandfathering** is one such formula, in which permits are distributed pro rata to those countries already emitting most CO_2. As might be expected, there has been much disagreement as to the allocation mechanism, with developing countries for example arguing that 'grandfathering' disadvantages them unfairly.

The efficiency gains via allowing CO_2 emissions permits to be traded across countries are indicated in Table 12.5.

By allowing a market in permits to develop in which countries with higher abatement costs purchase permits from countries with lower abatement costs, there is a move towards greater equality in marginal abatement costs.

Table 12.5 Costs of Kyoto in 2010, with and without tradeable permits.

	Change in real income (%)	
	Without tradeable permits	With tradeable permits
USA	−0.33	−0.40
Japan	−0.24	−0.19
European Union	−0.77	−0.33
Other OECD	−0.68	−0.64
OECD total	−0.48	−0.34

Source: Adapted from OECD (1999)

More on negotiation The idea here is that if we assign property rights to the polluters giving them the right to pollute, or to the sufferers giving them the right not to be polluted, then **bargains** may be struck whereby pollution is curbed. For instance, if we assign these property rights to the polluters, then those who suffer may find it advantageous to compensate the polluter for agreeing *not* to pollute. The suggestion is that compensation will be offered by the sufferers as long as this is less than the value of the damage that would otherwise be inflicted upon them. Alternatively, if the property rights are assigned to the sufferers, who then have the right not to be polluted, then the polluters may find it advantageous to offer the sufferers sums of money that would allow the polluters to continue polluting. The suggestion is that the polluters will offer compensation to the sufferers as long as this is less than the private benefits obtained by expanding output and thereby increasing pollution. Under either situation, Coase (1960) has shown that clearly assigned property rights can lead to 'bargains' that bring about output solutions closer to the social optimum than would otherwise occur.

The principle of 'sufferer pays' is already in evidence. For example, Sweden assists Poland with reducing acid rain because the acid rain from Poland damages Swedish lakes and forests. Similarly, the Montreal Protocol aims at protecting the ozone layer, and includes provisions by which China, India and other developing countries are to be compensated by richer countries for agreeing to limit their use of chlorofluorocarbons (CFCs). On this basis, Brazil argues that it is up to the developed countries to compensate it for desisting from exploiting its tropical rainforests, given that it is primarily other countries that will suffer if deforestation continues apace.

Non-market-based instruments: regulations

Many current environmental policies make use of **regulations**. Standards are set for air or water quality, and the polluter is then left free to decide on how best to achieve these minimum standards. The regulator then monitors the environmental situation and takes action against any producers found to be in violation of the standards set.

In the UK, the Environmental Protection Act (1989) laid down minimum environmental standards for emissions from over 3,500 factories involved in chemical processes, waste incineration and oil refining. The factories have to meet these standards for all emissions, whether into air, water or onto land. Factory performance is monitored by a strengthened HM Inspectorate of Pollution, the costs of which are paid for by the factory owners themselves. The Act also provided for public access to information on the pollution created by firms. Regulations were also established on restricting the release of genetically engineered bacteria and viruses, and a ban was imposed on most forms of straw and stubble burning from 1992 onwards. Stricter regulations were also imposed on waste disposal operations, with local authorities given a duty to keep public land clean. On-the-spot fines of up to £1,000 were instituted for persons dropping litter.

Regulations have also played an important part in the five Environmental Action Programmes of the EU, which first began in 1973. For example, specific standards have been set for minimum acceptable levels of water quality for drinking and for bathing. As regards the latter, regular monitoring of coastal waters must take place, with as many as 19 separate tests undertaken throughout the tourist season.

Of course regulations may be part of an integrated environmental policy, which also involves market-based incentives. We have already seen how the tradeable permits system in the USA is working in tandem with the standards imposed by the US Clean Air Act.

▓ The carbon tax: case study of a market-based instrument

We have noted the efficiency case for a **carbon tax**. In fact, rather than seek to measure and tax *carbon emissions*, governments can simply impose a tax on the three fossil fuels – coal, oil and gas – in proportion to their *carbon content*. The proposed EU carbon tax was to be a tax on the carbon content of fossil fuels *and* a tax on all non-renewable forms of energy. Although intended to help the EU meet its commitment at the Rio Summit of 1992 to stabilise carbon dioxide emissions at 1990 levels by the end of the century, it has failed to be ratified. Nevertheless Germany, Italy, Austria, Norway, Sweden, Finland, Denmark and the Netherlands have some form of carbon tax (OECD 1999), though the link with the carbon content of energy is usually weak. In any case, the carbon tax as initially proposed provides a useful study of a market-based policy instrument, in this case an environmental tax. The fossil fuels such as gas, coal and oil were to bear a tax made up of two components, one related to carbon content, the other to energy content. Other non-renewable energy forms (e.g. nuclear power) were to be subject to the energy part of the tax but not the carbon part. The idea was to combine the two parts in equal proportions, with half the tax related to the carbon content and half to the energy content, and to start the tax at $3 per barrel of oil-equivalent in 1993, moving in annual $1 increments to $10 per barrel of oil-equivalent in the year 2000.

Higher private costs A $10 tax per barrel of oil-equivalent would have its main initial impact on industry and power stations making direct use of fossil fuels. Such users would have to pay 58% more for hard coal, 45% more for heavy fuel oil, and 34% more for natural gas.

Higher prices for consumers Higher producer costs would shift the supply curve upwards (and to the left), causing a rise in market prices. It has been estimated that the proposed carbon tax, when fully implemented, would raise the price of petrol by 6% and the price of diesel fuels by 11%. For domestic heating purposes, the tax would be equivalent to a 16% increase in light fuel oil prices and a 14% increase in natural gas prices.

Substitution effects The tax on carbon emissions would cause some substitution *within* the fossil fuels. Coal has a higher carbon content than oil, which in turn has a higher carbon content than gas. A carbon tax would therefore penalise coal most. We have seen how the proposed carbon tax was expected to raise the prices of hard coal, fuel oil and natural gas by 58%, 45% and 34% respectively. This would encourage users to substitute gas and oil for coal, thereby reducing carbon emissions. There would also be substitution effects *between* fossil and non-fossil fuels. Alternative (and renewable) energy sources that do not emit carbon would now be relatively cheaper than fossil fuels for any given amount of energy provision. Wind, wave, solar and nuclear energy sources could all expect to benefit.

In practice these substitution effects were likely to be small. Various studies suggest that the price elasticities of demand for energy are low. For example, the UK price elasticity of demand for energy has been estimated (Rajah 1992) at only (−)0.1% in the short run and (−)0.3% in the long run (after 10 years). This implies that there would need to be rather substantial carbon taxes in place in order to have a significant effect on carbon usage.

The greater use of renewable energy sources would contribute to a *conservation effect*. Even the carbon-emitting fossil fuels would benefit from this effect, as any wasteful use of such fuels now becomes more expensive.

Finally, a *dynamic technological effect* could be expected to result from a carbon tax that penalises carbon emissions pro rata. Any fossil fuels that could be burned in ways that emit less carbon per unit of energy would then pay less tax. This will give an incentive for research and development expenditure on carbon reduction technologies or into finding ways of taking gas from coal, instead of burning coal directly, and so on.

Income effects Any tax will increase withdrawals from the circular flow of income and thereby depress levels of income and expenditure generally. The proposed carbon tax would, it was estimated, only marginally curb economic growth rates of the (then) 11 main EU countries (Table 12.6) – cutting them by only 0.9% over the forecasting period to 2010. The inflationary impact of a tax rise would also depress real levels of income and expenditure. In the case of the proposed carbon tax, the *additional* price rises have been estimated as being 3% over the period to 2010. These were again relatively modest, as was the fall in EU employment at around 0.8%.

Table 12.6 **Economic effects of a policy package to reduce CO_2 emissions via phased CO_2/energy tax of $US 10 per barrel of oil-equivalent: EU-11.**

Volumes	%
Private consumption	−0.9
Total fixed investment	0.0
Exports	−1.9
Imports	−1.3
GNP	−0.9
Employment	−0.8
Prices	
CPI	3.0

Source: Adapted from *European Economy* (1992)

Equity effects Fuel consumption takes a larger share of the expenditures of the poor than of the rich. A carbon tax would therefore be regressive. Some of the tax revenue raised from the tax would therefore be needed to offset some of the impacts on poorer households. However, in doing so, their consumption of carbon-releasing fuels might then increase.

Despite our conclusions of the efficiency advantages of a carbon tax, there were clearly practical problems involved in its implementation, although most of these could have been overcome with careful forethought.

Transport: market and non-market policy instruments

Here we focus on the environmental implications of various scenarios envisaged for the growth of transport, and the various policy instruments that might be applied to influence transport outcomes.

That transport has moved to centre-stage as regards environmental concern in the UK is amply illustrated by the plethora of major reports on transport and the environment (e.g. Royal Commission 1994, 1997; House of Commons 1994). This is hardly surprising given facts such as the following and our earlier discussions on global warming and climatic change:

● Total UK carbon dioxide emissions fell by 10% between 1970 and 1990, but emissions from transport increased by 65%.

- Transport accounts for the whole of the net increase projected in UK carbon dioxide emissions between 1970 and 2020 (an increase of 39 million tonnes of carbon a year).
- Two-thirds of that projected increase in carbon dioxide emissions is accounted for by private cars.

Nor is there any longer much doubt as to the serious impact of the negative externalities associated with road transport, as Table 12.7 usefully indicates. This table excludes congestion costs (see Chapter 11) and a number of other environmental costs, yet still calculates the environmental costs of road transport at between £10 billion and £18.3 billion per annum. This is equivalent to between 2% and 3% of UK GDP per annum. Even allowing for the uncertainty indicated by the lower and upper ranges of the calculations, negative externalities of such magnitude have forced transport to the forefront of environmental debate.

Table 12.7 Transport and environmental costs (£bn per annum/1994 prices).

Costs attributable to road transport are shown in parentheses	Lower end of range		Upper end of range	
Air pollution	2.4		6.0	
Climate change	1.8	(4.6)	3.6	(12.9)
Noise and vibration	1.2		5.4	
Accidents	5.5	(5.4)	45.5	(5.4)
Total quantified environmental costs	**10.9**	**(10.0)**	**20.5**	**(18.3)**

Note: Among environmental costs for which it has not been possible to estimate a money value and which are not therefore included above are: losses of land; loss of access to land; visual intrusion; severance of communities; loss or disruption of habitats.
Source: Adapted from Royal Commission on Environmental Pollution (1994)

The Royal Commission on Environmental Pollution (1994) set a range of *targets* for transport-related pollutants at specific future dates: for example, to limit emissions of carbon dioxide from surface transport in the year 2000 to the 1990 level, and in the year 2020 to no more than 80% of the 1990 level. To achieve such targets it has proposed a range of *policy instruments*, which includes a blend of market-based and non-market-based instruments.

Market-based instruments

There is a clear preference for using such instruments wherever feasible, yet a recognition that other approaches may sometimes be needed.

> Although economic instruments utilising the price mechanism are not a complete alternative to direct regulation, they tend to be more efficient. (Royal Commission 1994: 106)

The Commission reviewed a number of possible road charges that relate the amount paid to the environmental costs imposed by journeys or movements. These included charges related to distance travelled, to use of road space (road pricing), to pollutants emitted, to parking space, and to fuel used. The 'pollutant emitted' charge was attractive to the Commission as it would correspond to the Pigouvian environmental tax previously discussed (p. 470). A German proposal is for data on the use of the vehicle during the year to be stored in an electronic management system, displayed during an annual test on emissions and passed on to the tax authorities. The technology and necessary EU legislation for such a tax are not immediately available, and this was considered of interest for the medium term. For the present, the focus of attention became the charge on fuel used.

Fuel duty was regarded as having a number of advantages as an economic instrument for influencing decisions about additional journeys:

- *The amount of tax paid varies with the environmental costs*. The amount of fuel used and duty paid is in the main proportional to the amount of carbon dioxide emitted, and (for any given vehicle) is closely reflected in the quantities of other substances emitted. Fuel consumption is substantially higher in congested urban traffic, and is therefore correlated to some degree with situations in which a vehicle is contributing to higher concentrations of pollutants, and where there is a higher exposure to the noise and vibration it is producing.
- *It is simple to administer*. It costs little to collect, is difficult to avoid or evade, and can easily be modified.
- *Road users have discretion about how to respond*. Road users may respond either by reducing the number or length of their journeys or by reducing their use of fuel in other ways, such as switching to smaller or more fuel-efficient vehicles or driving in a more fuel-efficient way.
- *It is possible to vary the rate of fuel duty to provide an incentive to use environmentally less damaging forms of fuel,* as in the case of the existing small differentials in favour of diesel and unleaded petrol.
- *A fuel duty already exists*.

Empirical studies have indicated that variations in fuel duty do indeed have an *effect* on road transport use. The Department of Transport has estimated that a 10% increase in the price of fuel in real terms would lead to a fall in fuel use of up to 3%, of which half would be the result of reduced vehicle use. The Royal Commission concluded that in order to meet the target of limiting carbon dioxide emissions from road transport to 1990 levels by this means alone, the price of fuel would need to double, relative to the price of other goods, by the year 2005. This would require an increase in fuel duty of some 9% per year (in real terms) for 10 years (a further 4% above the government's already stated intention of 5% a year).

Certainly there is international evidence to indicate the effectiveness of higher fuel prices in deterring fuel use by road vehicles, as can be seen in Fig. 12.17.

Non-market-based instruments

The Royal Commission's recommended measures for achieving its CO_2 targets for the years 2000 and 2020 are set out in Table 12.8. These clearly involve a mix of market- and non-market-based instruments. For example, emissions of various pollutants (including CO_2) increase fairly rapidly at vehicle speeds over 55 mph, as do car accidents. There is therefore a recommendation for stricter enforcement by the regulatory authorities of the speed limits on various roads. Note that *all* the measures in Table 12.8 are needed to meet the target of carbon dioxide being at 80% of 1990 levels by the year 2020.

Fig. 12.17
Relationship
between fuel price
and fuel use by road
vehicles.

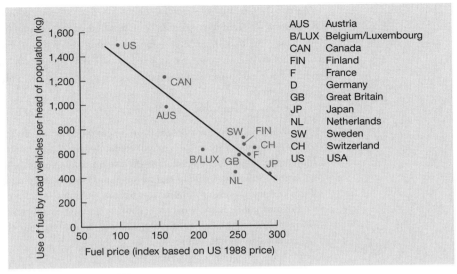

Source: Royal Commission (1994)

Table 12.8 **Combined
effect of
recommended
measures on carbon
dioxide emissions
from surface
transport, million
tonnes carbon/year.**

		Cars	Road	Total	% of 1990
	1990	19.7	30.5	32.3	100
Baseline	2000	22.4	34.7	36.4	113
Doubling of fuel prices by 2005		20.2	31.3	33.2	103
Enforcement of 60 mph and 70 mph speed limits		19.1	30.1	32.0	99
40% improvement in fuel efficiency of new cars by 2005		18.4	29.1	31.1	97
Halving of growth of car traffic in urban areas		18.2	28.9	30.9	96
Baseline	2020	26.9	42.9	44.7	138
Doubling of fuel prices by 2005		18.2	29.5	32.0	99
Enforcement of 60 mph and 70 mph speed limits		17.1	28.4	30.9	96
40% improvement in fuel efficiency of new cars by 2005		13.1	23.8	26.3	82
Halving of growth of car traffic in urban areas		12.6	23.2	25.7	80

Source: Adapted from Royal Commission (1994), Appendix D

Many other subsidiary *regulations* also underly these recommendations: for example, 'that more stringent standards be applied in the emissions element of the annual MOT test, and that this element become obligatory for all cars a year after registration' (instead of 3 years as at present). This recognises the fact that there is a tendency for pollution emissions to increase with age of vehicle, for any given distance travelled.

As the Royal Commission concludes:

> Government must use an appropriate combination of direct regulation and economic instruments to force the pace of technological development and foster markets for new products. In the case of noise levels and the emission of pollutants, direct regulation in the form of EU legislation should continue to be the primary method used to reduce the environmental impact of vehicles. Direct regulation should extend beyond compliance with limits for new vehicles to include much more effective enforcement of environmental standards applying to the existing fleet. (Royal Commission, 1994: 144)

Implementation of policy types

The World Bank (1992) has concluded that 'regulatory policies, which are used extensively in both industrial and developing countries, are best suited to situations that involve a few public enterprises and non-competitive private funds.' It also concludes that economic incentives, such as charges, will often be less costly than regulatory alternatives (see Table 12.9). For instance, to achieve the *least-cost* or *efficient* solution of point B in Fig. 12.16 above (p. 498) is estimated as costing some 22 times more in the USA if particulate matter is abated by regulations, rather than by using market-based instruments. Similarly, achieving this least-cost solution by regulating sulphur dioxide emissions in the UK is estimated as costing between 1.4 and 2.5 times as much using regulations as compared to using market-based instruments.

Table 12.9
Simulation studies of alternative policies for controlling air pollution.

Pollutant	Geographic area	Ratio of costs of regulatory policies to those of least-cost policy (%)
Sulphates	Los Angeles, Calif.	110
Nitrogen dioxide	Baltimore, Md.	600
Particulate matter	Baltimore, Md.	420
Sulphur dioxide	Lower Delaware Valley	180
Particulate matter	USA	2,200
Hydrocarbons	All US Dupont plants	420
Sulphur dioxide	Five regions of the USA	190
Sulphur dioxide	United Kingdom	140–250

Source: Adapted from World Bank (1992)

However, regulatory policies are particularly appropriate when it is important not to exceed certain thresholds, e.g. emissions of radioactive and toxic wastes. In these cases it is clearly of greater concern that substantial environmental damage be avoided than that pollution control be implemented by policies that might prove to be more expensive than expected. However, where the social costs of environmental damage do *not* increase dramatically if standards are breached by small margins, then it is worthwhile seeking the least-cost policy via market incentives rather than spending excessive amounts on regulation to avoid any breach at all.

With market-based policies, all resource users or polluters face the same price and must respond accordingly. Each *user* decides on the basis of their own utility/profit preferences whether to use fewer environmental resources or to pay extra for using more. On the other hand, with regulations it is the regulators who take such decisions on the behalf of the users: e.g. *all* users might be given the same limited access to a scarce environmental resource. Regulators are, of course, unlikely to be well informed about the relative costs and benefits faced by users or the valuations placed on these by such users.

Market-based policies have another advantage, namely that they price environmental damage in a way that affects all *polluters*, providing uniform 'prices' to which all polluters can respond (see Fig. 12.16), thereby yielding 'efficient' or 'least cost' solutions. By contrast, regulations usually affect only those who fail to comply and who therefore face penalties. Further, regulations that set minimising standards give polluters no incentives to do better than that minimum.

Our review of environmental concerns and possible remedial policies has, of necessity, been selective. We have considered the competing claims of market- and non-market-based incentives towards achieving socially efficient solutions. Market-based incentives often help to avoid the necessity of external bodies seeking to evaluate marginal abatement cost and marginal damage cost curves. This is certainly an advantage in an area where such valuations are notoriously difficult. Nevertheless there are situations where regulations, or a judicious mix of markets and regulations, may be the most appropriate way forward. In any case all the interdependencies of any proposed solution must be fully taken into account before any final decisions are made.

Key terms		
	Adverse selection	Negative externality
	Carbon tax	Non-exclusivity
	Coase theorem	Non-rivalry
	Common property resources	Pigouvian tax
	Externalities	Property rights
	Information asymmetry	Public good
	Intertemporal budget line	Pure public goods
	Marginal abatement costs	Social marginal rate of time
	Merit goods	preference
	Moral hazard	Tradeable permits

Full definitions can be found in the 'Glossary of terms' (pp. 699–710)

Review questions

1. A competitive industry is composed of many small companies producing lead for car batteries. The industry's demand function is $Q_D = 180 - 2P$ and the supply function is $Q_S = 4P - 80$, where P is price per tonne and Q is output in 000s. Answer the following questions by using both algebraic and diagrammatic approaches at each stage, or whenever appropriate.

   (a) Derive the demand and supply curves for the lead industry.
   (b) Calculate the equilibrium price and quantity for the industry.
   (c) If the production of lead creates pollution costs of £0.75 per tonne, write down the equation for the supply curve including the social costs of production.
   (d) Calculate the socially optimum equilibrium price and quantity.
   (e) Locate, with the aid of the diagram, the area of welfare loss as a result of pollution costs and calculate the value of the loss.
   (f) What tax should the government need to impose on the lead industry in order to get the industry to produce the socially optimum quantity of the product? What would be the price obtained by lead producers at this level of output?
   (g) How does government behaviour described in (f) seem compatible with the Pigouvian 'Golden Rule'?

2. A local authority has made an attempt to quantify the social benefits and the social costs of estuary pollution in its area in an attempt to calculate the optimum acceptable level of pollution. The relevant functions have been graphed in Fig. 12.18. *MSB* refers to the marginal social benefits of waste dumping and *MSC* is the marginal social costs of waste dumping.

   Using Fig. 12.18 and giving monetary values to the answers where possible:

   (a) Explain clearly the *economic* meaning of the *MSB* and *MSC* functions. What would be the shape of the *MSC* curve if a certain amount of waste could be dumped without any harmful effect?
   (b) If the environment could absorb all the waste dumped without apparent social cost, what area would represent the resources saved, i.e. the total social benefits?

Fig. 12.18

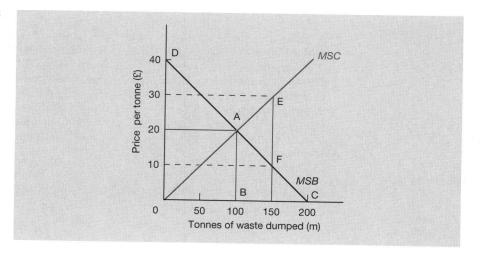

(c) What is the level of optimum pollution? Why is the level of 150 million tonnes of waste dumped not an optimal situation?

(d) Explain what areas 0DA and 0AB on Fig. 12.18 represent. Use them to explain why those who insist on zero pollution (i.e. no waste dumping) may not have understood the economic arguments underlying the debate.

3. There are two consumers of a good X. The marginal private benefit that consumer A derives from the consumption of X (MPB_{AX}) is $25 - \frac{5}{6}Q$ and the marginal private benefit that consumer B derives from the consumption of X (MPB_{BX}) is $30 - \frac{5}{10}Q$. The marginal social cost (MSC) is assumed to be $5 + \frac{5}{4}Q$ where Q is the quantity produced. With the aid of graph paper and measuring quantity on the horizontal axis and private and social benefits in pounds on the vertical axis:

(a) Draw the functions on one diagram.

(b) Draw two marginal social benefit (MSB) lines (i.e. the sum here of the two marginal private benefit curves) on the assumption that:
(i) good X is a pure private good;
(ii) good X is a pure public good.

(c) What would be the approximate value of the price and output if the good was (i) private and (ii) public?

(d) Indicate which areas of the diagram illustrate the *net* social benefit for (i) a private good and (ii) a public good.

(e) How could you check the values you have calculated in (c) by the use of algebra? What are your more accurate algebraic answers?

4. There are two firms, Glasco plc and Dram Ltd, who are located within a few miles of each other. Glasco plc is a local coal-processing plant and Dram Ltd is an existing electronics company producing microchips. There is a problem in that the processing of coal causes air pollution, which is of great detriment to the production of microchips. The marginal private cost (MPC) function of processing coal per week to Glasco is $MPC = 10 + 0.5Q$ and the marginal social cost function MSC (which includes the externality cost to Dram Ltd) is $MSC = 15 + 0.75Q$. Here Q is the tonnes of coal processed per week in '000s and MPC and MSC are measured in £ per tonne. If Glasco is a price taker at a price of £30 per tonne of coal, answer the following questions with the use of graph paper.

(a) What would be the competitive and socially optimal level of coal processing given the above information?

(b) If the government became alarmed at the problems caused to the microchip company, what level of tax would be needed to reduce the *net* price of coal processing to the level that is socially optimal?

(c) If, on the other hand, Glasco plc has property rights to use the air as it wishes, how could it produce the socially optimum level and still benefit? In your explanation show, on the diagram, the area of lost profits to Glasco plc from producing the socially optimum instead of the private optimum. Compare this with the maximum amount that Dram Ltd would have to pay to discourage Glasco from increasing its coal processing from the social to the private optimum level of coal processing. How is this analysis related to the Coase theorem?

5. An insurance company, Medidoc plc, specialises in medical insurance and has issued a million policies to the public. The company has grouped its policyholders into two main categories – those who smoke and those who do not smoke – and has assigned the probabilities of their becoming ill as being 0.9 and 0.1 respectively.

   (a) What is Medidoc's weighted average probability of illness if half the policyholders smoke and the other half do not?

   (b) If the cost of each illness to Medidoc plc is £1,000, what insurance premium should be charged to at least cover all cost? If the company does not divulge the above market information to its policyholders (i.e. there is information asymmetry between the company and policyholders), what would happen in the short run?

   (c) If the information from (a) is leaked to the press, what would you predict would result, and why? In the longer run, how should Medidoc plc try to overcome the problems created by the leak?

   (d) How can Medidoc plc try to cope with the concept of 'moral hazard' in the medical insurance business?

■ Further reading

Intermediate texts

Baumol, W. J. (1977), *Economic Theory and Operations Analysis*, 4th edn, Ch. 21, Prentice Hall, Hemel Hempstead.

Browning, E. and Browning, J. (1992), *Microeconomic Theory and Applications*, 4th edn, Ch. 20, HarperCollins, London.

Dobson, S., Maddala, G. S. and Miller, E. (1995), *Microeconomics*, Ch. 16, McGraw-Hill, Maidenhead.

Hope, S. (1999), *Applied Microeconomics*, Ch. 17, Wiley, Chichester.

Katz, M. and Rosen, H. (1998), *Microeconomics*, 3rd edn, Chs 16 and 17, Irwin, Boston, Mass.

Koutsoyiannis, A. (1979), *Modern Microeconomics*, 2nd edn, Ch. 23, Macmillan, Basingstoke.

Laidler, D. and Estrin, S. (1995), *Introduction to Microeconomics*, 4th edn, Chs 31 and 32, Harvester Wheatsheaf, Hemel Hempstead.

Maddala, G. S. and Miller, E. (1989), *Microeconomics: Theory and Application*, Chs 19 and 20, McGraw-Hill, New York.

Nicholson, W. (1997), *Intermediate Microeconomics and its Application*, 7th edn, Chs 22 and 23, Dryden Press, Fort Worth.

Pindyck, R. and Rubinfeld, D. (1998), *Microeconomics*, 4th edn, Chs 17 and 18, Macmillan, Basingstoke.

Varian, H. (1999), *Intermediate Microeconomics*, 5th edn, Chs 13 and 32–34, Norton, New York.

Advanced texts

Gravelle, H. and Rees, R. (1992), *Microeconomics*, 2nd edn, Chs 18 and 22, Longman, Harlow.

Mas-Colell, A., Whinston, M. D. and Green, J. R. (1995), *Microeconomic Theory*, Chs 11, 13 and 15–22, Oxford University Press, Oxford.

Akerlof, G. (1970), 'The Market for Lemons: Qualitative Uncertainty and the Market Mechanism', *Quarterly Journal of Economics*, 84.

Coase, R. (1960), 'The Problem of Social Cost', *Journal of Law and Economics*, III October.

Articles and other sources

Dobes, L. (1999), 'Kyoto: tradeable greenhouse emission permits in the transport sector', *Transport Review*, 19, 1.

European Economy 'The climate challenge, economic aspects of the Community's strategy for limiting CO_2 emissions', 51, May 1992.

House of Commons (1994), *Transport-Related Air Pollution in London*, 1, Report, Minutes of Proceedings and Appendices.

Ingham, A. and Ulph, A. (1991), 'Economics of global warming', *The Economic Review*, 9, 2.

Nordhaus, W. (1991), 'To slow or not to slow: the economics of the greenhouse effect', *Economic Journal*, 101.

O'Doherty, R. (1994), 'Pricing environmental disasters', *Economic Review*, 12, 1.

OECD (1998), 'The economics of climate change', *Economic Outlook*, 63, June.

OECD (1999), 'Policy challenges arising from climate change', *Economic Outlook*, 65, June.

Pearce, D. (1991), 'Economics and the environment', *Economics*, XXVII, (Pt. 1), 113.

Rajah, N. (1992), 'The European carbon tax – a solution to global warming?', *The Economic Review*, 10, 1.

Royal Commission on Environmental Pollution (1994), *Transport and the Environment*, Eighteenth Report.

Royal Commision on Environmental Pollution (1997), *Transport and the Environment*, Twentieth Report.

Shmalensee, R. *et al.* (1998), 'An interim evaluation of sulphur dioxide emissions trading', *Journal of Economic Perspectives*, 12, 3.

Spence, M. (1973), *Market Signalling: Information Transfer in Hiring and Related Economic Processes*, Harvard University Press, Harvard.

Turner, R. K. (1991), 'Environmental economics', *Developments in Economics: An Annual Review*, 7.

Turner, R. K. *et al.* (1994), *Environmental Economics*, Harvester Wheatsheaf, Hemel Hempstead.

Turner, R. K. *et al.* (1998), 'Green taxes, waste management and political economy', *Journal of Enviromental Management*, 53, 2.

Willis, K. (1991), 'The priceless countryside: the recreational benefits of environmental goods', *The Royal Bank of Scotland Review*, 172, December.

World Bank (1992), 'Development and the environment', *World Development Report*.

Chapter 13

Regulation, deregulation and public policy

Introduction and review

We have already touched on some of the issues relevant to regulation and deregulation in previous chapters. For example in Chapter 6 (pp. 254–7) we considered the efficiency of a competitive market as compared with specified types of intervention by government, including regulations as to maximum or minimum prices, etc. Again in Chapter 7 we examined the impacts of various types of market power (such as monopoly) on the competitive market, and the impacts of attempts to regulate such monopoly power *directly* (p. 295) or influence it *indirectly* via contestable markets (p. 263). We also considered aspects of regulation in the context of a 'natural monopoly' (p. 296). Attempts to regulate oligopolistic industries were touched upon in Chapters 8 and 9, and the 'general equilibrium' case for competitive markets was the focus of Chapter 10. In this chapter we take these earlier analyses further and look in some detail at the key policy issues of *privatisation*, the roles of regulators and the emergence of *internal* or *quasi-markets*.

Remember that the context of much of our discussion is that of a second-best economy (p. 442), in which more than one type of market failure exists. As a result simple first-best policy prescription (e.g. marginal cost pricing) can no longer be regarded as necessarily appropriate to raising economic or social efficiency. We must then consider each case on its merits, and seek pragmatic rather than ideological solutions to firm and industry problems and circumstances.

Attempts to **deregulate** an industry have often involved the notion of **privatisation** where the previous form of regulation has involved an element of state ownership and control. It may be useful at the outset of this chapter to review some of the arguments commonly advanced both for and against privatisation.

Initially much of the discussion is in the context of the UK, though issues of privatisation, deregulation and quasi-markets are equally applicable elsewhere. Later in the chapter (p. 534) we specifically consider empirical materials with an international focus.

The case for privatisation

The suggestion here is that privatisation exposes industries to market forces that would benefit consumers by giving them choice, and also lower prices as a result of efficiency gains within the privatised companies. This increased exposure to market forces could, it is often argued, bring benefits in terms of product, factor and capital markets (Wall 1999).

Market forces **Product market** The breaking of a state monopoly (e.g. as regards UK telecommunications, Cable & Wireless competing with BT) would, in this view, enable consumers to choose whichever company produced the product (good or service) they preferred. That company would then generate more profit and expand in response to consumer demand, while competitive pressure would be put on the company losing business to improve its service or go into liquidation. BT's progressive reductions in telephone charges have clearly been at least partly in response to competition. The pressure to meet such external competitive requirements should also improve internal efficiency (X-efficiency) as changes can be justified to workers and managers by the need to respond to the market. The old public corporations in the UK had increasingly been seen as producer led, serving the interests of management and workers rather than those of consumers and shareholders (in this case taxpayers). Privatisation arguably introduces market forces, which help to stimulate a change of organisational culture.

Factor markets Trade unions can be expected to discover that previous customs and work practices agreed when in the public sector are now challenged by privatisation as the stance taken by management changes from when it was in the state sector, in an attempt to raise corporate efficiency. Similarly competition in the product market will, in this view, force moderation in wage demands and increased attention to manning levels, again raising efficiency. Privatisation contributes in these various ways to the creation of flexibility in labour markets, higher productivity and reduced unit labour costs.

Capital markets The privatised company now has to rely on capital markets for the raising of finance. Poor performance in meeting consumer preferences or in utilising assets may now result in a share price that underperforms the rest of the stock market and undervalues the company's assets, ultimately leaving it vulnerable to takeover by a company able to make better use of the assets. Supporters of privatisation argue that in these ways the capital markets are likely to be better judges for allocating scarce investment finance to 'efficient' companies than public officials in state owned corporations.

Wider share ownership By 1998, share ownership in the UK had spread to 22% of the adult population, having been only 7% as recently as 1981. The total number of UK shareholders is about the same as the number of trade unionists. This increase in shareholding is, it is argued, due largely to privatisation. New groups of shareholders have been attracted and have become participants in the 'enterprise culture'. Additionally 90% of the employees in the privatised companies have become shareholders in the companies they work for, at least initially. Worker share-ownership is advocated as a means of involving workers more closely with their companies and achieving improved industrial relations. This has been taken further by selling companies to their managers or to consortiums of managers and workers.

Funding the Exchequer

In the UK, privatisation has been seen as a way of cutting the public sector borrowing requirement (PSBR). Privatisation has also been seen as a way in which the PSBR can be cut, at a stroke! The finance of external borrowing by the nationalised industries is regarded in accounting terms as being part of public expenditure, which then ceases when these industries become privately owned. Sales of assets or shares also increases government revenue, again reducing the PSBR in the year of the sale. Over the period 1979–99 the UK Treasury gained £70 billion from asset sales. Privatisation made a very significant contribution to the budget surpluses of the late 1980s and to curbing the size of the budget deficits of the 1990s. Privatisation proceeds reduced the PSBR as a proportion of GDP by more than 1.5% during the 1980s and by a still significant, if smaller, percentage in subsequent years.

Access to new sources of finance

The activities of state-owned organisations are constrained by their relationship with the government. They often lack financial freedom to raise investment capital externally because the government is concerned about restraining the growth of public expenditure, since expenditure based on such borrowing would be counted in the public expenditure total. Privatisation is then seen as increasing the prospects for raising investment capital, thereby increasing efficiency and lowering prices.

Indeed government control of investment expenditure by public corporations in the UK involves not only setting investment limits, but also the need for official approval for specific capital projects of more than £20 million. Supporters of privatisation argue that civil servants are not the best people to participate in essentially commercial decisions, and that the process is unwieldy and time consuming for top managers.

Removal of the financial controls on nationalised industries is *not* seen here as a satisfactory alternative to privatisation, largely because the nationalised industries would then gain an unfair advantage against private sector competitors in that losses would ultimately be underwritten by the tax payer. The Green Paper *The Future of the Postal Service* (HMSO 1994c) claimed that the removal of financial controls would create 'risk free' businesses, which would compete unfairly against private sector companies for funds in the capital market. Furthermore, the nationalised industries would also compete with other public sector services, such as health and education, for a share of public expenditure. On these grounds the Green Paper favoured instead of financial liberalisation, selling 51% of Royal Mail and Parcel Force to effectively remove them from the public sector, while retaining a close link between government and the Royal Mail consistent with the 'important role the Royal Mail plays in our life'. In 1999 the UK government announced plans for the Post Office that were very similar to these earlier proposals.

A further limitation on nationalised industries is the political near-impossibility of diversification. In many cases this would be the sensible corporate response to poor market prospects, but it is not an option likely to be open to a nationalised concern. Since privatisation, however, companies have been able to freely exploit market opportunities. So, for example, most of the regional electricity companies have become suppliers of gas as well as electricity.

The 'globalisation' of economic activity also, in this view, leaves nationalised industries at a distinct disadvantage. For example, no private oil company would follow the nationalised British Coal in confining its activities to one country where it happened to have reserves. This international perspective is an important reason why the Post Office management have seen privatisation as 'the only (option) which offers us the freedom to fight off foreign competition'. In the postal services, increased competition is expected from the Dutch Post Office, which has been privatised, and from further liberalisation of other national postal services expected within the European single market. The difficulties of an international strategy for nationalised industries are shown by the failure of the attempted Renault–Volvo merger in 1993. The then nationalised status of Renault contributed substantially to Swedish (Volvo) shareholder opposition to the merger.

Privatisation, then, is seen by its supporters as a means of greatly improving economic performance.

The case against privatisation

Privatisation may be opposed for a number of reasons. Both the rationale of the policy and its manner of implementation have been criticised.

Absence of competition

Privatisation is essentially about a change of *ownership and control*, from state to private individuals and companies respectively. As we note on p. 519 such a change of ownership does not necessarily equate with a change in the degree of competitive exposure. It may merely represent, in the extreme case, a change from state monopoly to private monopoly.

Externality considerations

As we have seen (p. 469), externalities occur when economic decisions create costs or benefits for people other than the decision taker: these are called external costs or external benefits. In other words, society is forced to bear part of the cost of private industrial activity. Sometimes those who impose external costs in this way can be controlled by legislation (pollution controls, Clean Air Acts), or penalised through taxation. The parties affected might be compensated, using the revenue raised from taxing those firms creating external costs. On the other hand, firms creating external benefits may be rewarded by the receipt of subsidies. In other cases public ownership is a possible solution. If the industry is run in the public interest, it might be expected that *full account* will be taken of any externalities. For instance, it can be argued that railways reduce road usage, creating social benefits by relieving urban congestion, pollution and traffic accidents. This was one aspect of the case for subsidising the then British Rail through the passenger service obligation grant. The grant enabled British Rail to continue operating some loss-making services. Public ownership is one means of exercising public control over the use of subsidies when these are thought to be in the public interest.

Public interest consideration

Related to the considerations already discussed, there are many situations where commercial criteria, with their focus on profitability, may be at odds with a broader view of the *public interest*, and in such cases public ownership is one solution. For instance, the Post Office aims to make a profit overall, but in doing so makes losses on rural services, which are subsidised by profits made elsewhere — a *cross-subsidy* from one group of consumers to another. Some object to cross-subsidisation in that it interferes with the price mechanism in its role of resource allocation when some consumers pay less than the true cost of the services they buy, while others pay more than the true cost. However, in the case of the Post Office cross-subsidisation seems reasonable, if only because we may all want to send letters to outlying areas from time to time, and all derive benefit from the existence of a full national postal service. A private sector profit-oriented firm might not be prepared to undertake the loss-making Post Office services.

In the electricity industry the UK government, controversially, decided in 1990 that the continued generation of electricity by nuclear power was in the public interest, and established Nuclear Electric as a public corporation while privatising the rest of the industry. In taking this decision it rejected the verdict of the markets, which, all over the world, have baulked at both the safety risks and the full financial costs of the nuclear industry. The government's view was that nuclear power offers strategic advantages as an alternative to fossil fuels and also environmental benefits in that it does not contribute to the greenhouse effect. The safety risks are said to be acceptable. Chernobyl, it is argued, could not happen in the UK.

State ownership may also be a means of promoting the public interest when entire businesses are about to collapse. The state has sometimes intervened to prevent liquidation, as in 1970 when the Conservative government decided to rescue Rolls-Royce rather than see the company liquidated. Prestige, strategic considerations, effects on employment and on the balance of payments, all played a part in the argument as the judgement of the market was rejected in favour of a broader view of the public interest. In the long run the markets were proved wrong and the decision to intervene commercially correct, as the company is now a world leader in aero-engine technology and has been successfully returned to the private sector.

Natural monopoly argument

The *natural monopoly* argument is often advanced in favour of public ownership of certain industries. Economies of scale in railways, water, electricity and gas industries are perhaps so great that the tendency towards monopoly can be termed 'natural'. Competing provision of these services, with duplication of investment, would clearly be wasteful of resources. The theory of the firm suggests that monopolies may enjoy supernormal profits, charging higher prices and producing lower output than would a competitive industry with the same cost conditions. However, where there are sufficient economies of scale, the monopoly price could be lower and output higher than under competition (see Chapter 7, Fig. 7.4). Monopoly might then be the preferred market form, especially if it can be regulated. Public ownership is one means of achieving such regulation. We consider others on p. 522.

In the next section we consider in more detail the theoretical underpinnings for some of the views outlined above. We also look at issues of *deregulation*, such that the newly privatised firm is forced to compete on roughly equal terms with other firms. We use the term 'deregulation' to refer to situations in which conscious decisions are taken to link any change in ownership (e.g. privatisation) with changes in the degree of competition.

Theoretical developments

As Jackson and Price (1994) point out, the activities involved in *privatisation* can include any combination of the following:

- the sale of public assets;
- deregulation;
- opening up of state monopolies to greater competition;
- contracting out;
- private provision of public services;
- joint capital projects using public and private finance;
- reducing public subsidies and introducing or increasing user charges.

This is clearly a diverse set of activities, each of which can merit detailed examination in its own right. The general benefits and costs of engaging in a broad subset of these activities have been considered in the previous section. In this section we focus on a number of *discrete* activities, which may either be involved in the privatisation process itself or be introduced as a consequence of that process:

- economic regulation of privatised monopolies;
- regulation versus deregulation;
- establishment of quasi- or internal markets.

In this section our main concern will be with the theoretical underpinnings of these activities. The next section will consider empirical aspects of the implementation of these activities.

Economic regulation of privatised monopolies

The transformation of public sector monopolies into private monopolies has been an important feature of the privatisation process in many countries. We noted in Chapter 7 (p. 286) that a profit-maximising monopoly need not be detrimental to the public interest. Indeed the existence of sizeable scale economies, together with adequate incentives (contestability!) to exploit them, could lead the monopoly to exhibit lower prices and higher output than a competitive industry. Nevertheless the presence of 'market power' may be exploited by a private monopolist in ways previously avoided when the monopoly was under public sector control. Similarly any negative externalities may be less readily acknowledged or addressed by the private monopolist than by its public sector predecessor. It is for such reasons that economic regulation may be introduced subsequent to the creation of privatised monopolies in order to counteract any potential abuse of market power or undesirable negative externality situations.

Objectives of regulators

Regulators have two fundamental objectives. First, they attempt to create the constraints and stimuli that companies would experience in a competitive market environment. For example, companies in competitive markets must bear in mind what their competitors are doing when setting their prices, and are under competitive pressure to improve their service to consumers in order to gain market share. Regulation can stimulate the effects of a competitive market by setting price caps (see p. 522) and performance standards. Second, regulators have the longer-term objective of encouraging actual competition by easing the entry of new producers and by preventing privatised monopoly power from maintaining barriers to entry. An ideal is the creation of markets sufficiently competitive to make regulation unnecessary. The market for gas has moved substantially in this direction. British Gas, when first privatised, had an apparent classic natural monopoly in the supply of gas to industry, but by the end of 1998 the British Gas market share was below 30% for industrial users, and since 1998 the company has faced nationwide competition in the supply of gas to domestic consumers. Similarly, the Regulator has insisted on the introduction of competition into the supply of electricity to domestic consumers since 1998.

Problems facing regulators Regulators have an unenviable role as they try to create the constraints and stimuli of a competitive market. Essentially they are arbitrating between the interests of consumers and those of producers. Other things being equal, attempts by regulators to achieve improvements in service levels will cause increases in costs and so lower profits, while price caps on services with inelastic demand will also reduce profits by preventing the regulated industries from raising prices and therefore revenue. Lower profits, and the expectation of lower profits, have immediate implications for dividend distributions to shareholders and so for share prices. At this point other things are unlikely to remain equal. The privatised company subject to a price cap may well look for ways of lowering costs to allow profits to be at least maintained, or perhaps raised. In most organisations there are economies to be gained by reducing staffing levels, and the utility companies have dramatically reduced their numbers of employees. Investment in new technology may also enable unit costs to be lowered so that profits are greater than they otherwise would have been.

In the UK, four previously public monopolies have been privatised since 1984, and subsequently regulated to curb the potential exploitation of market power. These include the telecommunications, gas, water and electricity industries. A common characteristic of such utilities is that they involve delivery of services through fixed networks (wires, pipes, etc.) to consumers. Clearly substantial *scale economies* are present here, and arguably elements of natural monopoly (see Chapter 7, p. 286) whereby costs can only be minimised by the avoidance of duplication. This argument in favour of a degree of monopoly being 'desirable' is reinforced if *economies of scope* (Chapter 4, p. 179) are also taken into account, whereby the cost of producing a *variety* of products by a large, integrated firm is arguably lower than the cost of making each product separately. Substantial sectors of the four industries (utilities) identified could be regarded as *natural monopolies* from this standpoint, though of course other sectors of these industries could arguably benefit from competitive pressures.

As we note later, the role of the regulator is inevitably complicated by the need to regulate natural monopoly sectors of such industries yet also ensure competitive practices in other sectors. The latter may involve securing access to the network for new entrants in situations where the incumbent monopolist owns that network and may seek to curb the emergence of competitors.

Given the complexity of regulation in such circumstances no single model can hope to capture all the relevant parameters. However, Fig. 13.1 overleaf is useful in highlighting some of the key features of regulation. Train (1991) suggests the following guiding principle for the regulator faced with the situation of Fig. 13.1: 'Effective regulation establishes a situation in which the outcome that is socially optimal also generates most profit for the firm, such that the firm chooses it voluntarily.'

In other words, Train is advocating that the regulator creates incentives/penalties such that the (assumed) profit-maximising private monopolist, of its own volition, seeks out the socially optimum solution. Following Price (1994), we can use Fig. 13.1 to illustrate the targets the regulator might seek if guided by the following objectives:

1. enabling the industry to capture economies of scale through monopoly production;
2. preventing abuse (high price and restricted output) of the consequent monopoly power;
3. encouraging productive efficiency (low operating costs);
4. minimising the regulatory costs of supervision.

In Fig. 13.1, for diagrammatic simplicity constant returns to scale are assumed. This assumption implies no loss of generality in the subsequent discussions, even though we are concerned here with increasing returns via natural monopoly elements. C_{obs} represents the observed costs; C_{min} represents the minimum achievable costs.

Price P_{po} and output q_{po} are the 'targets' that would seem most nearly to correspond to the four objectives we established for the regulator. Let us now seek to explain why these might be the *productive optimum* price and output targets for the regulator.

Without regulation, the (profit maximising) monopolist can be expected currently to set price and output at P_m/q_m. However, the regulator might be seeking to maximise industry 'welfare', seen as the weighted sum of consumer surplus and profit. If we apply an equal weight to each of these, then only *marginal cost pricing* can maximise such welfare. With the regulator observing costs C_{obs}, the implied target might then be P_{ae}/q_{ae}. The outcome could be regarded as an allocatively efficient outcome, in terms of maximising welfare (as we have defined it) given the level of costs currently observed.

Fig. 13.1 Identifying the price/output target that the regulator might seek to achieve.

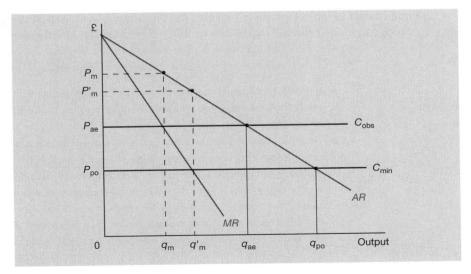

However, provided the regulator is aware that the industry can potentially achieve lower costs than those observed ($C_{min} < C_{obs}$), then the price/output target that would be both productively and allocatively efficient is P_{po}/q_{po} as previously indicated. *Without* regulation, the (profit maximising) private monopolist might be expected to set price and output P'_m/q'_m even if C_{min} had been achieved.

[Note that if the *weights* for consumer surplus and profits in the regulator's objective function for welfare were *not* equal, then different welfare-maximising outcomes would be required. Generally, the greater the weight given to consumer surplus in the regulator's objective function for welfare, the lower the price target relative to that currently specified, and vice versa.]

Methods of regulation

In seeking to achieve an appropriate outcome, the regulator may adopt one of a number of approaches or methods.

Rate of return regulation

Here the regulator restricts the company's rate of profit to some prescribed *proportion* of its capital investment. The so-called Averch–Johnson effect has been widely observed with this method, whereby companies apply 'excessive' amounts of capital in the productive process in order to secure higher *absolute* levels of profit. Another disadvantage of this method involves the regulator being drawn into having to decide which specific costs can be deducted (allowable and non-allowable capital expenditures) prior to calculating profit.

In terms of the four regulatory objectives outlined on p. 521, *rate of return regulation* arguably fails to meet 1, 3 and 4 respectively. In other words, over-capitalisation may take firms beyond the optimum scale of production, raise operating costs above the minimum achievable, and involve considerable regulatory costs of supervision.

Price control regulation

Some of the above problems can be avoided by this method of regulation. The regulated firm that faces some form of price cap or ceiling will have the incentive to cut costs in order to raise profits. It can therefore be expected to seek the *least-cost* combination of inputs.

However, a number of regulatory concerns may exist as regards the price cap policy:

- In order to minimise costs as the primary means to higher profit the *quality* of output might be compromised, which, should a lack of alternative suppliers exist, may impact adversely on consumers.
- Periodic price cap reviews may induce a non-optimal input combination in the current period. This is particularly likely where the industry believes that the regulator will vary the cap according to firm performance in the previous period. In practice regulators may have few, if any, price comparators available and therefore rely on some rate of return criterion with which to assess the appropriateness of the cap in the previous period. Firms will then adapt their behaviour accordingly. If they believe that the disclosure of excessive rates of return will lower the price cap in the next

period to the benefit of consumers rather than themselves, they may seek to depress the measured rate of return in the current period. This may again result in overuse of capital in the current period and a resulting inefficient input combination.

- The sector coverage of the price cap must be carefully selected. Price (1994) argues that it should be restricted to sectors where both competition and its prospects are absent. If the price cap is more generally applied as some weighted average over prices from *all* sectors of firm operation, then distortions might readily occur. For example, a firm with a monopoly in one sector of operation but facing competition in another sector may seek to stay within the *overall* price cap by *predatory pricing* (below cost) in the competitive sector and *exploitation pricing* in the monopolistic sector. Prices (and outputs) would diverge from the 'efficient' levels in each sector, resulting in an *inappropriate product mix*.

- The availability of *cost pass through* exemptions may create distortions in a price cap regime. It has been widely recognised in the UK that some costs are beyond the industry's control and cannot reasonably be reduced or absorbed. For example, British Airways may pass on 85% of costs incurred by government imposed safety regulations. Many such input costs can be passed through to consumers in whole or in part. However, the consequences may be to diminish the attention paid by producers to keep such costs to the minimum. As a result of such exemptions prices may be allowed to rise above the welfare-maximising P_{po} (and output fall below q_{po}) in Fig. 13.1 (p. 521).

Price regulation in the UK

Table 13.1 outlines the method of price capping used in the UK for the four privatised utilities previously discussed, each of which has its own regulatory body. Those parts of each industry that are regulated and those parts that are unregulated are indicated in the table.

We can see that the price-setting/capping formula adopted involves restricting the percentage increase in prices to that experienced for the retail price index (RPI) as a whole, plus or minus certain other specified percentages:

- X: the negative 'X factor' reflects the regulator's view as to reductions in costs that can be anticipated via new technology and other productivity improvements. These are to be passed directly through to consumers by curbing price increases below general inflation.

- Y: the positive 'Y factor' reflects the *cost pass through* previously discussed. Increases in costs that the regulator deems to be beyond the control of producers (e.g. costs of gas supplies from oil producers to British Gas, costs of fuel to electricity generators, etc.) can be passed through to consumers. Unlike X, the value of Y is *not* specified in advance of the regulatory period, but can vary to reflect actual changes in costs.

- K: the positive 'K factor' applies specifically to the water companies. The regulator permits such companies to pass on to consumers a specified percentage rise in price to cover the anticipated costs of environmental improvements in water quality. Some of these improvements are 'imposed' on the industry by outside agencies, such as the Environmental Agency or the European Union.

Table 13.1
Regulations of UK privatised utilities.

Industry	Regulatory body	Parts regulated	Formula		Parts unregulated
Telecoms (British Telecom)	Office of Telecommunications (OFTEL)	Switched calls (national and international), line rentals	RPI – 3 RPI – $4\frac{1}{2}$ RPI – $6\frac{1}{4}$ RPI – $7\frac{1}{2}$ RPI – $4\frac{1}{2}$	(1984–89) (1989–91) (1991–93) (1993–98) (1997–2000)	Payphone calls, customer premises equipment, telex, mobile radio, leased lines, etc.
Gas (British Gas/TransCo, independent gas producers and suppliers)	Office of Gas Supply (OFGAS)	Gas supplied to domestic users (up to 1998); pipeline charges by TransCo to suppliers	RPI – 2 + Y RPI – 5 + Y *Pipeline charges* RPI – 5 RPI – $6\frac{1}{2}$	(1987–92) (1992–97) (1995–97) (1997–2001)	Price of gas supplied to industrial and commercial users to 1998; all supply from 1998, connection charges, appliance sales
Electricity (Generators: National Power, PowerGen, Nuclear Electric. Distributors: 12 regional companies. Grid: National Grid Company.)	Office of Electricity Regulation (OFFER)	Prices for transmission, distribution and supply > 1 megawatt per annum up to 1994 > 0.1 megawatt per annum from 1994	Distribution: RPI – 0 + Y to RPI – 17 + Y depending on company RPI – 3 + Y Supply: RPI – 0 + Y RPI – 2 + Y	 (1991–97) (1997–2000) (1991–94) (1994–98)	Generation business, overall prices to customers consuming > 1 megawatt per annum up to 1994 > 0.1 megawatt per annum from 1994, electrical contracting appliances, etc.
Water (29 water and sewerage companies)	Office of Water Services (OFWAT) (pricing) Environment Agency (environmental control)	Standard domestic and non-domestic supply	RPI + Y + K	(1989–2005)	Bulk supplies to other users. Water infrastructure charges (sewers, reservoirs, etc.)

■ Regulation and deregulation

Regulation may be defined as the various rules set by governments or their agencies that seek to control the operations of firms. We have already discussed the role of the regulators for the privatised industries who themselves are part of this broad regulatory process.

Regulation is one of the mechanisms available to governments when dealing with the problem of 'market failure'. Of course market failure can take many forms although, as Stewart (1997) points out, four broad categories can usefully be identified:

- *Asymmetric information*. Here the providers may have information not available to the purchasers. For example, in recent cases involving the mis-selling of pensions the companies involved were found to have withheld information from purchasers. Stricter regulation of the sector has been the government's response to this situation.
- *Externalities*. In the case of negative externalities, regulations may be used to bring private costs more closely into line with social costs (as with environmental taxes) or to restrict social costs to a given level (as with environmental standards).
- *Public goods*. Regulation may be required if such goods are to be provided at all. The idea of a public 'good' (which may, of course, be a service) is that it has the characteristics of being non-excludable and non-exhaustible, at least in the 'pure' case. Non-excludable refers to the difficulty of excluding those who do not wish to pay for the 'good' (e.g. police or defence); non-exhaustibility refers to the fact that the marginal cost of providing an extra unit of the 'good' is effectively zero (e.g. an extra person covered by the police or defence forces). The non-excludability condition prevents a private market from developing, since it is difficult to make 'free riders' actually pay for the public good. The non-exhaustibility condition implies that any price that is charged should, for allocative efficiency (see Chapter 12, p. 468), equal marginal cost and therefore be zero. Private markets guided by the profit motive are hardly in the business of charging zero prices! Both conditions imply that the 'good' is best supplied by the public sector at zero price, using general tax revenue to fund provision (in the 'pure' public good case).
- *Monopoly*. Regulation may be required to prevent the abuse of monopoly power. In Chapter 7 on 'monopoly' Fig. 7.9 (p. 294) was used to show that regulations involving the Monopolies and Mergers Commission may help to prevent or modify certain proposed mergers that are arguably against the public interest (e.g. where gains in 'productive efficiency' are more than offset by losses in 'allocative efficiency').

The forms of regulation are too innumerable to capture in a few headings. The various rules can involve the application of maximum or minimum prices, the imposition of various types of standards, taxes, quotas, procedures, directives, etc., whether issued by national bodies (e.g. UK government or its agencies) or by international bodies (e.g. EU Commission, World Trade Organisation).

Although a strict classification of the numerous types of regulation would seem improbable, McKenzie (1998) makes a useful distinction:

- regulation aimed at protecting the consumer from the consequences of market failure;
- regulations aimed at preventing the market failure from happening in the first place.

In terms of the financial sector, the Deposit Guarantee Directive of the EU is of the former type. This protects customers of accredited EU banks by restoring at least 90% of any losses up to £12,000 that might result from the failure of a particular bank. In part this is a response to asymmetric information, since customers do not have the information to evaluate the credit-worthiness of a particular bank, and might not be able to interpret that information even if it was available.

The **Capital Adequacy Directive** of the EU is of the latter type. This seeks to prevent market failure (such as bank collapse) by directly relating the value of the capital that a bank must hold to the riskiness of the business. The idea here is that the greater the value of capital available to a bank, the larger the buffer stock that it can use to absorb any losses. Various elements of the Capital Adequacy Directive force the banks to increase their capital base if the riskiness of their portfolio (indicated by various statistical measures) is deemed to have increased. In part this is in response to the potential for negative externalities in this sector. One bank failure can invariably lead to a 'domino effect' and risk system collapse with incalculable consequences for the sector as a whole.

In these ways the regulatory system for EU financial markets is seeking to provide a framework within which greater competition between banks can occur, while addressing the fact that greater competition can increase the risks of bank failure. It is seeking both to protect consumers should any mishap occur and to prevent such a mishap from actually occurring.

Overall we can say that those who support any or all of these forms of regulation, in whatever sector of the economy, usually do so in the belief that they improve the allocation of resources in situations characterised by one or more types of market failure.

Deregulation   The term **deregulation** has been broadly interpreted in economic literature, and is regarded by many as an elusive concept. Nevertheless the central issue clearly involves the question as to whether, and to what extent, government regulation should be replaced by market forces in guaranteeing 'appropriate' industry outcomes. In other words deregulation involves efforts to *remove* the various rules set by governments or their agencies that seek to control the operation of firms.

Weyman-Jones (1994) suggests that there are two broad theoretical platforms from which the deregulation issue can be analysed:

- *Public interest theory*. The prevailing view here is that regulation or deregulation can be analysed as to whether or not it raises net economic welfare in such a way that gainers can potentially compensate losers (see also Chapter 11, p. 447). Whether or not a particular regulatory framework should be retained or abandoned then depends on an evaluation of its net impact on 'economic welfare', however defined.
- *Public choice theory*. The suggestion here is that producers, consumers and regulators act as competing coalitions, seeking to achieve a regulatory framework most likely to secure the goals of that coalition. In other words, the respective coalitions devote resources to achieving a set of regulations most likely to maximise the economic rent of the members of that coalition.

We now consider each of these approaches in turn.

Public interest theory and deregulation

One of the major arguments in favour of deregulation involves 'public interest theory'. The suggestion here is that regulations should be removed whenever it can be shown that this will remove or reduce the 'deadweight loss' typically shown to result from various types of market interference (see also Chapter 6, pp. 254–7, and Chapter 7, pp. 310–15).

Figure 13.2 can be used to show how a particular market regulation, here a quota scheme, can result in a 'deadweight loss'. In this analysis economic welfare is defined as consumer surplus plus producer surplus. The consumer surplus is the amount that consumers are willing to pay over and above the amount they need to pay; the producer surplus is the amount that producers receive over and above the amount they need for them to supply the product.

In Fig. 13.2 we start with an initial demand curve DD and supply curve SS giving market equilibrium price P_1 and quantity Q_1. However, the regulation here is that should the market price fall below a particular level P_2, then the government is directed to intervene. It is required to use a quota arrangement to prevent market price from falling below P_2; in other words P_2 is a *minimum price* that is set by regulation at a level that is above the free market price P_1. In terms of Fig. 13.2 the quota is set at Q_2: then the effective supply curve becomes SvS^1, since no more than Q_2 can be supplied whatever the price. The result is to raise the 'equilibrium' price to P_2 and reduce the 'equilibrium' quantity to Q_2. However, the quota regulation has resulted in a *loss of economic welfare* equivalent to the area B plus area C. The reduction in output from Q_1 to Q_2 means a loss of area B in consumer surplus and loss of area C in producer surplus. However, the higher price results in a gain of area A in producer surplus that exactly offsets the loss of area A in consumer surplus. This means that the net welfare change is negative: i.e. there is a 'deadweight loss' of area B + area C.

Public interest theory is therefore suggesting that deregulation should occur whenever the net welfare change of *removing regulations* is deemed to be positive. In terms of Fig. 13.2 it might be argued that removing the regulation whereby the government (or its agent) seeks to keep price artificially high at P_2 will give a net welfare change that is positive, namely a net gain of area B + area C. In other words, allowing the free market equilibrium price P_1 and quantity Q_1 to prevail restores the previous deadweight loss via

Fig. 13.2 Welfare loss with a quota scheme $0Q_2$ raising price (P_2) above the market-clearing level P_1.

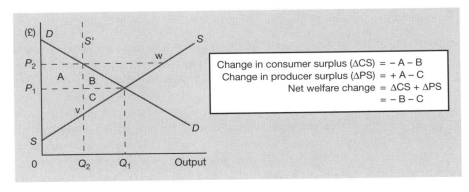

Change in consumer surplus (ΔCS) = $-A - B$
Change in producer surplus (ΔPS) = $+A - C$
Net welfare change = $\Delta CS + \Delta PS$
= $-B - C$

regulation. Put another way, public interest theory is suggesting that deregulation should occur whenever the outcome is a net welfare gain, so that those who gain can, at least potentially, more than compensate those who lose.

Of course a similar analysis can be carried out in the terms of other types of regulation incurring a deadweight loss *vis-à-vis* the free market equilibrium. In Chapter 6 we saw how the operation of price support schemes using central purchasing arrangements by the Common Agricultural Policy of the EU can incur deadweight loss, when intervention prices are set above the world market price for certain agricultural products.

However, such a 'broad brush' approach to public interest theory is rather simplistic, and a more detailed analysis would focus on the *type* of regulation currently in force and the potential gains/losses which might follow from its removal.

Three broad types of regulation are commonly identified:

- limitations involving market entry/exit;
- product specifications, particularly as regards quality;
- formulae for setting the prices of products.

We might usefully consider the form of market failure that each type of regulation seeks to redress.

Licensing arrangements

These are the most common form of limitation on entry to, or exit from, a market. The producer is delegated some form of legal authority to produce and sell a particular product. The official body responsible for issuing the **licence** may prohibit *new* suppliers from setting up in competition with the licensee and/or *existing* suppliers from entering some newly defined segment of the market. Often the licence will also specify certain obligations of the licensee, such as a minimum period before contemplating any exit from the market (or minimum quality provision, see later). The argument for regulation in the form of entry and exit licensing is that without a monopoly franchise, the firm will be unwilling to undertake the capital investment required to provide the product or service. The market failure that this form of regulation seeks to overcome is the risk of extensive investment of a fixed-cost variety failing to generate sufficient revenues to cover fixed and variable costs, including an 'adequate' return. As Weyman-Jones points out, in a first-best economy an insurance market of some form would permit risk-averse suppliers to 'trade' future risks with a risk-neutral population. In the absence of such a market, guaranteed monopoly franchises permit the risk-averse producer(s) to 'trade' with the licensing authority, which acts on behalf of a risk-neutral population.

Quality regulations

These forms of **quality regulation** often occur as part of a *minimum services/quality obligation* attached to the issue of a licence. For example, a specific air route may be awarded to a particular carrier on condition that a minimum number of flights are provided calling at prescribed destinations en route, and that these continue for a given period of time. Alternatively, the provision of certain types of appliance (e.g. electrical) must meet certain minimum safety requirements. The market failure that this form of regulation seeks to overcome often involves asymmetric information and the related problem of adverse selection (see p. 483). The suggestion here is that consumers are not fully aware (as producers are) of the quality of product available, whether service or good. There is a risk in such situations that suppliers will compromise on quality and, when more than one supplier is involved, that the quality will fall to the lowest common denominator. There may then only be limited, if indeed any, choices available to consumers in terms of variability of price and quality of output. The term *pooling equilibrium* is often used to refer to this common level of quality provision. The aim of quality of supply regulations is to ensure that all supplies reach an acceptable standard as regards this 'pooling equilibrium'.

Price regulation
We have already considered some of the possible **price regulations** involving maximum or minimum prices, or maximum rates of return. The market failure that this form of regulation seeks to overcome is the exploitation by incumbents of monopolistic or oligopolistic power. The consequence of such market failure is *allocative inefficiency*, via prices departing from marginal costs, and *X-inefficiency* via firms failing to achieve the minimum feasible costs give the absence of competitive constraints.

As we have noted, the public interest theory would see the continued use of such regulations as defensible if, and only if, they increase *net* economic welfare. Put another way, **deregulation** will be preferred if the alleged market failures that the regulations have sought to avoid do not in fact materialise on their abandonment, or are more than offset by gains elsewhere.

Public choice theory and deregulation

This approach to deregulation is quite different from the public interest theory previously considered. The suggestion here is that all parties to regulation are 'rent seekers' in that each is seeking a partial form of regulation that maximises its *own* objective function. This is seen as being the case for producers, consumers and even the regulators themselves, though of course the objective functions differ in each case.

Public choice theory is therefore suggesting that once regulations are established they will be difficult to remove. Indeed the 'rents' induced by regulations may already have been utilised by the parties involved and may in that sense be irrecoverable. For example, some of the rents will have been spent in securing the continuation of regulations deemed to be favourable. The benefits of *removing regulations* may therefore be less than is commonly supposed. As Weyman-Jones notes, deregulation is then most likely to occur in industries where maintaining the rent-inducing regulations requires continued expenditure on the part of incumbents.

Much of the theoretical underpinnings of public choice theory can be related to the work of the 'Chicago school', including contributions from Stigler (1971), Peltzman (1976) and Becker (1983). According to Peltzman (1989), the implications of the Chicago theory are that compact, well-organised groups (frequently but not always producers) will tend to benefit more from regulation than will broad, diffuse groups (frequently consumers). Regulatory policy will seek to preserve a politically optimal *distribution* of the rents resulting from regulation across these various coalitions, but it will be the well-organised groups that will have the greater visible and political impact, thereby receiving a disproportionately large share of that distribution. Peltzman goes on to argue that deregulation can be supported on the grounds that the losses to the well-organised group that benefited from and support regulation will tend to fall short of the gains to groups that support deregulation and are less formally organised within society.

Overall, these two broad theories of *public interest* and *public choice* tended to suggest that deregulation would enhance efficiency in one of two ways:

- Inefficient operations that developed because of regulations and because firms were insulated from actual and potential competitions would be curtailed.
- Rents that accrued to well-organised groups benefiting from regulation (generally producers and labour) would be dissipated by unregulated competition.

In the next section we consider some empirical work on the experience of deregulation, with the earlier deregulations in the USA proving a useful testbed for others contemplating the deregulatory process.

Contestability and deregulation

The notion of **contestability** (Chapter 6, p. 263) has been used by public interest theory advocates of deregulation. Creating contestable markets is seen here as an alternative mechanism to the present regulatory framework, and one that can generate still greater net economic welfare.

The suggestion here is that the *threat* of entry could, in the case of *perfect contestability* (see p. 263), result in monopolists (or oligopolists) setting prices equivalent to average costs and making only normal profits. This would even be the case for industries with increasing returns to scale, i.e. those possessing natural monopoly characteristics.

As we saw in Chapter 6, the essential characteristic of **contestable markets** is that there is free entry and exit from any production activity. For *free entry* to exist, a potential entrant must be faced with no cost disadvantage as compared with incumbents when providing the factors of production required to supply the product. Nor must there be any real, or perceived, differences in the quality of the entrant's product. *Free exit* implies costless exit from any production process that a firm might consider entering. Indeed this is a requirement for free entry: if a firm *cannot* costlessly exit from a production activity, then the firm is likely to regard such exit costs as being part of the costs of entry. This is connected to the problem of sunk costs (see p. 181) in the means of production. If sunk costs exist that cannot be recovered should a firm wish to leave an industry, then these costs become a barrier to (cost of) entry. Therefore, for a market to be perfectly contestable, any capital committed to the entry process must be capable of being resold or reused in other types of production.

As McDonald (1987) points out, it is this stress on free entry and exit that is at the heart of *contestable market theory*. Although this assumption is also necessary to obtain the *perfect competition* results, it is an implicit and rather subsidiary assumption. The key assumption in perfect competition is that of price-taking behaviour. What has been done in contestable market theory is to make free entry and exit both central and explicit. By doing this, several of the restrictive assumptions of perfect competition can be dropped. Price-taking behaviour is no longer necessary; neither is the existence of a large number of small firms, each producing a homogeneous product along 'U' shaped cost curves. The comparison of necessary assumptions for perfect competition and perfectly contestable market theories are listed in Table 13.2.

Table 13.2 Assumptions of perfect competition and contestable market theory.	Necessary assumptions	Competitive market	Contestable market
	(a) Profit maximisation	Yes	Yes
	(b) No barriers to entry or exit	Yes	Yes
	(c) Perfect mobility of inputs	Yes	Yes
	(d) Perfect information for all traders	Yes	Yes
	(e) Large number of small firms acting as price takers	Yes	Not required
	(f) Homogeneous product	Yes	Not required
	(g) All firms (or potential firms) are faced with the same cost functions	Yes	Yes
	(h) Average cost curves are U-shaped	Yes	Not required

The attraction of the concept of contestable market lies in the less restrictive assumptions necessary for achieving some of the outcomes of the competitive model. It is clearly more realistic to imagine an industry approaching perfect contestability than perfect competition, especially given assumption (e) in Table 13.2. In contestable markets there is no requirement for a large number of small (price-taking) firms to be already operating in the industry. It is the *potential* for entry and exit by firms (or a firm), as profitable opportunities dictate, that is vital here. The essence of contestable markets is that there exists the *potential* for hit-and-run entry: i.e. a firm can freely enter an industry, reap any profits that are available, then costlessly leave when such profitable opportunities disappear.

Figure 13.3 illustrates the case of perfect contestability in the case of a firm initially facing industry demand curve D_1. At this level of demand the industry could effectively be regarded as a natural monopoly, since the average cost of a single firm is still declining at any feasible price/output combination set by the firm. For example, at prices ranging between P^* and P_1 the firm earns above normal or normal profits, with associated outputs q^* to q_1. Yet the output equivalent to minimum average cost (MES) occurs at q_{MES}, to the right of any of these feasible price/output combinations.

The possible *average cost* pricing equilibria for perfect contestability are indicated in Fig. 13.3, with the firm earning only normal profit at each of these equilibria, despite its (natural) monopoly characteristics.

- P_1/q_1 is a *feasible* and *sustainable* equilibrium with industry demand D_1. Even with free entry, the normal profits earned will provide no attractions to new firms competing with the incumbent. Note that by setting price $> P_1 < P^*$ the firm can earn supernormal profits, but new entrants might be able to set still lower prices and capture segments of its market. Prices in this range are *not*, therefore, regarded as sustainable equilibrium outcomes.

- P_1/q_2 is a *feasible* but *non-sustainable* equilibrium with industry demand D_2. The suggestion here is that industry demand has increased to D_2 and the incumbent firm has continued with its average cost (normal profit) pricing policy. However, in this case a new entrant faced with similar costs to the incumbent might now be able to capture a share of the (increased) market between and q_1 and q_2 and still make supernormal

Fig. 13.3 Natural
monopoly in
a perfectly
contestable market.

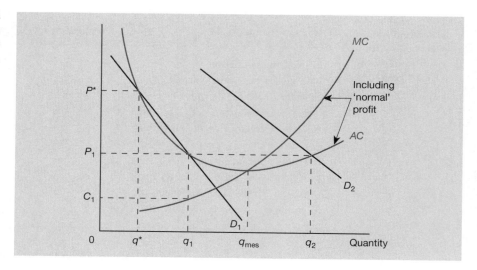

profits by charging a price below P_1 but above its average costs. The average cost pricing equilibrium P_1/q_2, while feasible for a contestable market, is therefore a non-sustainable equilibrium as it could only persist via the erection of some type of entry barrier. An alternative description of a **sustainable equilibrium** here is an average cost pricing equilibrium consistent with free entry. Markets for which the *only* feasible equilibrium when entry is free is a *sustainable equilibrium* can be regarded as **perfectly contestable**.

We have now seen that if the industry is **perfectly contestable** then although we do not have the first-best allocative solution (since price > MC: i.e. $P_1 > C_1$ in Fig. 13.3) we do have a situation where the *threat* of entry leads to normal profits and a single sustainable equilibrium (P_1/q_1) in Fig. 13.3.

However, in terms of public interest theory we do not need a *perfectly* contestable market in order to yield a net welfare gain as compared with the current regulatory framework. Indeed in the natural monopoly case it is likely that there would be considerable sunk costs in terms of infrastructure, etc. that are non-recoverable on exit and therefore act as barriers to entry. Nevertheless **deregulation** with potential or actual new entry may result in solutions in the vicinity of P_1/q_1 in Fig. 13.3 and which increase positive net economic welfare as compared with the regulatory alternative. Indeed the state could conceivably abandon the current regulatory framework and itself bear the sunk costs of the system, which could then be franchised/hired out to potential operators. Many pragmatic alternatives to regulation exist, and under public interest theory the net welfare outcomes of each of these might be evaluated in comparison with the current regulatory framework. Where deregulation *is* evaluated as yielding net welfare benefits, then deregulation can be supported.

Expressing the same idea in terms of costs, Noll (1989) points out that according to public interest theory an industry will be deregulated when the costs of regulation (in terms of benefits forgone) *exceed* the transactions costs of repealing that regulatory framework *plus* the costs of any remaining (post deregulation) market failure.

Quasi-markets

The provision of many services is increasingly being undertaken by what might be called **quasi-markets** or **internal markets** instead of being controlled or regulated by a government department, as previously. In many cases the state ceases to provide the services in question, relying instead on independent institutions to compete against each other to win contracts for supply. As well as competition on the supply side there is usually a purchasing aspect on the demand side of the quasi-market, often state funded. Since outcomes (in terms of allocations of resources) are determined by the interaction of supply and demand, typical of any market, we can reasonably use the term 'market' to describe these emerging mechanisms of welfare provision. However, there are a number of aspects of both the supply and demand sides that are untypical of any market – hence the term *quasi*.

- *Many types of service provider*. On the supply side there is a wider variety of types of service provider than is usual in a market – for example, private 'for profit' organisations, registered charities, or other voluntary sector organisations. There is therefore a greater diversity of ownership structures and organisational objectives than is typical of more conventional markets.
- *Use of vouchers or budgets rather than cash*. On the demand side, consumer purchasing power is often expressed in terms of *vouchers*, or *budgets* allocated for specific purposes, rather than in terms of cash changing hands.
- *Use of agents or intermediaries in purchasing*. On the demand side, instead of market preferences being expressed by the consumer directly, as in normal markets, the consumers, preferences are often expressed indirectly by an agent or intermediary (e.g. a GP, health authority, or care manager).

Many advocates of these emerging quasi-markets argue that they promote greater efficiency in supply, respond more rapidly to consumer preferences, and are more accountable to those who fund their operation. Critics argue that the market conditions necessary for such favourable outcomes do not exist in most welfare sectors. As a consequence movements towards quasi-market provision will increase administrative and other transaction costs and lead to greater inequalities amongst recipients of such services. Before considering the operation of these quasi-markets in the particular sectors of health care, education and housing, it may be useful to consider the contribution of conventional economic theory to an understanding of their operation. Indeed, economic theory suggests a number of conditions that must be met if the more favourable outcomes claimed for quasi-markets are to occur (Le Grand 1992):

- *The market structure must be competitive in both supply and demand, with many providers and many purchasers*. If markets are to operate efficiently, in terms of price, output and quality, dissatisfied purchasers must be able to seek alternative sources of supply (i.e. absence of monopoly in supply). Similarly suppliers must not be dependent on a few, powerful purchasers, otherwise price can be kept artificially low and many potentially efficient suppliers can be driven out of business (i.e. absence of monopsony in demand).
- *Accurate, easily accessible information on the cost and quality of provision must be available to both suppliers and purchasers*, otherwise suppliers will be unable to cost and price their activities appropriately, and purchasers will be unable to monitor the price and quality of the services they receive. Market failure in respect of this condition could, for

example, lead to suppliers reducing costs by lowering the quality of services without purchasers being aware of the fact.

- *Profit must be a significant factor in motivating suppliers.* Price is a key signal in markets, and if suppliers do not respond to the signal of higher prices and profits by increasing supply, because profit is not a motivating factor, then resource allocation will be impaired. It follows that an over-representation of voluntary and charitable bodies in provision, pursuing various 'praiseworthy' aims, may lead to unpredictable and arguably inefficient responses by suppliers to market signals.

- *There must be few opportunities in the market for 'adverse selection' or its opposite, 'cream skimming'.* Both are the consequence of a lack of symmetry in the information available to sellers and buyers, and may inhibit the existence of a market. In the case of adverse selection, purchasers who know themselves to be bad risks but who are not known to be so by providers may be over-represented in the market. This will reduce profitability for providers and may even cause the welfare provision to cease as suppliers make excessive losses. On the other hand 'cream skimming' can impair market efficiency by permitting providers to use information available only to themselves to select purchasers who are good risks, thereby raising profits. In this case welfare services may fail to reach those who most require them.

We shall refer back to some of the aspects of quasi-markets considered in this section as we look in more detail at the provision of particular welfare services in the next section (p. 544).

Applications and evidence

Deregulation: US experience

In 1977, 17% of US GNP was derived from the output of fully regulated industry; by 1988 that figure had been reduced to only 6.6%, and current estimates suggest a figure below 5%. As Winston (1993) notes, such a major switch to change the market conditions under which some $600 billion of US output was provided could only have occurred with a strong consensual support from opinion formers, not least from the contributions of microeconomists.

Table 13.3(a) outlines the *economic distortions* allegedly created by the regulatory framework operating in the USA *prior* to the deregulatory activities beginning in the mid to late 1970s. Table 13.3(b) outlines the *characteristics* of the deregulatory measures applied to the various industries.

Winston (1993) reviews a wide range of empirical studies into the impacts of deregulation in the USA. Table 13.4 compares the *predictions* made at the time of various deregulations of the quantitative impacts on prices and service quality, with assessments of the *actual outcomes* some time later. Such comparisons are clearly useful in reflecting on the extent to which the benefits allegedly rising from a proposed deregulation were actually secured, with of course the obvious caveat that other economic and social variables will also have been changing in often unpredictable ways in intervening time periods.

Table 13.3(a) Economic distortions created by regulations.

Industry	Distortion
Airlines	(a) Fares were set by a formula developed by the CAB that generally elevated fares above marginal costs for medium- and long-haul trips and below marginal costs for short-haul trips (*). (b) Carriers could not enter or exit routes and thus engaged in intensive service competition, in particular increasing flight frequency and reducing load factors (*). (c) Carriers were generally unable to adjust fares, route structures, equipment, or levels and wages of factors of production, which raised their operating costs and lowered revenues (*). (d) Regulation created dynamic inefficiencies: in particular, it encouraged a suboptimal fleet mix and stymied network development.
Trucking	(a) Rates were regulated by the ICC. Rate structures were complex, but generally rates were above marginal costs especially in the less-than-truckload sector, where shippers had no recourse to private carriage and rail alternatives available to truckload shippers (*). (b) Certain carriers were restricted to carrying particular commodities; some others were restricted to following designated routes. The restrictions increased carrier operating costs (*). (c) Regulation stymied productivity growth, technology change, and management quality.
Railroads	(a) Rates were regulated by the ICC. Rate structures were complex but generally rates were above the marginal costs for most commodities and possibly below marginal costs for a few others (*). (b) Carriers were generally unable to adjust rates, exit and consolidate routes, or fully shed excess labour costs, which raised operating costs and lowered revenues (*). (c) Regulation stymied productivity growth, technological change, and management quality.
Telecom-munications	(a) Interstate rates were regulated by the FCC and kept above marginal costs to cross-subsidize local service rates, which were regulated by the state public utility commissions and kept below marginal costs (*). (b) Regulation stymied technological change and productivity by allowing AT&T and other large phone companies to control equipment.
Cable television	(a) The FCC limited programme services that could be offered by cable systems (*). (b) Municipalities regulated rates and required franchise fees (or services in lieu of fees) that raised consumers' costs.
Banking	(a) Regulation put ceilings on deposit interest rates depriving consumers of market rates of return (*), and in times of financial distress causing disintermediation, to the detriment of sectors (e.g. housing) relying on depositories for finance. (b) Interstate banking operations were restricted, thus impeding competition and increasing risk (*). (c) Regulation placed restrictions on banks' asset investments and the range of services they could offer consumers.
Brokerage	Regulation fixed brokerage rates, depriving investors of the benefits of price competition (*).

Table 13.3(a) Contd

Industry	Distortion
Petroleum	(a) Regulation put a price ceiling on domestic crude oil and petroleum products, forcing prices below free market levels (*). (b) Regulation discouraged the development of long-run petroleum supplies.
Natural gas	(a) The wellhead price of natural gas was regulated, forcing prices below short-run market levels (*). (b) Regulation discouraged the development of long-run natural gas supply, creating artifical shortages that elevated prices to final users relative to unrestricted price levels (*).

Note: An asterisk after the effect indicates that its magnitude was estimated and used as a basis for predicting the effects of deregulation.
Source: Winston (1993)

Table 13.3(b) Characteristics of the deregulatory measures.

Industry	Major initiatives	Impact
Airlines	CAB Liberalization of Entry and Discount Fare Experiments (mid 1970s) Airline Deregulation Act (1978)	Set in motion complete deregulation of the industry. Since 1982 entry has been granted to all carriers that are fit, willing and able. In 1983, all regulations on fares were eliminated.
Trucking	ICC Liberalization of Truck Rates (late 1970s) Motor Carrier Reform Act (1980)	Led to substantial but not complete deregulation of the industry. Entry could only be denied if it was shown to be inconsistent with public convenience and necessity. Rates could be set independently but still had to be filed at the Interstate Commerce Commission (ICC). Private and contract carriers could compete directly with common carriers.
Railroads	ICC Liberalization of Rail Rates and Contracting (late 1970s) Staggers Rail Act (1980)	Added considerable force to previous regulatory reforms designed to promote railroad competition but did not completely deregulate the industry.Railroads were free to set their own rates without ICC involvement for many commodities and could negotiate contract rates for all commodities. Rates for certain commodities were subject to market dominance and rate reasonableness guidelines. The Act also made it much easier for railroads to abandon routes and to merge with other carriers.
Telecommunications	Federal Communications Commission (FCC) Court Decisions (late 1960s-mid 1970s) Execunet Decision (1977) AT&T Settlement (1982)	A series of court decisions that changed the nature of competition in telecommunications but still left large parts of the industry regulated. AT&T provides long-distance service but not local. AT&T's rates are subject to regulation; some rate flexibility has been granted over time. Its interstate rivals are not subject to rate regulation and face little entry regulation. Local service is provided by the former Bell operating companies, restructured into seven regional holding companies that operate a number of state-regulated companies. AT&T can compete in the telecommunications equipment market. The local service operating companies are restricted from competing in this market and interstate long distance. Following divestiture the operating companies were not allowed to offer content-based information services. They are now permitted to do so.

Table 13.3(b) Contd

Industry	Major initiatives	Impact
Cable television	FCC Rulemakings and other Regulatory Proceedings (late 1970s) Cable Television Deregulation Act (1984)	Provided for complete price deregulation of cable television subject to standards for effective competition, which are primarily based on the number of over-the-air broadcast stations in a city. Entry is granted by a city through a franchise arrangement. Cable television companies that are awarded a franchise in a city that meets the standards for effective competition are not subject to price regulation by the city. Markets that do not meet the standards are subject to basic service price regulation by local governments.
Brokerage	Securities Acts Amendments (1975)	Introduced price competition in brokerage services by instructing the Securities and Exchange Commission (SEC) to outlaw fixed brokerage rates on the New York Stock Exchange.
Banking	Depository Institution Deregulation and Monetary Control Act (1980) Garn-St. German Depository Institutions Act (1982)	These Acts enabled banks and thrifts to expand their activities and led to greater competition in financial services. Among other things, the first Act eliminated all interest rate ceilings (except on demand deposits) and permitted all depository institutions to offer NOW accounts. Both Acts expanded asset powers and activities for thrifts; the second Act allowed state chartered thrifts to offer variable rate mortgages.
Petroleum	Decontrol of crude oil and refined petroleum products (executive orders beginning in 1979)	Phased out controls on domestic crude oil prices. Full decontrol occurred in 1981. Windfall profit taxes were enacted in 1980 but were phased out beginning January 1988.
Natural gas	Natural Gas Policy Act (1978)	Specified a phased deregulation of the price at which a producer sells gas gas to a pipeline at the wellhead. The Act did not deal with the regulation of pipelines or of local distribution companies.

Source: Winston (1993)

Prices and beneficial service quality

We have already noted in Table 13.3(a) that regulatory price structures often overruled cost considerations and certain consumers at the expense of others. The third column of Table 13.4 outlines the *predicted impacts* of the deregulatory measures introduced into the various US industries. All figures are valuations, in constant 1990 (billion) dollars, of the net welfare gains or losses predicted at the time of deregulation. The fourth column of Table 13.4 outlines the *assessed outcomes* of the deregulatory measures some 10 years after the changes were introduced. Where a *range* of predictions for outcomes is available, the lowest and highest figures are given in brackets.

As regards *prices*, economists predicted that regulatory reform would usually lead to lower prices and significant welfare gains to consumers. In Table 13.4 Winston reports the *aggregate welfare effects* of price changes (e.g. consumers gain $1 billion) instead of average percentage changes in prices (e.g. air fares fall, on average, by 10%) because it facilitates comparisons with the effects of deregulation on service quality and profits. These predictions were generally accurate. The specific predictions, although often made more than a decade apart by different researchers, are surprisingly close to assessments as to actual outcomes. For example, empirical *predictions* of the annual economic benefits

Table 13.4 **Predicted versus assessed outcomes of deregulatory measures.**

Industry	Effect	Predicted	Assessed
Airlines	Fares	(2.7, 6.6)	(4.3, 6.5)
	Service frequency	(−0.40, −0.61), (0.32, 0.57)	8.5
	Travel time	Not predicted	(−1.0, +1.8)
	Travel restrictions	Not predicted	−3.0
Railroads	Rates	(−5.8, −11.5)	(−2.1, + 0.43)
	Service time and reliability	Not predicted	9.3
Trucking	Common carrier rates	9.8	7.8
	Private carrier costs	(0.43, 4.3)	6.0
	Common carrier service time and reliability	Not predicted	1.6
Telecomm- unications	Rates	(2.5, 6.0)	(0.73, 1.6)
	Service and equipment	Not predicted	Not assessed
Cable Television	Price and service	0.60	(0.37, 1.3)
Banking	Price and service	8.1	Positive
Brokerage	Prices	0.63	0.14
	Service	Reduce quantity but improve quality of brokerage research	No significant change discerned
Petroleum	Prices	−11.6	Ambiguous
Natural Gas	Prices	3.4 (by 1975), 1.5 (by 1980)	Substantial gains to consumers

Note: Figures in parentheses refer to a range of estimates − lowest and highest.

to travellers from airline fare deregulation range from $2.7 billion to $6.6 billion (1990 dollars). Empirical assessments of the *outcomes* for these benefits range from $4.3 billion to $6.5 billion (1990 dollars).

One exception to the general accuracy of the forecasts is the prediction that under deregulation railroad shippers, especially of bulk commodities, would face significantly higher rates as the railroad industry sought greater financial viability under a now dereg- ulated fares regime. The lower end of the assessed range of rate changes partially validates this prediction, but the upper end suggests that shippers may have actually *gained* from deregulation. The source of the conflicting assessments is that shippers gain from deregulation when their shipment sizes and lengths of haul are appropriately increased to capture the rate savings available from railroads' deregulated rate schedules. When these adjustments are *not* made, shippers appear to lose from rate deregulation. This illustrates a significant weakness in regulatory research that is more widespread in predictions of service changes: economists found it difficult to predict, or even consider, changes in firms' operations and technology, and consumers' responses to these changes, that developed in response to regulatory reform.

As Table 13.4 indicates, as regards *quality of service*, economists had more difficulty in even predicting quantitative changes likely to be caused by deregulation. For example, economists failed to make any quantitative predictions as to the value of several important service changes caused by deregulation. Notable omissions in this respect include improvements in the mean and variance of railroad and motor carrier service time, and the widely acknowledged benefits (as yet unquantified) from new telecommunications services and equipment. Even when such quantitative predictions *were* made as to impacts of deregulation on quality of service, they were often in error. For example, the important prediction of deregulation's effect on airline service frequency grossly underestimated the benefits from deregulation. As previously noted, the poor predictions reflect the failure to develop and apply a theory as to how the deregulated firm might anticipate the effects of regulatory reform on operations and technological change. The accelerated development of airlines' 'hub and spoke' operations (see p. 193) in combination with the use of more efficient propeller planes for local service and the development of computerised yield (fare) management systems have influenced outcome in quality of service provision for air travel in ways not predicted at the time of deregulation.

Winston (1993) further compares *predictions* at the time of deregulation with *outcomes* for profits, wages and employment in the industries presented in Table 13.4.

Table 13.5 seeks to evaluate the overall welfare impacts of deregulation, by industry and apportioned between consumers (additional consumer surplus via lower prices, etc.) and producers (gains/losses in producer surplus via lower costs/lower prices, etc.).

Table 13.5 **Welfare effects of deregulation.**

Industry	Consumers	Producers	Total	Additional benefits if deregulation achieves optimality[a]	Public support for deregulation
Airlines	(8.8, 14.8)[b]	4.9	(13.7, 19.7)	4.9	69%
Railroads	(7.2, 9.7)	3.2	(10.4, 12.9)	0.45	n.a.
Trucking	15.4	−4.8	10.6	0.0	n.a.
Telecommunications	(0.73, 1.6)	–	(0.73, 1.6)	11.8	52%
Cable television	(0.73, 1.6)	–	(0.37, 1.3)	(0.4, 0.8)	47%
Brokerage	0.14	−0.14	0.0	0.0	n.a.
Natural gas	–	–	–	4.1	n.a.
Total	(32.6, 43.0)	3.2	(35.8, 46.2)	(21.65, 22.05)	

Notes: [a]The additional welfare gains are based on assuming that regulatory reform actually generates optimal pricing and, where appropriate, optimal service. These benefits need not be generated by the market: that is, they could be achieved by optimising regulatory rate setting.
[b] Figures in parentheses refer to a range of estimates — lowest and highest.
Source: Winston (1993)

The total figure for all industries suggests that society has gained at least $36–46 billion (1990 dollars) annually from deregulation, primarily in the transportation industries (pending further evolution of and complete quantification of the benefits from deregulation of the other industries). This amounts to a 7–9% improvement in the part of GNP affected by regulatory reform. The bulk of the benefits are estimated to go to the consumer, but are not seen as being at the expense of producers or labour. Indeed producers are seen as *gaining* overall from the efficiency aspects of deregulation.

Table 13.5 suggests that regulatory reform could generate some $20 billion in additional benefits if it achieved optimal (first-best or, where appropriate, second-best) pricing and service. The final column of the table suggests that the public has not always shared the economics profession's enthusiasm for deregulation. As the table indicates, despite the large actual and potential benefits from airline, telecommunications, and cable television deregulation, only airline deregulation enjoyed a substantial majority of support.

■ Deregulation: UK bus industry

Ison (1999) considers the impacts of deregulating the bus industry in the UK. Prior to 1930, the local urban and rural bus industry operated in a competitive market structure with no government regulation. There was fierce competition between rival bus companies (using surplus war vehicles), and this period was associated with a high number of accidents, unscheduled and irregular intervention by 'pirate' operators at peak times, and other types of wasteful duplication.

Before deregulation It was for these reasons that, in 1930, the Road Traffic Act was introduced, which was to form the basis of bus industry regulation for 50 years. Under the Act, Traffic Commissioners were responsible for the issue of road service licences (a licence being required for each route operated), the quality of vehicles, and the level of fares.

The period 1930–80 was therefore a restrictive one for the local bus service industry. A comprehensive public transport network was provided under a protectionist system, with a licence acting as a barrier to entry, since a licence gave the operator a monopoly on a particular route for the duration of the licence. In 1930 the industry was dominated by private bus operators but, as it developed, the state took a progressively larger role, as with the formation in 1968 of the National Bus Company (NBC) and the Scottish Bus Group (SBG). This meant that by 1986 the industry consisted of state-owned operators, the local authority sector, and independent companies, which operated mainly in the contract hire sector (including school bus provision).

Changes were regarded as necessary by the mid 1980s. There had been a steady decline in patronage, with bus and coach passenger travel falling from 42% of total travel in 1953 to 8% in 1983. The growth in the use of the private car, fare increases in excess of the inflation rate, increased operating costs and the decline in the service provided, were seen as the chief reasons for the decline in bus/coach travel.

The Conservative government started on the changes with the 1980 Transport Act, which abolished road service licences for long-distance express coach travel, and with the decision to establish the 'trial areas' of Devon, Hereford and Worcester, and Norfolk, for local bus service deregulation. For long-distance coach travel, the Act allowed companies that met certain safety standards to enter the market and to offer whatever service they chose. By 1989, passenger prices on the main trunk roads were 15% lower in real terms, and coach frequency 70% higher, compared with the position prior to deregulation (Thompson and Whitfield 1990).

The 1984 White Paper on Buses stated:

> The total travel market is expanding. New measures are needed urgently to break out of the cycle of rising costs, rising fares, reducing services, so that public transport can win a bigger share of this market. We must get away from the idea that the only future for bus services is to contract painfully at large cost to taxpayers and ratepayers as well as travellers. Competition provides the opportunity for lower fares, new services, more passengers. For these great gains, half measures will not be enough. Within the essential framework of safety regulation and provision for social needs, the obstacles to enterprise, initiative and efficiency must be removed.

The White Paper led to the 1985 Transport Act, through which (by October 1986) road service licensing requirements were abolished outside London. Provision was also made in the Act for the privatisation of the National Bus Company. The Passenger Transport Executives operating in metropolitan areas were to be converted into independent companies, still owned by the local authorities but which now had the option to privatise them. Local bus operators had to register their routes and times and give sufficient notice of withdrawal of services. There was also the introduction of competitive tendering for the unprofitable bus routes.

So the main objective of the 1985 Act was to introduce competition into the bus sector, providing the opportunity for independent bus operators that did not offer licenced services before 1986, now to do so. It was envisaged that there would be a number of benefits from deregulation:

- Increased competition should allow greater choice for the consumer and provide a service that was more responsive to the preferences of the consumer.
- There should now be a closer relationship between bus operating costs and the fares charged, the reason for this being the ending of cross-subsidisation, whereby certain routes were overcharged in order to subsidize non-profitable routes. This was helped, of course, by the freedom of entry for new operators after 1986, which in principle should compete away any 'monopoly profits' from charging excessive fares on route, unrelated to costs.
- There would be a greater potential for innovation in bus travel under deregulation, which was less likely in the absence of competition. One such innovation following deregulation has been the introduction of minibus services.
- There would be a reduction in the subsidies obtained by bus operators to undertake unprofitable services. The revenue support from government had increased from £10 million in 1972 to £520 million in 1982. It could be argued that such subsidies created a protective wall behind which bus operators could operate inefficient services.

There were, however, reservations as to the likely success of bus deregulation, most notably the view that it could lead to a wasteful duplication of services on the profitable routes, especially at peak periods, with a resulting increase in the level of congestion in a number of urban areas. Further, it was feared that the intended reduction in the level of subsidy to the bus sector after deregulation might lead to a rise in the level of fares, thereby diminishing bus use.

Bus services
since deregulation
In terms of local bus services in England (outside London), there has in fact been an increase in annual bus-kilometres travelled; in 1985–86, the year before deregulation, 1,423 million bus-kilometres were undertaken, whereas by 1996–97 1,863 million bus-kilometres were recorded, an increase of 31%. Care must, however, be taken when interpreting these figures. In evidence to the House of Commons Transport Committee (1993) on the government's proposals for the deregulation of buses in London, two reasons were suggested as to why the recorded increase in bus-kilometres might be misleading:

> First, there has been a growth in the proportion of small buses, which may in some cases increase the probability of passengers not being able to get on the first bus to come; second, some proportion of the mileage run by competing bus companies is attributable to one bus closely following another, and in this case a rise in total vehicle mileage does not bring proportionate benefits to passengers. (HMSO 1993)

Nevertheless it is likely that there has indeed been some increase in the provision of local bus services.

Although there has been an *increase in bus-kilometres travelled* since deregulation, there has also been a *decrease in passenger journeys* over the period of some 4% per annum. There is little doubt that deregulation has been a contributing factor to the decline in bus use by passengers. One reason, at least immediately after deregulation, was the confusion that passengers experienced due to the changes in service times, routes and operators resulting from deregulation. Higher fares may also have played a part in the reduction in passenger journeys. For local bus services (outside London) an index of fares reveals an increase of 26% in real terms over the last decade. A factor in these price increases was the reduction in local authority subsidies for bus services, which fell by over £520 million in real terms between 1986 and 1997. Another factor in the recorded price increases was the ending of the 'cheap fares policies' by the Public Transport Executives (PTEs) in metropolitan areas. Of course the reduction in passenger use of buses has been a trend over a long period of time, closely related to the increase in car ownership and use.

Deregulation of buses can also be assessed in terms of its impact on operating costs. Over the period 1985–86 to 1996–97, bus operating costs fell from 153p per vehicle-kilometre to 81p per vehicle-kilometre in real terms, a reduction of 47%. This has been due in part to a reduction in the number of staff employed by the bus operators and in part to a reduction in real wages.

Many small bus operators were formed following deregulation, notably through management and employee buy-outs. Initially there was a fragmentation of the sector but this has subsequently been consolidated, with five major operators remaining within the sector. Many of the previously small companies have been taken over by the larger operators, and further takeovers are likely. What has developed is, in effect, an oligopolistic market with a number of the larger operators possessing local monopolies. In some instances this has led to the intervention of the Office of Fair Trading and the involvement of the Monopolies and Mergers Commission in investigating alleged anti-competitive behaviour and industry mergers.

Deregulation: UK electricity supply

In 1998 the electricity market in England and Wales was opened up to full competition, with all consumers now allowed to choose their electricity supplier independently of the geographical region in which they happened to be located. A number of studies have been conducted into the potential benefits and costs of such deregulation. Table 13.6 summarises the estimated benefits and costs (OFFER 1997) that lay behind the decision to deregulate.

Table 13.6 **Offer's estimates of the benefits and costs of deregulations.**

Benefits	
More efficient purchasing	£300 million p.a.
Lower generation costs: franchise	£100–200 million p.a.
Lower generation costs: non-franchise	£100–200 million p.a.
Additional consumer surplus	£100 million p.a.
New services	?
Total benefits	£600–800 million p.a.
Costs	
Set-up costs	£150–517 million
Operating costs	£22.5–83 million p.a.

Source: Adapted from OFFER (1997)

Overall, the estimates suggest that the projected additional annual benefits from deregulation of electricity supply would exceed the projected additional annual operating costs by a considerable margin (over £500 million per annum using respective 'low' estimates and over £700 million per annum using respective 'high' estimates). Against these ongoing *net* benefits from operating the new system a one-off set-up cost of £150–517 million would need to be deducted. We might usefully consider these various benefits and costs in more detail.

Three main benefits were identified as a result of electricity supply deregulation:

- lower costs of distributing electricity, via competitive pressure in electricity distribution, forcing the Regional Electricity Companies (RECs) who supply electricity to cut their costs, via efficiency gains;
- lower costs of generating electricity, via competitive pressure in electricity generation as the RECs seek lower input costs, forcing generators in turn to cut their costs via efficiency gains;
- lower prices to consumers resulting from these competitive pressures having reduced both the costs of electricity supply and the profit margins on such supply. Lower prices to consumers result in additional consumer surplus.

These various benefits were quantified, in discounted present value terms, as leading to some £600–800 million per annum in benefits from deregulation. In fact the figure was expected to be still higher as companies now try to provide improved services, such as more convenient payment methods or better advice on the efficient use of electricity, in this deregulated market. Such 'new service' benefits were left unquantified in Table 13.6.

As regards costs, it was accepted that there would be a significant one-off 'set-up' cost, for example in converting electricity meters to the needs of a deregulated market. A new system of meters would now be needed for small consumers based on infrequent meter readings, with consumption allocated to individual half-hour periods to reflect load profiles in the 'pooling system' (see Chapter 7, p. 326). The extra 'operating costs' of running this new metering system would need to be added to the set-up costs, but on an ongoing basis.

A separate study by Green and McDaniel (1998) also concluded that the deregulation of electricity supply was likely to provide net welfare gains as compared with continuing with the pre-1998 system.

Quasi-markets: education and training

Clearly this is an area of wide scope and considerable complexity, which merits an in-depth analysis. Here we consider only those aspects of education and training particularly relevant to the debate on market versus non-market means of resource allocation.

Additional education or training can clearly be regarded, in part, as yielding *consumption benefits*, e.g. positive utility or pleasure to those directly involved in the process of gaining knowledge or acquiring skills. However, the main motivation to both suppliers and purchasers of education and training is likely to take the form of *investment benefits*: in other words, the use of scarce resources by suppliers (labour, capital) and purchasers (time, energy, money, income expended, income forgone, etc.) to yield higher future returns.

At the *micro level* this return on human capital investment may originate from a rightward shift in the marginal revenue product curve (see Chapter 10). This rightward shift raises the value of labour input to both the firm and (via higher wages) the individual undertaking the education or training. At the *macro level* such investment is seen as shifting the production possibilities frontier for the economy to the right, i.e. raising what is often referred to as *sustainable growth*. This is growth that can be attained *without* running into capacity constraints, causing inflationary or balance of payments pressures. The term *endogenous growth* is also sometimes given to investment in education or training: 'endogenous' meaning here 'growth that develops from within'. Research by Robert Barro, for example, suggests that a 10% increase in educational attainment increases growth of GDP by 0.2% per year.

To what extent is the market capable of providing an appropriate level of educating or training? What role might there be for an internal or quasi-market in this area? Before seeking to address these issues it may be useful to review the circumstances under which the purchaser or provider, respectively, might be induced to invest in a given amount of education or training.

In Fig. 13.4, suppose the individual can leave school without training at 16 years and progress along the income pathway $S_1 S_1'$. Alternatively the individual can invest in $0A$ years of training, paying directly the sum $0ACD$ as costs for this training. On completion, the higher marginal revenue product of the employee raises his/her earning potential to $S_2 S_2'$. In addition the (full time) training period has meant an opportunity cost of $0AXS_1$

Fig. 13.4 **The
decision to invest in
education.**

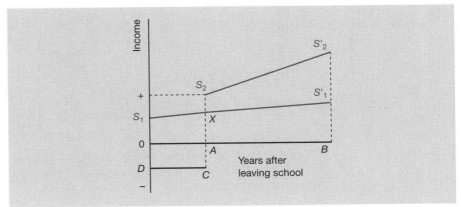

income forgone during the training period. Only if lifetime benefits exceed the lifetime costs of training is it likely that the investment in training will be regarded as worthwhile. In other words the extra benefits $X S_1' S_2' S_2$ must be greater than the extra costs $0ACD + 0AXS_1$. All sums must, since they occur at different times, be discounted to a present value equivalent.

**Problems for a
pure market**

It is unlikely that a pure market will lead to an efficient level of provision for education or training. This can be illustrated in Fig. 13.5. Suppose untrained labour has a marginal revenue product of MRP_0 to the firm, and is paid the wage ($=MRP_0$) of W_0. Suppose also that the firm that provides the training does so at a cost of ($V - W_0$) per week. The total cost to the firm of providing training during the training period is therefore given by area A. However, at the end of the training period, suppose the marginal revenue product rises to MRP_1 ($>MRP_0$). To recoup the training costs the firm will now need to pay a wage *below* MRP_1 (say W_1). The minimum condition necessary to make it worthwhile for the firm to support training is that

Area B		Area A
(Excess of MRP after	$=$	(Cost of training
training over wage paid)		during training period)

Again, of course, this equation must be expressed in present value terms, with all future sums involved discounted to their present value equivalents.

A problem for *a pure market* to be established in training would be the risks of 'poaching'. For example, a rival firm could offer to pay the trained worker at the end of the training period between W_1 and MRP_1 and still find this transaction profitable since it has not itself incurred the training costs A. If the worker leaves the company that has funded the training before sufficient time has elapsed for area B (in present value terms) to at least equal area A, then the company has lost at the expense of its rival. Such poaching, if extensive, would negate any incentives for individual firms themselves to offer an appropriate level of training opportunities.

Many of the reforms proposed for enhancing access to education and training involve aspects of the quasi-markets discussed earlier.

Fig. 13.5 **The firm's decision to train labour.**

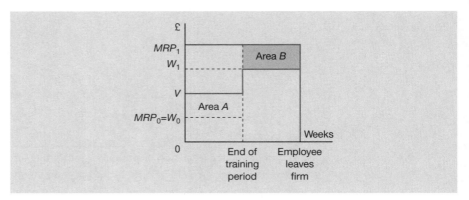

Fig. 13.5 **The firm's decision to train labour.**

On the *provider* side, a centralised state agency (Department for Education and Employment or Department of Trade and Industry) is being progressively replaced by market-type mechanisms for resource allocation. In the schools, inducements have been provided for schools to opt out of local authority control and to receive direct grants from central government. Budgets are increasingly allocated to schools according to their individual characteristics (formula funding) – if more pupils are attracted, more income is received. Schools have also been given greater opportunities for managing their own budgets (local management of schools – LMS), becoming in effect semi-independent providers.

On the *purchaser* side, under open enrolment parents have greater choice, within limits, of the school to which they send their child. Training and Enterprise Councils (TECs) can act as agents for consumers, selecting the educational institutions or training bodies they will fund to provide particular vocational or training courses, or even providing such courses themselves. Greater awareness of the results of different educational institutions (e.g. national league tables) are aimed at giving purchasers better information on the quality of service provision. In total, many of these reforms have similarities with a *voucher system*, whereby parents, students or TECs choose a particular provider, and a budget allocation directly follows that choice. Indeed, it is intended that education and training vouchers be allocated to students directly to a given value, which can then be spent on courses of their choice.

As in the case of health care, the government view is that increased competition of providers for the vouchers/expenditure of purchasers will raise both the efficiency of supply and the choice of consumers. We now consider a number of broad issues raised by the development of such quasi-markets in education and training.

Problem for quasi-market provision

'Cream skimming' and adverse selection   As with health care, the extent of efficiency gains from quasi-markets depends upon providers being unable to 'cream-skim' by taking only those most likely to succeed. If certain schools *are* able to do this, other (non-opted-out) schools will have a progressively adverse pool from which to draw their pupils, and disparities between schools will widen rather than narrow. There is evidence to suggest that a quasi-market in which only a minority of schools opt out is indeed likely to result in elements of selection. For example Mortimore *et al.* (1988) and

Rutter (1979) found in their detailed studies that only about 5% of what actually takes place in schools affects 'outcomes' (e.g. exam results). Over 64% of the variance in pupil achievements could be explained by initial attainment and social background. With such a large part of the likely outcomes for pupils outside the direct influence of the schools, Glennerster (1993) concludes that 'any school entrepreneur acting rationally would seek to exclude pupils who would drag down the overall performance of the school, its major selling point to parents'.

Poor information and externalities Following on from the previous point, a selective system might (say critics) create rather misleading information and a variety of negative externalities as compared with an initially non-selective system. This is in line with the earlier point (p. 533) that in quasi-markets there needs to be symmetry of information between providers and purchasers. In a competitive and selective system, educational providers may have incentives not to reveal relevant factors, and parents (purchasers) may be unable to extract that information. Of course such secrecy may also be the case in non-selective schools as a defence mechanism for teachers. In any case parents' charters and national league tables may help to remedy information deficiencies by ensuring that schools reveal specific aspects of information about themselves. 'Value-added' league tables may give still more relevant information to parents (prospective purchasers).

Selectivity may also lead to certain *negative externalities*: for example, the loss of local community ties fostered by non-selective local schools; the loss of the improved educational outcomes attributed to average and below average children in non-selective schooling (Glennerster and Law 1990). Opponents of this view would cite the *positive externalities* that selection might give to brighter children able to progress more rapidly in a cohort of children with similar ability.

Sunk costs A quasi-market will lead to winners and losers, with some schools expanding and others contracting. The corollary of this is that there will be more frequent entry to, and exit from, individual schools by children. *Sunk costs* are costs that cannot be recovered on exit from a market, and arguably these will be high in an educational context where schools have become part of a community. Any closure of the less successful schools will then incur substantial sunk costs. Similarly the disruption costs to children from frequent upheaval will be considerable. Critics of this view would argue that the decline and even closure of inadequate schools is a price worth paying for higher standards.

As in the case of health care, there can be no presumption that quasi-markets in education and training must of necessity create greater efficiency and choice. The issues are complex, and require thorough analysis and empirical investigation. Certainly the momentum is towards extending such quasi-markets, with recent reports such as Social Justice (1994) recommending the creation of individual learning accounts (i.e. transferable vouchers) for both pupils and employees. However, the Social Justice report recognised that pure market solutions will not work in the case of training (see also p. 545), so that it also proposes that *minimum standards* be set for all employers. For instance all employers, whether providing training or not, might be required to set aside up to 2% of payroll, reclaimable in part or full depending on the amount of training they themselves actually provide. Employers unable or unwilling to provide that level of training themselves would be required to put the difference into their employees' individual learning accounts or to pay the TECs to reimburse companies who do provide such training. Again the aim is to use quasi-markets rather than pure markets to redress a situation in which nearly two thirds of UK employers invest less than 2% of payroll costs in training, whereas three quarters of French employers invest more than 2% and in Germany an average of 3.5% of payroll is given towards training related programmes (Social Justice 1994).

Key terms		
	Contestable markets	Public choice theory
	Deregulation	Public interest theory
	Internal markets	Quality regulation
	Perfectly contestable markets	Quasi-markets
	Price regulation	Sustainable equilibrium
	Privatisation	
	Full definitions can be found in the 'Glossary of terms' (pp. 699–710)	

Review questions

1. An industry dominated by one large company produces a basic bulk chemical, ethydrene. The demand curve is represented by $P = 1,000 - 25Q$, where Q represents millions of tonnes of ethydrene and P the price per tonne. The total cost function for ethydrene is $TC = 400 + 580Q + 10Q^2$.

    (a) Determine the price, output and total profits that the company earns from its sale of ethydrene.
    (b) If the government imposes pollution control standards on ethydrene production that change the industry's cost curve to $TC = 500 + 650Q + 10Q^2$ then examine the impact of the new regulation on the price, output and profits of the monopoly producer.
    (c) What is the effect of stricter control standards on the company's rate of return on sales?

2. The recent privatisation of an electricity utility has posed dilemmas for government regulators. The new private company that now provides the electicity has a total cost curve $TC = 5 + 3Q$ and a demand curve $P = 10 - Q$, where costs and prices are in pence per kilowatt-hour and Q is measured in kilowatts (00s of millions) generated per week. Since privatisation the company has acted like a pure monopoly, charging a single price and limiting output. The regulator is trying to decide on various strategies to control the potentially powerful private monopoly.

    Answer the following questions using a diagram and simple algebra.

    (a) Draw the average and marginal cost functions and comment on their nature.
    (b) The government is thinking of requiring the electicity company to charge a price that reflects marginal cost of production. Draw the relevant demand and marginal revenue curves, and comment on the problems that will be created for the company if this pricing policy is adopted.

(c) The regulator has decided that the problems created by (b) can be solved by adopting a two-tier price. It will ask the company to charge a price of 6 pence per kilowatt-hour to consumers who are less price sensitive and charge the rest at the marginal cost rate. Explain whether this policy will help to maintain the viability of the company.

(d) Explain why the situation described in (c) is a second-best position for the electricity company. Suggest reasons why the regulators may decide to retain the two-tier pricing system even though such a policy gives the company nearly monopoly-type profits.

3. Figure 13.6(a) and (b) relate to contestability, industrial structure and market equilibrium. Using these diagrams and any other relevant information from Chapter 13, answer the following questions.

(a) Briefly explain the main assumptions underlying contestable markets.

(b) In Fig. 13.6(a) the market demand curve is denoted by D. Also, AC_A and MC_A are the average and marginal costs of a large company A operating within that market. If this figure operates under contestable market conditions:
   (i) Explain why firms would enter this market if the price were above $0P$.
   (ii) If we assume that the market demand is D and the output that minimises average cost is $1Q$ for the average firm, what would be the number of firms in the industry? Does the result surprise you given what you know about the nature of contestability?

(c) In Fig. 13.6(b) we have market demand (D) and market marginal revenue curves (MR) as in Fig. 13.6(a). However, in this instance we have a monopolist, M, who is operating under decreasing average costs (AC_M) up to and beyond the point where the AC_M curve crosses the market demand curve, D.
   (i) Locate the competitive output position. Can the monopoly operate effectively at this level?
   (ii) Locate the normal monopoly output position. Could this position be sustained in a contestable market?
   (iii) Locate the most likely output position for this monopoly firm given the constraints of contestability.

Fig. 13.6

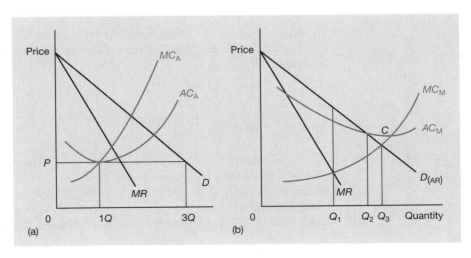

4. A regional bus service was run for 20 years as a local authority monopoly with price being set on a marginal cost basis. The demand curve for bus services was $P = 7 - 0.9Q$, where P is the average price per mile of journey (in pence) and Q is the number of passenger journeys per year (in millions). The marginal cost function was $MC = 3$. However, when the bus service was eventually privatised it was found that the change of ownership had merely shifted power from a public to a private monopoly. With the aid of a diagram:

   (a) Calculate the number of passenger journeys generated when the bus service was local authority controlled.
   (b) The privatisation of the bus services has meant that while demand for services has remained constant, the shareholders in the new company want better returns. The effect of this has been for company management to raise prices to monopoly levels while engaging in cost-cutting exercises.
      (i) What is the new private sector average price per mile of journey and the number of passenger journeys generated, given that the cost-cutting exercise produced a new marginal cost function of $MC = 2$?
      (ii) Calculate the *productive efficiency* gain as a result of the cost reduction and the *allocative* loss due to monopoly power. Is there a net gain or loss of welfare from the privatisation of bus services in this region?

5. A public utility water company has recently been privatised, but the government is worried that the company may use its regional monopoly of water supply to charge high prices. The demand curve for water is of the form $P = 8 - 0.8Q$, where P is price of water per thousand litres and Q is quantity of water in billions of litres per month. The marginal cost of the water supply is $MC = 0.5 + 0.375Q$.

   (a) If the water company had been allowed to charge the monopoly price and output, what would be their respective values?
   (b) To control any excessive prices, the government regulator is investigating two possible scenarios:
      (i) the adoption of a maximum price at the competitive market level;
      (ii) the adoption of a maximum price that would give the water company maximum revenue.

   Calculate the price and output values for these alternative solutions. Explain with the aid of a simple diagram the nature of the marginal revenue curve under condition (ii).

■ Further reading

Intermediate texts   Browning, E. and Browning, J. (1992), *Microeconomic Theory and Applications*, 4th edn, Chs 10 and 14, HarperCollins, London.
Dobson, S., Maddala, G. S. and Miller, E. (1995), *Microeconomics*, Ch. 16, McGraw-Hill, Maidenhead.
Hope, S. (1999), *Applied Microeconomics*, Ch. 12, Wiley, Chichester.

Katz, M. and Rosen, H. (1998), *Microeconomics*, 3rd edn, Ch. 18, Irwin, Boston, Mass.

Laidler, D. and Estrin, S. (1995), *Introduction to Microeconomics*, 4th edn, Chs 33–35, Harvester Wheatsheaf, Hemel Hempstead.

Maddala, G. S. and Miller, E. (1989), *Microeconomics*: *Theory and Application*, Ch. 12, McGraw-Hill, New York.

Nicholson, W. (1997), *Intermediate Microeconomics and its Application*, 7th edn, Ch. 19, Dryden Press, Fort Worth.

Noll, R. (1989), 'Conclusion: economics, politics and deregulation', *The Political Economy of Deregulation*, American Enterprise for Public Policy Research, Washington.

Pindyck, R. and Rubinfeld, D. (1998), *Microeconomics*, 4th edn, Ch. 9, Macmillan, Basingstoke.

Price, C. (1994), 'Economic regulation of privatised monopolies', in Jackson, P. M and Price, C. *op. cit.*

Varian, H. (1999), *Intermediate Microeconomics*, 5th edn, Ch. 23, Norton, New York.

Advanced texts

Gravelle, H. and Rees, R. (1992), *Microeconomics*, 2nd edn, Ch. 11, Longman, Harlow.

Mas-Colell, A., Whinston, M. D. and Green, J. R. (1995), *Microeconomic Theory*, Chs 12 and 22, Oxford University Press, Oxford.

Articles and other sources

Becker, G. (1983), 'A theory of competition amongst pressure groups for political influence', *Quarterly Journal of Economics*, 98.

Bishop, M., Kay, J. and Mayer, C. (1995), *The Regulatory Challenge*, Oxford University Press, Oxford.

Boardman, A. and Vining, A. R. (1989), 'Ownership and performance in competitive environments. A comparison of private, mixed and state-owned enterprises', *Journal of Law and Economics*, 32, April.

Byatt, I. (1997), 'Taking a view on price review: a perspective on economic regulation in the water industry', *National Institute Economic Review*, 1, 159.

Glennerster, H. and Law, W. (1990), 'Education', in J. Hills (ed.) *The State of Welfare*, Clarendon Press, Oxford.

Glennerster, H. (1993), 'The Economics of education', in N. Barr, and D. Whynes, *The Economics of the Welfare State*, Weidenfeld and Nicolson.

Green, R. and Newbery, D. (1997), 'Competition in the electricity industry in England and Wales', *Oxford Review of Economic Policy*, 13, 1.

Green, R. and McDaniel, T. (1998), 'Competition in electricity supply: will 1998 be worth it?', *Fiscal Studies*, 19, 3.

Helm, D. (1994), 'British utility regulation: theory, practice and reform', *Oxford Review of Economic Policy*, 10, 3.

House of Commons Transport Committee (1993), Fourth Report, *Roads for the Future*, 1, 198, HMSO.

HMSO (1993), Fourth Report, *The Government's Proposals for the Deregulation of Buses in London*.

Ison, S. (1999), 'Transport', in A. Griffiths and S. Wall (eds), *Applied Economics*, 8th edn, Longman, Harlow.

Jackson, P. M. and Price, C. M. (eds) (1994), *Privatisation and Regulation*, Longman, Harlow.

Jaffe, A. B., Peterson, S. R. and Portney, P. R. (1995), 'Environmental regulation and the competitiveness of US manufacturing. What does the evidence tell us?', *Journal of Economic Literature*, XXXIII, March.

Le Grand, J. (1992), 'Quasi markets in welfare,' *The Economic Review*, November.

McDonald, F. E. (1987), 'Contestable markets – a new ideal model', *Economics*, Spring.

Mahini, A. (1993), 'The three faces of European deregulation,' *The McKinsey Quarterly*, No 3.

McKenzie, G. (1998), 'Financial regulation and the European Union', *The Economic Review*, April.

Mortimore, P. *et al.* (1988), 'The Junior School Project: Understanding School Effectiveness', ILEA Statistics Section.

Newbery, D. and Pollitt, M. (1997), 'The restructuring and privatisation of Britain's CEGB: was it worth it?', *Journal of Industrial Economics*, 45.

OECD (1997), 'The economic benefits of regulatory reform', *OECD Economic Studies*, 1, 28.

OFFER (1997), 'The competitive electricity market from 1998: price restraints', Office of Electricity Regulation.

Parker, D. (1995), 'Has privatisation improved performance?' *Developments in Economics*', II.

Peltzman, S. (1976), 'Toward a more general theory of regulation', *Journal of Law and Economics*, 19 August.

Rutter, M. (1979), Secondary schools and their effects on children, Open Books.

Schwartz, G. and Lopes, P. S. (1993), 'Privatization: expectations, trade-offs and results', *Finance and Development*, June.

Social Justice (1994), *Strategies for National Renewal*, Vintage, London.

Stevens, B. (1991), 'Privatisation in OECD countries', *National Westminster Bank Review*, August.

Stigler, G. (1971), 'The theory of economic regulation', *Bell Journal of Economics*, 2.

Thompson, D. J. and Whitfield, A. (1990), 'Express Coaching: privatisation, incumbent advantage and the competitive process', Centre for Business Strategy, Working Paper, London Business School.

Train, K. (1991), *Optimal Regulation*: *The Economic Theory of Natural Monopoly*, MIT Press, Cambridge, Mass.

Wall, S. (1999), 'Privatisation and deregulation', A. Griffiths and S. Wall (eds), *Applied Economics*, 8th edn, Pearson, Harlow.

Weyman-Jones, T. (1994), 'Deregulation', in *Privatisation and Regulation*, Eds. Price and Jackson, op. cit.

Whynes, D. (1993), *Welfare State Economics*: *Studies in the UK Economy*, Heinemann, London.

Winston, C. (1993), 'Economic deregulation,' *Journal of Economic Literature*, XXXI, September, The Brookings Institution, Massachusetts.

Answers to review questions

Chapter 1   1. (a) To maximise total utility where there is more than one commodity, the condition to be satisfied is

$$\frac{MU_x}{P_x} = \frac{MU_y}{P_y} = \cdots \frac{MU_n}{P_n}$$

The first task is to calculate the utility/price ratios by dividing each marginal utility column by the price of the relevant ticket so that we obtain a matrix of ratio values, as seen in Table A.1.

Table A.1

No. of tickets	Cinema	Concert hall	Jazz club	Jazz club[a]
1	5.00	3.00	3.13	4.17
2	4.00	2.00	2.25	3.00
3	2.00	1.50	2.00	2.67
4	1.75	1.00	1.50	2.00
5	1.50	0.50	1.25	1.67
6	1.00	0.38	0.88	1.17
7	0.50	0.13	0.63	0.83
8	0.25	0.06	0.88	0.50

[a] With special offer of £6 per ticket

From this matrix it can be seen that there are two possible ratio solutions that satisfy the maximum utility condition, namely ratios of marginal utility per £ of 2 and 1.5. To find out which is the optimum solution we have to determine the combination of tickets that maximises total utility. When the ratio value of 2 is used, the utility of *three* cinema tickets is 22 utils (10 + 8 + 4), *two* concert hall tickets, 20 utils, and *three* jazz tickets, 59 utils – a total utility of 101 utils. Also, the total amount spent will be 3 × £2, 2 × £4, and 3 × £8, which is a total of £38. Therefore this fulfils the dual criterion that the ratios are equal and all the income is spent (i.e. within the budget constraint).

The other solution possible here would have been where all the ratios were 1.5. However, repeating the exercise noted above would have given a total utility of 125.5 utils, which is greater than that shown above (101 utils), but this would have cost £54, which is beyond the student's extra monthly allowance.

(b) If the student was able to buy only two jazz tickets rather than three, then there would be a surplus of £8 to divide between the cinema and concert hall tickets. The solution here may be found by investigating where the marginal utility to price ratios are the same for these two types of ticket, i.e. at 1.5 utils per £. In this case this would mean two more cinema tickets and one more concert hall ticket at a total extra cost of £8. The total utility as a result of the restricted combination would be cinema (28.5 utils), concert hall (26 utils) and jazz club (43 utils) – which is a second-best total of 97.5 utils. This means that the constraint on the purchase of the desired amount of jazz tickets has resulted in an overall loss of $101 - 97.5 = 3.5$ utils.

(c) To decide whether the student would have gained from the introductory offer for jazz tickets, it is necessary to divide the marginal utility function for jazz club tickets by the introductory price of £6. The result of these calculations can be seen in brackets in the last column of Table A.1. We can see that the only possible utility/price ratios that are now common to all three types of ticket are 2.0 and 0.5 utils per £.

When the ratio value of 2.0 is used, then the utility of *three cinema tickets* is 22 utils ($10 + 8 + 4$), *two concert hall tickets* 20 utils, and *four jazz tickets* 71 utils – a total utility of 113 utils. The money spent would have been $3 \times £2$, $2 \times £4$, and $4 \times £6$, which is a total of £38. Hence the dual criteria – that the utility/price ratios are the same and that all the income is spent – are fulfilled. Therefore, comparing these total utility figures with those in part (a) above, it appears that if the student had booked a few months earlier she could have increased her total utility by 12 utils ($113 - 101$).

The only other possible solution to the problem would have been where all the ratio values were 0.5 utils per £. Using similar calculations to those above, the total utility enjoyed would have been 159.5 utils: i.e. higher than any other previous figure, but at a cost of £82, which would have been far above the student's one-off windfall grant of £38.

2. (a) If we let Q_c be the quantity of clothes and Q_e the frequency of eating out, then the general budget expression that equates total expenditure with total income is

$$£12Q_c + £6Q_e = £60 \tag{1}$$

(b) To derive the budget equation from this expression divide by £12:

$$Q_c + 0.5Q_e = 5 \tag{2}$$

Subtract $0.5Q_e$ from both sides:

$$Q_c = 5 - 0.5Q_e \tag{3}$$

(c) The vertical intercept is where Q_e is zero, i.e. Q_c is 5. The horizontal intercept is where Q_c is zero and Q_e is 5/0.5 or 10. The slope of the budget line can be read off directly from equation (3) since this is the equation for a straight line with a slope of 0.5. Another way of obtaining the information is from the intercepts calculated above. The vertical intercept is 5 and the horizontal intercept is 10, so the slope of the line must be 5/10 or 0.5. It could also be calculated from the basic knowledge that the slope of the budget line is P_e/P_c, i.e. £6/£12 or 0.5.

3. (a) The condition for the consumer to be in equilibrium is where the budget line is tangential to the indifference curve. At this point the consumer will have achieved maximum satisfaction given the constraints of the budget. The solution can be obtained by equating the two functions and solving for Q_y and Q_x.

Where the indifference curve is tangential to the budget line then:

$$12 - Q_x = \frac{36}{Q_x} \tag{1}$$

Multiply both sides by Q_x:

$$12Q_x - Q_x^2 = 36 \tag{2}$$

Rearrange into a quadratic equation and solve for Q_x:

$$Q_x^2 - 12Q_x + 36 = 0$$
$$(Q_x - 6)(Q_x - 6) = 0$$
$$Q_x = +6 \tag{3}$$

At $Q_x = 6$ the budget line is tangent to the indifference line.

To obtain the value of Q_y substitute $Q_x = 6$ in the budget equation

$Q_y = 12 - Q_x$:

i.e. $Q_y = 12 - 6$
$$= 6 \tag{4}$$

(b) The indifference curve and the budget line touch where $Q_x = 6$ and $Q_y = 6$. To see that this is a point of tangency we must prove that the slopes of both lines are the same at the point where $Q_x = 6$.

First find the first derivative (slope) of the budget line $Q_y = 12 - Q_x$:

$$\frac{dQ_y}{dQ_x} = -1$$

Then find the slope of the indifference curve at $Q_x = 6$:

$$Q_y = \frac{36}{Q_x} \text{ or } 36Q_x^{-1} \text{ (since } 1/Q_x \text{ is the same as } Q_x{-1})$$

$$\frac{dQ_y}{dQ_x} = -36Q_x^{-2}$$

$$= \frac{-36}{Q_x^2}$$

where $Q_x = 6$ then $\dfrac{dQ_y}{dQ_x} = \dfrac{-36}{36} = -1$

Therefore the slope of the budget line is constant (straight line) with a value of -1. The slope of the indifference curve at $Q_x = 6$ is also -1. This means that both lines are tangential where $Q_x = 6$ with slopes of $-1°$ or $45°$.

4. (a) Draw the two indifference curves by joining the individual points with as smooth a curve as is feasible (Fig. A.1.)

(b) The first step after drawing the two indifference curves is to insert the budget line constraints. The budget line will cut the horizontal axis at 168 hrs – this being the total weekly hours available for leisure. The other end of the budget line will cut the vertical income axis at £336 i.e. (168 × £2) since this will be the position where leisure time will be zero and all week will be used as work time. The optimum satisfaction position will be where indifference curve I_1 is tangential to the budget line, and this will be at approximately 83 hours of leisure (85 hours work) and an income of £170 (85 × £2).

(c) If the government subsidises wages such that the wage rate per hour rises to £6, then the budget line will pivot at 168 hours and cut the vertical axis at £1,008 (168 × £6). When this budget line is drawn, it will be tangential to the second indifference curve at approximately 75 hours of leisure (93 hours work) a week

Fig. A.1

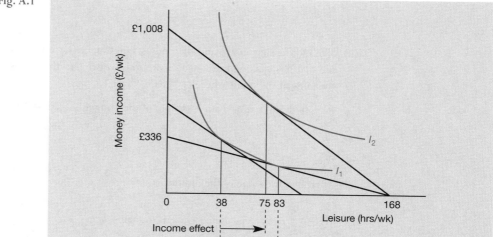

with an income level of some £558 (93 × £6). This means that the rise in wage rate from £2 to £6 per week has increased the number of hours worked by approximately 8 hours, and increased weekly income by some £388.

(d) To show the Hicksian income and substitution effects it is necessary to shift the £6 per week budget line downward to the left until it is tangential to the first indifference curve. This will put the worker back onto the original indifference curve but at the new wage rate of £6 (the compensated budget line). Leisure time will be approximately 38 hours (work 130 hours) and income £336. This means that the substitution effect of an increase in wage from £2 to £6 per hour is to increase the number of hours worked by 45 hours (83 − 38), and the income effect leads to a fall in the number of hours worked by 37 hours (75 − 38). As a result, the net increase in hours worked as a result of the rise in wage rate is only 8 hours.

What has happened here is that the large increase in hourly wage rate has had two effects. The first effect, i.e. the substitution effect, led to a substantial substitution of work for leisure involving 45 more hours worked. However, the large increase in wage rates also meant that the worker could earn an increased 'acceptable' level of income without losing too much leisure (i.e. without having to work too many extra hours). This income effect led to a fall of 37 hours worked per week.

As a result of both income and substitution effects, the final increase in hours worked was only 8 hours. The supply curve for labour in this case is upward sloping and fairly steep since it takes a largish increase in wage rates to induce the worker to work more hours.

5. (a) The first task is to find the expression for the budget constraint. We know that the maximum budget available is £95 and that P_x is £10 and P_y is £5. Therefore the equation for the budget constraint is (excluding the £ sign)

$$10Q_x + 5Q_y = 95 \tag{1}$$

(b) To enable the budget constraint to be used in the Lagrangian function we need to equate it to zero, i.e.

$$95 - 10Q_x - 5Q_y = 0 \tag{2}$$

The next step is to substitute this in the Lagrangian function given in the question:

$$L = Q_x + 8Q_y - Q_x^2 - Q_xQ_y - Q_y^2 + \lambda(95 - 10Q_x - 5Q_y) \tag{3}$$
$$L = Q_x + 8Q_y - Q_x^2 - Q_xQ_y - Q_y^2 + 95\lambda - 10\lambda Q_x - 5\lambda Q_y \tag{4}$$

To maximise L we set the partial derivatives of L with respect to Q_x, Q_y and λ equal to zero.

Differentiating L with respect to Q_x:

$$\frac{\partial L}{\partial Q_x} = 1 - 2Q_x - Q_y - 10\lambda = 0 \tag{5}$$

Differentiating L with respect to Q_y:

$$\frac{\partial L}{\partial Q_y} = 8 - Q_x - 2Q_y - 5\lambda = 0 \tag{6}$$

Differentiating L with respect to λ:

$$\frac{\partial L}{\partial \lambda} = 95 - 10Q_x - 5Q_y = 0 \tag{7}$$

We can compute the values of Q_x and Q_y that maximise the consumer's utility by using equations (5) and (6). Multiplying (6) by 2 and subtracting it from (5) we get:

$$
\begin{array}{lr}
1 - 2Q_x - Q_y - 10\lambda & = 0 \\
16 - 2Q_x - 4Q_y - 10\lambda & = 0 \\
\hline
-15 \qquad +3Q_y & = 0 \\
\qquad\qquad 3Q_y & = 15 \\
\qquad\qquad Q_y & = 5
\end{array}
$$

To find the value of Q_x, substitute $Q_y = 5$ in equation (2):

$$
\begin{array}{r}
95 - 10Q_x - 25 = 0 \\
10Q_x = 70 \\
Q_x = 7
\end{array}
$$

To calculate the value of λ, substitute the values of Q_x and Q_y in (5):

$$
\begin{array}{r}
1 - 14 - 5 - 10\lambda = 0 \\
10\lambda = -18 \\
\lambda = -1.8
\end{array}
$$

In this case λ measures the marginal effect on the value of the objective function resulting from a one-unit change in the constraint. In other words it measures how much more would be added to total utility if the budget were increased by £1. It is, in fact the ratio of marginal utility to price.

Chapter 2　1. (a) (i) The graph of the data can be seen in Fig. A.2.

(ii) When the price is £6 per edition, then a line PC can be drawn across at this level that shows that the quantity of editions demanded per month will be 500 units. Consumer surplus, as we saw in Chapter 1, is the area between the demand curve and the price line, i.e. the area APC. The area of the triangle APC (as with all triangles) is $\frac{1}{2}$ PC × AP, so that the total monthly consumer surplus is $\frac{1}{2}$ (500) × £5 = £1250.

(iii) As we saw in Chapter 2 , the point price elasticity of demand (*PED*) can be expressed as $PED = (P/Q) \times K$, where K is the reciprocal of the slope of the demand curve. The slope of the demand curve is 11/1100 or 1/100, and therefore its reciprocal is 100. Since we know that $P = $ £6 and $Q = 500$, then

Fig. A.2

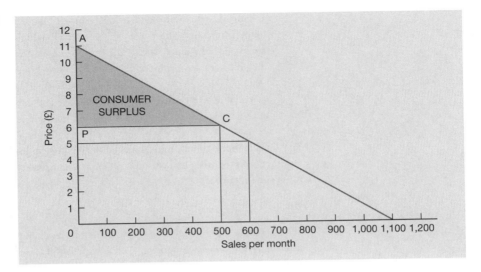

applying the formula we get $(6/500) \times 100 = 1.2$. When the price is £6 per journal, demand is therefore relatively elastic with a value of 1.2. The same process can be repeated for the price of £5, remembering that in the expression for point price elasticity of demand the value of K will be the same but P/Q will have changed, i.e. the new PED $= (5/600) \times 100 = 0.8$ (approx.).

(iv) The arc price elasticity of demand is defined in Chapter 2 as $(P+P_1)/ (Q + Q_1) \times (\Delta Q/\Delta P)$. Substituting the figures for P and Q when P rises from £5 to £6 gives the expression $11/1100 \times 100/1 = 1$. In this case the arc price elasticity of demand is unity or 1 (strictly speaking –1). We can see when we compare this answer with those obtained in (iii) above that the arc elasticity of demand is really an average of the two point elasticity measures of 1.2 and 0.83. When price changes are *discrete*, i.e. are relatively large (in this case from £5 to £6), then the arc measure may be a more appropriate technique to use. The point elasticity measurement calculated in (iii) above is based on *continuous* variables, with extremely small changes in price, an assumption that is often unrealistic in practice.

(b) (i) If Sci-publishers' price elasticity of demand is –1 and the firm increases its price by 4%, then sales will change by $-1 \times 4\% = -4\%$. Since it is assumed that consumers' income will rise by 3% and income elasticity of demand is 2, then total sales should increase by 6% as a result of income changes. Also, if Electype's price falls by 2% and the cross-elasticity of demand is –2 , then Sci-publishers should experience a fall in sales equivalent to $-2 \times 2 = -4\%$. The *net effect* of an increase in Sci-publishers' price by 4% in 2001 should be a fall in sales of –2% (i.e. –4% +6% –4%). Therefore the monthly sales of its journal in the year 2001 would be 550 (0.98) = 539 units.

(ii) *Without* an increase in the price of Sci-publishers' journal, there will be an increase in expected sales (given the assumptions made about the income and cross-elasticities of demand) of 6% – 4% = 2%. In order to keep sales unchanged, sales will need to be reduced by 2%. Sci-publishers could do this by increasing the price of its journal, which under normal circumstances should reduce sales. Since the price elasticity of demand is −1 then Sci-publishers should increase price by 2%, which would then lead to a fall in sales of −1 x 2% = −2%. This fall in sales would cancel out the rise of 2% in sales as a result of the combined income and cross-elasticity effects, leaving monthly sales at the original level of 550 journals per month.

2. (a) The total revenue function (*TR*) can be derived by multiplying quantity and price together, and the marginal revenue (*MR*) can be calculated *at* each output level by using the formula

$$MR = P\,(1 + 1/e)$$

(This formula incorporates the negative sign for *e*; change + to − inside parenthesis if we ignore negative sign for *e*.) The completed table will then be as shown in Table A.2.

Table A.2

Price	Quantity	Elasticity	TR	MR
£6	0		0	0
£5	300	−5	1500	4
£4	600	−2	2400	2
£3	900	−1	2700	0
£2	1200	−0.5	2400	−2
£1	1500	−0.2	1500	−4
£0	1800	0	0	0

(b) Plotting the above data in Table A.2 will result in the diagram in Fig. A.3.

(c) From the table and figures it can be seen that there is a clear relationship between the variables. When price falls towards £3, elasticity is above unity, total revenue rises and marginal revenue (which is the change in total revenue) is positive. At price of £3, elasticity reaches unity, the total revenue is a maximum, and marginal revenue becomes zero. Finally, when price falls below £3, the elasticity of demand becomes less than 1 and total revenue falls while marginal revenue becomes negative.

(d) The equation for any straight line when price is on the vertical axis and quantity demanded is on the horizontal axis is given by $P = a + bQ$, where *a* is the intercept on the vertical axis and *b* is the slope of the line. Using this definition and taking the relevant data from Fig. A.3(b) we can see that for the demand curve, *a* = 6, b = − 6/1800 (meals are in '00s), so that the equation is $P = 6 − 0.0033Q$. Using the same method, the equation for the *MR* is $MR = 6 − 0.0066Q$. Comparing *AR* with *MR* we can clearly identify the well-known fact that the marginal revenue curve is twice as steep as the demand curve.

Fig. A.3

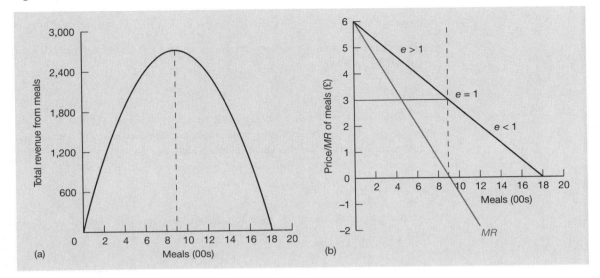

(a)

(b)

3. (a) The number of sweaters purchased per year declines by 40 units for each £1 increase in the price of sweaters (P_w), increases by 0.8 units for each £1 increase in advertising expenditure on sweaters (A), and increases by 0.1 units for every £1 increase in per capita income (Y).

(b) To find the value of Q substitute the relevant values for $(P_w, A, $ and Y in the demand function:

$$Q_w = 100 - 40(50) + 0.8(6,000) + 0.1(20,000)$$
$$= 100 - 2,000 + 4,800 + 2,000$$
$$= 4,900$$

(c) The equation for the demand curve can be obtained from the demand function by relating Q_w to P_w, all other factors remaining constant. To do this we substitute into the estimated demand function the values of the explanatory variables with the exception of P_w. In other words,

$$Q_w = 100 - 40P_w + 4,800 + 2,000$$
$$= 6,900 - 40P_w$$

To convert this demand curve into the normal form with P_w on the left-hand side and Q_w on the right-hand side merely subtract 6,900 from both sides:

$$Q_w - 6,900 = -40P_w$$

Divide both sides by 40 and rearrange:

$$Q_w/40 - 6,900/40 = -P_w$$
$$P_w = 6,900/40 - Q_w/40$$
$$P_w = 172.5 - 0.025Q_w$$

This equation is the normal way of expressing the demand curve, with 172.5 being the intercept on the vertical price axis and 0.025 being the slope of the demand curve.

(d) To calculate the point price elasticity of demand we need to understand that the normal definition is

$$\partial Q_w / \partial P_w \cdot P_w / Q_w$$

We know from the demand function that $\partial Q_w / \partial P_w$ is, in fact, 40 since this is the coefficient of P_w in the demand equation and measures the effect of demand per unit change in price. We also know that the values of P_w and Q_w are 50 and 4,900 respectively. Therefore, substituting in the elasticity definition we get

$$40 \times 50 / 4{,}900 = 0.408$$

Similarly, to obtain the value of income elasticity of demand we have

$$0.1 \times 20{,}000 / 4{,}900 = 0.408$$

In this case both price and income elasticity of demand happen to coincide at 0.408, which means that the price and income elasticities of demand are relatively inelastic.

(e) To derive the total revenue function we know that total revenue obtained from the sales of the sweaters equals the price of each sweater times the quantity sold, i.e. $TR_w = P_w \cdot Q_w$. Since we know the demand curve is $P_w = 172.5 - 0.025 Q_w$, we can substitute for P_w in the total revenue equation:

$$\begin{aligned} TR_w &= (172.5 - 0.025 Q_w) \, Q_w \\ &= 172.5 Q_w - 0.025 Q_w^2 \end{aligned}$$

To derive the marginal revenue expression we need to differentiate the TR function with respect to Q_w:

$$MR \, (dTR_w / dQ_w) = 172.5 - 0.050 Q_w$$

We could also have arrived at this conclusion from a knowledge of the fact that the slope of the MR curve is twice that of the demand curve.

4. (a) To find the intersection points take the demand equation and, in turn, let P_L and Q_L be equal to 0. For example, when $Q_L = 0$ then $P_L = 50$. When $P_L = 0$ then $Q_L = 80$ (50/0.625). Therefore the demand curve cuts the vertical price axis at £50 and the horizontal sales axis at 80 pairs of jeans.

(b) We know that point elasticity of demand is defined as $P_L / Q_L \cdot \partial Q_L / \partial P_L$. Since the slope of the demand curve i.e. $\partial P_L / \partial Q_L$ is -0.625 (i.e. $-5/8$), then its inverse, $\partial Q_L / \partial P_L$, will be -1.6 (i.e. $-8/5$). To calculate the elasticity at point 40/16 merely substitute the values in the equation for elasticity, i.e. $(40/16) \times (-8/5) = -4$. Similarly, at point 16/80, the elasticity measure will be $(16/80) \times (-8/5) = -0.32$.

(c) From the definition of elasticity we know that the value of $\partial Q_L / \partial P_L$ is $-8/5$. If the elasticity is to be unity then the other part of the elasticity definition, i.e. P_L / Q_L, must be in the ratio of $5/8$. The only possible combination of price and sales is £25/40 since here the ratios are $5/8$. These values are at the mid points of the respective axes, as can be seen by comparing these figures with the intercept calculations in answer (a). Since the demand curve forms a right-angled triangle with the axes, it can be proved using congruent triangles that the price/sales combination of £25/£40 will not only be at the mid points of the respective axes but will also be at the mid point of the demand curve.

(d) To solve this problem we need to understand that the maximising level of output is where $MR = MC$. We can calculate MR in two ways. First, we know from elementary theory that the slope of the MR curve is twice that of the demand (AR) curve (i.e. 2×0.625), so that the equation for MR curve is $MR = 50 - 1.25Q_L$. Another way to do this would be by using simple calculus. We know that total revenue $TR_L = P_L . Q_L$ and that $P_L = 50 - 0.625Q_L$ from our demand equation. Simply substitute $50 - 0.625Q_L$ for P_L in the total revenue equation:

$$TR_L = 50 - 0.625Q_L \ (Q_L)$$
$$= 50Q_L - 0.625Q_L^2$$
$$\frac{dTR_L}{dQ_L} = 50 - 1.25Q_L$$

Since we know that the MC of each pair of jeans is £20 then we can find the profit-maximising price and sales level by equating $MR = MC$:

$$50 - 1.25Q_L = 20$$
$$50 - 20 = 1.25Q_L$$
$$30 = 1.25Q_L$$
$$24 = Q_L$$

To find the price of the jeans, substitute $Q_L = 24$ in the demand equation $P_L = 50 - 0.625Q$. This leaves $P_L = 50 - 0.625 \times 24$, which equals £35. Therefore the profit-maximising price and quantity are £35 and 24 pairs of jeans respectively.

5. (a) The first task is to draw the axes with smoothness on the vertical axis and flavour on the horizontal axis (see Fig. A.4). Then the relevant attribute rays can be drawn with the following ratios (slopes): Parma, $2/1$, Yama, $1/2$ and Mano, $1/1$. The next stage is to locate the attainable combination of the desired attributes given the budget constraint. For the Parma brand, the number of bars that can be bought is £10/0.75 = 13.33. Since each bar gives 10 units of smoothness, the total units of smoothness obtained will be $13.33 \times 10 = 133.3$ units, which is then measured off on the smoothness axis. A similar calculation would give 66.6 (5×13.3) units of flavour, which is then plotted on the flavour axis. Repeating the procedure for the Yama brand would give 83.3 units of attribute on the smoothness axis and 166.6 units of attribute on the flavour axis respectively. The next stage is to draw the efficiency frontier between the Parma and Yama

Fig. A.4

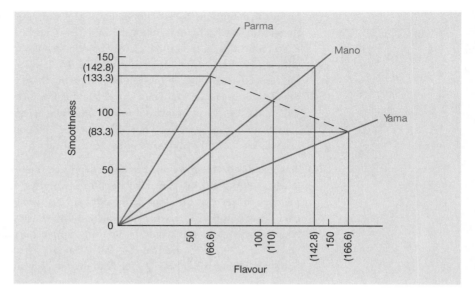

attribute rays given the above budget constraints: i.e. join the maximum attainable point of smoothness/flavour on the Parma ray (133.3/66.6) to the similar maximum attainable point on the Yama ray (83.3/166.6).

(b) The problem asks us to look at the Mano brand in such a way that the combination of attributes that it has lies on the efficiency frontier. In other words, it is at the point where the Mano ray cuts the efficiency frontier. An approximate reading on the smoothness and flavour scale gives a value of 110 units. From the calculations we made in (a), we know the income (£10), the units of attribute (10) per bar, and the maximum allowable units on the frontier (110) – the only variable not known is the price for Mano that satisfies these criteria. Using the same methodology as the calculations in (a) we can derive a formula for the maximum price per bar of Yama that can be charged given the flavour constraint of 110. Hence we get £10/$P \times 10$ =110. Therefore $P = 100/110 = 0.91$ or 91p.

(c) If however, the Mano brand was priced at 70p then we could find the maximum combination of attributes possible on the Mano ray. As in (a) this is £10/.70 $\times$ 10 = 142.8 units of both smoothness and flavour. This can then be plotted on the graph. We can see that the consumer would shift from Parma to Mano because Mano gives more smoothness *and* flavour attribute units than Parma. However, when we compare Mano with Yama we find that Mano has more smoothness attributes but less flavour units than Yama so that some consumers who prefer smoothness may shift to Mano but not all. The marginal rate of substitution of smoothness for flavour is 23.8 (166.6 − 142.8) to 59.5 (142.8 − 83.3), i.e. the MRS is 59.5/23.8 = 2.5. Therefore the Yama consumer will only shift to Mano if the MRS of smoothness for flavour rises above 2.5.

Chapter 3   1. (a) We know that the standard deviation of a portfolio consisting of one risky and one risk-free asset is

$$\sigma_P = b\sigma_m \text{ or } b = \sigma_P/\sigma_m$$

where σ_P is the standard deviation of the portfolio, b is the fraction of the portfolio invested in the risky asset, and σ_m is the standard deviation of the risky asset.

The value of b can be obtained by substituting the values of σ_P (0.018) and σ_m (0.09) in the above equation, i.e. $b = 0.018/0.09 = 0.2$. This means that 20% of the portfolio should be invested in more risky steel shares and 80% in safer Government stock.

The expected return on the total portfolio is

$$R_P = bR_m + (1 - b)R_f$$

Therefore, substituting $b = 0.2$, $R_m = 0.12$, and $R_f = 0.08$ in the equation will give the value of the expected returns from the whole portfolio:

$$
\begin{aligned}
R_P &= (0.2) \times 0.12 + (1 - 0.2) \times 0.08 \\
&= 0.024 + 0.064 \\
&= 0.088
\end{aligned}
$$

(b) Rearranging the expected return equation in (a), we can express the total expected return R_P in the following way:

$$R_P = R_f + b (R_m - R_f)$$

Substituting the relevant values in the equation and remembering that R_m has fallen to 0.10 we get

$$
\begin{aligned}
0.088 &= 0.08 + b (0.10 - 0.08) \\
0.088 &= b (0.02) \\
b &= 0.008/0.02 = 0.4
\end{aligned}
$$

In other words, the investor would have to increase his share of investment in steel to 0.4 (40%) of the total portfolio in order to retain the same overall expected return given the fact that the expected rate of return on steel shares (R_m) was to fall from 0.12 to 0.10.

(c) To answer this question we need to understand that, for an optimum portfolio, the return that the investor needs in order to accept a further increase in risk, i.e. the price of the risk, must be equal to the marginal rate of substitution (MRS) between the risk-free and the risky assets, i.e. between government shares and steel shares. The price of the risk is the so-called budget line or the trade-off between risk and expected return. We saw that the slope of the budget or trade-off line is expressed as $(R_m - R_f)/\sigma_m$. Substituting the relevant values in the expression gives $(0.12 - 0.08)/0.09 = 0.44$. For an optimum portfolio, the MRS must also be 0.44.

2. (a) In order to determine what sort of risk taker the manufacturer is, we need to know what happens to the marginal utility of money as profits in Deutschmarks vary. To do this we need to differentiate the total utility function with respect to D. For example, we know that the total utility function is

$$U = 300D - 2D^2$$

Differentiate U with respect to D to obtain the marginal utility (MU) of money:

$$MU = \frac{dU}{dD} = 300 - 4D$$

We see that the marginal utility function is a straight line with a negative slope of −4, indicating that as marginal utility falls, profits in money terms rises.

This conclusion could have been obtained in a simpler way by taking the utility function and substituting values for D and then calculating the resultant value of U. For example, if the values of D are 1 and 2 then the values of U would be

$$U = 300D - 2D^2$$
$$U = 300(1) - 2(1)^2 = 300 - 2 = 298 \text{ utils}$$
$$U = 300(2) - 2(2)^2 = 600 - 8 = 592 \text{ utils}$$

In other words, when D doubles, the total utility *does* increase but by *less* than in proportion to *D:* i.e. the marginal utility of money falls and the exporter is said to be risk averse.

(b) From the relationship in (a) we have seen that if the exporter has a diminishing marginal utility of money then this means that he will suffer more from a Deutschmark lost (moving back on the total utility curve) than he will derive from a Deutschmark gained (moving forward on the total utility curve). Since risk taking means, in essence, that a given future outcome may turn out to be lower than expected, it is unlikely that the German exporter will want to take this risk if the marginal utility gained from the export profits is decreasing.

(c) To find out whether the exporter should lease or not lease new equipment we have to calculate the expected profits from leasing and not leasing under different demand conditions (see Table A.3).

Table A.3

Demand	Probability	Profits		Expected profits	
		Leased	Not leased	Leased	Not leased
Above normal	0.25	80	60	20	15
Normal	0.50	50	34	25	17
Below normal	0.25	0	20	0	5
Expected profits				45	37

The expected profits columns in Table A.3 are obtained by multiplying the probability figures for each demand situation by profits, both leased and not leased. From the table we can see that in terms of expected profits, it would be better for the exporter to lease new equipment since the expected profits are 45,000 DM as compared with 37,000 DM.

(d) If the exporter's objective is to maximise utility, then the situation would appear as in Table A.4.

Table A.4

Demand	Probability	Utility		Expected utility	
		Leased	Not leased	Leased	Not leased
Above normal	0.25	92	76	23	19
Normal	0.50	40	60	20	30
Below normal	0.25	0	20	0	5
Expected utility				43	54

The expected utility columns are obtained by multiplying the probability figures for each demand situation by the associated utility levels, both leased and not leased. From these figures it appears that the exporter should not lease the intended capital equipment because the expected utility from not leasing (54,000 utils) is greater than that of leasing (43,000 utils).

3. (a) The first step is to calculate the net present value of the two gaming machines. Using the standard formula and substituting the values for machine 1 we get

$$\sum_{t=1}^{t=4} \frac{£4,250}{(1.10)^t} - £10,000$$

To obtain the discount factor for machine 1 we need to consult the present value tables for years 1, 2, 3 and 4 using the discount rate of 10%. In other words, the discount rate gives us the value of $1/(1.10)^t$ in this equation for each of the four years starting with $t=1$. The final calculations are shown in Table A.5.

Table A.5

Year	Cash income(£)	Discount factor (10%)	Present value (£)
1	4,250	0.9091	3,863.68
2	4,250	0.8264	3,512.20
3	4,250	0.7513	3,193.03
4	4,250	0.6830	2,902.75
			Total 13,471.66

NPV = £13,471.66 − £10,000
    = £3,471.66

To calculate the NPV for machine 2, the procedure is repeated using the relevant cash flow and life span figures (Table A.6).

Table A.6

Year	Cash income (£)	Discount factor (10%)	Present value (£)
1	6,000	0.9091	5,454.60
2	6,000	0.8264	4,958.40
3	6,000	0.7513	4,507.80
			Total 14,920.80

NPV = £14,920.80 – £10,000
= £4,920.80

From the figures in Table A.6 it can be seen that the most favourable investment that the landlord should make is to buy machine 2, since its NPV is higher than for machine 1.

(b) The landlord feels that technological change is faster in the machine 2 sector and thus adjusts the discount rate to reflect this risk premium. If the discount rate chosen is 20%, then the exercise is repeated using new discount factors obtained from present value tables (see Table A.7).

Table A.7

Year	Cash income (£)	Discount factor (10%)	Present value (£)
1	6,000	0.8333	4,999.80
2	6,000	0.6944	4,166.40
3	6,000	0.5787	3,472.20
			Total 12,638.40

NPV = £12,638.40 – £10,000
= £2,638.40

As a result of the risk adjustment being made to machine 2, it shows that the preferred investment under these conditions is machine 1. Machine 1 still gives a return of £3,471.66, which is greater than the risk-adjusted £2,638.40 of machine 2.

4. (a) The expected level of profits from each strategy can be obtained by summing the expected profit at each sales level as seen in Tables A.8 and A.9. To calculate the expected profit at each sales level we first need to calculate the profit (by multiplying sales figures by 50%, i.e. the management's profit to sales ratio) and then multiply this profit data by the probabilities.

Table A.8

Strategy: Modify body design			
Sales (ecu m)	Profit (ecu m)	Probability	Expected profit (ecu m)
10	5	0.2	1.00
14	7	0.6	4.20
18	9	0.2	1.80

Expected profit = 1.0 + 4.2 + 1.8 = 7.0 million ecus

Table A.9

Strategy: Modify engine specifications			
Sales (ecu m)	Profit (ecu m)	Probability	Expected profit (ecu m)
10	5	0.3	1.50
12	6	0.4	2.40
14	7	0.3	2.10

Expected profit = 1.5 + 2.4 + 2.1 = 6.0 million ecus

(b) The standard deviation of the profit rates measures the dispersion or spread of expected profits for each strategy. This measure can be used to assess the riskiness of a strategy, since the greater the dispersion of profits, the greater the riskiness of the strategy and vice versa. The equation for this is

$$\sqrt{\sum_{i=1}^{n} (X_i - \bar{X})^2 P_i}$$

For the purposes of our problem, P_i represents the probability figures; X_i represents each profit outcome and $\bar{X}$ is the expected value or the mean of the distribution (since the expected profit is the weighted average of all possible profit levels). The figures in Tables A.10 and A.11 are calculated to two decimal places.

Table A.10

Strategy: Modify body design			
$X_i - \bar{X}$	$(X_i - \bar{X})^2$	P_i	$(X_i - \bar{X})^2 \cdot P_i$
5 − 7	4	0.2	0.80
7 − 7	0	0.6	0.00
9 − 7	4	0.2	0.80

Sum of last column (variance) = 1.60
Standard deviation = $\sqrt{1.60}$ = 1.26

Table A.11

Strategy: Modify engine specification			
$X_i - \bar{X}$	$(X_i - \bar{X})^2$	P_i	$(X_i - \bar{X})^2 \cdot P_i$
5 − 6.0	1.00	0.3	0.30
6 − 6.0	0.00	0.4	0.00
7 − 6.0	1.00	0.3	0.30

Sum of last column (variance) = 0.60
Standard deviation = $\sqrt{0.60}$ = 0.77

(c) From the figures in Tables A.10 and A.11 we see that the company is still in some dilemma, in that the strategy of modifying the body design is more profitable but it is also more risky because the standard deviation, i.e. the dispersion of profits, is higher. Therefore we have a situation where the management may have to make a trade-off between profit and risk, and that may depend on management views of the future.

(d) To help the management decide on the most suitable course of events, it would be useful to measure the risk per ecu of profit obtained: i.e to calculate the coefficient of variation for each strategy (which is defined as the standard deviation/expected profit, i.e. the value of the risk/expected profit). Using the information obtained: from our previous calculations, the results would be as follows:

Modify body design = 1.26/7.0 = 0.18
Modify engine spec. = 0.77/6.0 = 0.13

(e) Since the risk per ecu of profit is less for modifying engine specification, it is best to decide on that strategy. Confirmation of the decision is made more meaningful by looking at the probability distributions of profit from Tables A.8 and A.9. The tables show that probability distribution of profits under the modifying engine specifications strategy (0.3 − 0.4) was also smaller than for the body design strategy (0.2 − 0.6).

5. (a) The tree diagram can be seen in Fig. A.5. Following the information in Table 3.13, we first set up the interest rate combinations and probabilities for each strategy. Then we add the demand scenarios and their probabilities. The next major column is the calculated value of the joint probabilities. These are the probabilities associated with the interest rates multiplied by the probabilities assigned to each demand condition. This column is followed by the present value of the cash flows obtained from the table. Finally the expected values of the cash flows are calculated by multiplying the present values of the cash flows by the joint probability values.

(b) The expected net present values of both schemes are seen in Fig. A.5. They are obtained by summing the expected value of the cash flow for each of the two potential building strategies and deducting the cost of the investment that was

Fig. A.5

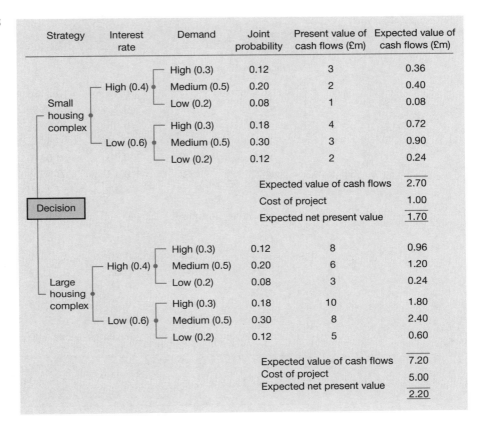

Strategy	Interest rate	Demand	Joint probability	Present value of cash flows (£m)	Expected value of cash flows (£m)
Small housing complex	High (0.4)	High (0.3)	0.12	3	0.36
		Medium (0.5)	0.20	2	0.40
		Low (0.2)	0.08	1	0.08
	Low (0.6)	High (0.3)	0.18	4	0.72
		Medium (0.5)	0.30	3	0.90
		Low (0.2)	0.12	2	0.24

Expected value of cash flows	2.70
Cost of project	1.00
Expected net present value	1.70

Decision

Strategy	Interest rate	Demand	Joint probability	Present value of cash flows (£m)	Expected value of cash flows (£m)
Large housing complex	High (0.4)	High (0.3)	0.12	8	0.96
		Medium (0.5)	0.20	6	1.20
		Low (0.2)	0.08	3	0.24
	Low (0.6)	High (0.3)	0.18	10	1.80
		Medium (0.5)	0.30	8	2.40
		Low (0.2)	0.12	5	0.60

Expected value of cash flows	7.20
Cost of project	5.00
Expected net present value	2.20

given in the original table. The figures can then be compared. In this case, the expected net present value of the smaller housing scheme is approximately £1.70 million while that of the larger scheme is £2.20 million. On this basis, the larger scheme seems to be the more favourable.

(c) The range of outcomes from these schemes can be obtained from Fig. A.5 by subtracting the cost of the relevant scheme from the present value of cash flows in each demand situation. For example, for the small scheme, with high interest rates and high demand, the outcome is £3 million – £1 million = £2 million. Once these figures have been calculated for both schemes we can see that the range of outcomes varies between £0 million and £3 million in the small scheme and –£2 million to £5 million in the larger scheme. Therefore, although the net expected return is greater in the larger scheme there is also a greater spread of outcomes so that there may be a possibility of greater risk in this scheme. To determine if this is so we need to calculate the coefficient of variation.

(d) This is done in Table A.12 using data in Fig. A.5. Here, the first column is obtained by subtracting the individual present value of cash flows from the total expected value of the cash flows. For example, if we take the high interest, high demand situation for the small housing complex, then the present value of cash flow is £3 million (X_1) and the expected value of cash flows for the whole complex is £2.7

Table A.12

$(X_i - \bar{X})$	$(X_i - \bar{X})^2$	P	$(X_i - \bar{X})^2 \cdot P$
Small housing complex			
0.3	0.09	0.12	0.0108
−0.7	0.49	0.20	0.0980
−1.7	2.89	0.08	0.2312
1.3	1.69	0.18	0.3042
0.3	0.09	0.30	0.0270
−0.7	0.49	0.12	0.0588
		Variance =	0.7300
Large housing complex			
0.8	0.64	0.12	0.0768
−1.2	1.44	0.20	0.2880
−4.2	17.64	0.08	1.4112
2.8	7.84	0.18	1.4112
0.8	0.64	0.30	0.1920
−2.2	4.84	0.12	0.5808
		Variance =	3.9600

	Standard deviation	Expected net present value	Coefficient of variation
Small housing complex	0.85	1.70	0.5
Large housing complex	1.99	2.20	0.9

million $(\bar{X})$ so that by subtraction the first figure $(X_1 - \bar{X})$ is £0.3 million. Similarly the second figure down that column will be £2 million – £2.7 million = −£0.7 million. Note that at the bottom of Table A.12, the standard deviation column is the square root of the variance figure calculated in the table, and the expected net present value column was obtained from Fig. A.5. The coefficient of variation is merely the former divided by the latter. When this exercise is completed, we find the values are 0.5 for the small scheme and 0.9 for the large scheme, which indicates that the large scheme is somewhat more risky since the coefficient is higher. Therefore, although the large scheme provides more expected net present value, it is also slightly more risky. The decision-making process is therefore not as straightforward as first thought.

(e) The risk differences between the two schemes make the decision process more complicated. To try to overcome this problem, we could assign utility values to each of the figures in the 'present value of cash flows' column of Fig. A.5 making it then possible to calculate expected utility instead of expected cash flow. Thus the project with the highest expected utility would then be chosen.

Alternatively, the 'risk adjusted' discount method could be used to calculate the 'present values of cash flows' column and this could then be used to decide on the best strategy: i.e the scheme that offered the larger 'risk adjusted', expected net present value.

Chapter 4   1. (a) After the relevant calculations have been completed, the table should be as in Table A.13.

Table A.13

Q	TFC	TVC	TC	AFC	AVC	ATC	MC
0	1,200	0	1,200	0	0	0	0
10	1,200	600	1,800	120	60	180	60
20	1,200	800	2,000	60	40	100	20
30	1,200	900	2,100	40	30	70	10
40	1,200	1,040	2,240	30	26	56	14
50	1,200	1,400	2,600	24	28	52	36
60	1,200	2,100	3,300	20	35	55	70
70	1,200	3,010	4,210	17	43	61	91

(b) Graphing the figures in Table A.13 would give cost functions similar to those shown in Fig. A.6.

Fig. A.6

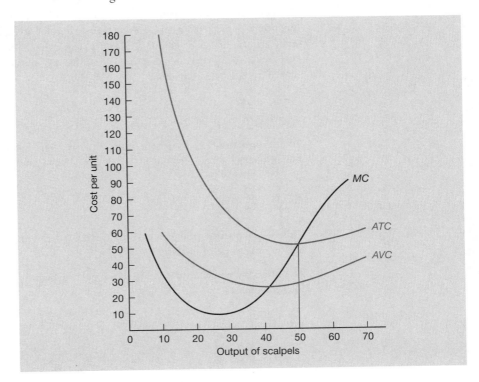

(c) (i) From Table A.13 and Fig. A.6 we can see that the cost functions are of the short-run type. The fact that there was a cost figure of £1,200 when output was zero indicates that there are fixed costs to take into consideration. We are therefore dealing with short-run cost, since in the long run all costs are variable.

(ii) The AVC curve is U-shaped, indicating greater productive efficiency point as increasing returns to the variable factors are enjoyed and average variable cost fall. However, beyond 40 units of output, productive efficiency begins to fall as diminishing returns set in, resulting in a rise in average variable cost. The ATC curve still falls beyond 40 units of output since AFC is falling faster than AVC is rising, so ATC (= AFC + AVC) still falls. This continues up to an output of 50 units, when ATC starts to rise. Note that AFC is the vertical distance between AVC and ATC.

(iii) From Fig. A.6 we can see that production will be at its optimum efficiency when ATC is at its lowest, i.e. at an output of approximately 50 scalpels. At this output, the average cost per unit is around £52. If the market price of the scalpels were £40 each, then Fabrication Ltd would not be able to cover all its costs whatever the output level it chose to produce. The company could continue to operate at 50 units *in the short run* because at a price of £40 it is covering all its variable costs and making some contribution to its fixed costs. However, in the long run it is failing to cover all its costs and would therefore have to decide to leave this area of production unless the market price rose to cover all costs, i.e. approximately £52.

2. (a) The general equation for the isocost curve can be obtained from the total cost function $C = wL + rK$, where C = total cost, L and K are labour and capital, and w and r are the prices of labour and capital respectively. The expression for total cost can then be rearranged into an isocost curve by subtracting wL from each side of the total cost equation:

$$C = wL + rK \tag{1}$$
$$C - wL = rK \tag{2}$$

Divide equation (2) by r and move K to the left-hand side of the equation for simplicity:

$$K = \frac{C}{r} - \frac{wL}{r} \tag{3}$$

This is the equation of the isocost line with C/r being the intercept on the K axis and w/r the slope of the line.

(b) To obtain the actual equation for the isocost, substitute the values of C, w and r into equation (3):

$$K = \frac{1,200}{60} - \frac{20L}{60} \tag{4}$$
$$= 20 - \tfrac{1}{3} L \tag{5}$$

We can now draw the isocost as seen in Fig. A.7 because we know that the intercept on the vertical K axis is 20, and the slope of the isocost line (i.e. K/L) is $\frac{1}{3}$ so that the intercept on the horizontal L axis will be $3 \times 20 = 60$. (Another way to obtain this figure would be to show what the L intercept will be when $K = 0$, i.e. $20 - \frac{1}{3}L = 0$ giving $L = 60$.) If the price of renting machines halves, then r will be 30 and the vertical intercept will then be $1,200/30 = 40$. The value L on the horizontal axis remains the same at 60 because the price of labour has not changed. The slope of the isocost curve (K/L) will then be $\frac{2}{3}$ $(40/60)$.

(c) Draw the production isoquants, using the data shown in the production table. The isocost line with $w = £20$ and $r = £60$ will be tangential to the 18 units production isoquant where $K = 10$ and $L = 30$. If the cost of renting machinery halves then the new isocost line will be tangential to the 30 units of production isoquant so that 30 units will be the optimal weekly production amount, using $30L$ and $20K$.

(d) It is known that the marginal rate of technical substitution $(MRTS)$ is the slope of the production isoquant at any given point. In our example, it is the rate at which labour can be substituted for machinery. At the optimum point, the slopes of the isocost line and the production isoquant will be the same, so taking the value of the slopes of the two isocost curves, $MRTS$ will be $\frac{1}{3}$ at the 18 unit isoquant and $\frac{2}{3}$ at the 30 unit isoquant.

(e) When we look at the two optimum positions on the 18 and 30 unit isoquants it appears that labour productivity has increased because, with the same amount of labour (30), output has increased from 18 to 30 units. However, we can see that this increase in output is also due to employing more machinery (i.e. up from 10 to 20 units). In other words, much of the apparent increase in labour productivity may be attributable to an increased capital intensity of production.

Fig. A.7

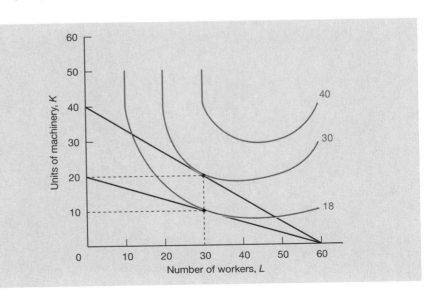

3. (a) In this problem we are given the production function and the amount of output required. Thus, the equation is in the form

$$100 = L^{3/5} K^{1/5} \tag{1}$$

K can then be expressed as a function of L by dividing both sides of equation (1) by $L^{3/5}$ and rearranging (remember that $1/L^{3/5}$ is $L^{-3/5}$)

$$K^{1/5} = 100 L^{-3/5} \tag{2}$$

Multiplying each side by the power of 5:

$$K = 100^5 L^{-3} \tag{3}$$

To find the marginal rate of technical substitution ($MRTS$) we need to calculate the first derivative of this function:

i.e. $$\dfrac{\partial K}{\partial L} (MRTS) = (-3)\,100^5\,L^{-4} \tag{4}$$

The fact that this is a negative value indicates that K and L are substitutable because a fall in labour input is associated with a rise in capital input.

(b) The equation for total cost using the wage and rental figures given in the question is $C = 4L + 5K$. Thus to find the combination of K and L that minimises the total costs of producing the 100 units needed, we merely take the total cost function and substitute the value of K that we derived in equation (3) above:

$$C = 4L + 5\,(\,100^5 L^{-3}) \tag{5}$$

To derive the minimum cost we differentiate equation (5) with respect to L and equate it to zero:

$$\dfrac{\partial C}{\partial L} = 4 + 5\,(-3 \times 100^5 L^{-4}) = 0$$

i.e. $15 \times 100^5 L^{-4} = 4$

$$L = \left(\dfrac{15 \times 100^5}{4}\right)^{\frac{1}{4}}$$
$$= 440 \text{ man-hours}$$

Given this value of L all we now need to do to find K is to substitute for L in equation (3), i.e. $K = 100^5 L^{-3}$:

$$K = 100^5 \times (440)^{-3}$$
$$= 100^5 \times 1/(440)^3$$
$$= 117 \text{ machine-hours}$$

(c) Another way of solving the problem would be to use the knowledge that the optimal cost-minimising situation will be where the production isoquant and the isocost line are tangential. Therefore we need to find the values of K and L that make the slope of both the production and cost functions identical.

The first step is to substitute the relevant figures into the general total cost equation, $C = wL + rK$. This gives $100 = 4L + 5K$, and by rearranging we can obtain the isocost equation i.e. $K = 20 - \frac{4}{5}L$. This means that the slope of the isocost line is $-\frac{4}{5}$. The slope of the production isoquant ($K = 100^5 L^{-3}$) at any point on its length can be obtained by finding the first derivative of the production isoquant i.e. $\partial K/\partial L$, and then equating this to $-\frac{4}{5}$, i.e.

$$\frac{\partial K}{\partial L} = (-3)\ 100^5 L^{-4} = -4/5$$

$$= \left(\frac{15 \times 100^5}{4}\right)^{\frac{1}{4}}$$

$$= 440 \text{ man-hours}$$

Substitute for L in the equation $K = 100^5\ L^{-3}$ to obtain the answer of 117 machine-hours.

4. (a) To calculate the value of Q given $L = 200$ and $K = 100$ then merely substitute those values in the production equation, i.e.

$$\begin{aligned} Q &= 4 \times 200^{0.75} \times 100^{0.25} \\ &= 4 \times (53.19) \times (3.16) \\ &= 672 \end{aligned}$$

(b) After capital equipment has been substituted for labour the value of the production function would be

$$\begin{aligned} Q &= 4 \times 190^{0.75} \times 180^{0.25} \\ &= 4 \times (51.18) \times (3.66) \\ &= 749 \end{aligned}$$

The substitution of capital for labour has raised Q by 77 units per year.

(c) If the company decided to double the input of labour and capital, we can show this by adjusting the production function seen here, i.e.

$$Q = 4\ L^{0.75}\ K^{0.25}$$

If we double the input of L and K then we have

$$Q = 4\ (2L)^{0.75}\ (2K)^{0.25}$$

Multiplying the equation out fully:

$$Q = 4 \times 2^{0.75} \times L^{0.75} \times 2^{0.25} \times K^{0.25}$$

Rearranging the equation:

$$Q = 2^{0.75+0.25} \times 4(L^{0.75}\ K^{0.25})$$

The second part of this rearrangement is in fact Q, so the equation becomes

$$= 2 \times Q$$
i.e. $2Q$

Therefore, a doubling of L and K would have led to a doubling of output, which means that the company is operating under constant returns to scale.

(d) To derive the marginal product of labour we need to find the first derivative of the production function, i.e. the change that occurs in output as a result of a unit change in labour input:

$$Q = 4L^{0.75} K^{0.25}$$

$$\frac{\partial Q}{\partial L} = 3L^{-0.25} K^{0.25}$$

To show that it diminishes with output we must take the second derivative and investigate its sign:

$$\frac{\partial^2 Q}{\partial L^2} = -0.75L^{-1.75} K^{0.25}$$

Since the sign is negative it means that the marginal product of labour diminishes as more labour is applied to production, i.e. diminishing returns to labour.

(e) To answer this part of the question we need to use the equation that we have derived for the marginal product of labour (i.e. $3L^{-0.25} K^{0.25}$) and substitute the values of L and K for the two years. Rounding off the figures we get:

Year 1 $\dfrac{\partial Q}{\partial L} = 3 \times 200^{-0.25} \times 100^{0.25} = 3 \times (0.266) \times (3.162)$
$$= 2.52$$

Year 2 $\dfrac{\partial Q}{\partial L} = 3 \times 190^{-0.25} \times 180^{0.25} = 3 \times (0.269) \times (3.662)$
$$= 2.96$$

The change in the marginal product is $2.96 - 2.52 = 0.44$. The percentage change is $0.44/2.52 \times 100 = 17.5\%$.

Since changes in the marginal product of labour are equal to the change in wages, then the percentage change in wages is also 17.5%.

5. (a) The value of the fixed costs can be obtained easily because these are costs that do not vary with output in the short run. If we let $Q = 0$ in the total cost equation then $TC = 300$. Since this is the value of total costs when no output has yet been produced, it must represent the fixed costs.

The average total cost is obtained by dividing the TC function by Q:

$$ATC = \frac{TC}{Q} = \frac{300}{Q} + 50 - 10Q + Q^2$$

The total variable cost is equal to the total cost minus the fixed cost element of 300, i.e.

$$TVC = 50Q - 10Q^2 + Q^3$$

The average variable cost function is obtained by dividing the TVC by Q:

$$AVC = \frac{TVC}{Q} = 50 - 10Q + Q^2$$

The *MC* function measures the change in the total cost (*TC*) function, and is the first derivative of the *TC* function with respect to Q, i.e.

$$TC = 300 + 50Q - 10Q^2 + Q^3$$

$$MC = \frac{d(TC)}{dQ} = 50 - 20Q + 3Q^2$$

(b) To show that the *AVC* is U-shaped it is necessary to find the turning point of the *AVC* function and equate this to zero because this will be a point where *MC* is neither falling nor rising. Therefore we need to find the first derivative of the *AVC* function and equate it to zero:

$$AVC = 50 - 10Q + Q^2$$

$$\frac{d(AVC)}{dQ} = -10 + 2Q = 0$$

$$Q = 5$$

Therefore there is a turning point where $Q = 5$. To decide whether the turning point is a minimum we have to investigate the second-order condition, i.e.

$$\frac{d_2(AVC)}{dQ^2} = +2$$

This is a positive number, which confirms that it is a minimum point and that the curve is, in fact, U-shaped.

We now have to show that *MC* cuts *AVC* at the lowest point of the latter. To do this we need to equate the expression for *MC* with that of *AVC*:

$$50 - 10Q + Q^2 = 50 - 20Q + 3Q^2$$
$$2Q^2 - 10Q = 0$$
$$Q(2Q - 10) = 0$$
$$Q = 0 \text{ or } 5$$

Since both *AVC* and *MC* cut at $Q = 5$, and we know that at $Q=5$ the *AVC* is at its minimum, therefore *MC* must cut *AVC* at the latter's minimum point.

(d) The quantity of nitrates that minimises *AVC* is 5 tonnes/hour, which has already been calculated, and the cost per tonne can be obtained by substituting $Q = 5$ in the equation for the *AVC*:

$$AVC = 50 - 10(5) + (5)^2$$
$$= 50 - 50 + 25$$
$$= 25$$

Therefore the minimum cost per tonne of fertiliser is £25 at an output of 5 tonnes per hour.

Chapter 5   1. (a) The break-even points occur where total revenue (*TR*) is equal to total cost (*TC*). Therefore to identify these points we need to equate the two functions, i.e.

$$150Q - 0.5Q^2 = 1,750 - 12Q + 0.5Q^2$$

Rearranging we get

$$Q^2 - 162Q + 1,750 = 0$$

This is a quadratic equation which can be solved by using the equation

$$\frac{-b \pm \sqrt{b^2 - 4ac}}{2a} \quad \text{where } a = 1, b = -162, c = +1,750$$

Applying this equation to the quadratic function, we obtain the following results:

$$\frac{162 \pm \sqrt{(-162)^2 - 4(1,750)}}{2}$$

equals:

$$\frac{162 + 138.7}{2} \quad \text{or} \quad \frac{162 - 138.7}{2}$$

$$= 150.4 \quad \text{or} \quad 11.65$$

The lower break-even point is at 11.65 or 11,650 medical books per year while the upper break-even point is at 150.4 or 150,400 books per year.

(b) The profit-maximising output will be where the difference between total revenue and total costs (i.e. profits) is a maximum. To get the expression for the total profit (π) we use total revenue (*TR*) minus total cost (*TC*):

$$\pi = 150Q - 0.5Q^2 - (1,750 - 12Q + 0.5Q^2)$$
$$= 162Q - Q^2 - 1,750$$

To obtain the profit-maximising output (i.e. the turning point) we need to find the first derivative of the profit function and equate it to zero:

$$\frac{d\pi}{dQ} = 162 - 2Q = 0$$
$$162 = 2Q$$
$$81 = Q$$

The total yearly output to maximise profits will be 81,000. To calculate the total profits at this level we substitute *Q* = 81 in the total profit equation:

$$\pi = 162(81) - (81)^2 - 1,750$$
$$= 13,122 - 6,561 - 1,750$$
$$= 4,811$$

Therefore the total profits at the profit-maximising output will be £4.811 million.

The price per book can be obtained by finding the total revenue at the output of 81,000 and dividing it by the number of books produced. To find the total revenue at this output we substitute $Q = 81$ in the TR function (remember that the equations are in 000s so that 81,000 is 81 for the substitution).

$$TR = 150(81) - 0.5(81)^2$$
$$= 12,150 - 3,280.5$$
$$= 8,869.5$$

Divide by 81 to get the average price of the medical books, i.e. £8,869.5/81 = £109.5. (The answer would be the same if we converted the figures into thousands, i.e. 8,869,500/81,000.)

When the company is operating at the profit-maximising output we can prove that $MR = MC$ by first deriving the expressions for MR and MC from the respective TR and TC curves. All we need do is differentiate the TR and TC with respect to Q:

$$TR = 150Q - 0.5Q^2 \qquad\qquad TC = 1,750 - 12Q + 0.5Q^2$$

$$\frac{dTR}{dQ}\ (MR) = 150 - Q \qquad\qquad \frac{dTC}{dQ}\ (MC) = -12 + Q$$

To find whether MR and MC are equal at the profit-maximising level of 81 merely equate MR and MC and find the value of Q. This will give a Q value of 81, which provides the proof we needed that MR will be equal to MC at the profit-maximising output.

(c) If the company decide to produce at the sales maximisation level then we can find this level since it is where TR is a maximum. Therefore we need to differentiate the TR function and equate it to zero:

$$TR = 150Q - 0.5Q^2$$

$$\frac{dTR}{dQ} = 150 - Q = 0$$

$$Q = 150$$

The sales-maximising output is therefore 150 or 150,000 copies a year. The price of a book at the sales-maximising level can be obtained by dividing the total revenue at this level by the number of books printed. The total revenue at this output can be obtained by substituting $Q = 150$ (the equation is in 000s) in the TR equation:

$$TR = 150(150) - 0.5(150)^2$$
$$= 225,000 - 11,250$$
$$= 11,250$$

The price per copy is this figure divided by 150, i.e. £75. (The solution would be the same if the figures were converted into their real values, i.e. 11,250,000/150,000.)

The level of output of 150,000 books per year is only slightly less than the upper break-even point, indicating that the sales-maximising output is close to a zero profits level. To check on this we could have substituted the value of $Q = 150$ in the profit equation and derived the answer of 50 or a mere £50,000 profit as compared with the substantial £4.811 million at the profit-maximising level.

2. (a) To find the new profit-maximising output level after the introduction of the new colour printer investment we need to find the new profit function and then find the output when this function is a maximum. The new profit function is the difference between total revenue and the new total cost, i.e.

$$\pi = 150Q - 0.5Q^2 - (1{,}850 - 12Q + 0.5Q^2)$$
$$= 162Q - Q^2 - 1{,}850$$

Differentiate with respect to Q and let the result equal zero:

$$\frac{d\pi}{dQ} = 162 - 2Q = 0$$

$$Q = 81$$

In other words, the increase in costs has *not* altered the profit-maximising output level of 81,000 books. To calculate profits after the new investment, then we need to substitute $Q = 81$ in the new profit equation.

$$\pi = TR - TC$$
$$= 150Q - 0.5Q^2 - (1{,}850 - 12Q + 0.5Q^2)$$
$$= 162Q - Q^2 - 1{,}850$$

Substitute $Q = 81$ in the previous equation:

$$\pi = 162(81) - (81)^2 - 1{,}850$$
$$= 13{,}122 - 6{,}561 - 1{,}850$$
$$= 4{,}711$$

In other words, the total profit is £4.711 million. If we refer back to question 1 we saw that the original profit before the introduction of the new printer was £4.811 million. Therefore profits have fallen by £0.1 million or £100,000. This is equivalent to the rise in fixed element of the cost function from £1,750 to £1,850, i.e. by £100.00 (the figures are in thousands so that the difference between the two fixed cost elements, £1,850,000 – £1,750,000, is £100,000). This result is understandable in terms of economic theory because the introduction of the new printer increased the company's fixed costs only. To change the equilibrium output position as a result of a cost change would have required changes in the *variable* costs. If only fixed costs are changed, the equilibrium output stays the same and profits fall by exactly the same amount as the increase in fixed costs.

(b) If the new investment goes ahead, then we need to use the new profit function and equate this to £1 million in order to find the maximum sales level possible given the profit constraint.

$$\pi = 162Q - Q^2 - 1,850 \text{ where } \pi = 1,000$$

(remember that the equation figures are in 000s, so that £1 million is denoted by 1,000 in the equation)

$$1,000 = 162Q - Q^2 - 1,850$$
$$Q^2 - 162Q + 2,850 = 0$$

Using the standard equation (see p. 580) to solve the quadratic equation we get

$$\frac{162 \pm \sqrt{(-162)^2 - 4(2850)}}{2}$$

$$= \frac{162 + 121.8}{2} \qquad \text{or} \qquad \frac{162 - 121.8}{2}$$

$$= 141.9 \qquad \text{or} \qquad 20.1$$

The maximum solution of the two available is 141.9, so that the maximum number of medical books that the company can sell, given the profit constraint, is 141,900 copies per year.

3. (a) We can use the range of G values suggested in the question to plot both functions. The result can be seen in Fig. A.8.

The valuation constraint function shows the typical shape associated with this type of relationship, and the managerial function has the usual convex indifference curve shape.

Fig. A.8

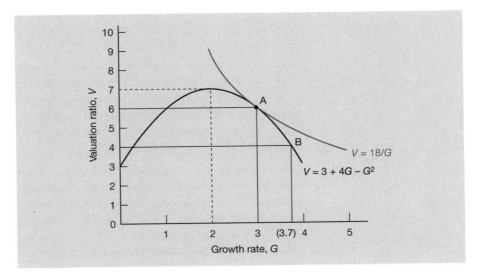

The rate of growth that maximises the valuation ratio can be read directly from Fig. A.8. This occurs where the growth rate is 2% and the valuation ratio is 7. This maximum position can be checked using simple calculus: we take the valuation function and differentiate it with respect to G. This is then equated to zero:

$$V = 3 + 4G - G^2$$

$$\frac{dV}{dG} = 4 - 2G = 0$$

$$G = 2$$

(We can check whether this is a maximum position by finding the second derivative of the V function. If this is a minus figure then the valuation rate will be at its maximum.)

$$\frac{d^2V}{dG^2} = -2 \text{ (i.e. this is a maximum position for } V\text{)}$$

To get the value of V at its maximum point, merely substitute $G = 2$ in the valuation function, i.e.

$$V = 3 + 4(2) - (2)^2$$
$$= 7$$

(b) From Fig. A.8 we can see that the maximum medium-term managerial utility function is tangential to the valuation constraint function at point A where the growth rate is 3% and the valuation ratio is 6. To substantiate that there is a tangency or equilibrium solution at A we need to prove that the slopes of both functions are equal when $G = 3$. First calculate the first derivative of both functions with respect to G:

$$V = 3 + 4G - G^2 \qquad \text{and} \qquad V = 18/G \text{ (or } V = 18G^{-1})$$

$$\frac{dV}{dG} = 4 - 2G \qquad \text{and} \qquad \frac{dV}{dG} = \frac{-18}{G^2} \text{ (or } -18G^{-2})$$

Substitute $G = 3$ in the above expressions and we obtain the value of -2. In other words, the slopes of the two functions are identical so that there is an equilibrium solution. The rate of substitution of V for G is 2, which means that for every 1 unit increase in growth, the valuation ratio falls by two units. This is a valid equilibrium position because the valuation ratio at the point of tangency (6) is above the critical level to prevent takeover (4).

(c) The profit-maximising firm would operate at a growth rate below 3%. To understand this fact we need to realise that the maximum valuation ratio is where growth is 2%, but the peak of the valuation ratio tends to occur after the peak of the profit rate curve (see Fig. 5.5, p. 210). When profits rise, the demand for shares increases and their prices rise. However, when profits start to fall, the demand for shares will fall after a short lag, thus resulting in the fall in the price of shares. This fall in share prices leads to a fall in the valuation ratio. In other words, the profit rate peak will be before the valuation ratio peak. This means that the profit peak will be reached at a growth rate that is below 2% (the valuation peak). On the other hand, to maximise managerial utility, the desired growth rate should be 3%, i.e. a rate that is above both the valuation and profit-maximising growth rates.

(d) If the managers had a free choice of growth rates with only a minimum takeover constraint of 4, then they would *prefer* to have a growth rate of approximately 3.7%, i.e. at B in Fig. A.8, where the line from a valuation rate of 4 crosses the general valuation constraint curve. A more precise method to find the point would be to take the valuation constraint function and equate this to 4. We then get a quadratic equation, which can be solved using the familiar formula:

$$V = 3 + 4G - G^2$$
$$4 = 3 + 4G - G^2$$
$$G^2 - 4G + 1 = 0$$

Using the formula for solving the quadratic equation shown above, we get two values, $G = 0.27$ and 3.7. The solution that maximises growth when $V = 4$ is the higher one, i.e. 3.7%. Obviously, managers would *prefer* a higher growth rate if possible, but *in practice* they could achieve this position only if the managerial utility function (or indifference curve) shifted down the valuation constraint curve from A to B.

4. (a) The production manager in this example is geared to a profit-maximising philosophy in order to use the profits to reinvest. Therefore the task is to find the price and output that will meet this criterion. First we need to write out the total revenue function. Since total revenue is merely price (average revenue) times quantity produced, Q, then $TR = P$ (or $80 - 0.5Q$) multiplied by Q, i.e.

$$TR = 80Q - 0.5Q^2$$

and we know that total cost (TC) is

$$TC = 160 + 10Q + 0.2Q^2$$

Therefore profits (π) is $TR - TC$, or

$$\pi = 80Q - 0.5Q^2 - (160 + 10Q + 0.2Q^2)$$
$$\pi = 70Q - 0.7Q^2 - 160$$

To find the level of monthly output that maximises profits we need to differentiate the profit function with respect to output and equate this to zero:

$$\frac{d\pi}{dQ} = 70 - 1.4Q = 0$$

$$70 = 1.4Q$$
$$50 = Q$$

To find the price at this level of output, substitute for Q in the demand equation:

$$P(AR) = 80 - 0.5(50)$$
$$P = 55$$

For the total profit we merely substitute the value of Q in the profits equation:

$$= 70(50) - 0.7(50)^2 - 160$$
$$= 3,500 - 1,750 - 160$$
$$= 1,590$$

Therefore the profit-maximising monthly output is 50 boxes at a price of £55 per box and a total profit of £1,590.

(b) The sales manager with one eye on the market share would want to maximise sales. To calculate the sales maximisation point we have to find the point at which the total revenue is a maximum, i.e. find the first derivative of the TR function and equate this to zero:

$$TR = 80Q - 0.5Q^2$$

$$\frac{d(TR)}{dQ} = 80 - 1Q$$

For maximisation

$$80 - 1Q = 0$$
$$Q = 80$$

Substitute $Q = 80$ in the demand curve equation to obtain P:

$$P(AR) = 80 - 0.5(80)$$
$$P = 40$$

The total profit is obtained, as previously, by substituting for Q in the total profit equation:

$$= 70(80) - 0.7(80)^2 - 160$$
$$= 5,600 - 4,480 - 160$$
$$= 960$$

Therefore the monthly sales-maximising output is 80 boxes at a price of £40 per box and a profit of £960.

(c) The managing director wants to ensure a minimum profit of £1,080 per month. This means we need to equate the total profits equation to 1,080 and then calculate quantity and price levels. This means that

$$70Q - 0.7Q^2 - 160 = 1,080$$
$$70Q - 0.7Q^2 - 1,240 = 0$$

This is a quadratic equation, and we have to solve for Q. The standard definition for the solution of this kind of equation is

$$\frac{-b \pm \sqrt{b^2 - 4ac}}{2a} \quad \text{where } a = -0.7, b = 70, c = -1,240$$

Applying this equation to the profit function we have

$$\frac{-70 \pm \sqrt{(70)^2 - 4(-0.7 \times -1,240)}}{2(-0.7)}$$

$$= \frac{-70 + 37.8}{-1.4} \quad \text{or} \quad \frac{-70 - 37.8}{-1.4}$$

$$= 23 \qquad \text{or} \qquad 77$$

We have two potential solutions. We assume that the managing director would naturally take the larger of the two figures, i.e. $Q = 77$. To obtain the price level, substitute $Q = 77$ in the demand equation:

$$P(AR) = 80 - 0.5(77)$$
$$= 41.5$$

Therefore the monthly quantity produced under the profit constraint criterion would be 77 boxes at £41.5 per box.

5. (a) To decide on the location of production, we need to find the equilibrium output and price that Intersound would charge US customers if it produced the amplifiers in the UK and, alternatively, if it built a plant in the USA to supply that market. We know that the demand curve for the amplifier in the USA is $P = 100 - 0.001Q$, so it is possible to obtain an expression for the marginal cost curve. This will be $P = 100 - 0.002Q$ since the marginal revenue curve always has the same intercept point as the demand curve (100) and has twice the slope of the demand curve (0.002).

The marginal cost of producing amplifiers in the UK and shipping them to the USA would be made up of the marginal production costs plus the transport and tariff costs per unit. This amounts to £15 + £15 = £30. The equilibrium price and quantity produced in the UK for shipment to the USA would be where the marginal cost equals marginal revenue. We have the expression for marginal revenue and we have the value of the marginal cost, so all we need to do is to equate them:

$$MR = MC$$

$$100 - 0.002Q = 30$$
$$0.002Q = 70$$
$$Q = 35,000$$

To find the price of the amplifiers, substitute $Q = 35,000$ in the demand curve equation:

$$P = 100 - 0.001 (35,000)$$
$$= 100 - 35$$
$$= 65$$

Total revenue from producing in the UK and shipping to the USA would be £65 × 35,000 = £2.27 million and the total cost would be £30 × 35,000 = £1.05 million. Therefore gross profits would be £2.27 million − £1.05 million = £1.22 million. Since the fixed cost of setting up production facilities in the UK is £0.5 million, then the net profit would be £0.72 million per month.

We now have to consider the price and output positions had Intersound decided to produce in the USA. In this case, the demand and marginal revenue curves are the same but the marginal cost curve will be £15 since the company is producing in the USA and has no international transport or tariff costs to consider. Therefore, in this case, we need to equate the marginal revenue curve to the domestic USA marginal cost of £15, i.e.

$$MR = MC$$

$$100 - 0.002Q = 15$$
$$0.002Q = 85$$
$$Q = 42,500$$

To find the price in the USA we substitute for Q in the demand curve equation, i.e.

$$P = 100 - 0.001 (42,500)$$
$$= 100 - 42.5$$
$$= 57.5$$

The total revenue per month of producing in the USA would be £57.5 × 42,500 = £2.44 million and the total costs £15 × 42,500 = £0.64 million. Therefore the gross profits would be £2.44 million − £0.64 million = £1.8 million. Net profits after payment of fixed costs would be £1.8 million − £0.7 million = £1.1 million per month.

Since the net profits per month of producing in the USA (£1.1 million) are greater than the net profits of producing in the UK (£0.72 million), then, other things being equal, the company will decide to produce in the USA.

(b) (i)   If US tariff rates on imports were abolished, leaving only a transport charge of £2 per unit then the total marginal costs per unit of producing in the UK and selling to the USA would be £15 + £2 = £17. We now need to equate the marginal revenue curve to the new marginal cost of £17, i.e.

$$100 - 0.002Q = 17$$
$$0.002Q = 83$$
$$Q = 41,500$$

The price at this level of output can be obtained by substituting for Q in the demand curve:

$$P = 100 - 0.001(41,500)$$
$$= 100 - 41.5$$
$$= 58.5$$

The total revenue from this operation will be £58.5 × 41,500 = £2.43 million and the total cost will be £17 × 41,500 = £0.71 million. The gross profit would therefore be £1.72 million. The net profit after payment of fixed costs is £1.72 million – £0.5 million = £1.12 million.

Therefore, the abolition of tariffs has increased the monthly net profit rate of producing the amplifier in the UK to £1.12 million per month as compared with the profit per month of £1.1 million if the amplifiers were produced in the USA. As a result, net profits are very similar in both locations. In this case, the decision on what to do depends on the future course of some critical variables. For example, the projections of future demand in the USA could affect the decision of whether to shift production back to the UK. Also, the nature of technological change in the two countries and its effects on relative costs in each country would have to be investigated. Also, any changes in the organisation of the company might be relevant. For example, the formation of a clearer divisional structure in Intersound based on product lines might streamline international control, thus making it easier and cheaper to set up in the USA. Since Intersound plc decided to produce in the USA in the first instance, it may be unlikely for it to change its strategy in the short run despite the more recent shift in competitiveness towards UK production.

(ii)   If the fixed costs of setting up in the USA fell from £0.7 million to the UK level of £0.5 million, then the location decision would become clearer since the costs of producing in the USA would be the gross profits of producing in the USA, i.e. £1.8 minus £0.5 (the decreased costs of setting up in the USA). This leaves a monthly net profit of £1.3 million, which makes producing in the USA even more profitable since the net profits of producing in the UK under the post tariff changes would only be £1.12 million per month.

Therefore, if we take the whole scenario we find that the first decision under (a) was to locate in the USA. When conditions changed (b)(i) we found that net profit in both countries was very similar, making it unclear whether production should shift back to the UK. The lowering of fixed costs in the USA reaffirmed the original decision to produce the amplifiers in the USA.

Chapter 6   1. (a) Since the question gives a demand *function*, it is necessary to convert it into the form of a demand *curve* by rearranging the equation to leave P on the left-hand side of the expression, i.e.

$$Q = 400 - 4P$$
$$4P = 400 - Q$$
$$P = 100 - 0.25Q$$

This is the equation for the demand curve for the industry. The supply curve for the same industry will be

$$P = 40 - 0.05Q$$

This equation is the supply curve for the industry because if each firm is operating at minimum average cost, i.e. $P = AC_{min}$, then in a competitive industry this will also be the industry's supply price. We can therefore equate P to the equation for AC, as we have seen. The industry supply curve is downward sloping (= negative slope of –0.05) so that the industry is experiencing decreasing costs.

(b) To calculate the equilibrium quantity and price we need to equate the supply and demand curves, i.e.

$$100 - 0.25Q = 40 - 0.05Q$$
$$0.2Q = 60$$
$$Q = 300$$

To find the price, substitute for Q in the demand equation:

$$P = 100 - 0.25Q$$
$$= 100 - 0.25\,(300)$$
$$= 25$$

Therefore the equilibrium price is 25 pence per screw and the equilibrium output is 300,000 screws (output was expressed in 000s).

(c) If a maximum price of 30 pence was placed on the screws, then there would be no consequences for the price and output combination since this price is above the equilibrium. However, if the minimum price of 30 pence was placed on the screws, the output would then be limited by the demand curve, i.e. using the demand curve and substituting $P = 30$:

$$P = 100 - 0.25Q$$
$$30 = 100 - 0.25Q$$
$$0.25Q = 70$$
$$Q = 280$$

In other words, there will be a downward pressure on the government's minimum price since the quantity demanded at the minimum price of 30 pence (280,000) is less than at the equilibrium (300,000).

2. (a) Under perfectly competitive conditions, the equilibrium condition for the firm is $P = MC$. If the price per bag is £30 then this can be equated to the MC function and the value of Q determined, i.e.

$$30 = 10 + 0.5Q$$
$$20 = 0.5Q$$
$$40 = Q$$

Therefore the short-run equilibrium number of bags that should be produced is 40.

(b) To calculate profit at the equilibrium level of output we need to derive the total variable cost and the total fixed cost and compare these with total revenue. The equation for the total variable costs (TVC) can be derived by multiplying the AVC function by output Q:

$$AVC = 10 + 0.25Q$$

Multiply by Q to obtain TVC:

$$TVC = 10(Q) + 0.25Q(Q)$$
$$= 10Q + 0.25Q^2$$

At the equilibrium output of 40 bags, the value of TVC can be obtained by substituting Q = 40 in the previous equation:

$$TVC = 10(40) + 0.25(40)^2$$
$$= 400 + 400$$
$$= 800$$

To calculate the profit at this level of output it is necessary to subtract the total revenue from the total cost. We know that the total revenue curve is merely the price times the quantity, i.e. £30 × 40 = £1,200. Total cost is made up of total variable and total fixed costs, i.e. £800 + £1,000 = £1,800. Therefore the farmer is making a loss of £1,200 − £1,800 = −£600.

(c) The market for carrots is not in long-run equilibrium because the farmer and others like him are making a loss of £600 each on an output of 40 bags. Whether the farmer produces in the short run depends on the relationship between P and AVC. Therefore, to answer this question we need to calculate the value of AVC at the equilibrium level of output. Since the AVC function is 10 + 0.25Q we can find the value of AVC at the equilibrium output by substituting the value Q = 40 in the AVC equation, i.e.

$$AVC = 10 + 0.25(40)$$
$$= 20$$

In the short run, the farmer may decide to continue producing for a while because price is greater than average variable cost (P > AVC). market price is £30 per bag while the AVC at the equilibrium output of 40 bags was calculated at £20 per bag. Therefore, this price covers average variable costs and contributes £10 to fixed costs. However, the farmer still has problems. For example, the total cost for 40 bags is £1,800 as calculated in (b) so that the average total cost (ATC) of 40 bags is £1,800/40 =£45. In other words, the price would have to be £45 per bag to cover all costs, i.e. variable and fixed costs. However, the market price is £30 per bag, so the farmer would continue to lose £15 per bag, and this is not sustainable in the long run.

3. (a) Under perfectly competitive conditions, the optimum output in the long run would be at the bottom point of the long-run average cost curve. Equilibrium conditions would be P = LAC = LMC. Therefore since LAC is equal to LMC at this

optimum output, we can take the expressions for *LAC* and *LMC* in the question and equate them:

$$Q + \frac{225}{Q} = 2Q$$

Multiply both sides by Q:

$$Q^2 + 225 = 2Q^2$$
$$225 = Q^2$$
$$15 = Q$$

We know from the question that $LMC = 2Q$. Substituting the value of $Q = 15$ in this equation we find that at the long-run marginal cost, $LMC = £30$. However, at the point of long-run equilibrium, P is also equal to £30 ($P = LMC$) since under conditions of perfect competition each small firm is a 'price taker'. Therefore the long-run equilibrium price for each firm is also £30.

(b) The market demand function during the period when all the firms are producing their optimum output of 15 units each is defined as $Q = 6,000 - 50P$. Therefore, to calculate the market demand we need to substitute $P = 30$ in the equation

$$Q = 6,000 - 50P$$
$$= 6,000 - 50(30)$$
$$= 6,000 - 1,500$$
$$= 4,500$$

If each firm produces 15 lampshades then the number of firms in the industry will be 4,500/15, which is 300.

(c) The market demand rises so that the new equation is $Q = 7,000 - 50P$. However, in the short run, the industry cannot increase the output of shades so that the maximum number is still only 4,500. Hence it is necessary to equate the new demand function to 4,500 and then calculate the value of P:

$$4,500 = 7,000 - 50P$$
$$50P = 2,500$$
$$P = 50$$

Therefore, in the short run the price will rise to £50 per shade. To find the total short-run abnormal profits made by each firm we subtract the short-run price from the equilibrium price and multiply the number of shades produced by each small firm, i.e. ($£50 - £30) \times 15 = £300$.

4. (a) To calculate the market-clearing price and output it is necessary to equate the demand and supply functions and solve for Q and P, i.e.

$$2P - 300 = 800 - 0.5P$$
$$2.5P = 1,100$$
$$P = 440$$

(1)

To obtain Q, substitute for P in either the demand or the supply equation:

$$Q_S = 2\,(440) - 300 \qquad\qquad Q_D = 800 - 0.5\,(440)$$
$$= 880 - 300 \qquad\qquad\qquad = 800 - 220$$
$$= 580 \qquad\qquad\qquad\qquad = 580$$

The initial market-clearing price and quantities are £440 and 580,000 units respectively (output in 000s).

(b) If the market for the product doubles then the demand function will double, i.e. from $Q_D = 800 - 0.5P$ to $Q_D = 1,600 - P$. This is because, at each price, twice the amount would be bought compared with previously. (If you are in doubt about the validity of the 'doubling' of the values of the demand function shown, then convert the demand functions into demand curves and draw them on a graph.) To obtain the new equilibrium price and quantities we need to equate the new demand function with the original supply function, i.e.

$$2P - 300 = 1,600 - P \qquad\qquad\qquad\qquad\qquad\qquad (2)$$
$$3P = 1,900$$
$$P = 633.3$$

To obtain the equilibrium levels of Q, substitute in the demand or supply equations:

$$Q_S = 2\,(633.3) - 300 \qquad\qquad Q_D = 1,600 - 633.3$$
$$= 1,266.6 - 300 \qquad\qquad\qquad = 966.6$$
$$= 966.6$$

After the changes in demand, the market will settle down at a market-clearing price of £633.30 at output levels of 966,600.

(c) (i) If the government decides to place a special tax of t on suppliers for each computer sold, then this will affect the supply curve. To see the effect of the tax on price we need to rearrange the supply *function*, so that we express it in the more familiar supply *curve* format. (Please remind yourself of the difference between the two.)

$$Q_S = 2P - 300$$
$$2P = Q_S + 300$$
$$P = 0.5Q_S + 150 \qquad\qquad\qquad\qquad\qquad\qquad (3)$$

If the government places a tax of t on the computers then suppliers will need to add this amount onto the previous supply price if they are to offer the same amount as before. In other words, the supply *curve* will be shifted up by an amount t as a result of the tax. This can be shown on the supply curve by adding t so that we get the supply curve:

$$P = 0.5Q_S + 150 + t \qquad\qquad\qquad\qquad\qquad\qquad (4)$$

In order to express the supply *function* incorporating t, it is necessary to rearrange equation (4):

$$P = 0.5Q_S + 150 + t$$

Multiply both sides by 2 and rearrange:

$$2P = Q_S + 300 + 2t$$
$$Q_S = 2P - 300 - 2t \qquad (5)$$

This is the supply function including the tax element.

(ii) To find the final equilibrium position and therefore the price in terms of t we equate the new demand curve with the new, after tax, supply curve. We will then obtain a value for P in terms of t:

$$1,600 - P = 2P - 300 - 2t$$
$$3P = 1,900 + 2t$$
$$P = 633.3 + 0.66t \qquad (6)$$

Taking the supply equation (5) and substituting for P, which we obtained in (6), we then have the quantity supplied in terms of t:

$$
\begin{aligned}
Q_S &= 2(633.3 + 0.66t) - 300 - 2t \\
&= 1,266.6 + 1.33t - 300 - 2t \\
&= 966.6 - 0.66t \qquad (7)
\end{aligned}
$$

(iii) The value assigned to t is 0.66, which means that as a result of the final post-tax equilibrium situation, the final price will have been raised by $0.66t$ or 66% of the original tax imposed. In other words, 66% of the tax is borne by the consumers, and 33% by the suppliers.

(iv) If the special tax is £50 per computer then we substitute 50 for t in equations (6) and (7):

$$
\begin{array}{ll}
P = 633.3 + 0.66(50) & Q_S = 966.6 - 0.66(50) \\
 = 633.3 + 33 & = 966.6 - 33 \\
 = 666.3 & = 933.6
\end{array}
$$

Therefore the final post-tax price and output combination will give a price of £666.30 and a quantity demanded and sold of 933,600 (remember that sales are in thousands). Out of interest, notice that the price rose from £633.30 to £666.30, i.e. by £33 as a result of a £50 tax: the burden borne by the consumer is £33/£50 or 66%. This confirms the fact that the consumer burden was, in fact, $0.66t$.

5. (a) A firm's (proportionate) demand curve DD is based on the assumption that all the firms in the industry have the same perception of the market and therefore vary their prices in the same way and at the same time. In other words, if each firm acts exactly like all the others then every firm will have a demand curve

shaped like *DD*. On the other hand, the (expected) demand curve *dd* represents demand conditions where a 'representative' firm's expectation may differ from other firms in the industry. For example, a 'representative' firm may opt for a price–quantity combination that is different from those of other firms on the assumption that the others will not change their pricing strategy. The *dd* curve will be more elastic than the *DD* curve because in the former case the firm hopes to gain more of the market from the others as a result of its different perceptions of the market.

(b) If we look at the generalised demand equation we can use our knowledge of the form of any simple demand curve to identify that *A* is merely the point at which the demand curve for the whole sector, *DD*, cuts the price axis, i.e. it is the price intercept for the sector. The symbol *b* is the slope of the demand curve *dd* of the representative firm, and measures the change in output produced by that firm on the assumption that the other firms hold their output constant. Finally, the symbol *a* represents the amount by which the representative firm's *dd* curve shifts down, i.e. decreases, for each extra unit produced by other firms in the market. In other words if other firms increase their share of the whole market, then the representative firm with the *dd* curve will lose part of the market equivalent to proportion *a* of the amount gained by the other firms in the industry.

(c) The generalised equation is in the form

$$P = A - (n-1)aq^o - bq \tag{1}$$

To obtain the *DD* curve we know that all firms act in the same way so that $q^o = q$, i.e. they all produce the same output levels. Therefore the equation becomes

$$\begin{aligned} P &= A - (n-1)aq - bq \\ &= A - q[(n-1)a - b] \end{aligned} \tag{2}$$

Interestingly, this is the equation of a straight line *DD* with the price intercept at *A* and a slope of $-[(n-1)a - b]$.

If we now substitute the values of $n = 101, A = 120, b = -1$, and $a = 0.01$ we get

$$P = 120 - 2q \tag{3}$$

which is the equation for the (proportionate) *DD* curve.

The equation for the *dd* curve is the same as the generalised one, i.e.

$$P = A - (n-1)aq^o - bq \tag{4}$$

with the expression $[A - (n-1)aq^o]$ being the vertical intercept since q^o is a constant (all other firms' output is assumed unchanged). Applying the values for *A*,*b*, *n* and *a* in the above equation, we get

$$P = (120 - q^o) - q \tag{5}$$

which is the equation for the *dd* curve.

(d) In short-run equilibrium, each firm must be maximising profits and the output of each firm in the industry will be equal to one another, i.e. $q^o = q$ (otherwise output adjustments would be taking place and the firms would not be in equilibrium). Also, the normal equilibrium conditions apply, i.e. $MR = MC$. It is possible to derive the expression for MR from the demand curve dd in equation (5) since the price intercept is $120 - q^o$ and the slope is -1 (value of b). The equation for the MR curve will be $[120 - q^o] -2q$ because the slope of the MR is always twice that of the demand curve. Since we know the MC curve for each firm is $MC = 50 + 0.5q$, then equilibrium will be where these two expressions are equal, i.e.

$$(120 - q^o) -2q = 50 + 0.5q$$

Since $q^o = q$ in equilibrium, then

$$120 - 3q = 50 + 0.5q$$

$$3.5q = 70$$
$$q = 20$$

Each firm will be generating 20 pension contracts per week. The charge or price for each contract can be obtained by substituting for q in the equation for DD or dd. For example, if we take DD in equation (3) and substitute the value $q = 20$ then the price of each contract will be £80, i.e.

$$P = 120 - 2 (20)$$
$$= £80$$

(e) Since $MC = 50 + 0.5q$ then the expression for AVC must be $50 + 0.25q$. Since MC is a straight line with an intercept of 50 and a slope of 0.5, the AVC curve will also have an intercept of 50, but the slope is half that of the MC curve, i.e. 0.25. The equation for the AVC is therefore $50 + 0.25q$. To calculate whether the short-run equilibrium is also a long-run equilibrium situation we need to prove that at an output of 20, each firm is earning normal profits, i.e. that average total cost (ATC) is also where $q = 20$ and $P = £80$.

ATC is made up of average fixed costs (AFC) and average variable costs (AVC). The total fixed costs are 500 so that the AFC is $500/q$. We can now substitute all the information provided in this section in the well-known cost relationship

$$ATC = AFC + AVC$$

By substituting we get

$$ATC = (500/q) + (50 + 0.25q)$$

When $q = 20$ then

$$ATC = (500/20) + [50 + 0.25 (20)]$$
$$= £80$$

In other words, when output is 20 then ATC is £80, which is the same level as the price. In short, when each firm is producing 20 pension contracts per week, then $P = ATC$ and therefore the whole industry is also in long-run equilibrium at this level of output.

Chapter 7   1. (a) From Chapter 2 we know that the relationship between marginal revenue MR and elasticity is $MR = P(1 - 1/e)$, where P is price and e is the price elasticity of demand. In equilibrium, the monopolist equates MR with MC so that the equation becomes $MC = (P - 1/e)$. This equation can be rearranged (as seen earlier in this chapter) to the following relationship:

$$\frac{P - MC}{P} = \frac{1}{e} \tag{1}$$

This means that the mark-up (which is the expression on the left-hand side of equation (1)) is equal to the reciprocal of the price elasticity. The first task is to express the price in relation to MC in order to obtain the mark-up ratio and then find the value of P from our knowledge of e and MC. For example, if the price elasticity of demand in the USA is 2 (strictly −2 but the form of equation (1) has taken this into consideration so we only need to use 2) then substitute this in equation (1) and cross-multiply, i.e.

$$\frac{P - MC}{P} = \frac{1}{2}$$

$$P = 2P - 2MC$$
$$P = 2MC \tag{2}$$

This means that the price charged is twice the marginal cost so that the mark-up must be 100%. To calculate the price P all we need to know is the value of MC. Since we are given the total cost curve, we can find MC by finding the first derivative of the total cost function:

$$TC = 1{,}000 + 200Q \tag{3}$$

$$MC = \frac{\mathrm{d}TC}{\mathrm{d}Q} = 200 \tag{4}$$

Substituting for $MC = 200$ in equation (2) we get

$$P = 2(200)$$
$$= 400$$

Therefore in the US market the mark-up is 100%, and the price charged would be £400 per filter.

(b) In the European market the elasticity of demand is 6 so that the equation is

$$\frac{P - MC}{P} = \frac{1}{6}$$

Cross-multiplying we get

$$P = 6P - 6MC$$
$$5P = 6MC$$
$$P = 1.2MC \tag{5}$$

In this case the price is 0.2 or 20% above MC and therefore the mark-up is 20%. The price charged in this market can be obtained as before by substituting $MC = 200$ in equation (5):

$$P = 1.2(200)$$
$$= 240$$

Therefore in the European market the mark-up is 20% and the price is £240 per filter.

(c) It is obvious from these calculations that the greater the price elasticity of demand, the smaller is the mark-up and the price charged. This is understandable since if the market is relatively inelastic (USA), it will be less sensitive to price changes. This means that higher prices and mark-ups can be obtained. At the relatively higher elasticity level (Europe), demand is more sensitive to price changes so that high prices cannot be charged and mark-ups will therefore be lower.

(d) If research in the Asian market found that the price elasticity was 0.5, then using the same technique we can say

$$\frac{P - MC}{P} = \frac{1}{0.5}$$

$$P = 0.5P - 0.5MC$$
$$0.5P = -0.5MC$$
$$P = -MC \tag{6}$$

This would give negative mark-up on marginal cost, which indicates a non-viable situation. It illustrates the well-known point about a monopolist, i.e. that it will not operate in situations where the elasticity drops below unity because marginal revenue becomes negative.

2. (a) The total revenue function is quadratic in form, i.e. a function in which one or more of the independent variables are squared. Since the Q^2 term has a negative parameter value, the function increases at low levels of output but then begins to fall after a certain maximum point. Since there is no intercept term, the function will start at the origin. On the other hand, the total cost function is also quadratic but has a positive intercept on the vertical cost axis (c) and the curve has an ever-increasing upward trend since the Q^2 term has a positive parameter value.

(b) (i) After the tax, the cost structure will change so that we have to add the total tax (tQ) to the original total costs (C) to obtain the post-tax total costs (C^*), i.e.

$$C^* = C + tQ \tag{1}$$

Since we know the value of C (i.e. total cost TC), then substitute it in equation (1):

$$C^* = C + tQ$$
$$= (c + bQ + aQ^2) + tQ$$
$$= c + (b + t)Q + aQ^2 \tag{2}$$

(ii) To find the expression for the monopolist's equilibrium output we need to equate the post-tax marginal cost with the marginal revenue, and so we need to find the expressions for these. The post-tax marginal cost MC^* is merely the first derivative of the post-tax total cost function in equation (2), i.e.

$$MC^* = \frac{dC^*}{dQ} = b + t + 2aQ \tag{3}$$

Similarly the marginal revenue MR is the first derivative of the total revenue function TR, i.e.

$$TR = \beta Q - \alpha Q^2$$

$$MR = \frac{dTR}{dQ} = \beta - 2\alpha Q \tag{4}$$

(iii) The monopolist equilibrium output is where $MC^* = MR$. This means equating the two equations (3) and (4) and solving for Q:

$$MC^* = MR$$
$$b + t + 2aQ = \beta - 2\alpha Q$$

$$2Q(a + \alpha) = \beta - b - t$$
$$Q = \frac{\beta - b - t}{2(a + \alpha)} \tag{5}$$

Now that we have the expression for Q, we need to substitute this in the government tax function $T = tQ$ to get

$$T = tQ$$
$$= \frac{t(\beta - b - t)}{2(a + \alpha)} \quad \text{or} \quad \frac{t\beta - tb - t^2}{2(a + \alpha)} \tag{6}$$

(c) To obtain the maximum value for t we need to satisfy the first-order condition: we must find the first derivative of T, i.e. differentiate equation (6) with respect to t, and equate it to zero.

$$\frac{dT}{dt} = \frac{\beta - b - 2t}{2(a + \alpha)} = 0 \tag{7}$$

Since the expression will be zero only if the numerator is zero, we can simply set $\beta - b - 2t = 0$ and then deduce from this equation the revenue-maximising tax rate:

$$\beta - b - 2t = 0$$
$$2t = \beta - b$$
$$t = \frac{\beta - b}{2} \tag{8}$$

The final stage is to check whether this tax rate is a maximum tax rate. To do this it is necessary to find the sign of the second derivative of the tax function. To get this we have to differentiate equation (7) once more:

$$\frac{dT}{dt} = \frac{\beta - b - 2t}{2(a + \alpha)}$$

Taking the second derivative we have

$$\frac{d^2T}{dt^2} = \frac{-2}{2(a + \alpha)} = \frac{-1}{a + \alpha} \tag{9}$$

Since this is a negative quantity it proves that the tax rate t actually does maximise total tax T.

3. (a) The demand function is $Q = 80 - 4P$. To obtain the demand *curve* we need to rearrange this function and divide throughout by 4, i.e.

$$Q = 80 - 4P$$
$$4P = 80 - Q$$
$$P = 20 - 0.25Q \tag{1}$$

(b) To calculate the marginal revenue we first have to obtain the expression for the total revenue. It is known that total revenue is price times quantity, i.e. $TR = P \times Q$. Since we have the expression for P from equation (1) we can substitute this in the equation for TR:

$$TR = P \times Q$$
$$= (20 - 0.25Q)Q$$
$$= 20Q - 0.25Q^2 \tag{2}$$

To obtain the equation for MR we need to differentiate the TR function shown in equation (2) with respect to Q:

$$MR = \frac{dTR}{dQ} = 20 - 0.5Q \tag{3}$$

Equation (3) is in the typical form of a straight line with a slope of -0.5, i.e. a downward-sloping demand curve. To confirm this, it is necessary to take the second derivative of the TR function, i.e. differentiate equation (3) (the MR curve) once more:

$$\frac{d^2TR}{dQ^2} = -0.5$$

Since this is a negative number, the curve is downward sloping, i.e. has a negative slope.

(c) Profit is the difference between total revenue and total costs. We know that total revenue, $TR = 20Q - 0.25Q^2$. Total cost can be expressed as average cost times output, i.e. $TC = AC \times Q$. We know that $AC = 40Q^{-1} + 6$ (or $40/Q + 6$). Therefore

$$TC = (40/Q + 6)Q$$
$$= 40 + 6Q \tag{4}$$

Total profit, π, is total revenue (equation (2)) minus total cost (equation (4)), i.e.

$$\pi = TR - TC$$
$$= (20Q - 0.25Q^2) - (40 + 6Q)$$
$$= 20Q - 0.25Q^2 - 40 - 6Q$$
$$= 14Q - 0.25Q^2 - 40 \tag{5}$$

The maximum profits will be where the first derivative of the total profit function (equation (5)) is zero, i.e.

$$\text{Max profit} = \frac{d\pi}{dQ} = 14 - 0.5Q = 0$$

$$0.5Q = 14$$
$$Q = 28$$

This means that the maximum profit is where output of ink is 28,000 litres per month. To find the price at this level of output we need to substitute 28 for Q in the demand equation (1):

$$P = 20 - 0.25Q$$
$$= 20 - 0.25(28)$$
$$= 13$$

Therefore the profit-maximising output is 28,000 litres per month and the optimum price is £13 per litre. To find the level of profits all that is necessary is to substitute for Q in the total profit equation (5):

$$= 14Q - 0.25Q^2 - 40$$
$$= 14(28) - 0.25(28)^2 - 40$$
$$= 392 - 196 - 40$$
$$= 156$$

In other words, the total profit is £156,000 per month.

(d) To calculate the price elasticity of demand at the profit-maximising point on the demand curve we need to write down the expression for point price elasticity of demand, i.e.

$$E_d = \frac{\partial Q}{\partial P} \cdot \frac{P}{Q}$$

where $\partial Q / \partial P$ is the reciprocal of the slope of the demand curve ($\partial P / \partial Q$) i.e. $-1/0.25 = -4$ and P/Q is the price and quantity combination at the point on the demand curve, i.e. 13/28.

Therefore the value of the price elasticity of demand is

$-4 \times 13/28 = -1.85$.

(e) If the government imposes a lump sum tax of £20,000 on the monthly output of ink, then this means that the total costs, TC, will increase by £20,000. Because the cost equations are expressed in 000s of units we therefore increase TC by 20, i.e.

$TC = 40 + 6Q + (20)$
$\quad = 60 + 6Q$ (6)

To calculate the new level of profits we need to use the expression

$\pi = TR - TC$
$\quad = 20Q - 0.25Q^2 - (60 + 6Q)$
$\quad = 20Q - 0.25Q^2 - 60 - 6Q$
$\quad = 14Q - 0.25^2 - 60$ (7)

To find the profit-maximising output and price, we repeat the stages starting from equation (5). The maximum profits will be where the first derivative of the total profit function (equation (7)) is zero, i.e.

Max. profit $= \dfrac{d\pi}{dQ} = 14 - 0.5Q = 0$
$\qquad\qquad\qquad 0.5Q = 14$
$\qquad\qquad\qquad\quad Q = 28$

This means that the maximum profit is where output is 28,000 litres per month. To find the price at this level of output, we need to substitute 28 in the demand curve:

$P = 20 - 0.25Q$
$\quad = 20 - 0.25(28)$
$\quad = 13$

From these calculations we can see that despite the imposition of a lump sum tax, the price and output levels have not changed, i.e. have stayed at £13 and 28,000 litres respectively. To find out what has happened to profits we need to substitute the values of 13 and 28 in equation (7):

$\pi = 14Q - 0.25Q^2 - 60$
$\quad = 14(28) - 0.25(28)^2 - 60$
$\quad = 392 - 196 - 60$
$\quad = 136$

This means that post-tax profits will be £136,000 or £20,000 down on the original profits of £156,000. In other words, the effect of the tax is to decrease profits by exactly the amount of the tax while leaving price and output undisturbed.

(*Note*: Remember when attempting this question that the value of the tax at £20,000 has to be converted to 20 when placed in equation (6) because the equation is in units of a thousand. Then once the results of the equations are calculated they can be reconverted to actual amounts by multiplying by 1,000, with the exception of price, which was in single units. All the information about the units in which price and quantities were measured was given in the question.)

4. (a) If we first take the domestic market, we know that the demand function is $Q_1 = 20 - 0.4P_1$. This function needs to be converted into the form of a demand curve:

$$Q_1 = 20 - 0.4P_1$$
$$0.4P_1 = 20 - Q_1$$
$$P_1 = 50 - 2.5Q_1 \qquad (1)$$

We now have the demand curve for the domestic market but we also need to obtain the marginal revenue (MR) curve for the market. If we look at the demand curve, it is possible to write down the equation for the marginal revenue curve from our knowledge of the relationship between the demand and MR. In other words, both curves will have the intercept at 50 and the MR curve has twice the slope of the demand curve, i.e. 0.5. Therefore the equation for MR_1 is $50 - 0.5Q_1$. However, if we need to be more precise in our methodology we should calculate the total revenue (TR_1) and then differentiate that function in order to obtain MR_1:

$$\begin{aligned} TR_1 &= P_1 \times Q_1 \\ &= (50 - 2.5Q_1)\,Q_1 \\ &= 50Q_1 - 2.5Q_1^2 \end{aligned} \qquad (2)$$

MR_1 can be obtained by finding the first derivative of TR_1:

$$MR_1 = \frac{dTR_1}{dQ_1} = 50 - 5Q_1 \qquad (3)$$

To enable us to calculate the price and output levels in the *domestic market* we need to equate the MR_1 of the domestic market with the MC of actually producing the part in the UK plant. We know that total cost (TC) is $30Q + 20$, where Q is the total output of parts. From this information we can obtain the marginal cost by differentiating this function with respect to Q, i.e.

$$TC = 30Q + 20 \qquad (4)$$

$$MC = \frac{dTC}{dQ} = 30 \qquad (5)$$

Therefore the marginal cost of producing the part at the factory is 30. If we equate this MC to the MR_1 of the domestic market we will obtain the information we need:

$$\begin{aligned} MR_1 &= MC \\ 50 - 5Q_1 &= 30 \\ 5Q_1 &= 20 \\ Q_1 &= 4 \end{aligned}$$

To find the price in the domestic market, substitute for Q_1 in the demand curve (equation (1)):

$$P_1 = 50 - 2.5Q_1$$
$$= 50 - 2.5(4)$$
$$= 40$$

This information when translated into actual amounts indicates that in the domestic market the price per engine part is 40 ecus and the quantity produced is 4,000.

To calculate the total profit in the domestic market we need to subtract the total revenue from the total cost:

$$TR_1 = P_1 \times Q_1$$
$$= 40 \times 4$$
$$= 160$$

$$TC = 30Q + 20$$
$$= 30(4) + 20$$
$$= 140$$

The total profit in the domestic market is $160 - 140 = 20$, and since the figures are in thousands this means £20,000.

The next step is to repeat the same process for the *overseas market* since we need to know the demand and marginal revenue curves in this market. We then equate the MR in the overseas market (i.e. MR_2) with the MC of producing the engine part in order to find out the price and output for that market. First we take the demand function and convert it into a demand curve:

$$Q_2 = 5.5 - 0.05P_2$$
$$0.05P_2 = 5.5 - Q_2$$
$$P_2 = 110 - 20Q_2 \qquad (6)$$

To obtain the total and marginal revenue curves for the overseas market we need to write down the expression for TR_2 and substitute equation (6), i.e for P_2, into that expression:

$$TR_2 = P_2 \times Q_2$$
$$= (110 - 20Q_2)Q_2$$
$$= 110Q_2 - 20Q_2^2$$

Differentiate this expression with respect to Q:

$$MR_2 = \frac{dTR_2}{dQ_2} = 110 - 40Q_2 \qquad (7)$$

To find the quantity Q_2, equate MR_2 of the overseas market with the MC of producing the part in the sole UK plant:

$$MR_2 = MC$$
$$110 - 40Q_2 = 30$$
$$40Q_2 = 80$$
$$Q_2 = 2$$

Substitute $Q_2 = 2$ in the overseas demand curve (equation (6)):

$$P_2 = 110 - 20Q_2$$
$$= 110 - 20(2)$$
$$= 70$$

In other words, the price in the overseas market is 70 ecus and the quantity produced is 2,000 parts.

To calculate the profit in the overseas market we must go back to the original equations and deduct the total revenue from the total costs. The total revenue will be 70×2 or 140 while the total costs can be obtained by substituting $Q = 2$ in the total cost function (equation (4)), i.e. $30(2) + 20 = 80$. Therefore the total profit from the overseas market is $140 - 80 = 60$. Since the figures in the equations are in thousands, the total profit is 60,000 ecus.

We now summarise this section and provide a full picture of the amounts, etc. (remember that the Qs are in 000s). The Airocraft company will charge a lower price (40 ecus) and produce a higher output (4,000) in the domestic market than in the overseas market, where the price will be 70 ecus and the output 2,000. The profits in the domestic market were 20,000 ecus and in the overseas market 60,000 ecus, totalling 80,000 ecus in all.

(b) The next stage is to calculate what the price and profit levels would have been if Airocraft had *not* engaged in price discrimination, i.e if the output of the two markets had been sold at one single price. To do this we need to construct the total demand function for the engine part by summing the two separate markets and remembering that $P_1 = P_2$. Letting the common price be P and total output Q, we get

$$\text{Total market demand } Q = Q_1 + Q_2$$
$$= (20 - 0.4P) + (5.5 - 0.05P)$$
$$= 25.5 - 0.45P \qquad (8)$$

To derive the total demand curve we need to rearrange equation (8):

$$Q = 25.5 - 0.45P$$
$$0.45P = 25.5 - Q$$
$$P = 56.66 - 2.22Q \qquad (9)$$

The expression for the total revenue or the whole operation can be obtained by substituting equation (9) in the usual expression for TR, i.e.

$$TR = P \times Q$$
$$= (56.66 - 2.22Q)Q$$
$$= 56.66Q - 2.22Q^2$$

The marginal revenue curve for the whole market can be obtained by finding the first derivative of the TR function, i.e.

$$MR = \frac{dTR}{dQ} = 56.66 - 4.44Q \tag{10}$$

We know that the MC is 30 (equation (5)) so that if we equate MR with MC we will obtain the equilibrium price and output levels:

$$MR = MC$$

$$56.66 - 4.44Q = 30$$
$$4.44Q = 26.66$$
$$Q = 6$$

This output of 6 (i.e. 6,000) comes as no surprise because it is the combined output of the home and overseas markets, both of which were produced in the single UK plant. The price discrimination strategy merely distributed this amount over two markets. However, to obtain the price level for the single market we can substitute $Q = 6$ in the overall market demand curve (equation 9):

$$
\begin{aligned}
P &= 56.66 - 2.22Q \\
&= 56.66 - 2.22(6) \\
&= 56.66 - 13.33 \\
&= 43.33
\end{aligned}
$$

The total profit for the unified market is $TR - TC$ as usual. In this case $TR = 6 \times 43.33 = 260$ while, using the total cost equation (equation (4)), $TC = 30(6) + 20 = 200$. The profits are therefore 60. Because the quantities are measured in 000s, the profits are, in fact, 60,000 ecus.

(c) The price discrimination strategy of Airocraft plc has been beneficial because by introducing price discrimination its profits have been maximised. The profits from discrimination were 80,000 ecus while a single overall market would have produced only 60,000 ecus.

A glance at the demand curves of the separate market would explain why there was distinct potential for price discrimination. The slope of the overseas demand curve was −20 (equation (6)) while that of the domestic market was −2.5 (equation (1)). Therefore the overseas market has a larger or steeper slope, i.e. is relatively inelastic, compared with the domestic market. The natural thing for a monopolist to do is to distribute its output in such a way as to charge a higher price in the relatively inelastic overseas market and a lower price in the domestic market. We can see in this case that Airocraft plc followed this pattern, which is the classic strategy of a discriminating monopolist.

5. (a) (i) The profit-maximising output and price are determined where the marginal cost equals marginal revenue. We therefore need to derive these relationships from the information given. Taking the revenue side, we know that the market demand curve for the sleeping pills is

$$P_M = 80 - 0.001Q_M \tag{1}$$

Since we know that the total revenue is price multiplied by quantity, then the total revenue (*TR*) for the sleeping pills can be expressed as $P_M \times Q_M$. Substituting for P_M in this relationship we get

$$TR = (80 - 0.001Q_M)\, Q_M$$
$$= 80Q_M - 0.001Q^2_M \tag{2}$$

To obtain the marginal revenue curve we need to differentiate the above equation with respect to Q_M, i.e.

$$MR_M = \frac{dTR}{dQ_M} = 80 - 0.002Q_M \tag{3}$$

We also need to derive the marginal cost curve for the sleeping pills, and this can be done by finding the first derivatives (*MCs*) of the production and marketing divisions and adding them together. Taking the marketing division,

$$C_M = 200{,}000 + 10Q_M$$

$$MC_M = \frac{dC_M}{dQ_M} = 10 \tag{4}$$

Similarly, for the production division:

$$C_P = 400{,}000 + 10Q_P + 0.001Q^2_P$$

$$MC_P = \frac{dC_P}{dQ_P} = 10 + 0.002Q_P \tag{5}$$

Therefore to obtain the total marginal cost curve we must add the marginal cost curves of the production and marketing divisions, recognising that $Q_M = Q_P$ since the production division sells all of its production to the marketing department (i.e. no external market). We can substitute the Q_M term when we see Q_P, i.e.

$$MC = MC_M + MC_P$$
$$= 10 + 10 + 0.002Q_M$$
$$= 20 + 0.002Q_M \tag{6}$$

We can now calculate the profit-maximising market output by equating *MC* to the MR_M already calculated (equation (3)), i.e.

$$MR_M = MC$$

$$80 - 0.002Q_M = 20 + 0.002Q_M$$
$$60 = 0.004Q_M$$
$$15{,}000 = Q_M$$

Since $Q_M = Q_P$, the output for the production division should also be 15,000. To obtain the market price and output merely substitute for Q_M in the demand equation (1):

$$P_M = 80 - 0.001Q_M$$
$$= 80 - 0.001(15,000)$$
$$= 65$$

The profit-maximising market price is 65 ecus per pack and the output is 15 million (since Q_M is in 000s). This means that to maximise profits, Pharma's market output will be 15 million packs and the market price should be 65 ecus per pack.

(ii) The optimal transfer price at which the production division should sell its sleeping pills to the marketing division is equal to the marginal cost of producing the pills at the optimal level of output. We know the equation for the marginal cost of the production division and we have just calculated the optimum output, so that we can substitute 15,000 in equation (5):

$$MC_P = 10 + 0.002Q_P$$
$$= 10 + 0.002 (15,000)$$
$$= 40$$

Therefore the intra-company price at which the production division should sell to the marketing division is 40 ecus per pack.

(b) (i) In the second part of this question we are told that there is an external market for the sleeping pills. In other words, the production department can sell the pills to the marketing department or directly to the perfectly competitive external wholesale market for 45 ecus per pack equivalent. The task is to calculate the profit-maximising output for the production and marketing divisions and the optimal transfer price for intra-company sales, given that there is an external wholesale market.

The production division can sell as much output as it wants to the external market for a price of 45 ecus per pack equivalent, so that the marginal revenue (MR_P) will also be 45 ecus (since $P(AR) = MR$ in a perfectly competitive market). The optimum output for the production division will be where MR_P is equal to MC_P:

$$MR_P = MC_P$$

Substituting the values of the two marginal revenues in the above equation we obtain

$$45 = 10 + 0.002Q_P$$
$$35 = 0.002Q_P$$
$$17,500 = Q_P$$

This provides us with the information that the production division will produce 17.5 million packs given the fact that there is an external perfectly competitive market in operation.

To calculate the optimum output for the marketing division we need to calculate the marginal cost of the marketing division (MC_t). This is composed of the pure marginal marketing costs (MC_M) plus the cost per unit of the 'intermediate product' (i.e. the pills prior to packaging) bought from the production division, i.e. $MC_t = MC_M + 45$. The value 45 in ecus is, of course, the price of the intermediate product as sold by the production division to the marketing division. The production department will not sell its intermediate product to the marketing division for less than 45 ecus because it can get this price in the external market. Therefore 45 ecus represents the optimal transfer price.

If we want to calculate the optimal output for the marketing division we first need to calculate MC_t ($MC_M = 10$ from equation (4)):

$$MC_t = MC_M + 45$$
$$= 10 + 45$$
$$= 55$$

To find the profit-maximising output then this will be where the marginal cost of the marketing department is equal to the marginal revenue of the marketing department (equation (3)), i.e.

$$MC_t = MR_M$$

$$55 = 80 - 0.002Q_M$$

$$0.002Q_M = 25$$

$$Q_M = 12,500$$

In other words, the profit-maximising output that is sold by the marketing department is 12.5 million packs.

(b) (ii)   We can conclude by saying that, to maximise profits, Pharma's production division should produce the equivalent of 17.5 million (Qs are in 000s) packs. It should then sell 12.5 million packs internally to the marketing department and sell the remainder, i.e. 5 million packs, on the open market. The marketing department should therefore sell 12.5 million packs through its retail outlets. The optimal transfer price for the intra-company sales is the price in the competitive market, i.e. 45 ecus.

Chapter 8   1. (a)   To plot the two demand curves, it is necessary to find the points where the two demand curves cut the price and quantity axes. This can be done by taking both demand equations and working out the value of P when Q is zero (the value on the P axis will then be given) and the value of Q when P is zero (the value on the Q axis will then be given). We can then draw the demand curves by joining these points for each curve, i.e. for a price fall ($P = 12$, $Q = 60$) and for a price rise ($P = 9$, $Q = 180$). As noted in the question, it is unnecessary to draw an extended horizontal axis to accommodate the 180 value for Q_A; we need only draw the Q_A function up to 70. This can be done by substituting the value of 70 in the Q_A equation and getting a P value of £5.5. Then the Q_A demand curve will extend from £9 on the vertical axis to point £5.5/70 when output is 70. After drawing these curves, it will be seen that both intersect at a price of £8. Only *certain parts* of each demand curve are relevant to the oligopoly situation. These are the Q_A part of the demand curve to the left of the intersection, and the Q_B part of the demand curve to the right of the intersection. Erase the parts of the curves that are not needed, and we shall then see the 'kink' in the composite demand curve. To draw the relevant marginal revenues all that we need to know is that the position of the marginal revenue curve is always midway between the demand curve and the vertical axis. These can then be drawn, leaving on the diagram only those relevant parts of the marginal revenue that correspond to the composite demand curve. When this has been done, the kink will look as shown in Fig. A.9.

Price often remains at the 'kink' in an oligopoly situation because the logical assumption is made that if Safelock increases its price from that position then its competitor, Securol, is *not likely* to follow it by raising price; rather it is more likely to remain at the old price in order to gain market share for itself. In this case Safelock is likely to lose customers if it puts up price, and thus its demand curve will then be relatively elastic. On the other hand if Safelock reduces its price from the kink position, then Securol *is likely* to follow Safelock in order to avoid losing market share to Safelock. In this case, the company will not gain as much as it would like, i.e. its demand curve will be relatively inelastic. Therefore, because Safelock will lose market share rapidly if it raises price and gains little market share when it decreases price, there is little incentive for it to move from the 'kink' position. Notice that the kink in the demand curves has also resulted in a composite marginal revenue curve with a vertical segment of the *MR* curve extending downwards from £7 to £4.

(b) Plotting the SAC_1 and SMC_1 curves allows us to find the equilibrium output position. The condition for equilibrium is $MR = SMC_1$, where price is £8 per clip and quantity is 20, i.e. 20,000 clips (Q is in 000s units). The profit per unit at this level of output is denoted by the difference between P and SAC_1. In this case it is £8 − £5 = £3 per unit. Since there are 20,000 units, the total profit will be £60,000.

Fig. A.9

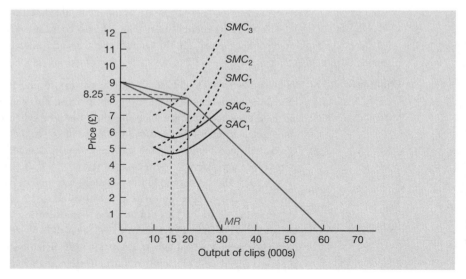

(c) If Safelock's costs rise as a result of an increase in price of raw materials, then we need to draw the curves for SAC_2 and SMC_2 onto the graph paper. When this has been done, the new equilibrium position can be found where $MR = SMC_2$: i.e. the price will still be at £8 and the output at 20 (20,000). In this case the profit per clip will be $P - SAC_2$ or £8 − £6 = £2. The total profits will have fallen to £2 × 20,000 = £40,000.

(d) Trade union bargaining at Safelock has increased marginal costs to SMC_3. By drawing this curve and equating MR and SAC_3 we can see that Safelock has been forced to decrease its equilibrium output from 20 to 15 (000), and price has risen from £8 to £8.25 per clip. Safelock was prepared to keep price and output steady at £8 and 20 (000) respectively when costs were rising upward along the vertical part of its MR curve, i.e. from £4 to £7. This was because it preferred to experience a rise in *known* costs and a fall in *known* total profits rather than change price and *gamble* on the reaction of competitors. However, when marginal costs rose beyond £7 per unit at the 20,000 output, Safelock was forced to adjust its price upwards to £8.25, resulting in a fall in sales to 15,000 clips.

2. (a) To draw the demand curve we need to take the demand function $Q = 12 - P$ and let Q and P be zero in turn. This will leave us with $Q = 12$ when P is zero and $P = 12$ when Q is zero. Plotting this on a graph will produce the D curve in Fig. A.10. The marginal revenue curve can be drawn since, as we have seen earlier in Chapter 2 (p. 55) (see also Fig. 8.2, p. 334), the MR curve lies at half the distance between the price axis and the demand curve. Fastfoods will maximise its profits where $MR = MC$, but since MC is zero, MR will also be zero. This profit-maximising equilibrium will be at output 6 (000) meals per week and a price of £6 per meal. Fastfoods' total profits would be 6,000 × 6 = £36,000 per week (there are no costs to consider here). Notice that where $MR = 0$ the profit-maximising output will be at 6 (000) meals, which is exactly half ($Q/2$) the market demand at $P = 0$.

Fig. A.10

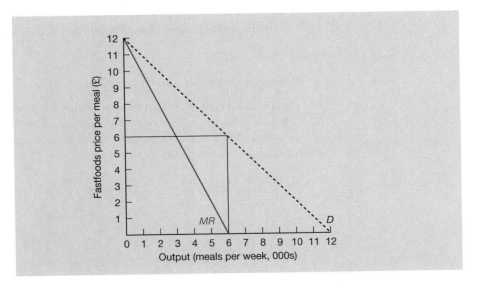

(b) Under the Cournot model Fastfoods assumes that Easymeal will not change its output if Fastfoods decides to change its own output. Similarly, Easymeal assumes that Fastfoods will not change its output if Easymeal decides to change its own output. In other words, each firm chooses an output level on the assumption that the others firm's output will *not be adjusted*. If we assume that the market outputs of the firms are denoted by Q_F and Q_E then the Cournot model theorises that Fastfoods will choose output Q_F on the assumption that the output of Easymeal will be fixed at Q_E and will not be adjusted in response to Fastfood's actions.

The total market output, Q, is composed of $Q_F + Q_E$, so that the market demand function is

$$Q_F + Q_E = 12 - P \tag{1}$$

If we assume that Q_E is fixed, then the demand function facing Fastfoods is

$$Q_F = (12 - Q_E) - P \tag{2}$$

This means that if a portion Q_E of the market is taken by Easymeal, then Fastfoods makes its choice from what is left of the market, i.e. Q_F. Now we know that the profit-maximising output will be where $MR = 0$, i.e. half the distance from the demand curve to the price axis. It follows that Fastfoods' profit-maximising reaction curve will be

$$Q_F = (12 - Q_E)/2 \tag{3}$$

Notice that compared with equation (2), equation (3) does not have a P term, and the remaining expression $(12 - Q_E)$ has been divided by 2. This is because Fastfoods will be at a profit-maximising equilibrium where its $MR = 0$ (remember the assumptions that $MC = 0$) and therefore P must also be zero. The divisor 2 comes from the well-known assumption that when $MR = 0$ the profit-maximising output will be at a level of half the demand when $P = 0$. In this context, Q_F will be at half the output remaining $(12 - Q_E)$, which we noted in part (a) of this answer.

We can do the same process for Easymeal as we did for Fastfoods and get Easymeal's profit-maximising reaction function as

$$Q_E = (12 - Q_F)/2 \tag{4}$$

If we graph equations (3) and (4) we get Fig. A. 11.

(c) From Fig. A.11, the Cournot equilibrium is at A where both reaction curves (lines) intersect, i.e. both companies produce 4 (000) meals per week. This graphical solution could have been obtained through simple algebra by substituting equation (4) into equation (3), giving

$$Q_F = \frac{12 - (12 - Q_F)/2}{2}$$

$$= \frac{12 - 6 - Q_F/2}{2}$$

$$= 3 - (Q_F/4) \tag{5}$$

Fig. A.11

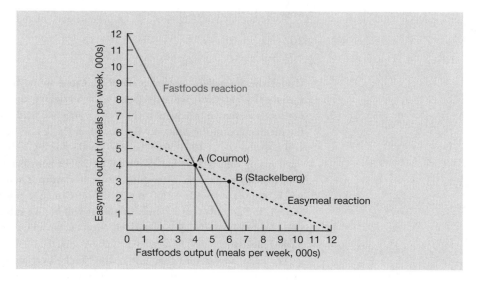

We can multiply both sides of this equation by 4 so that we get

$$4Q_F = 12 - Q_F$$
$$Q_F = 4 \text{ (or 4,000 meals per week)}$$

To get the value of Q_E merely substitute the value of 4 for Q_F in equation (4), which gives $Q_E = 4$ (000) meals per week. In other words, both companies produce $4 + 4 = 8$ (000) meals per week. This is the total market demand (Q) of meals per week.

Fastfoods' total profits in this situation will be market price (P) times output (Q_F). To find the market price, P, we need to substitute the value for Q (i.e. 8) into the market equation $Q = 12 - P$. Therefore $P = 12 - 8 = £4$ per meal. The total profit under the duopoly will therefore be $£4 \times 8,000 = £32,000$, i.e. £16,000 each for Fastfoods and Easymeal. Therefore a shift from the monopoly to the duopoly situation has brought total profits down from £36,000 to £32,000. The reason why profits are less in a duopoly is because it is difficult to coordinate the actions of two companies to achieve the highest possible profits. Only if the two companies collude as if they were one company, i.e. a monopoly, could market profits rise to the levels shown when Fastfoods was operating on its own.

(d) If Fastfoods recognises that Easymeal reacts to its output as given by equation (4) above, then it can increase its profits by making use of this knowledge. In other words, by substituting equation (4) into (2) above, we get

$$Q_F = (12 - Q_E) - P$$
$$= [12 - (12 - Q_F)/2] - P$$
$$= 6 + Q_F/2 - P$$

Multiply both sides by 2:

$$2Q_F = 12 + Q_F - 2P$$
$$Q_F = 12 - 2P \tag{6}$$

Under the *Stackelberg leadership model* we can assume that Fastfoods will know Easymeal's reaction; we have been able to derive the demand function for Fastfoods as shown in equation (6) above. Since we made the assumption that in the profit-maximising situation $MR = 0$, then P will also be zero and equation (6) will become $Q_F = 12$. But we have to divide this figure by 2 because the profit-maximising output is at half the total output at zero price, giving a figure of 6 (000) meals per week. Therefore Fastfoods' output will be 6,000 meals per week, compared with 4,000 meals in the Cournot position (see answer (c) above). To find out what Easymeal's output will be, we substitute for Q_F in equation (4) above, which is Easymeal's reaction curve, and we get $Q_E = (12-6)/2 = 3$ (000 meals).

We have now found that under the Stackelberg conditions Fastfoods has increased its share of output over its Cournot situation from 4,000 to 6,000 meals and Easymeal has experienced a fall in its output of meals from 4,000 to 3,000. In Fig. A.11 this is shown as a move from the Cournot equilibrium at A to the Stackelberg equilibrium with Fastfoods as the sophisticated leader, at B.

The final task is to calculate the respective profit levels of each company, but before that we have to calculate the market price for meals under these new conditions. As previously noted, we know that the market demand function is $Q = 12 - P$ and that, in this case, $Q = 9$ (i.e. $6 + 3$). This means that the equilibrium price of meals is $12 - 9 = 3$, i.e. £3 each. Total profits per company will be £3 × 6,000 or £18,000 for Fastfoods and £3 × 3,000 or £9,000 for Easymeal. Therefore by using its knowledge of Easymeal's reaction function, Fastfoods has been able to increase its total profits from the previous £16,000 (see (c) above) to a new £18,000 level, while Easymeal has suffered a fall in profits from £16,000 to £9,000.

3. (a) (i) The condition for equilibrium in a competitive market is where price equals marginal cost, i.e. $P = MC$. Since we are given both of these values we can equate them and solve for Q and P:

$$P = MC$$
$$1,000 - Q_M = 100$$
$$Q_M = 900$$

To find the competitive price substitute $Q = 900$ in the demand equation:

$$P = 1,000 - Q_M$$
$$= 1,000 - 900$$
$$= 100$$

Therefore the competitive quantity is 900 units at a price of 100 ecus each.

(ii) To obtain the equilibrium price and output on the assumption that the industry was in the hands of one company we need to equate marginal revenue with marginal cost. We know that marginal cost is 100 but we need to derive the marginal revenue curve for the industry. This means that it is necessary to find the expression for the total revenue (*TR*) function and then calculate the first derivative of this function, which will then give us the marginal revenue (*MR*) function. First we know that the expression for total revenue is

$$TR = P \times Q_M$$

Substituting for *P*:

$$\begin{aligned} TR &= (1,000 - Q_M)\, Q_M \\ &= 1,000 Q_M - Q_M^2 \end{aligned} \tag{1}$$

Differentiate this function with respect to Q_M:

$$MR = \frac{dTR}{dQ_M} = 1,000 - 2Q_M \tag{2}$$

(This part of the calculation could have been done quickly from the knowledge that the marginal revenue curve has twice the slope of the demand curve.)

Profit-maximising equilibrium under monopoly will be where

$$MR = MC$$

Substitute the values of *MR* and *MC*:

$$\begin{aligned} 1,000 - 2Q_M &= 100 \\ Q_M &= 450 \end{aligned}$$

The equilibrium price can be obtained by substituting $Q_M = 450$ in the demand equation given in the question, i.e.

$$\begin{aligned} P &= 1,000 - Q_M \\ &= 1,000 - 450 \\ &= 550 \end{aligned}$$

In other words, if the industry was under monopoly conditions the quantity produced would be 450 units and the price would be 550 ecus per unit.

(b) Since the two companies are in a Cournot-type duopoly situation, we need to provide the expressions for both the demand and marginal revenue curves for both Avionics and Engineering Enterprises. If we let the output of Avionics and Engineering Enterprises be Q_A and Q_E respectively we know that the demand curve for the industry can be expressed as

$$P = 1,000 - (Q_A + Q_E) \tag{3}$$

(remember that $Q_M = Q_A + Q_E$)

From Avionics' perspective, the demand curve for its portion of the market can be written as

$$P_A = (1,000 - Q_E) - Q_A \tag{4}$$

This is merely that part of the demand curve that is left after assuming that Engineering Enterprises produces Q_E and continues to do so under the Cournot assumptions. To obtain Avionics' marginal revenue curve we can take the 'short cut' and merely double the angle for the demand curve (equation (4)), giving

$$MR_A = (1,000 - Q_E) - 2Q_A \tag{5}$$

The other way is to find the expression for total revenue and differentiate that expression to obtain the marginal revenue, i.e.

$$TR_A = P_A \times Q_A$$

Substitute the values of P_A (equation (4)):

$$TR_A = [(1,000 - Q_E) - Q_A] Q_A$$
$$= (1,000 - Q_E) Q_A - Q_A{}^2$$

Differentiating this function we get

$$MR_A = \frac{dTR_A}{dQ_A} = (1,000 - Q_E) - 2Q_A$$

Using the same methodology as for Avionics, the demand curve for Engineering Enterprises will be

$$P_E = (1,000 - Q_A) - Q_E \tag{6}$$

The marginal revenue would follow as

$$MR_E = (1,000 - Q_A) - 2Q_E \tag{7}$$

(c) To obtain the reaction curve for Avionics from the marginal revenue curve we assume that Avionics maximises profits independently from Engineering Enterprises (as assumed in the Cournot model) by setting its marginal revenue equal to marginal cost. Therefore its reaction curve will be where $MR_A = MC_A$, i.e.

$$MR_A = MC_A$$

Substituting the values for marginal revenue (equation (5)) and marginal cost $MC_A = 100$ (given) in this equation we get

$$1,000 - Q_E - 2Q_A = 100$$
$$2Q_A = 900 - Q_E$$
$$Q_A = 450 - 0.5Q_E \tag{8}$$

Similarly, the reaction curve for Engineering Enterprises would be where the value of marginal revenue (equation (7)) is equal to the marginal cost $MC_A = 100$.

$$MR_E = MC_E$$

Substituting the relevant values in the equation:

$$1,000 - Q_A - 2Q_E = 100$$
$$2Q_E = 900 - Q_A$$
$$Q_E = 450 - 0.5Q_A \qquad (9)$$

The equilibrium level of output at which both Avionics and Engineering Enterprises maximise profits and reach the Cournot solution is where the two reaction curves intersect. To obtain the solution points we can take, say, the reaction curve for Avionics (equation (8)) and substitute the value of Q_E, i.e. equation (9):

$$Q_A = 450 - 0.5Q_E$$

Substitute the expression for Q_E into this equation:

$$Q_A = 450 - 0.5 (450 - 0.5Q_A)$$
$$= 450 - 225 + 0.25Q_A$$
$$0.75Q_A = 225$$
$$Q_A = 300$$

To find Q_E, substitute $Q_A = 300$ in the equation for Q_A (equation(8)):

$$Q_A = 450 - 0.5(300)$$
$$= 300$$

To conclude, we have calculated that the two companies would produce an equilibrium output of 300 units each under the profit-maximising hypothesis and reaction assumptions of the Cournot model. Incidentally, this would be a third of the competitive market output of 900 units calculated in (a).

(d) If Avionics decided to leave the market, then Engineering Enterprise would behave in the same way as a monopolist, and as we saw in (a) it would produce 450 units. This result can also be obtained by using equation (9), $Q_E = 450 - 0.5Q_A$, since in this case the output of Avionics, Q_A, would be zero, so that Q_E is 450 units.

4. (a) In this example, the dominant or more sophisticated firm is Engineering Enterprises plc. Because of its strength, it is able to maximise profits knowing that whatever output it chooses to produce will be accepted by Avionics. In other words, Engineering Enterprises can anticipate the reaction curve of Avionics and incorporate it in its own demand curve to determine its output and market price. Avionics will then produce the difference between the market demand and what Engineering Enterprises produces at the price dictated by the dominant company.

From the functions provided in question 3 (equation (3)) we know that the market demand is given by

$$P = 1,000 - (Q_A + Q_E)$$
$$= 1,000 - Q_A - Q_E \qquad (1)$$

Since Avionics' reaction curve is known to be of the form $Q_A = 450 - 0.5Q_E$ (see Answer 3, equation (9)), Engineering Enterprises can take this reaction into consideration when deriving its own demand curve. Basically all we need to do is substitute for Q_A in the market demand equation (1), to obtain the demand equation for Engineering Enterprises, i.e.

$$
\begin{aligned}
P_E &= 1,000 - (450 - 0.5Q_E) - Q_E \\
&= 1,000 - 450 + 0.5Q_E - Q_E \\
&= 550 - 0.5Q_E
\end{aligned}
$$

Therefore Engineering Enterprises' demand equation is

$$P_E = 550 - 0.5Q_E \tag{2}$$

(b) To determine the output and price that Engineering Enterprises will choose in order to maximise profits we must equate MR_E with MC_E. First we need to obtain the expression for the marginal revenue MR_E of Engineering Enterprises, from the demand curve. This can be done the simple way by using the fact that the slope of the marginal revenue curve is twice that of the demand curve while the intercept remains the same, i.e.

$$
\begin{aligned}
\text{since} \quad P_E &= 550 - 0.5Q_E \\
\text{then} \quad MR_E &= 550 - Q_E
\end{aligned} \tag{3}
$$

To obtain the profit-maximising output level for Engineering Enterprises, the dominant firm, we need to equate MR_E with MC_E (which was given as 100 in question 3). Therefore

$$
\begin{aligned}
MR_E &= MC_E \\
550 - Q_E &= 100 \\
Q_E &= 450
\end{aligned}
$$

The price at this level of output can be obtained by substituting $Q_E = 450$ in the demand equation (2), i.e.

$$
\begin{aligned}
P_E &= 550 - 0.5Q_E \\
&= 550 - 0.5(450) \\
&= 325
\end{aligned}
$$

(c) Since the dominant firm has decided to produce 450 units at a price of 325 ecus then this price will be the market price as it has been dictated by Engineering Enterprises owing to its strong market position. To calculate how much output Avionics will produce we need to use the market demand curve $P = 1,000 - Q_A - Q_E$ and substitute the values $P = 325$ and $Q_E = 450$:

$$
\begin{aligned}
P &= 1,000 - Q_A - Q_E \\
325 &= 1,000 - Q_A - 450 \\
Q_A &= 225
\end{aligned}
$$

Therefore Avionics produces what is left of the total market demand after Engineering Enterprises has decided on its output/price combination. The total size of the market is $450 + 225 = 675$ units at the price of 325 ecus per unit.

5. (a) Plotting the variables on graph paper would result in three functions: the market demand curve, D_M, the marginal cost curve for International Chemicals, MC_I, and the composite marginal cost curve of the smaller firms, ΣMC_0. Once we have these functions it becomes possible to derive the leader's demand and marginal revenue curves. We know that the leader sets the price and that the output produced by the smaller firms at that price will be given by the ΣMC_0 curve, since these companies are behaving as if they were in a competitive environment, i.e. 'price takers'. In this case, output will be where P is equal to ΣMC_0. Once we know how much the small firms sell at a given price, we can find the demand curve for the leader by subtracting the small firms' combined outputs from the market demand curve. For example, when price is £7 per kg then the small companies will supply *all* the market, since at that price ΣMC_0 intersects with the market demand curve. The leader would of course supply a zero amount, and therefore the relevant position of its demand curve would be on the vertical price axis when P is £7, technically, point (£7,0 million kg). If price was lower at, say, £6, then the market demand (D_M) would be 6 million while the amount supplied by the small firms would be 4 million (read off from the ΣMC_0 curve). The amount left for the leader to produce would be the difference, i.e. 2 million. Therefore we have a point (£6, 2 million). By moving down the price scale we can get more points to plot, resulting in a demand curve, D_I, for International Chemicals, the dominant firm. To draw the dominant firm's marginal cost curve, all we have to do is draw a line from the £7 point on the vertical axis, at half the distance between the dominant firm's demand curve, D_I, and the vertical price axis. If we do this we will have MR_I.

Fig. A.12

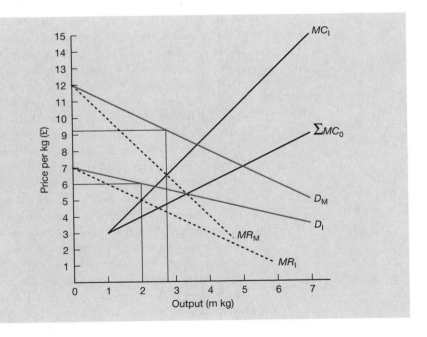

(b) We can now read off the price that International Chemicals will charge for the soda by noting the price at which MR_I equals MC_I, i.e. £6. In this case, market demand will be 6 million kg and International Chemicals will produce 2 million kg (33.3% of the market), while the 20 other smaller companies will produce 4 m llion kg (66.7% of the market). The smaller companies would be likely to foll w the leader's price for fear of cut-throat retaliation from International Chemicals, which would make life difficult for the smaller companies. Also, if the smaller companies 'tacitly' accept the leadership of the large company, then the market actually acts like an informal cartel, in which both large and small companies are happy with the 'understanding'.

(c) If the smaller companies created problems for International Chemicals, it could decide to use its dominant power to push the smaller firms out, thus leaving itself as a monopolist producer of soda. In this case we know that the market demand curve, D_M, will now be International Chemicals' demand curve, and the marginal revenue curve, MR_M, can be drawn half way between the D_M curve and the price axis. In this case International Chemicals will produce where MR_M equals MC_I. This will result in a market price of approximately £9.2 per kg at an output of 2.8 million kg.

Chapter 9 1. (a) A 'zero sum' game is the simplest form of game strategy. In the crisp industry, for example, it assumes that the gain of market share by Summer Delight is exactly matched by the losses of market share by Golden Dawn, and vice versa.

The maxi-min and mini-max solutions emerge from the assumptions made by Summer Delight about the response of Golden Dawn to any of its strategies and vice versa. Von Neumann and Morgenstern suggested that it is reasonable to assume that a firm such as Summer Delight that embarks on a certain strategy should expect its rival, Golden Dawn, to choose the most damaging counter-strategy available to it. Therefore Summer Delight should adopt a strategy that chooses the best out of the worst possible options available to it. For example, when Summer Delight introduces its three flavours, tomato, chicken and onion, it looks for the worst outcomes that could happen to it given Golden Dawn's responses because it knows that Golden Dawn will react with the most damaging strategy. Then it chooses the best (maxima) of these worst (minima) possible outcomes. In a zero-sum game, we also know that the best outcome for Summer Delight is the worst for Golden Dawn. Therefore as far as Golden Dawn is concerned, it responds to Summer Delight's various strategies by choosing the worst (minima) of the best (maxima) of Summer Delight's strategies (i.e. the best that Golden Dawn can hope for in the circumstances).

(b) We see in Table A.14 that the clearest way to see the various outcomes of the matrix is to add a vertical or 'minimum' column on the right, which will be used to find the best (maximum) out of a range of worst (minimum) possible outcomes from Summer Delight's strategy. The horizontal or 'maximum' column will be used to find the worst (minimum) outcome out of a range of best (maximum) of Summer Delight's strategies. This worst outcome for Summer Delight will, of course, be the best for Golden Dawn. (The discussion in the next

Table A.14

		Summer Delight's gain (+) or loss (−) of market share (%)			
		Golden Dawn			**Minimum**
		Cheese	Bacon	Curry	
Summer	Tomato	+5	−1	−4	**−4**
Delight	Chicken	+3(+1)	+1(+3)	+9	**+1**
	Onion	+4	−2	−6	**−6**
	Maximum	**+5**	**+1(+3)**	**+9**	

paragraph excludes the bracketed figures because these relate to a problem introduced in part (d) of the question.)

What we have done in the vertical column labelled 'minimum' is to look across, for example, at the tomato crisp strategy of Summer Delight and then work out, given the various possible responses of Golden Dawn, what the minimum benefit would be to Summer Delight. For example, if Summer Delight introduced its tomato-flavoured crisp the worst scenario for Summer Delight would be if Golden Dawn responded with a curry-flavoured crisp. In this case, Summer Delight would lose 4% of the market. If we follow this method for the chicken and onion flavours we get the vertical row on the right of the table. This column indicates the three worst scenarios that Summer Delight should expect, given that Golden Dawn will always try to find the most damaging counter-strategy. From this exercise we can see that Summer Delight's strategy will be to choose the bacon flavour option in the +1 box. In other words, this is the *best* of the worst possible outcomes for Summer Delight, i.e the maxi-min.

From Golden Dawn's point of view, it will be looking to minimise Summer Delight's best possible outcomes, and the result of these combinations is seen in the 'maximum' line at the bottom of Table A.14. For example, if Golden Dawn decides to introduce its own cheese flavour, then Summer Delight can react by introducing tomato-, chicken-, or onion-flavoured crisps. The best outcome for Summer Delight will be to respond with the tomato flavour since it will gain 5% of the market. If this exercise is repeated as Golden Dawn introduces its bacon and curry flavours then the results will be as seen in the bottom line of Table A.14. This gives the best outcomes for Summer Delight as a result of Golden Dawn introducing its three crisp flavours. Golden Dawn will then naturally choose the *worst* of these best Summer Delight figures: i.e. the mini-max condition will have been determined. From this exercise we can see that Golden Dawn's strategy will be to choose the bacon flavour option in the +1 box since this is the worst of Summer Delight's best or maximum possible outcomes, and by definition the best for Golden Dawn.

(c) As a result of this process we see that the maxi-min solution is +1 and the mini-max is also +1, i.e. what is called a 'saddle-point'. In conclusion, we have a situation where Summer Delight will launch its chicken flavour with Golden Dawn responding with bacon flavour, giving Summer Delight a 1% increase in market share and a 1% decrease in market share for Golden Dawn. Both companies recognise that neither can do better than this combination since both strategies provide a common solution. They therefore have no incentive to change their strategy since even if either Summer Delight or Golden Dawn knew the other's choice in advance they would also realise that neither could do better than the 'saddle-point' where the maxi-min is equal to the mini-max.

(d) If the values of the market share in the cheese/chicken and bacon/chicken boxes were reversed (as seen with the figures in brackets), then we would have the same maxi-min value (i.e. +1) but the mini-max would now be +3 (i.e. the bottom of the bacon column) with Summer Delight gaining 3% of the market. Since the maxi-min and the mini-max are not coincidental, i.e. not in the same box, it means that there is no 'saddle-point' and Golden Dawn would then change its strategy, if it knew Summer Delight's strategy in advance. For example, if Golden Dawn knew that Summer Delight was going to introduce chicken-flavoured crisps then it would be best to introduce cheese flavour since it would give Summer Delight only an increased market share of 1% instead of 3% if it had stuck with bacon flavour. However, if Summer Delight knew that Golden Dawn would introduce its cheese flavour it would produce its tomato-flavoured crisps in order to gain 5% of the market. Similarly, if Golden Dawn knew that Summer Delight would introduce the tomato flavour, it would introduce its curry flavour in order to gain 4% (−4) of Summer Delight's market, and so on.

In other words, when we do not have a stable situation, i.e. no saddle-point, it means that a company that sticks to its usual strategy will lose out since the other company will gain the vital information (i.e. that the original company will not change its strategy) and use it to modify its own strategy in order to gain an advantage. In our example, this leads to a mixed strategy where Summer Delight and Golden Dawn may engage in a period of competition when strategies change at random from one to another in an attempt to confuse the competition.

2. (a) From the top right-hand square of the pay-off matrix it can be seen that if Westgram did not enter the industry, then Saltco could charge a high monopoly price and earn £200 million profit. Even if the company decided to charge a lower price to benefit consumers, the profit would still be £80 million. However, if Westgram entered the industry and Saltco kept its prices high, then Saltco would earn £100 million, while Westgram would earn £20 million (i.e. £100 million − £80 million cost of new plant). This situation can be seen in the upper left-hand square. If, on Westgram's entry, Saltco decided to engage in price warfare, then this would decrease its profits to £60 million and cause Westgram to earn negative profits (£60 million − £80 million = − £20 million), as seen in the bottom left-hand square.

(b) If Saltco threatened a price war (i.e. low-price competition) to try to keep Westgram out, and Westgram *believed* the threat, then it would not enter because it would experience a negative profit of −£20 million as seen in the bottom left-hand square. However, Westgram may not believe Saltco's threat because, if it did enter the industry, it would still be in Saltco's interest to charge a high price, thus allowing Westgram to make a profit. This is because, as far as Saltco is concerned, the entry of Westgram would leave it with the choice of either £100 million profit if it charged the high price or a lower profit of £60 million if it carried out its threat to engage in a price war. As a result, Saltco's threat of warfare may not be a credible one, and Westgram might realise this and so enter the industry. In the end we might find that both companies would occupy the top left-hand square, with both Saltco and Westgram earning profits.

(c) In this case Saltco has invested £60 million in new capacity *before* Westgram's entry in order to bring down the market price. Assuming that Saltco's policy remains a high-price one and Westgram does not enter, then Saltco's profits will fall to £140 million (£200 million – £60 million). However, if Westgram does enter, Saltco's profits will be £40 million (£100 million – £60 million). From the bottom left-hand square of the new pay-off matrix we can see that installing the new capacity (probably lowering costs per unit) has enabled Saltco to improve its competitiveness and maintain its profits while Westgram still makes a loss. In this situation Westgram now knows that entry will definitely result in price warfare because Saltco's net profit is higher if it engages in price warfare (low prices) than if it charges high prices (£40 million compared with £60 million) while Westgram will still experience negative profits in this situation. This new strategic investment decision by Saltco may therefore prove a credible deterrent to Westgram. Saltco will then continue alone in the industry earning its £140 million profits, as seen in the top right-hand square.

(d) One way for Saltco to deter entry *without* investing in the new capacity-creating equipment is to get a reputation for being rather irrational and aggressive. For example, Saltco may have engaged in aggressive price cutting *in the past* when threatened by competitors, and been successful despite profit losses in the short run. This may be enough to ensure that potential new entrants might think twice before deciding to engage in the heavy investment (sunk costs) necessary to enter the industry.

3. (a) A dominant strategy for Lever would be one that is optimal for that company irrespective of Proctor's strategy. Similarly the dominant strategy for Proctor would be the one that is optimal for it, irrespective of Lever's strategy. On the other hand, the Nash equilibrium is where Lever is carrying out its optimal strategy given what Proctor is doing. Likewise, Proctor is carrying out its optimal strategy given what Lever is doing. In a way, the dominant strategy is a *special case* of a Nash equilibrium.

(b) The dominant strategy for Lever would be to advertise, because whatever Proctor does, advertising still proves to be the most profitable strategy for Lever. For example, when Proctor advertises, Lever makes £11 million profit if it also advertises, but only £7 million if it doesn't advertise. If Proctor does not advertise then Lever earns £16 million profits by advertising, but only £11 million if it doesn't advertise. In this case, advertising is a dominant strategy for Lever. Let us now check to see what strategy is best for Proctor. If Lever decides to advertise, then the best strategy for Proctor is also to advertise, because it will earn £6 million profits instead of £0 million if it does not. If Lever does not advertise, then it will still be best for Proctor to advertise because it will get £9 million profit instead of the £3 million if it doesn't advertise. The above argument shows that whatever Lever or Proctor's strategic response to each other, it still pays both of them to advertise. Thus advertising is a dominant strategy for *both* companies, and the outcome would be the top left-hand square, where both companies undertake to advertise.

(c) If we now use the new profit pay-offs in part (b), we can see that Proctor still has advertising as a dominant strategic response. For example, if Lever advertises then Proctor will benefit from advertising because it will gain £6 million rather than the £0 million it would get by not advertising. If Lever does not advertise then Proctor will still benefit from advertising because it will gain £9 million instead of the £2 million it would earn if it didn't advertise. However, in the new scenario it does not seem as if Lever has a dominant strategy. If Proctor advertises, then Lever will gain £11 million if it also advertises and £7 million if it doesn't: i.e. advertising still seems the best strategy. However, if Proctor decides not to advertise, Lever will gain £16 million if it advertises but will gain more, £22 million, if it decides not to advertise. In this case, Lever does not have a dominant strategy because advertising is not the best course of action taking *both* of Proctor's strategies into consideration. In other words, Lever *should* advertise if Proctor advertises but Lever *should not* advertise if Proctor decides not to advertise.

What should Lever do in this situation? Lever will know that Proctor will have the dominant strategy of advertising whatever Lever does, so that by looking at the matrix it would seem best for Lever to also advertise, because if it does advertise it will gain £11 million profit instead of the £7 million it would get if it decided not to advertise. The equilibrium will be that *both firms* will advertise.

4. (a) If the two companies colluded, then from Table 9.15 we can see that the best output/net profit combination would be where they produce a total amount of 1,250 units per week between them and share out a joint profit maximising profit of £35,000 per week.

(b) The profit pay-off matrix would consist of nine boxes, as shown in Table A.15.

(c) From this matrix one can see that the Nash equilibrium would be in the middle square, where each company would produce 750 units per week and the weekly net profits would be £15,000 each. The Nash equilibrium is a position from which neither company wants to deviate, *taking the other company's behaviour as given*. In other words, if for one or both companies it is best to move from a particular square, then that square is *not* a Nash equilibrium. However, if *both* companies do not want to move from a particular square, then that square *is* a Nash equilibrium. If Deckord dropped its weekly output from 750 to 500 then its profit would fall from £15,000 to £14,000 per week, and if it increased its weekly output to 1,000 then its net profit would fall from £15,000 to £12,000 per week. Likewise for Tapemech: if it moved from producing 750 to producing

Table A.15
Deckord/Tapemech
profit pay-off matrix.

Deckord weekly output

		500	750	1,000
Tapemech weekly output	500	Deckord £16,000 Tapemech £16,000	Deckord £21,000 Tapemech £14,000	Deckord £20,000 Tapemech £10,000
	750	Deckord £14,000 Tapemech £21,000	Deckord £15,000 Tapemech £15,000	Deckord £12,000 Tapemech £9,000
	1,000	Deckord £10,000 Tapemech £20,000	Deckord £9,000 Tapemech £12,000	Deckord £5,000 Tapemech £5,000

500 (given that Deckord would produce its usual 750) its profit would fall from £15,000 to £14,000 per week. If it produced 1,000 then it would land up in the bottom middle square with net profits falling from £15,000 to £12,000 per week. If all the boxes are checked in turn it will be found that it is only the *middle square* that fulfils the Nash criterion. At first glance it might look as though the 500/500 box, the top left-hand corner square, shows that both companies could get £16,000 of net profit each, which is greater than the £15,000 each from the middle square. However, this square is *not* a Nash equilibrium because Deckord would want to move from this square to the top middle square, because its profits would then rise from £16,000 to £21,000 per week.

(d) If the companies announce their strategy *sequentially*, i.e. if, in this case, Deckord announces its strategy *before* Tapemech, then Deckord has to find the best strategy assuming that Tapemech will choose an optimal response for itself once it knows Deckord's move. In terms of the pay-off matrix, we are saying that Deckord will choose the appropriate *column* on the assumption that Tapemech will look for the best *row* for itself. If Deckord chooses to produce 500 units, which means it is operating in the first column, then Tapemech will pick its favourite square from the three rows in the first column. This would be 750 units, giving it £21,000 net profit, because this is better than the other squares in that column, which give £16,000 and £20,000 profit. If Deckord chooses to produce 750 units, thus operating in the second column, then one would expect Tapemech to pick the square in the second row of that column, because this gives it the maximum profit of £15,000, which is above the other possibilities of £14,000 and £12,000 in that column. Finally if Deckord decides to produce 1,000 units, thus operating in the third column, then Tapemech will pick the square in the top row of that column (i.e. top right-hand box), where its profit would be £10,000, because this figure is higher than the £9,000 or £5,000 profit it could earn in the other rows in that column.

After the process described above, we have three possible options for Deckord given Tapemech's optimum responses. These are the middle two squares of the first two columns and the top square of the third column. The combination of

Deckord/Tapemech net profits would be (14,000/21,000), (15,000/15,000) and (20,000/10,000) respectively. Deckord will choose the best of these three positions: i.e. it will choose the top right-hand box, giving it a profit of £20,000 to Tapemech's £10,000. In this case the situation ends here, and this position is sometimes known as a *Stackelberg equilibrium*. This is because it defines a situation where one company commits to a strategy at the outset, on the assumption that the other firm will follow by choosing its own optimal response position.

(e) If Deckord and Tapemech are located in the top right-hand box, as described above, but then Deckord decides to break this commitment, then it is most likely to decide to move to the square on its left and produce 750 units at a net profit of £21,000, which is greater than the £20,000 profit in the top right-hand square. Now if Tapemech foresees this move, it will look in the middle column for the square with its highest net profit, i.e. the middle square. Because Deckord broke its commitment to stay in the top right-hand square, it has therefore found itself in the Nash equilibrium in the centre square, resulting in a fall in its profits from £20,000 to £15,000. Ironically, it would have been better for Deckord to have assured Tapemech that it was committed to producing 1,000 units rather than to try to retain flexibility and make a 'run for it' (i.e. by producing 750).

5. (a) A non-zero sum game means that the winnings and losses of both Metal Trades Ltd and Building Supplies Ltd can add up to a positive or a negative number. In other words, Metal Trades' gain is not necessarily Building Supplies' loss, and vice versa. This is different from the situation in a zero-sum game (which we encountered in question 1), where the sum of the winnings and losses equals zero: i.e. Metal Trades Ltd's gain would, in that case, be Building Supplies Ltd's loss, and vice versa. Under the conditions of the non-zero game situation that we are given in Table A.16, it is obvious that *both* firms will try to maxi-min, i.e. to maximise the minimum benefits as indicated by the Von Neumann/Morgenstern assumption in order to try to get a net advantage over each other.

(b) (i) If we look at the original table given in the question (which is the same as Table A.16 excluding the two minimum entries) in a logical fashion then we can say that if there was complete trust and the two companies were happy not to break the agreement they would both earn £5 million profit each. However, if Metal Trades keeps to the agreement, but Building Supplies breaks the agreement, then Building Supplies will gain by obtaining £6 million profits instead of £5 million. In the meantime Metal Trades' profits will have fallen from £5 million to £2 million. When Metal Trades realises this, it will also break the agreement because it can raise its profits from £2 million to £4 million.

Taking the other aspect, if Building Supplies Ltd sticks to the agreement but Metal Trades Ltd decides to break the agreement, then Metal Trades will benefit because its profits will rise from £5 million to £6 million while Building Supplies' profits will fall from £5 million to £2 million. This strategy will cause Building Supplies to break the arrangement also because it can increase its profits from £2 million to £4 million. Therefore, given the

Table A.16

	Metal Trades Ltd (profits £m)			
Building Supplies Ltd (profit £m)		Maintain agreement	Break agreement	**Minimum**
	Maintain agreement	5 \ 5	6 \ 2	2
	Break agreement	2 \ 6	4 \ 4	4
	Minimum	2	4	

conditions shown in Table A.16 there is a short-run incentive for both companies to cheat. But if they do so, they will finally arrive in the bottom right-hand quadrant of Table A.16 with £4 million profit apiece when if they had kept the agreement they would have both stayed in the top left-hand quadrant with £5 million profits apiece. This situation is the typical 'prisoners dilemma', where both companies try to get the best for themselves but fail to achieve it because of their distrust or lack of cooperation between the parties to the arrangement.

(ii) Since this is a non-zero-sum game, we shall be looking for the maximin strategies for both Metal Trades Ltd and Building Supplies Ltd. We can do this by adding vertical and horizontal columns to the original table and then calculating the two maxi-min positions. This is shown in Table A.16.

As we noted before, the maxi-min criterion for Building Supplies is obtained by choosing the best of the worst outcomes for Building Supplies. Since the two worst outcomes are £2 million and £4 million (right-hand column), then the best of those is £4 million. Similarly, for Metal Trades we look for the worst outcomes, which are £2 million and £4 million (bottom line), so the best of those is £4 million. Therefore the final solution to this problem is that both companies are likely to follow the maxi-min approach and break the cartel agreement. This will lead to the final position in the lower right-hand quadrant, with both companies earning £4 million each.

(c) As noted earlier, the final position would be where both are encouraged to cheat, i.e. to break the agreement – thus resulting in a profit of £4 million each. If they had maintained the agreement they would be in a position denoted by the upper left-hand quadrant, i.e. £5 million profit each.

(d) If the cartel was new and only likely to exist for one period only, then the situation would follow that we have described. If, however, the cartel has a longer history and the decision to change price (i.e. to break the agreement in order to improve profits) has had to be made very often in the course of the life of the cartel, then the solution to the cartel problem might be to maintain the agreement. This is because the repetitive 'game' of whether or not to break the agreement will soon mean that the companies learn that although each may enjoy higher profits in the short run, they will both lose out in the long run by finding themselves in the bottom right-hand quadrant. Thus they will learn that it is not in their interest to cheat, but to maintain the cartel agreement and stay in the top right-hand quadrant.

The best overall strategy for these repeated 'games' is for the companies to play the 'tit for tat' game, where each company should do on one occasion what the other company did on the previous occasion. In other words, both companies should follow each other by not cheating, but if one cheats, the other should follow and cheat. Robert Axelrod, using computer analysis, argues that the 'tit for tat' strategy is the most effective approach to this sort of dilemma.

Chapter 10 1. (a) Since we know the equation for the supply or average labour cost function, we can derive the marginal labour cost equation. To do this we first derive the expression for the total labour costs and then take the first derivative of that function. Total labour costs (TC_L) are the average labour costs times the quantity of labour, i.e.

$$TC = (100 + Q_L)Q_L$$
$$= 100Q_L + Q_L^2 \tag{1}$$

Differentiating TC_L with respect to Q_L we get marginal labour costs, MC_L:

$$MC_L = \frac{dTC_L}{dQ_L} = 100 + 2Q_L \tag{2}$$

(b) The demand or marginal revenue product is the *value* to the hospital of employing an additional maintenance worker, while the marginal cost of labour is the *cost* to the hospital of hiring each additional maintenance worker. The monopsonist's (i.e. hospital's) profit-maximising rule is to employ maintenance workers up to the point where marginal revenue product of such workers equals their marginal cost. Since we have this information, we can now equate both, i.e.

$$MRP_L = MC_L$$
$$1{,}000 - Q_L = 100 + 2Q_L$$
$$900 = 3Q_L$$
$$300 = Q_L$$

The profit-maximising weekly employment level for maintenance workers will be 300. To find the weekly wage level we need to substitute the value of 300 into the supply or average labour cost equation (see Chapter 10, Fig. 10.3):

$$S = 100 + Q_L$$
$$= 100 + 300$$
$$= 400$$

The hospital, acting as a monopsonistic buyer of maintenance workers, will hire 300 maintenance workers at an average weekly wage of £400. If we wish to know how much each maintenance worker contributes to the hospital revenue all we have to do is to substitute 300 into the MC_L equation (equation (2)), i.e.

$$MC_L = 100 + 2Q_L$$
$$= 100 + 2(300)$$
$$= 700$$

In other words, the hospital is receiving £700 worth of revenue from employing each of the 300 maintenance workers while only paying them £400 – a surplus of £300 per worker.

(c) If the market for maintenance workers was perfect, then the equilibrium level of employment would be where demand or marginal revenue product was equal to supply, i.e.

$$D(MRP) = S$$

$$1,000 - Q_L = 100 + Q_L$$
$$900 = 2Q_L$$
$$450 = Q_L$$

This means that 450 maintenance workers would have been employed. To find the wage rate we need to substitute the value 450 into the supply (or demand) equation:

$$D = 1,000 - 450$$
$$= 550$$
$$S = 100 + 450$$
$$= 550$$

Under perfectly competitive labour market conditions, the wage of maintenance workers would have been £550 per week and employment at 450. This means that when the hospital acts as a monopsonist buyer of maintenance workers, it pays them less and hires fewer workers than under perfect competitive conditions.

2. (a) To obtain the competitive clearing wage and employment levels we need to equate the demand and supply curves, i.e.

$$760 - 0.1Q_e = 60 + 0.04Q_e$$
$$700 = 0.14Q_e$$
$$5,000 = Q_e$$

The wage rate at this equilibrium level of employment can be obtained by substituting 5,000 into the demand curve:

$$D_e = 760 - 0.1(5,000)$$
$$= 260$$

Therefore the competitive wage level would be £260 at the employment level of 5,000.

(b) (i)   If a union is introduced and it aims to get the maximum total income for its engineering workers, then the union can be viewed just like a company that is trying to maximise revenue from selling its product. Following this reasoning, the union will try to maximise its members' total income (i.e. its revenue) by selling its product (labour) up to the point where the market demand for labour has an elasticity of unity. At this point, we also know that the marginal revenue to the union from selling labour will be zero.

We need to obtain an expression for the marginal revenue function and then equate this to zero to find the employment and wage level that the union will demand in order to maximise its total revenue (i.e. wages to workers). To do this it is necessary to find the total revenue from selling labour (TR_e), then calculate the first derivative (MR_e) and equate it to zero, i.e.

$$TR_e = w \times Q_e$$

This means that the total revenue that the union will obtain by selling its labour is equal to the wage (w) multiplied by employment level (Q_e). We know that the expression for w is in fact the demand curve for labour. Therefore substituting this in the equation we get

$$TR_e = 760 - 0.1Q_e(Q_e)$$
$$= 760Q_e - 0.1Q_e^2$$

To find the marginal revenue that the union receives for selling its labour we have to differentiate the equation and then equate this to zero, since this is the point where elasticity of demand for labour will be unity:

$$\frac{dTR_e}{dQ_e} (MR_e) = 760 - 0.2Q_e = 0$$

$$760 = 0.2Q_e$$
$$3,800 = Q_e$$

To obtain the wage rate at this level of employment we need to substitute 3,800 for Q_e in the demand (i.e. wage) equation:

$$D_e = 760 - 0.1(3,800)$$
$$= 760 - 380$$
$$= 380$$

To maximise the total wage bill, the union would attempt to push up wages to £380 per week at an employment level of 3,800.

(ii) If the union wanted to get the highest wage possible it would try to attain a point where the union's marginal revenue from 'selling' engineers was equal to the union's marginal cost of supplying engineers. Since the supply curve is the marginal cost curve, all we have to do is equate the union's supply curve (marginal cost curve) to its marginal revenue curve:

$$MC_e = MR_e$$
$$60 + 0.04Q_e = 760 - 0.2Q_e$$
$$0.24Q_e = 700$$
$$Q_e = 2,917 \text{ approx.}$$

To obtain the wage rate we substitute 2,917 in the demand curve:

$$D_e = 760 - 0.1\, Q_e$$
$$= 760 - 0.1(2,917)$$
$$= 760 - 292$$
$$= 468 \text{ approx.}$$

The 'rent maximising' wage will be approximately £468 and the employment level will be about 2,917 engineers. If a diagram of this problem is constructed then the total rent will be the area between the rent-maximising wage of £468 and the supply curve up to 2,917 engineers. In the normal way, the supply curve illustrates the transfer earnings, i.e. what the engineer could have obtained in his/her next-best occupation.

Therefore we see that the presence of a union on a competitive labour market tends to increase wages above the competitive level and decrease employment. A union strategy that aims to set a rent-maximising wage for its members will provide the highest wage and lowest employment. The union that wants to maximise total labour income will choose a lower wage but higher employment position.

3. (a) To draw the demand curve, D, on the diagram we need to know where the demand curve cuts the P_L and Q_L axes. It cuts the P_L axis when Q_L is zero: i.e. $P_L = 80 - 0.1(0)$ or $P_L = 80$. Similarly if we take the same demand curve, then when P_L is zero, Q_L will be 800. Since we know that S_1 is perfectly inelastic at 400 then we can draw both demand D_1 and supply curve S_1 as in Fig. A.13.

Demand and supply of the specialist labour will be in equilibrium at a wage rate of £40 per hour. The total economic rent element will be $40 \times 400 = £16,000$. Since the supply of specialist labour is completely inelastic there is no transfer earnings element so that the *whole* of the wage is economic rent.

Fig. A.13

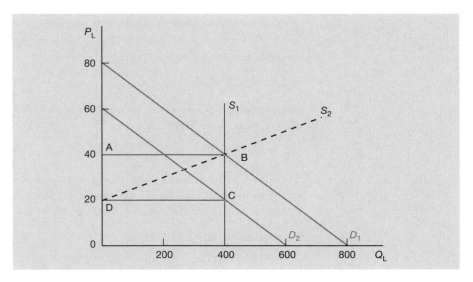

(b) If the demand curve changes so that it is now $P_L = 60 - 0.1Q_L$ then we can repeat the procedure already described and find the positions on the axes where P_L and Q_L are zero. The relevant demand line will cut the P_L axis at 60 and the Q_L axis at 600. The position will be as D_2 in Fig. A.13 above with an equilibrium wage rate of £20 per hour and a total economic rent of $20 \times 400 = £8,000$. In other words, the decrease in demand has halved the economic rent element.

(c) If the supply function becomes more 'normal', i.e. $P_L = 20 + 0.05Q_L$, then we need to draw this function. We know that it will cut the P_L axis where Q_L is zero, i.e. at 20, and it will have a slope of 0.05. Drawing this function on Fig. A.13 we get the dotted supply line S_2. To calculate the economic rent at the old demand curve position, D_1, we need to take the area between the equilibrium price level of 40 and the supply curve (which represents the transfer earnings). This is half the area of the rectangle ABCD. The value of the area of the rectangle is $20 \times 400 = £8,000$ so that the total economic rent has fallen to £4,000. This is logical because the fact that the supply curve has become more elastic means that there is now an element of transfer earnings to be considered. This means that the economic rent element decreases as the labour loses its specificity.

4. (a) The income/expenditure per day is the wage rate, w, multiplied by the number of hours worked, H, so that the value of the goods, G, that can be bought is

$$G = wH \tag{1}$$

Similarly, the person's hours of work per day is the total available hours minus leisure time, L, i.e.

$$H = 24 - L \tag{2}$$

(b) The utility function that needs to be maximised is

$$\text{Max } U(G, L) \tag{3}$$

This means that to maximise utility it is necessary to maximise the functions G and L. We know what the values of G and L are from equations (1) and (2), so we can substitute these values in equation (3), giving

$$\text{Max } U(wH, 24-H)$$

Differentiating with respect to H and setting the result equal to zero we can find the maximum utility condition, i.e.

$$U_G w + U_L(-1) = 0 \tag{4}$$

Therefore, at the optimum, the person equates the marginal benefit of work ($U_G w$) to the marginal cost of the leisure forgone (U_L), i.e. $U_G w = U_L$. If we express both benefits and costs in terms of goods we have

$$w = \frac{U_L(wH, 24-H)}{U_G(wH, 24-H)} \tag{5}$$

In other words, the real wage rate, w (i.e. the rate at which goods can be transformed into leisure), is equated to the rate of substitution between goods and leisure (U_L/U_G). Situation (5) is the supply curve for labour since it gives the relationship between the wage rate (w) and the number of hours worked (H).

(c) If the person has a utility function $U = G + 2L^{1/2}$ then differentiating the function with respect to L and following the reasoning in part (b) of this answer will give

$$\frac{U_L}{U_G} = L^{-1/2} = w \tag{6}$$

but $L = 24-H$, from (2), so substituting this in (6) we get $H = 24 - w^{-2}$ or $H = 24 - (1/w^2)$, which is the equation for the supply of labour since it relates hours worked (H) to the wage rate (w).

Chapter 11   1. (a) Figure A.14 incorporates all the information relating to this question. First, the information about the production isoquants can be drawn into an Edgeworth–Bowley box diagram with L measured on the horizontal axis and K on the vertical axis.

(b) (i) After plotting the isoquants we see that point I is where isoquant B_1 intersects isoquant A_1. We can see that $5L$ and $55K$ are used to produce A_1, and the remainder of the resources, i.e. $55L$ and $15K$, are used to produce B_1 (remember that the total resources available were $60L$ and $70K$). Point I is a resource equilibrium point but is *not* the most efficient point because a move along A_1 from I to X would mean that the same amount of A could be produced but more B, i.e. B_3 (instead of B_1 at I). Similarly, we could move along B_1 from I to Z, which would again be more efficient because at Z the

Fig. A.14
**Edgeworth–Bowley
production box.**

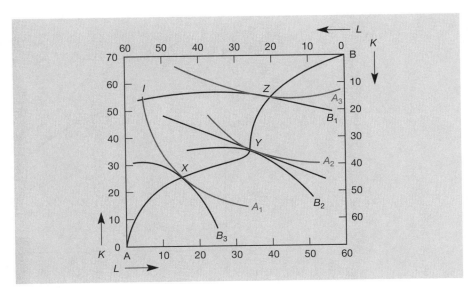

same amount of B would be produced but more A, i.e. A_3 (instead of A_1 at I). Finally we could have an even better position if the economy moved from I to Y because more A (A_2) *and* B (B_2) could be produced at Y than at I $(A_1$ and $B_1)$ with the same resources. As a result of this rationale, position I is clearly a sub-optimal position.

Points of tangency between the production isoquants are optimal positions because any move from the tangency point means that the output of A cannot be increased without reducing the output of B, and vice versa. When the economy was at I it was possible to increase the output of either A or B without decreasing the output of the other.

(ii) If the coordinates of the tangency line are $(25K, 55L)$ and $(22.5K, 50L)$ from the A and B origins respectively, then the marginal rate of technical substitution, $MRTS_{LK}$, or common slope of both isoquants A_2 and B_2 is $25K - 22.5K/55L - 50 L$, which is $2.5/5 = 0.5$.

(c) To draw the production box contract curve all that is necessary is to join the points of tangency, i.e. X, Y and Z. If production occurs anywhere along the production contract curve then this is an optimum position because there is no further gain to be achieved by transferring some K and L between the production of A and B. This is exactly why point I was *not* an equilibrium point because a gain (more of one good, no less of the other good) could be made by shifting resources away from I.

2. (a) The transformation curve (production frontier) is the contract curve of question 1. It can be obtained using the values of the A and B isoquants and plotting the optimum points X, Y and Z of question 1. This means that the coordinates of point X would be (A_1, B_3), i.e. $(40, 90)$, point Y (A_2, B_2), i.e. $(100, 60)$ and finally, point Z (A_3, B_1), i.e. $(120, 30)$. Sketching in the transformation curve we get something like Fig. A.15.

Fig. A.15

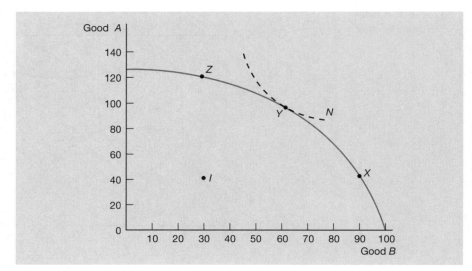

The transformation curve is important to general equilibrium theory because it shows the optimum combinations of two goods or commodities that can be produced with a given set of resources. The slope of the transformation curve at any point measures the marginal rate of physical transformation ($MRPT$) of one good (A) into another good (B). This measures by how much the economy has to reduce its output of A in order to release enough K and L to produce one more unit of B.

(b) The location of point I in question 1 can be identified because the coordinates are (A_1, B_1), i.e. (40A, 30B). This point is within the transformation curve, and indicates that if production occurs here, the economy will be underutilising its resources because more of both A and B can be produced: e.g. one can reach point Y on the transformation curve.

(c) If we take the two commodities A and B, then the economy's $MRPT_{AB}$ is given by the slope of the transformation curve (production frontier). But for general equilibrium it is essential that both production and consumption are in equilibrium. Efficiency in consumption requires that the marginal rate of substitution (MRS_{AB}) for all consumers is identical. Efficiency in production requires that $MRPT_{AB}$ is identical for all firms. Therefore, for general equilibrium MRS_{AB} must be equal to $MRPT_{AB}$. However, the MRS_{AB} in aggregate is the slope of the community indifference curve or social welfare function, so that for general equilibrium the slopes of the community indifference curve (MRS_{AB}) and transformation curve ($MRPT_{AB}$) should be equal. This can be illustrated by drawing a community indifference curve N tangential to the transformation curve at Y in Fig. A.15.

3. (a) From the question it is obvious that we need to find the expression for the slope of the A and B isoquants and express these in relation to marginal productivities. If we start with A then what we need to do is to totally differentiate the production function, i.e.

$$X^A = f(K^A L^A)$$

$$= \frac{dX^A}{dL^A} = \frac{df}{dK^A} \cdot \frac{dK^A}{dL^A} + \frac{df}{dL^A} \cdot \frac{dL^A}{dL^A} \tag{1}$$

but $(df/dK^A) = f^A{}_K$, which is equal to the change in output of A as a result of a change in capital. In other words it is the marginal product of capital. Similarly from equation (1) we know that df/dL^A or f_L^A is the marginal product of labour in the production of commodity A. If we now substitute these expressions in (1) while understanding that $dL/dL = 1$ then the expression for equation (1) becomes

$$\frac{dX^A}{dL^A} = f^A{}_K \cdot \frac{dK^A}{dL^A} + f^A{}_L \tag{1}$$

Also, since output, X, is constant on any isoquant then $dX^A/dL^A = 0$, and therefore

$$f^A{}_K \cdot \frac{dK^A}{dL^A} + f^A{}_L = 0$$

$$-\frac{dK^A}{dL^A} \cdot f^A_K = f^A_L$$

$$-\frac{dK^A}{dL^A} = \frac{f^A_L}{f^A_K} \tag{2}$$

The expression in equation (2) indicates that the slope of the isoquant relating K and L to A is $-dK^A/dL^A$, and that this is equal to the ratio of the marginal product of labour divided by the marginal product of capital (f^A_L/f^A_K), i.e. the marginal rate of technical substitution of labour for capital, $MRTS^A_{LK}$.

We can now repeat the process by finding the total derivative of the B iso-quant, starting from the production function $B = f(K^B, L^B)$. When we have done this we will find that the slope of the B isoquant will be $-(dK^B/dL^B) = f^B_L/f^B_K$, i.e. the $MRTS^B_{LK}$.

(b) The efficiency criterion for production is where the two isoquants in the Edgeworth–Bowley box diagram are tangential to each other. This means that $MRTS^A_{LK} = MRTS^B_{LK}$, or

$$\frac{f^A_L}{f^A_K} = \frac{f^B_L}{f^B_K} \tag{3}$$

(c) If the isoquants cut at any other position, i.e. meet but are not tangential, then the slopes of the two isoquants will be different and the $MRTS$ will also be differ-ent. Here we assume that production is at an inefficient point and that factors are being used in the same proportions in both industries producing A and B. Let us take an example. If the $MRTS^A_{LK} > MRTS^B_{LK}$ then

$$\frac{f^A_L}{f^A_K} > \frac{f^B_L}{f^B_K} \tag{4}$$

Rearranging we get

$$\frac{f^A_L}{f^B_L} > \frac{f^A_K}{f^B_K} \tag{5}$$

Equation (5) means that the ratio of the marginal product of labour in A to labour in B is higher than the corresponding ratio for capital. In other words, labour has a comparative advantage in producing A: i.e. it is relatively more efficient at pro-ducing A than is capital. If the factors are employed in the same proportions in both industries, then this difference in comparative advantage is not exploited. To do this we need to allocate more labour to A and more capital to B so that each factor is being allocated towards the industry in which it has a comparative advantage. When this happens, the ratio f^A_L/f^B_L will fall and the ratio f^A_K/f^B_K will rise, bringing about the equality of $MRTS^A_{LK}$ and $MRTS^B_{LK}$ and thus arriving at the most efficient position where there is no incentive to alter the allocation of factor inputs.

4. (a) If the equation for the production frontier or transformation curve is $X^2 + 9Y^2 = 100$ then we can obtain an expression for the marginal rate of physical transformation into X of Y ($MRPT_{XY}$), i.e. the slope of the curve, by rearranging the equation and finding the first derivative of the function. (Notice that a function to the power of $\frac{1}{2}$ is the square root of that function.)

$$X^2 + 9Y^2 = 100$$
$$9Y^2 = 100 - X^2$$
$$Y^2 = \frac{100 - X^2}{9}$$

$$Y = \tfrac{1}{3}(100 - X^2)^{1/2} \tag{1}$$

Differentiating with respect to X by using the 'function of a function' rule (p. 668) we get

$$\frac{\mathrm{d}Y}{\mathrm{d}X} = \tfrac{1}{2} \times \tfrac{1}{3}(100 - X^2)^{-1/2} \cdot (-2X)$$

$$= \tfrac{1}{6} \times (100 - X^2)^{-1/2} \cdot (-2X)$$
$$= -\tfrac{1}{3}(100 - X^2)^{-1/2} \cdot (X)$$

$$= -\frac{X}{3}(100 - X^2)^{-1/2} \tag{2}$$

Equation (2) gives the equation for the $MRPT_{XY}$, i.e. the slope of the production frontier or transformation curve.

(b) To prove that the production frontier or transformation curve is concave to the origin we need to show that the second derivative of equation (1) is positive, i.e.

$$\frac{\mathrm{d}^2Y}{\mathrm{d}X^2} = -\tfrac{1}{2}(100 - X^2)^{-3/2} \times -\tfrac{1}{3}$$

$$= \tfrac{1}{6}(100 - X^2)^{-3/2} \tag{3}$$

Since the expression is positive, it means that increasing amounts of Y have to be given up for each additional unit of X as X increases.

(c) We know that one of the equilibrium points on the consumption contract curve obtained from an Edgeworth–Bowley box diagram (where the $MRS^A_{XY} = MRS^B_{XY}$) has a value of $-\frac{4}{7}$. This means that this particular equilibrium point on the consumption contract curve, i.e. the exchange equilibrium, has a slope of $-\frac{4}{7}$. To achieve *simultaneous* equilibrium of both exchange and production then the slope of the production frontier or transformation curve must also be $-\frac{4}{7}$. In other words we have to let the first derivative, equation (2), be equal to $-\frac{4}{7}$, i.e.

$$-\frac{X}{3} \cdot (100 - X^2)^{-1/2} = -\tfrac{4}{7}$$

$$\frac{X}{3} \cdot (100 - X^2)^{-1/2} = \tfrac{4}{7}$$

Squaring both sides we get

$$\frac{X^2}{9} \cdot (100 - X^2)^{-1} = \frac{16}{49}$$

$$(100 - X^2)^{-1} = \frac{144}{49X^2}$$

$$100 - X^2 = \frac{49X^2}{144}$$

$$14,400 - 144X^2 = 49X^2$$

$$14,400 = 193X^2$$

$$74.61 = X^2$$

$$8.64 = X$$

To find the value of Y we need to substitute $X = 8.64$ in equation (1):

$$\begin{aligned} Y &= \tfrac{1}{3}(100 - 8.64^2)^{1/2} \\ &= \tfrac{1}{3}(100 - 74.61)^{1/2} \\ &= \tfrac{1}{3}(25.39)^{1/2} \\ &= 1.68 \end{aligned}$$

Therefore the values of X and Y that would be needed to achieve simultaneous equilibrium of both production and exchange would be where X is 8,640 and Y is 1,680 (since X and Y are measured in 000s).

5. (a) The three social welfare functions or community indifference curves are drawn as in Fig. A.16.

The social welfare functions show the various combinations of U_A and U_B that provide society with the same levels of welfare. The higher the social welfare functions (e.g. $SW_3 > SW_2 > SW_1$), the greater the levels of welfare, and vice versa.

Fig. A.16

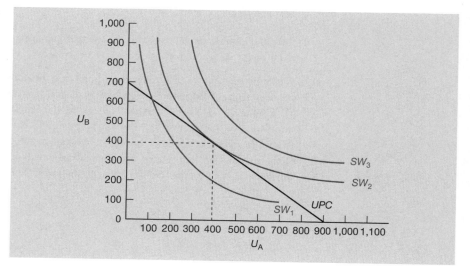

Note that the movement along a social welfare function makes one individual better off and another worse off, so in order to construct such a curve, the society must make explicit value judgements, i.e. interpersonal comparisons of utility.

(b) In a simple two-commodity, two-consumer society the consumption contract curve is a locus of all points where the marginal rate of substitution, *MRS*, in the consumption of the two goods is the same for both consumers (i.e. all the points where the two indifference curves are tangential). Each indifference curve not only has a quantity value attached to it, but also has a utility value. Therefore if we wish to draw a utility possibility curve we must give each indifference curve its utility value, and then plot the utility values of the respective consumers at each point where the indifference curves are tangential. In other words, each consumption contract curve has an associated utility possibility curve. We know that the criterion for equilibrium in both production and consumption is where the slope of the production frontier or transformation curve *MRPT* is equal to *MRS* for each consumer. Therefore, this specific position can be plotted on the utility possibility curve.

(c) The grand utility possibility curve takes us a step further. We know that there is a unique point on the utility possibility curve that also corresponds to a single point of the transformation curve, i.e. where there is Pareto optimality between consumption and production. However, if we pick another point on the transformation curve we shall have a different Edgeworth–Bowley consumption box diagram (see Fig. 11.7 in Chapter 11) and therefore a different consumption contract curve and utility possibility curve. The grand utility possibility curve is the locus of *all* Pareto-optimal points of production and consumption (exchange). In other words it takes all the optimal combinations of positions on the transformation curve and their associated equilibrium positions on the consumption contract/utility possibility curves.

Therefore the grand utility possibility curve gives a *range* of Pareto-optimal points of production and consumption (exchange). We cannot know which of those Pareto optimum positions is best for society unless we have a welfare function for society. The point of maximum social welfare will be where the grand utility possibility curve is tangential to the highest social welfare function.

(d) We assume for simplicity a straight-line grand utility possibility curve. Therefore if we draw the relationship $U_B = 700 - \frac{7}{9}U_A$ onto Fig. A.16, we shall find that the grand utility possibility curve (*UPC*) will be tangential to the social welfare indifference curve SW_2, showing that the values of U_B and U_A at which social welfare is maximised are 400 for both *A* and *B*.

Chapter 12   1. (a) To derive the demand and supply curves from the demand and supply functions we need to rearrange the two equations to show *P* on the right-hand side, i.e.

$$Q_D = 180 - 2P$$
$$2P = 180 - Q_D$$
$$P = 90 - 0.5Q_D \qquad\qquad (1)$$

Similarly:

$$Q_S = -80 + 4P$$
$$4P = 80 + Q_S$$
$$P = 20 + 0.25Q_S \qquad (2)$$

(b) Once we have done this it is possible to find the equilibrium price and output by either drawing the supply and demand curves D and S_1 as in Fig. A.17 or by using simple algebra. If we draw the curves then we know that the P intercept for the demand curve will be 90 and the slope of the line will be -0.5. For the supply curve, the P intercept will be 20 and the slope will be $+0.25$.

To solve the problem with algebra we merely need to equate the demand and supply curves remembering that at equilibrium $Q_D = Q_S$, i.e.

$$90 - 0.5Q_D = 20 + 0.25Q_S$$
$$70 = 0.75Q$$
$$93.33 = Q$$

To find the equilibrium price, substitute for Q in the demand curve:

$$P = 90 - 0.5\,(93.33)$$
$$= 90 - 46.67$$
$$= 43.33$$

Therefore the equilibrium price will be £43.33 per ton and the output will be 9,333 tonnes (figures in 00s tonnes).

(c) The production of lead creates a pollution problem so that the true social cost comprises the production costs *and* the pollution costs. Since pollution costs are £0.75 per tonne, the social costs can be expressed as £0.75Q_S (since costs rise by

Fig. A.17

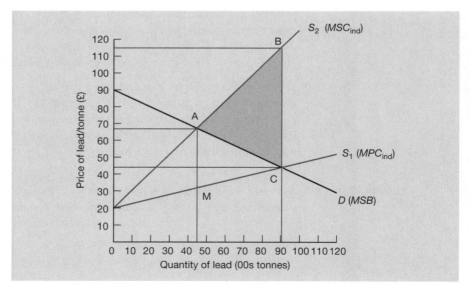

£0.75 for every unit increase in quantity supplied). The new supply curve will be the old one plus £0.75, i.e.

$$P = 20 + 0.25Q_S + 0.75Q_S$$
or
$$P = 20 + Q_S$$

(d) We can now draw the new supply curve, S_2, which includes pollution costs, and note the new socially optimum price and quantity in Fig. A.17. The algebraic solution would be obtained by equating the demand curve to the new supply curve, i.e.

$$90 - 0.5Q_D = 20 + Q_S$$
$$70 = 1.5Q$$
$$46.66 = Q$$

To find the equilibrium price we substitute for Q in the demand equation:

$$\begin{aligned} P &= 90 - 0.5(46.66) \\ &= 90 - 23.33 \\ &= 66.67 \end{aligned}$$

The socially optimum price and quantity will be £66.67 per tonne and 4,666 tons respectively.

(e) The area of welfare loss will be the triangle ABC marked on Fig. A.17. To calculate this area we need to know the distance BC. We know that C = £43.33 since it is the initial equilibrium price. To find B we need to either read it off from Fig. A.17 or use the new supply curve and find the value of S_2 when Q is 93.33, i.e. price (or C) = 20 + Q where Q = 93.33, i.e. point B will be £113.33. Therefore the distance BC is 113.33 − 43.33 = £70. The area of any triangle ABC is expressed as $\frac{1}{2}$ base of the triangle × height, i.e. $\frac{1}{2}$ of 70 times (93.33 − 46.66). This is 35 × 46.67 = £1,633.45. Since the Q figures are in 00s this loss of welfare is the equivalent of about £163,345.

(f) The tax that needs to be imposed to induce the lead companies to produce at the socially optimum level would be equivalent to a vertical shift of the supply curve from S_1 to S_3 in Fig. A.18. To find the vertical distance we can read it off from Fig. A.18 or calculate distance AM. We know that A is £66.66, i.e. the equilibrium price including pollution costs, so all we need to do is to calculate the price at point M and subtract them. To find the price at M we need to take the original S_1 curve and substitute the value of Q = 46.66, i.e. M = 20 + (0.25) 46.66 = £31.66. This means that the distance AM is 66.66 − 31.66 = £35. The price obtained by the producer is of course the price at M on the supply curve, i.e. £31.66.

To summarise, the tax that needs to be imposed on lead producers is £35 per tonne and the price obtained by the lead producers is £31.66 per tonne.

(g) The Pigouvian 'golden rule' indicates that in order to maximise total economic welfare, all divergences between any activity's marginal social benefit and marginal social cost must be eliminated. A government, Pigou would argue, could

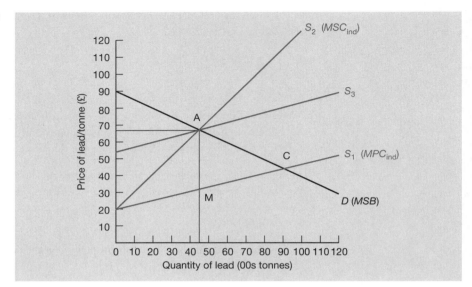

remove the gap BC in Fig. A.17 (which is the difference between the marginal social cost and marginal social benefit) by imposing a per-unit tax equal to AM on producers. This tax would raise the marginal private cost curve from S_1 to S_3 in Fig. A.18. As a result price would rise to £66.66 and quantity produced would fall to 46.66. Producers would produce less because they get a lower net price (from point C to point M) in Fig. A.17 and consumers would buy less because of the higher price (point C to point A). Both producers and consumers would have been made aware of their negative behaviour on other people in society, and marginal social benefit would once more be equal to marginal social cost.

2. (a) As demonstrated by Fig. 12.18 (p. 510), the marginal social benefit (*MSB*) measures the marginal benefit of a certain activity as seen from the viewpoint of society as a whole. In this case, the *MSB* curve measures the benefit to society of waste dumping. As we can see, the marginal benefit of waste dumping decreases as the quantity of waste dumped increases. At first sight it is difficult to think about the fact that there may be any *benefit* associated with waste dumping, so the best way to understand the situation is as follows. If there is only a little waste to be dumped, then the fixed costs etc. to the polluter and society of setting up plants to eliminate this small amount of waste would be high. Therefore there are high benefits to the producer and society from *not* introducing pollution equipment because the money saved can be used to produce other, more worthwhile goods or services. When there is a larger amount of waste to be dumped, then it becomes more meaningful for polluters to introduce pollution control equipment because the cost per unit of pollution control equipment is cheaper so that the benefit of *not* introducing pollution equipment is low. The marginal benefit curve therefore measures the benefits derived from *not* having to spend resources on waste disposal control. As the amount of waste increases, these benefits fall.

The main thing to remember is that everything has an opportunity cost. If waste dumping is low, then it is not worth building a waste disposal plant since, for such a small amount of waste, the opportunity cost of building the plant would be high. Therefore by *not* building the plant, those opportunity costs are saved and become benefits. However, when waste dumping becomes high, it is more efficient and less costly to treat a given amount of waste. In this case it is worthwhile introducing pollution equipment and the opportunity cost of building the control equipment is relatively lower, so the benefits (*MSB*) arising from *not* building the plant are small.

The line *MSC* represents the rising marginal cost of waste dumping. As the amount of waste increases, the damage to the estuary in terms of damage to property, fish and health also increases. If there was an amount of waste that could be dumped without harm (e.g. if the environment could easily absorb a certain amount of waste), then the *MSC* curve would start at the origin 0 and coincide with the horizontal axis until a point on the waste axis representing the amount of waste that could be absorbed without effect on the environment, i.e. without cost. From then onwards, as waste dumping began to create positive costs for the environment, the *MSC* curve would begin to slope upwards.

(b) If the environment could absorb *all* the waste without apparent cost then the resources saved by society from *not* having to build waste control equipment would be the area of the triangle D0C, which would be equivalent to $100 \times 40 = 4,000$, i.e. £4,000 million (area of a triangle $= \frac{1}{2}$ base $\times$ height).

(c) The level of optimum pollution would be at 100 million tonnes of waste, where $MSB = MSC$. If the amount of waste dumped was 150 million tonnes, then at this level the marginal social cost to society (*MSC*) would be greater than the marginal social benefits. The area AEF, which shows the net loss, would be equivalent to $10 \times 50 = £500$ million.

(d) The area 0DA represents the net benefits to society from dumping the goods at the optimum level of waste. It is derived from subtracting the total amount of benefits 0DAB from the cost of pollution 0AB. In money terms it is worth £2,000 million (area of triangle method).

If people insist on zero pollution, then they see the argument in terms of absolutes. In the real world some level of pollution may be inevitable as production occurs. The aim of the economist is to find the *optimum* level of pollution given certain criteria of costs and benefits. The economist would say that up to 100 million tonnes, there are *net* benefits to be derived from the dumping of waste. Those who insist on zero pollution are asking society to sacrifice this net gain, equivalent to the area 0DA. However, since anti-pollution arguments are often based on *normative* statements of what *should* be, it is sometimes difficult to reconcile the difference between economists and zero pollution activists.

3. (a) As demonstrated by Fig. A.19, to draw the functions MPB_{AX} and MPB_{BX} we need to find the points where these functions cut the vertical and horizontal axes. In other words, take the equations for MPB_{AX} and MPB_{BX} in turn and let Q be zero. This will give the vertical intercepts. Then take the same equations and put

MPB_{AX} and MPB_{BX} equal to zero to obtain the intercepts on the Q axis. Once this has been done, the points for MPB_{AX} (25,30) and MPB_{BX} (30,50) can be obtained and the lines drawn. The MSC line can be drawn by finding the vertical intercept (let Q be zero) and drawing a line upwards at an angle of 1.25: i.e. for every four units horizontally, the vertical distance increases by five units. Once these basic lines have been drawn it is possible to go to the next stage.

(b) (i)   The next stage is to draw the marginal social benefit for a pure private good (MSB_{Pr}). This is relatively easy because it is the same as for an ordinary market demand curve: i.e. add MPB_{AX} and MPB_{BX} *horizontally*. To do this we start down the MPB_{BX} curve until we reach the point opposite where MPB_{AX} starts (point A). From here on we need to add MPB_{BX} and MPB_{AX} together in a horizontal fashion. The easiest thing to do is to realise that the combined line will end at the horizontal axis at 80 (i.e. 30 (MPB_{AX}) + 50 (MPB_{BX})). This is point B. Join point B to point A and we have the MSB_{Pr} for the private good.

(ii) To obtain the marginal social benefit for the pure public good (MSB_{Pu}) it is essential to understand that since a pure public good can be consumed by *everyone*, then MSB_{Pu} is the sum of the marginal benefits reaped by all consumers. Therefore we have to add MPB_{AX} and MPB_{BX} *vertically*. (Please check that you understand this fact from the text.) To do this we need to start at point E and move up the MPB_{BX} curve until we come to point C opposite where MPB_{AX} starts. From this point onwards, add MPB_{AX} *vertically* to MPB_{BX}. Again, the easiest way to do this is to find point D, which is adding MPB_{AX} (25) to MPB_{BX} (30) on the vertical axis, and then join DC.

(c) The equilibrium value for the private good is where MSC intersects with line AB. The approximate values would be around 14 units and a value of £23 per unit. For the public good the intersection of MSC with DC would give approximately 18 units at a value of £28 per unit. In this case more of a public good would have been produced but at a higher equilibrium quantity and value (price) than for the private sector.

Fig. A.19

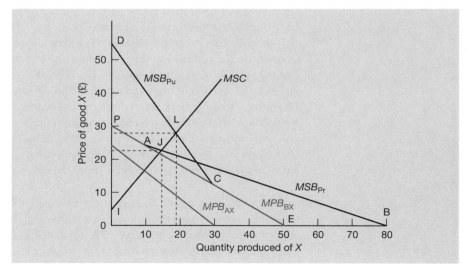

(d) The *net* social benefit from the private and public goos is the area between their respective *MSB*s and the *MSC* line. In the case of the private good this is area PAJI, and for the public good, it is DLI – indicating that in the example given, the *net* social benefit under a public good situation is greater than for a private good.

(e) To check on the rough values that have been calculated from the diagram in (c), it is possible to work out the exact values using algebra. To find the private good solution we need to add *horizontally* the two curves MPB_{AX} and MPB_{BX}. To do this we must express the functions shown in the question in terms of Q (not MPB_{AX} or MPB_{BX} as in the question). Once this has been done, merely add these two equations and then rearrange the resulting combined equation with relation to P not Q. This can be equated with *MSC* to find the required values. The answers ahould come to £14.3 and 22.9 units. To find the public good solution we need only add the functions in the form shown in the question and equate this to the *MSC* since they are all expressed in terms of P. The answers will be £28.3 and 18.7 units.

4. (a) As demonstrated in Fig. A.20, the first task is to draw the *MPC* and *MSC* functions, using a vertical scale illustrating coal processing costs per tonne and a horizontal axis representing thousands of tonnes processed per week. For *MPC*, the intercept on the vertical axis will be 10 with a slope of 0.5 ($\frac{1}{2}$), while for *MSC* the intercept will be 15 and the slope 0.75 ($\frac{3}{4}$). The price can then be added as a horizontal line at the level of £30. Remember that in this case the price illustrates the demand curve, which is also equal to the marginal public and private benefit (*MPB*) to Glasco.

Once these lines have been drawn, the equilibrium output for the competitive industry can be read from the axis. In this case it would be where the MSB_1 or 'price' line cuts the *MPC* line, i.e. at 40 (or 40,000 tonnes of coal processing per week). The social optimum output level of output would be where the MSB_1 or price line cuts *MSC*, i.e. at 20 (or 20,000 tonnes of coal processed per week).

Fig. A.20

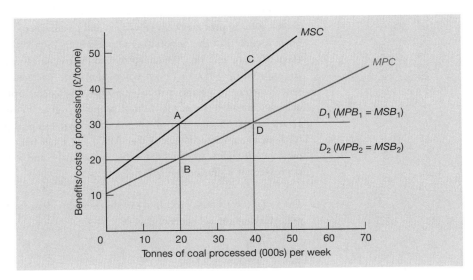

(b) If the government were alarmed about the problems confronted by Dram Ltd, then it would need to impose a tax on Glasco that would put the *net* price of coal processing below the current level. In this case the tax needed at the social optimum output of 20 would be £10 per tonne, i.e. the distance AB in Fig. A.20.

(c) If Glasco had 'property rights' over the air around the processing plant, then one would assume that it would merely produce the competitive output of 40,000 tonnes per week and not worry about the problems caused to Dram. However, it might be possible for Glasco and Dram to *negotiate* over these property rights so as to get Glasco to decrease its output below the competitive level (i.e. less air pollution) and still have a net benefit. This could happen if it sold some of its property rights to Dram (which wants cleaner air for its chip production) and could still have a surplus benefit.

In effect, part of the cost to Glasco of processing coal should include the value of its property rights, i.e. what it *could* get from Dram if it sold its property rights of the surrounding air to that company (a form of opportunity cost). Therefore Glasco should include this opportunity cost in its marginal social cost line (*MSC*). If Glasco produced at the socially optimum level instead of its natural competitive level, then it would lose profits/surpluses equivalent to the area ABD. However, Glasco could get a maximum payment or compensation from Dram of ABDC for producing at the socially optimum level, i.e. for not processing so much coal and therefore relinquishing some of its property rights on the surrounding air and selling them to Dram.

As far as this problem is concerned, the area of loss to Glasco is the area ABD = 10 × 10 = 100 or £100,000 (since the quantities are in 000s). The maximum amount that Dram would pay to avoid Glasco producing so much coal processing pollution ACDB is triangles ABD + ACD. The area of triangle ACD equals 15 × 10 = 150 (or £150,000) plus area ABD of £100,000, which equals £250,000. If this is the case then we can see that there would be a potential maximum net benefit to Glasco of the area ACD, i.e. £150,000.

Using our present example, Ronald Coase's theorem states that assuming that the bargaining process between Glasco and Dram has no transaction costs, i.e. no costs incurred in the negotiating process etc., then the pollution-creating firm (Glasco) may have the *same* incentives to choose an efficient output level as does the injured firm (Dram) even where there are externalities involved. In other words, even in a competitive economy, the social optimum output may be achieved through the negotiation of property rights. In our example, we see that Dram can pay compensation for Glasco's ownership of property rights, which leads to a net gain to Glasco (area ACD) and a net benefit to Dram since it can now produce its microchips more efficiently and cheaper because of the decreased air pollution levels.

5. (a) The weighted average probability of illness or accident for the whole of Medidoc's policyholders can be expressed as

$$P = P_H \cdot \frac{H}{H+L} + P_L \cdot \frac{L}{H+L}$$

We are given the relevant information in the question to calculate P. Since $P_H =$ 0.9, $P_L = 0.1$, and H and L are 0.5 each, then

$$P = 0.9(0.5) + 0.1(0.5)$$
$$= 0.5$$

Therefore the weighted average probability is 0.5.

(b) The minimum insurance premium should follow the equation $I \geq C \times P$, where I is the premium level and C is cost of each line to Medidoc plc.

Substituting the relevant values we get

$$I \geq £1,000 \times 0.5 = £500.$$

If Medidoc does not divulge its information to policyholders, then nothing will happen in the short run since the low-risk non-smokers will not know that the insurance company is operating with an illness probability of 0.5 and therefore charging *all low risk policyholders* an inflated premium (I).

(c) If the information is leaked to the press then the non-smoking policyholders will realise that the probability of 0.5 calculated by the company to cover *all* policyholders is far in excess of the 0.1 probability assigned to non-smokers only. The non-smoking policyholders would leave in search of a premium that better reflects their lower probabilities of being ill. On the other hand, more smokers would apply for policies because they know the company is working on a probability of 0.5 when their probability of being ill is calculated to be 0.9: i.e. the premium they pay is charged on a much lower probability of being ill (0.5) than the actual likelihood of their being ill (0.9). Basically, the process described has led to *adverse selection*, where the 'high quality' participants, i.e. the non-smokers, are being driven out of the market.

Medidoc plc could offer different policies where non-smokers are given a fixed amount of cover at a low premium while the smokers are provided with any amount of insurance but at an expensive rate. Thus both markets are separated and each market can break even on each group. The problem with this is that non-smokers are not allowed to buy as much insurance as they want. The reason for this limitation is because it might induce smokers to claim they are non-smokers to get the low rate *and* an 'unlimited' amount of insurance.

(d) 'Moral hazard' is the incentive of an individual to take more risks when he or she is insured. In this case, smokers who have been covered by insurance might feel that they can increase their consumption of tobacco because they could get early hospital treatment through private insurance. To counteract this, Medidoc could introduce clauses in its insurance policies to disclaim any maximum payment of medical benefits if smokers are found to consume in excess of a certain amount of cigarettes. Alternatively, the company can send out leaflets to show the dangers of smoking and the advantages of exercise.

Chapter 13   1. (a) Since the industry is dominated by a monopoly producer, the condition for equilibrium is where marginal revenue equals marginal costs. To derive the marginal revenue curve we can, for simplicity, use the well-known fact that the marginal revenue curve has the same intercept point on the vertical price axis as the demand curve, but has twice the slope, i.e. the equation for the marginal revenue curve is

$$MR = 1{,}000 - 50Q \tag{1}$$

To find the equation for the marginal cost curve we need to find the first derivative of the total cost function:

$$TC = 400 + 580Q + 10Q^2$$

$$\frac{dTC}{dQ} \ (MC) = 580 + 20Q \tag{2}$$

The equilibrium condition will be where $MR = MC$, i.e. we need to equate equations (1) and (2):

$$1{,}000 - 50Q = 580 + 20Q$$

$$70Q = 420$$

$$Q = 6$$

To obtain the price of ethydrene we need to substitute for Q in the demand equation:

$$
\begin{aligned}
P &= 1{,}000 - 25Q \\
&= 1{,}000 - 25(6) \\
&= 850
\end{aligned}
$$

The profits earned will be equal to total revenue minus total costs at this output and price.

$$TR = P \times Q = 6 \times 850 = 5{,}100$$
$$TC = 400 + 580(6) + 10(6)^2 = 4{,}240$$

Therefore, to summarise, the monopolist producer of ethydrene will produce 6 million tonnes per year at a price of £850 per tonne. The total profits will be $5{,}100 - 4{,}240 = 860$ or £860 million per year (quantities are in millions).

(b) If the Government introduces pollution control standards so that the total cost function rises to $TC_1 = 500 + 650Q + 10Q^2$ then we have to repeat the exercise already described. First we need to equate the marginal revenue curve to the new marginal cost curve. The new marginal cost curve, MC_1, will be the first derivative of the new total cost curve, i.e.

$$TC_1 = 500 + 650Q + 10Q^2$$

$$\frac{dTC_1}{dQ} \ (MC_1) = 650 + 20Q$$

Equate this to the equation for the marginal revenue curve (equation (1)):

$1,000 - 50Q = 650 + 20Q$

$70Q = 350$

$Q = 5$

To find the price merely substitute for Q in the demand curve:

$P_1 = 1,000 - 25Q_1$
$= 1,000 - 25(5)$
$= 875$

The new profit level is the difference between the new total revenue and the new total cost.

$TR_1 = P_1 \times Q_1 = 5 \times 875 = 4,375$
$TC_1 = 500 + 650(5) + 10(5)^2 = 4,000$

To summarise, the new price and output after government regulations are £850 per tonne and 5 million tonnes respectively. The new profit level will be $4,375 - 4,000 = 375$ or £375 million per year. The effect of tighter control is to increase the price and decrease both the quantity sold and the profit of the monopoly producer of ethydrene.

(c) The rate of return on sales (total revenue) can be defined by the ratio total profits/total sales. In the first instance the profit/sales ratio was 860/5,100 or 16.9% while in the second situation the ratio was 375/4,375 or 8.6%. Therefore the effect of stricter government standards would be to halve the rate of return that the company earns on its sales.

2. (a) As described in Fig. A.21, the first step is to take the cost function and convert it into the form that is needed. If $TC = 5 + 3Q$, then average cost (AC) is total cost divided by Q: i.e. $AC = 5/Q + 3$. This form indicates that the company is operating under conditions of falling average cost. We now need to calculate marginal cost (MC), and we can do this in two ways. We can take the total cost function, TC, and let Q be 1, 2, 3, etc. and calculate the difference in total cost as Q increases by one unit, or we can differentiate the TC function with respect to Q. Whichever method is preferred the answer will be 3. In other words, the MC curve is a constant and is shown to be a horizontal line parallel to the horizontal axis at a value of 3 pence per kilowatt-hour. The average cost curve can be drawn by substituting the values of $Q = 1, 2, 3, 4, 5$ etc., into the equation for AC. Plotting the values of AC and MC onto a graph, we get the lines shown as AC and MC in Fig. A.21. We see here that the company exhibits diminishing average costs over a broad range of output levels, and that MC lies below AC.

(b) If the regulator wishes to introduce a pricing system where price accurately reflects the marginal cost of production, then we can see the implication of this by drawing the demand curve $P = 10 - Q$, where 10 is the intercept on the price axis with a slope of unity, i.e. 45°. The demand curve cuts the MC curve (i.e. the

Fig. A.21

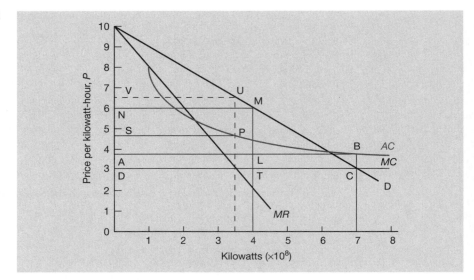

$P = MC$ criterion) at an output of 7 million kilowatts. Unfortunately, at this level, the average cost will be 3.71 pence per kilowatt-hour (substitute $Q = 7$ in the average cost equation), which is above the marginal cost-based price of 3 pence. The result is a loss of 0.71 pence per kilowatt-hour. The total loss for the monopolist would be the area ABCD, which is $0.71 \times 7 = 4.97$. Since the units are in 00s of millions, this means a loss of £4.97 million. Therefore if the regulator forces a monopolist who is operating under decreasing average costs (i.e. where marginal costs are below average costs) to charge at 'efficiency' price of $P = MC$, the monopolist will run at a loss.

(c) If the regulator requires the company to charge 6 pence per kilowatt-hour to less price-sensitive consumers, they will consume 4 (we will convert the units on the horizontal axis into their real value later). Other users, who are more price sensitive, would be charged 3 pence per kilowatt-hour, i.e. the lower, marginal cost-based price, and they would consume $7 - 4 = 3$. The average cost of generating the total amount of electricity, i.e. 7, is 3.71 pence per kilowatt-hour. Therefore the profit made by the monopolist electricity company would be the area ALMN, i.e. $2.29 \times 4 = 9.16$. The loss experienced by the company when it sells at the marginal cost level is area LBCT or $0.71 \times 3 = 2.13$. The net benefit to the company would be $9.16 - 2.13 = 7.03$. Since all the figures are in 00s of millions, the sum is equivalent to £7.03 million. Therefore the regulator's pricing decisions have brought the electricity company into profit.

(d) This is still a 'second best' for the electricity producer because its first choice would have been to produce at the point where $MR = MC$. We have drawn MC on our graph, so all we need to do is draw MR. Since the equation for MR has the same intercept, 10, but at twice the angle of the demand curve, i.e. $2Q$, then the equation for MR is $10 - 2Q$. If we draw this line and equate it to MC we find from Fig. A.21 (or from simple algebra) that the optimum price for the electricity company would be 6.5 pence per kilowatt-hour with an output of 3.5. Profits would be the area VUPS, which equals the quantity of electricity, 3.5, multiplied by the difference between the price and average cost (*AC*) at output 3.5. To find the precise level of *AC* substitute the value $Q = 3.5$ in the equation for *AC*, i.e. $(5/Q + 3) = 4.428$. This means that the profit per kilowatt-hour is $6.5 - 4.428 = 2.072$p. The total profit will be area VUPS, i.e. $2.072 \times 3.5 = 7.252$ or £7.252 million (since figures are in 00s of million kilowatts). Comparing the two-tier price system with the pure monopoly situation means that the monopolist would have gained £7.252 million − £7.03 million = £0.222 million if allowed to operate a pure, one-price, monopoly system.

In this sense it was a second-best situation. However, the regulator may be relatively happy because even though the electricity company is still earning close to monopoly profits through the two-tier price system, the regulator may have succeeded in forcing the company to split the market so that the more sensitive consumers can be charged a 'subsidised' price at the marginal cost level. This may be particularly important if the low price is charged to the more economically vulnerable people in society and if the government wants to see some element of marginal cost pricing introduced into the industry. Also, the output of electricity made available is much higher than would have been the case if the company was allowed freedom to limit output as a pure monopoly. Finally, the government could tax the excess profits created as a by-product of their two-tier system, thus redressing any excessive profits created by such a policy. Since these profits are supra-normal, a tax placed on them will not alter the price and output policy of the monopolist given the nature of a monopolist and the control set up by the regulators.

3. (a) The main assumptions of the theory of contestability are the following. First, entry into an industry is absolutely free and exit from that industry is absolutely costless. This means that firms can enter the industry even if conventional theory describes the industry as being made up of a small number of dominant firms, e.g. oligopolistic or monopoly. In other words, even if a market contains only a few firms, the fact that it is a contestable market means that it will be forced to operate like a competitive market because of the threat of entry. Second, and as a consequence of the threat of entry, each firm in the industry is made to produce where $P = MC = AC$, i.e. at zero economic profits. Third, the industry is liable to 'hit and run' competition, where firms can enter briefly to take advantage of transient profit opportunities. Thus, as noted above, the theory also stresses the effect of *potential* entrants, i.e. 'hit and run', on the behaviour of *existing* firms in the market. This means that firms already in the industry are pressurised to operate at minimum average costs in order to prevent other firms from entering the industry. Fourth, tactics such as collusive behaviour by firms already in the industry to try to keep other firms out cannot be successful because entry is costless and the barriers to entry usually set up by collusive behaviour will not work in a contestable market.

(b) (i) Firms would enter the industry if the market price rose above OP because positive economic profits would be made as price rises above minimum average costs. Even if firm A in this diagram were a large, apparently powerful firm, the fact that entry is free will encourage firms to enter and charge a price just below the existing firm but above minimum average cost. Obviously after a short time period sufficient firms would enter on a hit and run basis to bring price charged by existing firm/s in the market down to the minimum average cost levels shown by firm A in Figs. 13.6 (a) and (b), (see p. 549).

(b) (ii) At the price of OP the market demand would be $3Q$ but the average firm's output at which $P = MC = AC$ is Q. Therefore, the number of firms in the industry is $3Q/Q$ or 3. On the surface, this result seems contradictory because, under normal conditions, three firms in an industry seems to invite oligopolistic behaviour including excess profits and collusion. However, if the market is contestable, these benefits are not open to these few firms because entry into the industry is easy and free, thus forcing the existing firms to operate at their minimum efficient cost levels.

(c) (i) The competitive position would be where $P = MC_M$, i.e. at output Q_3. Since the demand or average revenue curve (AR) is below the average cost curve AC_M at output Q_3, the company would be operating at a loss.

(ii) The normal monopoly situation is where $MR = MC_M$ so the equilibrium level of output would be Q_1. At this level of output AR would be greater than AC and positive economic profit would be made. In a contestable market, firms would be lured into the industry, and any benefit to existing firms would be short run.

(iii) The most likely position for the monopoly firm is to produce an output of Q_2 where average cost is equal to average revenue and where zero economic profits are made. Any price above this level would encourage outside firms to enter: i.e. the *threat* of entry keeps the monopolist at the zero profits point. The monopolist will not operate at the lowest-cost position (C) because there is insufficient market demand to merit this solution. Interestingly, contestability provides an invisible hand that guides market equilibrium even under a decreasing-cost monopoly situation towards a perfectly competitive type of equilibrium.

4. (a) Since the local authority imposed a pricing system based on marginal costs, the number of passenger miles provided can be obtained by equating the demand curve (P) with the marginal cost curve, i.e.

$$7 - 0.9Q = 3 \qquad \text{(To answer this question using a diagram, draw}$$
$$4 = 0.9Q \qquad \text{the relevant functions, as in Fig. A.22.)}$$
$$4.44 = Q$$

The number of bus passenger miles provided under local authority control is 4.44 million per year at a price of 3 pence per mile.

(b) (i) To calculate the new private sector monopoly price and output we need to equate the marginal revenue to the new post-privatisation marginal cost. To find the equation for the marginal revenue curve, we take the same intercept point (7) as for the demand curve and double the slope of the demand curve, i.e. $MR = 7 - 1.8Q$. To find the price and passenger miles under the new conditions we need to equate MR and the new MC, i.e.

$$7 - 1.8Q = 2$$
$$5 = 1.8Q$$
$$2.77 = Q$$

The price at this level of output can be obtained by substituting for Q in the demand equation

$$P = 7 - 0.9(2.77)$$
$$= 7 - 2.49$$
$$= 4.51$$

The new private sector price will be 4.51 pence per mile and 2.77 million passenger miles provided. As a result of the privatisation, the number of passenger miles provided has decreased and the price per mile has increased.

(ii) The *productive efficiency* gained by the lowering of marginal cost from 3 to 2 pence per mile is the cost savings per mile times the number of passenger miles offered under the new private monopoly, i.e. the area ABCD in Fig. A.22. In this case it is 2.77 million multiplied by 1 pence, i.e. 2.77 million pence, or £27,770. The *allocative loss* resulting from the exercise of monopoly power by the new privatised company is equivalent to the area MBF, i.e. the area between the demand curve and the marginal cost under the local authority control. This area or deadweight loss is defined as $\frac{1}{2}$ BF $\times$ MB, which gives $\frac{1}{2}$ (4.44 − 2.77) $\times$ (4.51 − 3). This gives a 1.26 million pence or £12,600 loss. In this case, privatisation has increased economic welfare by £27,770 − £12,600 = £15,170.

Fig. A.22

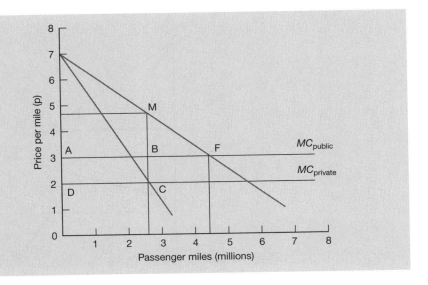

5. (a) If the water company was acting as a monopolist supplier of water it would equate its marginal cost with its marginal revenue. We therefore equate marginal cost with marginal revenue, i.e. $MC = MR$. We are given the marginal cost but we need to calculate the marginal revenue. To do this we can take the demand curve and convert it into a marginal revenue curve by merely keeping the same price intercept 8, and doubling the value of the slope of the demand curve, i.e. $0.8 \times 2 = 1.6$. The equation for the marginal revenue curve is therefore $MR = 8 - 1.6Q$. To find the equilibrium values of price and output we can draw the functions as in Fig. A.23 or use algebra.

$$MR = MC$$
$$8 - 1.6Q = 0.5 + 0.375Q$$
$$7.5 = 1.975Q$$
$$3.8 = Q$$

To find the price at this level of output substitute for Q in the demand equation, i.e.

$$P = 8 - 0.8(3.8)$$
$$= 4.96$$

The water company's monopoly price would be £4.96 per 1,000 litres and would supply 3.8 billion litres per month.

(b) (i) If the government regulator is thinking of a maximum price at the competitive level, then this will be where $P = MC$. Substituting the relevant equations we get

$$8 - 0.8Q = 0.5 + 0.375Q$$
$$7.5 = 1.175Q$$
$$6.4 = Q$$

Fig. A.23

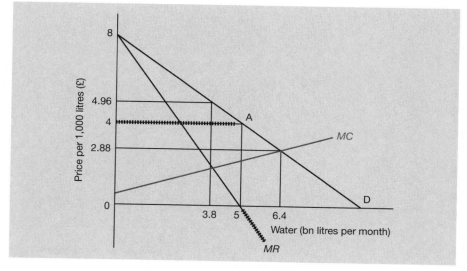

Substituting in the demand equation for price we get

$$P = 8 - 0.8(6.4)$$
$$= 2.88$$

This means that if the government decided on a price and quantity at the competitive level, then the water company would charge only £2.88 per 1,000 litres and supply 6.4 billion litres per month.

(ii) If the government regulator was thinking of a maximum price that would provide the maximum revenue for the water company then this would be where MR is zero because this is where total revenue (TR) is a maximum. To find the output level where $MR=0$ we take the MR curve:

$$MR = 8 - 1.6Q = 0$$
$$8 = 1.6Q$$
$$5 = Q$$

To find the price at this level of output substitute for Q in the demand equation, i.e.

$$P = 8 - 0.8(5)$$
$$= 4$$

In other words, if the government decided to place a maximum price at the maximum revenue level, the price would be £4 per 1,000 litres and the quantity supplied would be 5 billion litres per month.

Fig. A.23 shows a sketch of the relevant curves. As we can see, if the government placed a maximum price of £4 per 1,000 litres on the water, then the demand curve above A would not be relevant and the new demand curve (and therefore the marginal revenue curve) would be the horizontal line (hatched). Then at A, the demand curve becomes AD so that the relevant MR curve for that part of the demand curve would be the portion that is in the negative quadrant (hatched). The new MR curve is therefore the two hatched lines, i.e. horizontal to A and then in the negative quadrant beyond output 5 billion litres per month.

Mathematical foundations

In this appendix we briefly review the key mathematical techniques underpinning much of the microeconomic analysis at intermediate level. Those wishing to consider a particular mathematical technique in still more detail, or take it further, will be helped by the guided reading list presented at the end of the appendix.

Function

A **function** is a rule describing the relationship between variables. Using the notation $y = f(x)$, we are indicating, in a type of shorthand, that the variable y *depends upon* (is a function of) some other variable x. We could then say that y is the **dependent variable** and x the **independent variable**, though our study of economics will alert us to the fact that relationships between variables are rarely in single direction only.

The function or rule describing the relationship between variables may be specified more precisely. Thus $y = f(x) = 3x + 2$, will tell us that y takes the value 2 when $x = 0$ and rises by 3 units for every unit rise in x. This is an example of a *linear function*, of the general form $y = mx + c$, where c is the vertical intercept and m the slope of gradient.

- Where the highest power of the independent variable is 1, as in $y = 3x^1 + 2$, then we have a **linear function** or relationship. A *graph* or picture of this linear relationship between the variables is shown in Fig. X.1.
- Where the highest power of the independent variable is 2, as in the case of $y = ax^2 + bx + c$, then we have a **quadratic function** or relationship. A graph of such a quadratic relationship between the variables is shown in Fig. X.2. The shape of this graph is termed a *parabola*, and will be $\cup$-shaped where a is positive and $\cap$-shaped where a is negative. The vertical intercept will again be determined by the value of c.
- Where the highest power of the independent variable is 3, as in the case of $y = ax^3 + bx^2 + cx + d$, then we have a **cubic function** or relationship. A graph of such a cubic relationship between the variables is shown in Fig. X.3.

You should, of course, be familiar with other functional relationships:

- **exponential**: of the form $y = a^x$, where a is any constant >1 and x any variable. Figure X.4 graphs the exponential relationship $y = 2^x$ over the values $x = 1$ to 5.
- **reciprocal (hyperbolic)**: of the form $y = \frac{a}{x}$, where a is any constant and x any variable. Figure X.5 graphs the reciprocal (hyperbolic) relationship of $y = \frac{6}{x}$ over the values $x = 1$ to 6.

Fig. X.1 **Linear function.**

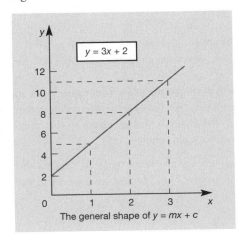

$y = 3x + 2$

The general shape of $y = mx + c$

Fig. X.2 **Quadratic function.**

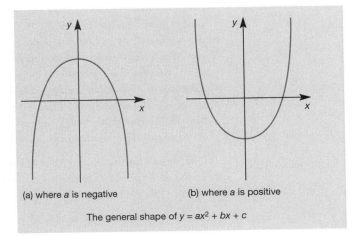

(a) where a is negative

(b) where a is positive

The general shape of $y = ax^2 + bx + c$

Fig. X.3 **Cubic function.**

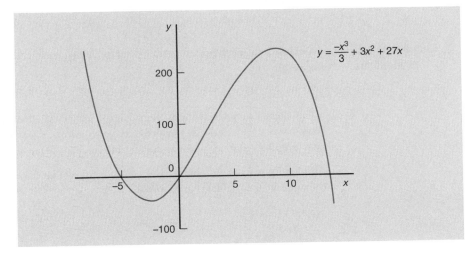

$y = \dfrac{-x^3}{3} + 3x^2 + 27x$

Fig. X.4 **Exponential function.**

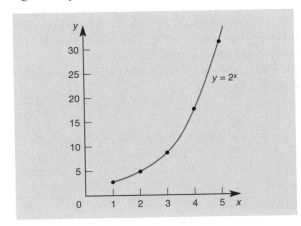

$y = 2^x$

Fig. X.5 **Reciprocal (hyperbolic) function.**

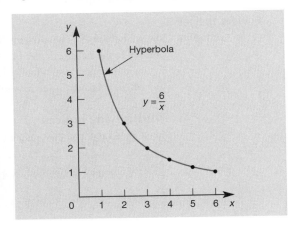

Hyperbola

$y = \dfrac{6}{x}$

- **logarithmic**: logarithmic functions involve the idea of *exponents* and are therefore considered later (p. 660) after reviewing some rules concerning exponents (sometimes known as *powers* or *indices*).
- **monotonic**: a functional relationship that always increases or always decreases. A *positive monotonic function* always increases as *x* increases; a *negative monotonic function* always decreases as *x* increases.
- **inverse**: in mathematical terms, a function is a unique mapping from elements in an initial set (the *domain*) to an image set (the *range*). An **inverse** of a function is that function or rule that returns elements from the image set (range) back to the initial set (domain). The notation of an inverse function is often shown as f^{-1}.

One way to find an inverse (if it exists) is to change the function to an *equation* and then *change the subject* of the equation as appropriate. Thus, to find the inverse of the function $y = f(x) = 3x - 1$:

Write the function as an equation: $y = 3x - 1$

Change the subject from y to x: $x = \dfrac{y + 1}{3}$

Equations and identities

- An **equation** is where a function is set as being equal to some particular number, for example:

$$3x = 9, x^2 = 16$$

The *solution* to an equation is the value (or values) of *x* that satisfy the equation. In these cases $x = +3$ and ± 4 are respective solutions. Clearly an equation will only hold true for specified values of the variable (here *x*).

- An identity is where a function is set in such a way that it holds true for *all* values of the variable or variables. For example:

$$3(x + 1) \equiv 3x + 3$$

$$(x + y)^2 \equiv x^2 + 2xy + y^2$$

The special symbol $\equiv$ indicates that the left-hand side of the identity will equal the right-hand side for *all* values of the variable or variables inserted in either side.

Powers, indices or exponents

As we have seen, the **power** (**index** or **exponent**) of the independent variable will influence the nature of any functional relationship. Here is a brief review of some of the 'rules of indices' with which you should be familiar. You will find these particularly helpful when *differentiating* or *integrating* functions.

Multiplying indices

$$4^3 \times 4^2 = (4 \times 4 \times 4) \times (4 \times 4) = 4 \times 4 \times 4 \times 4 \times 4 = 4^5$$

To multiply, just add the indices

i.e. $x^a \times x^b = x^{a+b}$

Dividing indices

$$3^5 \div 3^2 = \frac{3 \times 3 \times 3 \times 3 \times 3}{3 \times 3} = 3 \times 3 \times 3 = 3^3$$

> To divide, just subtract the indices
>
> i.e. $x^a \div x^b = x^{a-b}$

Variables to the power zero

e.g. $2^3 \div 2^3 = 2^{3-3} = 2^0$

but $2^3 \div 2^3 = \frac{8}{8} = 1$

so $2^0 = 1$

> $x^0 = 1$

Variables with negative powers

e.g. $3^1 \div 3^3 = 3^{1-3} = 3^{-2}$

but $3^1 \div 3^3 = \frac{3}{27} = \frac{1}{9} = \frac{1}{3^2}$

so $3^{-2} = \frac{1}{3^2}$

> $x^{-a} = \frac{1}{x^a}$

Variables with fractional powers

Fractional powers will be used to indicate roots

$x^{\frac{1}{2}} = \sqrt{x}$

$x^{\frac{1}{3}} = \sqrt[3]{x}$

> $x^{\frac{1}{n}} = \sqrt[n]{x}$

and $x^{\frac{3}{2}} = \sqrt{x^3} = (\sqrt{x})^3$

while $x^{\frac{2}{3}} = \sqrt[3]{x^2} = (\sqrt[3]{x})^2$

> $x^{\frac{m}{n}} = \sqrt[n]{x^m} = (\sqrt[n]{x})^m$

Logarithms   These **common logarithms** have been constructed to the base 10. A logarithm is simply the power, or exponent, to which 10 has to be raised to equal any given number. Thus

$$
\begin{array}{lll}
1000 = 10^3 \text{ therefore} & \log_{10}1000 = & 3.0000 \\
100 = 10^2 & \log_{10}100 = & 2.0000 \\
10 = 10^1 & \log_{10}10 = & 1.0000 \\
1 = 10^0 & \log_{10}1 = & 0.0000 \\
0.1 = 10^{-1} & \log_{10}0.1 = & -1.0000 \\
\text{usually written} & & \bar{1}.0000 \\
0.01 = 10^{-2} & \log_{10}0.01 = & \bar{2}.0000 \\
\end{array}
$$

(The table can of course be continued in both directions.)

A logarithm is composed of two parts: the number before the decimal point, which is known as the *characteristic*, and the number following the decimal point, called the *mantissa*.

Logarithms to other bases   It is, of course, possible to construct logarithms to any base. For example, if 2 is the base

$$
\begin{array}{lll}
1 = 2^0 \text{ therefore} & \log_2 1 & = 0 \\
2 = 2^1 & \log_2 2 & = 1 \\
4 = 2^2 & \log_2 4 & = 2 \\
8 = 2^3 & \log_2 8 & = 3 \\
16 = 2^4 & \log_2 16 & = 4 \\
32 = 2^5 & \log_2 32 & = 5 \\
64 = 2^6 & \log_2 64 & = 6 \\
128 = 2^7 & \log_2 128 & = 7 \\
\end{array}
$$

and so on.

Rules for the use of logarithms

It follows that:

if $N = a^x$

$\log_a N = x$

Two special cases are

$\log_a 1 = 0 \ (a^0 = 1)$

$\log_a a = 1 \ (N = a)$

The following 'rules' or 'laws' of logarithms can be generally applied:

- **The logarithm of a product:**
  $\log_a MN = \log_a M + \log_a N$

- **The logarithm of a quotient:**
  $\log_a \dfrac{M}{N} = \log_a M - \log_a N$

- **The logarithm of a power:**

$$\log_a N^p = p \log_a N$$

- **The change of base in a logarithm:**

$$\log_a N = \log_b N \log_a b$$

Logarithmic functions Any *exponential function* of the form $y = a^x$ noted earlier will have an *inverse function* that will be a **logarithmic function**. For example, if $y = 8^x$ then $x = \log_8 y$; in other words x equals the power to which 8 must be raised to give y.

In general a logarithmic function is of the form

$$x = \log_a y \; (a > 1)$$

where a is the *base* of the logarithmic function.

Since the graphs of all logarithmic functions can be obtained by inverting axes for the corresponding exponential function (see Fig. X.4), then the graphs of logarithmic functions will be as in Fig. X.6.

All such graphs will intersect the y-axis when $y = 1$. Further:

as $y \to 0, x \to -\infty$
as $y \to \infty, x \to \infty$

Note the characteristic shape of a logarithmic function, whereby a constant *absolute* increase in x leads to a *declining rate of growth* in y. This is because logarithmic scales reflect *proportional changes*. Thus a change in x from 1 to 2 represents an increase of 100%, but the same absolute change in x from 2 to 3 represents an increase of only 50%. So a graph of the form $x = \log_a y$ shows a declining growth rate.

Fig. X.6
A logarithmic
function.

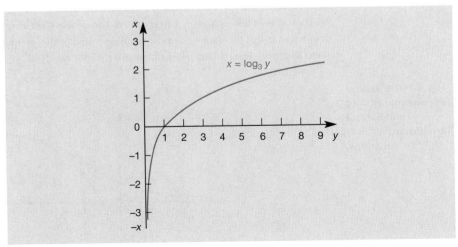

Note: Remember $x = \log_3 y$ is the *inverse* of the exponential function $y = 3^x$. In other words x equals the power to which 3 must be raised to give a particular value of y. So when $x = 2, y = 9$; and so on.

Natural logarithms

The exponential and logarithmic functions most widely used by economists are those for which the constant a in $y = a^x$ takes a value approximately equal to 2.71828. This is usually given the symbol e, so that the equation for **natural logarithms** becomes

$$y = e^x \quad e \simeq 2.71828$$

This function is often referred to as the *natural exponential function* or the exponential function, and its logarithmic form as the *natural logarithmic function*.

From Fig. X.7 we can see that, as previously explained, the natural exponential function $y = e^x$ is represented in logarithmic form by its *inverse*, $y = \ln x$.

Notice from the figure that:

- $\ln x$ does not exist for negative values of x
- $y = 0$ when $\ln x = 1$
- As $x \rightarrow \infty$ then $\ln x \rightarrow \infty$
- As $x \rightarrow 0$ then $\ln x \rightarrow -\infty$

Differentiation

Differentiation refers to the process whereby we calculate the gradient to a curve at any point. Clearly for a *linear function* or equation $y = mx + c$ the gradient, m, is a constant at every point. In Fig. X.1 (p. 657) the gradient of the curve $y = 3x + 2$ is clearly $+3$ at all points along that curve.

However, to find the gradient to a *non-linear function*, we would need to draw a straight line touching the curve at each particular point (the tangent to that point) and then find the slope (gradient) of that tangent. Clearly in Fig. X.2(a) and (b) gradients to these non-linear (quadratic) functions will be changing at each and every point (i.e. for different values of x). It would be extremely tedious to draw and measure the gradients to a large number of points along non-linear functions.

We can short-circuit this whole process by using the technique of **differentiation**. We can then establish a formula that will give the value of the tangent drawn to any point on the curve. This formula is often referred to as the **first derivative** of the curve. So important is this technique to understanding much of the analysis underpinning intermediate microeconomics that we shall consider it in some detail.

Fig. X.7 **The natural exponential ($y = e^x$) and natural logarithmic ($y = \ln x$) functions.**

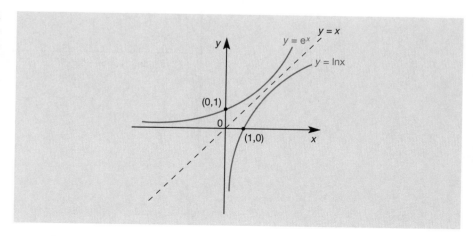

Gradients and limits

The idea of *limits* is central to understanding the process of differentiation. In fact we shall see that the slope of a *tangent* just touching a curve is in fact the **limit** of the slope of a *chord* joining two points along that curve. In Fig. X.8 we can connect two separate points on the curve, namely P and Q, by drawing the straight line PQ. This chord can easily be depicted as the hypotenuse of the right-angled triangle PQR, and from trigonometry we know that the tangent of angle QPR will give us the slope of the chord.

Slope of chord PQ $=$ tan QPR

$$= \frac{\text{side opposite}}{\text{side adjacent}}$$

$$= \frac{\text{QR}}{\text{PR}}$$

Now as Q approaches (gets nearer to) P along the curve, the slope of the *chord* PQ gets closer and closer to the slope of the *tangent* at P, namely PT. Of course another way of expressing the idea of Q approaching P is to say as PR (the base of the triangle) tends to zero, i.e. PR $\rightarrow$ 0. Of course as long as P and Q are separate points along the curve, PQ will never actually equal PT, but it will become so close to the value of PT that for all intents and purposes it can be regarded as identical. We can use the following shorthand to express this idea

$$\text{Slope of tangent PT} = \begin{array}{c} \text{limit slope of chord PQ,} \\ \text{as Q approaches P} \end{array}$$

i.e. Slope of tangent PT $= \displaystyle\lim_{\text{PR} \to 0} \left(\frac{\text{QR}}{\text{PR}}\right)$

We now apply these ideas to curves involving the dependent variable y and the independent variable x. For purposes of exposition we actually use the simple *quadratic* relationship $y = x^2$ as in Fig. X.9. The symbol Δ refers to a *change* in any variable.

We construct a chord PQ connecting point P (with coordinates x^*, y^*) and point Q (with coordinates $x^* + \Delta x, y^* + \Delta y$).

Fig. X.8 **Gradient and limits.**

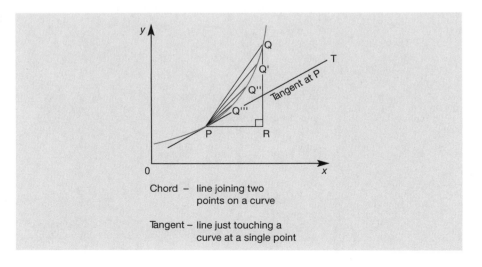

Chord – line joining two points on a curve

Tangent – line just touching a curve at a single point

Fig. X.9 **Process of differentiation.**

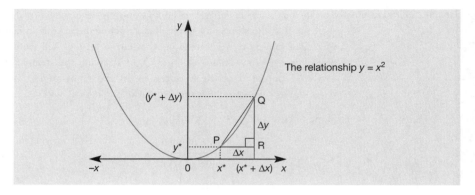

Following our earlier reasoning we can state the following:

$$\text{Gradient of curve at P} = \frac{\text{limit}}{\text{PR} \to 0}\left(\frac{\text{QR}}{\text{PR}}\right)$$

$$= \frac{\text{limit}}{\Delta x \to 0}\left(\frac{\Delta y}{\Delta x}\right)$$

$$= \frac{dy}{dx}$$

The expression $\frac{dy}{dx}$ is termed the **first derivative**. Put another way we have **differentiated** the variable y with respect to x. Of course what we have done is to find an expression for the gradient of the *tangent* to any point on the curve as being the limit of a known expression for the slope of a *chord* to that curve.

From Fig. X.9 we can show that for the curve $y = x^2$, the first derivative will always be $\frac{dy}{dx} = 2x$ at each and every point on that curve. The workings behind this solution are indicated in the box below.

The relationship $y = x^2$ (see Fig X.9, p. 664)

or
$$y^* + \Delta y = (x^* + \Delta x)^2$$
$$y^* + \Delta y = x^{*2} + 2x^*\Delta x + (\Delta x)^2$$

but $\qquad y^* = x^{*2}$

Subtracting: $\qquad \Delta y = 2x^*\Delta x + (\Delta x)^2$

and dividing throughout by Δx:

gives $\qquad \dfrac{\Delta y}{\Delta x} = 2x^* + \Delta x$

and $\quad$ limit $\quad \dfrac{\Delta y}{\Delta x} = 2x^*$
$\qquad \Delta x \to 0$

i.e. $\qquad \dfrac{dy}{dx} = 2x^*$

Note:
$(x^* + \Delta x)(x^* + \Delta x)$
$x^{*2} + x^*\Delta x + x^*\Delta x + \Delta x.\Delta x$
$x^{*2} + 2x^*\Delta x + (\Delta x)^2$

This extremely powerful result tells us that for any given value of x we can find the slope of the tangent to the curve at that point. Thus for $x = 1$, $\frac{dy}{dx} = 2(1) = 2$; for $x = 2$, $\frac{dy}{dx} = 2(2) = 4$; and so on.

If we repeat this process for other curves then we shall see that a *pattern* emerges that forms the basis for an important formula used in differentiation.

Suppose we differentiate (find $\frac{dy}{dx}$ for) the curve $y = 3x^2$ using our earlier approach. As we can see from the box below, the solution will be that $\frac{dy}{dx} = 6x$.

Thus for $x = 1$, the slope of the tangent to the curve $y = 3x^2$ at this point is $\frac{dy}{dx} = 6(1) = 6$; for $x = 2$, $\frac{dy}{dx} = 6(2) = 12$; and so on.

The relationship $y = 3x^2$

$$y^* + \Delta y = 3(x^* + \Delta x)^2$$

or

$$y^* + \Delta y = 3x^{*2} + 6x^* \Delta x + 3(\Delta x)^2$$

but $\qquad\qquad\quad y^* = 3x^{*2}$

Subtracting: $\qquad \Delta y = 6x^* \Delta x + 3(\Delta x)^2$

and dividing throughout by Δx

gives $\qquad\qquad\quad \dfrac{\Delta y}{\Delta x} = 6x^* + 3\Delta x$

and $\qquad\qquad \underset{\Delta x \to 0}{\text{limit}}\ \dfrac{\Delta y}{\Delta x} = 6x^*$

i.e. $\qquad\qquad\quad \dfrac{dy}{dx} = 6x^*$

General formula   In fact the pattern that will always result from such differentiation will give us the following **general formula**.

$$\text{If } y = ax^n$$
$$\text{where } a = \text{any constant}$$
$$x = \text{any variable}$$
$$n = \text{any power}$$
$$\text{then } \frac{dy}{dx} = nax^{n-1}$$

Thus if $y = 1x^2$

$$\frac{dy}{dx} = 2.1x^{2-1} = 2x$$

and if $y = 3x^2$

$$\frac{dy}{dx} = 2.3x^{2-1} = 6x$$

and so on.

This extremely powerful result will allow us to find (in the limit) the slope of the tangent drawn to any point on a particular curve.

Turning points Clearly the ideas of *maxima* and *minima* (i.e. **turning points**) are vital to many micro-economic analyses. As we can see from Fig. X.10(a), the value of the **first derivative** will be zero for any turning point, whether maximum or minimum. In other words we can differentiate the equation of the curve $y = x^3$ by finding $\dfrac{dy}{dx}$. If we plot $\dfrac{dy}{dx} (= 3x^2)$ against x, as in Fig. X.10(b), set $\dfrac{dy}{dx} = 0$ and solve for x, then for a quadratic equation we can expect two solutions, x_1 and x_2.

Unfortunately we shall not, at this stage, be able to distinguish between the maximum and minimum solutions. However, by taking **second derivatives** (i.e. finding the gradient to the gradient), we can distinguish between the different turning points.

Figure X.10(c) shows the gradient $\left(\dfrac{dy}{dx}\right)$ of the gradient $\left(\dfrac{dy}{dx}\right)$ displayed in Fig. X.10(b). This is known as finding the *second derivative* and is expressed as $\dfrac{d^2y}{dx^2} \left(\dfrac{dy}{dx} \text{ of } \dfrac{dy}{dx}\right)$.

Fig. X.10 Using differentiation to identify turning points.

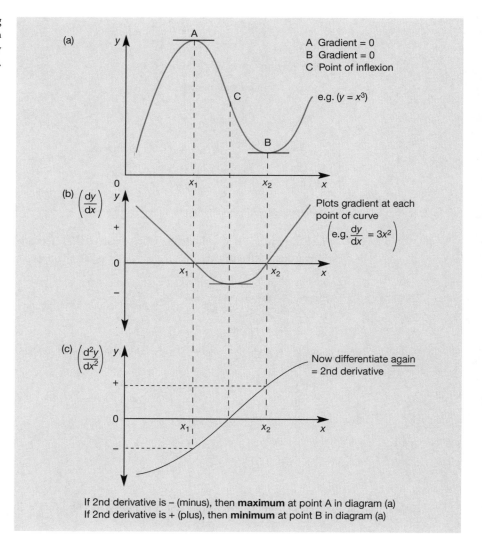

If 2nd derivative is − (minus), then **maximum** at point A in diagram (a)
If 2nd derivative is + (plus), then **minimum** at point B in diagram (a)

- Where we have the **maximum** at x_1, the value of the *first derivative* is zero, and the value of the *second derivative* (at x_1) is negative.
- Where we have the **minimum** at x_2, the value of the *first derivative* is zero, and the value of the *second derivative* (at x_2) is positive.

The following worked example illustrates this approach.

Example:

$$y = x^3 - 27x + 3$$

Find the turning points for this equation.
Distinguish between maximum and minimum turning points.

$$\frac{dy}{dx} = 0 \text{ at a turning point}$$

i.e. $\dfrac{dy}{dx} = 3x^2 - 27 = 0$ (applying our general formula for differentiation to each term separately)

$$3x^2 = 27$$
$$x^2 = 9$$
$$x = +3 \text{ or } -3 \text{ are the turning points.}$$

$$\frac{d^2y}{dx^2} = 6x \text{ (second derivative)}$$

At $x = +3$, second derivative $= +18$
   $x = +3$ is a minimum
At $x = -3$, second derivative $= -18$
   $x = -3$ is a maximum

Rules of
differentiation

The derivative of a sum or difference

If $y = u + v$ (where u and v are functions of x)

$$\frac{dy}{dx} = \frac{du}{dx} + \frac{dv}{dx}$$

Example:

$$y = 2x^4 - 4x^2$$
$$\frac{dy}{dx} = 8x^3 - 8x$$

The derivative of a product

If $y = uv$ (where u and v are functions of x)

$$\frac{dy}{dx} = u\frac{dv}{dx} + v\frac{du}{dx}$$

Example:

$$y = (3x + 1)(3x^2) \quad \left[u = 3x + 1, \frac{du}{dx} = 3 \right.$$
$$\left. v = 3x^2, \frac{dv}{dx} = 6x \right]$$

$$\frac{dy}{dx} = (3x + 1).(6x) + (3x^2).(3)$$

$$\frac{dy}{dx} = 18x^2 + 6x + 9x^2$$

$$\frac{dy}{dx} = 27x^2 + 6x$$

The derivative of a quotient

$$y = \frac{u}{v} \quad \text{(where } u \text{ and } v \text{ are functions of } x)$$

$$\frac{dy}{dx} = \frac{u\dfrac{dv}{dx} - v\dfrac{du}{dx}}{v^2}$$

Example

$$y = \frac{3x - 2}{5x + 3} \quad \left[u = 3x - 2, \frac{du}{dx} = 3 \right.$$
$$\left. v = 5x + 3, \frac{dv}{dx} = 5 \right]$$

$$\frac{dy}{dx} = \frac{(3x - 2) \times (5) - (5x + 3) \times (3)}{(5x + 3)^2}$$

$$= \frac{15x - 10 - 15x - 9}{25x^2 + 30x + 9}$$

$$= \frac{-19}{25x^2 + 30x + 9}$$

The derivative of a function of a function

If $y = f(u)$ where $u = f(x)$

$$\frac{dy}{dx} = \frac{dy}{du} \cdot \frac{du}{dx}$$

Example:

$$y = (3x^2 + 2)^4 \quad \left[y = u^4, \frac{dy}{du} = 4u^3 \right.$$
$$\left. u = 3x^2 + 2, \frac{du}{dx} = 6x \right]$$

$$\frac{dy}{dx} = 4u^3 \times 6x$$

$$= 24x \times u^3$$

$$= 24x \times (3x^2 + 2)^3$$

The derivative of a logarithmic function

Logarithms to the base e

It can be shown that for the function

$$y = \log_e x$$

$$\frac{dy}{dx} = \frac{1}{x}$$

Now suppose that we have

$$y = \log_e u$$

where $u = f(x)$, e.g. $y = \log_e(3x^2 + 2x - 1)$

We know from our rule for the differentiation of a function of a function that

$$\frac{dy}{dx} = \frac{dy}{du} \cdot \frac{du}{dx}$$

In this case, where $y = \log_e u$ we have that $\dfrac{dy}{du} = \dfrac{1}{u} = \dfrac{1}{f(x)}$ and so

$$\frac{dy}{dx} = \frac{1}{u}\frac{dy}{dx} = \frac{1}{f(x)} \frac{d}{dx} f(x)$$

$$= \frac{f'(x)}{f(x)}$$

where we use $f'(x)$ to denote $\dfrac{d}{dx} f(x)$

Example

$$y = \log_e(3x^2 + 2x - 1)$$

Here we have that

$$f(x) = (3x^2 + 2x - 1)$$

and so

$$f'(x) = \frac{d}{dx} f(x) = 6x + 2$$

Therefore,

$$\frac{dy}{dx} = \frac{f'(x)}{f(x)} = \frac{6x + 2}{3x^2 + 2x - 1}$$

Logarithms to any base

Although we have seen how to differentiate a logarithm to the base e, we have not yet considered how to differentiate a logarithm to some other base. This is done quite simply by remembering that

$$\log_a x = \frac{\log_e x}{\log_e a}$$

It follows immediately from this that

$$\frac{d}{dx} \log_a x = \frac{1}{x \log_e a}$$

And it is not difficult to deduce that

$$\frac{d}{dx} \log_a f(x) = \frac{f'(x)}{f(x) \log_e a}$$

For example, if we have that $y = \log_{10}(3x^2 + 5x)$, then

$$\frac{dy}{dx} = \frac{6x + 5}{(3x^2 + 5x) \log_e 10}$$

Partial differentiation Many functions have *more than one* independent variable. A function with two independent variables could be expressed

$$y = f(x,z)$$

Similarly, a function with three independent variables could be expressed

$$y = f(w,x,z)$$

If we differentiate the function with respect to *one* of these variables, keeping *all other variables constant*, we are using the process of **partial differentiation** and are finding the **partial derivatives**.

We can illustrate the idea of partial differentiation using Fig. X.11, which shows a situation where the variable y depends upon two variables, x and z. Clearly we now have a three-dimensional diagram.

When we partially differentiate y with respect to x, we use the terminology $\frac{\partial y}{\partial x}$, replacing the letter d with ∂ to indicate partial differentiation. Essentially we are seeking to find the rate of change of y with respect to x, everything else (in this case z) assumed constant. Suppose z is assumed to be constant at the specific value OG, then we are finding the gradient (rate of change) to segment DE of the surface at each value of x. On the other hand, if z is assumed to be constant at the specific value 0 (zero) then we are finding the gradient (rate of change) to segment CB of the surface at each value of x.

Fig. X.11 Partial differentiation.

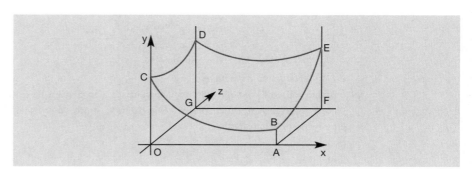

Alternatively we may be seeking to partially differentiate y with respect to z, using the terminology $\frac{\partial y}{\partial z}$. In this case we are seeking to find the rate of change of y with respect to z, everything else (in this case x) assumed constant. Suppose x is assumed to be constant at the specific value OA, then we are finding the gradient (rate of change) to segment BE of the surface at each value of z. On the other hand, if x is assumed to be constant at the specific value 0 (zero), then we are finding the gradient (rate of change) to segment CD of the surface at each value of z.

As we noted in demand theory, finding *own-price elasticities of demand* often involves the 'other things equal' assumption for variables other than the price of the product in question, and is therefore a partial elasticity. The same is true of calculations involving *cross-elasticities of demand*, where only the price of the other product is allowed to change.

Here the dependent variable (y) depends upon two independent variables (x and z).

Calculating partial derivatives

To differentiate a function with respect to *one* of its variables, treat the remaining variables as constants and proceed in the usual way already considered for differentiation.

Examples:

(a) Give the partial derivatives of

$$y = x^2 + 3xz - 4z^2$$

$$\frac{\partial y}{\partial x} = 2x + 3z$$

$$\frac{\partial y}{\partial z} = 3x - 8z$$

(b) Give the partial derivatives of

$$y = w^3 - w^2x + x^2z - z^2$$

$$\frac{\partial y}{\partial w} = 3w^2 - 2wx$$

$$\frac{\partial y}{\partial x} = -w^2 + 2xz$$

$$\frac{\partial y}{\partial z} = x^2 - 2z$$

Partial derivatives and total derivatives

So far we have seen that if y is a function of x and z, i.e. $y = f(x,z)$ then:

- $\frac{\partial y}{\partial x}$ measures the rate of change of y with respect to x when z is held constant; and

- $\frac{\partial y}{\partial z}$ measures the rate of change of y with respect to z when x is held constant.

Here we consider the problem of finding how y changes when both x and z vary *simultaneously* at given rates.

Suppose, now, that it takes a time t for each of these variables, y, x and z to change. Then in the limit we can say that, for the relationship $y = f(x, z)$:

$$\frac{dy}{dt} = \frac{\partial y}{\partial x} \cdot \frac{dx}{dt} + \frac{\partial y}{\partial z} \cdot \frac{dz}{dt}$$

We call $\frac{dy}{dt}$ the **total derivative** of y with respect to t. It is total in the sense that it takes into account all the partial variations of y, making no presumption that other variables remain unchanged (constant).

We might also note that if Δy, Δx and Δz are very small, but are still large enough to be measured, then it is *approximately* true that for the relationship $y = f(x,z)$:

$$\Delta y = \frac{\partial y}{\partial x} \cdot \Delta x + \frac{\partial y}{\partial z} \cdot \Delta z$$

Constrained maximisation (Lagrangian multipliers)

Often we are faced with maximising some variable subject to one or more *constraints* for example maximising consumer utility subject to a given level of income. Problems of this type can be solved using the idea of **Lagrangian multipliers**, as we shall see.

Suppose that we wish to maximise z, a function of the n variables $x_1, x_2, \ldots, x_n$, subject to the condition that $u = 0$ where u is another function of the same variables.

For example, we may wish to maximise

$$z = w^2 + x^2 + y^2$$

subject to the condition that

$$u = w + x + y = 0$$

To do so we consider a new function F, which is defined to be

$$F = z + \lambda u$$

where λ is a new variable, independent of the xs.

Now since $u = 0$, the values of x_i (i.e. the values of $x_1, x_2, \ldots, x_n$) that make F a maximum must also make z a maximum. We now seek to find these values of x_i.

This process involves two conditions:

(i)   that all the *first derivatives* of F equal zero;
(ii) that the value of the *determinant* formed from the second derivatives of F and the first derivatives of u in $F = z + \lambda u$ should fall within a prescribed range, together with the value of its principal minor(s).

Here we focus on the first of these two conditions. A more detailed exposition involving the second condition can be found elsewhere (see 'Further reading', pp. 679–80).

> **All the first derivatives of *F* must equal zero for a turning point (maximum or minimum).**

This condition will determine the values of the *n* xs and of λ that give *F* a turning point.

In order that the first derivatives of *F* (which is a function of the *n* xs and of λ) may all be zero, we have that

$$\frac{\partial F}{\partial x_i} = \frac{\partial z}{\partial x_i} + \lambda \frac{\partial u}{\partial x_i} = 0$$

for all values of *i* (giving *n* equations in all),

and that

$$\frac{\partial F}{\partial \lambda} = u = 0$$

We may write the first of these equations in the form

$$z_i + \lambda u_i = 0 \qquad (i = 1, \ldots, n)$$

where we understand that z_i is simply a convenient way of writing $\partial z / \partial x_i$. This equation

$$z_i + \lambda u_i = 0 \qquad (i = 1, \ldots, n)$$

is really, of course, *n* equations: one for each value of *i*. We have that

$$z_i + \lambda u_i = 0$$
$$z_2 + \lambda u_2 = 0$$

and so on.

We also have that $\dfrac{\partial F}{\partial \lambda} = 0$

where $u = 0$

This means that we have $n + 1$ equations from which to determine the *n* values of x_i and the value of λ that make *F* a maximum or minimum; and then these same values of x_i will make *z* a maximum or minimum subject to $u = 0$.

The first step in the determination of a maximum or minimum is therefore to solve the $n + 1$ equations summarised by

and

$$z_i + \lambda u_i = 0$$
$$u = 0$$

We refer to λ as an *undetermined multiplier*, since we multiply *u* by it before we have determined its value.

Example:

Suppose that we wish to find the maxima and minima of

$$z = x^2 + y^2$$

subject to the condition

$$u = 3x + 2y - 6 = 0$$

To do so we take a new function

$$F = z + \lambda u = x^2 + y^2 + \lambda (3x + 2y - 6)$$

where λ is the undetermined multiplier. We now maximise F, treated as a function of x, y and λ. We have

$$F_x = 2x + 3\lambda$$
$$F_y = 2y + 2\lambda$$
$$F_\lambda = u = 3x + 2y - 6$$

For F (and therefore z) to be stationary

$$F_x = F_y = F_\lambda = 0$$

Therefore

$$2x + 3\lambda = 0$$
$$2y + 2\lambda = 0$$
$$3x + 2y - 6 = 0$$

Clearly $x = \dfrac{-3\lambda}{2}$ and $y = -\lambda$, whence

$$3(\dfrac{-3\lambda}{2}) + 2(-\lambda) - 6 = 0$$

Giving $-\dfrac{9\lambda}{2} - 2\lambda - 6 = 0$

$$-\dfrac{13}{2}\lambda = 6$$

$$\lambda = -\dfrac{12}{13}$$

So that $x = 1\frac{5}{13}$ and $y = \frac{12}{13}$.

At these values of x and y we have a turning point for F (and therefore z) subject to $u = 0$.

Of course, having identified a turning point, we must turn to the second condition to determine whether we have a maximum or minimum value (or indeed a point of inflexion).

Integration   This is the opposite process to differentiation. It involves the continuous summing of changes in a function $f(x)$ over an interval of the variable x.

Rules of integration

The integral of Ax^n with respect to $x = \dfrac{Ax^{n+1}}{n+1} + C$ where A and n are real numbers and C is a constant.

This is usually written as

$$\int Ax^n \, dx = \frac{Ax^{n+1}}{n+1} + C$$

Examples:

(i) $\int 3x^7 \, dx = \frac{3x^8}{8} + C$

(ii) $\int (5 + 6x) \, dx = 5x + \frac{6x^2}{2} + C = 5x + 3x^2 + C$

(iii) $\int x^{-3} \, dx = \frac{x^{-2}}{-2} + C = -\frac{1}{2x^2} + C$

Your simple check, of course, is to differentiate your final answer to see that you get back what you started with.

To find out the value of C you need to use more information. Look at the following worked example.

Example:

Find the equation of the curve whose gradient at the point (1, 1) is given by $1 - 3x^2$.

Since $\dfrac{dy}{dx} = 1 - 3x^2$ then $y = \int (1 - 3x^2) dx$

$$= x - \frac{3x^3}{3} + C$$

$$y = x - x^3 + C$$

When $x = 1$, $y = 1$ so $1 = 1 - 1 + C$

giving $C = 1$

The equation of the curve then is $y = x - x^3 + 1$

Area under a curve

The area between a curve $y = f(x)$, the x axis and the lines $x = a$, $x = b$ is defined by

$$\int_a^b f(x) \, dx$$

**Fig. X.12
Integration.**

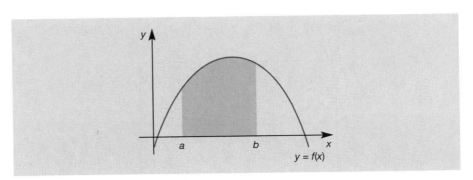

The worked example that follows illustrates the use of integration in such situations.

Example:

Find the area included between the curve $y = 2x + x^2 + x^3$, the x-axis and the lines $x = 1$ and $x = 2$.

$$\text{Area} = \int_1^2 (2x + x^2 + x^3)\,dx$$

$$= \left[\frac{2x^2}{2} + \frac{x^3}{3} + \frac{x^4}{4} \right]_1^2 = \left[x^2 + \frac{x^3}{3} + \frac{x^4}{4} \right]_1^2$$

$$= \left(4 + \frac{8}{3} + \frac{16}{4} \right) - \left(1 + \frac{1}{3} + \frac{1}{4} \right)$$

$$= 9 \tfrac{1}{12} \text{ unit}^2$$

Matrices and input/output analysis

A **matrix** is a rectangular array of numbers satisfying certain rules. The usual notation for a matrix with m rows and n columns (called a matrix of order $m \times n$) is

$$A = \begin{bmatrix} a_{11} & a_{12} & \cdots & a_{1n} \\ a_{21} & a_{22} & \cdots & a_{2n} \\ a_{m1} & a_{m2} & \cdots & a_{mn} \end{bmatrix}$$

Here a_{ij} denotes the element in the ith row and jth column. The transpose of A, written A', is formed by interchanging the rows and columns of A. A' is a matrix of order $(n \times m)$ and

$$A' = \begin{bmatrix} a_{11} & a_{21} & \cdots & a_{m1} \\ a_{12} & a_{22} & \cdots & a_{m2} \\ a_{1n} & a_{2n} & \cdots & a_{mn} \end{bmatrix}$$

The matrix is called *square* if $m = n$.

A particularly important application of matrix notation occurs in the context of **input–output analysis.**

Input–output is often used in micro and macro-planning. The UK produces input–output tables.

Technology matrix shows the inputs needed to produce one unit of output of various products. Here we illustrate using a 2×2 technology matrix (Table X.1) (i.e. 2 rows and 2 columns). It contains the elements a_{ij}, where i is the row (input) and j the column (output).

Table X.1

Output Input	Steel	Iron
Steel	0.5	0.6
Iron	0.25	0.1

$$\begin{bmatrix} a_{11} & a_{12} \\ a_{21} & a_{22} \end{bmatrix}$$

Technology matrix $= A$

Net output	$=$	Gross output	$-$	Intermediate inputs

$$y = x - Ax$$

$$\begin{bmatrix} y_1 \\ y_2 \end{bmatrix} = \begin{bmatrix} x_1 \\ x_2 \end{bmatrix} - \begin{bmatrix} a_{11} & a_{12} \\ a_{21} & a_{22} \end{bmatrix} \begin{bmatrix} x_1 \\ x_2 \end{bmatrix}$$

$$y_1 = x_1 - (a_{11} x_1 + a_{12} x_2)$$

$$y_2 = x_2 - (a_{21} x_1 + a_{22} x_2)$$

> *Note:*
> Multiply matrices/vectors of same order at right angles. Add the products of elements

Net output of steel	$=$	Gross output of steel	$-$	$\left(\begin{array}{c}\text{Amount of steel needed to produce steel}\end{array} + \begin{array}{c}\text{Amount of steel needed to produce iron}\end{array}\right)$
Net output of iron	$=$	Gross output of iron	$-$	$\left(\begin{array}{c}\text{Amount of iron needed to produce steel}\end{array} + \begin{array}{c}\text{Amount of iron needed to produce iron}\end{array}\right)$

Input–output analysis can be used to answer two types of question:

1. Given the *net output* you require, find the *gross outputs* that must be produced.
2. Given the *gross outputs* you intend to produce, find the *net outputs* you will end up with.

Question 1 A planner wishes the company to produce 500 units of steel and iron *net*. What must be the total (*gross*) output of each product?

$$y = x - A \cdot x$$

Net output	$=$	Gross output	$-$	Intermediate inputs

$$\begin{bmatrix} 500 \\ 500 \end{bmatrix} = \begin{bmatrix} x_1 \\ x_2 \end{bmatrix} - \begin{bmatrix} 0.5 & 0.6 \\ 0.25 & 0.1 \end{bmatrix} \begin{bmatrix} x_1 \\ x_2 \end{bmatrix}$$

$$500 = x_1 - (0.5x_1 + 0.6x_2)$$

$$500 = x_2 - (0.25x_1 + 0.1x_2)$$

Simplify:

$$500 = 0.5x_1 - 0.6x_2 \qquad (1)$$

$$500 = 0.9x_2 - 0.25x_1 \qquad (2)$$

Multiply (2) by 2, and rearrange:

$$1{,}000 = -0.5x_1 + 1.8x_2 \qquad (3)$$

$$(1) + (3) \text{ gives}$$

$$1{,}500 = 0 + 1.2x_2$$

$$\frac{1{,}500}{1.2} = x_2$$

$1,250 = x_2$

From (1):

$$500 = 0.5x_1 - 0.6(1,250)$$
$$500 = 0.5x_1 - 750$$
$$1,250 = 0.5x_1$$
$$2,500 = x_1$$

So, in order to produce 500 units of each product (net) the company needs to produce 2,500 units of steel (gross) and 1,250 units of iron (gross).

Question 2 The (gross) output levels of steel, gas and oil of a company are 4,000, 5,000 and 3,000 units respectively.

Each unit of *steel* requires inputs of 0.4 units of steel and 0.1 units of gas. Each unit of *gas* requires inputs of 0.3 units of steel and 0.1 units of oil. Each unit of *oil* requires inputs of 0.1 units of gas and 0.2 units of oil. Find the (net) steel, gas and oil potentially available for export.

We can summarise the information given in the question using the technology matrix in Table X.2.

Table X.2

Output			
Input	Steel	Gas	Oil
Steel	0.4	0.3	0
Gas	0.1	0	0.1
Oil	0	0.1	0.2

Remember

$$y \quad = \quad x \quad - \quad Ax$$

$$\text{Net output} \quad = \quad \text{Gross output} \quad - \quad \text{Intermediate inputs}$$

$$\begin{bmatrix} y_1 \\ y_2 \\ y_3 \end{bmatrix} = \begin{bmatrix} x_1 \\ x_2 \\ x_3 \end{bmatrix} - \begin{bmatrix} 0.4 & 0.3 & 0 \\ 0.1 & 0 & 0.1 \\ 0 & 0.1 & 0.2 \end{bmatrix} \begin{bmatrix} x_1 \\ x_2 \\ x_3 \end{bmatrix}$$

So

$$y_1 = x_1 - (0.4x_1 + 0.3x_2)$$
$$y_2 = x_2 - (0.1x_1 + 0.1x_3)$$
$$y_3 = x_3 - (0.1x_2 + 0.2x_3)$$

$$y_1 = 4,000 - (1,600 + 1,500) = 900$$
$$y_2 = 5,000 - (400 + 300) = 4,300$$
$$y_3 = 3,000 - (500 + 600) = 1,900$$

The company potentially has (net) 900 units of steel, 4,300 units of gas and 1,900 units of oil available for export.

▓ Further reading

Bancroft, G. and O'Sullivan, G. (1993), *Maths and Statistics for Accounting and Business Studies* (3rd edn), McGraw-Hill, Maidenhead.

Ch. 2	Graphs and equations
Ch. 4	Matrices
Ch. 5	Calculus
Ch. 12	Probability
Ch. 13	Decision theory analysis
Ch. 14	Probability

Burton, G., Carrol, G. and Wall, S. (1999), *Quantitative Methods for Business and Economics*, Longman Modular Texts in Business and Economics, Pearson Education, Harlow.

Ch. 5	Probability
Ch. 11	Calculus and business applications
Appendix 1	Basic mathematics

Curwin, J. and Slater, R. (1991), *Quantitative Methods for Business Decisions*, Chapman & Hall, London.

Ch. 6	Mathematical relationships
Ch. 7	Matrices
Ch. 8	Calculus
Ch. 10	Probability

Dinwiddy, C. (1989), *Elementary Mathematics for Economists*, Oxford University Press, Oxford.

Part 1	Elementary algebra
Part 2	Introduction to calculus
Part 3, Ch. 11	Logarithms
Ch. 12	Logarithmic and exponential functions
Part 4, Ch. 16	Introduction to matrices
Ch. 17	Further applications of matrices and determinants

Holden, K. and Pearson, A. W. (1992), *Introductory Mathematics for Economics and Business*, Macmillan, Basingstoke.

Ch. 1	Linear equations
Ch. 2	Elementary matrix algebra
Ch. 3	Non-linear equations
Ch. 4	Series
Ch. 5	Differential calculus
Ch. 6	Integral calculus
Ch. 7	Partial differentiation

Jacques, I. (1992), *Mathematics for Economics and Business*, Addison-Wesley, Wokingham.

Ch. 1	Linear equations
Ch. 2	Non-linear equations
Ch. 4	Differentiation
Ch. 5	Partial differentiation
Ch. 6	Integration
Ch. 8	Matrices

Lewis, J. P. (1969), *An Introduction to Mathematics for Students of Economics* (2nd edn), Macmillan, London.

Section 1	Algebra
Section 3	Calculus: functions of one variable
Section 4	Calculus: functions of many variables
Section 6	Linear algebra

Thomas, R. L. (1992), *Using Mathematics in Economics*, Longman, Harlow.

Ch. 1	Functions and equations
Ch. 7	Differentiation
Ch. 8	Higher order derivatives
Ch. 9	Integration
Ch. 10	Partial differentiation
Ch. 11	Total differentials and total derivatives
Ch. 12	Unconstrained and constrained optimization
Ch. 15	Exponential and logarithmic functions
Ch. 17	Matrix algebra

Timbrell, M. E. (1990), *Mathematics for Economists*, Blackwell, Oxford.

Part I	Simple mathematical concepts
Part III	Differential calculus
Part IV	Integral calculus
Part V	Multivariate calculus
Part VI	Matrix algebra

Waters, D. (1994), *Quantitative Methods for Business*, Addison-Wesley, Wokingham.

Ch. 2	Equations and graphs
Ch. 9	Forecasting
Ch. 10	Matrices
Ch. 12	Calculus
Chs 13 and 14	Probability

Statistical foundations

In this appendix we briefly review the key statistical techniques underpinning some of the microeconomic analysis frequently encountered at intermediate level. Those wishing to consider a particular statistical technique in still more detail, or take it further, will be helped by the guided reading list presented at the end of the appendix.

The following statistical techniques are frequently used with the intention of giving some meaning to raw (untreated) data.

Measures of central location
At least three types of average are in common use when seeking to describe a data set, namely arithmetic mean, median and mode. The formulae used in their derivation (and indeed elsewhere) make use of notations with which you should be familiar.

Notation

Σ = Greek letter Sigma = Sum of

When applied to some variable X_i, the range of values considered are indicated by the numbers imposed below and above the Sigma sign. For example, suppose X_i refers to the throws of a dice, and we wish to sum (add together) the scores on the first three throws, we would write:

$$\sum_{i=1}^{3} X_i = X_1 + X_2 + X_3$$
$$= 3 + 5 + 1 \text{ (say)}$$

Other possibilities might include the following:

$$\sum_{i=2}^{4} X_i = X_2 + X_3 + X_4$$
$$= 5 + 1 + 6 \text{ (say)}$$

$$\sum_{i=1}^{n} X_i = X_1 + X_2 + X_3 + \ldots + X_n$$

where n can be any number (of throws of the dice here)

Sometimes a particular score on the dice might occur once or more than once: in other words that particular score might occur with a *frequency* F_i. For n throws of the dice we might then write the total score as being given by

$$\sum_{i=1}^{n} F_i X_i = F_1 X_1 + F_2 X_2 + F_3 X_3 + \ldots + F_n X_n$$

Formulae   There are a number of formulae frequently used in the calculation of the various measures of central location that make use of this notation. These are outlined here and can be considered in more detail by referring to the guided reading list.

The arithmetic mean   This is the simple average of everyday use, and is often represented by the symbol $\bar{X}$.

Ungrouped data   Where individual or *ungrouped* data is available, the following formula is commonly used:

$$\bar{X} = \frac{\sum_{i=1}^{n} X_i}{n}$$

where $\bar{X}$ = arithmetic mean
    X_i = value of each item of data
    n = number of items of data.

Example:

Suppose the daily takings of a small corner shop are as shown in Table X.3.

Table X.3

	Mon	Tue	Wed	Thur	Fri
Daily sales (£)	420	560	630	580	810

Using the formula:

$$\bar{X} = \frac{\sum_{i=1}^{5} X_i}{5} = \frac{420 + 560 + 630 + 580 + 810}{5}$$

$$= \frac{3,000}{5} = £600$$

The average daily sales are £600, and this represents a typical figure around which the rest of the data will cluster.

Grouped data More unusually data is *grouped* into a **frequency table** various **class intervals**. To deal with such data the simplifying assumption must be made that *within any given class interval* the items of data fall on the *class mid-point*. This is equivalent to assuming that items of data are evenly spread within any given class interval.

We may now make use of the following formula:

$$\bar{X} = \frac{\sum\limits_{i=1}^{n} F_i X_i}{\sum\limits_{i=1}^{n} F_i} = \frac{F_1 X_1 + F_2 X_2 + \ldots + F_n X_n}{F_1 + F_2 + \ldots + F_n}$$

where F_i = frequency of ith class interval
X_i = mid-point of ith class interval
n = number of class intervals

Example:

Suppose that a survey of the prices of 50 items sold in a shop gives the results in Table X.4 (5 class intervals for prices).

Table X.4

Price of item (£)	Number of items sold
1.5–2.5	5
2.5–3.5	3
3.5–4.5	18
4.5–5.5	10
5.5–6.5	14

We can use our formula for grouped data to calculate the average (arithmetic mean) price of the items sold (Table X.5).

Table X.5

Price of item (£)	Class mid-points X_i	Number of items sold F_i	$F_i X_i$
1.5–2.5	2	5	10
2.5–3.5	3	3	9
3.5–4.5	4	18	72
4.5–5.5	5	10	50
5.5–6.5	6	14	84
		$\sum\limits_{i=1}^{5} F_i = 50$	$\sum\limits_{i=1}^{5} F_i X_i = 225$

$$\bar{X} = \frac{225}{50} = 4.5$$

The median This is the value that divides the data set into two equal halves with 50% of values lying below the median and 50% of values lying above the median.

Ungrouped data
To find this median:

1. Construct an *array* (i.e. place data in numerical order – whether ascending or descending).
2. Find median *position*.

$$\frac{n + 1}{2}$$

where n = number of values.

3. Find median *value*.

Example:

Table X.6

Machine output over 5-day period					
Daily output	210	240	260	220	230

Step 1 Place in an array: 210 220 230 240 260

Step 2 Find the median position using the equation $\dfrac{n + 1}{2}$

where n = the number of values

$$= \frac{5 + 1}{2} = \text{3rd item}$$

Step 3 Read the value of the 3rd item, i.e. 230 units.

NB Where there is an *even* number of items there will be *two* middle items. Take the *arithmetic mean* of these two items.

Grouped data The following steps can be use to arithmetically calculate the median value for data presented in a frequency table:

1. Find the median position.
2. Find the *class interval* in which the median observation lies.
3. Assume that all items in this class interval are equally spaced.
4. Estimate the median.

Example: From the data given in Table X.7:

$$\text{Median position} = \frac{n + 1}{2}$$

$$= \frac{20 + 1}{2}$$

$$= 10.5$$

The class interval in which this medium lies is 170–175.

Table X.7 **Grouped frequency distribution: heights of male students.**

Heights (cm) X_i	Frequency (number of students) F_i
150 and under 155	1
155 and under 160	1
160 and under 165	2
165 and under 170	3
170 and under 175	5
175 and under 180	2
180 and under 185	5
185 and under 190	1
	20

The median value can be found using the formula

$$\text{Median} = \text{LCB} + \left(\text{Class width} \times \frac{\text{Number of observations to median position}}{\text{Total number of observations in class interval}} \right)$$

where LCB = Lower class boundary (of median class interval).

$$\text{Median} = 170 \text{ cm} + (5 \text{ cm} \times \frac{3.5}{5})$$

$$\text{Median} = 173.5 \text{ cm}$$

The mode This is the value that occurs with greatest frequency. When data is grouped, then the *class interval* with the highest frequency if referred to as the modal class interval.

Both median and mode for grouped data can be estimated using *graphical methods* (see p. 686).

Normal and skewed distribution

When the set of data is distributed in a perfectly symmetrical way, as in Fig. X.13(a), then all three types of average have the same value. Such a symmetrical distribution is often referred to as a **normal distribution**. However, when, as is more usually the case, the set of data is **skewed** in one direction or another (Fig. X.13(b) and (c)), the three types of average will cease to be identical. In fact the arithmetic mean will always be most heavily influenced by the direction of skew, the direction being described by the tail of the distribution. In other words, the arithmetic mean will be most affected by a *few* extreme values, whether high (skewed to right) or low (skewed to left).

Fig. X.13 **Normal and skewed frequency distributions and measures of central location.**

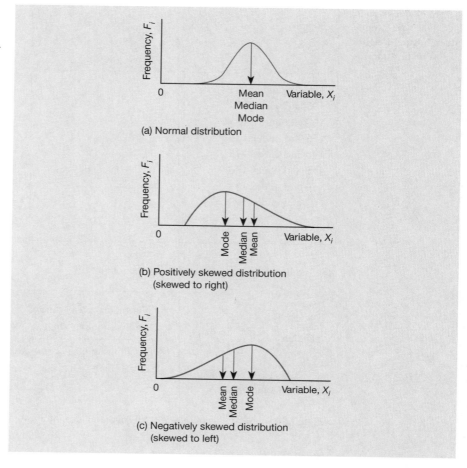

(a) Normal distribution

(b) Positively skewed distribution (skewed to right)

(c) Negatively skewed distribution (skewed to left)

Measures of dispersion

As well as measures of central tendency or average, it is helpful to have a measure of the extent of **dispersion** or spread around that average. The formulae and brief outline for the most widely used measures of dispersion are presented here, with guided reading to a more detailed consideration of these measures outlined in the reading list.

Mean deviation (MD)   Average of the deviation from the arithmetic mean, ignoring the sign of those deviations.

- *Ungrouped data* $\text{MD} = \dfrac{\sum\limits_{i=1}^{n} |X_i - \bar{X}|}{n}$

- *Grouped data* $\text{MD} = \dfrac{\sum\limits_{i=1}^{n} F_i |X_i - \bar{X}|}{\sum\limits_{i=1}^{n} F_i}$

where $| \; | = $ modulus (i.e. sign ignored)

Variance (S^2) Average of the squared deviations from the arithmetic mean. Result is expressed in square units. (*Note*: since all deviations are squared, all values are positive and we no longer require the modulus.)

- *Ungrouped data* $S^2 = \dfrac{\sum\limits_{i=1}^{n}(X_i - \bar{X})^2}{n}$

- *Grouped data* $S^2 = \dfrac{\sum\limits_{i=1}^{n}F_i(X_i - \bar{X})^2}{\sum\limits_{i=1}^{n}F_i}$

or $S^2 = \dfrac{\sum\limits_{i=1}^{n}F_i X_i^{\,2}}{\sum\limits_{i=1}^{n}F_i} - \left(\dfrac{\sum\limits_{i=1}^{n}F_i X_i}{\sum\limits_{i=1}^{n}F_i}\right)^2$

or $S^2 = \dfrac{\sum\limits_{i=1}^{n}F_i X_i^{\,2}}{\sum\limits_{i=1}^{n}F_i} - (\bar{X})^2$

Standard deviation (S) The square root of average of the square deviations from the arithmetic mean. The result is expressed in units.

$S = \sqrt{\text{variance}}$

for both ungrouped and grouped data.

We can use our earlier data on 20 male student heights (Table X.7) to Illustrate the calculation of variance and standard deviation as measures of dispersion.

$$\bar{X} = \dfrac{\sum\limits_{i=1}^{8}F_i X_i}{\sum\limits_{i=1}^{8}F_i} = \dfrac{3{,}455}{20} = 172.75 \text{ cm}$$

$$S^2 = \dfrac{\sum\limits_{i=1}^{8}F_i X_i^{\,2}}{\sum\limits_{i=1}^{8}F_i} - \left(\dfrac{\sum\limits_{i=1}^{8}F_i X_i}{\sum\limits_{i=1}^{8}F_i}\right)^2$$

$$\dfrac{598{,}525}{20} - \left(\dfrac{3{,}455}{20}\right)^2$$

$$29{,}926.25 - 29{,}842.56$$

$S^2 = $ Variance $= 83.69 \text{ cm}^2$

$S = $ Standard deviation $= \sqrt{83.69} \text{ cm}^2$

i.e. $S = 9.15 \text{ cm}$

Table X.8

Heights (cm)	Number of students F_i	Mid-points X_i	F_iX_i	$F_iX_i^2$
150 and under 155	1	152.5	152.5	23,256.25
155 and under 160	1	157.5	157.5	24,806.25
160 and under 165	2	162.5	325	52,812.50
165 and under 170	3	167.5	502.5	84,168.75
170 and under 175	5	172.5	862.5	148,781.25
175 and under 180	2	177.5	355	63,012.50
180 and under 185	5	182.5	912.5	166,531.25
185 and under 190	1	187. 5	187.5	35,156.25
	$\sum_{i=1}^{8} F_i = 20$		$\sum_{i=1}^{8} F_i X_i = 3,455$	$\sum_{i=1}^{8} F_iX_i^2 = 598,525$

Of course other, less sophisticated measures of dispersion might also be used and can be considered in the further reading.

- **Range**: difference between highest and lowest values.
- **Interquartile range**: difference between upper and lower quartiles. The *upper quartile* being that value corresponding to an item of data three-quarters of the way up the distribution; the *lower quartile* being that value corresponding to an item of data one quarter of the was up the distribution.
- **Quartile deviation**: the interquartile range divided by 2. Sometimes called *semi-interquartile* range.

Coefficient of variation

This is a widely used measure of **relative dispersion**. It relates an *absolute* measure of dispersion (the standard deviation) to the *absolute* value of the arithmetic mean around which the dispersion takes place. Clearly a data set A with a standard deviation (S) of 10 units and mean ($\bar{X}$) of 10 units has a *greater* relative dispersion than a data set B with a higher absolute standard deviation of 20 units but a still higher absolute mean of 50 units. We would say that:

$$C \text{ of } V_A = \frac{S}{\bar{X}} = \frac{10}{10} = 1.0$$

$$C \text{ of } V_B = \frac{S}{\bar{X}} = \frac{20}{50} = 0.4$$

The **coefficient of variation** (C of V) can be expressed (as here) as a decimal, or as a percentage (here 100% and 40% respectively). The data set with the highest coefficient of variation has the greater relative dispersion.

Regression analysis

Regression analysis involves establishing a relationship between two or more variables. Here we illustrate in terms of a *linear* relationship, although more sophisticated approaches can establish similar *non-linear* relationships. For purposes of exposition we shall assume two variables only: Y, the dependent variable, and X, the independent variable.

Least squares line

As we shall see, the **least squares line** is that (here straight) line that minimises the sum of the squared deviations of the actual observations from the line. The square (rather than the absolute value) of the deviations is used to avoid the problem of first having to identify, then ignore, the sign ($\pm$) of the deviations.

In terms of Fig. X.14 the least squares line will be such that $\sum_{i=1}^{n} d_i^2$ is a minimum.

The slope (m) and intercept (c) of this unique line can be found using either of the following two approaches. In either case the formulae outlined are obtained via diffentiating expressions in order to find those values of m and c that will maximise the sum of squared deviation from the (straight) line containing those values. Proofs of these formulae can be found elsewhere (see 'Further reading', pp. 697–8).

(i) Original data (X, Y)

$$m = \frac{n \sum_{i=1}^{n} X_i Y_i \;-\; \sum_{i=1}^{n} X_i \sum_{i=1}^{n} Y_i}{n \sum_{i=1}^{n} X_i^2 \;-\; (\sum_{i=1}^{n} X_i)^2}$$

$$c = \bar{Y} - m\bar{X}$$

Fig. X.14 Finding the least squares line (LSL) $Y = mX + c$.

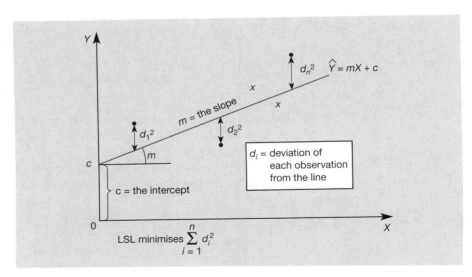

Fig. X.15 **Changing the origin from zero to the point of means** $(\bar{X}, \bar{Y})$ **to establish the coding formulae. Here a single observation (9, 8) is re-expressed as (4, 2) using the new axes** (x, y) **when** $\bar{X} = 5$ **and** $\bar{Y} = 6$.

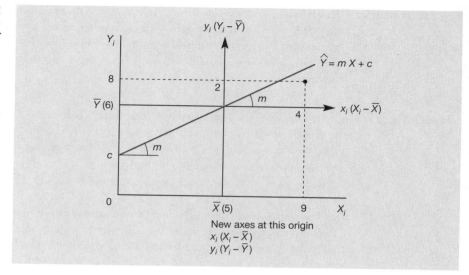

Rather simpler coding formulae can be derived using the fact that the regression (least squares) line must go through the point of means $(\bar{X}, \bar{Y})$. We can redefine the origin from zero to the point of means $(\bar{X}, \bar{Y})$, as in Fig. X.15, and use the resulting new axes (x, y) as the basis for our coding formulae.

(ii) Redefined data (x, y)

Here we change the origin from zero to the point of means $(\bar{X}, \bar{Y})$ and express new axes and data, $x_i (X_i - \bar{X})$ and $y_i (Y_i - \bar{Y})$

$$m = \frac{\sum\limits_{i=1}^{n} x_i y_i}{\sum\limits_{i=1}^{n} x_i^2}$$

$$c = \bar{Y} - m\bar{X}$$

Having calculated m (the slope of the least squares line) at the new origin, we revert to the zero origin to calculate c (the intercept). The slope, m, is of course identical at each of these origins for the linear least squares line.

The following simple worked example uses the *coding formulae* to calculate the least squares regression line. You could, of course, use the formulae involving *original data* to achieve an equivalent result.

Example:

Y_i	X_i	$\begin{array}{c}x_i\\(X_i-\bar{X})\end{array}$	$\begin{array}{c}y_i\\(Y_i-\bar{Y})\end{array}$	$x_i y_i$	x_i^2
2	1	−1.5	−1.5	2.25	2.25
3	2	−0.5	−0.5	0.25	0.25
4	3	0.5	0.5	0.25	0.25
5	4	1.5	1.5	2.25	2.25

$$\sum_{i=1}^{4} Y_i = 14 \qquad \sum_{i=1}^{4} X_i = 10 \qquad\qquad \sum_{i=1}^{4} x_i y_i = 5 \qquad \sum_{i=1}^{4} x_i^2 = 5$$

$$\bar{Y} = 3.5 \qquad \bar{X} = 2.5$$

$$m = \frac{\sum_{i=1}^{n} x_i y_i}{\sum_{i=1}^{n} x_i^2} = \frac{5}{5} = 1$$

$$c = \bar{Y} - m\bar{X} = 3.5 - 1\,(2.5) = 1$$
$$\hat{Y} = mX + c$$
$$\hat{Y} = 1X + 1$$

Fig. X.16

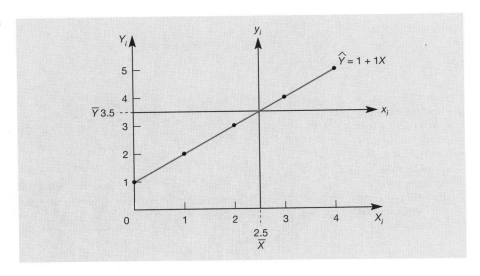

Correlation The idea here is to measure how well the regression line fits the actual data. Two key measures are frequently used in this respect:

- the coefficient of determination (R^2);
- the coefficient of correlation (R).

Before considering *formulae* for calculating these measures, it will be helpful to define the concepts of *deviation* and *variation* that underpin them. Figure X.17 will be used for illustration.

Deviation (d_i) is the difference between the actual value of an observation (Y_i) and its arithmetic mean $(\bar{Y})$. This deviation can be split into two separate parts: an *explained* part (d_e), which is predicted or accounted for by the regression line, and an *unexplained* part (d_u), which is *not* predicted or accounted for by the regression line.

Deviation $= d_i = Y_i - \bar{Y}$

Deviation = Explained deviation + Unexplained deviation.

$$d_i = d_e + d_u$$

Summing such deviations across all n observations gives **total deviation**.

Variation (d_i^2) is the *square* of the difference between the actual value of an observation (Y_i) and its arithmetic mean $(\bar{Y})$. As before, squaring the deviations avoids the problem of first identifying, then dropping, the sign $(\pm)$ of each deviation.

Summing the squared deviation across all n observations gives **total variation**.

It can be shown that

$$\text{Total variation} = \sum_{i=1}^{n} d_i^2 = \sum_{i=1}^{n} d_e^2 + \sum_{i=1}^{n} d_u^2$$

$$\frac{\text{Total}}{\text{variation}} = \frac{\text{Explained}}{\text{variation}} + \frac{\text{Unexplained}}{\text{variation}}$$

Fig. X.17 Deviation for each observation (d_i) is the actual value (Y_i) minus the arithmetic mean $(\bar{Y})$. This can be split into two parts: explained deviation (d_e) and unexplained deviation (d_u).

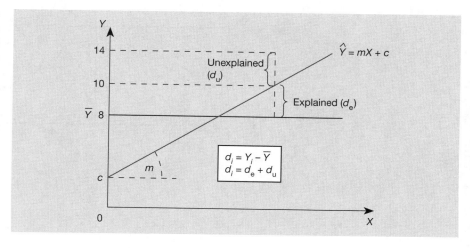

Coefficient of determination (R^2)

$$R^2 = \frac{\text{Explained variation}}{\text{Total variation}}$$

Clearly when $R^2 = 1$, as in Fig. X.18(a), then all the deviation and therefore variation can be explained or accounted for by the regression line. We have a perfect fit.

Similarly when $R^2 = 0$ (or close to 0) as in Fig. X.18(b), none of the deviation and therefore variation can be explained or accounted for by the regression line. We effectively have a random scatter of points, to which any regression line fits as well as any other.

The closer R^2 is to 1, the better the fit of the least squares line to the actual data.

Coefficient of correlation (R)

$$R = \sqrt{\frac{\text{Explained variation}}{\text{Total variation}}}$$

Just as R^2 varies between 1 and 0, so R varies between ± 1 and 0. 'Perfect correlation' implies a value for R of $+1$ when the relationship between Y and X is direct, and -1 when the relationship between Y and X is indirect (inverse).

As we saw earlier, two alternative approaches can be used to derive formulae for calculating R^2 and R.

(i) Original data (X, Y)

$$R^2 = \left[\frac{n\sum_{i=1}^{n} X_i Y_i - \sum_{i=1}^{n} X_i \sum_{i=1}^{n} Y_i}{\sqrt{[n\sum_{i=1}^{n} X_i^2 - (\sum X_i)^2] \times [n\sum_{i=1}^{n} Y_i^2 - (\sum Y_i)^2]}} \right]^2$$

$$R = \sqrt{R^2}$$

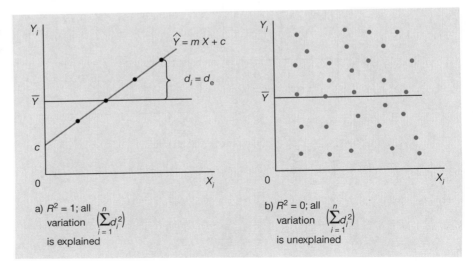

Fig. X.18 **Coefficient of determination (R^2).**

a) $R^2 = 1$; all variation $\left(\sum_{i=1}^{n} d_i^2\right)$ is explained

b) $R^2 = 0$; all variation $\left(\sum_{i=1}^{n} d_i^2\right)$ is unexplained

Alternatively, we can transfer the origin from zero to the point of means $(\bar{X}, \bar{Y})$ and use a coding formula for R^2 and R. In this case we make use of new axes $x_i = X_i - \bar{X}, y_i = Y_i - \bar{Y}$.

(ii) Redefined data

Here we can make use of calculations already undertaken in finding m and c for the regression line $Y = mX + c$ when using the coding formula:

$$R^2 = \frac{\sum_{i=1}^{n} x_i y_i}{\left(\sum_{i=1}^{n} x_i^2\right)\left(\sum_{i=1}^{n} y_i^2\right)}$$

where $\quad x_i = X_i - \bar{X}$
$\qquad\qquad y_i = Y_i - \bar{Y}$

$R = \sqrt{R^2}$

The following worked example uses the **coding formulae** to calculate both the regression line and the coefficients of determination and correlation for a data set containing six observations.

Example:

Y_i	X_i	x_i $(Y_i - \bar{Y})$	y_i $(X_i - \bar{X})$	$x_i y_i$	x_i^2	y_i^2
−4	0	−4.5	−2.5	11.25	6.25	20.25
−3	1	−3.5	−1.5	5.25	2.25	12.25
−1	2	−1.5	−0.5	0.75	0.25	2.25
2	3	1.5	0.5	0.75	0.25	2.25
3	4	2.5	1.5	3.75	2.25	6.25
6	5	5.5	2.5	13.75	6.25	30.25

$\sum Y = 3 \quad \sum X = 15 \qquad\qquad \sum xy = 35.5 \quad \sum x^2 = 17.50 \quad \sum y^2 = 73.50$
$\bar{Y} = 0.5 \quad \bar{X} = 2.5$

$m = \dfrac{\sum xy}{\sum x^2} \qquad R^2 = \dfrac{(\sum x_i y_i)^2}{(\sum x_i^2)(\sum y_i^2)}$

$\quad = \dfrac{35.5}{17.5} \qquad\quad = \dfrac{1{,}260.25}{1{,}286.25}$

$\quad = 2.03 \qquad\qquad = 0.98$

$\qquad\qquad\qquad\quad R = \sqrt{0.98}$

$\qquad\qquad\qquad\quad = 0.99$

$$C = \bar{Y} - m\bar{X}$$
$$= 0.5 - (2.03)\, 2.5$$
$$= -4.6$$
$$\hat{Y} = 2.03X - 4.6$$

Multiple regression analysis

Multiple regression analysis is used when the number of independent variables (X_i) is greater than 1. If, say $\hat{Y}$ was influenced by *three* independent variables, the equation would be

$$\hat{Y} = \alpha + \beta_1 X_1 + \beta_2 X_2 + \beta_3 X_3 + e$$

where α is the intercept and e is the error term (i.e. the difference between predicted and actual outcome). The technique of multiple regression is seeking to *estimate* values for α, and for the coefficient $\beta_1, \beta_2, \beta_3$ in this example. A number of problems are commonly associated with multiple regression analysis.

Multicollinearity This is a situation where two or more of the independent variables are *not* independent of each other, but rather are highly correlated. For example, in this equation it might be found X_1 and X_2 were dependent on each other: home ownership and family income provide this sort of difficulty. A firm might believe that whether a given family will buy its product is dependent, amongst other things, upon the family's income and whether the family owns or rents its home. Because families who own their own homes tend to have relatively high incomes, these two variables are highly correlated, with the result that the standard deviations of their respective regression coefficients (i.e. the βs) become large. It is possible to overcome this problem by dropping one of the independent variables in question, or extending the sample size, etc. However, it should be noted that provided any correlation between the independent variables persists into the future, the regression equation may still be used as a reliable guide to future trends.

Heteroscedasticity One of the assumptions made about the regression model is that the independent variables have a uniform variability or variance around the regression line. Heteroscedasticity occurs when the error term, e, increases (Fig. X.19(a)) or decreases (Fig. X.19(b)) as the value of the independent variable rises.

Thus the variance is not constant as demanded by the original assumptions. For example, consider a regression model in which savings by households are postulated to be a function of household income. In this case it is likely that more variability will be found in the savings of the high-income households compared with low-income households simply because high-income households have more money for potential savings. It is possible to offset this to an extent by using the log form of the data or by dividing all the variables in the equation by the independent variable that is believed to be causing the problem.

Autocorrelation In many regression equations, the dependent variable and independent variable(s) may be plotted through time. The assumption made in these models is that, over time, the error or disturbance term must be an independent random variable. In other words, the es should not show a predictable pattern over time. However, we can

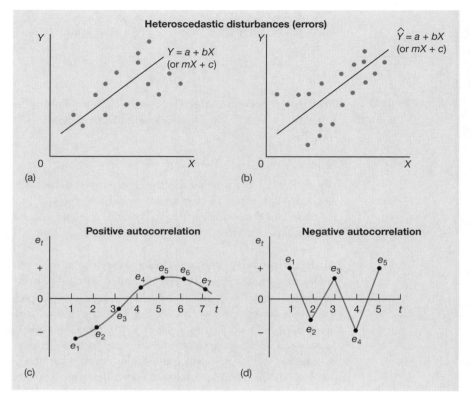

Fig. X.19 **Problems for multiple regression.**

see in Fig. X.19(c) that the positive or negative error respectively in one period is followed by another positive or negative error term respectively in the following period; this is known as **positive autocorrelation**. In Fig. X.19(d), however, the successive positive or negative errors are followed by errors of the *opposite* sign; this is known as **negative autocorrelation**. This means that there is a clear pattern to the *e*-terms, something that violates the assumptions of the regression equation.

Autocorrelation can result from, say, some cyclical or seasonal variations in economic variables that occur regularly over time. To test for this we use the **Durbin–Watson** statistic. In general, where the Durbin–Watson statistic (*d*) has a value of approximately 2, then this is taken to mean an absence of autocorrelation. Strictly speaking the calculated value of *d* should be compared with 'critical values' for *d* derived from the 'level of significance' used in the test (see, for example, Curwin and Slater, 1991, Ch. 19). Amongst other problems, the presence of autocorrelation means that the overall measures of fit of the regression line such as R^2 will not be reliable. It is possible to deal with this problem by introducing techniques to transform or remove these patterns, such as introducing a new linear trend or time variable into the equation.

Further reading Bancroft, G. and O'Sullivan, G. (1993), *Quantitative Methods for Accounting and Business Studies* (3rd edn), McGraw-Hill, Maidenhead..

Chs 6 and 7	Collecting and describing statistical data
Ch. 8	Measures of central location and dispersion
Ch. 9	Regression and correlation
Ch. 14	Probability distributions
Chs 15 and 16	Sampling and hypothesis testing

Barrow, M. (1992), *Statistics for Economics, Accounting and Business Studies*, Longman, Harlow.

Ch. 1	Descriptive statistics
Chs 3 and 4	Probability and probability distributions
Ch. 5	Estimation and confidence intervals
Chs 6, 7	Hypothesis testing and sampling
Ch. 9	Correlation and regression

Burton, G., Carrol, G. and Wall, S. (1999), *Quantitative Methods for Business and Economics*, Longman, Modular Texts in Business and Economics, Pearson Education, Harlow.

Ch. 1	Data presentation and collection
Ch. 2	Central location and dispersion
Ch. 3	Regression and correlation
Ch. 4	Time series and forecasting
Ch. 5	Probability
Ch. 6	Probability distributions
Ch. 7	Sampling and tests of hypotheses

Curwin, J. and Slater, R. (1991), *Quantitative Methods for Business Decisions* (3rd edn), Chapman & Hall, London.

Chs 1 and 2	Collecting and presenting statistical data
Ch. 3	Measures of location
Ch. 4	Measures of dispersion
Chs 10–12	Measures of uncertainty
Chs 13–16	Statistical inference
Ch. 17	Correlation
Ch. 18	Regression
Ch. 19	Multiple regression and correlation

Hannagan, T.J. (1986), *Mastering Statistics* (2nd edn), Macmillan, Basingstoke.

Chs 1–8	Collecting and presentation of data
Ch. 9	Measures of central location
Ch. 10	Measures of dispersion
Ch. 11	Probability and probability distributions
Ch. 13	Regression and correlation

Harper, W. M. (1991), *Statistics*, M and E Handbooks,

Chs 1–6	Collection and presentation of data
Chs 7–11	Frequency distributions
Chs 12–14	Regression and correlation
Chs 17–19	Probability distributions and sampling theory

Newbold, P. (1991), *Statistics for Business and Economics* (3rd edn), Prentice Hall, Hemel Hempstead.

Chs 1–2	Presenting and collecting data
Chs 3–6	Probability and probability distribution
Chs 7–8	Estimation
Chs 9–11	Hypothesis testing
Ch. 12	Linear regression and correlations
Ch. 13	Multiple regression
Ch. 14	Further regression analysis

Waters, D. (1994), *Quantitative Methods for Business*, Addison-Wesley, Wokingham.

Chs 3–6	Data collection and description
Ch. 8	Regression
Ch. 14	Probability distributions
Ch. 15	Sampling
Ch. 16	Testing hypothesis

Weiss, N. (1989), *Elementary Statistics* (2nd edn), Addison-Wesley, Wokingham.

Chs 2, 3	Collection and presentation of data
Ch. 4	Probability concepts
Ch. 5	Discrete random variables
Ch. 6	The normal distribution
Ch. 7	The sampling distribution of the mean
Chs 8–13	Inferential statistics
Chs 12,13	Regression and correlation

Whitehead, P. and Whitehead, G. (1992), *Statistics for Business*, Longman, Harlow.

Chs 1–7	Collecting and presenting data
Ch. 10	Measures of central tendency
Ch. 11	Measures of dispersion and skewness
Chs 13, 14	Probability and probability distributions
Ch. 16	Regression and correlation
Ch. 17	Sampling and significance testing

Glossary of terms

abatement costs The costs associated with abating (avoiding) a negative externality (e.g. pollution).

adverse selection The result of information asymmetry in which the true characteristics of agents/purchasers may be hidden from principals/suppliers. It may result in markets (e.g. insurance) being dominated by those presenting 'adverse' characteristics from the point of view of suppliers.

allocative efficiency This is often taken to mean setting price or output levels consistent with achieving Pareto-optimal resource allocations. For example, setting price equal to marginal cost is one of the conditions for a Pareto-optimal resource, where it is no longer possible to make someone better off without making someone else worse off.

arc elasticity of demand A measure of price elasticity of demand that uses the average of the initial and final values for price and quantity. It is the elasticity at the mid-point of the chord connecting the two points on the demand curve corresponding to the initial and final price levels.

average product of labour Output per unit of labour input; i.e.

$$\frac{\text{Total product}}{\text{Total labour input}} = \frac{Q}{L}$$

barometric-firm leadership Here the price leader is a small firm, recognised by others as having a close knowledge of prevailing market conditions.

barriers to entry Various deterrents to new firm entry into a market.

behavioural theories Theories that view the internal organisation and operation of companies as a key factor in explaining how firms take decisions in a modern, complex environment.

Bertrand-type equilibrium Price combination that achieves the objectives of the respective firms (firms take their rivals' *prices* as given).

beta value A measure used to assess the riskiness of shares. The variance of the returns on a particular share is related to the variance of shares in the market as a whole.

bilateral monopoly Usually refers to factor markets in which two monopolies are involved: one in purchasing the factor (e.g. labour), the other in supplying the factor.

budget line Describes the various combinations of two (or more) products that can be purchased if the whole household income is spent on these products.

capital-deepening technical progress Technical progress in which the marginal product of capital is raised by more than the marginal product of labour.

carbon tax A tax related in some way to the carbon content of the fossil fuels, namely coal, oil and gas.

cardinalist The cardinalist school supposed that utility could be measured, either in terms of some abstract quantity (e.g. utils) or in terms of money. In the latter case, utility is expressed in terms of the amount of money a consumer is willing to sacrifice for an additional unit of a commodity.

cartel A central body with responsibility for setting the industry price and/or output which most nearly meets some agreed objective.

certainty equivalent The sum of money, available with certainty, which would give the decision maker the same utility as if he had undertaken a more risky course of action.

coalition Any group which, at a given moment in time, shares a consensus as to the goals to be pursued.

Coase theorem The suggestion, following the work of R. Coase, that negotiation can be used to resolve externality problems. The nature of property rights is seen as primarily influencing the income distribution from any such negotiation.

coefficient of variation A measure of relative dispersion;

$$CV = \frac{\text{Standard deviation}}{\text{Arithmetic mean}}$$

collusive oligopoly Models of oligopoly behaviour which assume an element of formal collusion between firms.

collusive-price leadership Where a group of firms initiate, often informally, simultaneous price changes. Sometimes known as 'parallel pricing'.

common property resources Resources in which property rights are held in common rather than being assigned to individuals.

concave (to the origin) Bends towards the origin.

conditions of demand The variables which result in the demand curve shifting to the right (increase) or left (decrease).

conditions of supply The variables which result in the supply curve shifting to the right (increase) or left (decrease).

consumer surplus A measure, in monetary units, of the difference between the amount of money a consumer is willing to pay to buy a certain quantity of a commodity and the amount that he actually does pay for this quantity of the commodity.

contestable markets Markets in which the threat of new firm entry causes incumbents to act as though such potential competition actually existed.

contingency fee A fee, for services, based on the output achieved by an agent acting on behalf of the principal.

contingency theory Theory in which the optimal solutions to organisational problems are viewed as being derived from matching the internal structure and processes of the firm more closely to a set of characteristics present in its external environment.

contract curve In terms of profitability, the set of tangency points between the isoprofit curves of the respective firms. Corresponds to the set of outputs (or prices) that maximise industry profits. In terms of general equilibrium, the set of tangency points between the indifference curves of consumers (Edgeworth–Bowley consumption box) or isoquants of producers (Edgeworth–Bowley production box). Indicates resource allocations that are Pareto optimal.

convex (to the origin) Bends away from the origin.

cost-oriented multinationals Firms in which the search for cheaper or more secure inputs into the productive process is seen as the driving force for multinational activity.

cost gradient Represents the increase in costs as a result of the production (enterprise) unit being only a specified percentage of the optimum size.

Cournot-type equilibrium Output combination that achieves the objectives of the respective firms (firms take their rivals' *outputs* as given).

cross-elasticity of demand (CED) Indicates the responsiveness of demand for a product to changes in the price of some other product.

$$CED = \frac{\% \text{ change in quantity demanded of } X}{\% \text{ change in price of } Y}$$

Here we are considering shifts in the demand curve of the product.

deadweight loss The loss of economic welfare (producer and consumer surplus) that can be attributed to 'market failure'; here the existence of monopoly power.

demand curve Maps the relationship between the quantity demanded of some product and changes in its own price.

demand function Expresses the relationship between the quantity demanded of some product and the main variables that influence that demand.

deregulation The removal by government of one or more existing regulations affecting some industry or sector.

diminishing marginal rate of substitution Can refer to products (consumers) or factors (producers). In a two-product context, it suggests that consumers will be willing to sacrifice progressively less of one product (Y) for an extra unit of another product (X) the more of that product (X) they already consume (keeping utility unchanged). In a two-factor context, it suggests that producers will be able to replace progressively less of one factor (L) by an extra unit of another factor (K), the more of that factor (K) they already use (keeping output unchanged).

diminishing returns Usually refers to the short-run time period. The average/marginal product curves of a variable factor will eventually decline as more of the variable factor is applied to some fixed factor.

discount factor The value by which a future sum is multiplied to reduce it to a present value equivalent.

diseconomies of scale The suggestion that, in the long run, a proportionate increase in all factors will lead to a less than proportionate increase in output. As a result, long-run average costs rise.

dominant-firm leadership Situation in which the price leader is the dominant firm in the industry.

dominant strategy One in which the respective firms seek to do the best they can (in terms of the objectives set) irrespective of the possible actions/reactions of any rival(s).

economic rent A surplus payment to a factor of production in the sense of being over and above the minimum price at which that factor would be supplied.

economies of scale Changes in (long-run) average cost where proportionate changes in all the factors of production lead to more than proportionate changes in output. It describes the downward-sloping segment of the LRAC curve.

economies of scope Changes in average costs of production as a result of changes in the mix of output.

Edgeworth–Bowley consumption box A diagram showing the set of allocations of product between consumers that are Pareto optimal.

Edgeworth–Bowley production box A diagram showing the set of allocations of factor inputs between producers that are Pareto optimal.

endogenous variables Variables that are determined inside an economic system or model.

expected monetary value (EMV) For a particular course of action over n possible outcomes it can be defined as

$$EMV = \sum_{i=1}^{n} p_i \cdot X_i$$

where p_i = probability of ith outcome
X_i = value of ith outcome

and $\sum_{i=1}^{n} p_i = 1$

expected utility (EU) For a particular course of action over n possible outcomes it can be defined as

$$EU = \sum_{i=1}^{n} p_i \cdot U_i$$

where p_i = probability of ith outcome
U_i = utility of ith outcome

and $\sum_{i=1}^{n} p_i = 1$

expected value In an uncertain situation, expected value is a weighted average of the values (pay-offs) associated with each possible outcome, with the probabilities of each outcome being used as weights.

externalities Occur when economic decisions create costs or benefits for people other than the decision takers.

fair bet In the context of insurance, defined as one for which, should it be repeated an infinite number of times, both insured and insurer would expect to break even.

first-best economy An economy in which no market failure occurs.

first-degree price discrimination An extreme situation in which the firm charges a different price to every consumer, reflecting each consumer's willingness to pay.

first mover advantage If decisions can only be taken in sequence, an important issue is whether the firm making the first move can secure any advantage. Any such advantage might lie in anticipating the likely responses of the rival and channelling those responses in a particular direction.

full insurance Occurs where the lawyer (agent) is willing to pay a fee to the client (principal) to cover all the client's perceived risk.

gamble A choice (usually involving a money payment) between alternative outcomes in a situation of uncertainty.

general equilibrium Situation in which all markets clear (reach equilibrium) simultaneously.

Giffen goods Named after the nineteenth-century economist, Sir Robert Giffen, who claimed to identify an upward-sloping demand curve for certain inferior goods. To be a Giffen good it is necessary, but not sufficient, that the good be inferior.

Gini coefficient The ratio of the enclosed area between the Lorenz curve and the diagonal (perfect equality) to the total area beneath the diagonal. The smaller the ratio, the greater the equality, and vice versa. A Gini coefficient of 0 represents perfect equality, whereas 1 represents perfect inequality.

grandfathering A formula for distributing tradeable permits to countries in proportion to their existing levels of emissions of pollutants.

guaranteed minimum price A designated price floor, usually with mechanisms in place to prevent price from falling below some specified level.

identification problem Refers to problems associated with identifying the actual demand curve for a product when changes in the 'conditions of demand' occur at the same time as changes in the product's own price.

imperfect competition See *monopolistic competition*.

income consumption line A line which joins the set of tangency points between budget lines and highest attainable indifference curves.

income effect The additional purchasing power resulting from a fall in price of one or more products in the consumption bundle.

income elasticity of demand (IED) The responsiveness of demand for a product to changes in consumer (national) income.

$$IED = \frac{\% \text{ change in quantity demanded of } X}{\% \text{ change in income}}$$

Here we are considering shifts in the demand curve for the product.

increase/decrease (demand) Shifts to right/left in the demand curve, caused by changes in the 'conditions of demand'.

increase/decrease (supply) Shifts to right/left in the supply curve, caused by changes in the 'conditions of supply'.

increasing returns Usually refers to the short-run time period. The average/marginal product curves of a variable factor may at first rise as more of the variable factor is applied.

indifference curves Lines representing different combinations of commodities that yield a constant level of utility or satisfaction to the consumer.

industry MC curve The addition to total costs in the industry from an extra unit of output. If we aggregate the *MC* curves for each and every firm (summing horizontally), in a competitive industry, we derive the industry *MC* curve.

industry supply curve Maps the relationship between price and quantity supplied in an industry. By aggregating the *MC* curves of each firm in a competitive industry we are aggregating their supply curves, thereby deriving the industry supply curve.

inferior goods Cheap but poor-quality substitutes for other goods. As real incomes rise above a certain 'threshold', consumers tend to substitute more expensive but better-quality alternatives for certain products. In other words, inferior goods have negative income elasticities of demand over certain ranges of income.

information asymmetry Occurs when some agents in a market are better informed than others. A type of 'market failure'.

input–output (Leontief) isoquant Isoquant that assumes zero substitutability between the factors of production.

insurance premium The fee that a decision maker must pay at the beginning of a time period to guarantee some specified outcome in a situation of uncertainty.

isocost line/curve The various combinations of factors or production that can be purchased for a given expenditure.

isoprofit line/curve The various combinations of output yielding a given level of profit.

isoquant The various combinations of factor input that can produce a given level of output (in a technically efficient manner).

justified discrimination Often used as regards wage differentials that can be attributed to genuine differences in attributes or characteristics.

Kaldor criterion An attempt to rank allocations of resources that involve some 'winning' and some 'losing'. An allocation is regarded as preferred when it yields an overall net gain available to make some better off after any losers have been compensated.

labour-deepening technical progress Technical progress in which the marginal product of labour is raised by more than the marginal product of capital.

law of variable proportions Applied to the short–run (time period) when at least one factor of production is fixed. For example, when labour is the variable factor being applied to some fixed factor (such as land or capital), both the marginal and average products of labour at first rise but subsequently fall as the quantity of labour increases.

Lerner index A measure of monopoly power, reflecting the extent to which the monopoly can raise price (P) above marginal cost (MC). Lerner's index (L) can be expressed as follows:

$$L = \frac{(P - MC)}{P} = 1 - \frac{MC}{P}$$

limit price The highest price that the established firms (incumbents) believe they can charge without inducing entry.

linear isoquant Isoquant in which the marginal rate of (technical) substitution between factors is constant at all points.

load factor The ratio of average actual use to full–capacity use in a production process.

long run The period of time in which all factors of production can be varied.

Lorenz curve A curve relating the cumulative percentage values of two variables.

managerial theories Theories that focus on the separation of ownership and control in limited liability companies as giving management greater discretion in setting firm objectives; in particular, to pursue objectives other than pure profit maximisation.

marginal abatement costs The extra cost to the firm of avoiding emitting the last unit of pollutant (or other source of negative externality).

marginal physical product (MPP) The addition to total physical product (output volume) from using an extra unit of a factor. If labour is the factor, it refers to the additional (physical) output contributed by the last person employed.

marginal productivity theory Suggests that firms will continue to employ factors of production until the employment of the marginal unit of each factor adds as much to revenue as it does to costs. Predicts that factors will then receive the value of their marginal products (marginal revenue product).

marginal physical product of labour The addition to total (physical) output from employing the last unit of labour.

marginal rate of substitution between risk and return The trade-off, at the margin, for a portfolio holder between risk and the expected return.

marginal rate of substitution of X for Y (MRS$_{xy}$) The amount of product Y that the consumer is willing to give up for an extra unit of product X and still achieve the same level of satisfaction (i.e. be on the same indifference curve).

marginal rate of technical substitution of labour for capital (MRTS$_{LK}$) The amount of capital that can be replaced by one extra unit of labour, output remaining constant.

marginal revenue product (MRP) The additional value contributed by the last unit of factor input. Often refers to labour as factor input. In a perfectly competitive product market, MRP of labour is found by multiplying the MPP of labour by the price of the product. Sometimes called the value marginal product (VMP).

marginal utility The addition to total utility from consuming the last unit of a product.

market-oriented multinationals Firms in which the prospect of new markets and greater sales is seen as the driving force of multinational activity.

mark-up The difference between price and average cost; often expressed as a percentage of the average cost. Less usually, marginal cost is used instead of average cost.

maxi-min An approach in game theory whereby the firm selects from the best of the worst possible outcomes identified in a pay-off matrix.

maximising theories Theories that predict price (and/or output) on the assumption that firms seek to maximise a particular objective, such as profit, sales revenue, etc.

merit goods Goods/services that add to the quality of life but are not, strictly, public goods. For example, education/health care can be withheld from consumers (i.e. they do not possess the public good quality of non-excludability), and so private markets can be established to provide them.

M-form structure Multidivisional organisational structure in which a central office comprising (elite) staff committed to strategic development oversees a number of operating divisions, each of which is responsible for a group of related activities.

mini-max An approach in game theory whereby each firm selects the worst of the best possible outcomes identified in a pay-off matrix.

minimum efficient scale (MES) The level of output that results in the lowest attainable average cost. Usually refers to the long-run time period.

mixed public good A good/service that only possesses the characteristics attributable to a pure public good.

monopolistic competition A market structure which contains elements of both monopoly and competitive market forms. Differentiated (or non-homogeneous) products give firms an element of market power, but the existence of large numbers of relatively small firms, with freedom of entry/exit, provides an element of competition.

monopsony Occurs when a firm is a significant purchaser of labour. Any additional hiring of labour potentially forces up the price of labour against itself so that the marginal cost of labour lies above the average cost of labour.

moral hazard Information asymmetry may give agents superior information to principals. For example, hidden actions and motives by agents may make it difficult for principals to assess quality within the market.

multinational (transnational) A company that owns or controls production or service facilities in more than one country.

Nash equilibrium Occurs when each firm is doing the best that it can in terms of its own objective(s), given the strategies chosen by the other firms in the market.

natural monopoly Situation where the minimum efficient size of the productive unit or enterprise is so large that the industry can sustain only a single operator.

net present value (NPV) The present value of expected future receipts from a project minus the initial cost of the project.

neutral technical progress Technical progress in which the marginal products of both labour and capital are raised by the same percentage.

non-collusive oligopoly Models of oligopoly behaviour that assume no formal collusion between firms.

non-exclusivity An alternative phrase for non-excludability (see *public goods*).

non-rivalry An alternative phrase for non-exhaustibility (see *public goods*). If the marginal cost of an extra person consuming a good/service is zero because it is non-exhaustible, then consumers can be regarded as non-rivals.

normal profit That profit just sufficient to keep the firm in the industry in the long run.

one-shot game Where decisions as to price, output, advertising expenditure are made at the outset and remain unchanged during the course of the game.

ordinalist The ordinalist approach does not assume that consumer utility be measurable, merely that consumer preferences can be *ranked* in order of importance.

Pareto criterion An allocation of resources is regarded as 'Pareto preferred' when someone is made better off and no one worse off *vis-à-vis* some alternative allocation.

Pareto optimality A situation is said to be Pareto optimal when it is no longer possible to reallocate resources in such a way that we can make one person better off, without at the same time making someone else worse off.

partial equilibrium Situation in which only some subset of all the available markets clear (reach equilibrium).

pay-offs The expected values assigned to various combinations of strategy and counter-strategy in game theory situations.

peak period pricing Situation in which the price varies between different time periods (e.g. peak and off-peak). Such price variation is often related to variations in the costs of providing the product in the different time periods.

perfectly contestable market Situation in which no barriers to entry exist so that incumbent firms are constrained by the threat of new firm entry to keep prices at levels that, in relation to costs, earn only normal profits. Incumbents in perfectly contestable markets earn no supernormal profits, are cost efficient, and cannot cross-subsidise between products or set prices below costs in order to deter new entrants.

perfectly elastic demand Situation in which an infinitely small change in price of a product results in an infinitely large change in the quantity demanded of that product.

perfectly inelastic demand Situation in which demand for a product is totally unresponsive to changes in its own price: whatever the percentage change in price there is a 0% change in quantity demanded of the product.

Pigouvian tax A tax on the producer of an externality exactly equal to the net marginal external cost imposed.

point price elasticity of demand (PED) Measures the responsiveness of demand for a product to an infinitely small change in its own price.

portfolio planning Firms are seen as managing a 'portfolio' of products with different profiles in terms of market share and market growth. Terms such as 'cash cows', 'stars', 'question marks' and 'dogs' are attributed to different segments of the portfolio.

poverty trap Refers to the web of overlapping tax schedules and benefits. These may result in those with low earnings gaining little or nothing from any rise in earnings when this results in benefits being lost and tax paid.

price–consumption line A line joining the set of tangency points between budget lines representing a change in the price of the product and the highest attainable indifference curves.

price discrimination Situation in which different prices are charged for identical units of a product.

price elasticity of demand (PED) A measure of the responsiveness of demand for a product to changes in its own price.

$$PED = \frac{\% \text{ change in quantity demanded of } X}{\% \text{ change in price of } X}$$

PED indicates the extent of movement along a demand curve in response to a change in price of the product.

price elasticity of supply (PES) A measure of the responsiveness of supply of a product to changes in its own price.

$$PES = \frac{\% \text{ change in quantity supplied of } X}{\% \text{ change in price of } X}$$

price of risk See *marginal rate of substitution between risk and return*.

price regulation Regulations that involve some form of price cap or ceiling; often with a view to firms having to cut costs in order to raise profits.

principal–agent problem The suggestion that the separation of ownership and control in limited liability companies gives agents (managers) opportunities to pursue objectives that may not accord with the wishes of principals (owners, shareholders).

producer surplus The excess of revenue actually received by producers over and above the amount required to induce them to supply a given quantity of a product.

production function An expression relating the output of a product to various types of factor input.

production quota Maximum volume of output permitted for a product.

productive efficiency Involves identifying the least-cost method of producing a given level of output.

product life cycle The suggestion that products typically follow a 'life cycle' involving distinct stages: introduction, growth, maturity, and decline.

property rights The legal rules that determine what individuals or firms may do with their property.

proportionate demand curve A demand curve used in models of imperfect competition, derived from an assumption that if all firms charge the same price, they will receive identical market shares within a product group.

public choice theory The suggestion that producers, consumers and regulators act as competing coalitions, each seeking to achieve the regulatory framework most likely to secure the goals of that coalition.

public good A good (or service) that involves two key characteristics: non-excludability and non-exhaustibility. Non-excludability means that, once provided, it is difficult to exclude people from consuming the good/service. Non-exhaustibility means that consumption of an extra unit by one person does not diminish the amount available for consumption by others.

public interest theory An approach that seeks to assess the impacts of regulation or deregulation in terms of whether or not it raises economic welfare in such a way that gainers can potentially compensate losers. Usually involves the ideas of consumer and producer surplus.

pure public good A good/service that fully possesses the characteristics of non-excludability and non-exhaustibility. See *public good*.

quality regulations Regulations that seek to prescribe some form of minimum service/quality obligation as a means of securing a licence to operate.

quasi rent That part of the earnings of a factor of production that is economic rent in the short run but transfer earnings in the long run.

rate of return regulation Regulations that involve restricting the firm's rate of profit to some prescribed proportion of its capital investment.

reaction curves Show how a firm reacts to any price or output set by some other firm(s).

relatively price-elastic demand Occurs when a given percentage change in own price leads to a larger percentage change in quantity demanded of a product.

relatively price-inelastic demand Occurs when a given percentage change in own price leads to a smaller percentage change in quantity demanded of a product.

repeated game A game in which the firm can modify its strategy from one period to the next and respond to any changes in strategy by its rival.

risk An estimate of the chance of an event or series of events occurring.

risk-adjusted discount rate The risk-free discount rate plus an additional element to represent the risk factor.

risk averse Describes a person who prefers a situation in which a given income (pay-off) is certain to a situation that yields the same expected value for income but which involves uncertainty.

risk-free asset Asset for which the chances of default are minimal and the payments are known.

risk loving Describes a person who prefers a gamble with the same expected value for income as would occur in the certain (no gamble) situation.

risk neutral Decribes a person who is indifferent (same utility) between certain and uncertain outcomes that have the same expected value of income.

risk premium Measures the amount of income that an individual would give up to leave him/her indifferent between a risky choice and a certain one.

satisficing The pursuit of outcomes that are acceptable or satisfactory for the main internal groups comprising a company, rather than the pursuit of outcomes that are optimal for only one or a few groups in a company.

Scitovsky double criterion The suggestion that an allocation of resources is preferred to another only when both the move from the initial allocation to the new and the reverse move from the new allocation to the initial fulfil the Kaldor criterion.

second-best economy An economy in which more than one market failure occurs.

second-degree price discrimination Situation in which different prices are charged for different quantities or blocks of the same product.

sequential game A game in which the moves and countermoves take place in a defined order; one firm makes a move and only then does the rival decide how to react to that move.

short run That period of time in which at least one factor of production is fixed.

Slutsky equation An equation that expresses the pure substitution effect in terms of a movement along a given indifference curve.

social costs The cost to society of any particular action. Usually regarded as the sum of any private costs to the individuals undertaking that action and any associated external costs.

social welfare function The aggregation of individual indifference curves into a set of community indifference curves using explicit rules as regards interpersonal comparisons.

sophisticated leader A firm that develops a strategy to give it the best return (e.g. profit level) consistent with the reaction curve of its rival(s).

stable equilibrium Situation in which any movement away from an equilibrium initiates changes that move the situation back towards that equilibrium.

Stackelberg equilibrium Involves output combinations in which at least one firm does the best it can consistent with the anticipated reactions of its rival(s). The 'sophisticated leader' in this model recognises that the other firm(s) act on the Cournot assumption.

substitution effect The additional amount of a product purchased as a result of its price being cheaper relative to other substitutes in consumption.

sunk cost A cost of acquiring an asset, whether tangible (e.g. plant) or intangible (e.g. reputation), which cannot be recouped by selling that asset or redeploying it to some other use.

technical economies Reasons for economies of scale involving benefits from increasing the size of the production unit.

third-degree price discrimination Situation in which the market is separated into two or more groups of consumers, with a different price charged to each group.

tit-for-tat strategy A strategy in which a firm's reactions are deliberately imitative of the rival's initial actions.

total economic value A concept often applied to environmental assets and regarded as the sum of use value, option value and existence value.

total price effect The total impact on demand of a fall in price of the product, taking into account both income and substitution effects.

tradeable permits Permits that give the holders the right to emit a specific volume of pollution. These permits can be traded on markets.

transfer pricing Situation in which the price charged in a geographical location bears more relation to the tax regime in operation than to the true costs of provision.

two-part tariff Situation in which the firm charges an initial fixed fee (per time period) that on payment gives consumers the right to purchase the product at a uniform price per unit.

U-form structure Unitary organisational structure in which a chief executive officer (managing director) has responsibility for a number of functional areas of the firm (production, marketing, finance, etc.).

unemployment trap Refers to the web of overlapping tax schedules and benefits that may result in those moving out of unemployment into work gaining little or nothing in terms of net income.

union bargaining power The ability of unions to influence the bargaining process. Can be represented by the following ratio:

$$\frac{\text{Management costs of disagreeing (to union terms)}}{\text{Management costs of agreeing (to union terms)}}$$

unit elastic demand Situation in which a given percentage change in own price of a product leads to exactly the same percentage change in the quantity demanded of that product.

unjustified discrimination Refers to situations in which factors of production are rewarded differently in the market for identical attributes or characteristics provided.

valuation ratio The ratio of the market value of a share at any time to the capital or book value of that share.

value marginal product (VMP) An alternative name for the marginal revenue product of labour in a competitive product market. VMP can be found by multiplying marginal physical product (MPP) by price of the product.

variable sum game A game in which the gains for one or more players need not be offset by equivalent losses for some other player(s).

zero-sum game A game in which any gain for one or more players is offset by an equivalent loss for some other player(s).

Index